PATHFINDER®

VOLUME ONE

DARK WATERS RISING

PATHFINDER®

VOLUME ONE
DARK WATERS RISING

Written by	**JIM ZUB**
Illustrated by	**ANDREW HUERTA** (issues 1 through 6)
	JAKE BILBAO (issue 5)
	IVAN ANAYA (The Last Mosswood Goblin)
Colored by	**ROSS CAMPBELL** (issues 1 through 6)
	MOHAN (issue 5 and The Last Mosswood Goblin)
Lettered by	**MARSHALL DILLON**
Collection cover by	**MATTEO SCALERA**
Editor	**RICH YOUNG**
Collection design by	**GEOFF HARKINS**

Special thanks to ERIK MONA at Paizo Publishing

This volume collects Pathfinder issues #1-6 by Dynamite Entertainment.

ISBN 13: 978-1-5241-0421-4

10 9 8 7 6 5 4 3 2 1

Online at www.**DYNAMITE**.com
On Instagram /Dynamitecomics
On Twitter @dynamitecomics

On Facebook /Dynamitecomics
On Tumblr dynamitecomics.tumblr.com
On YouTube /Dynamitecomics

DYNAMITE.

Nick Barrucci, CEO / Publisher
Juan Collado, President / COO

Joe Rybandt, Executive Editor
Matt Idelson, Senior Editor
Anthony Marques, Associate Editor
Matt Humphreys, Assistant Editor
Kevin Ketner, Assistant Editor

Jason Ullmeyer, Art Director
Geoff Harkins, Senior Graphic Designer
Cathleen Heard, Graphic Designer
Alexis Persson, Graphic Designer
Chris Caniano, Digital Associate
Rachel Kilbury, Digital Assistant

Brandon Dante Primavera, V.P. of IT and Operations
Rich Young, Director of Business Development

Alan Payne, V.P. of Sales and Marketing
Keith Davidsen, Marketing Director
Pat O'Connell, Sales Manager

Contents

Secret Origin of the Pathfinder Iconics

It all started, appropriately enough, in a *dungeon*. Or more to the point, in a *Dungeon*. Years before we released the first volume of the Pathfinder Adventure Path, Paizo Publishing produced licensed magazines supporting the world's oldest fantasy roleplaying game. As part of a 2004 revamp of *Dungeon* magazine, I made two important editorial changes that would inform the birth of Pathfinder three years later.

The first change involved making our popular Adventure Path ongoing campaign adventures a monthly feature of the magazine, bringing a sense of continuity and shared experience to *Dungeon's* readership. Secondly, as part of an artistic revamp we created a host of "iconic characters" for each of the game's 11 character classes. These characters, designed by our favorite cover artist, Wayne Reynolds, appeared as proxies for the player characters of the readers in nearly every illustration published over the next several years. Readers demanded to know more about these characters. What were their names? How did they meet? How did they get along with one another?

The crushing monthly deadlines left us little time to contemplate these topics, and by the time demand for more information about them reached a clamor, the writing was already on the wall that Paizo would need to shift its business away from licensed support and into the creation of its own original monthly game products. We decided to expand the Adventure Path idea into the Pathfinder Adventure Path, complete with its own set of iconic characters. Pathfinder continues to this day, having produced more than 70 volumes since then. It's now the best-selling monthly RPG release, with players all over the world.

Unlike the *Dungeon* iconics, who had been created simply as a way to help artists understand what a "ranger" looked like without having to explain every aspect of their armor, gear, and abilities, these new Pathfinder iconics were designed with future expansion firmly in mind. Once again, we teamed up with Wayne Reynolds to design 11 iconic characters based on the races and classes inhabiting the world of Pathfinder. But this time, we had more ambitious plans for our iconics than making life a little easier on artists. This time, we knew we wanted to tell their stories.

Inspired by Wayne's illustrations, our in-house creative staff sketched out short bios for each character, tying their backgrounds into elements of our official Pathfinder world of Golarion. But RPGs are about *your* heroes, not ours. In the context of a Pathfinder RPG adventure, a picture of Valeros and Seoni slaying their way through a group of foes is really meant to be a stand-in for characters created by you and your friends. RPGs are about creating the framework for stories cooperatively developed by the players. It simply isn't the right medium.

The right medium is comics. Wayne's awesome character designs beg for amazing action scenes and suggest tons of stories about where the characters have been in the course of their adventuring life. Each scroll case, ring, weapon, pouch, and trinket incorporated into their costumes has a story waiting to be told. Pathfinder players have been adventuring along with the iconic characters since the beginning, but only with the transition to comics have they been able to see how they met, who they are, and how they think and work with one another.

Jim Zub is the perfect writer for the *Pathfinder* comic. We worked with him way back in Paizo's magazine era, and I knew from numerous conversations that he understood fantasy gaming. His creator-owned comic *Skullkickers*, itself a comedic send-up of the fantasy genre and tropes of tabletop gaming, proved that he knew how to handle characters and dialog. Once Dynamite signed on to produce the comic, we sent a pile of reference art and character bios to Jim, and he came back with the story collected here in this volume.

Artist Andrew Huerta was the last key ingredient in the Pathfinder comic potion. His kinetic action scenes and inventive page compositions bring a sense of energy and excitement to Jim's tale of goblins and demon cults, and his distinctive style manages both to reproduce intricate costume details and provide a fresh look at these familiar characters, all at the same time.

So take up your swords, your shields, and your 20-sided die, because the Pathfinder comic is ready to begin its first adventure!

Erik Mona
Publisher
Paizo Publishing

Dark Waters Rising
Chapter I

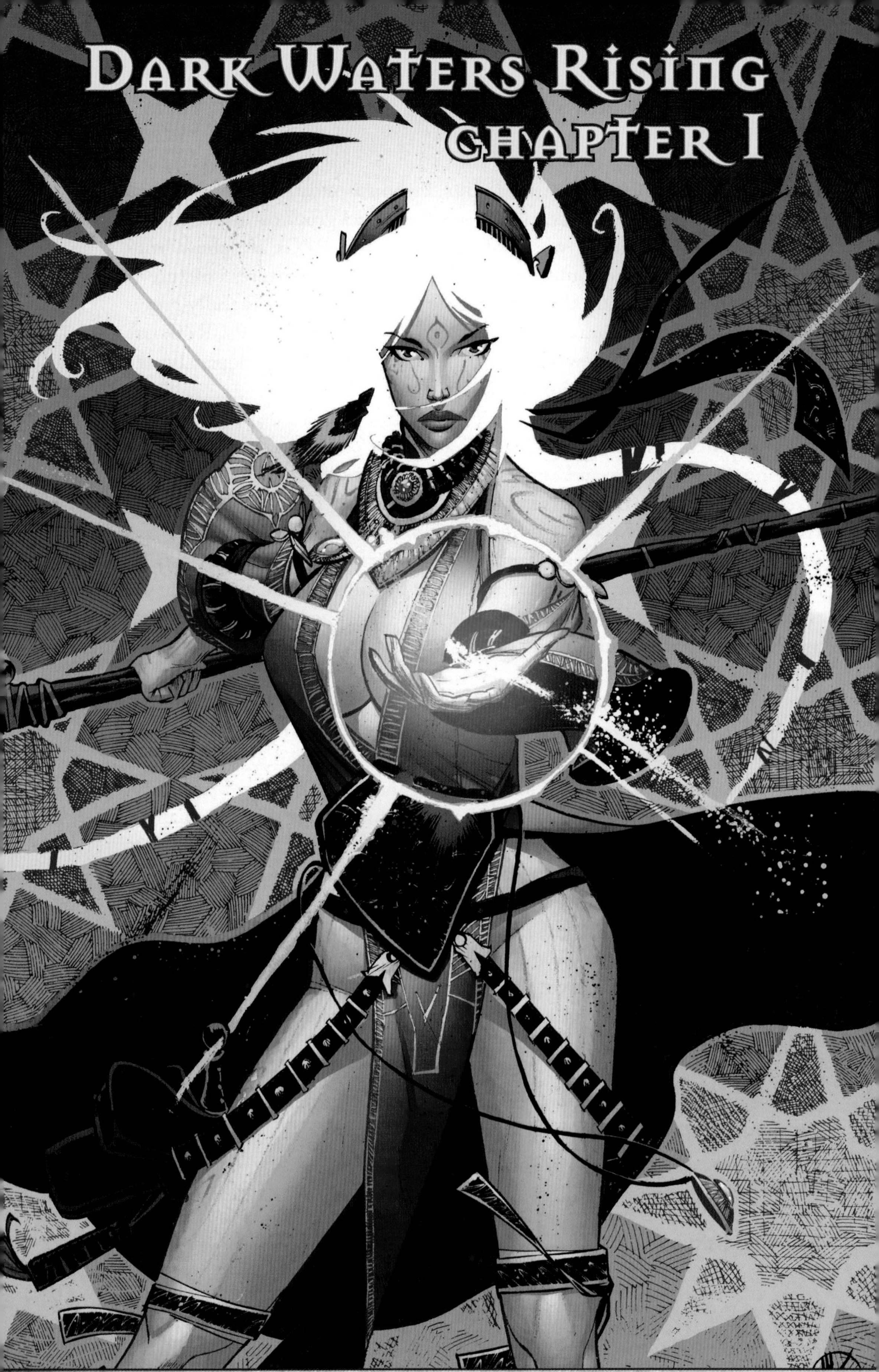

Issue #1 cover by MATTEO SCALERA

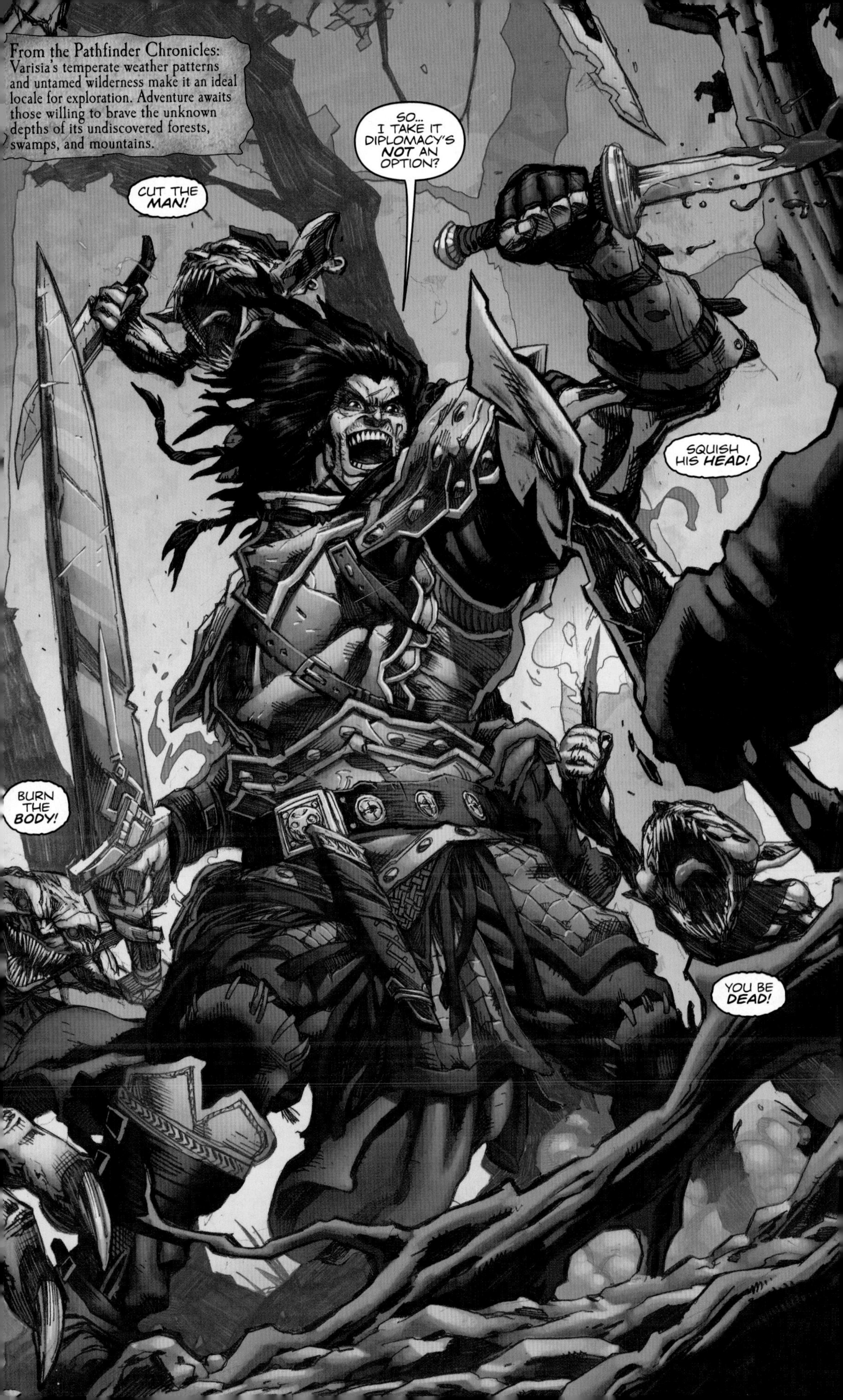
From the Pathfinder Chronicles:
Varisia's temperate weather patterns and untamed wilderness make it an ideal locale for exploration. Adventure awaits those willing to brave the unknown depths of its undiscovered forests, swamps, and mountains.
CUT THE MAN!
SO... I TAKE IT DIPLOMACY'S NOT AN OPTION?
SQUISH HIS HEAD!
BURN THE BODY!
YOU BE DEAD!

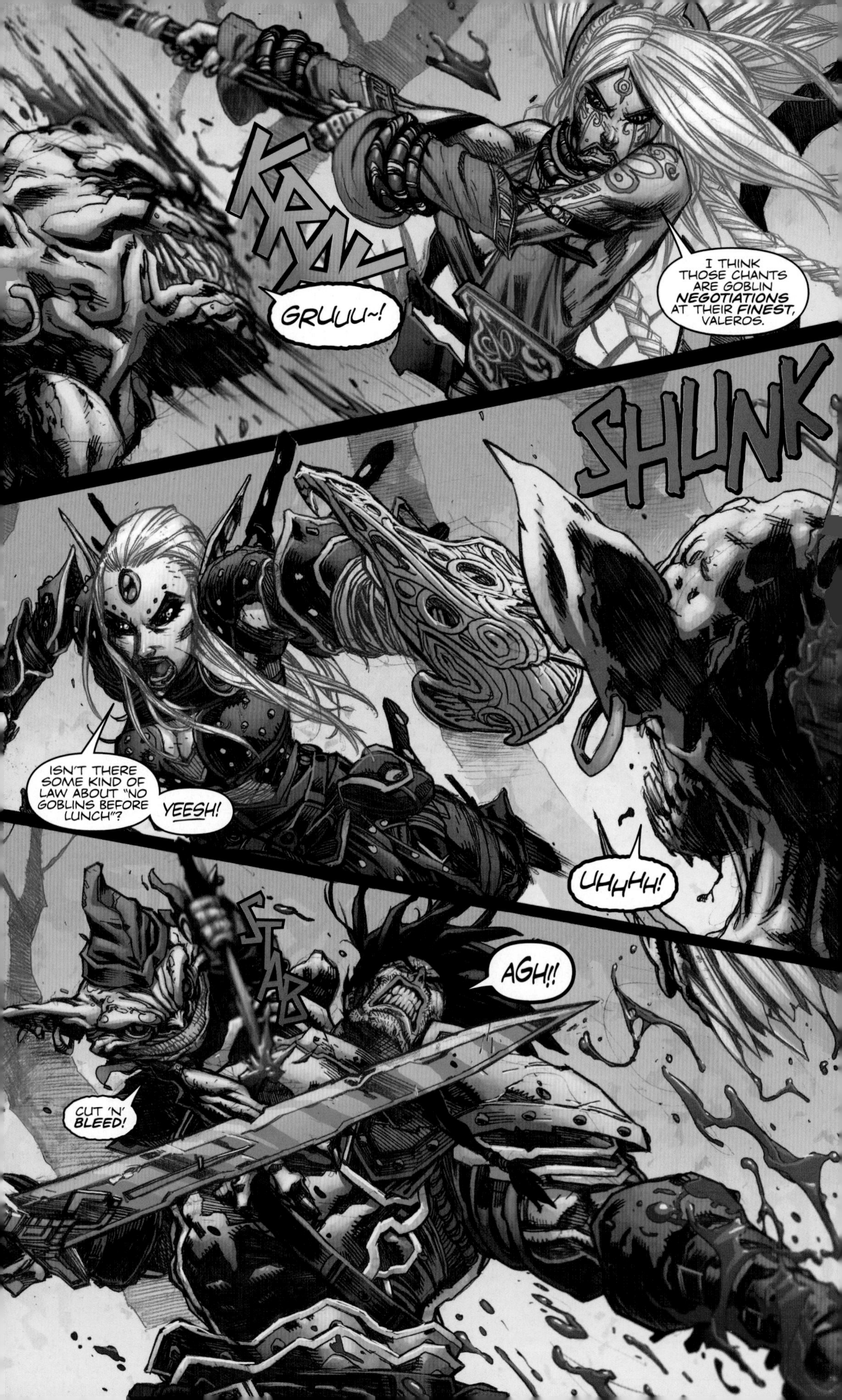
KRAK
GRUUU~!
I THINK THOSE CHANTS ARE GOBLIN NEGOTIATIONS AT THEIR FINEST, VALEROS.
SHUNK
ISN'T THERE SOME KIND OF LAW ABOUT "NO GOBLINS BEFORE LUNCH"?
YEESH!
UHHHH!
STAB
AGH!!
CUT 'N' BLEED!

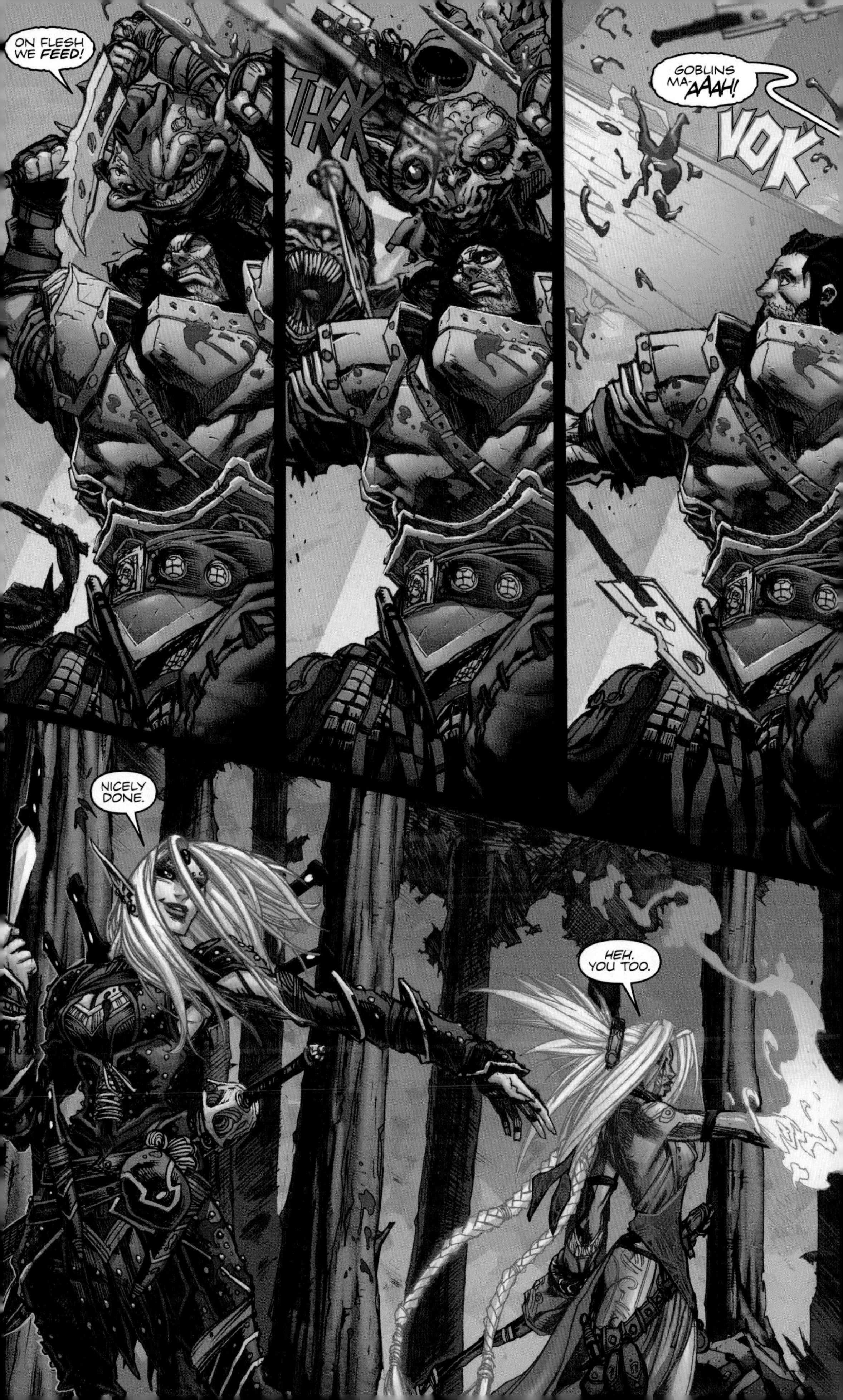
ON FLESH WE FEED!
THOK
GOBLINS MA-AAAH!
VOK
NICELY DONE.
HEH. YOU TOO.

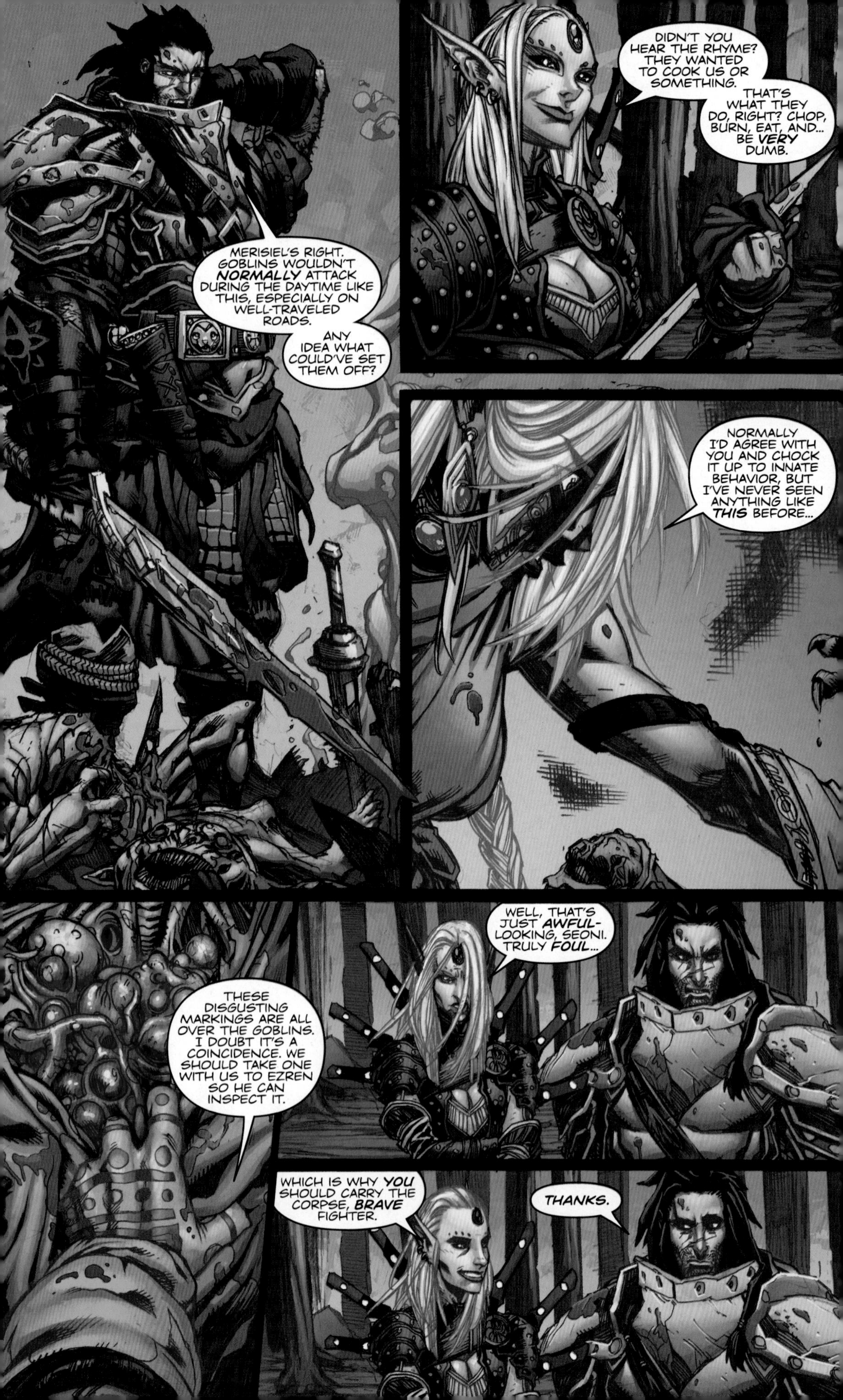
DIDN'T YOU HEAR THE RHYME? THEY WANTED TO COOK US OR SOMETHING.
THAT'S WHAT THEY DO, RIGHT? CHOP, BURN, EAT, AND... BE VERY DUMB.
MERISIEL'S RIGHT. GOBLINS WOULDN'T NORMALLY ATTACK DURING THE DAYTIME LIKE THIS, ESPECIALLY ON WELL-TRAVELED ROADS.
ANY IDEA WHAT COULD'VE SET THEM OFF?
NORMALLY I'D AGREE WITH YOU AND CHOCK IT UP TO INNATE BEHAVIOR, BUT I'VE NEVER SEEN ANYTHING LIKE THIS BEFORE...
WELL, THAT'S JUST AWFUL-LOOKING, SEONI. TRULY FOUL...
THESE DISGUSTING MARKINGS ARE ALL OVER THE GOBLINS. I DOUBT IT'S A COINCIDENCE. WE SHOULD TAKE ONE WITH US TO EZREN SO HE CAN INSPECT IT.
WHICH IS WHY YOU SHOULD CARRY THE CORPSE, BRAVE FIGHTER.
THANKS.

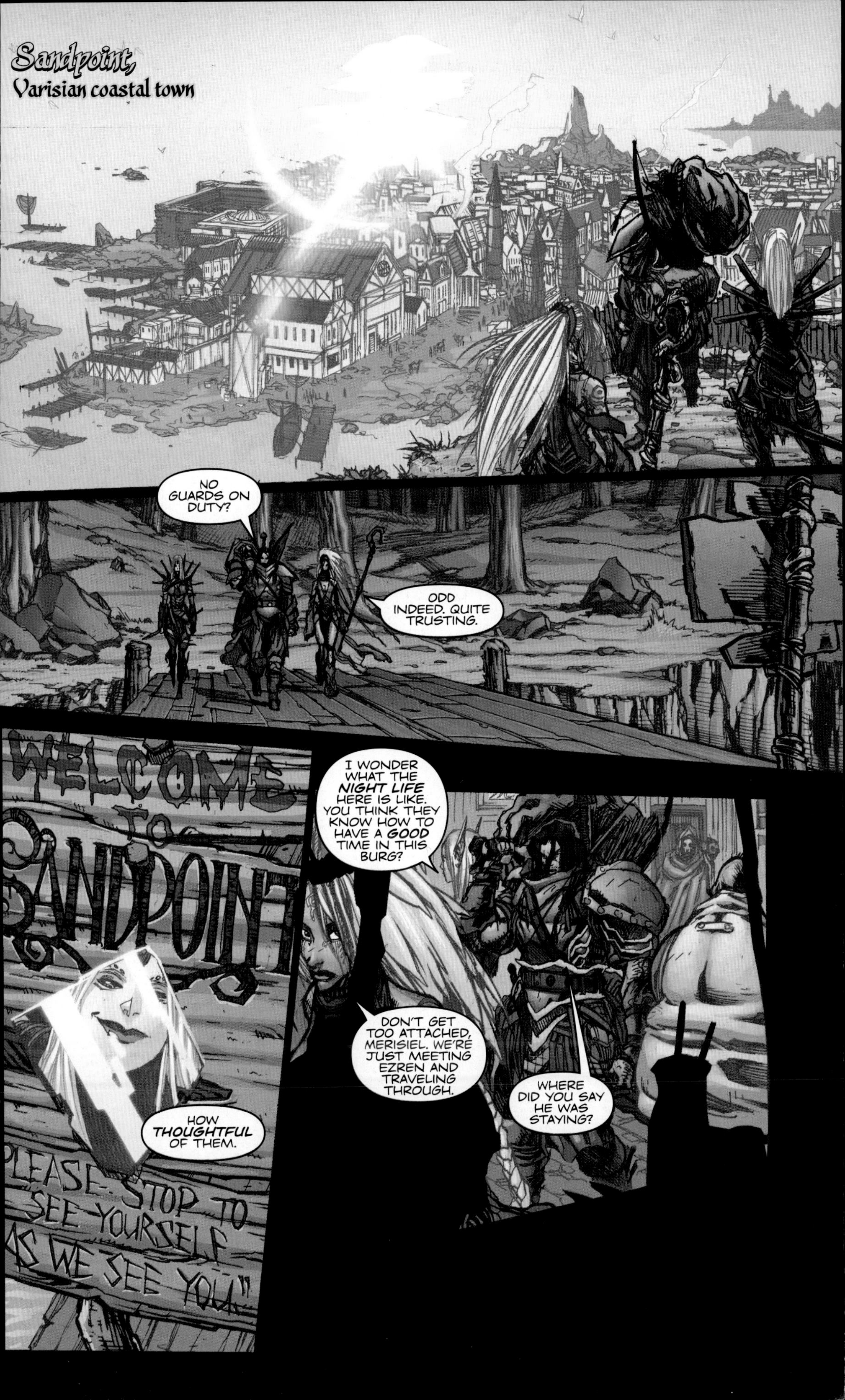

Sandpoint,
Varisian coastal town
NO GUARDS ON DUTY?
ODD INDEED. QUITE TRUSTING.
WELCOME TO SANDPOINT
PLEASE STOP TO SEE YOURSELF AS WE SEE YOU."
HOW THOUGHTFUL OF THEM.
I WONDER WHAT THE NIGHT LIFE HERE IS LIKE. YOU THINK THEY KNOW HOW TO HAVE A GOOD TIME IN THIS BURG?
DON'T GET TOO ATTACHED, MERISIEL. WE'RE JUST MEETING EZREN AND TRAVELING THROUGH.
WHERE DID YOU SAY HE WAS STAYING?

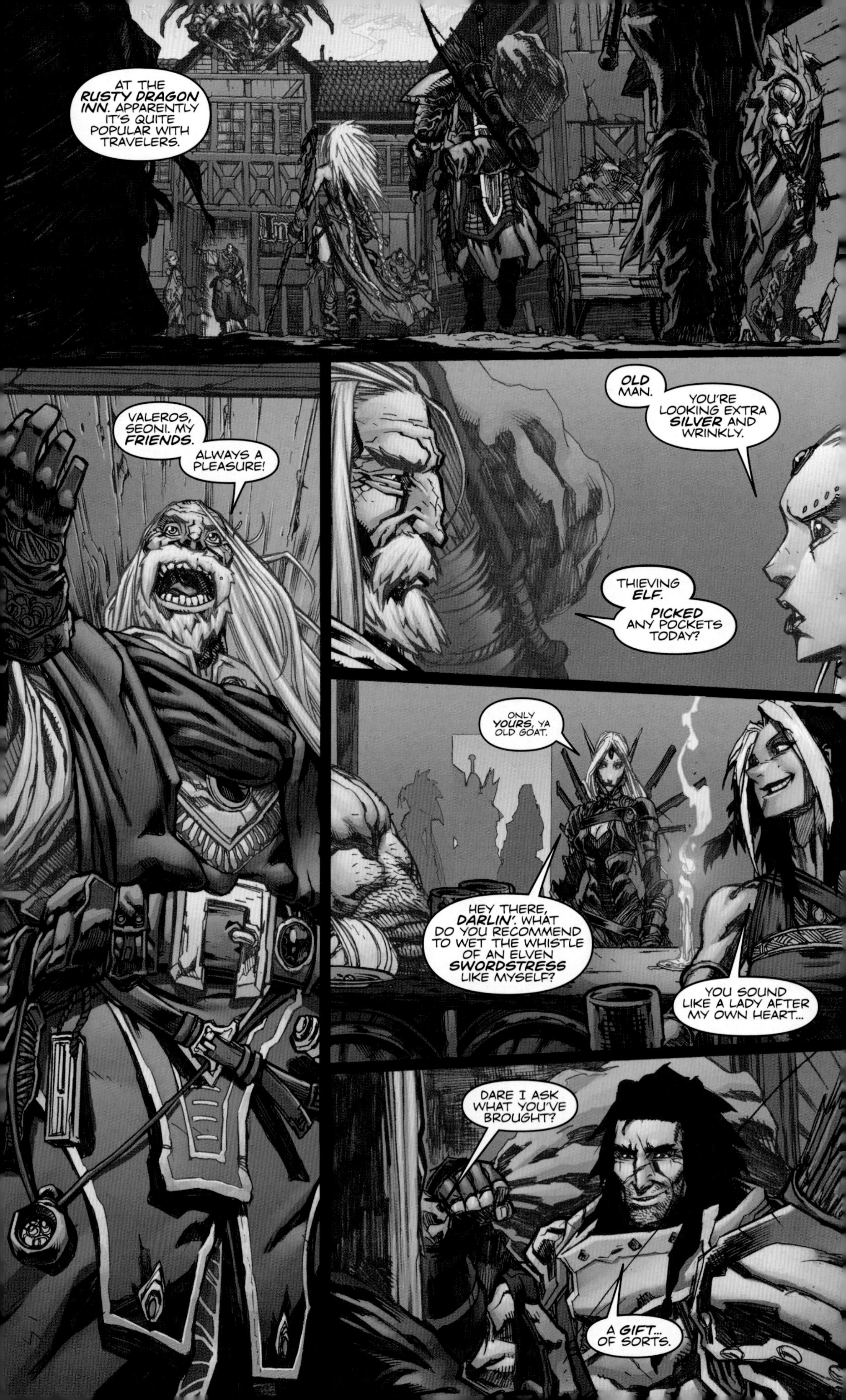
AT THE RUSTY DRAGON INN. APPARENTLY IT'S QUITE POPULAR WITH TRAVELERS.
VALEROS, SEONI. MY FRIENDS.
ALWAYS A PLEASURE!
OLD MAN.
YOU'RE LOOKING EXTRA SILVER AND WRINKLY.
THIEVING ELF.
PICKED ANY POCKETS TODAY?
ONLY YOURS, YA OLD GOAT.
HEY THERE, DARLIN'. WHAT DO YOU RECOMMEND TO WET THE WHISTLE OF AN ELVEN SWORDSTRESS LIKE MYSELF?
YOU SOUND LIKE A LADY AFTER MY OWN HEART...
DARE I ASK WHAT YOU'VE BROUGHT?
A GIFT... OF SORTS.

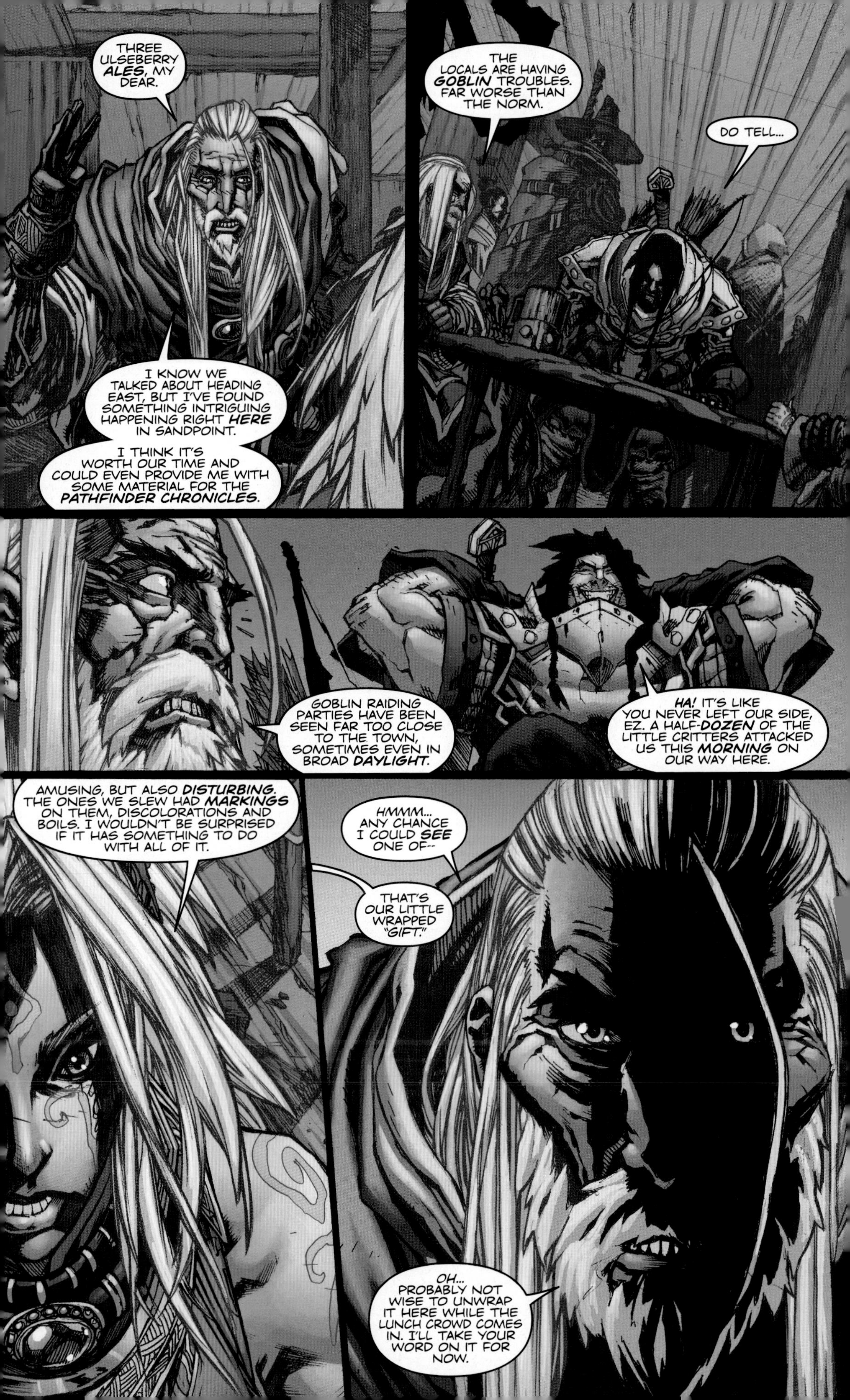
THREE ULSEBERRY ALES, MY DEAR.
I KNOW WE TALKED ABOUT HEADING EAST, BUT I'VE FOUND SOMETHING INTRIGUING HAPPENING RIGHT HERE IN SANDPOINT.
I THINK IT'S WORTH OUR TIME AND COULD EVEN PROVIDE ME WITH SOME MATERIAL FOR THE PATHFINDER CHRONICLES.
THE LOCALS ARE HAVING GOBLIN TROUBLES. FAR WORSE THAN THE NORM.
DO TELL...
GOBLIN RAIDING PARTIES HAVE BEEN SEEN FAR TOO CLOSE TO THE TOWN, SOMETIMES EVEN IN BROAD DAYLIGHT.
HA! IT'S LIKE YOU NEVER LEFT OUR SIDE, EZ. A HALF-DOZEN OF THE LITTLE CRITTERS ATTACKED US THIS MORNING ON OUR WAY HERE.
AMUSING, BUT ALSO DISTURBING. THE ONES WE SLEW HAD MARKINGS ON THEM, DISCOLORATIONS AND BOILS. I WOULDN'T BE SURPRISED IF IT HAS SOMETHING TO DO WITH ALL OF IT.
HMMM... ANY CHANCE I COULD SEE ONE OF--
THAT'S OUR LITTLE WRAPPED "GIFT."
OH... PROBABLY NOT WISE TO UNWRAP IT HERE WHILE THE LUNCH CROWD COMES IN. I'LL TAKE YOUR WORD ON IT FOR NOW.

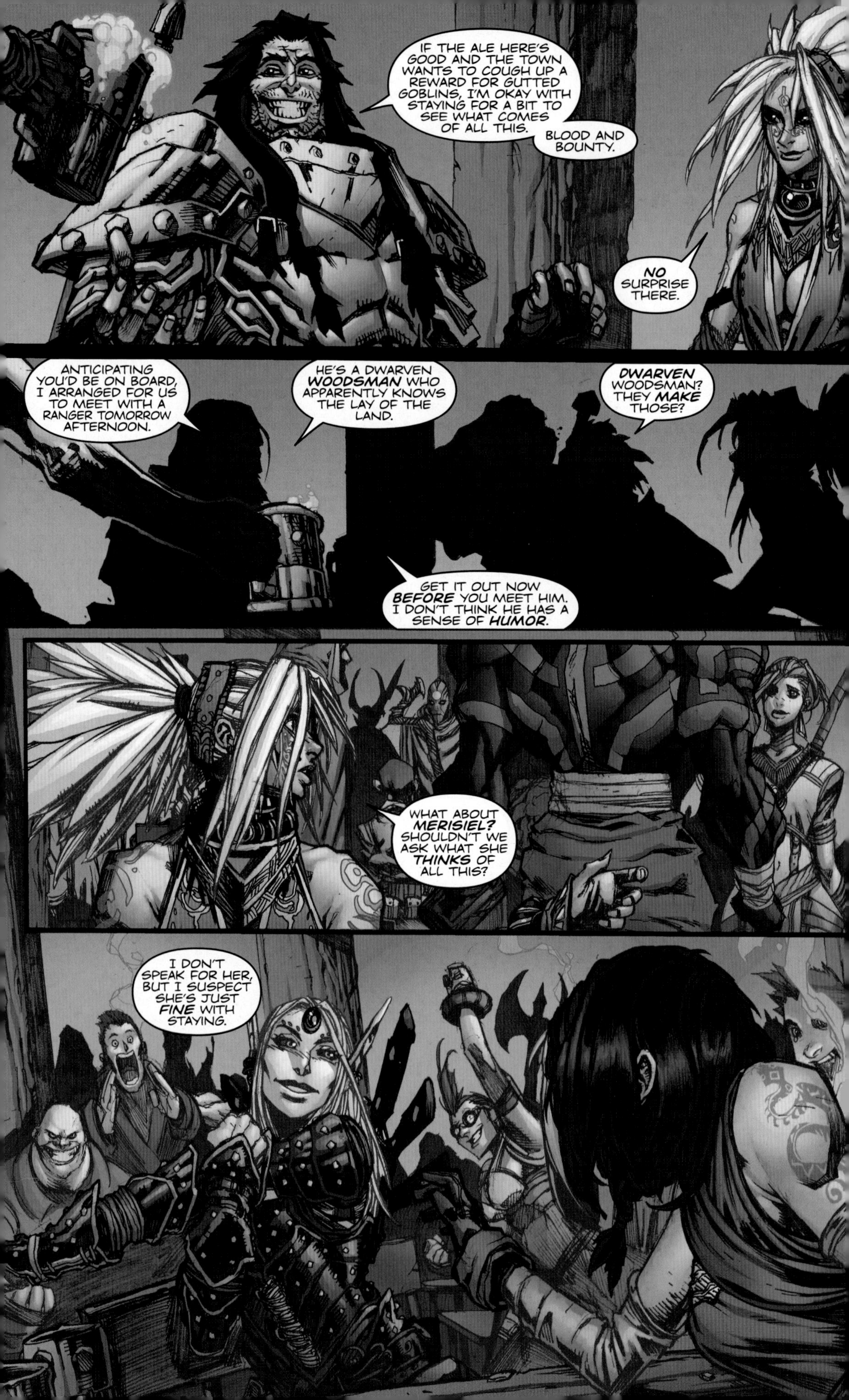
IF THE ALE HERE'S GOOD AND THE TOWN WANTS TO COUGH UP A REWARD FOR GUTTED GOBLINS, I'M OKAY WITH STAYING FOR A BIT TO SEE WHAT COMES OF ALL THIS.
BLOOD AND BOUNTY.
NO SURPRISE THERE.
ANTICIPATING YOU'D BE ON BOARD, I ARRANGED FOR US TO MEET WITH A RANGER TOMORROW AFTERNOON.
HE'S A DWARVEN WOODSMAN WHO APPARENTLY KNOWS THE LAY OF THE LAND.
DWARVEN WOODSMAN? THEY MAKE THOSE?
GET IT OUT NOW BEFORE YOU MEET HIM. I DON'T THINK HE HAS A SENSE OF HUMOR.
WHAT ABOUT MERISIEL? SHOULDN'T WE ASK WHAT SHE THINKS OF ALL THIS?
I DON'T SPEAK FOR HER, BUT I SUSPECT SHE'S JUST FINE WITH STAYING.

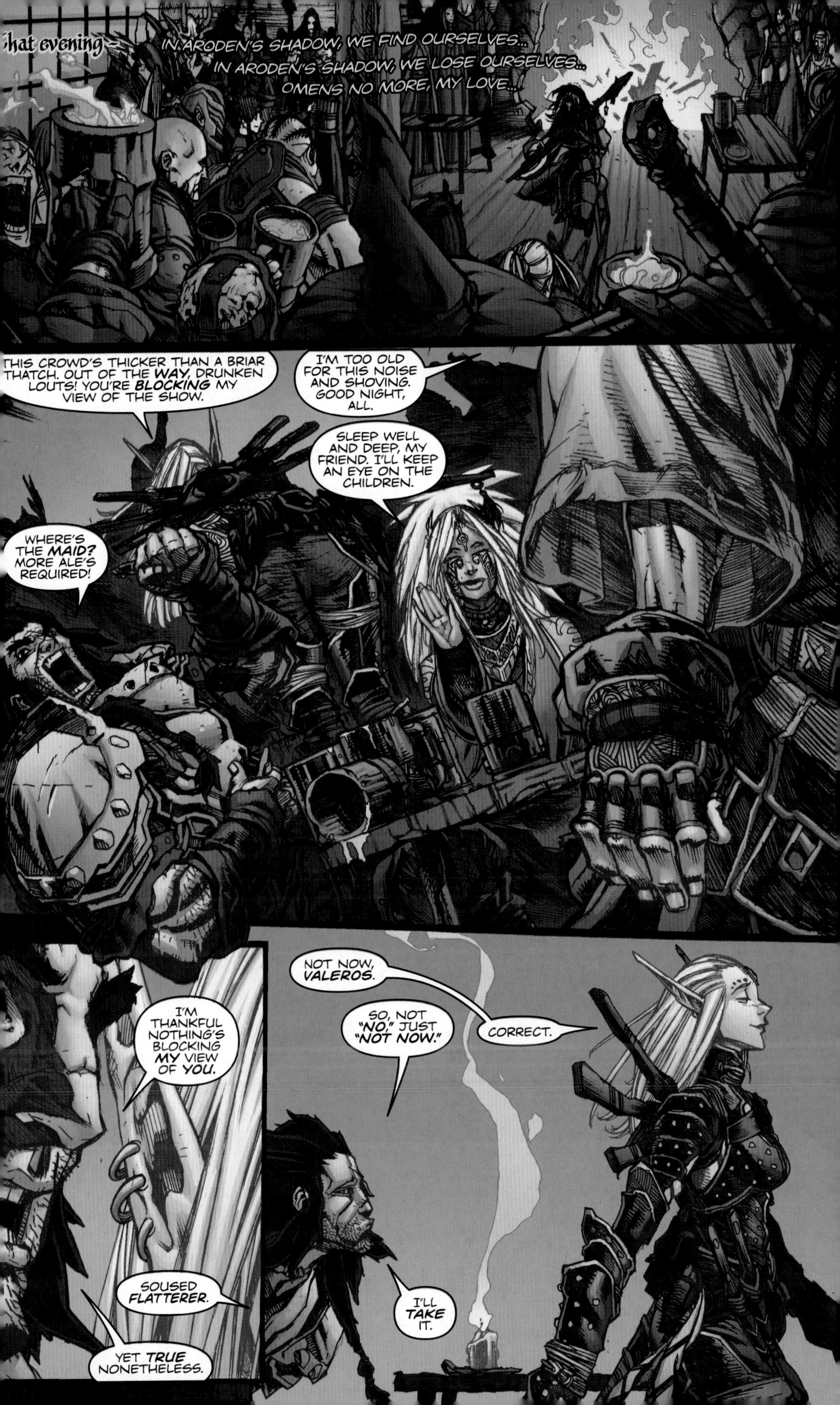

hat evening –
IN ARODEN'S SHADOW, WE FIND OURSELVES...
IN ARODEN'S SHADOW, WE LOSE OURSELVES...
OMENS NO MORE, MY LOVE...
THIS CROWD'S THICKER THAN A BRIAR THATCH. OUT OF THE WAY, DRUNKEN LOUTS! YOU'RE BLOCKING MY VIEW OF THE SHOW.
I'M TOO OLD FOR THIS NOISE AND SHOVING. GOOD NIGHT, ALL.
SLEEP WELL AND DEEP, MY FRIEND. I'LL KEEP AN EYE ON THE CHILDREN.
WHERE'S THE MAID? MORE ALE'S REQUIRED!
I'M THANKFUL NOTHING'S BLOCKING MY VIEW OF YOU.
SOUSED FLATTERER.
YET TRUE NONETHELESS.
NOT NOW, VALEROS.
SO, NOT "NO," JUST "NOT NOW."
CORRECT.
I'LL TAKE IT.

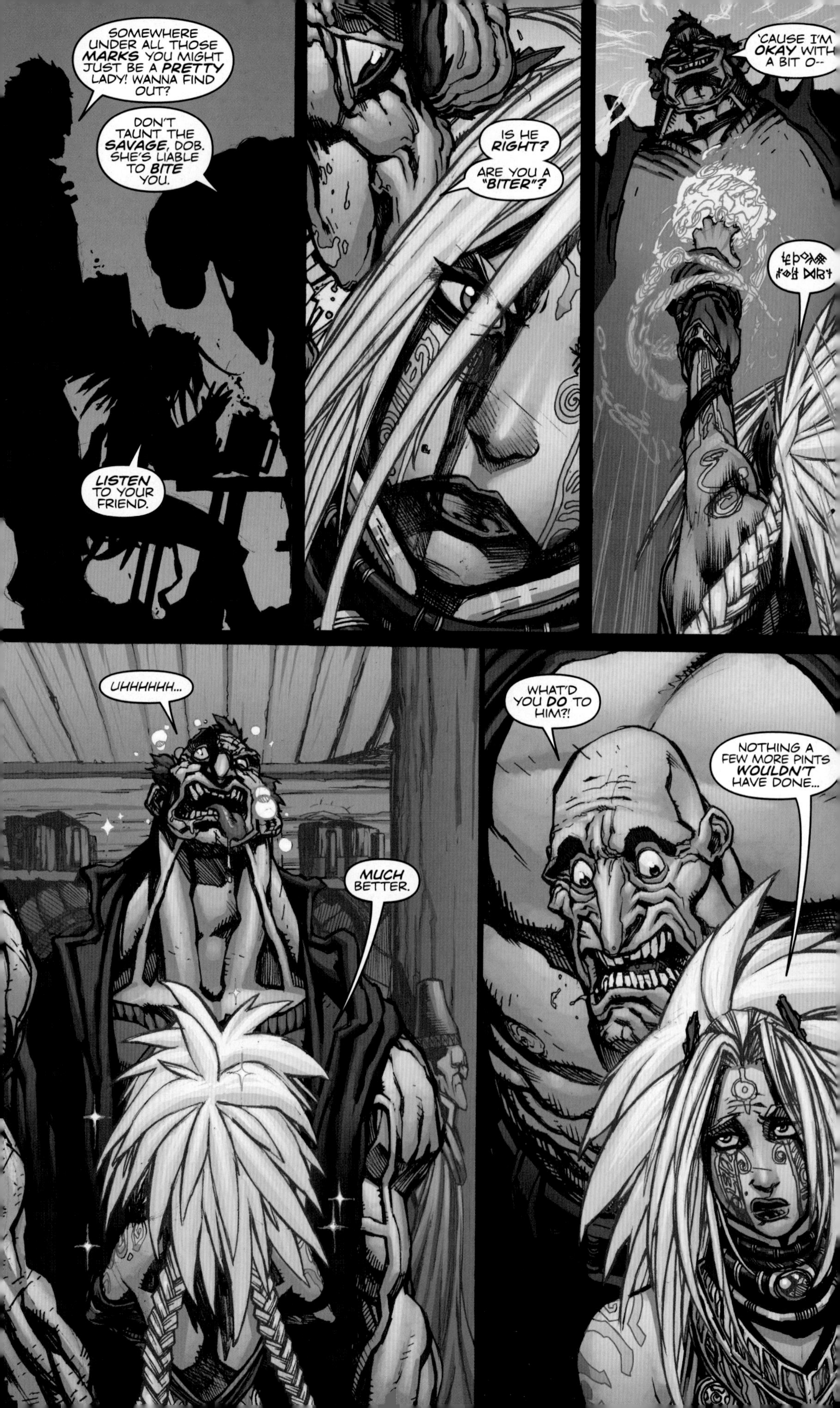
SOMEWHERE UNDER ALL THOSE MARKS YOU MIGHT JUST BE A PRETTY LADY! WANNA FIND OUT?
DON'T TAUNT THE SAVAGE, DOB. SHE'S LIABLE TO BITE YOU.
LISTEN TO YOUR FRIEND.
IS HE RIGHT?
ARE YOU A "BITER"?
'CAUSE I'M OKAY WITH A BIT O--
UHHHHHH...
MUCH BETTER.
WHAT'D YOU DO TO HIM?!
NOTHING A FEW MORE PINTS WOULDN'T HAVE DONE...

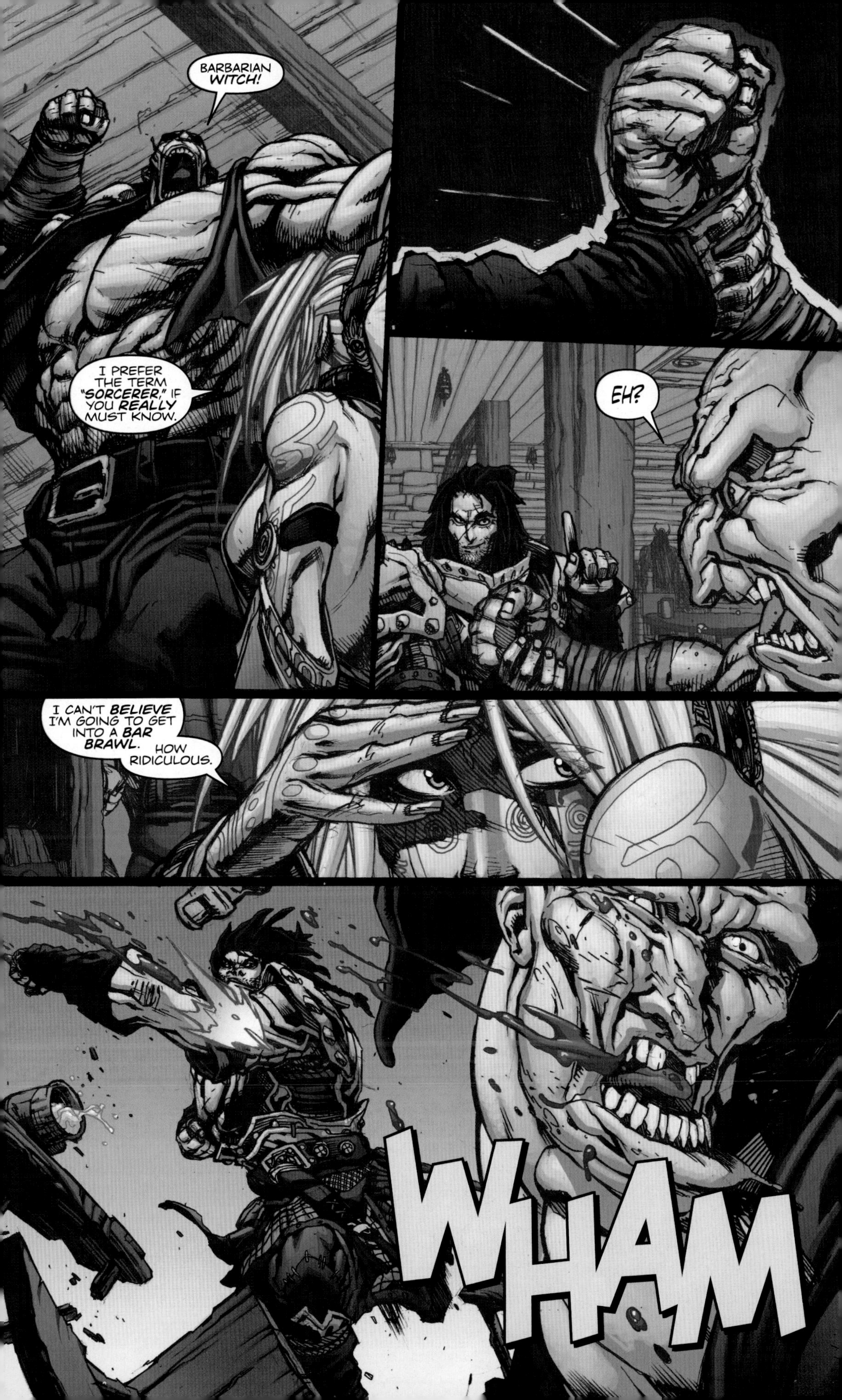
BARBARIAN WITCH!
I PREFER THE TERM "SORCERER," IF YOU REALLY MUST KNOW.
EH?
I CAN'T BELIEVE I'M GOING TO GET INTO A BAR BRAWL. HOW RIDICULOUS.
WHAM

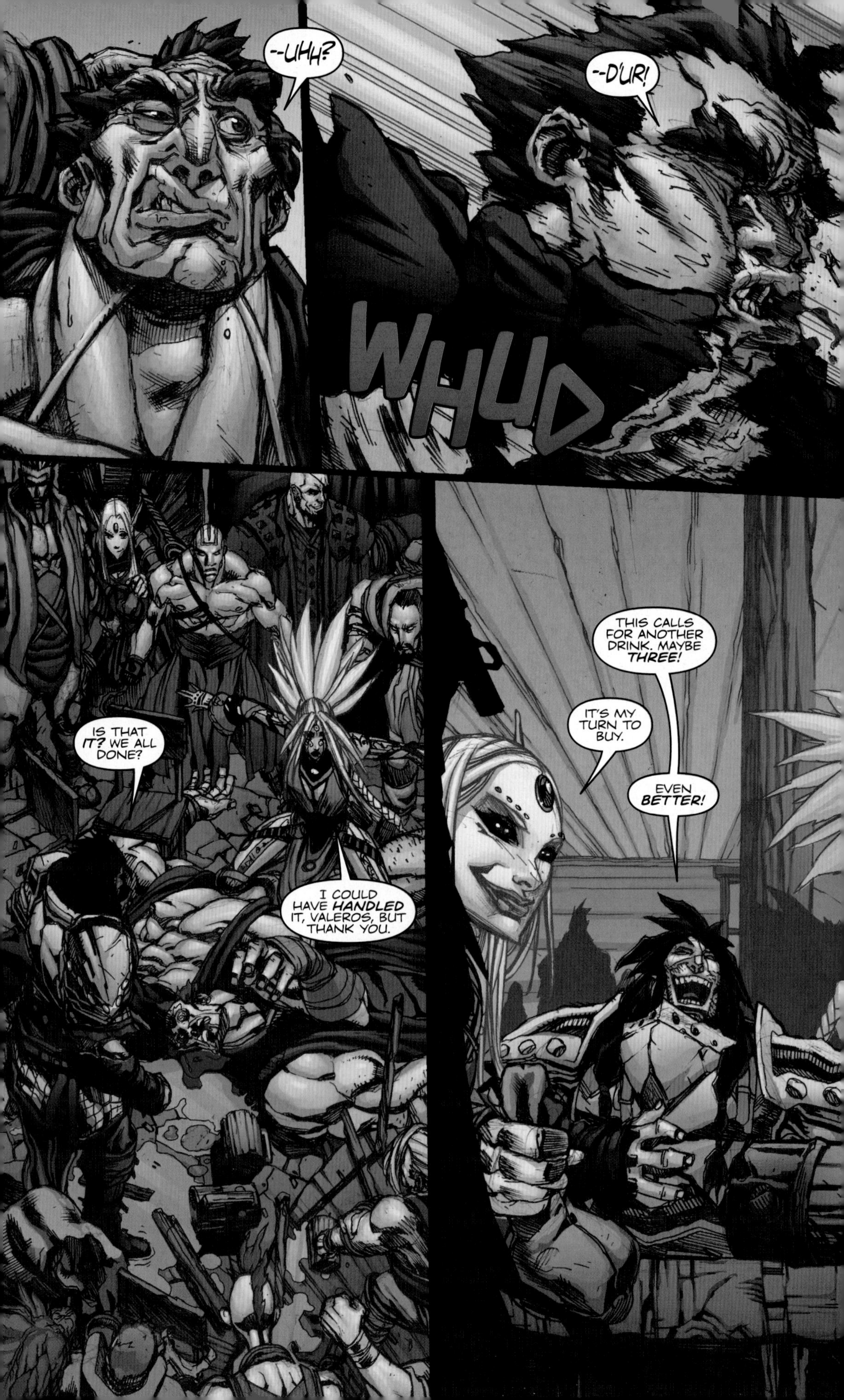
--UHH?
--D'UR!
WHUD
IS THAT *IT?* WE ALL DONE?
I COULD HAVE **HANDLED** IT, VALEROS, BUT THANK YOU.
THIS CALLS FOR ANOTHER DRINK. MAYBE ***THREE!***
IT'S MY TURN TO BUY.
EVEN ***BETTER!***

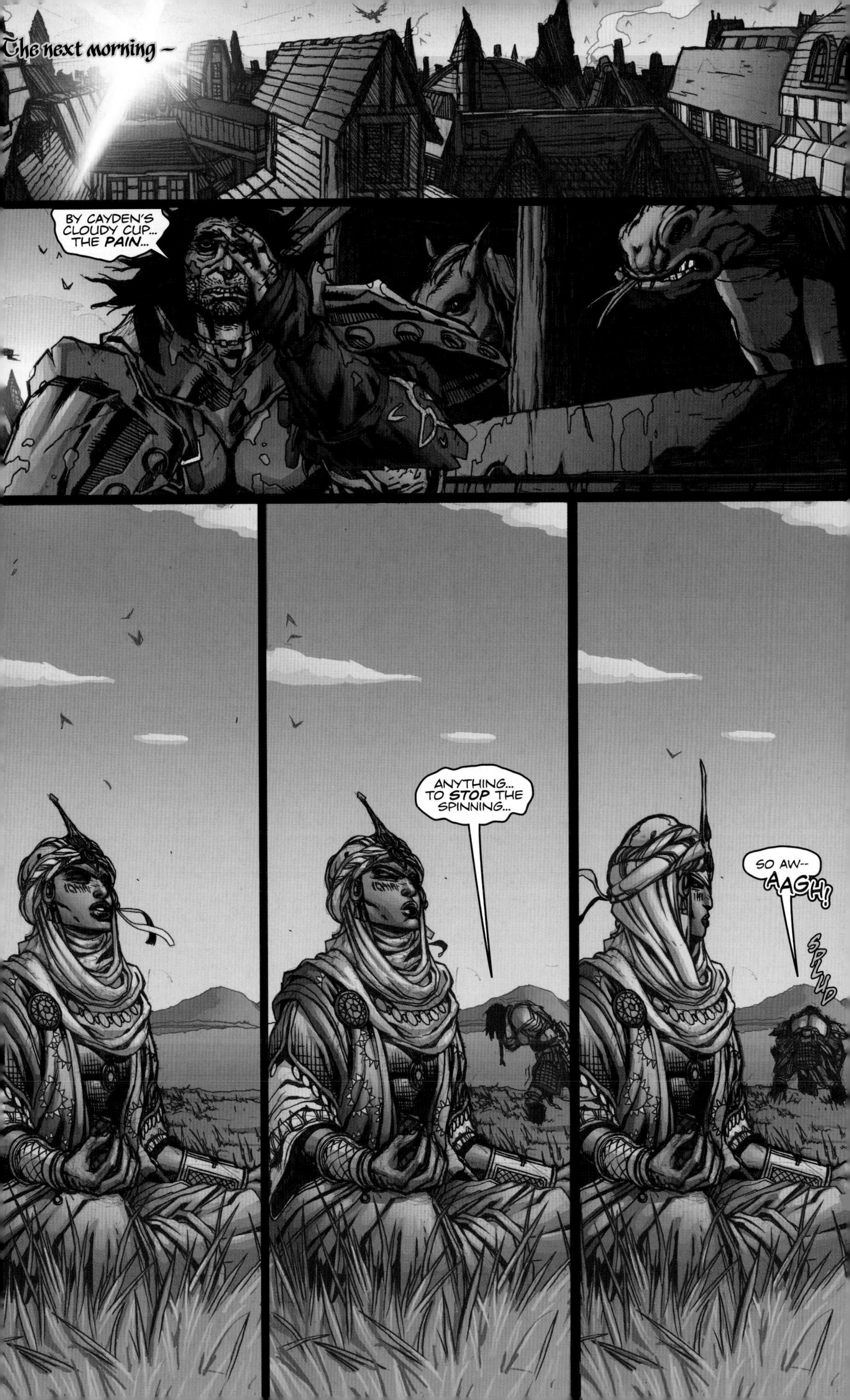
The next morning –
BY CAYDEN'S CLOUDY CUP... THE PAIN...
ANYTHING... TO STOP THE SPINNING...
SO AW--
AAGH!
SPLUD

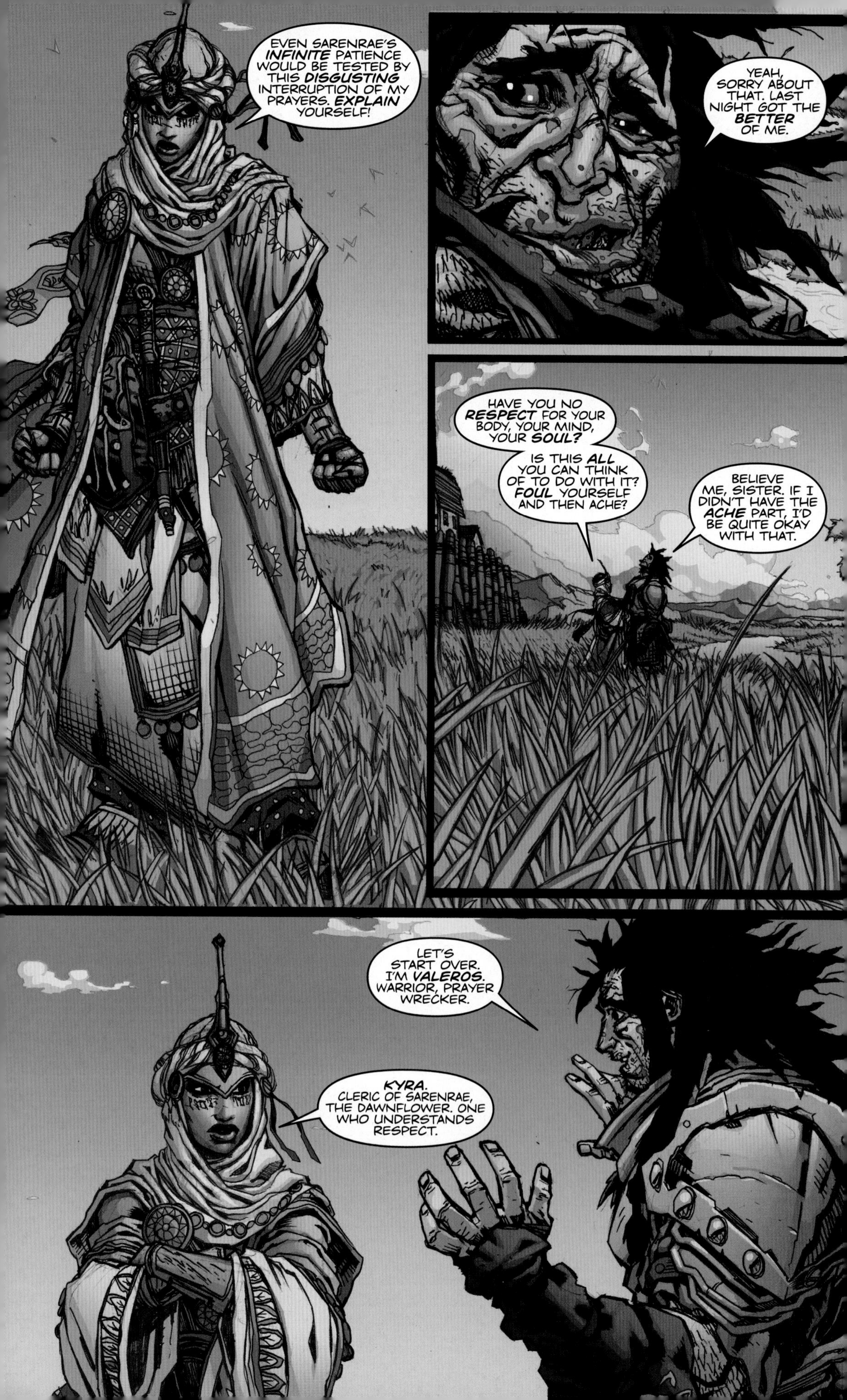
EVEN SARENRAE'S ***INFINITE*** PATIENCE WOULD BE TESTED BY THIS ***DISGUSTING*** INTERRUPTION OF MY PRAYERS. ***EXPLAIN*** YOURSELF!
YEAH, SORRY ABOUT THAT. LAST NIGHT GOT THE ***BETTER*** OF ME.
HAVE YOU NO ***RESPECT*** FOR YOUR BODY, YOUR MIND, YOUR ***SOUL?***
IS THIS ***ALL*** YOU CAN THINK OF TO DO WITH IT? ***FOUL*** YOURSELF AND THEN ACHE?
BELIEVE ME, SISTER. IF I DIDN'T HAVE THE ***ACHE*** PART, I'D BE QUITE OKAY WITH THAT.
LET'S START OVER. I'M ***VALEROS***. WARRIOR, PRAYER WRECKER.
KYRA. CLERIC OF SARENRAE, THE DAWNFLOWER. ONE WHO UNDERSTANDS RESPECT.

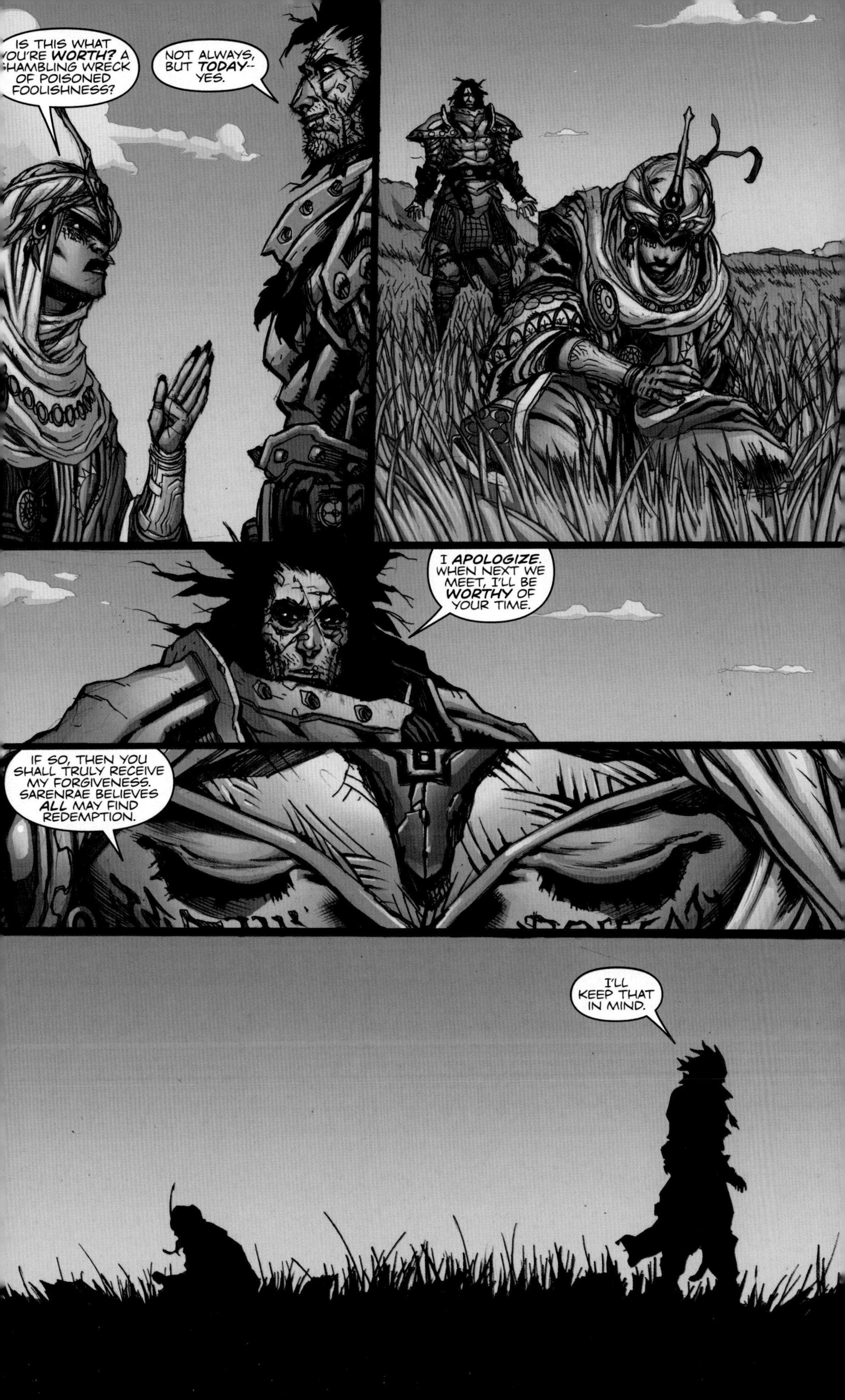
IS THIS WHAT YOU'RE **WORTH?** A SHAMBLING WRECK OF POISONED FOOLISHNESS?
NOT ALWAYS, BUT **TODAY**-- YES.
I **APOLOGIZE**. WHEN NEXT WE MEET, I'LL BE **WORTHY** OF YOUR TIME.
IF SO, THEN YOU SHALL TRULY RECEIVE MY FORGIVENESS. SARENRAE BELIEVES **ALL** MAY FIND REDEMPTION.
I'LL KEEP THAT IN MIND.

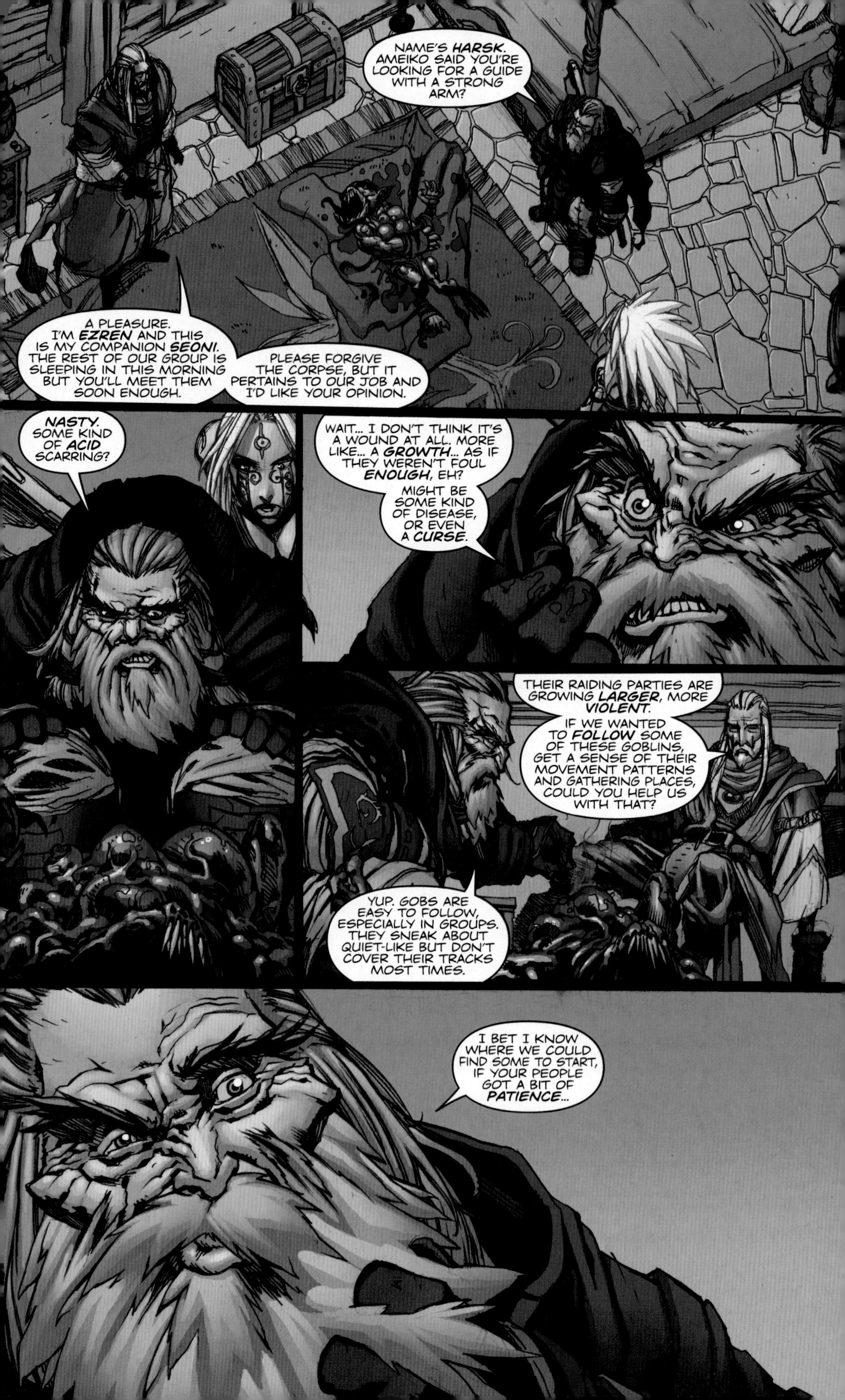
NAME'S HARSK. AMEIKO SAID YOU'RE LOOKING FOR A GUIDE WITH A STRONG ARM?
A PLEASURE. I'M EZREN AND THIS IS MY COMPANION SEONI. THE REST OF OUR GROUP IS SLEEPING IN THIS MORNING BUT YOU'LL MEET THEM SOON ENOUGH.
PLEASE FORGIVE THE CORPSE, BUT IT PERTAINS TO OUR JOB AND I'D LIKE YOUR OPINION.
NASTY. SOME KIND OF ACID SCARRING?
WAIT... I DON'T THINK IT'S A WOUND AT ALL. MORE LIKE... A GROWTH... AS IF THEY WEREN'T FOUL ENOUGH, EH?
MIGHT BE SOME KIND OF DISEASE, OR EVEN A CURSE.
THEIR RAIDING PARTIES ARE GROWING LARGER, MORE VIOLENT.
IF WE WANTED TO FOLLOW SOME OF THESE GOBLINS, GET A SENSE OF THEIR MOVEMENT PATTERNS AND GATHERING PLACES, COULD YOU HELP US WITH THAT?
YUP. GOBS ARE EASY TO FOLLOW, ESPECIALLY IN GROUPS. THEY SNEAK ABOUT QUIET-LIKE BUT DON'T COVER THEIR TRACKS MOST TIMES.
I BET I KNOW WHERE WE COULD FIND SOME TO START, IF YOUR PEOPLE GOT A BIT OF PATIENCE...

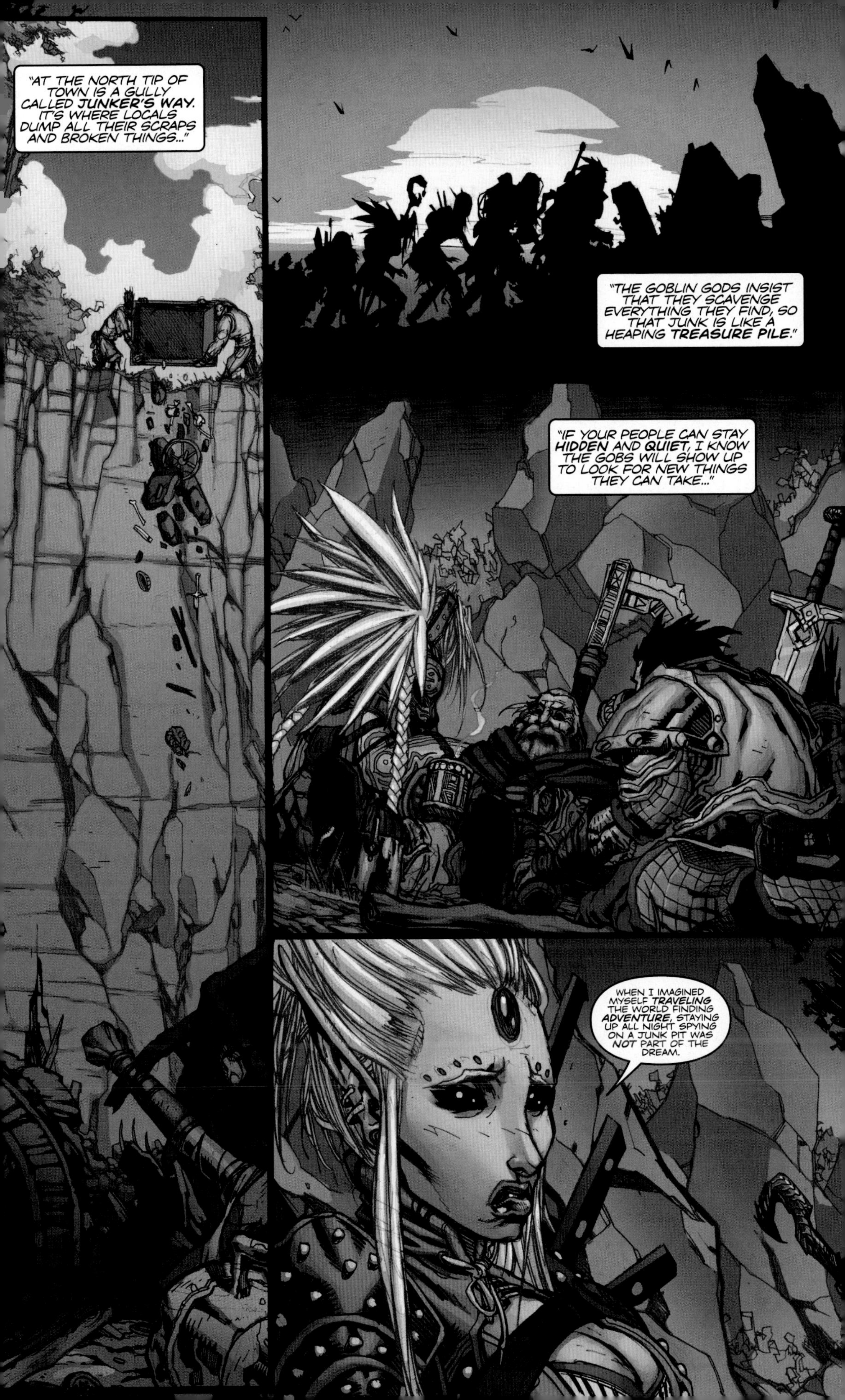
"AT THE NORTH TIP OF TOWN IS A GULLY CALLED JUNKER'S WAY. IT'S WHERE LOCALS DUMP ALL THEIR SCRAPS AND BROKEN THINGS..."
"THE GOBLIN GODS INSIST THAT THEY SCAVENGE EVERYTHING THEY FIND, SO THAT JUNK IS LIKE A HEAPING TREASURE PILE."
"IF YOUR PEOPLE CAN STAY HIDDEN AND QUIET, I KNOW THE GOBS WILL SHOW UP TO LOOK FOR NEW THINGS THEY CAN TAKE..."
WHEN I IMAGINED MYSELF TRAVELING THE WORLD FINDING ADVENTURE, STAYING UP ALL NIGHT SPYING ON A JUNK PIT WAS NOT PART OF THE DREAM.

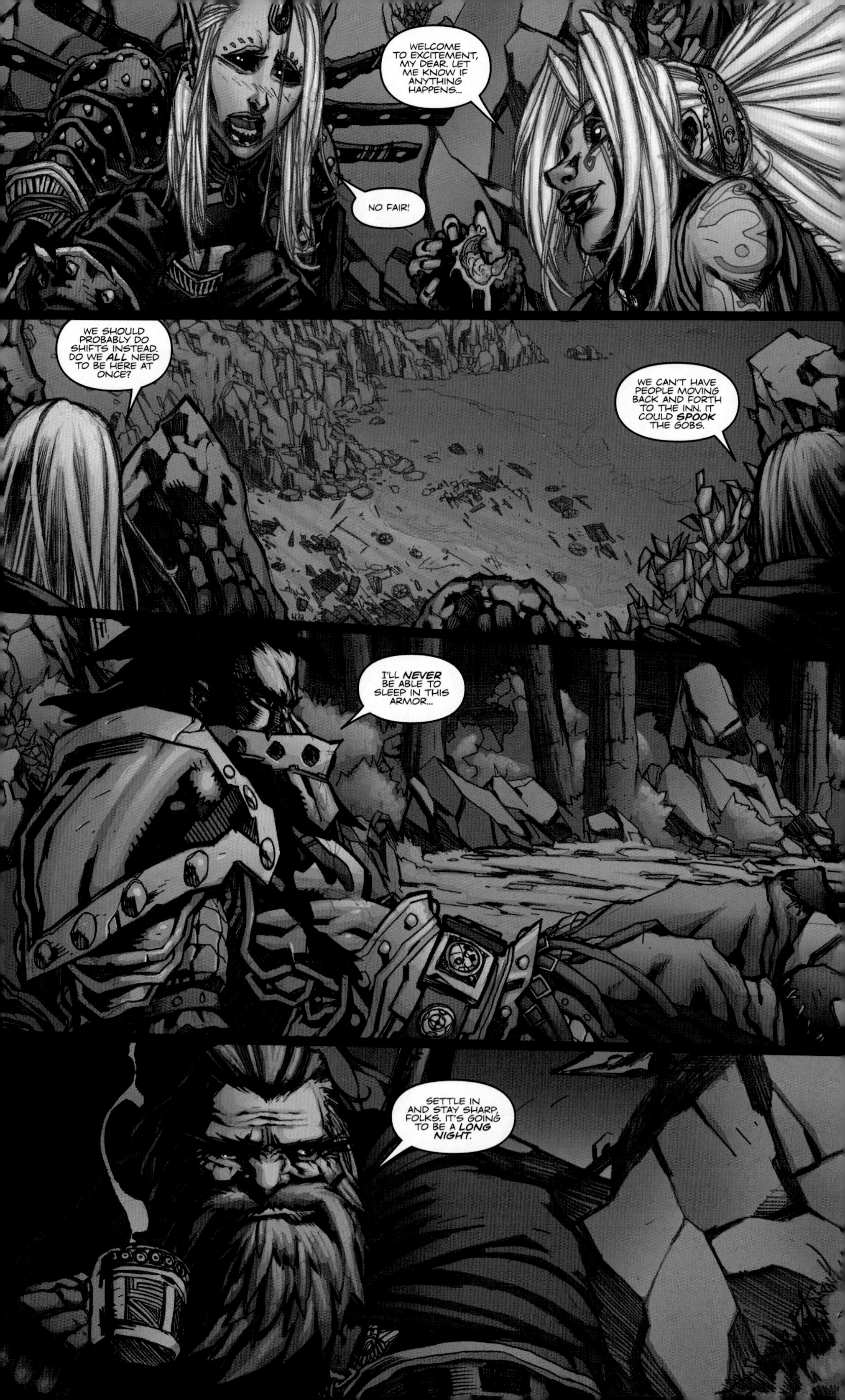
WELCOME TO EXCITEMENT, MY DEAR. LET ME KNOW IF ANYTHING HAPPENS...
NO FAIR!
WE SHOULD PROBABLY DO SHIFTS INSTEAD. DO WE ALL NEED TO BE HERE AT ONCE?
WE CAN'T HAVE PEOPLE MOVING BACK AND FORTH TO THE INN. IT COULD SPOOK THE GOBS.
I'LL NEVER BE ABLE TO SLEEP IN THIS ARMOR...
SETTLE IN AND STAY SHARP, FOLKS. IT'S GOING TO BE A LONG NIGHT.

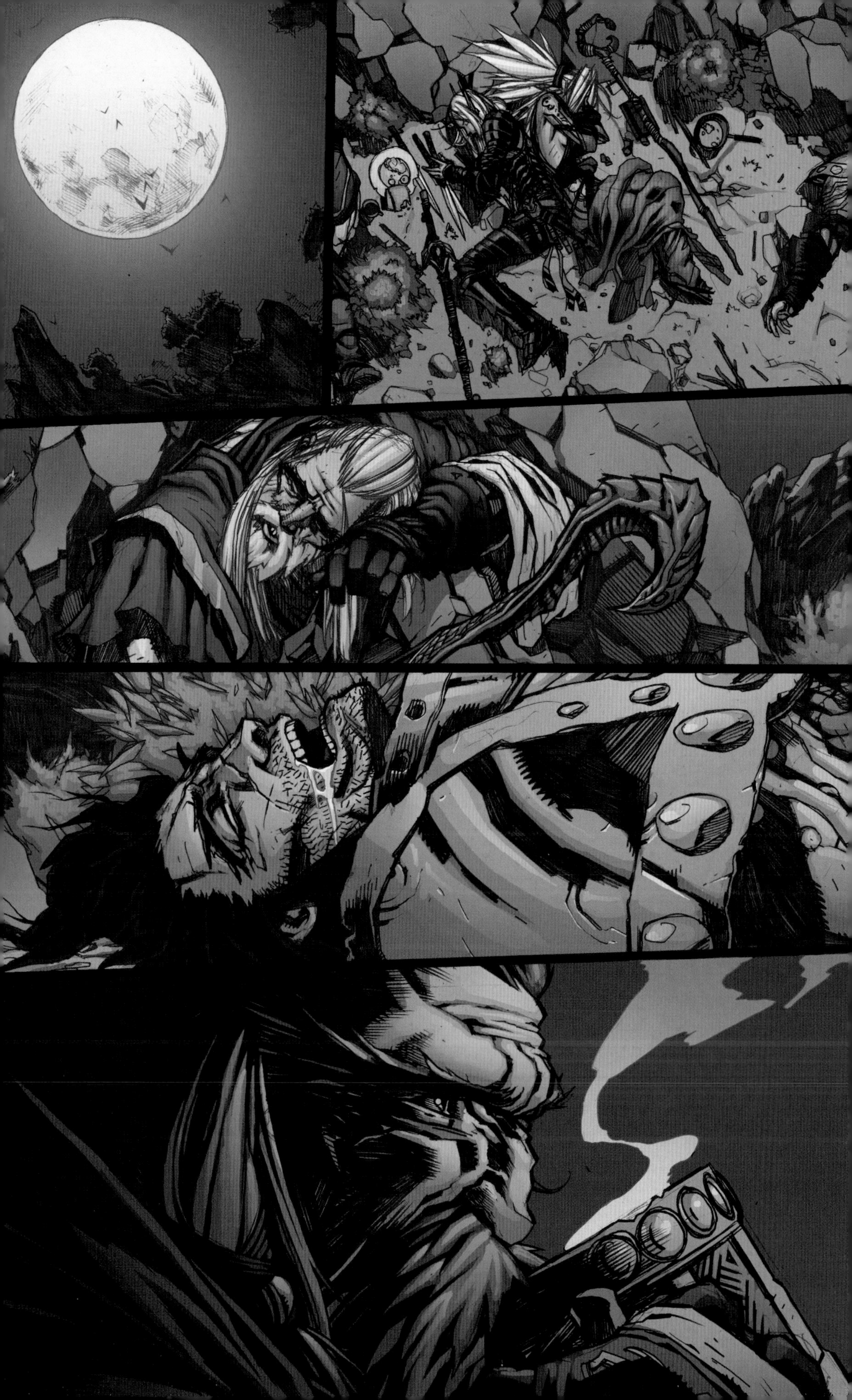

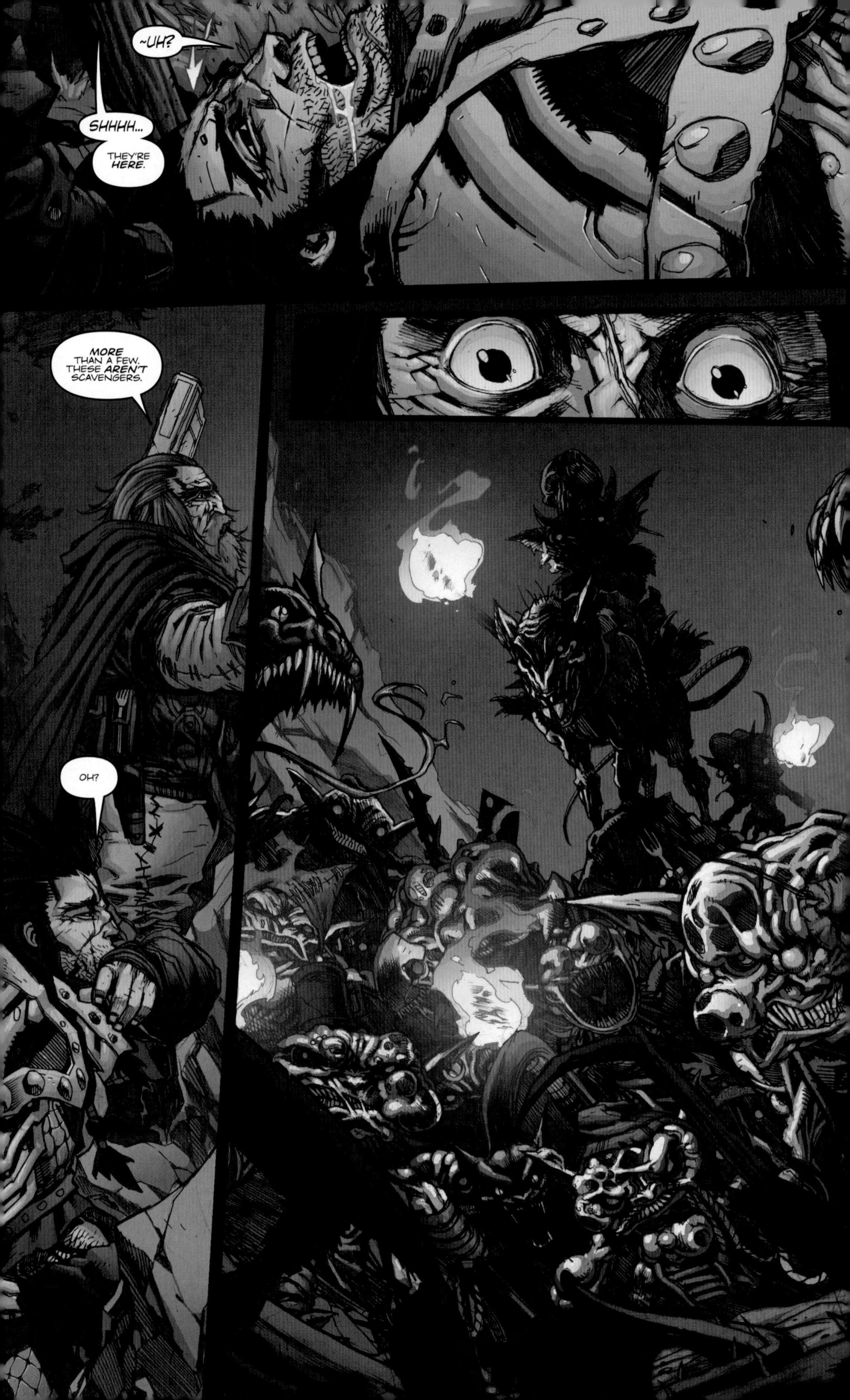
~UH?
SHHHH...
THEY'RE HERE.
MORE THAN A FEW. THESE AREN'T SCAVENGERS.
OH?

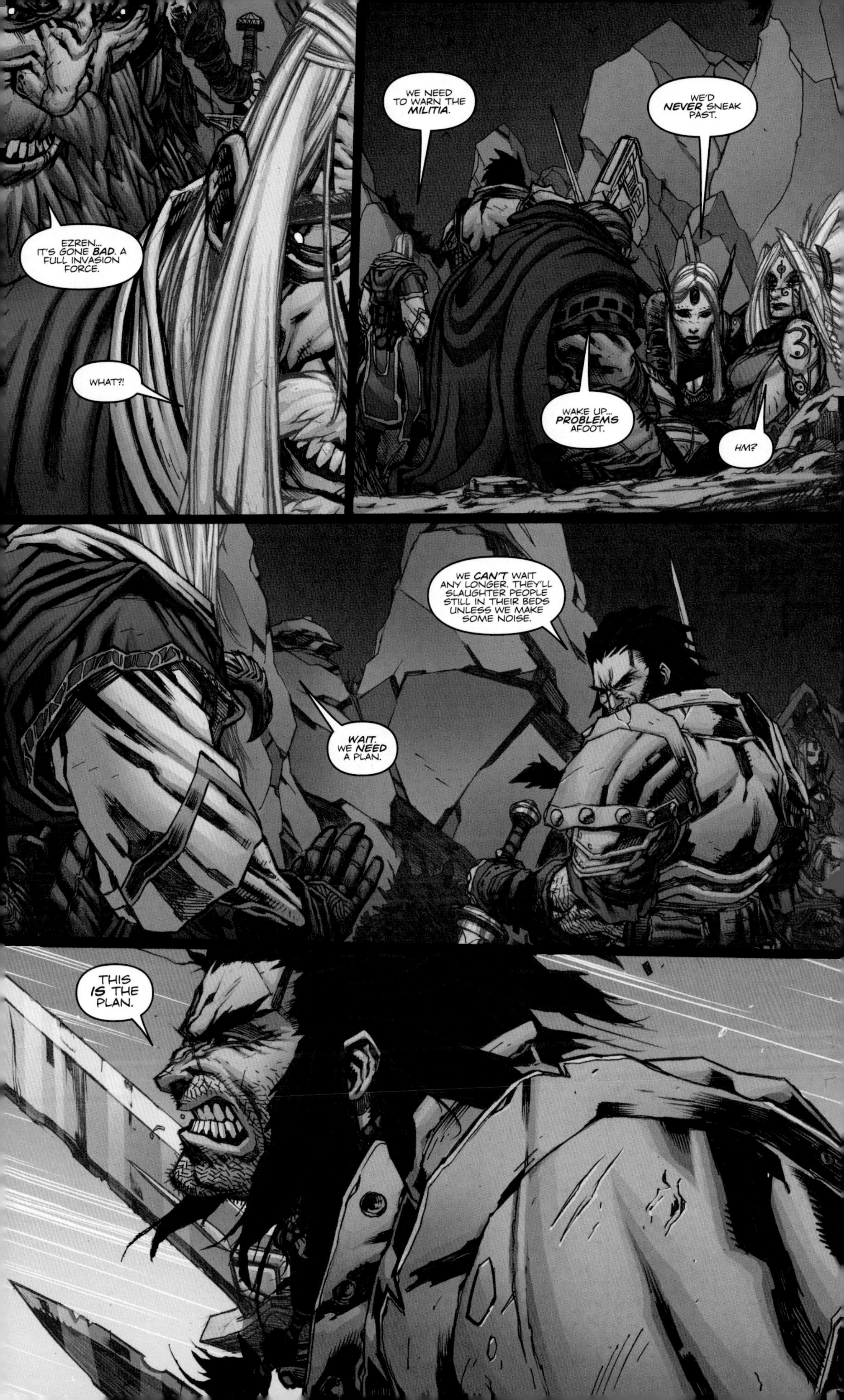
EZREN... IT'S GONE BAD. A FULL INVASION FORCE.
WHAT?!
WE NEED TO WARN THE MILITIA.
WE'D NEVER SNEAK PAST.
WAKE UP... PROBLEMS AFOOT.
HM?
WE CAN'T WAIT ANY LONGER. THEY'LL SLAUGHTER PEOPLE STILL IN THEIR BEDS UNLESS WE MAKE SOME NOISE.
WAIT. WE NEED A PLAN.
THIS IS THE PLAN.

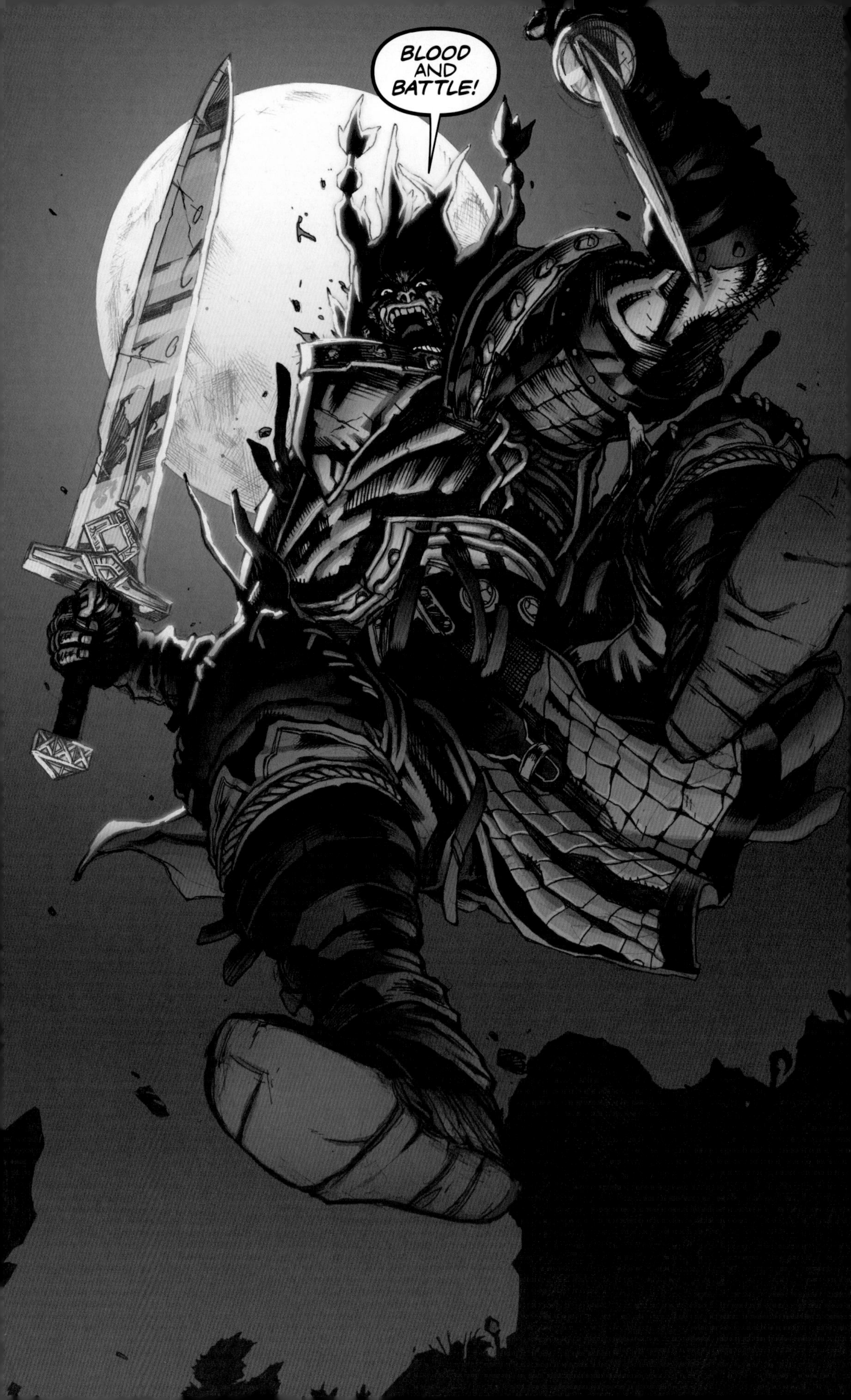
BLOOD AND BATTLE!

CHAPTER 2

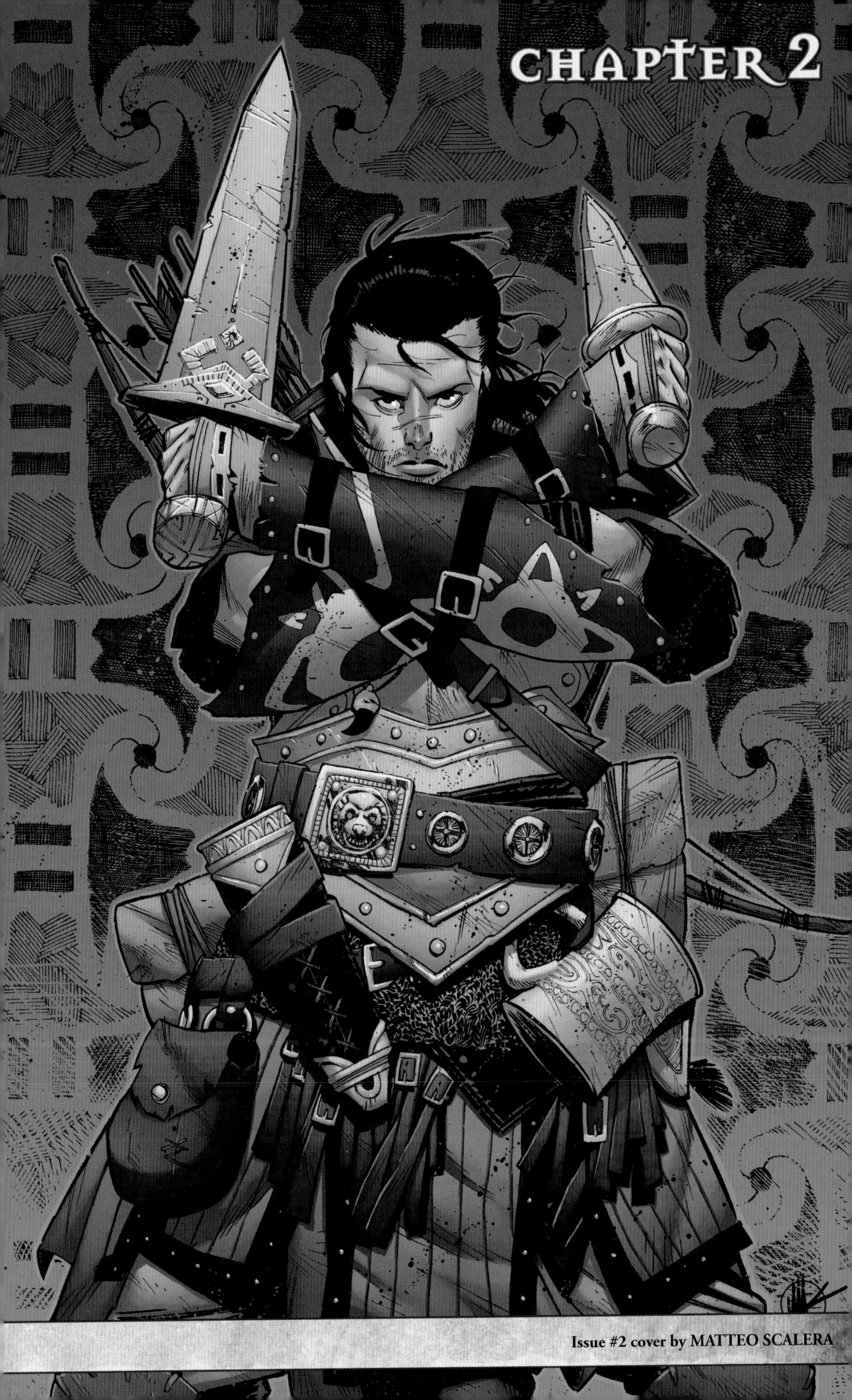

Issue #2 cover by MATTEO SCALERA

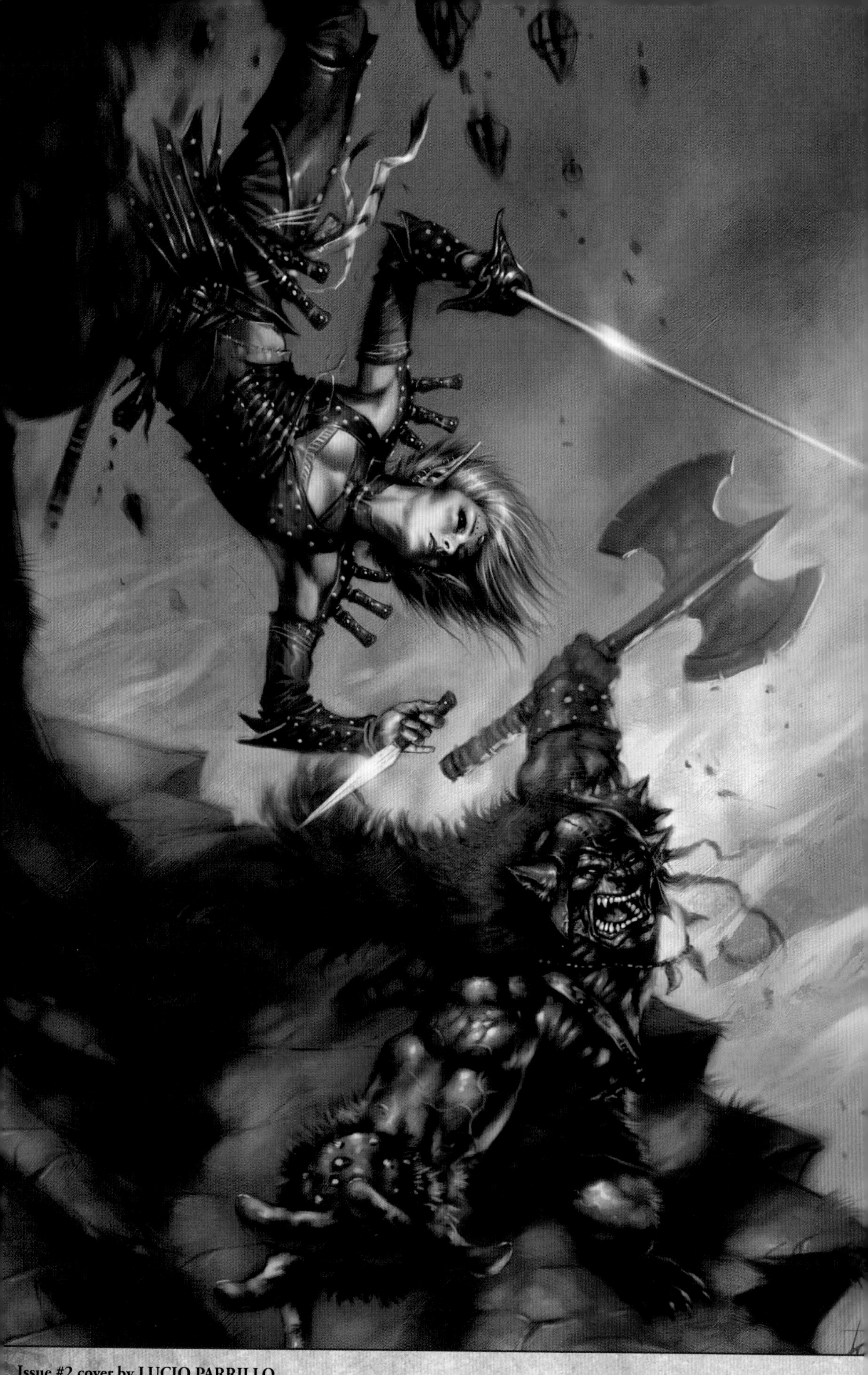

Issue #2 cover by LUCIO PARRILLO

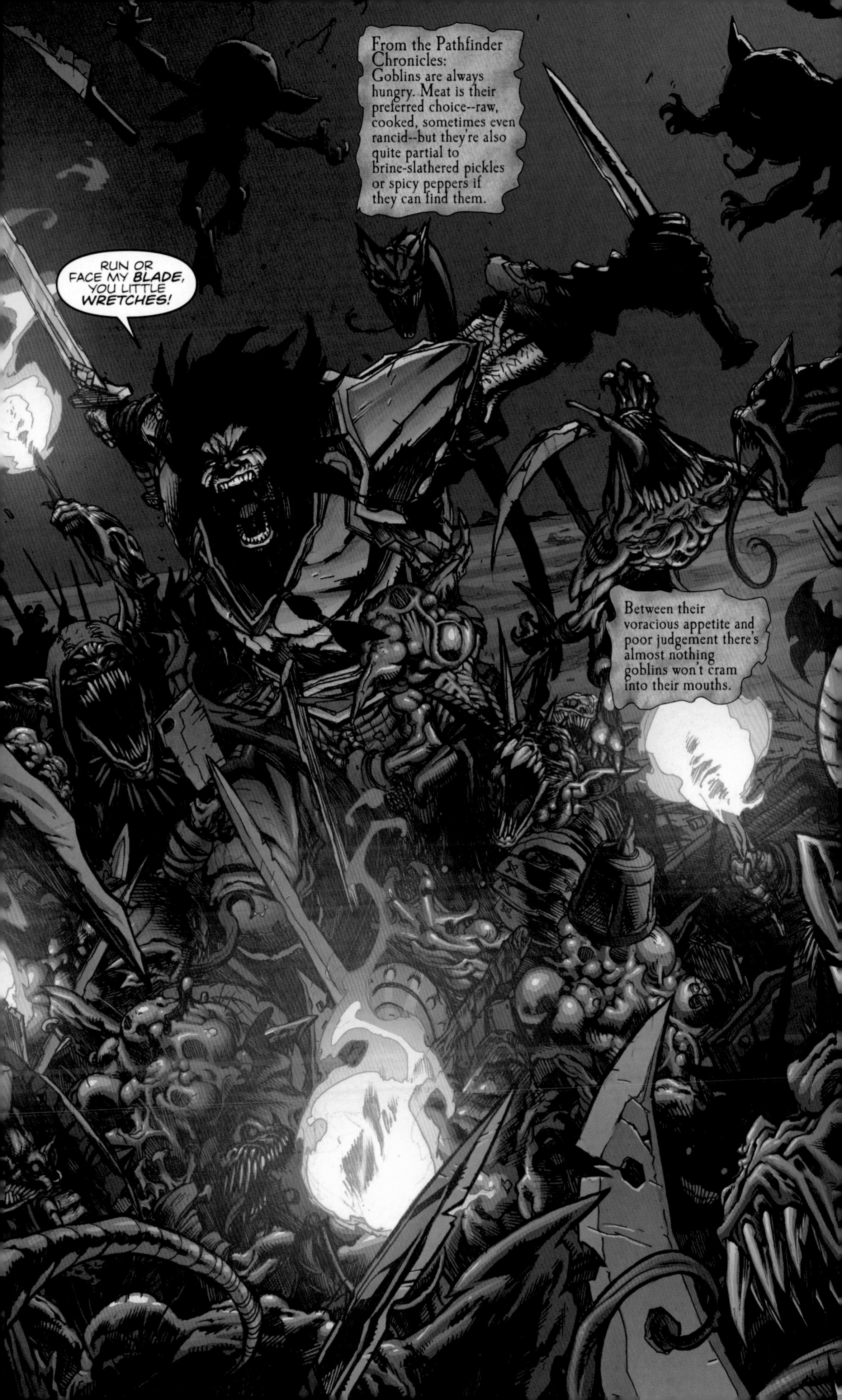
From the Pathfinder Chronicles:
Goblins are always hungry. Meat is their preferred choice--raw, cooked, sometimes even rancid--but they're also quite partial to brine-slathered pickles or spicy peppers if they can find them.
RUN OR FACE MY BLADE, YOU LITTLE WRETCHES!
Between their voracious appetite and poor judgement there's almost nothing goblins won't cram into their mouths.

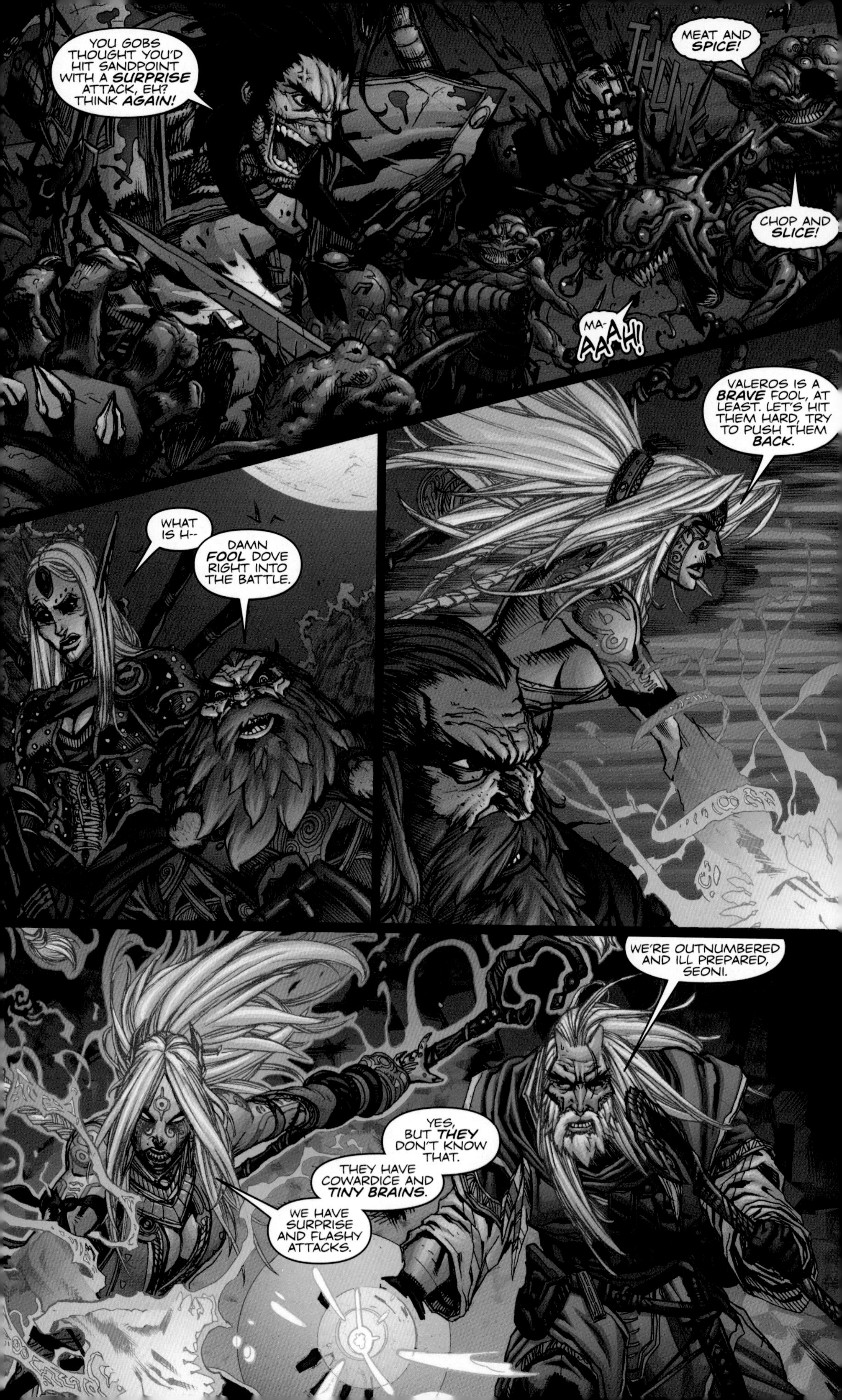
YOU GOBS THOUGHT YOU'D HIT SANDPOINT WITH A SURPRISE ATTACK, EH? THINK AGAIN!
THUNK
MEAT AND SPICE!
CHOP AND SLICE!
MA-AAAH!
VALEROS IS A BRAVE FOOL, AT LEAST. LET'S HIT THEM HARD, TRY TO PUSH THEM BACK.
WHAT IS H--
DAMN FOOL DOVE RIGHT INTO THE BATTLE.
WE'RE OUTNUMBERED AND ILL PREPARED, SEONI.
YES, BUT THEY DON'T KNOW THAT.
THEY HAVE COWARDICE AND TINY BRAINS.
WE HAVE SURPRISE AND FLASHY ATTACKS.

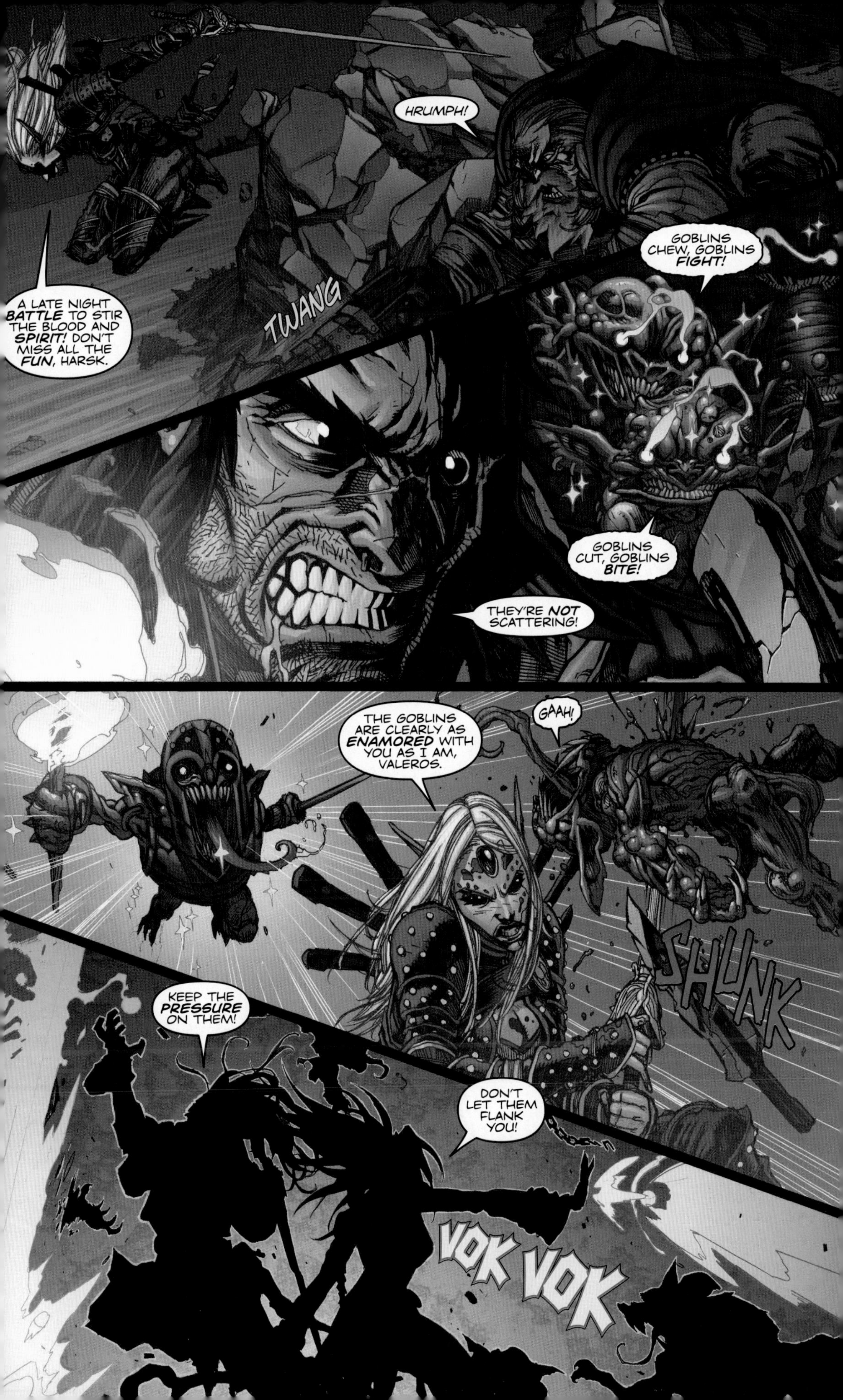

HRUMPH!
A LATE NIGHT BATTLE TO STIR THE BLOOD AND SPIRIT! DON'T MISS ALL THE FUN, HARSK.
TWANG
GOBLINS CHEW, GOBLINS FIGHT!
GOBLINS CUT, GOBLINS BITE!
THEY'RE NOT SCATTERING!
THE GOBLINS ARE CLEARLY AS ENAMORED WITH YOU AS I AM, VALEROS.
GAAH!
SHUNK
KEEP THE PRESSURE ON THEM!
DON'T LET THEM FLANK YOU!
VOK VOK

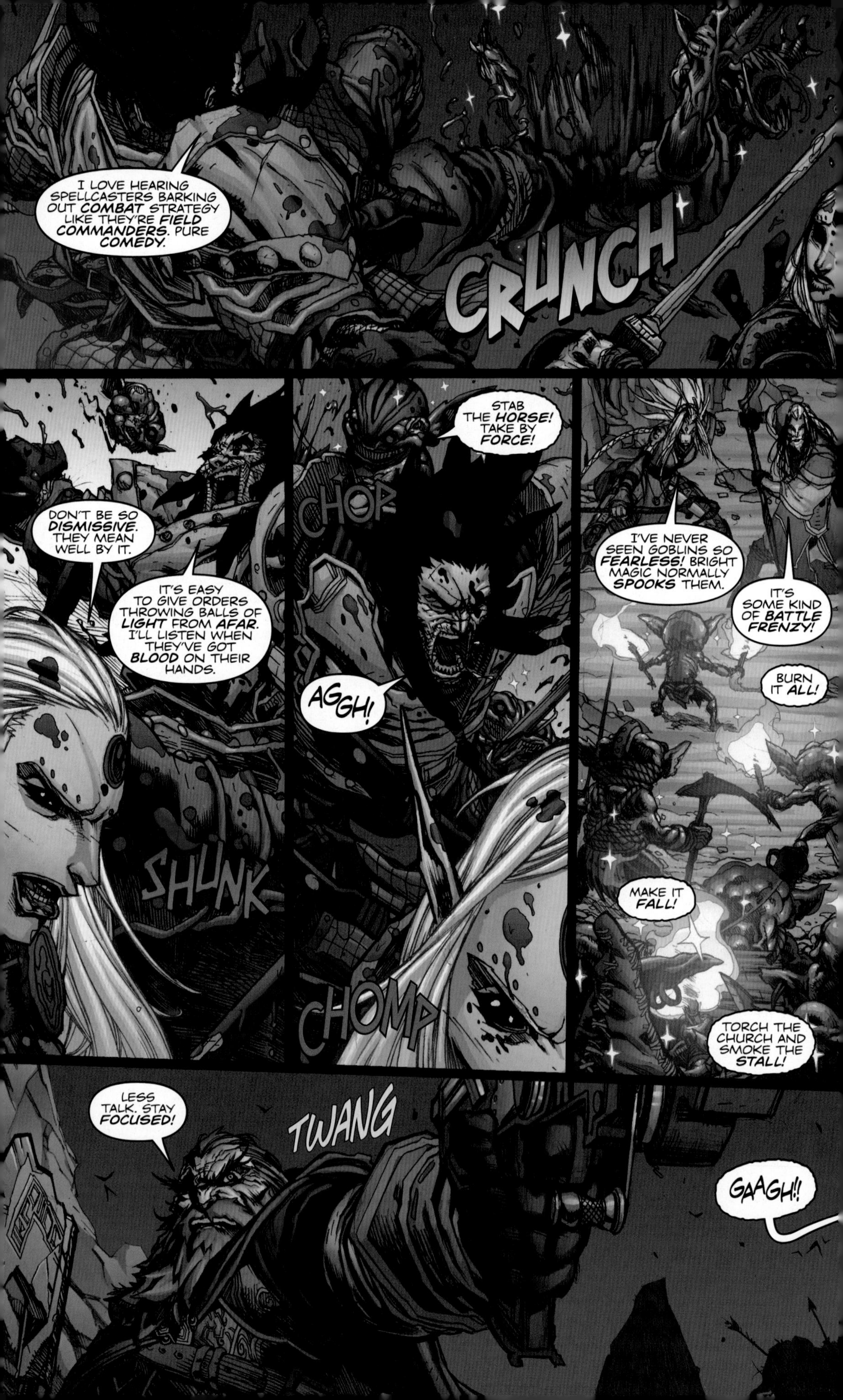
I LOVE HEARING SPELLCASTERS BARKING OUT **COMBAT** STRATEGY LIKE THEY'RE **FIELD COMMANDERS**. PURE **COMEDY**.
CRUNCH
DON'T BE SO **DISMISSIVE**. THEY MEAN WELL BY IT.
IT'S EASY TO GIVE ORDERS THROWING BALLS OF **LIGHT** FROM **AFAR**. I'LL LISTEN WHEN THEY'VE GOT **BLOOD** ON THEIR HANDS.
SHUNK
STAB THE **HORSE**! TAKE BY **FORCE**!
CHOP
AGGH!
CHOMP
I'VE NEVER SEEN GOBLINS SO **FEARLESS**! BRIGHT MAGIC NORMALLY **SPOOKS** THEM.
IT'S SOME KIND OF **BATTLE FRENZY**!
BURN IT **ALL**!
MAKE IT **FALL**!
TORCH THE CHURCH AND SMOKE THE **STALL**!
LESS TALK. STAY **FOCUSED**!
TWANG
GAAGH!!

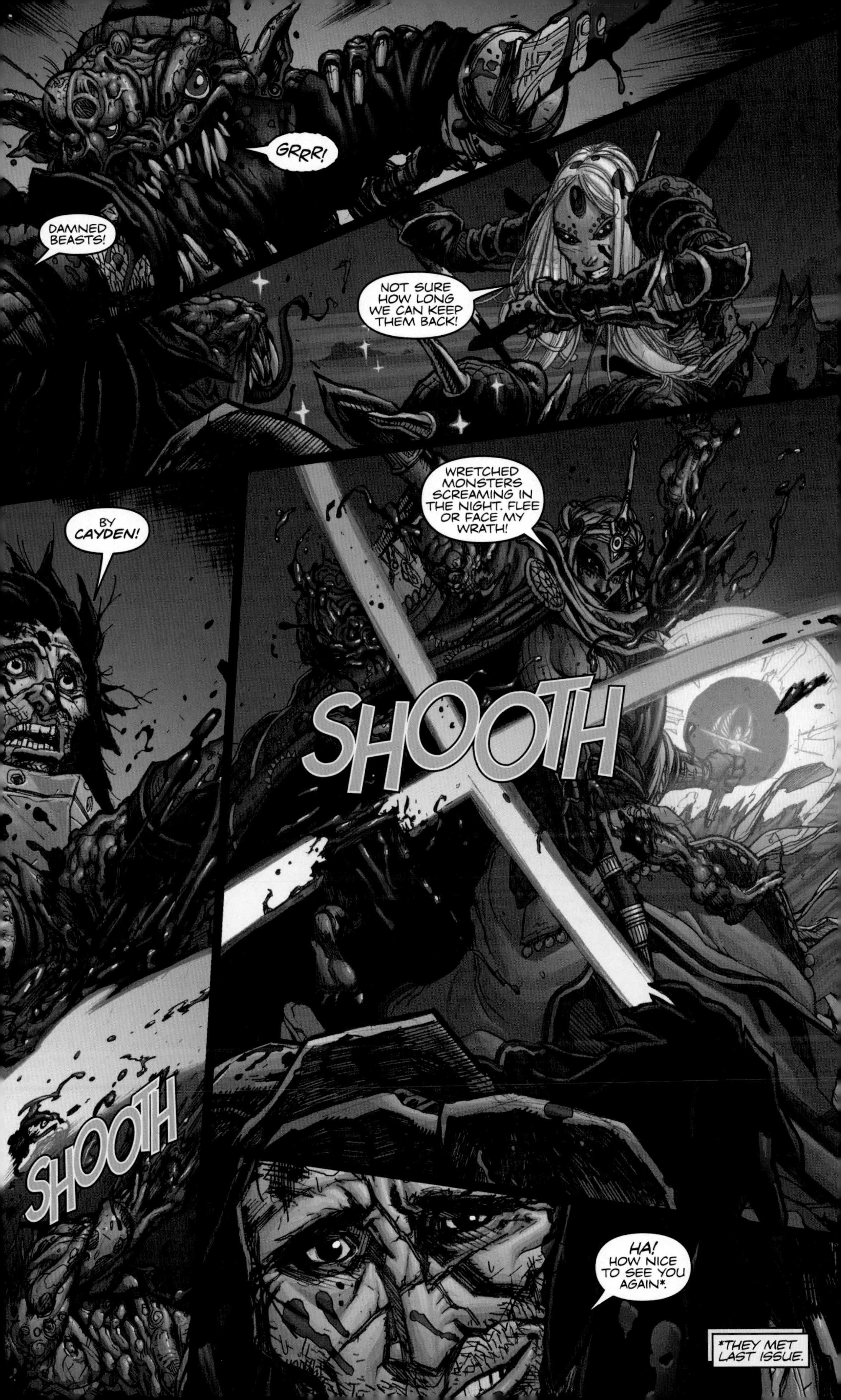
GRRR!
DAMNED BEASTS!
NOT SURE HOW LONG WE CAN KEEP THEM BACK!
BY CAYDEN!
WRETCHED MONSTERS SCREAMING IN THE NIGHT. FLEE OR FACE MY WRATH!
SHOOTH
SHOOTH
HA! HOW NICE TO SEE YOU AGAIN*.
*THEY MET LAST ISSUE.

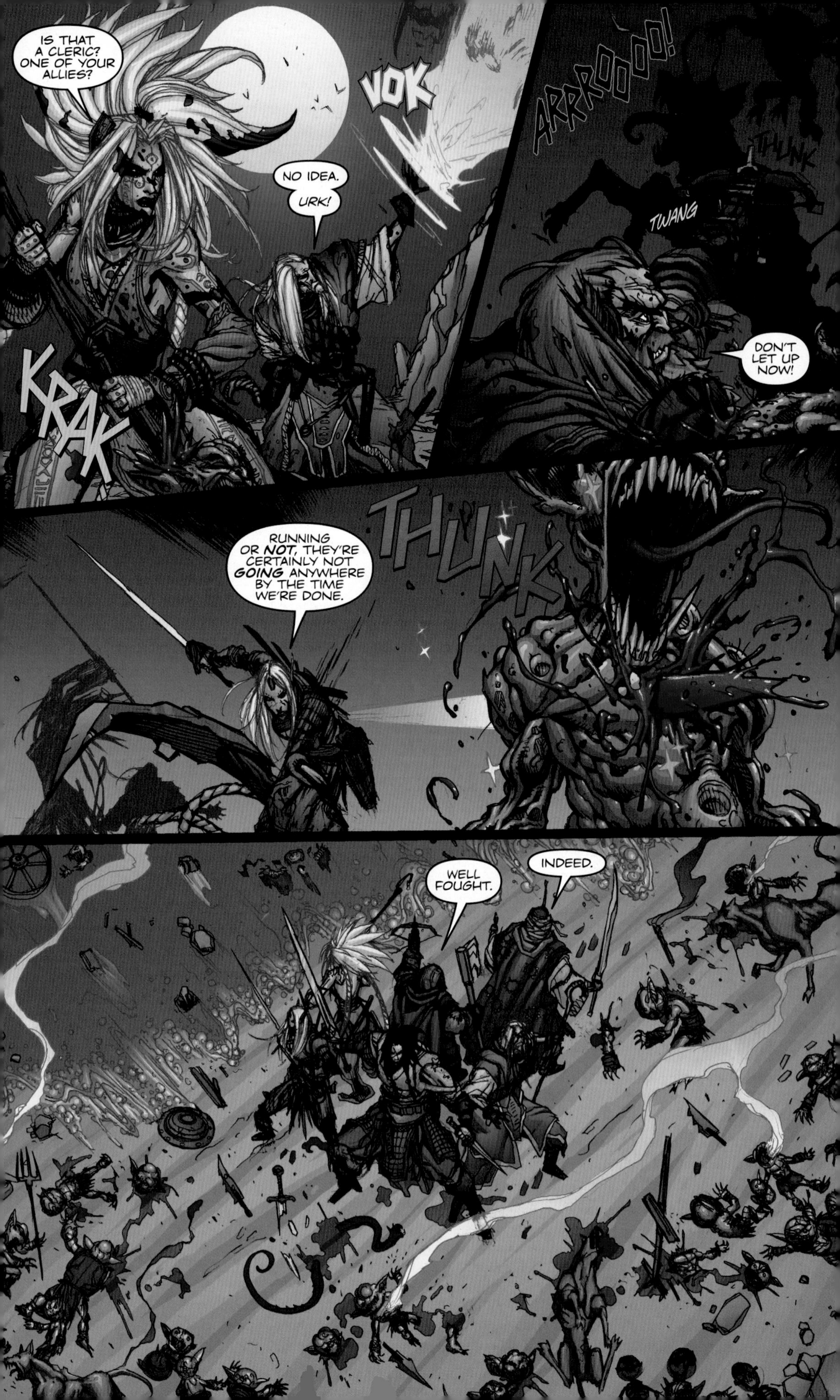
IS THAT A CLERIC? ONE OF YOUR ALLIES?
VOK
NO IDEA.
URK!
KRAK
ARRROOOO!
THUNK
TWANG
DON'T LET UP NOW!
THUNK
RUNNING OR **NOT**, THEY'RE CERTAINLY NOT **GOING** ANYWHERE BY THE TIME WE'RE DONE.
WELL FOUGHT.
INDEED.

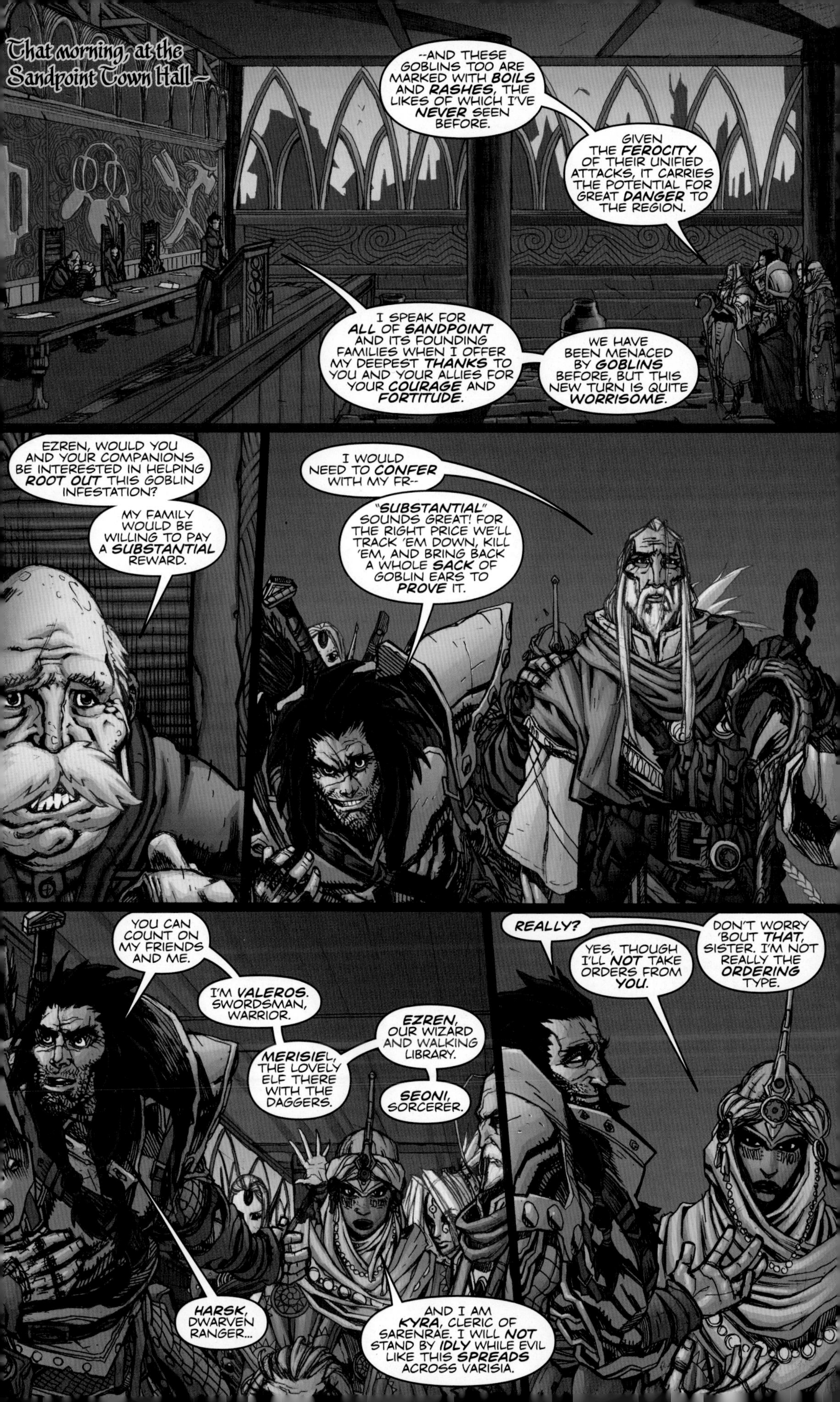
That morning, at the Sandpoint Town Hall—
--AND THESE GOBLINS TOO ARE MARKED WITH BOILS AND RASHES, THE LIKES OF WHICH I'VE NEVER SEEN BEFORE.
GIVEN THE FEROCITY OF THEIR UNIFIED ATTACKS, IT CARRIES THE POTENTIAL FOR GREAT DANGER TO THE REGION.
I SPEAK FOR ALL OF SANDPOINT AND ITS FOUNDING FAMILIES WHEN I OFFER MY DEEPEST THANKS TO YOU AND YOUR ALLIES FOR YOUR COURAGE AND FORTITUDE.
WE HAVE BEEN MENACED BY GOBLINS BEFORE, BUT THIS NEW TURN IS QUITE WORRISOME.
EZREN, WOULD YOU AND YOUR COMPANIONS BE INTERESTED IN HELPING ROOT OUT THIS GOBLIN INFESTATION?
MY FAMILY WOULD BE WILLING TO PAY A SUBSTANTIAL REWARD.
I WOULD NEED TO CONFER WITH MY FR--
"SUBSTANTIAL" SOUNDS GREAT! FOR THE RIGHT PRICE WE'LL TRACK 'EM DOWN, KILL 'EM, AND BRING BACK A WHOLE SACK OF GOBLIN EARS TO PROVE IT.
YOU CAN COUNT ON MY FRIENDS AND ME.
I'M VALEROS. SWORDSMAN, WARRIOR.
MERISIEL, THE LOVELY ELF THERE WITH THE DAGGERS.
EZREN, OUR WIZARD AND WALKING LIBRARY.
SEONI, SORCERER.
HARSK, DWARVEN RANGER...
AND I AM KYRA, CLERIC OF SARENRAE. I WILL NOT STAND BY IDLY WHILE EVIL LIKE THIS SPREADS ACROSS VARISIA.
REALLY?
YES, THOUGH I'LL NOT TAKE ORDERS FROM YOU.
DON'T WORRY 'BOUT THAT, SISTER. I'M NOT REALLY THE ORDERING TYPE.

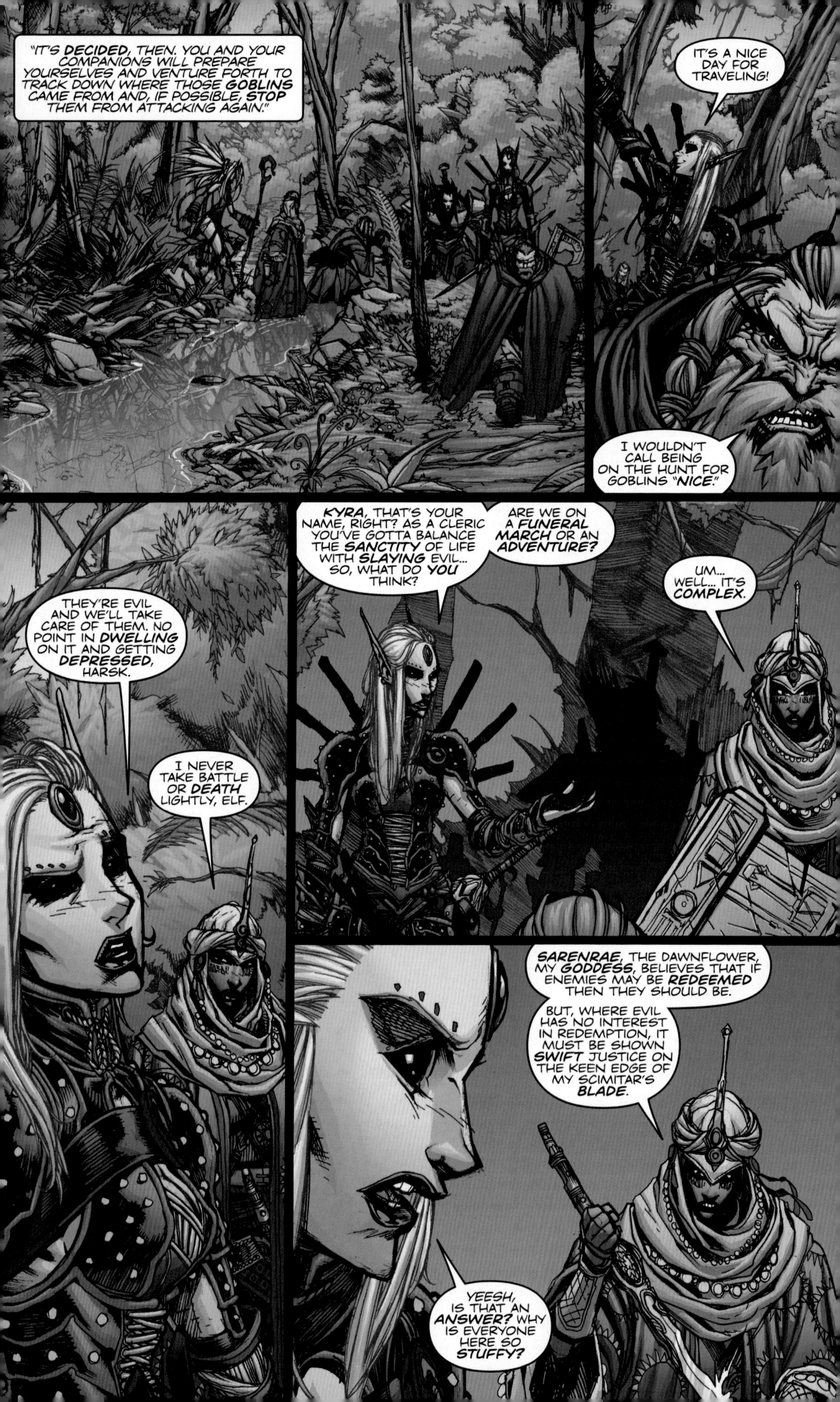
"IT'S DECIDED, THEN. YOU AND YOUR COMPANIONS WILL PREPARE YOURSELVES AND VENTURE FORTH TO TRACK DOWN WHERE THOSE GOBLINS CAME FROM AND, IF POSSIBLE, STOP THEM FROM ATTACKING AGAIN."
IT'S A NICE DAY FOR TRAVELING!
I WOULDN'T CALL BEING ON THE HUNT FOR GOBLINS "NICE."
THEY'RE EVIL AND WE'LL TAKE CARE OF THEM. NO POINT IN DWELLING ON IT AND GETTING DEPRESSED, HARSK.
I NEVER TAKE BATTLE OR DEATH LIGHTLY, ELF.
KYRA, THAT'S YOUR NAME, RIGHT? AS A CLERIC YOU'VE GOTTA BALANCE THE SANCTITY OF LIFE WITH SLAYING EVIL... SO, WHAT DO YOU THINK?
ARE WE ON A FUNERAL MARCH OR AN ADVENTURE?
UM... WELL... IT'S COMPLEX.
SARENRAE, THE DAWNFLOWER, MY GODDESS, BELIEVES THAT IF ENEMIES MAY BE REDEEMED THEN THEY SHOULD BE.
BUT, WHERE EVIL HAS NO INTEREST IN REDEMPTION, IT MUST BE SHOWN SWIFT JUSTICE ON THE KEEN EDGE OF MY SCIMITAR'S BLADE.
YEESH, IS THAT AN ANSWER? WHY IS EVERYONE HERE SO STUFFY?

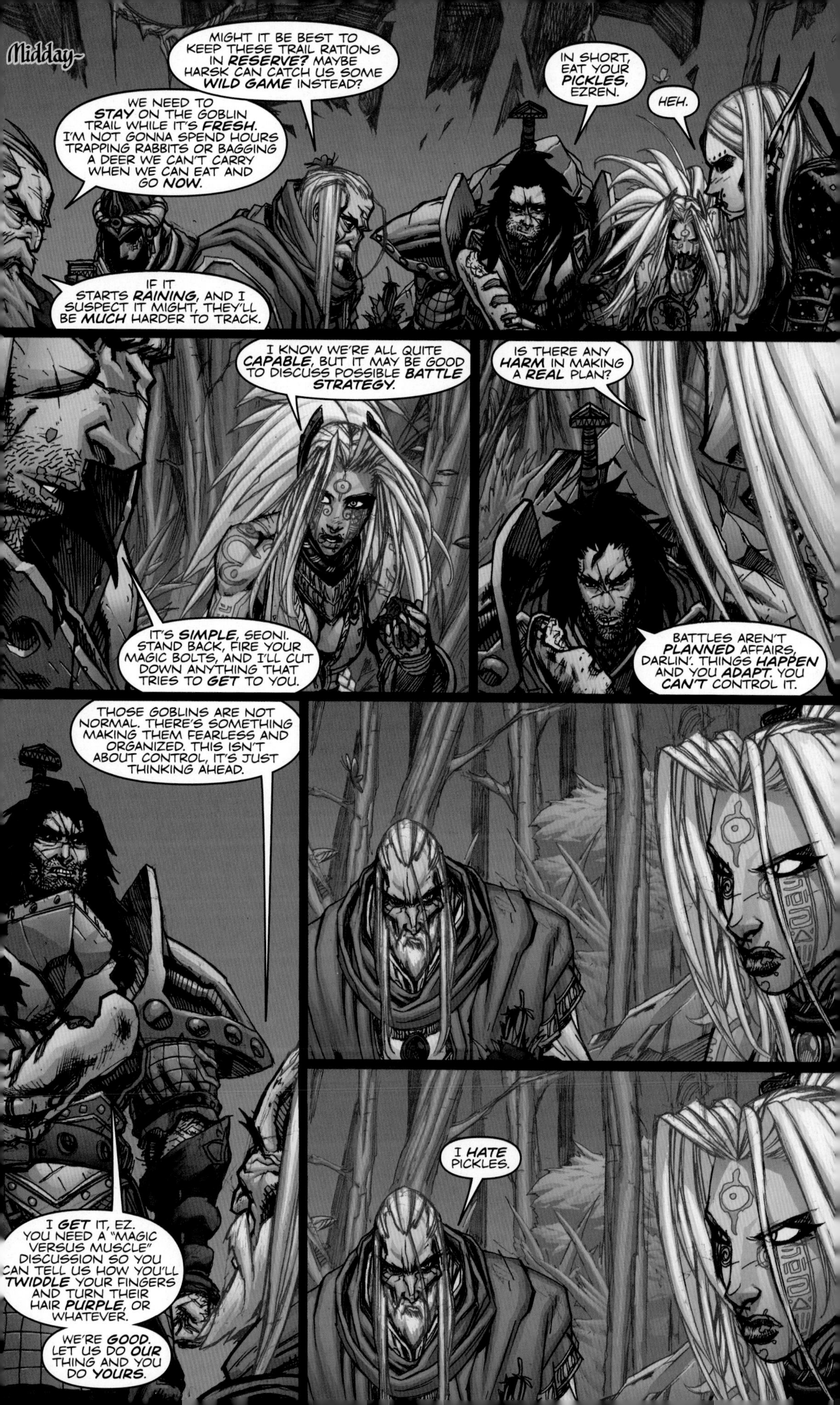
Midday~
MIGHT IT BE BEST TO KEEP THESE TRAIL RATIONS IN RESERVE? MAYBE HARSK CAN CATCH US SOME WILD GAME INSTEAD?
WE NEED TO STAY ON THE GOBLIN TRAIL WHILE IT'S FRESH. I'M NOT GONNA SPEND HOURS TRAPPING RABBITS OR BAGGING A DEER WE CAN'T CARRY WHEN WE CAN EAT AND GO NOW.
IN SHORT, EAT YOUR PICKLES, EZREN.
HEH.
IF IT STARTS RAINING, AND I SUSPECT IT MIGHT, THEY'LL BE MUCH HARDER TO TRACK.
I KNOW WE'RE ALL QUITE CAPABLE, BUT IT MAY BE GOOD TO DISCUSS POSSIBLE BATTLE STRATEGY.
IT'S SIMPLE, SEONI. STAND BACK, FIRE YOUR MAGIC BOLTS, AND I'LL CUT DOWN ANYTHING THAT TRIES TO GET TO YOU.
IS THERE ANY HARM IN MAKING A REAL PLAN?
BATTLES AREN'T PLANNED AFFAIRS, DARLIN'. THINGS HAPPEN AND YOU ADAPT. YOU CAN'T CONTROL IT.
THOSE GOBLINS ARE NOT NORMAL. THERE'S SOMETHING MAKING THEM FEARLESS AND ORGANIZED. THIS ISN'T ABOUT CONTROL, IT'S JUST THINKING AHEAD.
I GET IT, EZ. YOU NEED A "MAGIC VERSUS MUSCLE" DISCUSSION SO YOU CAN TELL US HOW YOU'LL TWIDDLE YOUR FINGERS AND TURN THEIR HAIR PURPLE, OR WHATEVER.
WE'RE GOOD. LET US DO OUR THING AND YOU DO YOURS.
I HATE PICKLES.

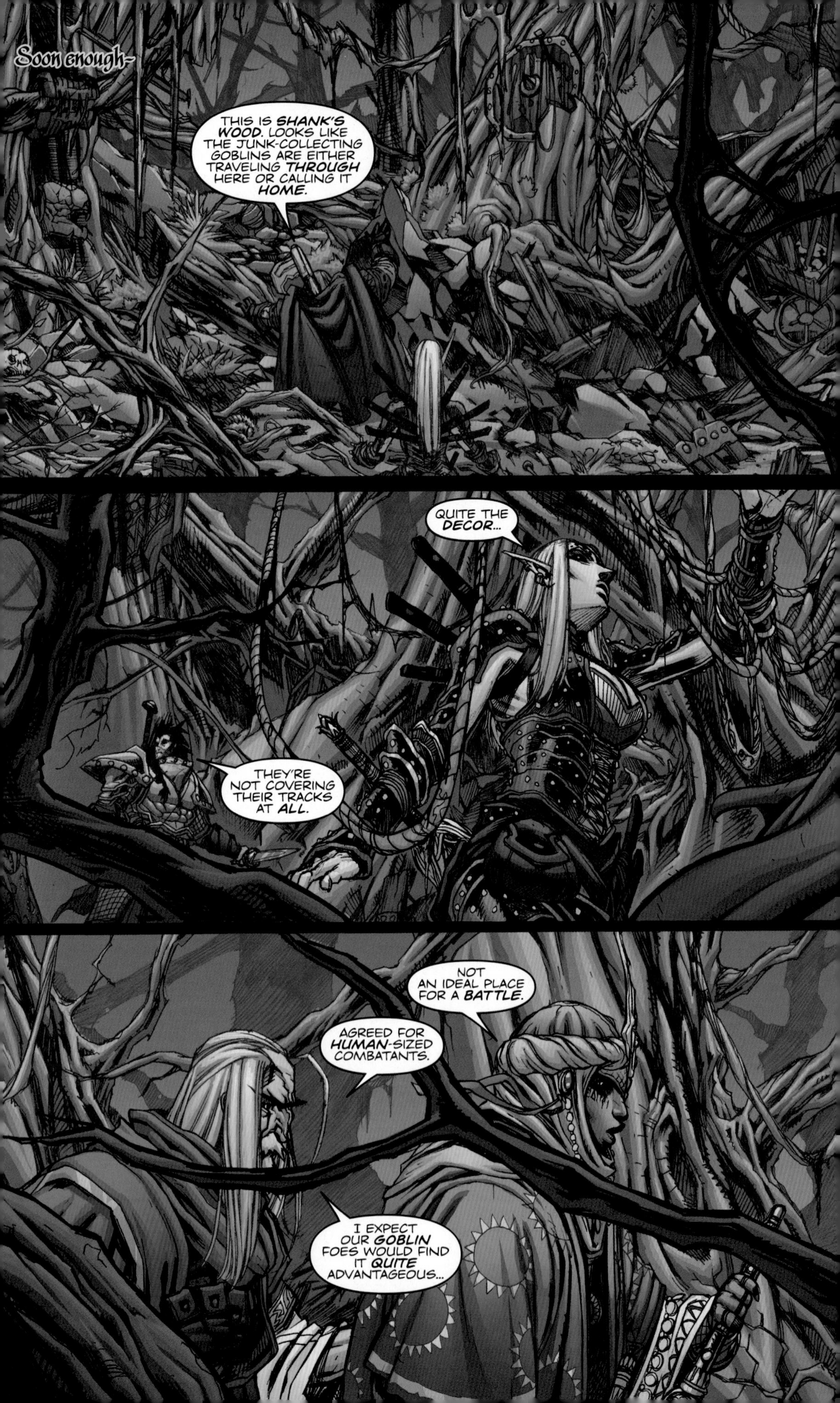
Soon enough-
THIS IS SHANK'S WOOD. LOOKS LIKE THE JUNK-COLLECTING GOBLINS ARE EITHER TRAVELING THROUGH HERE OR CALLING IT HOME.
QUITE THE DECOR...
THEY'RE NOT COVERING THEIR TRACKS AT ALL.
NOT AN IDEAL PLACE FOR A BATTLE.
AGREED FOR HUMAN-SIZED COMBATANTS.
I EXPECT OUR GOBLIN FOES WOULD FIND IT QUITE ADVANTAGEOUS...

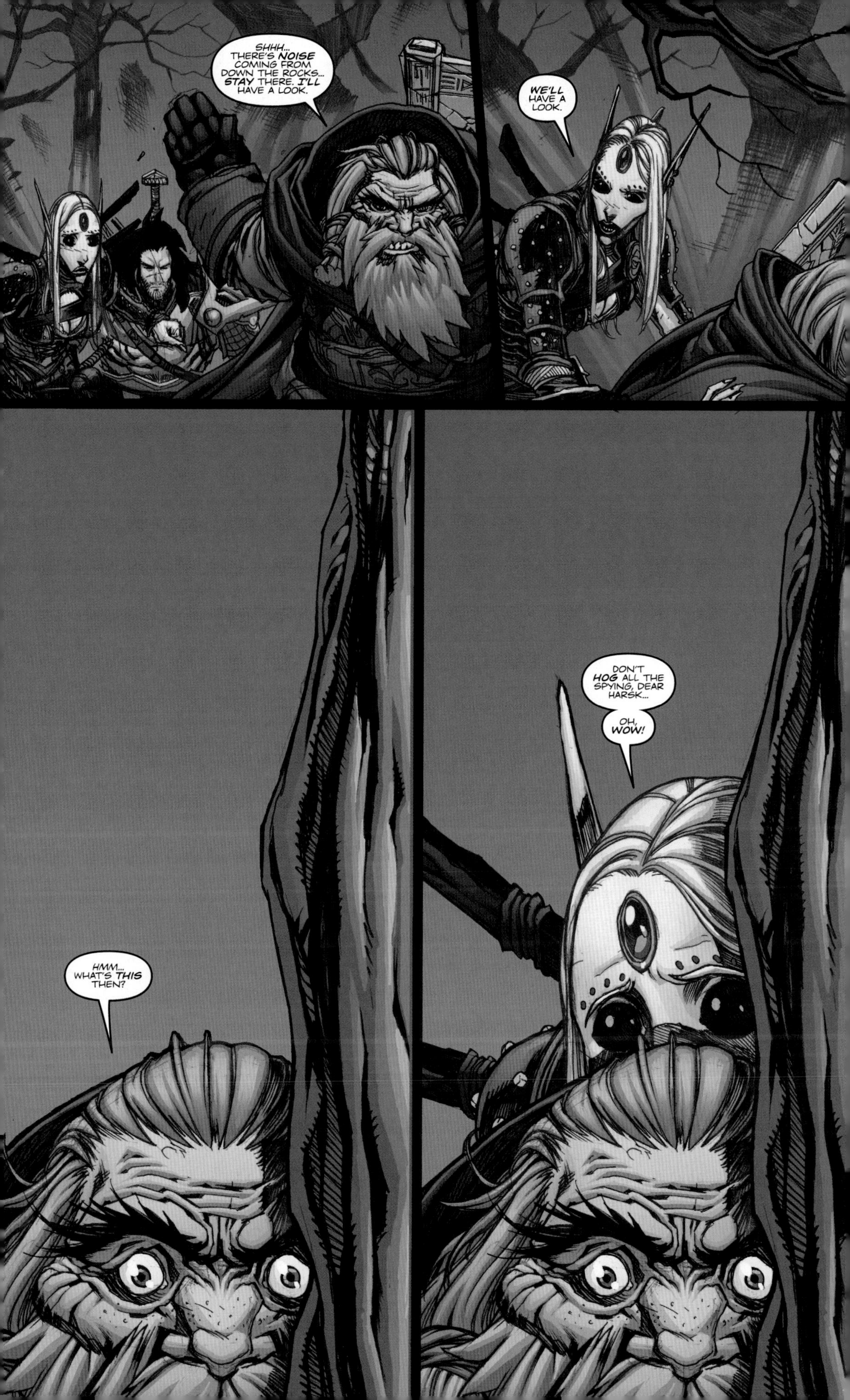

SHHH... THERE'S NOISE COMING FROM DOWN THE ROCKS... STAY THERE. I'LL HAVE A LOOK.
WE'LL HAVE A LOOK.
HMM... WHAT'S THIS THEN?
DON'T HOG ALL THE SPYING, DEAR HARSK...
OH, WOW!

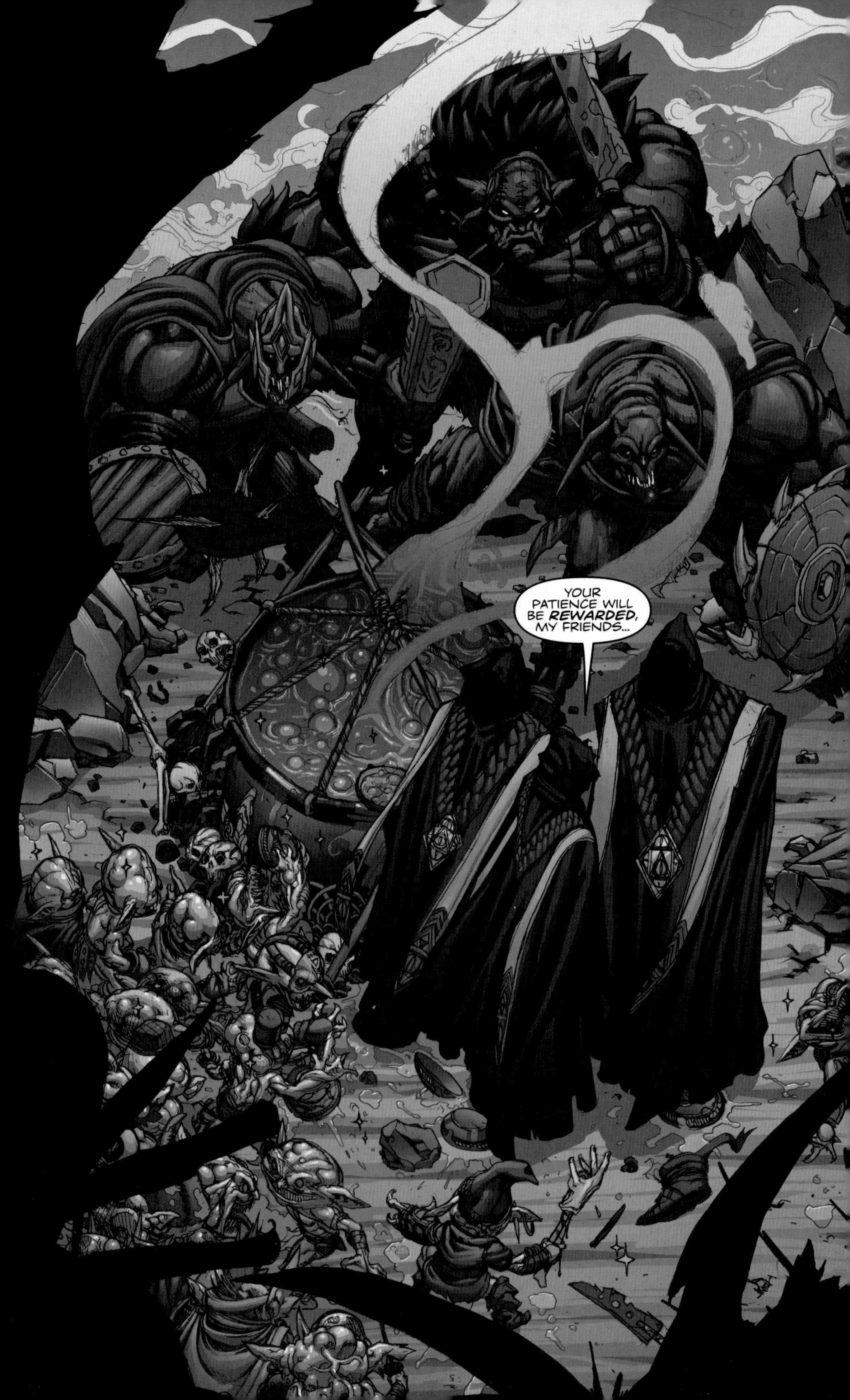
YOUR PATIENCE WILL BE REWARDED, MY FRIENDS...

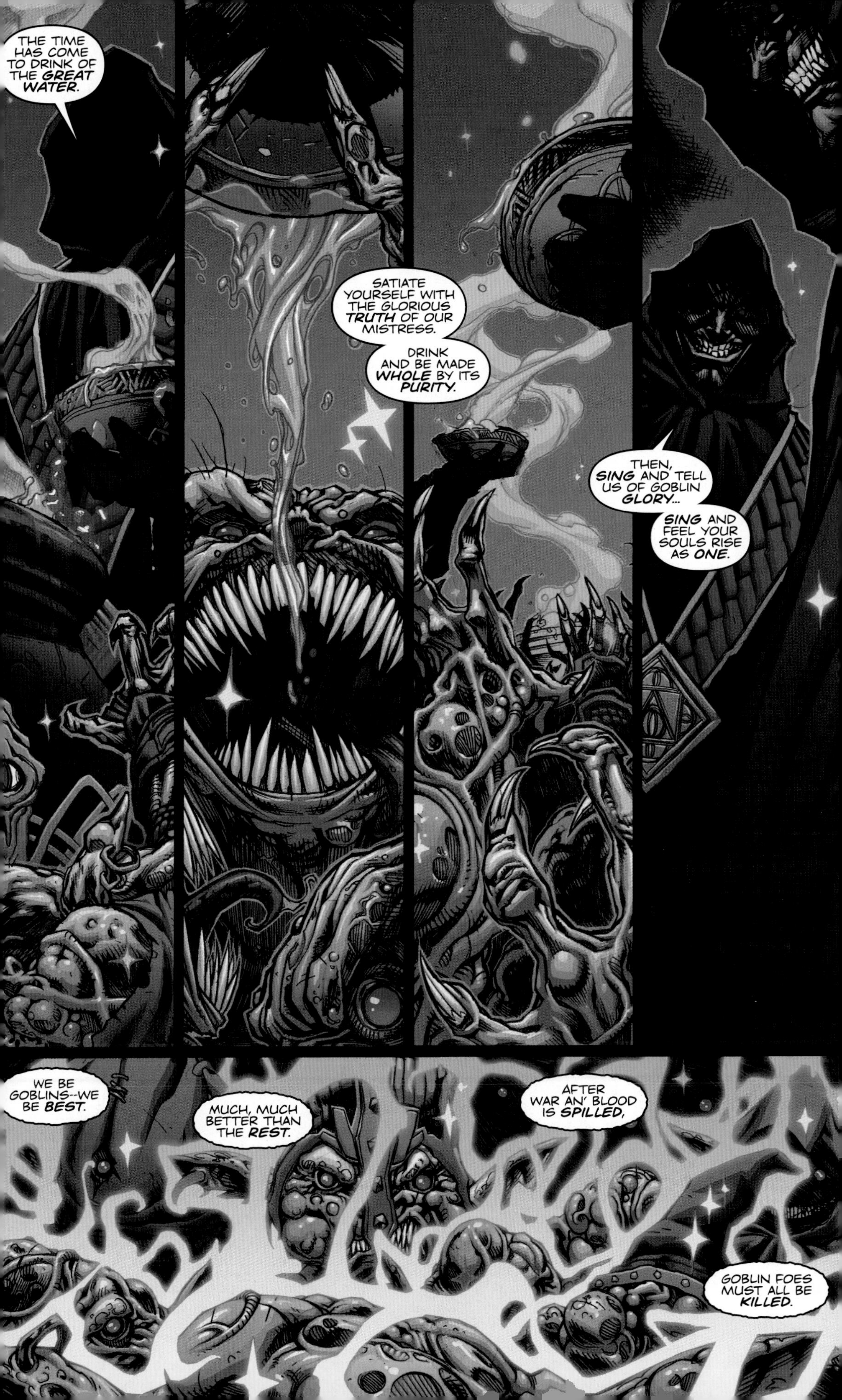

THE TIME HAS COME TO DRINK OF THE GREAT WATER.
SATIATE YOURSELF WITH THE GLORIOUS TRUTH OF OUR MISTRESS.
DRINK AND BE MADE WHOLE BY ITS PURITY.
THEN, SING AND TELL US OF GOBLIN GLORY...
SING AND FEEL YOUR SOULS RISE AS ONE.
WE BE GOBLINS--WE BE BEST.
MUCH, MUCH BETTER THAN THE REST.
AFTER WAR AN' BLOOD IS SPILLED,
GOBLIN FOES MUST ALL BE KILLED.

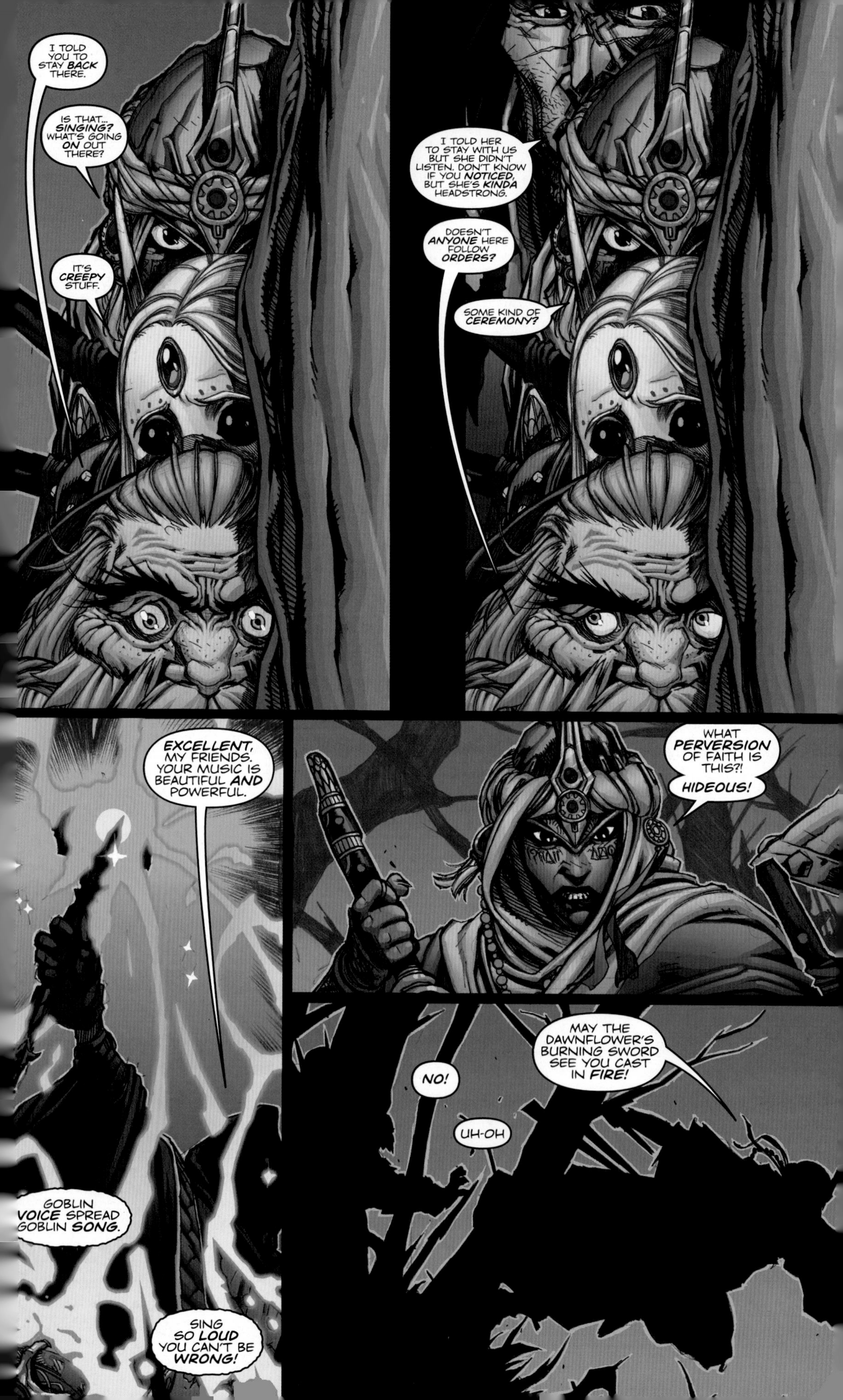

I TOLD YOU TO STAY BACK THERE.
IS THAT... SINGING? WHAT'S GOING ON OUT THERE?
IT'S CREEPY STUFF.
I TOLD HER TO STAY WITH US BUT SHE DIDN'T LISTEN. DON'T KNOW IF YOU NOTICED, BUT SHE'S KINDA HEADSTRONG.
DOESN'T ANYONE HERE FOLLOW ORDERS?
SOME KIND OF CEREMONY?
EXCELLENT, MY FRIENDS. YOUR MUSIC IS BEAUTIFUL AND POWERFUL.
GOBLIN VOICE SPREAD GOBLIN SONG.
SING SO LOUD YOU CAN'T BE WRONG!
WHAT PERVERSION OF FAITH IS THIS?! HIDEOUS!
MAY THE DAWNFLOWER'S BURNING SWORD SEE YOU CAST IN FIRE!
NO!
UH-OH

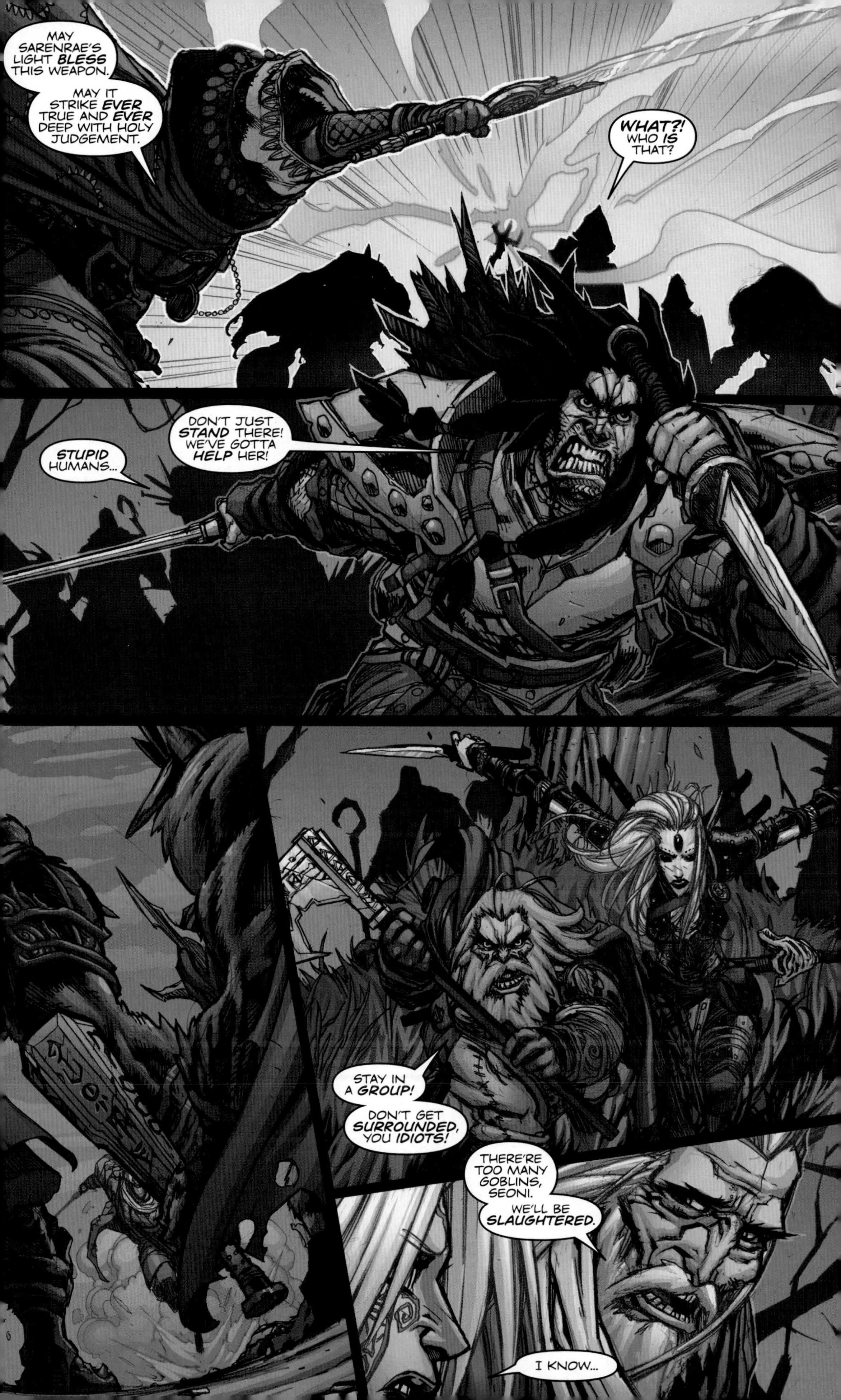
MAY SARENRAE'S LIGHT BLESS THIS WEAPON.
MAY IT STRIKE EVER TRUE AND EVER DEEP WITH HOLY JUDGEMENT.
WHAT?! WHO IS THAT?
DON'T JUST STAND THERE! WE'VE GOTTA HELP HER!
STUPID HUMANS...
STAY IN A GROUP!
DON'T GET SURROUNDED, YOU IDIOTS!
THERE'RE TOO MANY GOBLINS, SEONI.
WE'LL BE SLAUGHTERED.
I KNOW...

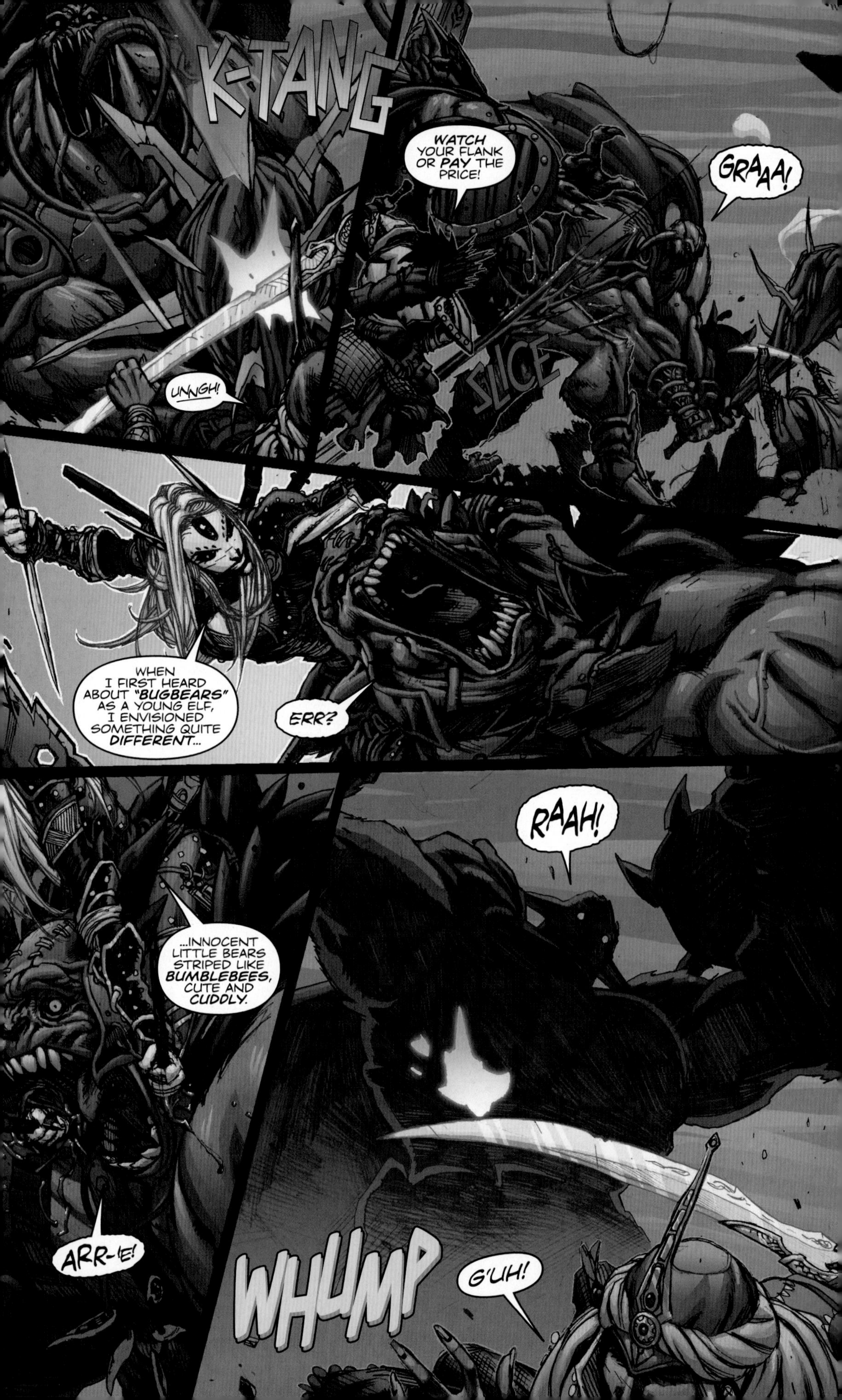
K-TANG
WATCH YOUR FLANK OR PAY THE PRICE!
GRAAA!
SLICE
UNNGH!
WHEN I FIRST HEARD ABOUT "BUGBEARS" AS A YOUNG ELF, I ENVISIONED SOMETHING QUITE DIFFERENT...
ERR?
RAAH!
...INNOCENT LITTLE BEARS STRIPED LIKE BUMBLEBEES, CUTE AND CUDDLY.
ARR-IE!
WHUMP
G'UH!

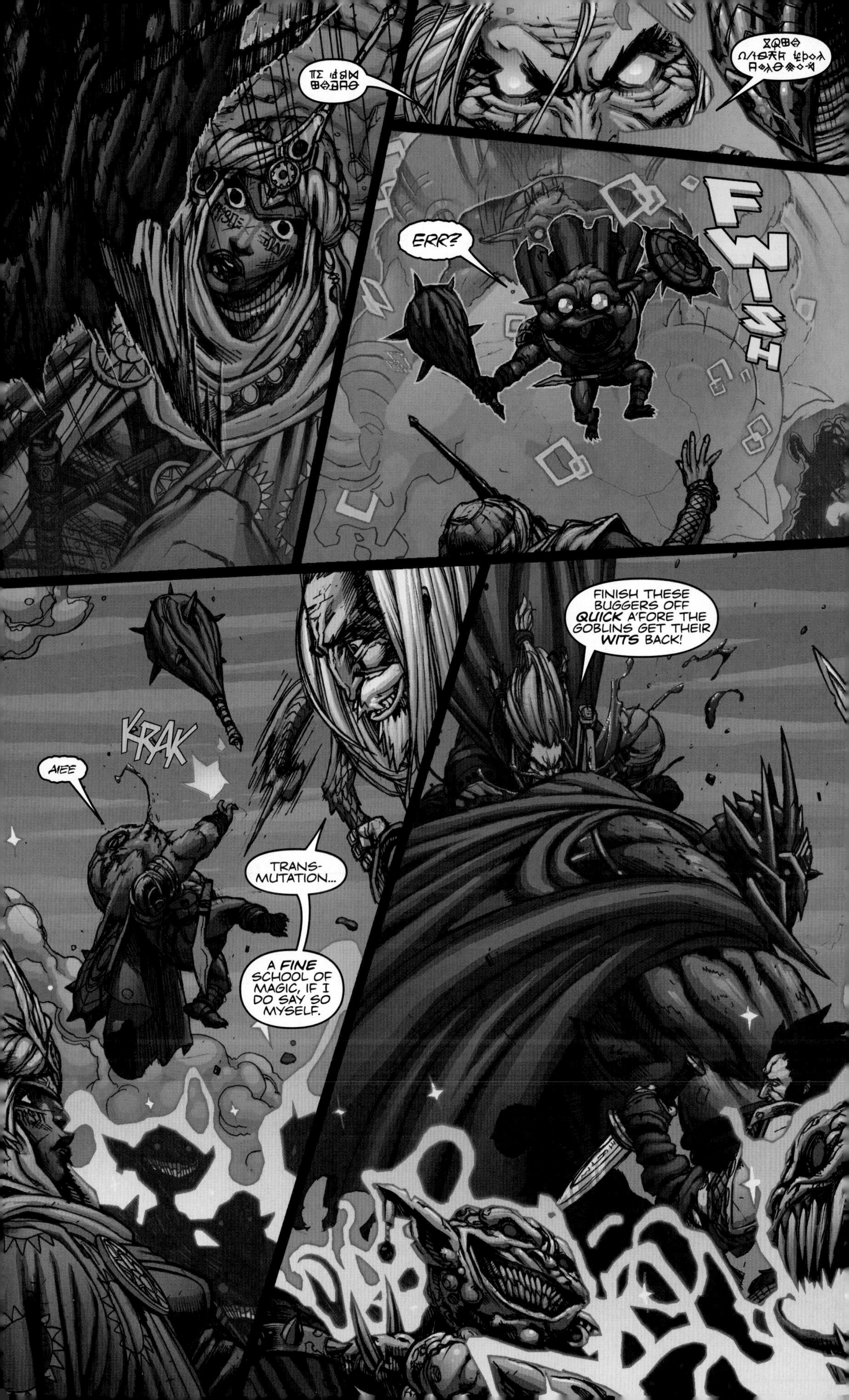

ERR?
FWISH
KRAK
AIEE
TRANS-MUTATION...
A FINE SCHOOL OF MAGIC, IF I DO SAY SO MYSELF.
FINISH THESE BUGGERS OFF QUICK A'FORE THE GOBLINS GET THEIR WITS BACK!

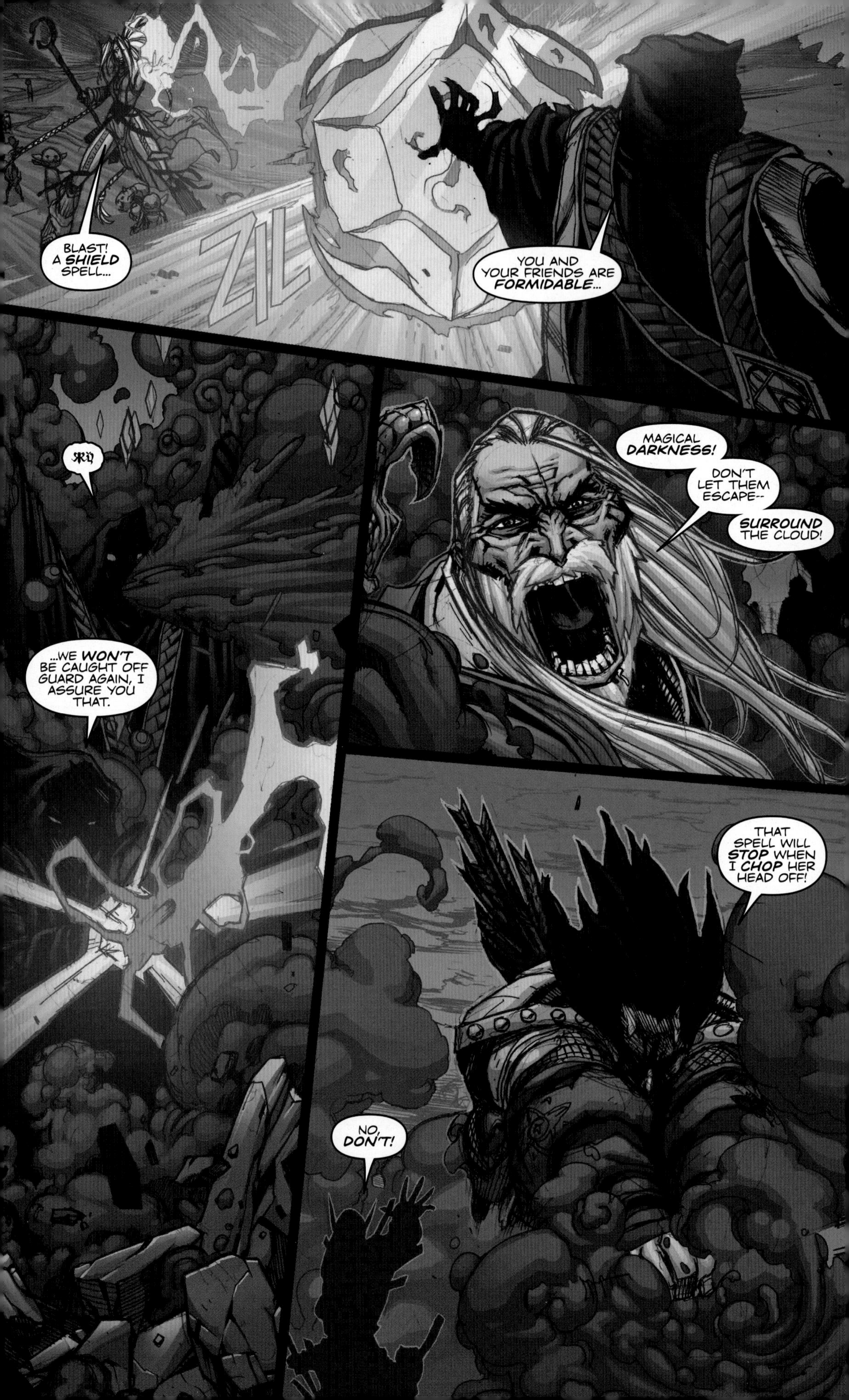

BLAST! A SHIELD SPELL...
YOU AND YOUR FRIENDS ARE FORMIDABLE...
ZIL
...WE WON'T BE CAUGHT OFF GUARD AGAIN, I ASSURE YOU THAT.
MAGICAL DARKNESS!
DON'T LET THEM ESCAPE--
SURROUND THE CLOUD!
THAT SPELL WILL STOP WHEN I CHOP HER HEAD OFF!
NO, DON'T!

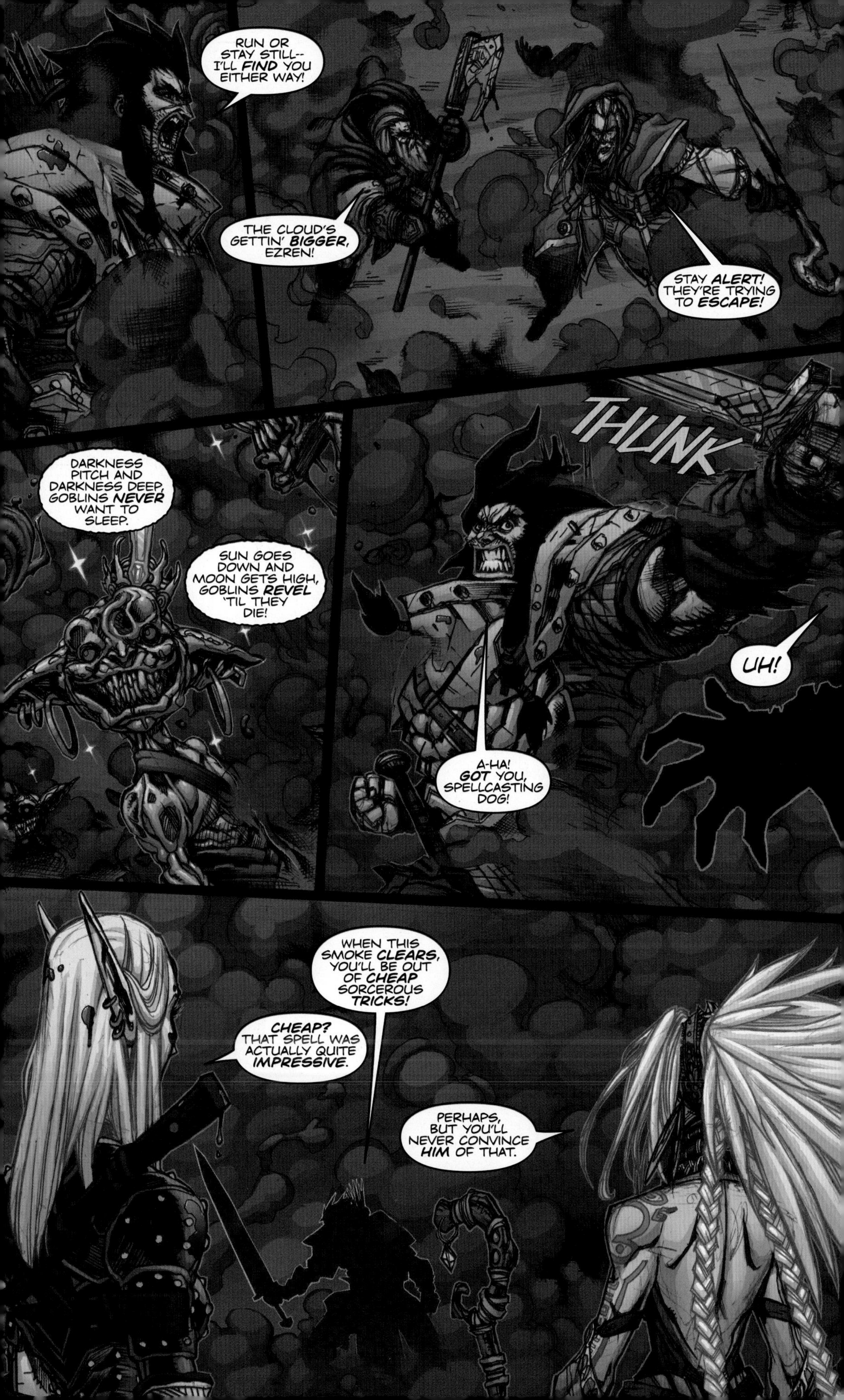
RUN OR STAY STILL-- I'LL FIND YOU EITHER WAY!
THE CLOUD'S GETTIN' BIGGER, EZREN!
STAY ALERT! THEY'RE TRYING TO ESCAPE!
DARKNESS PITCH AND DARKNESS DEEP, GOBLINS NEVER WANT TO SLEEP.
SUN GOES DOWN AND MOON GETS HIGH, GOBLINS REVEL 'TIL THEY DIE!
THUNK
UH!
A-HA! GOT YOU, SPELLCASTING DOG!
WHEN THIS SMOKE CLEARS, YOU'LL BE OUT OF CHEAP SORCEROUS TRICKS!
CHEAP? THAT SPELL WAS ACTUALLY QUITE IMPRESSIVE.
PERHAPS, BUT YOU'LL NEVER CONVINCE HIM OF THAT.

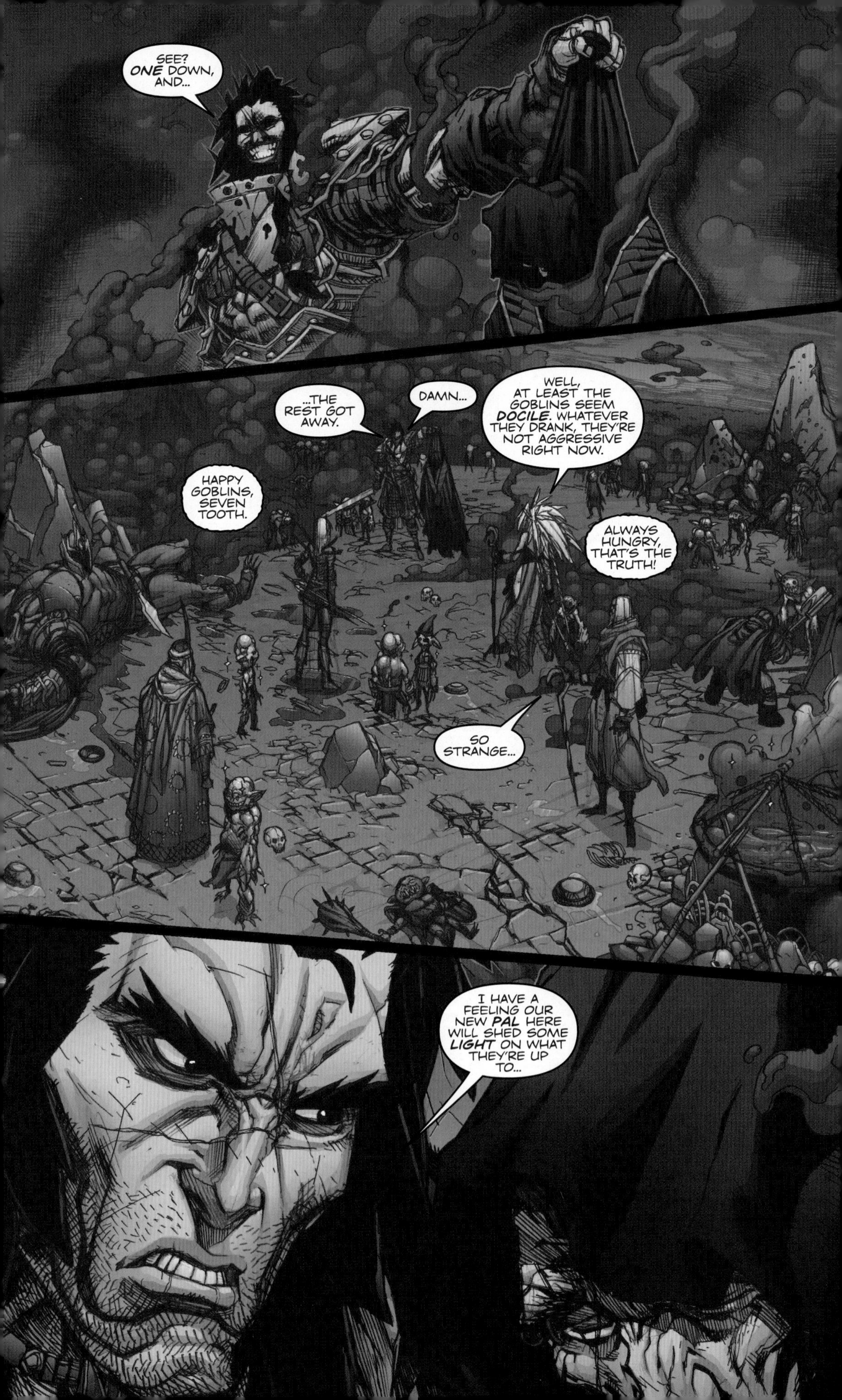
SEE? ONE DOWN, AND...
...THE REST GOT AWAY.
DAMN...
WELL, AT LEAST THE GOBLINS SEEM DOCILE. WHATEVER THEY DRANK, THEY'RE NOT AGGRESSIVE RIGHT NOW.
HAPPY GOBLINS, SEVEN TOOTH.
ALWAYS HUNGRY, THAT'S THE TRUTH!
SO STRANGE...
I HAVE A FEELING OUR NEW PAL HERE WILL SHED SOME LIGHT ON WHAT THEY'RE UP TO...

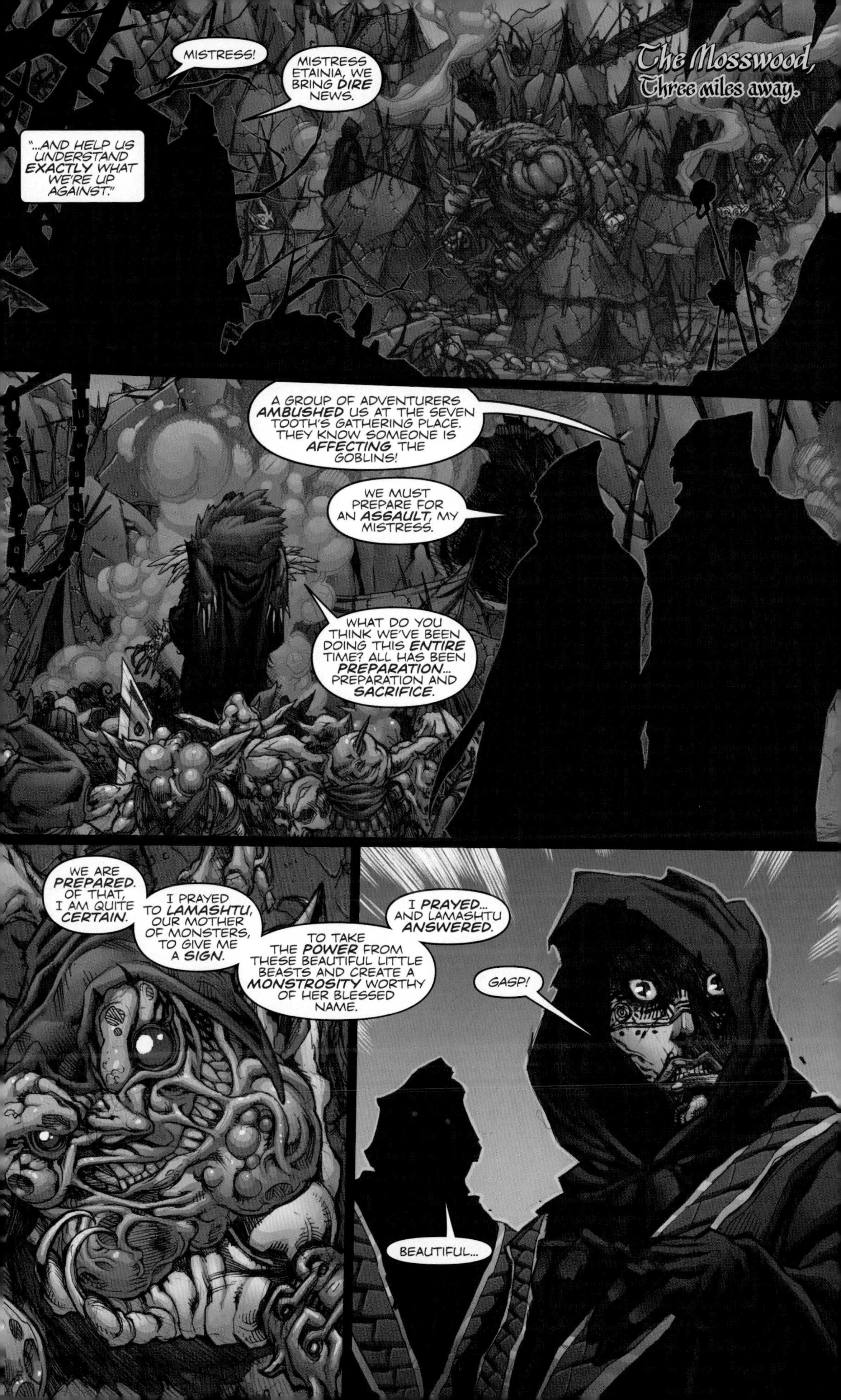
The Mosswood,
Three miles away.
"...AND HELP US UNDERSTAND EXACTLY WHAT WE'RE UP AGAINST."
MISTRESS!
MISTRESS ETAINIA, WE BRING DIRE NEWS.
A GROUP OF ADVENTURERS AMBUSHED US AT THE SEVEN TOOTH'S GATHERING PLACE. THEY KNOW SOMEONE IS AFFECTING THE GOBLINS!
WE MUST PREPARE FOR AN ASSAULT, MY MISTRESS.
WHAT DO YOU THINK WE'VE BEEN DOING THIS ENTIRE TIME? ALL HAS BEEN PREPARATION... PREPARATION AND SACRIFICE.
WE ARE PREPARED. OF THAT, I AM QUITE CERTAIN.
I PRAYED TO LAMASHTU, OUR MOTHER OF MONSTERS, TO GIVE ME A SIGN.
TO TAKE THE POWER FROM THESE BEAUTIFUL LITTLE BEASTS AND CREATE A MONSTROSITY WORTHY OF HER BLESSED NAME.
I PRAYED... AND LAMASHTU ANSWERED.
GASP!
BEAUTIFUL...

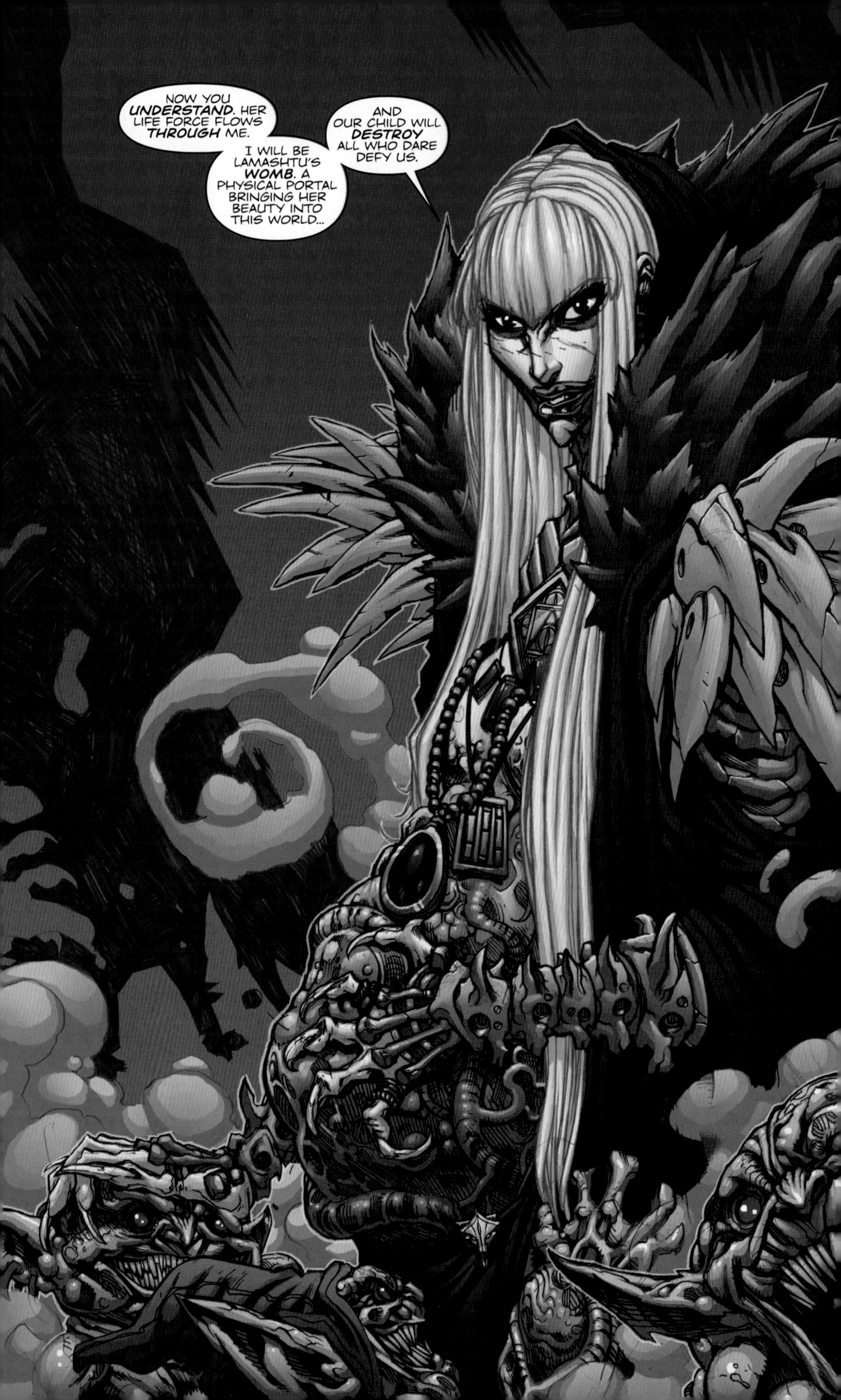
NOW YOU **UNDERSTAND**. HER LIFE FORCE FLOWS **THROUGH** ME.
I WILL BE LAMASHTU'S **WOMB**. A PHYSICAL PORTAL BRINGING HER BEAUTY INTO THIS WORLD...
AND OUR CHILD WILL **DESTROY** ALL WHO DARE DEFY US.

CHAPTER 3

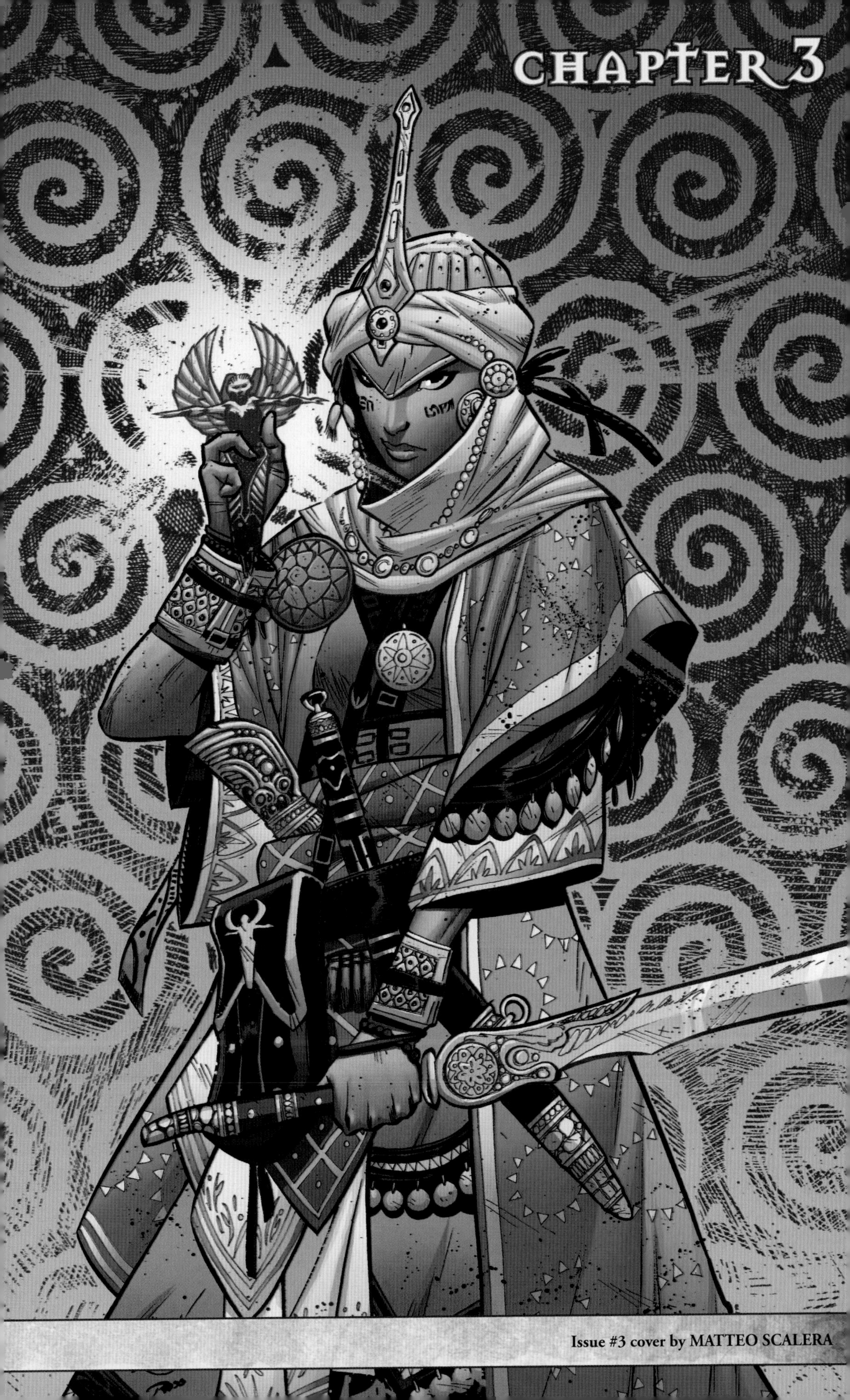

Issue #3 cover by MATTEO SCALERA

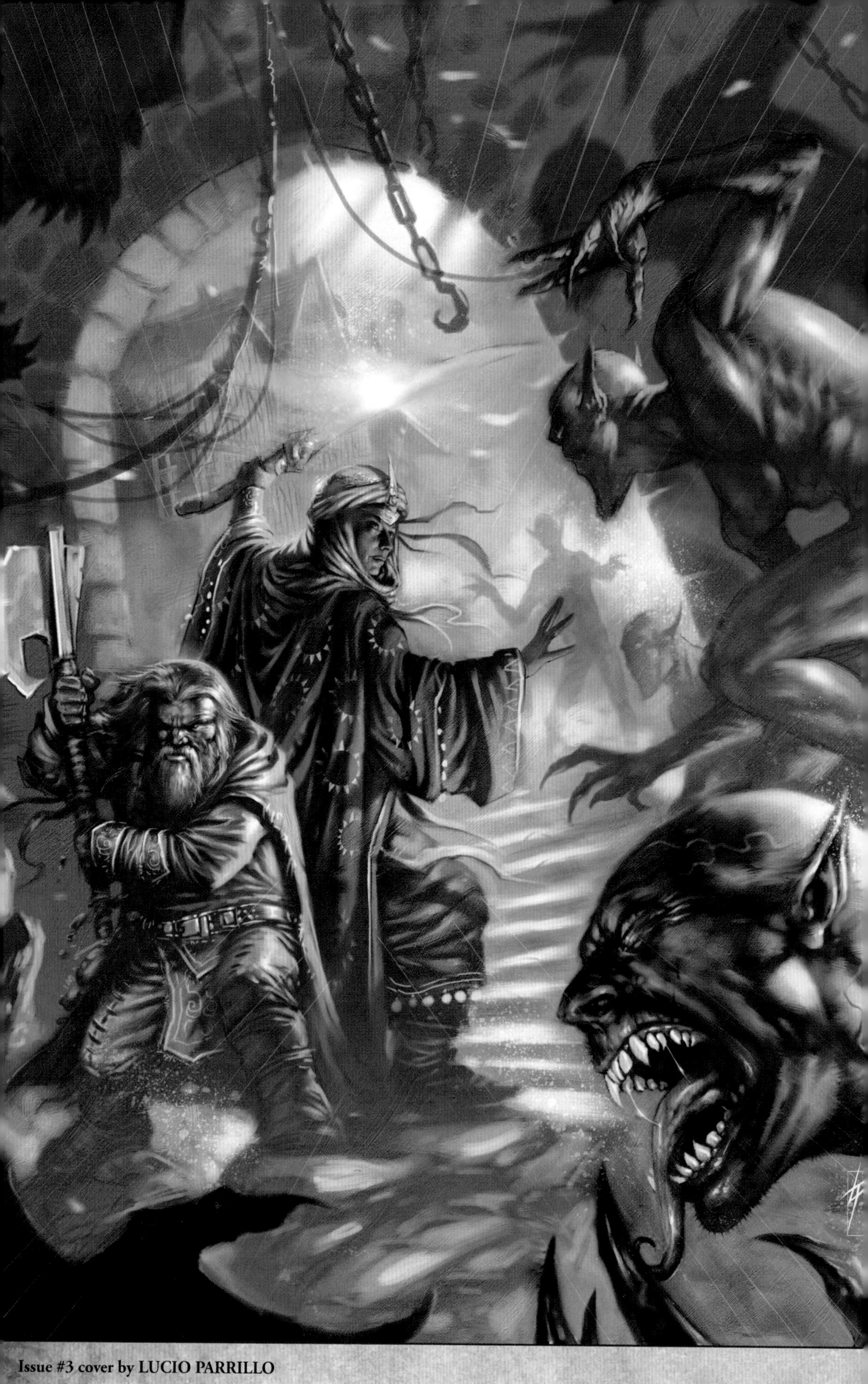

Issue #3 cover by LUCIO PARRILLO

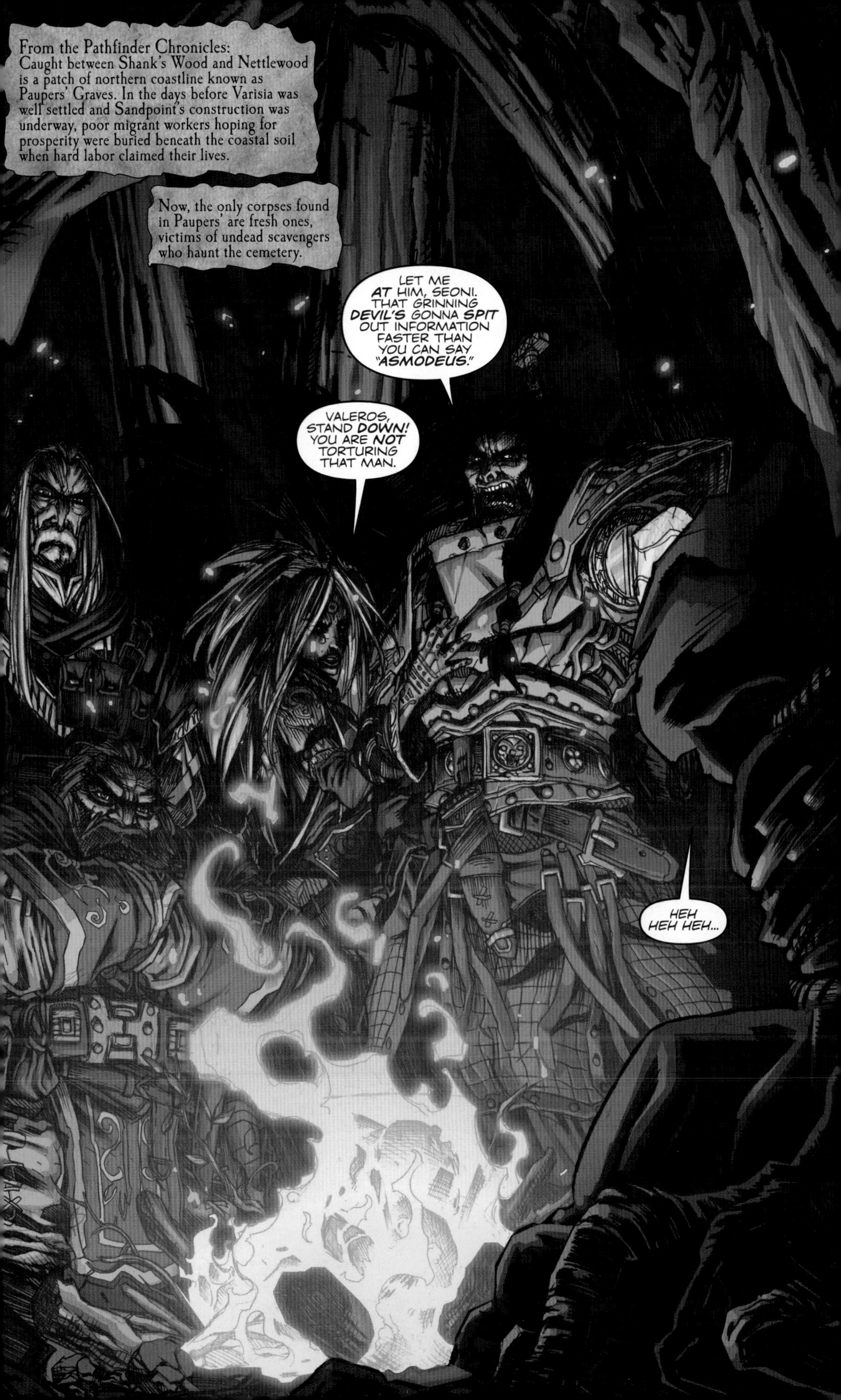
From the Pathfinder Chronicles:
Caught between Shank's Wood and Nettlewood is a patch of northern coastline known as Paupers' Graves. In the days before Varisia was well settled and Sandpoint's construction was underway, poor migrant workers hoping for prosperity were buried beneath the coastal soil when hard labor claimed their lives.
Now, the only corpses found in Paupers' are fresh ones, victims of undead scavengers who haunt the cemetery.
LET ME AT HIM, SEONI. THAT GRINNING DEVIL'S GONNA SPIT OUT INFORMATION FASTER THAN YOU CAN SAY "ASMODEUS."
VALEROS, STAND DOWN! YOU ARE NOT TORTURING THAT MAN.
HEH HEH HEH...

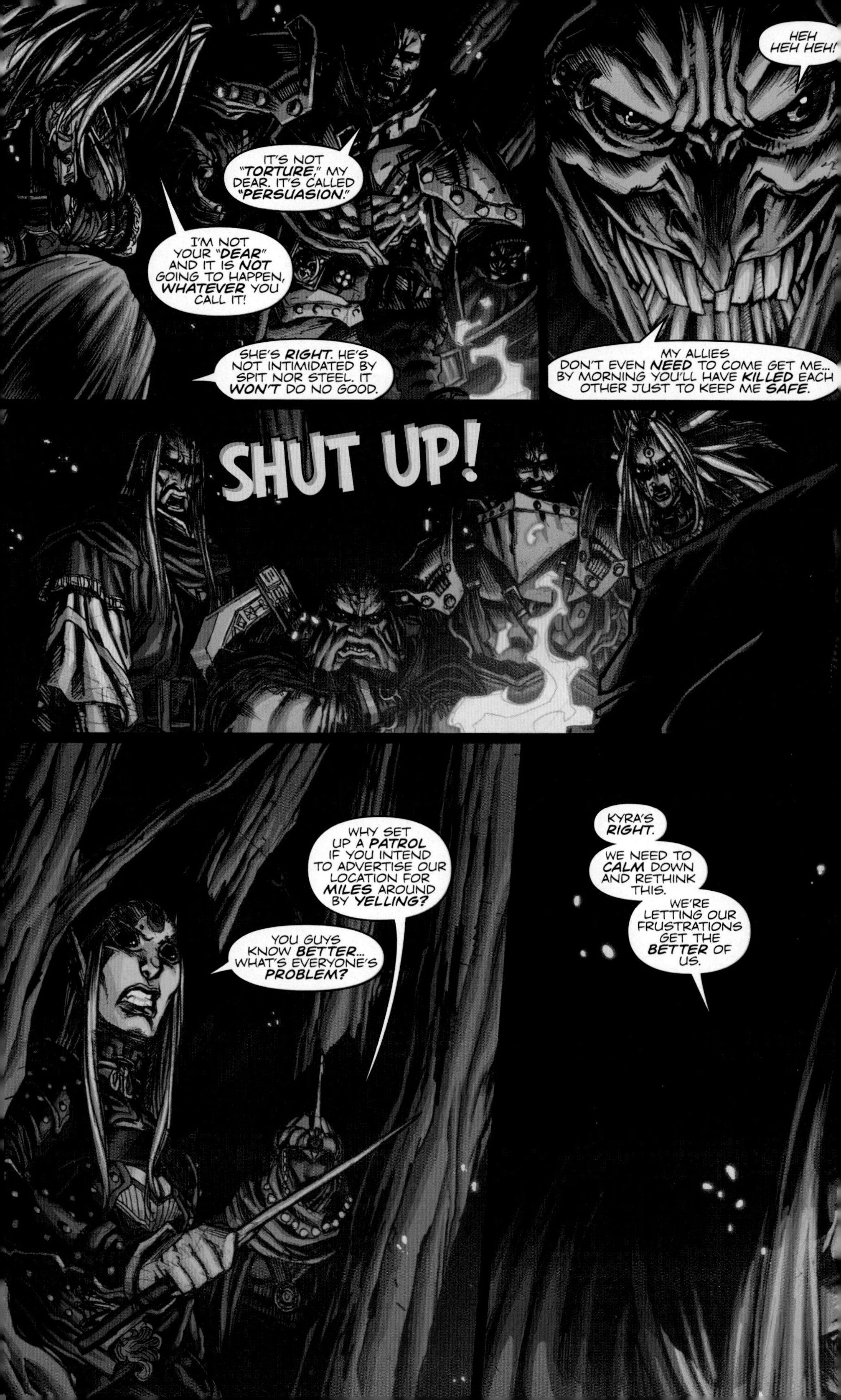
IT'S NOT "TORTURE," MY DEAR. IT'S CALLED "PERSUASION."
I'M NOT YOUR "DEAR" AND IT IS NOT GOING TO HAPPEN, WHATEVER YOU CALL IT!
SHE'S RIGHT. HE'S NOT INTIMIDATED BY SPIT NOR STEEL. IT WON'T DO NO GOOD.
HEH HEH HEH!
MY ALLIES DON'T EVEN NEED TO COME GET ME... BY MORNING YOU'LL HAVE KILLED EACH OTHER JUST TO KEEP ME SAFE.
SHUT UP!
WHY SET UP A PATROL IF YOU INTEND TO ADVERTISE OUR LOCATION FOR MILES AROUND BY YELLING?
YOU GUYS KNOW BETTER... WHAT'S EVERYONE'S PROBLEM?
KYRA'S RIGHT.
WE NEED TO CALM DOWN AND RETHINK THIS.
WE'RE LETTING OUR FRUSTRATIONS GET THE BETTER OF US.

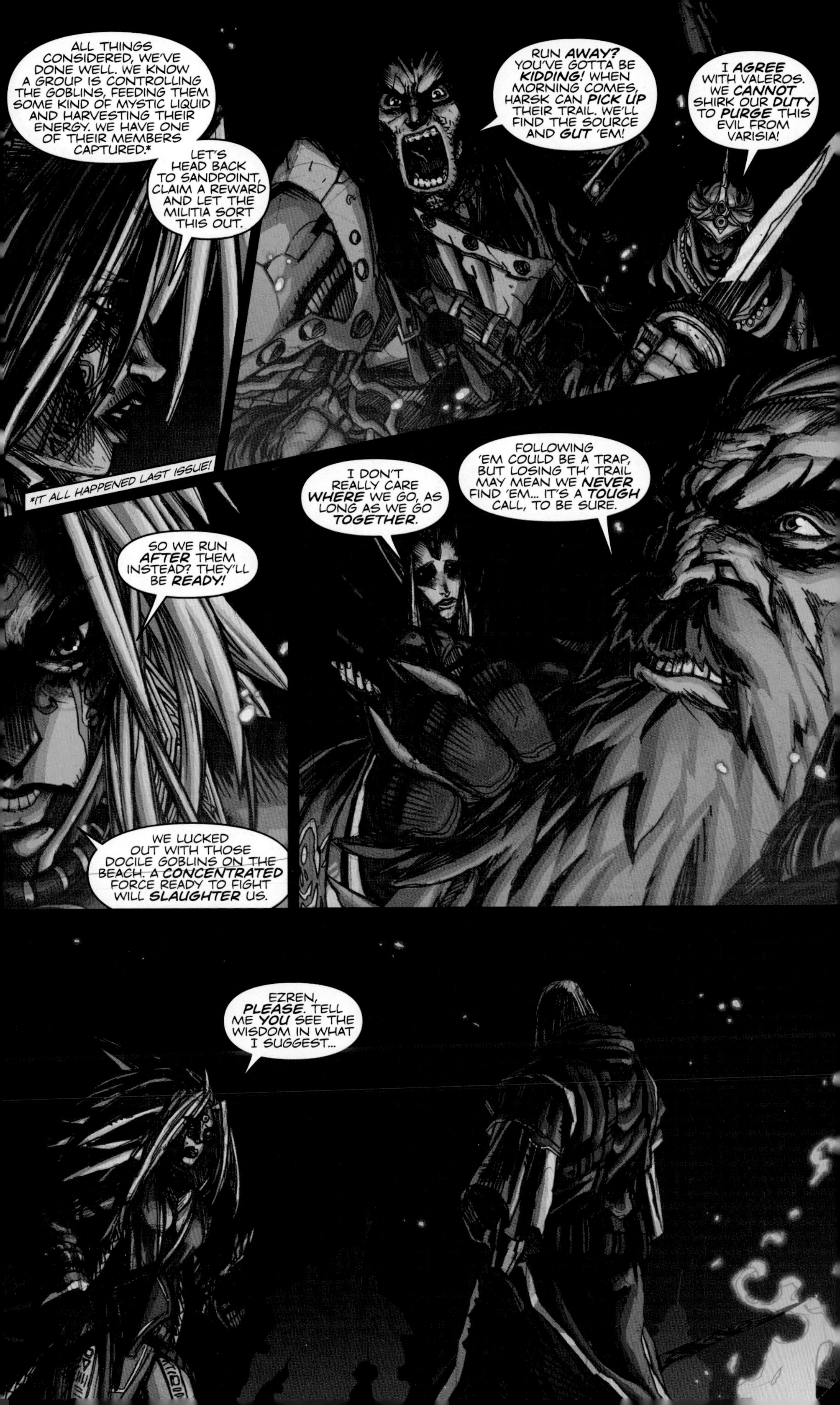

ALL THINGS CONSIDERED, WE'VE DONE WELL. WE KNOW A GROUP IS CONTROLLING THE GOBLINS, FEEDING THEM SOME KIND OF MYSTIC LIQUID AND HARVESTING THEIR ENERGY. WE HAVE ONE OF THEIR MEMBERS CAPTURED.*
LET'S HEAD BACK TO SANDPOINT, CLAIM A REWARD AND LET THE MILITIA SORT THIS OUT.
*IT ALL HAPPENED LAST ISSUE!
RUN AWAY? YOU'VE GOTTA BE KIDDING! WHEN MORNING COMES, HARSK CAN PICK UP THEIR TRAIL. WE'LL FIND THE SOURCE AND GUT 'EM!
I AGREE WITH VALEROS. WE CANNOT SHIRK OUR DUTY TO PURGE THIS EVIL FROM VARISIA!
SO WE RUN AFTER THEM INSTEAD? THEY'LL BE READY!
WE LUCKED OUT WITH THOSE DOCILE GOBLINS ON THE BEACH. A CONCENTRATED FORCE READY TO FIGHT WILL SLAUGHTER US.
I DON'T REALLY CARE WHERE WE GO, AS LONG AS WE GO TOGETHER.
FOLLOWING 'EM COULD BE A TRAP, BUT LOSING TH' TRAIL MAY MEAN WE NEVER FIND 'EM... IT'S A TOUGH CALL, TO BE SURE.
EZREN, PLEASE. TELL ME YOU SEE THE WISDOM IN WHAT I SUGGEST...

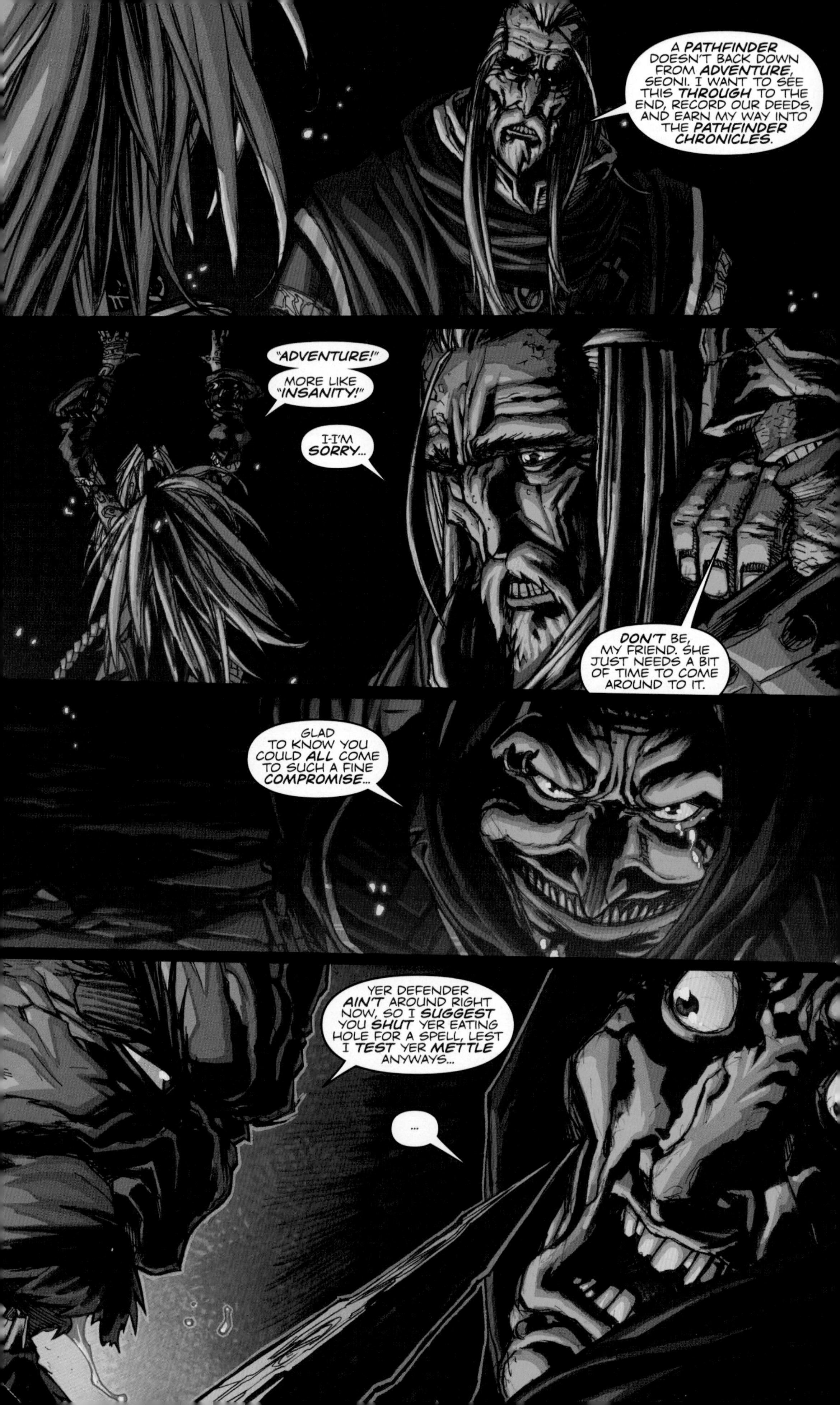

A PATHFINDER DOESN'T BACK DOWN FROM ADVENTURE, SEONI. I WANT TO SEE THIS THROUGH TO THE END, RECORD OUR DEEDS, AND EARN MY WAY INTO THE PATHFINDER CHRONICLES.
"ADVENTURE!"
MORE LIKE "INSANITY!"
I-I'M SORRY...
DON'T BE, MY FRIEND. SHE JUST NEEDS A BIT OF TIME TO COME AROUND TO IT.
GLAD TO KNOW YOU COULD ALL COME TO SUCH A FINE COMPROMISE...
YER DEFENDER AIN'T AROUND RIGHT NOW, SO I SUGGEST YOU SHUT YER EATING HOLE FOR A SPELL, LEST I TEST YER METTLE ANYWAYS...
...

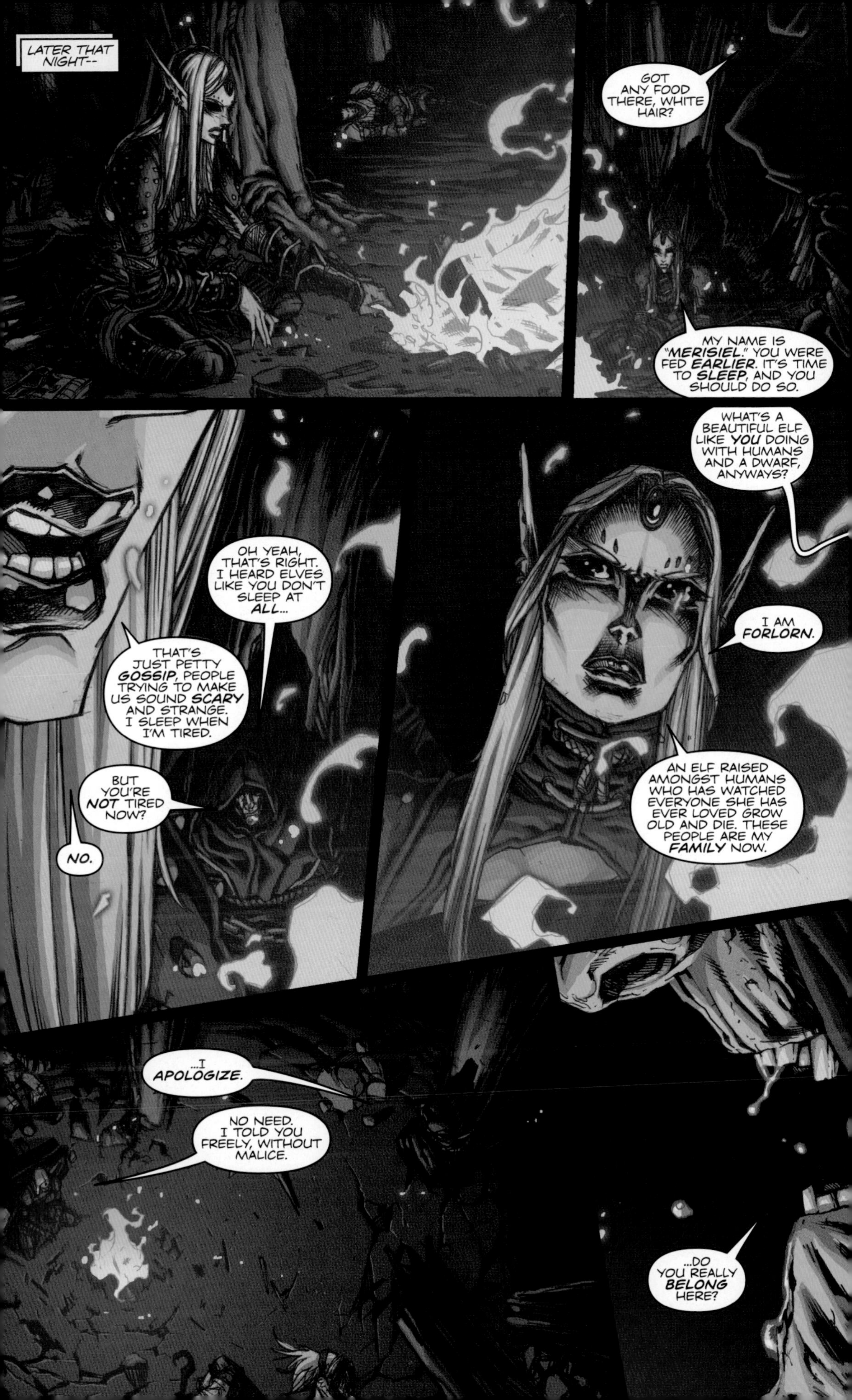
LATER THAT NIGHT--
GOT ANY FOOD THERE, WHITE HAIR?
MY NAME IS "MERISIEL." YOU WERE FED EARLIER. IT'S TIME TO SLEEP, AND YOU SHOULD DO SO.
OH YEAH, THAT'S RIGHT. I HEARD ELVES LIKE YOU DON'T SLEEP AT ALL...
THAT'S JUST PETTY GOSSIP, PEOPLE TRYING TO MAKE US SOUND SCARY AND STRANGE. I SLEEP WHEN I'M TIRED.
BUT YOU'RE NOT TIRED NOW?
NO.
WHAT'S A BEAUTIFUL ELF LIKE YOU DOING WITH HUMANS AND A DWARF, ANYWAYS?
I AM FORLORN.
AN ELF RAISED AMONGST HUMANS WHO HAS WATCHED EVERYONE SHE HAS EVER LOVED GROW OLD AND DIE. THESE PEOPLE ARE MY FAMILY NOW.
...I APOLOGIZE.
NO NEED. I TOLD YOU FREELY, WITHOUT MALICE.
...DO YOU REALLY BELONG HERE?

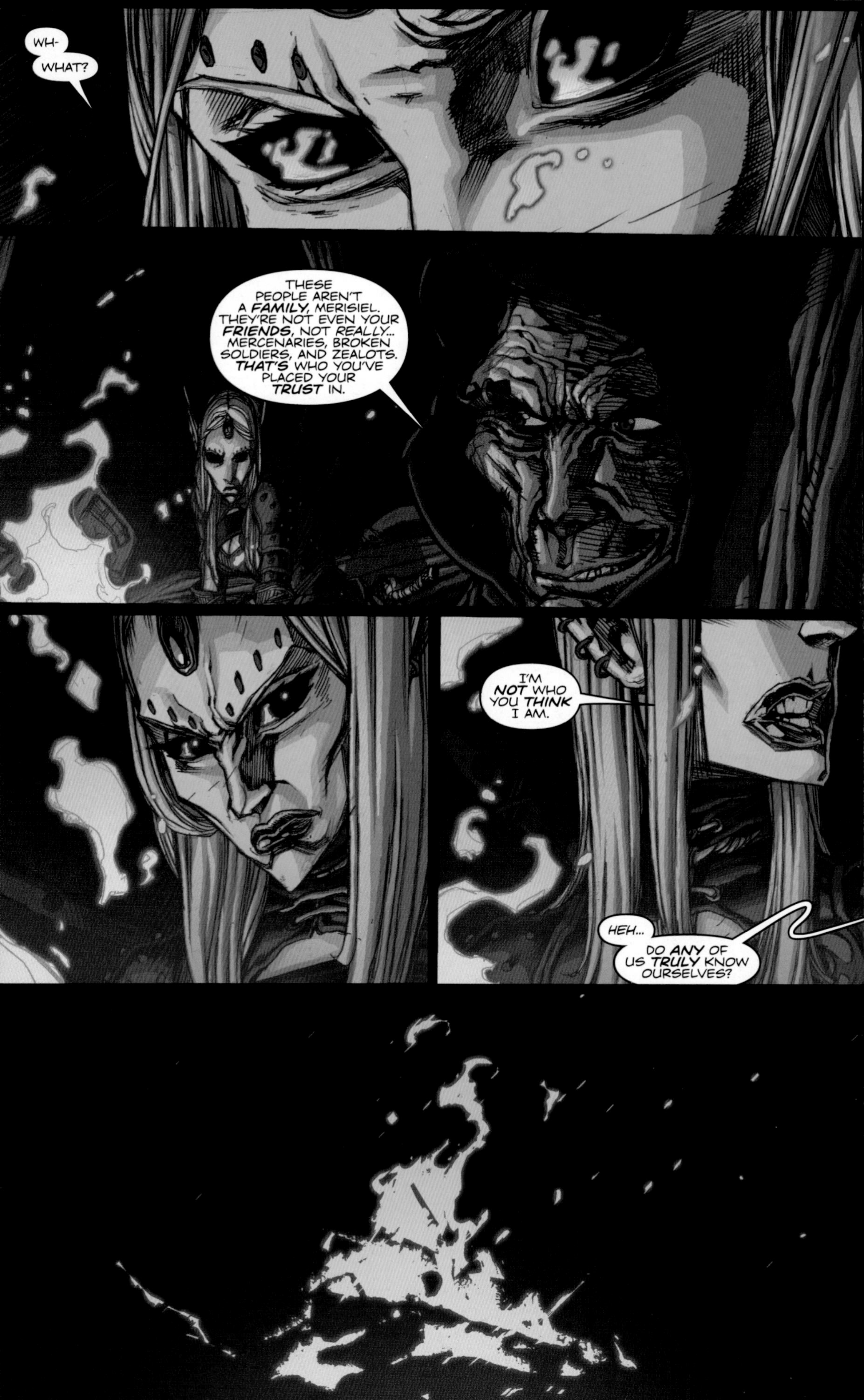
WH- WHAT?
THESE PEOPLE AREN'T A FAMILY, MERISIEL. THEY'RE NOT EVEN YOUR FRIENDS, NOT REALLY... MERCENARIES, BROKEN SOLDIERS, AND ZEALOTS. THAT'S WHO YOU'VE PLACED YOUR TRUST IN.
I'M NOT WHO YOU THINK I AM.
HEH... DO ANY OF US TRULY KNOW OURSELVES?

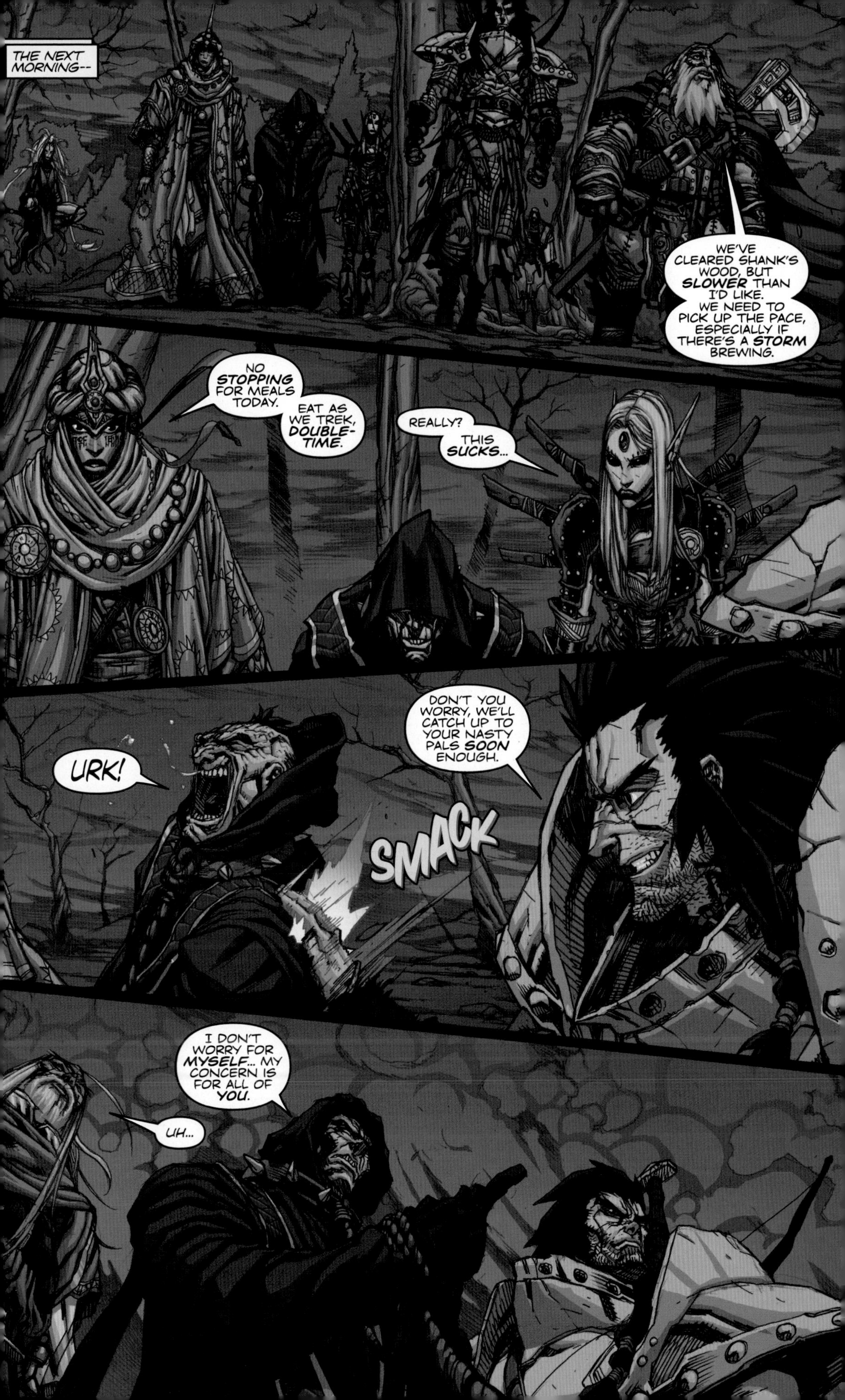
THE NEXT MORNING--
WE'VE CLEARED SHANK'S WOOD, BUT SLOWER THAN I'D LIKE. WE NEED TO PICK UP THE PACE, ESPECIALLY IF THERE'S A STORM BREWING.
NO STOPPING FOR MEALS TODAY.
EAT AS WE TREK, DOUBLE-TIME.
REALLY? THIS SUCKS...
DON'T YOU WORRY, WE'LL CATCH UP TO YOUR NASTY PALS SOON ENOUGH.
URK!
SMACK
I DON'T WORRY FOR MYSELF... MY CONCERN IS FOR ALL OF YOU.
UH...

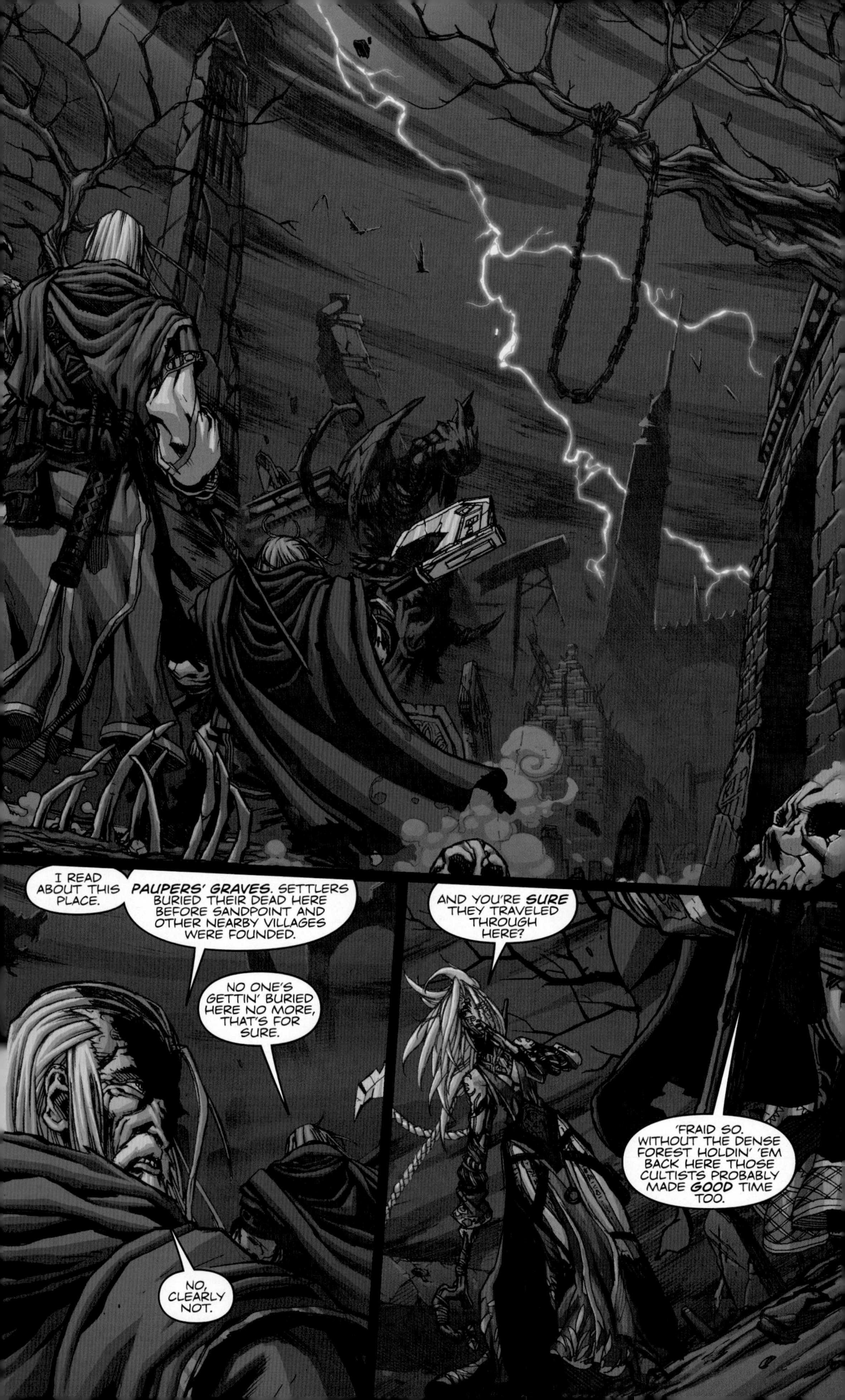
I READ ABOUT THIS PLACE.
PAUPERS' GRAVES. SETTLERS BURIED THEIR DEAD HERE BEFORE SANDPOINT AND OTHER NEARBY VILLAGES WERE FOUNDED.
NO ONE'S GETTIN' BURIED HERE NO MORE, THAT'S FOR SURE.
NO, CLEARLY NOT.
AND YOU'RE SURE THEY TRAVELED THROUGH HERE?
'FRAID SO. WITHOUT THE DENSE FOREST HOLDIN' 'EM BACK HERE THOSE CULTISTS PROBABLY MADE GOOD TIME TOO.

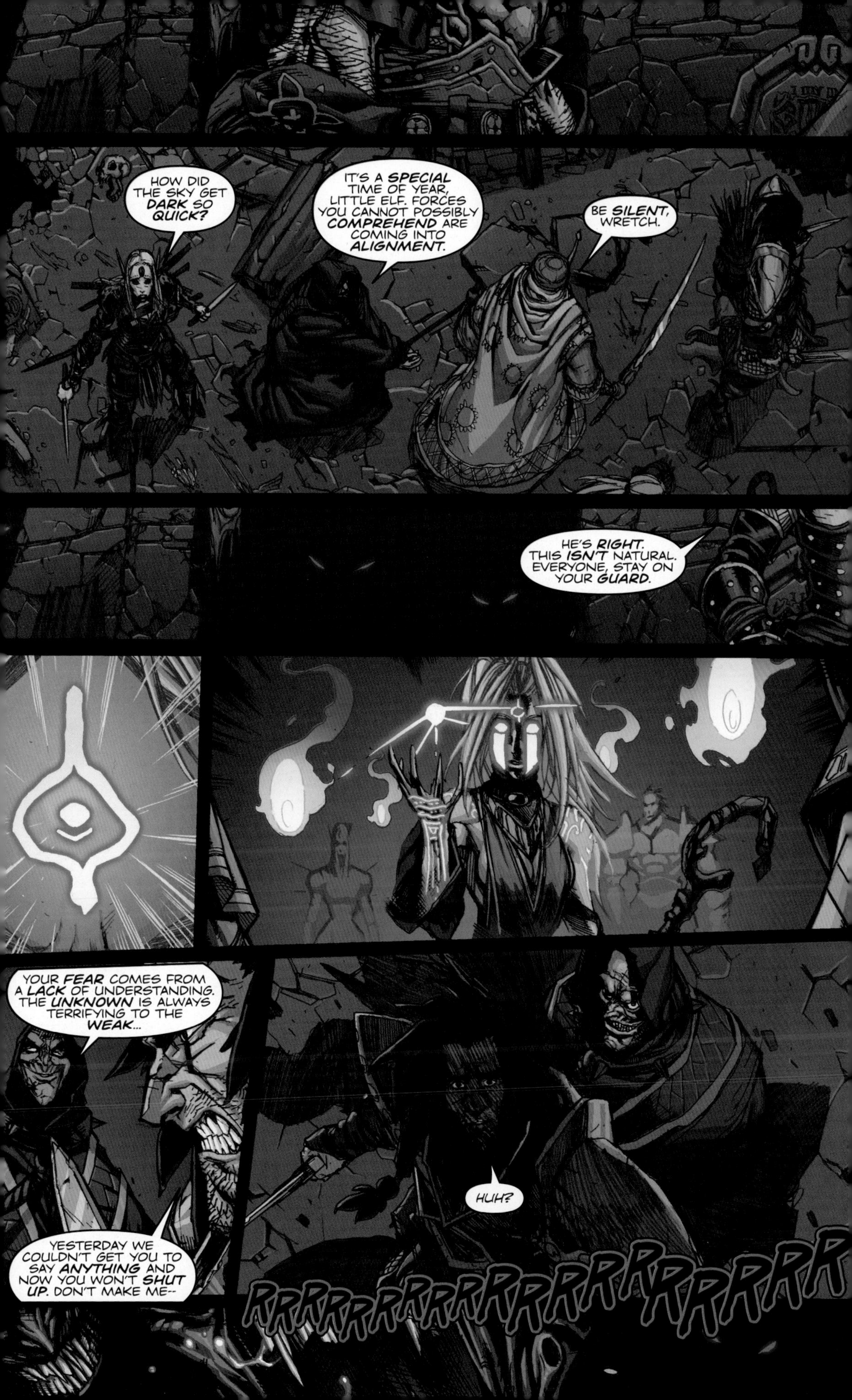
HOW DID THE SKY GET DARK SO QUICK?
IT'S A SPECIAL TIME OF YEAR, LITTLE ELF. FORCES YOU CANNOT POSSIBLY COMPREHEND ARE COMING INTO ALIGNMENT.
BE SILENT, WRETCH.
HE'S RIGHT. THIS ISN'T NATURAL. EVERYONE, STAY ON YOUR GUARD.
YOUR FEAR COMES FROM A LACK OF UNDERSTANDING. THE UNKNOWN IS ALWAYS TERRIFYING TO THE WEAK...
YESTERDAY WE COULDN'T GET YOU TO SAY ANYTHING AND NOW YOU WON'T SHUT UP. DON'T MAKE ME--
HUH?
RRRRRRRRRRRRRRRRRRRRRRR

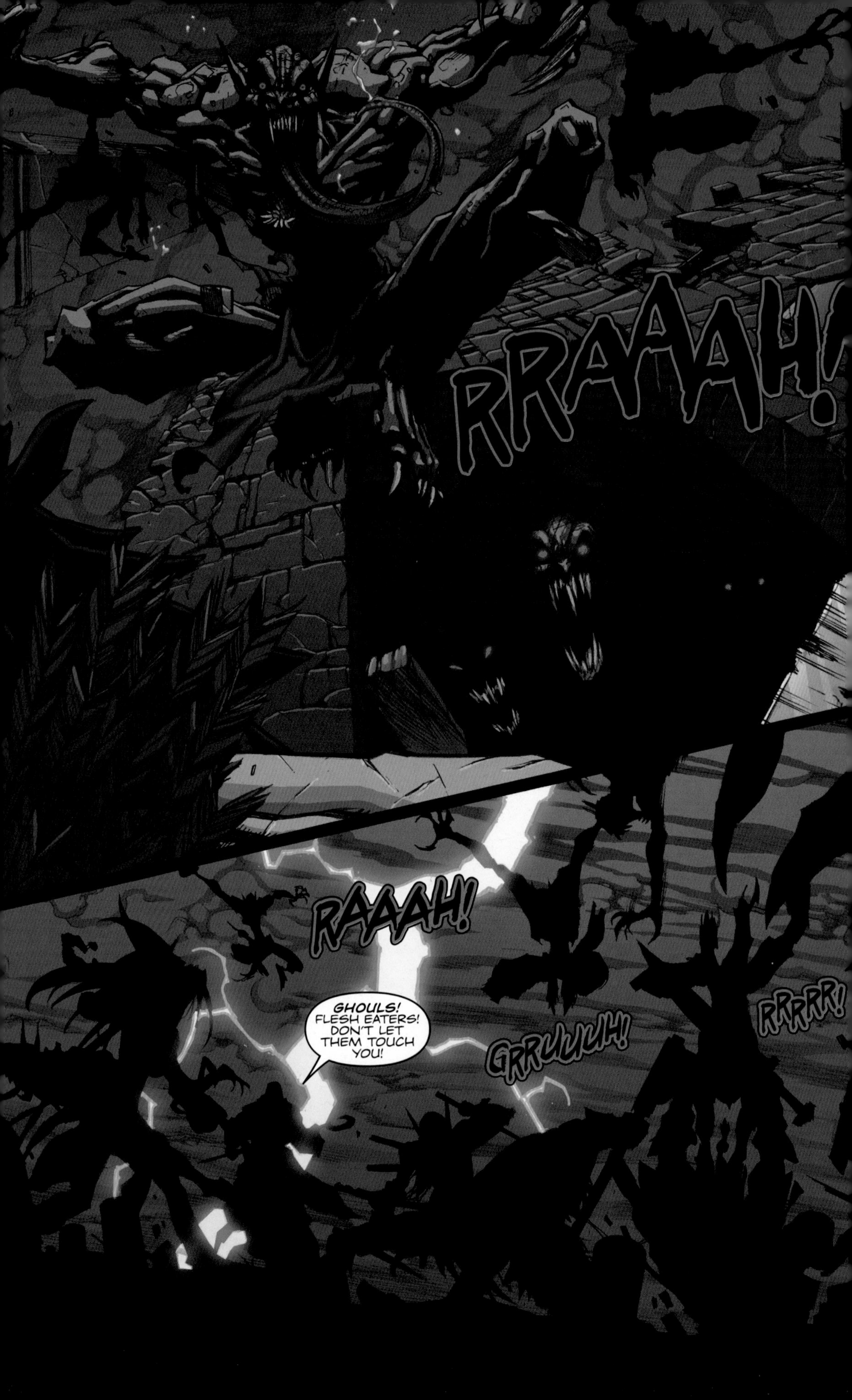
RRAAAAH!
RAAAH!
GHOULS! FLESH EATERS! DON'T LET THEM TOUCH YOU!
GRRULLUH!
RRRRR!

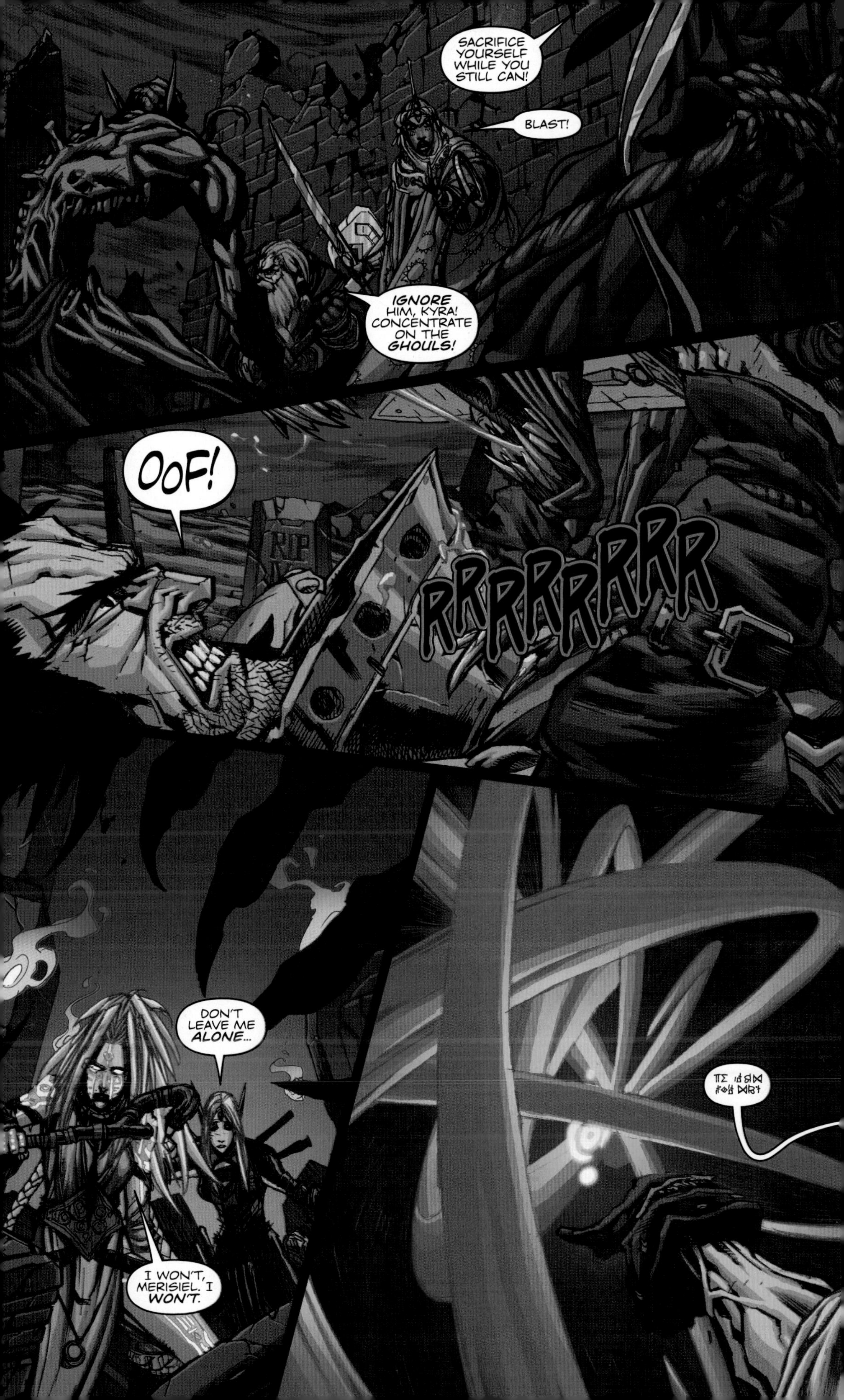
SACRIFICE YOURSELF WHILE YOU STILL CAN!
BLAST!
IGNORE HIM, KYRA! CONCENTRATE ON THE GHOULS!
OOF!
RIP
RRRRRRRR
DON'T LEAVE ME ALONE...
I WON'T, MERISIEL. I WON'T.

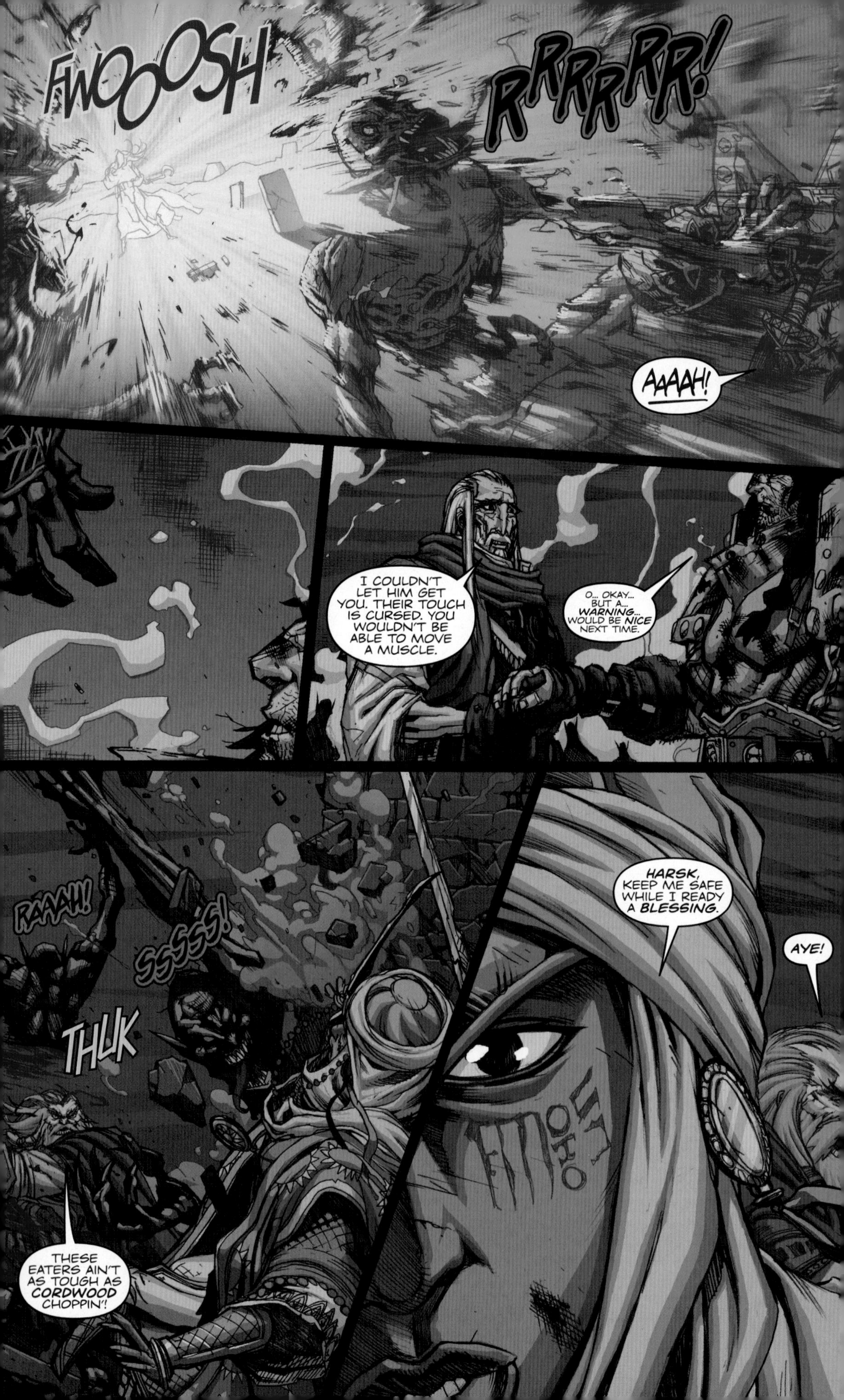
FWOOOSH
RRRRRR!
AAAAH!
I COULDN'T LET HIM GET YOU. THEIR TOUCH IS CURSED. YOU WOULDN'T BE ABLE TO MOVE A MUSCLE.
O... OKAY... BUT A... WARNING... WOULD BE NICE NEXT TIME.
RAAAH!
SSSSS!
THUK
THESE EATERS AIN'T AS TOUGH AS CORDWOOD CHOPPIN'!
HARSK, KEEP ME SAFE WHILE I READY A BLESSING.
AYE!

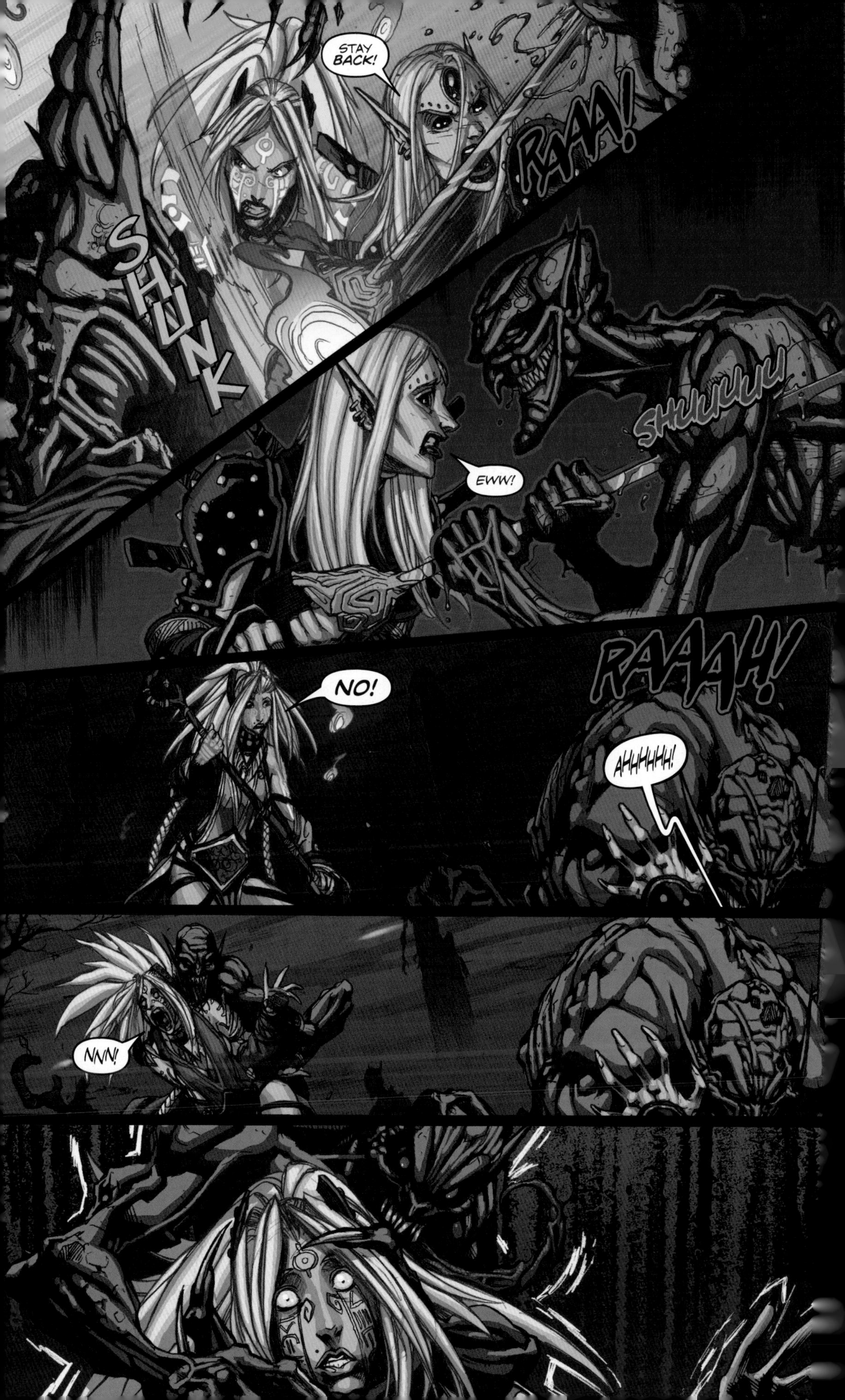
STAY BACK!
RAAA!
SHUNK
SHUUUUU
EWW!
RAAAH!
NO!
AHHHHHH!
NNN!

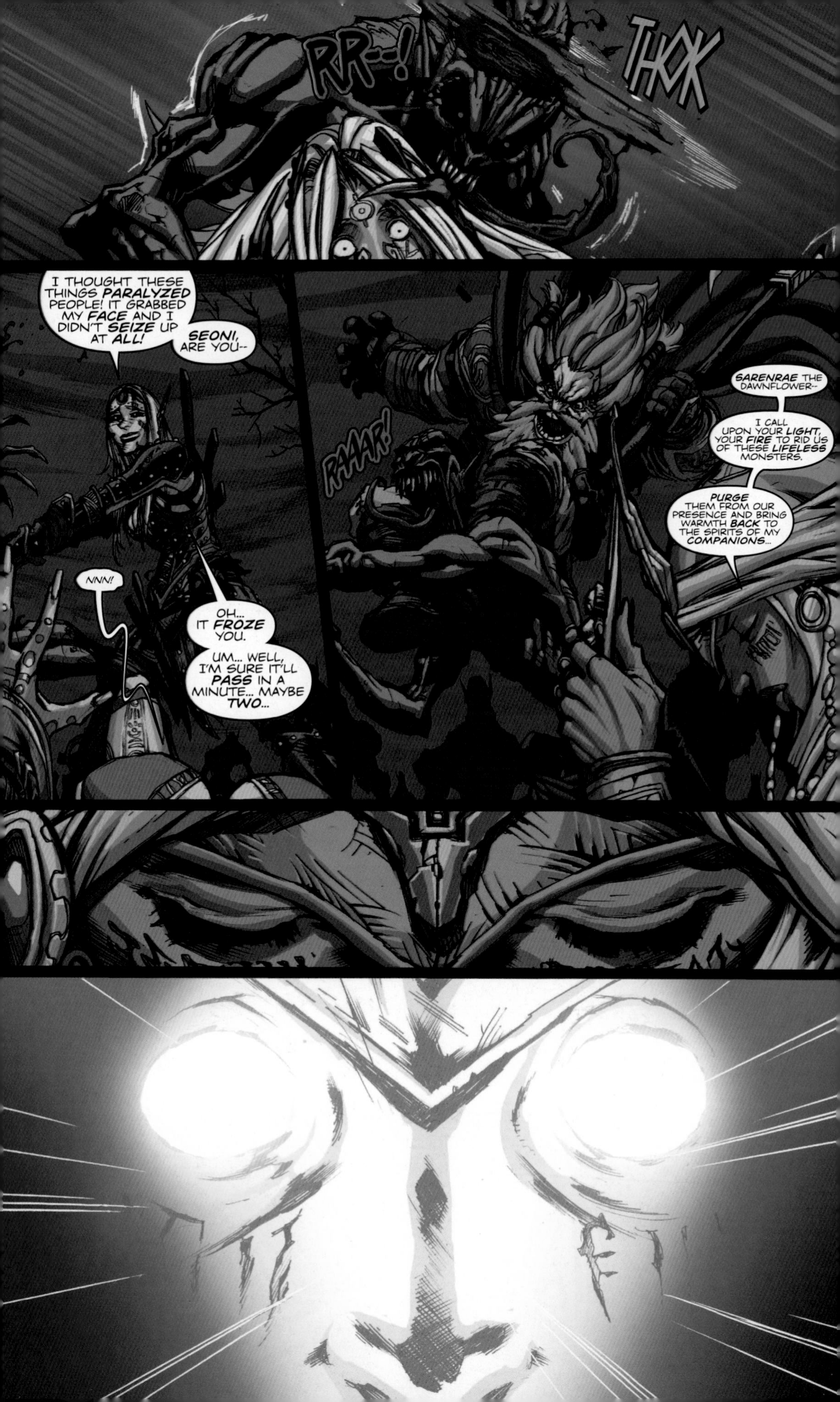

RR--!
THOK
I THOUGHT THESE THINGS PARALYZED PEOPLE! IT GRABBED MY FACE AND I DIDN'T SEIZE UP AT ALL!
SEONI, ARE YOU--
NNN!
OH... IT FROZE YOU.
UM... WELL, I'M SURE IT'LL PASS IN A MINUTE... MAYBE TWO...
RAAAR!
SARENRAE THE DAWNFLOWER--
I CALL UPON YOUR LIGHT, YOUR FIRE TO RID US OF THESE LIFELESS MONSTERS.
PURGE THEM FROM OUR PRESENCE AND BRING WARMTH BACK TO THE SPIRITS OF MY COMPANIONS...

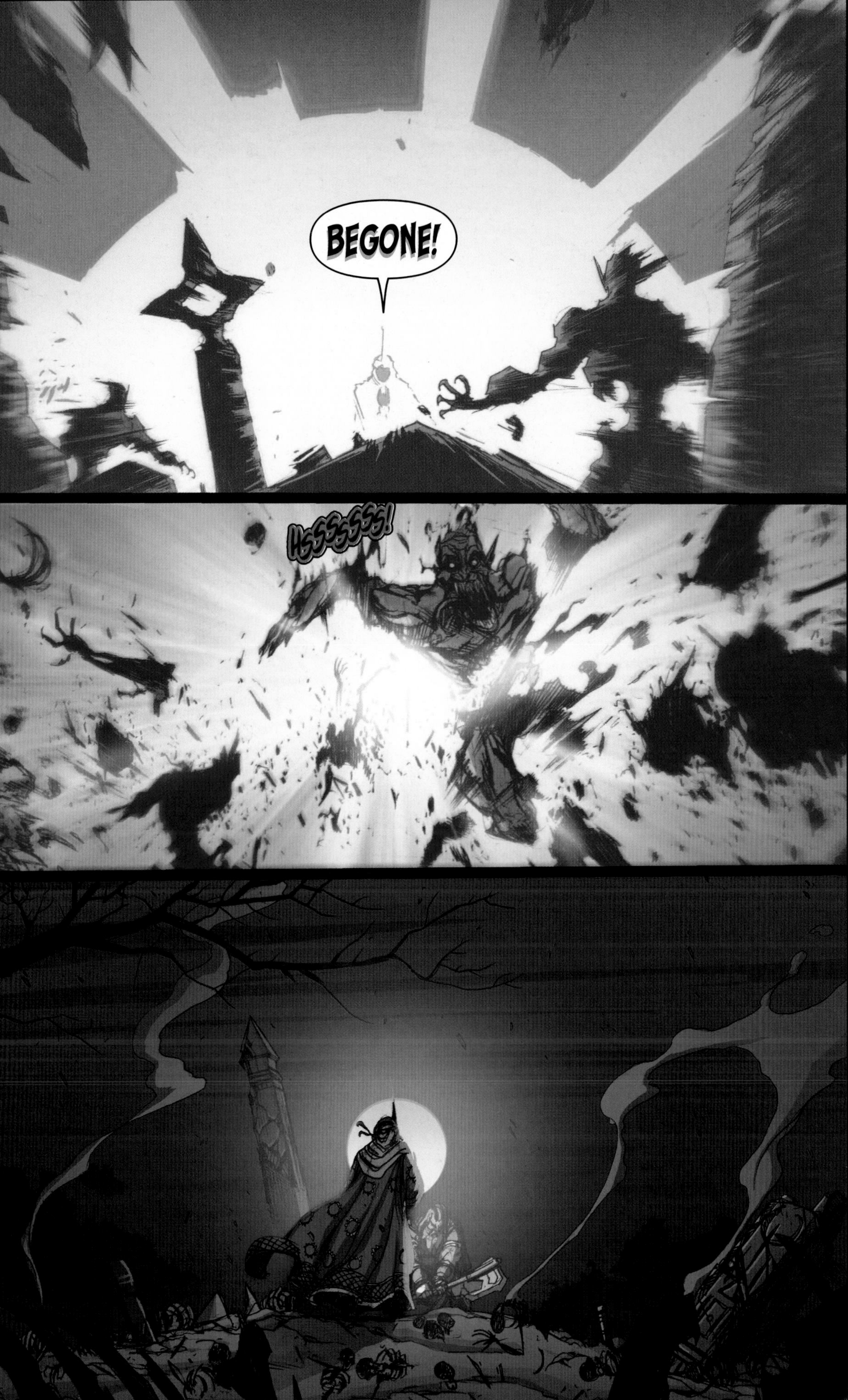
BEGONE!
HSSSSSSS!

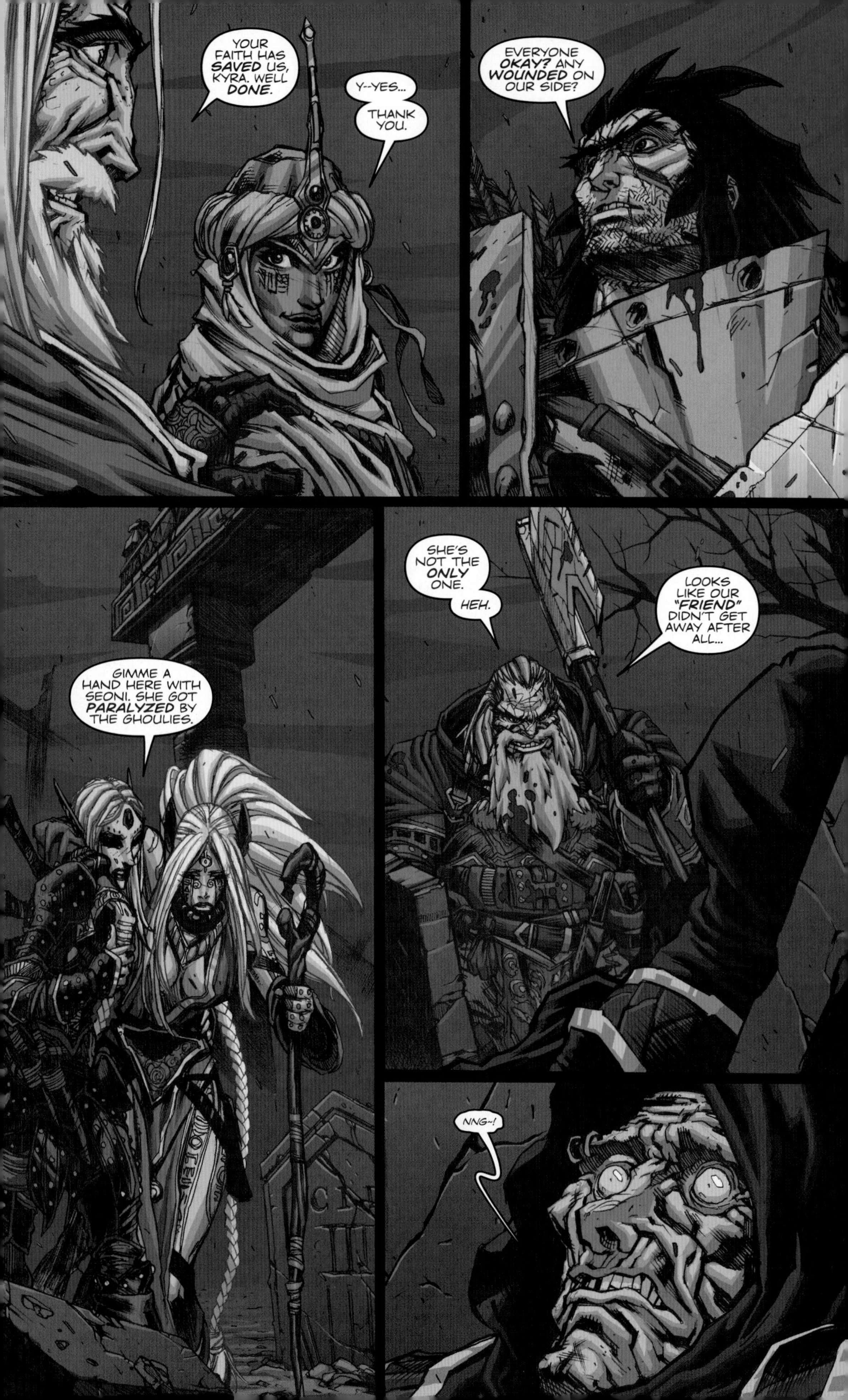
YOUR FAITH HAS SAVED US, KYRA. WELL DONE.
Y--YES...
THANK YOU.
EVERYONE OKAY? ANY WOUNDED ON OUR SIDE?
GIMME A HAND HERE WITH SEONI. SHE GOT PARALYZED BY THE GHOULIES.
SHE'S NOT THE ONLY ONE.
HEH.
LOOKS LIKE OUR "FRIEND" DIDN'T GET AWAY AFTER ALL...
NNG~!

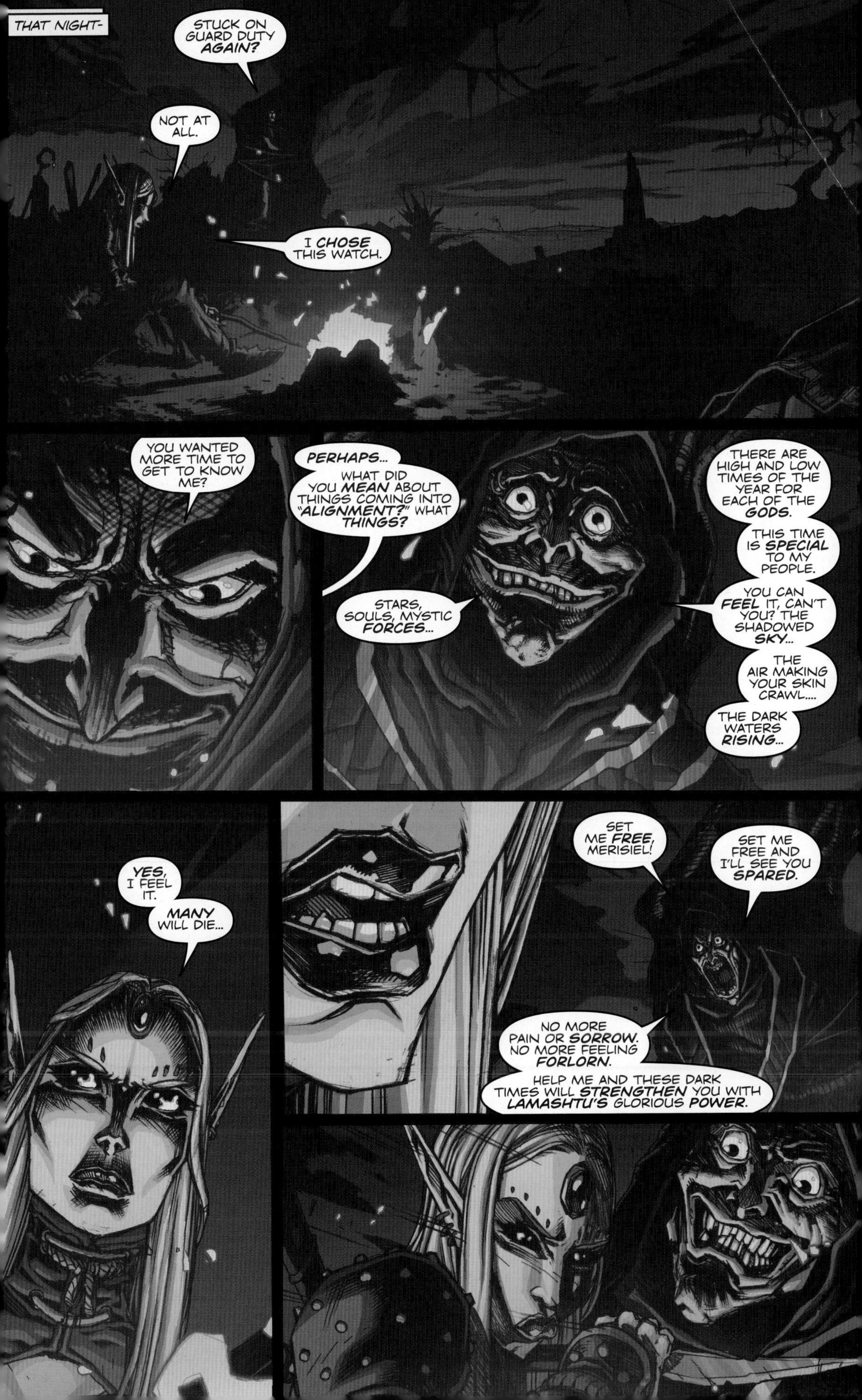
THAT NIGHT-
STUCK ON GUARD DUTY AGAIN?
NOT AT ALL.
I CHOSE THIS WATCH.
YOU WANTED MORE TIME TO GET TO KNOW ME?
PERHAPS... WHAT DID YOU MEAN ABOUT THINGS COMING INTO "ALIGNMENT?" WHAT THINGS?
STARS, SOULS, MYSTIC FORCES...
THERE ARE HIGH AND LOW TIMES OF THE YEAR FOR EACH OF THE GODS.
THIS TIME IS SPECIAL TO MY PEOPLE.
YOU CAN FEEL IT, CAN'T YOU? THE SHADOWED SKY...
THE AIR MAKING YOUR SKIN CRAWL....
THE DARK WATERS RISING...
YES, I FEEL IT.
MANY WILL DIE...
SET ME FREE, MERISIEL!
SET ME FREE AND I'LL SEE YOU SPARED.
NO MORE PAIN OR SORROW. NO MORE FEELING FORLORN.
HELP ME AND THESE DARK TIMES WILL STRENGTHEN YOU WITH LAMASHTU'S GLORIOUS POWER.

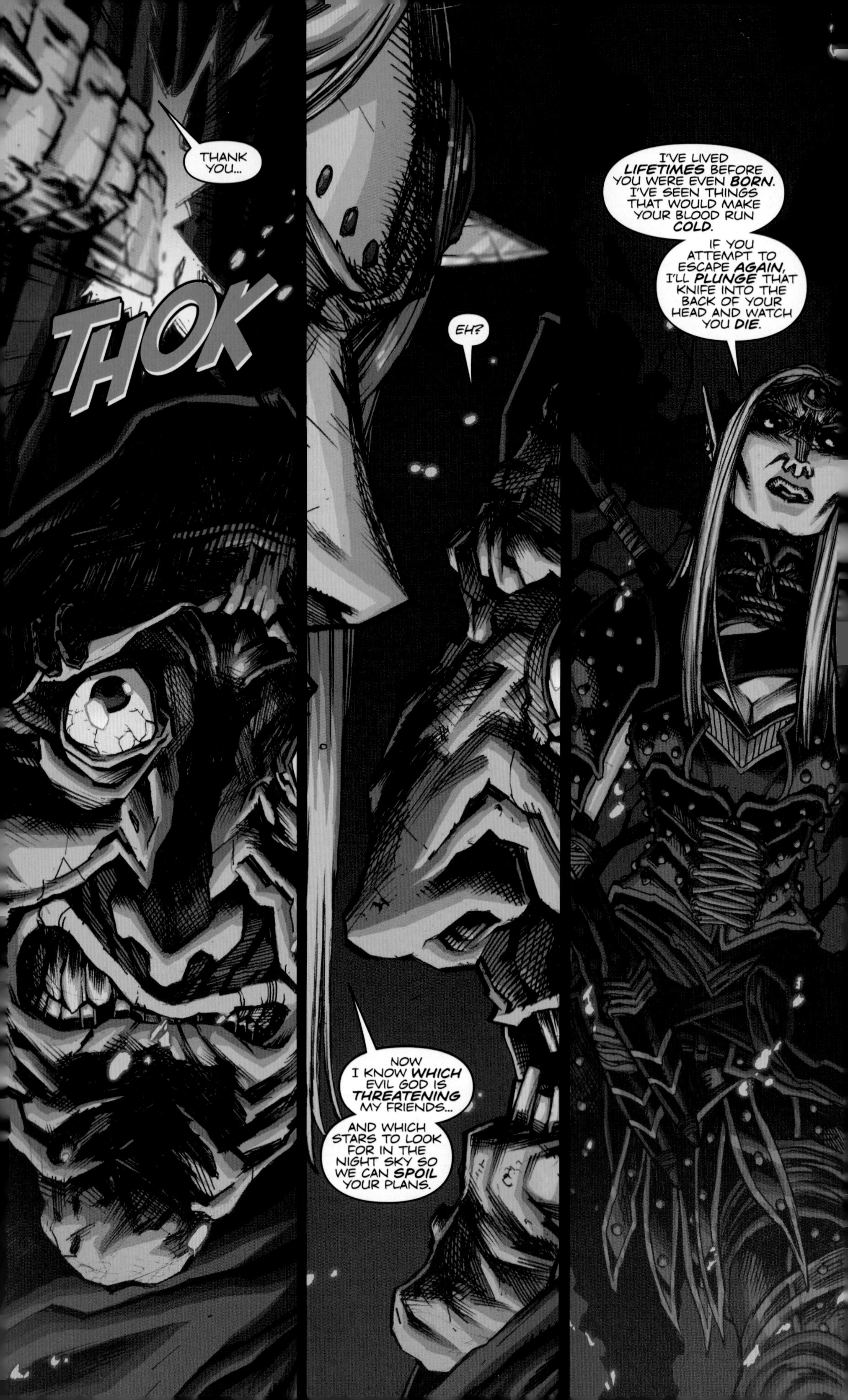
THANK YOU...
THOK
EH?
NOW I KNOW WHICH EVIL GOD IS THREATENING MY FRIENDS...
AND WHICH STARS TO LOOK FOR IN THE NIGHT SKY SO WE CAN SPOIL YOUR PLANS.
I'VE LIVED LIFETIMES BEFORE YOU WERE EVEN BORN. I'VE SEEN THINGS THAT WOULD MAKE YOUR BLOOD RUN COLD.
IF YOU ATTEMPT TO ESCAPE AGAIN, I'LL PLUNGE THAT KNIFE INTO THE BACK OF YOUR HEAD AND WATCH YOU DIE.

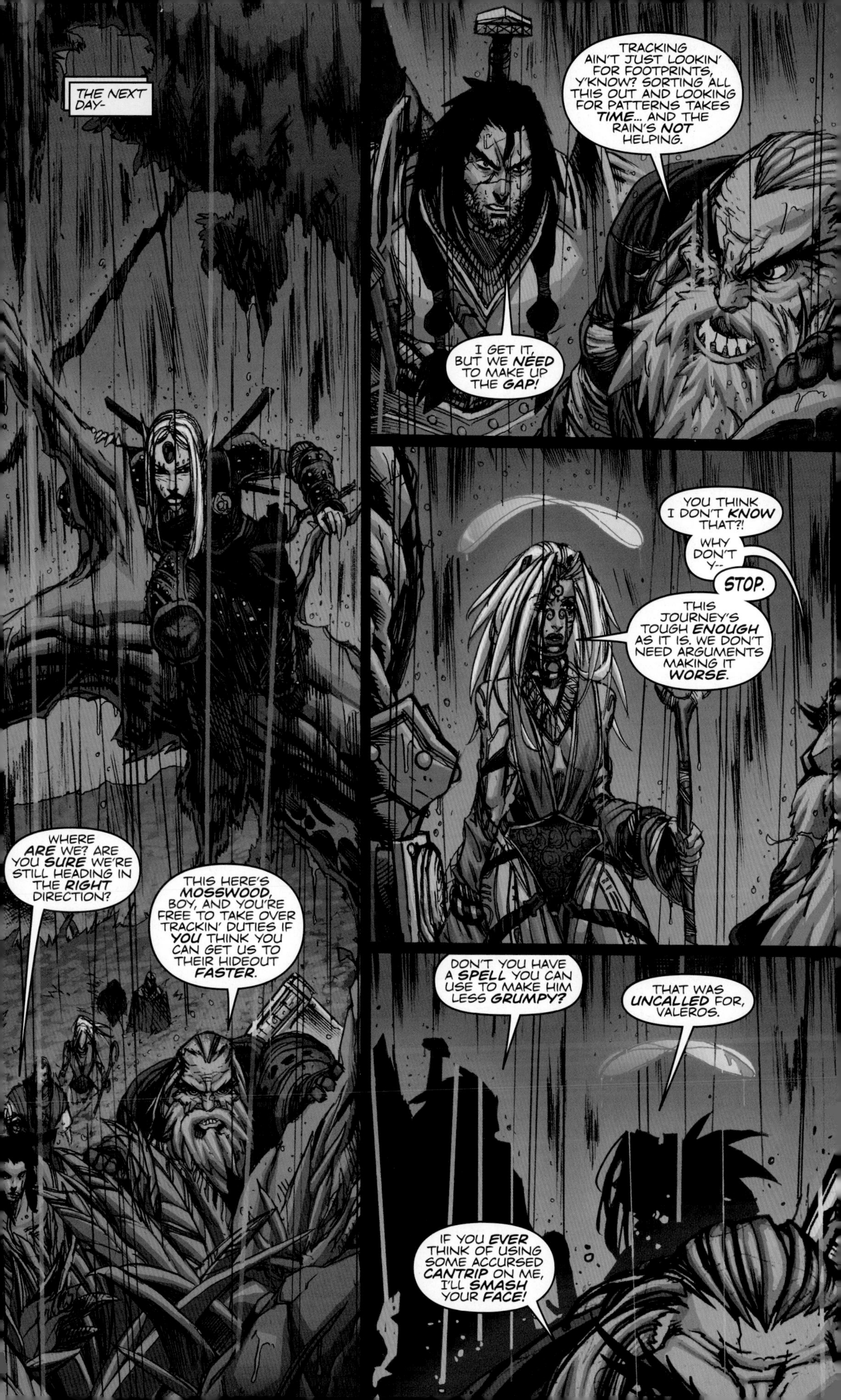

THE NEXT DAY-
WHERE ARE WE? ARE YOU SURE WE'RE STILL HEADING IN THE RIGHT DIRECTION?
THIS HERE'S MOSSWOOD, BOY, AND YOU'RE FREE TO TAKE OVER TRACKIN' DUTIES IF YOU THINK YOU CAN GET US TO THEIR HIDEOUT FASTER.
TRACKING AIN'T JUST LOOKIN' FOR FOOTPRINTS, Y'KNOW? SORTING ALL THIS OUT AND LOOKING FOR PATTERNS TAKES TIME... AND THE RAIN'S NOT HELPING.
I GET IT, BUT WE NEED TO MAKE UP THE GAP!
YOU THINK I DON'T KNOW THAT?!
WHY DON'T Y--
STOP.
THIS JOURNEY'S TOUGH ENOUGH AS IT IS. WE DON'T NEED ARGUMENTS MAKING IT WORSE.
DON'T YOU HAVE A SPELL YOU CAN USE TO MAKE HIM LESS GRUMPY?
THAT WAS UNCALLED FOR, VALEROS.
IF YOU EVER THINK OF USING SOME ACCURSED CANTRIP ON ME, I'LL SMASH YOUR FACE!

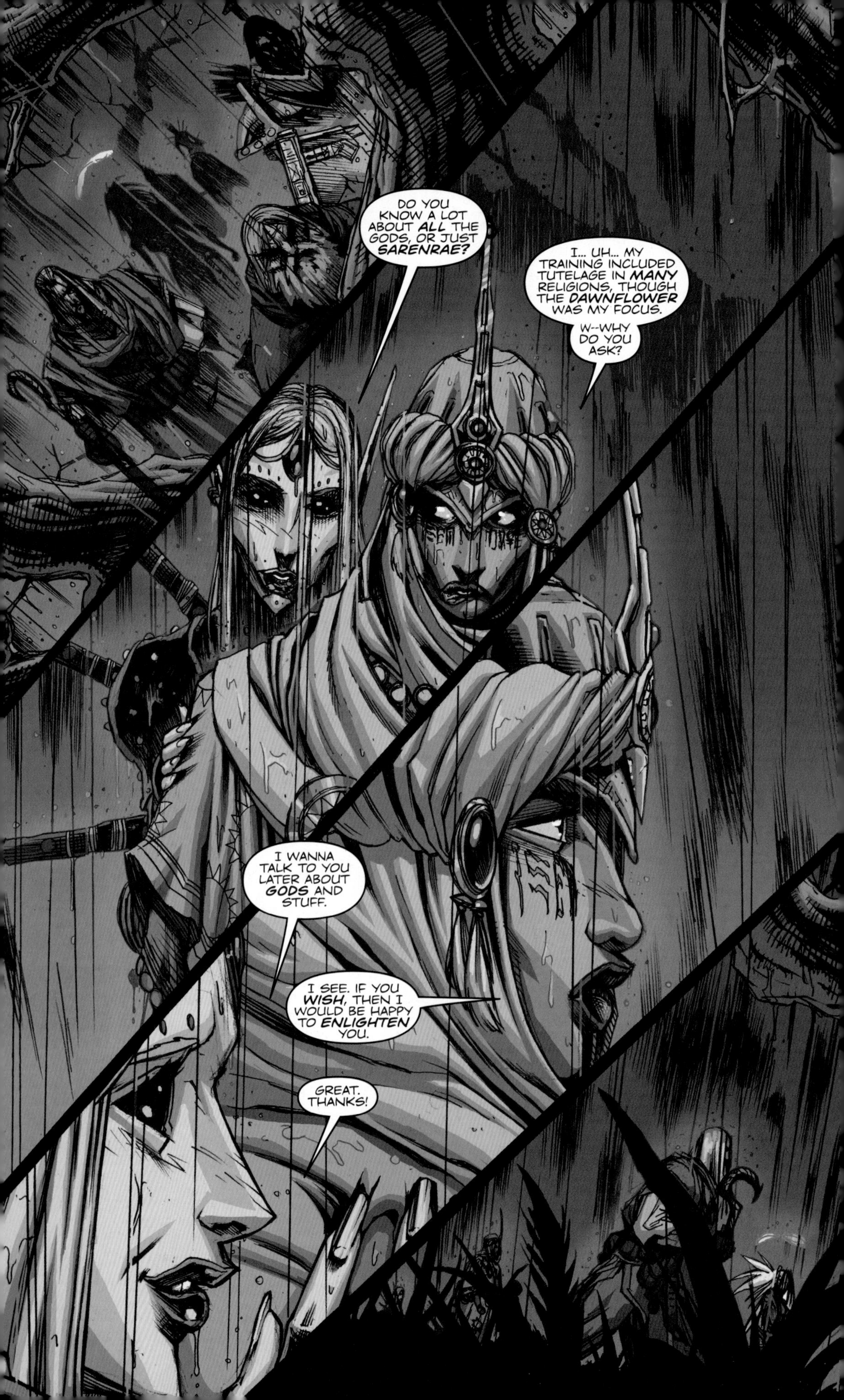
DO YOU KNOW A LOT ABOUT **ALL** THE GODS, OR JUST **SARENRAE?**
I... UH... MY TRAINING INCLUDED TUTELAGE IN **MANY** RELIGIONS, THOUGH THE **DAWNFLOWER** WAS MY FOCUS.
W--WHY DO YOU ASK?
I WANNA TALK TO YOU LATER ABOUT **GODS** AND STUFF.
I SEE. IF YOU **WISH**, THEN I WOULD BE HAPPY TO **ENLIGHTEN** YOU.
GREAT. THANKS!

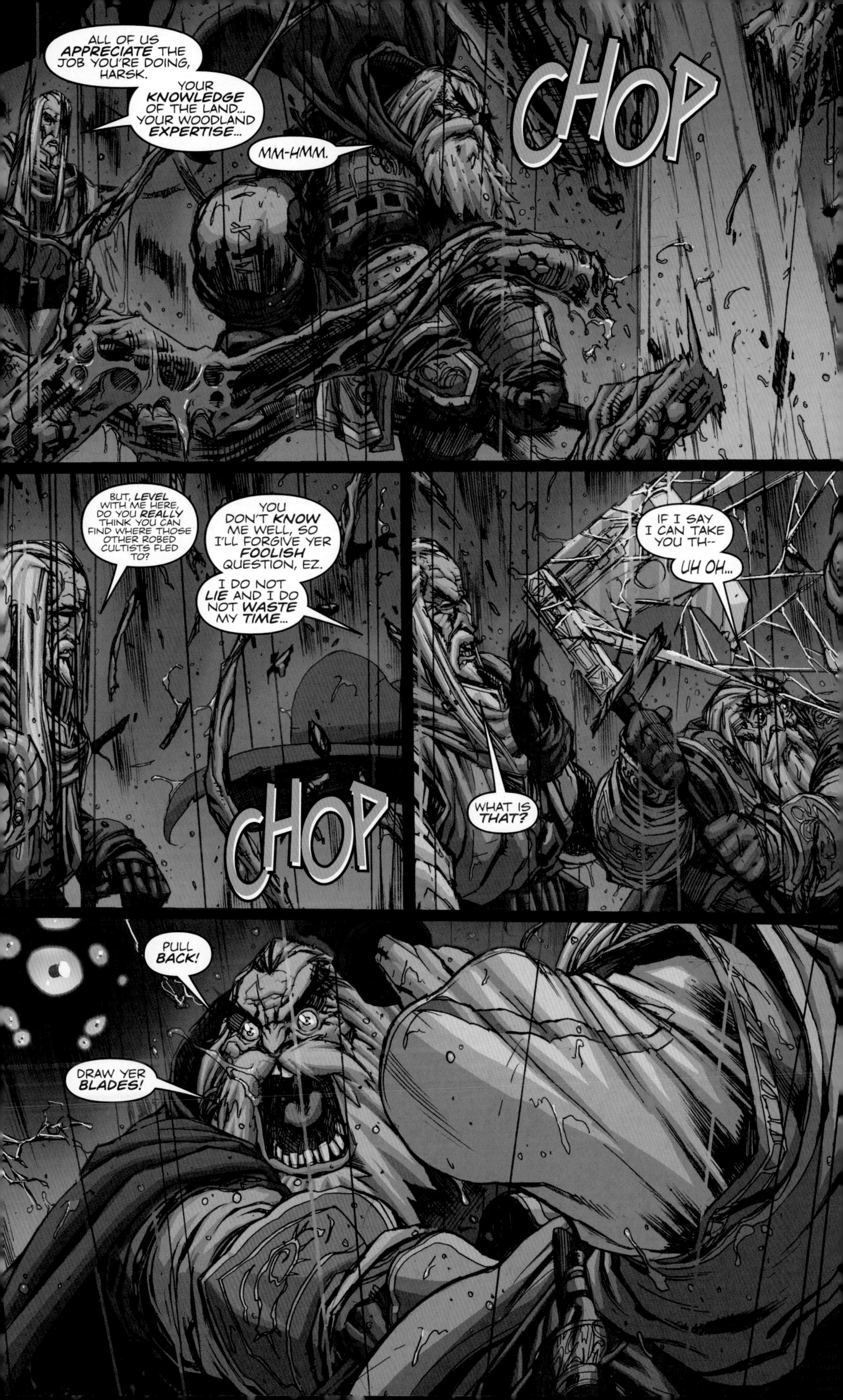
ALL OF US APPRECIATE THE JOB YOU'RE DOING, HARSK.
YOUR KNOWLEDGE OF THE LAND... YOUR WOODLAND EXPERTISE...
MM-HMM.
CHOP
BUT, LEVEL WITH ME HERE, DO YOU REALLY THINK YOU CAN FIND WHERE THOSE OTHER ROBED CULTISTS FLED TO?
YOU DON'T KNOW ME WELL, SO I'LL FORGIVE YER FOOLISH QUESTION, EZ.
I DO NOT LIE AND I DO NOT WASTE MY TIME...
CHOP
IF I SAY I CAN TAKE YOU TH--
UH OH...
WHAT IS THAT?
PULL BACK!
DRAW YER BLADES!

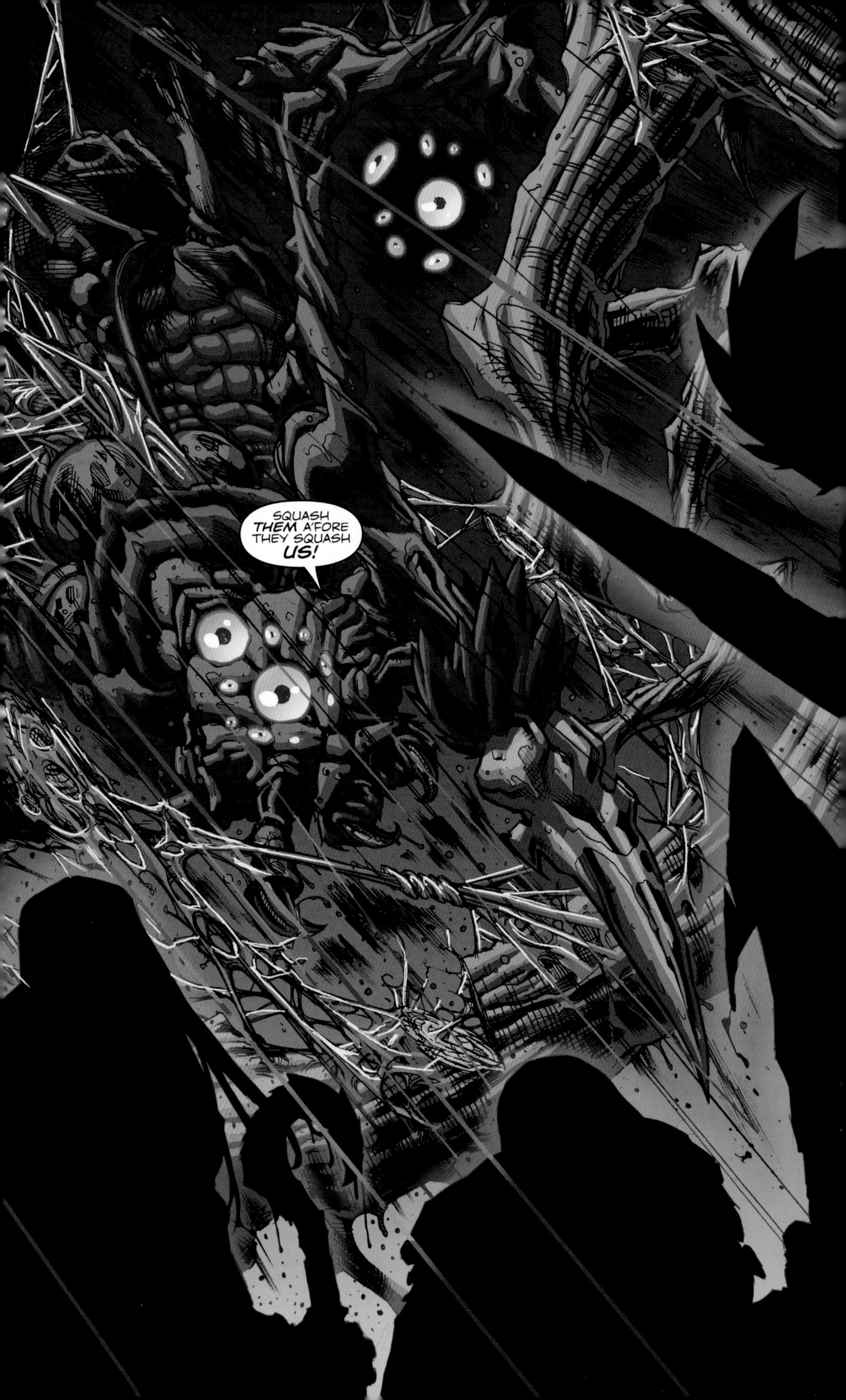
SQUASH THEM A'FORE THEY SQUASH US!

CHAPTER 4

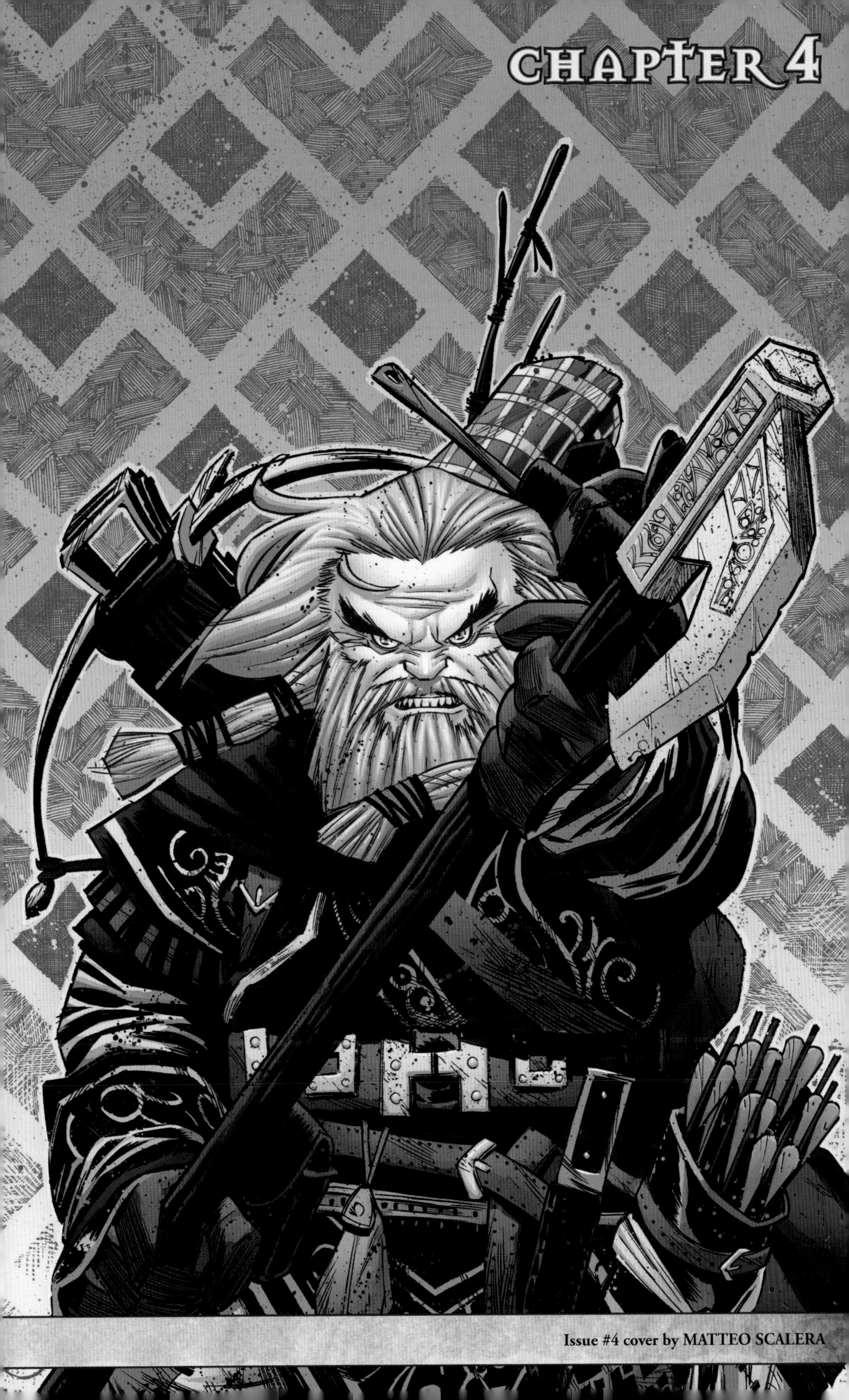

Issue #4 cover by MATTEO SCALERA

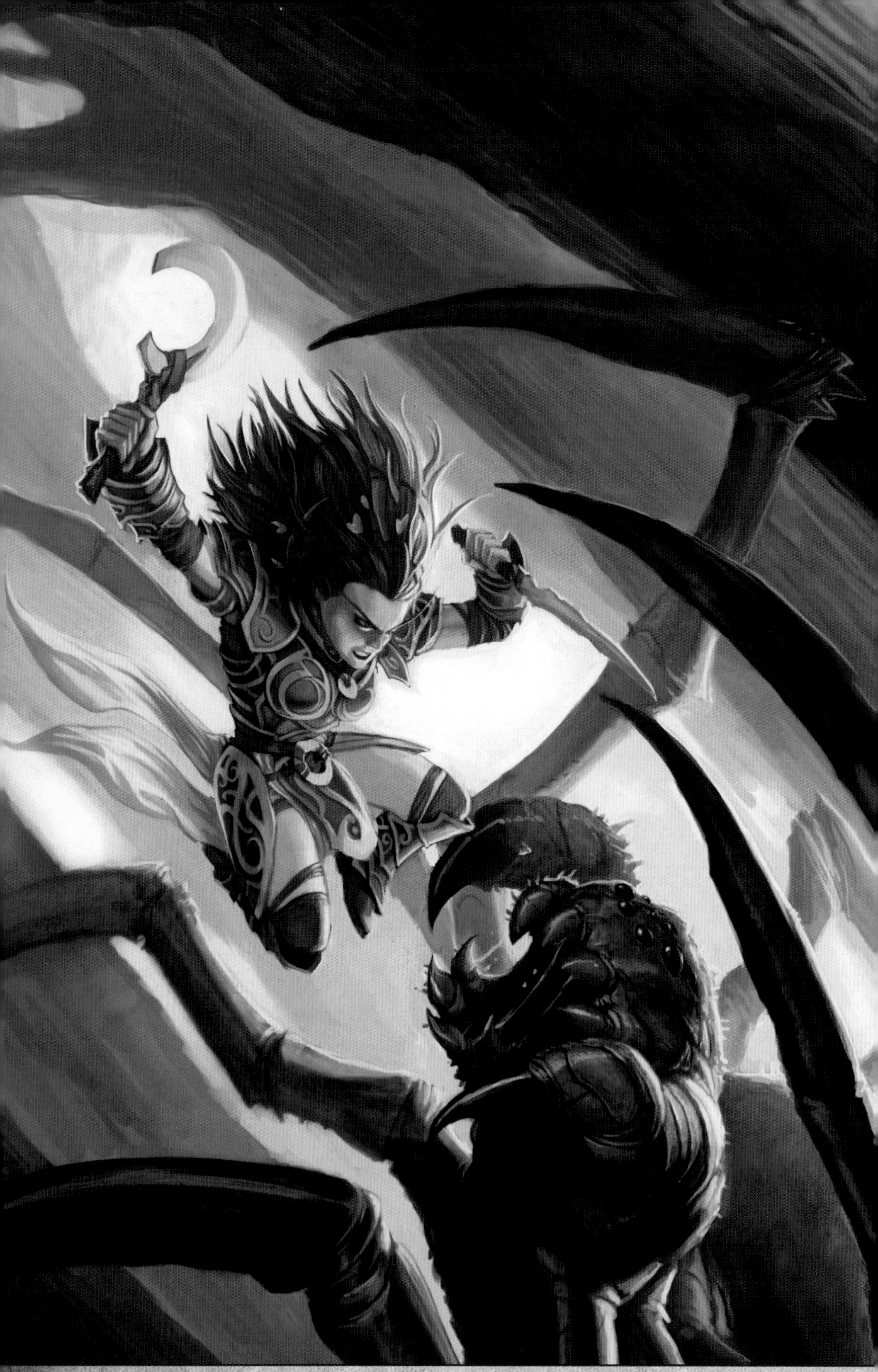

Issue #4 cover by TYLER WALPOLE

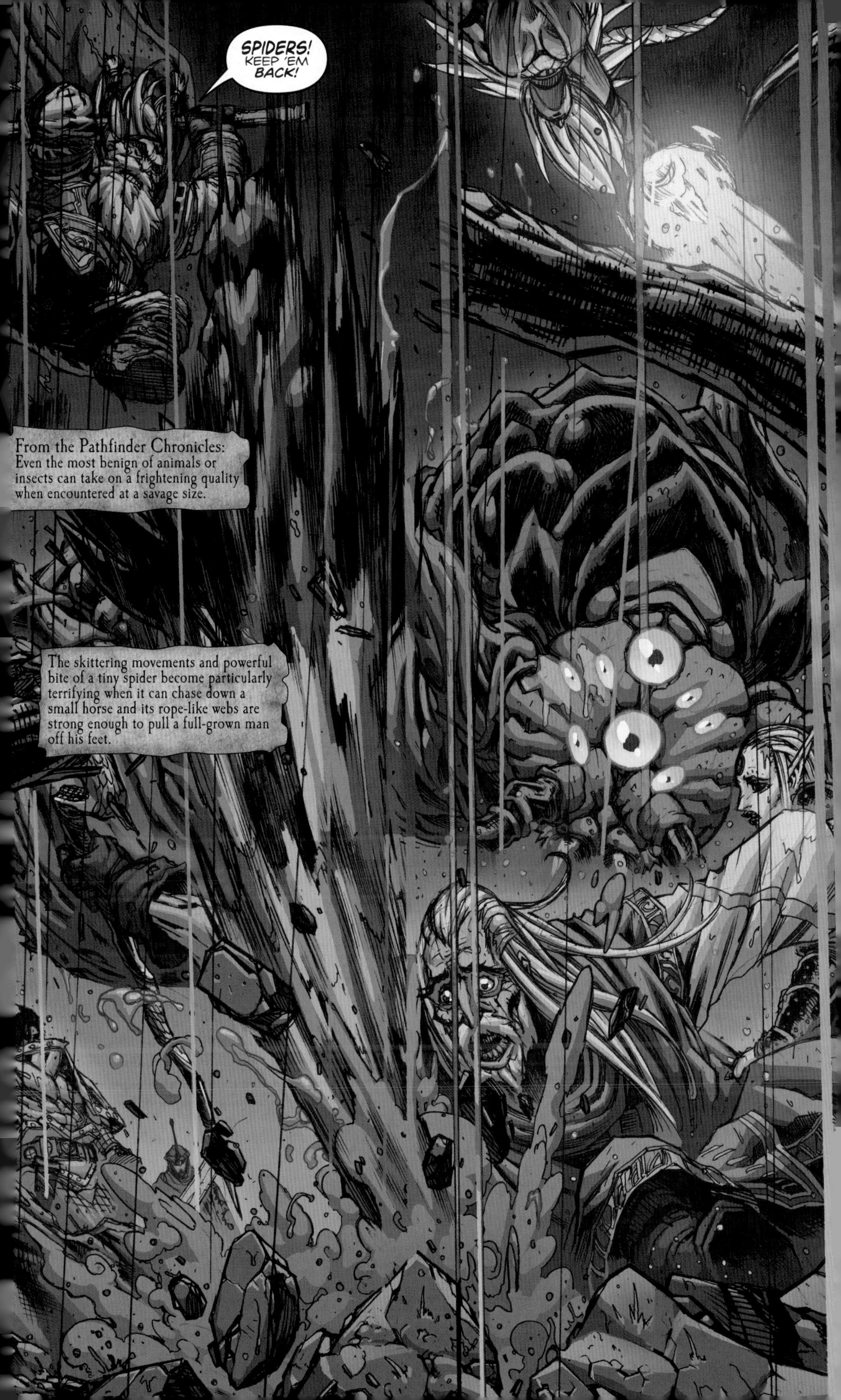
SPIDERS! KEEP 'EM BACK!
From the Pathfinder Chronicles:
Even the most benign of animals or insects can take on a frightening quality when encountered at a savage size.
The skittering movements and powerful bite of a tiny spider become particularly terrifying when it can chase down a small horse and its rope-like webs are strong enough to pull a full-grown man off his feet.

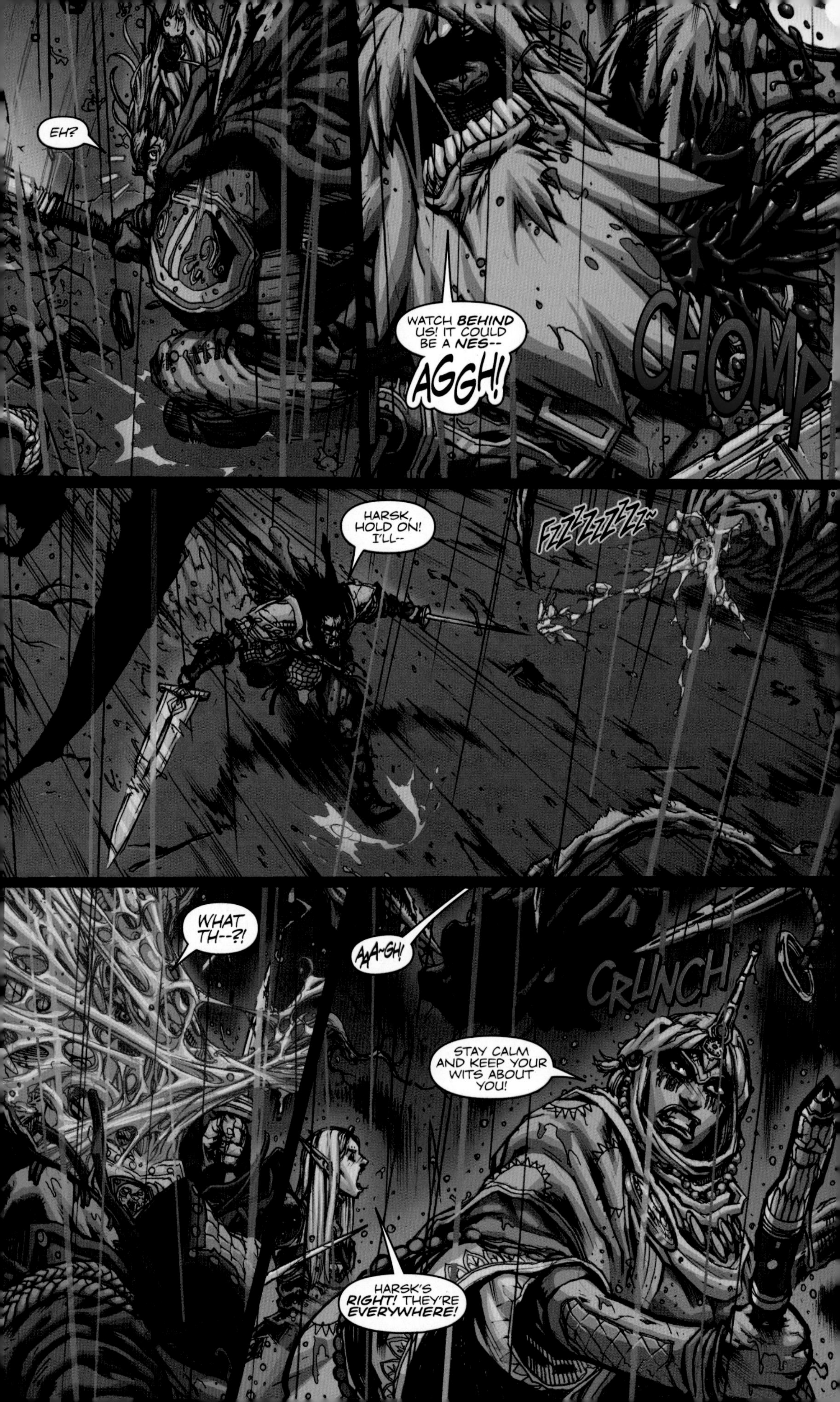
EH?
WATCH BEHIND US! IT COULD BE A NES--
AGGH!
CHOMP
HARSK, HOLD ON! I'LL--
FZZZZZZZZ~
WHAT TH--?!
AAAGH!
CRUNCH
STAY CALM AND KEEP YOUR WITS ABOUT YOU!
HARSK'S RIGHT! THEY'RE EVERYWHERE!

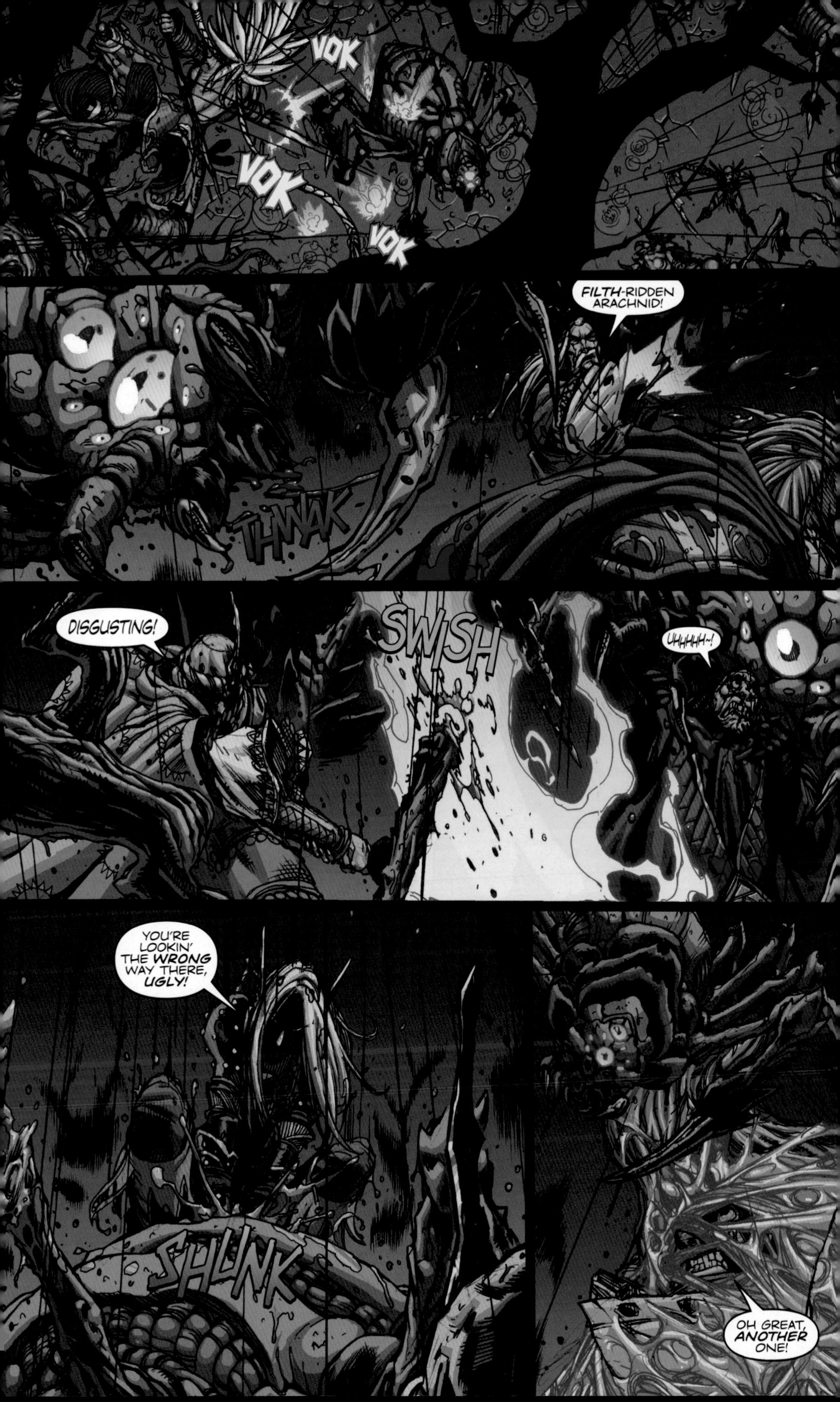
VOK
VOK
VOK
FILTH-RIDDEN ARACHNID!
THWAK
DISGUSTING!
SWISH
UHHHHH~!
YOU'RE LOOKIN' THE WRONG WAY THERE, UGLY!
SHUNK
OH GREAT, ANOTHER ONE!

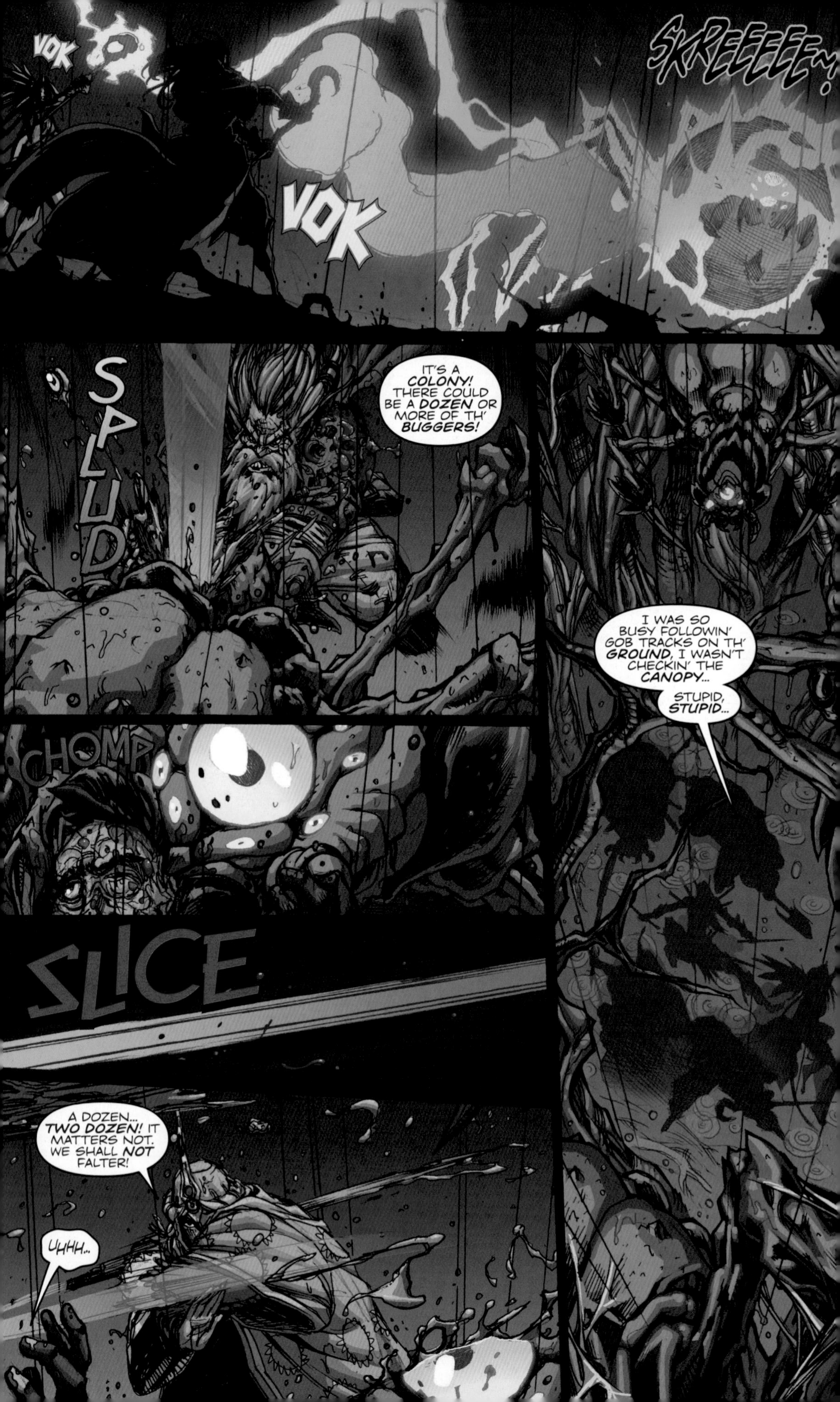
VOK
SKREEEEEE~!
VOK
SPLUD
IT'S A COLONY! THERE COULD BE A DOZEN OR MORE OF TH' BUGGERS!
I WAS SO BUSY FOLLOWIN' GOB TRACKS ON TH' GROUND, I WASN'T CHECKIN' THE CANOPY...
STUPID, STUPID...
CHOMP
SLICE
A DOZEN... TWO DOZEN! IT MATTERS NOT. WE SHALL NOT FALTER!
UHHH...

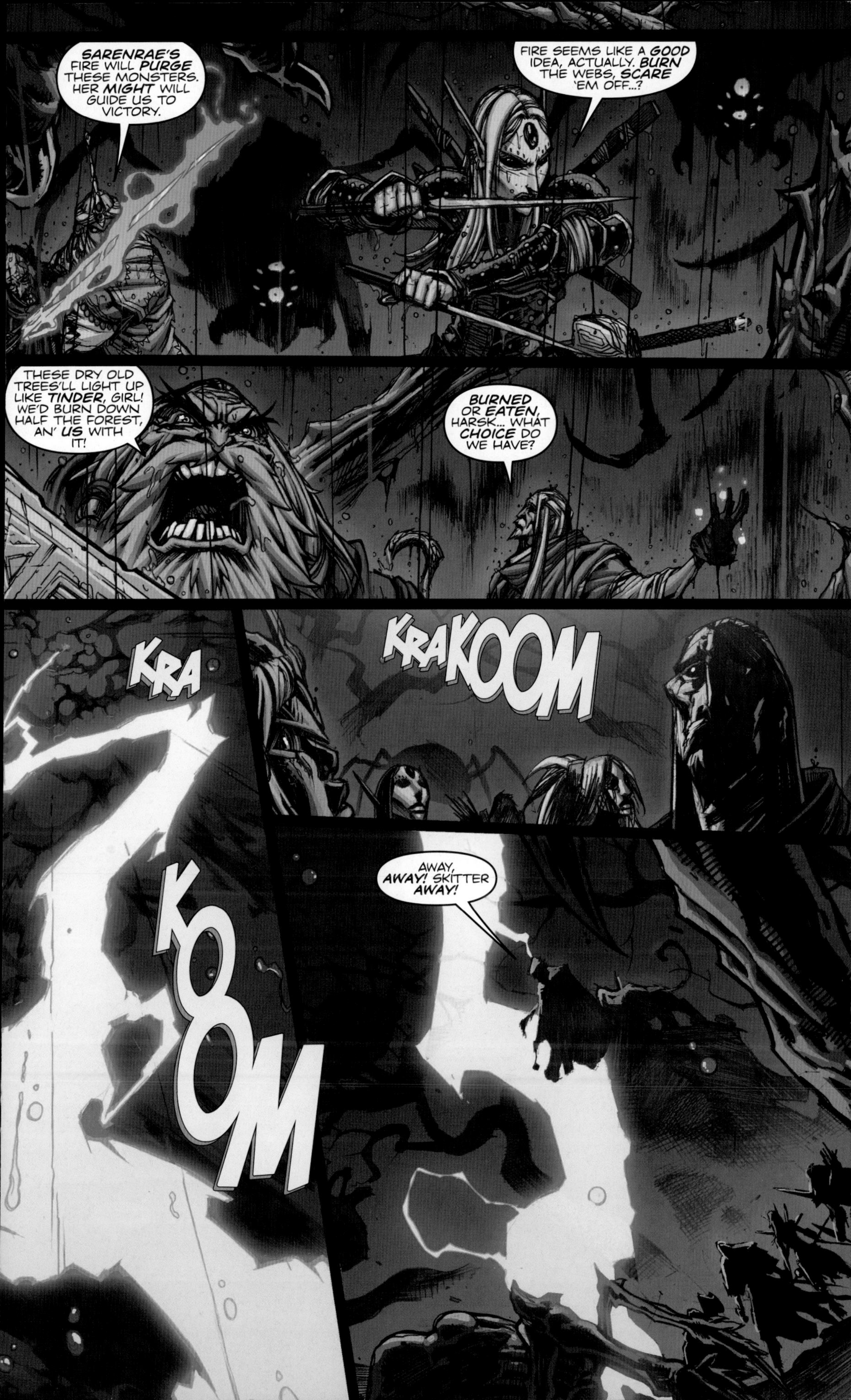
SARENRAE'S FIRE WILL PURGE THESE MONSTERS. HER MIGHT WILL GUIDE US TO VICTORY.
FIRE SEEMS LIKE A GOOD IDEA, ACTUALLY. BURN THE WEBS, SCARE 'EM OFF...?
THESE DRY OLD TREES'LL LIGHT UP LIKE TINDER, GIRL! WE'D BURN DOWN HALF THE FOREST, AN' US WITH IT!
BURNED OR EATEN, HARSK... WHAT CHOICE DO WE HAVE?
KRA
KOOM
KRAKOOM
AWAY, AWAY! SKITTER AWAY!

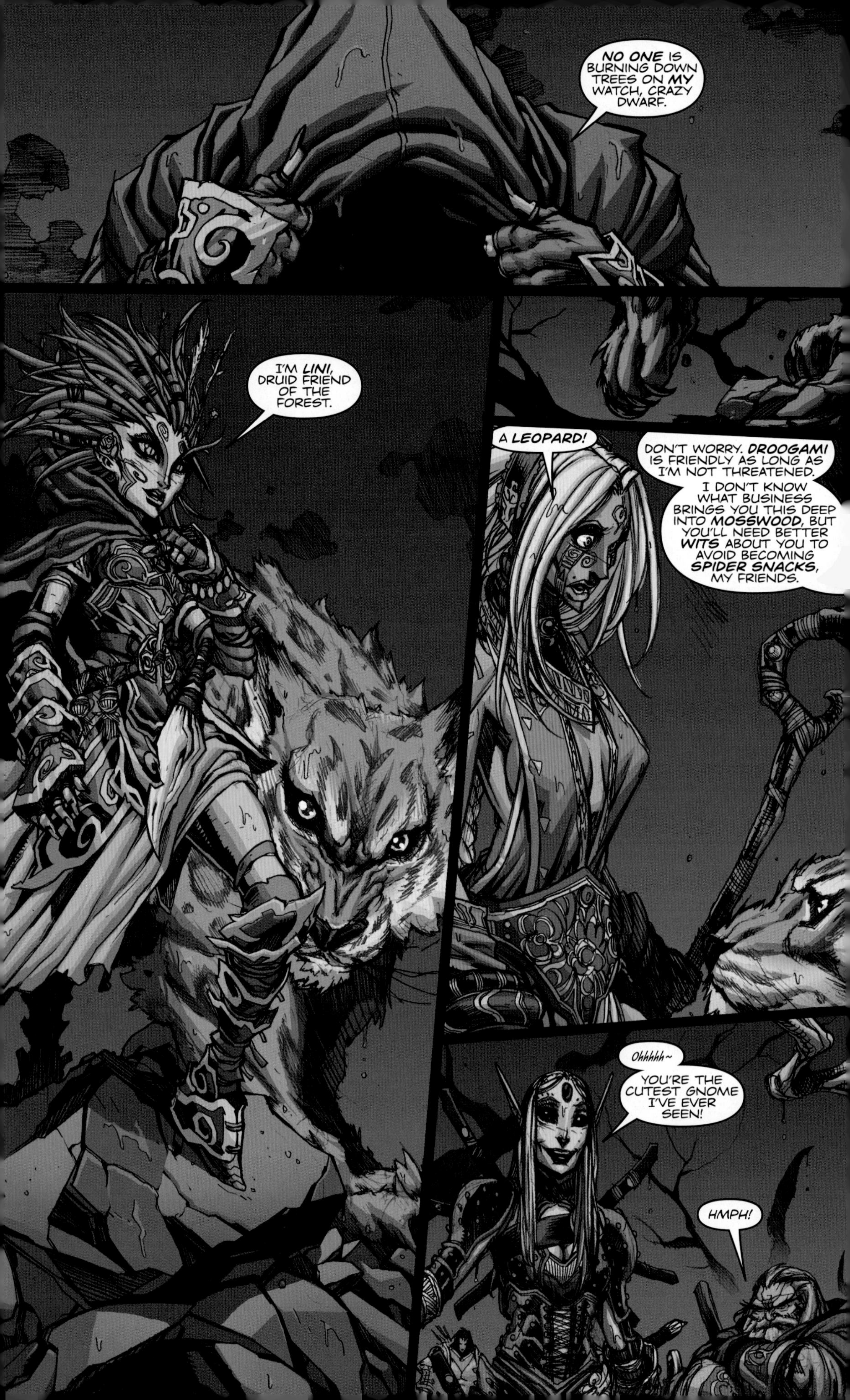
NO ONE IS BURNING DOWN TREES ON MY WATCH, CRAZY DWARF.
I'M LINI, DRUID FRIEND OF THE FOREST.
A LEOPARD!
DON'T WORRY. DROOGAMI IS FRIENDLY AS LONG AS I'M NOT THREATENED.
I DON'T KNOW WHAT BUSINESS BRINGS YOU THIS DEEP INTO MOSSWOOD, BUT YOU'LL NEED BETTER WITS ABOUT YOU TO AVOID BECOMING SPIDER SNACKS, MY FRIENDS.
Ohhhhh~
YOU'RE THE CUTEST GNOME I'VE EVER SEEN!
HMPH!

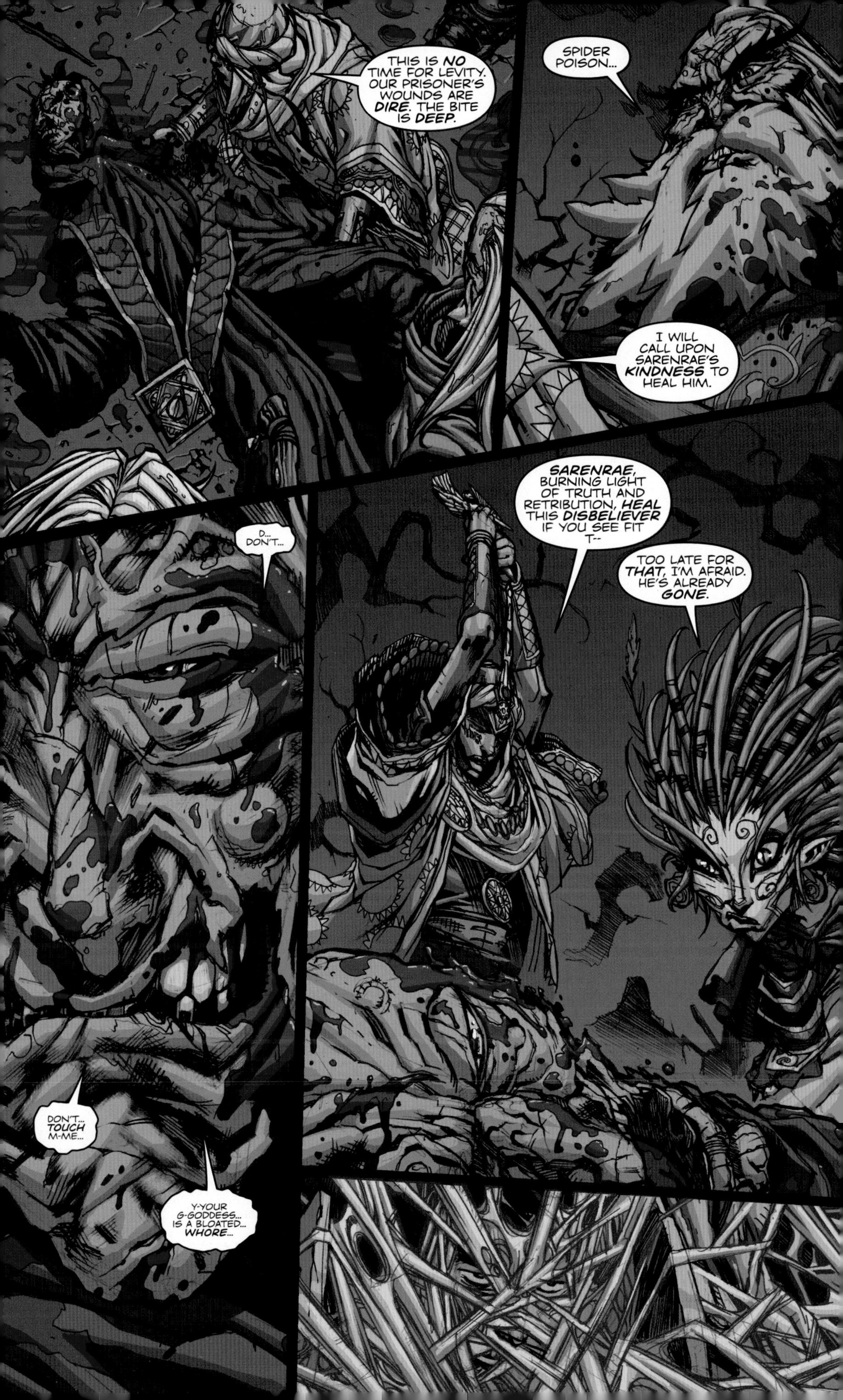

THIS IS **NO** TIME FOR LEVITY. OUR PRISONER'S WOUNDS ARE ***DIRE***. THE BITE IS ***DEEP***.
SPIDER POISON...
I WILL CALL UPON SARENRAE'S ***KINDNESS*** TO HEAL HIM.
D... DON'T...
DON'T... ***TOUCH*** M-ME...
Y-YOUR G-GODDESS... IS A BLOATED... ***WHORE***...
SARENRAE, BURNING LIGHT OF TRUTH AND RETRIBUTION, ***HEAL*** THIS ***DISBELIEVER*** IF YOU SEE FIT T--
TOO LATE FOR ***THAT***, I'M AFRAID. HE'S ALREADY ***GONE***.

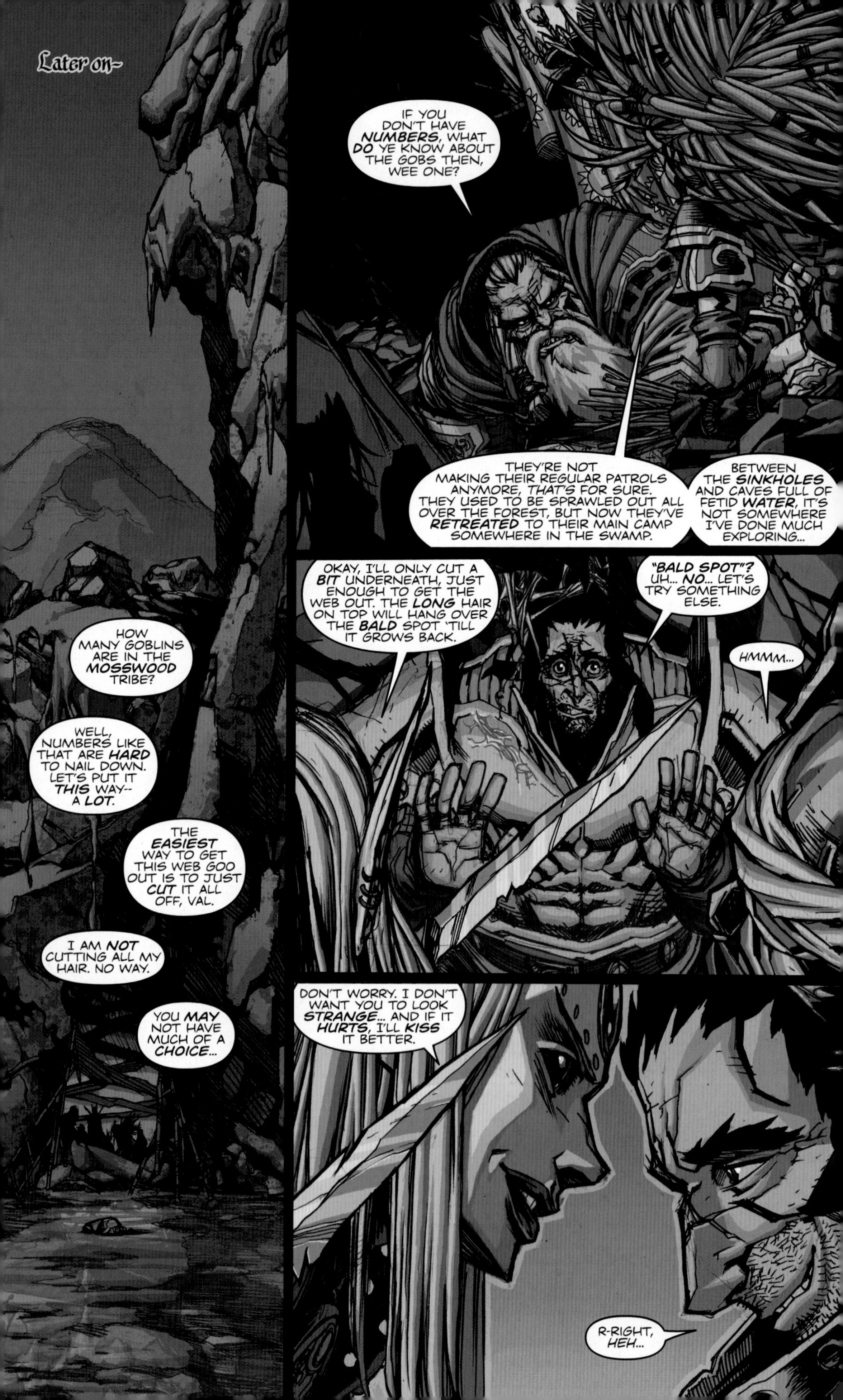
Later on~
IF YOU DON'T HAVE NUMBERS, WHAT DO YE KNOW ABOUT THE GOBS THEN, WEE ONE?
THEY'RE NOT MAKING THEIR REGULAR PATROLS ANYMORE, THAT'S FOR SURE. THEY USED TO BE SPRAWLED OUT ALL OVER THE FOREST, BUT NOW THEY'VE RETREATED TO THEIR MAIN CAMP SOMEWHERE IN THE SWAMP.
BETWEEN THE SINKHOLES AND CAVES FULL OF FETID WATER, IT'S NOT SOMEWHERE I'VE DONE MUCH EXPLORING...
HOW MANY GOBLINS ARE IN THE MOSSWOOD TRIBE?
WELL, NUMBERS LIKE THAT ARE HARD TO NAIL DOWN. LET'S PUT IT THIS WAY-- A LOT.
THE EASIEST WAY TO GET THIS WEB GOO OUT IS TO JUST CUT IT ALL OFF, VAL.
I AM NOT CUTTING ALL MY HAIR. NO WAY.
YOU MAY NOT HAVE MUCH OF A CHOICE...
OKAY, I'LL ONLY CUT A BIT UNDERNEATH, JUST ENOUGH TO GET THE WEB OUT. THE LONG HAIR ON TOP WILL HANG OVER THE BALD SPOT 'TILL IT GROWS BACK.
"BALD SPOT"? UH... NO... LET'S TRY SOMETHING ELSE.
HMMM...
DON'T WORRY. I DON'T WANT YOU TO LOOK STRANGE... AND IF IT HURTS, I'LL KISS IT BETTER.
R-RIGHT, HEH...

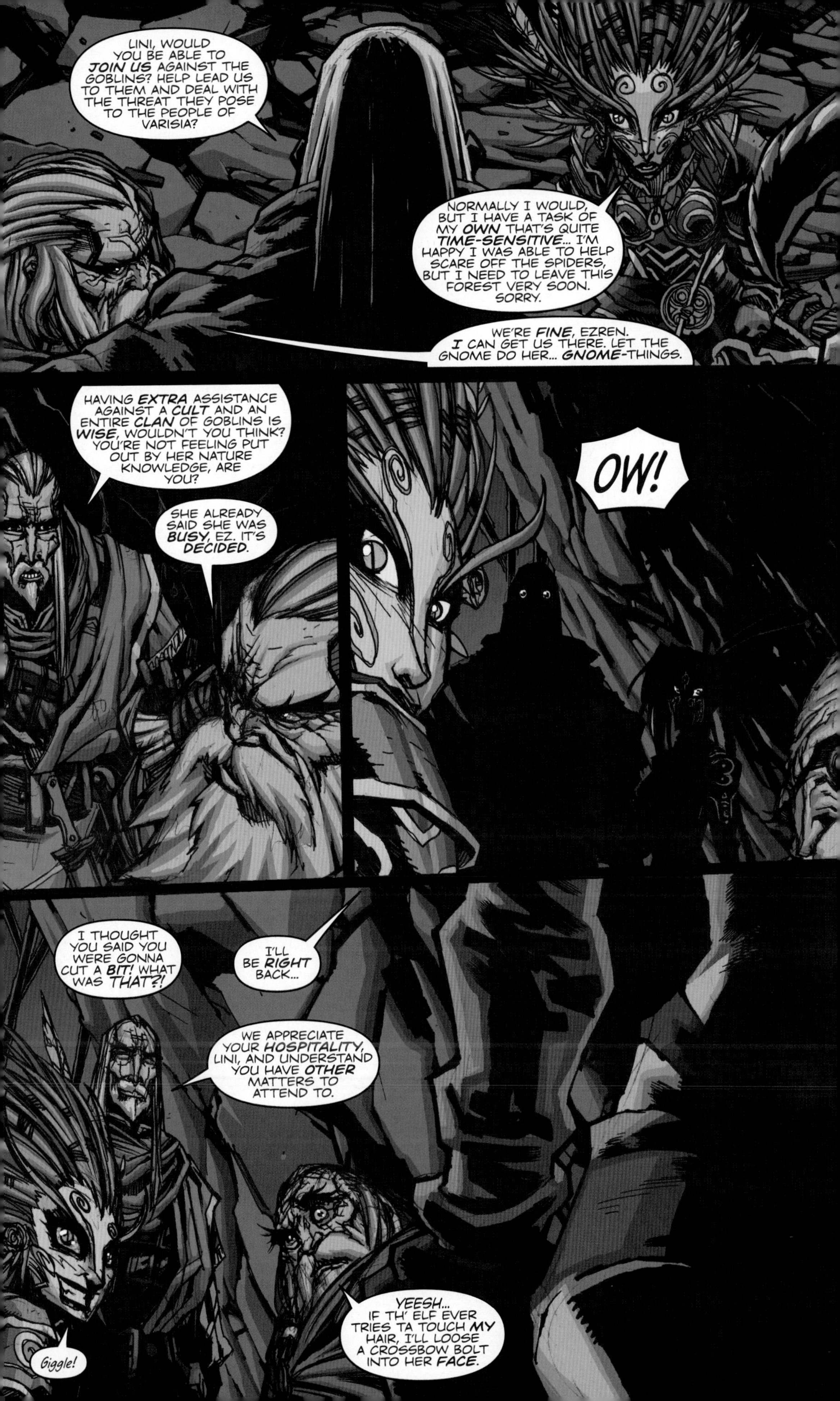

LINI, WOULD YOU BE ABLE TO JOIN US AGAINST THE GOBLINS? HELP LEAD US TO THEM AND DEAL WITH THE THREAT THEY POSE TO THE PEOPLE OF VARISIA?
NORMALLY I WOULD, BUT I HAVE A TASK OF MY OWN THAT'S QUITE TIME-SENSITIVE... I'M HAPPY I WAS ABLE TO HELP SCARE OFF THE SPIDERS, BUT I NEED TO LEAVE THIS FOREST VERY SOON. SORRY.
WE'RE FINE, EZREN. I CAN GET US THERE. LET THE GNOME DO HER... GNOME-THINGS.
HAVING EXTRA ASSISTANCE AGAINST A CULT AND AN ENTIRE CLAN OF GOBLINS IS WISE, WOULDN'T YOU THINK? YOU'RE NOT FEELING PUT OUT BY HER NATURE KNOWLEDGE, ARE YOU?
SHE ALREADY SAID SHE WAS BUSY, EZ. IT'S DECIDED.
OW!
I THOUGHT YOU SAID YOU WERE GONNA CUT A BIT! WHAT WAS THAT?!
I'LL BE RIGHT BACK...
WE APPRECIATE YOUR HOSPITALITY, LINI, AND UNDERSTAND YOU HAVE OTHER MATTERS TO ATTEND TO.
Giggle!
YEESH... IF TH' ELF EVER TRIES TA TOUCH MY HAIR, I'LL LOOSE A CROSSBOW BOLT INTO HER FACE.

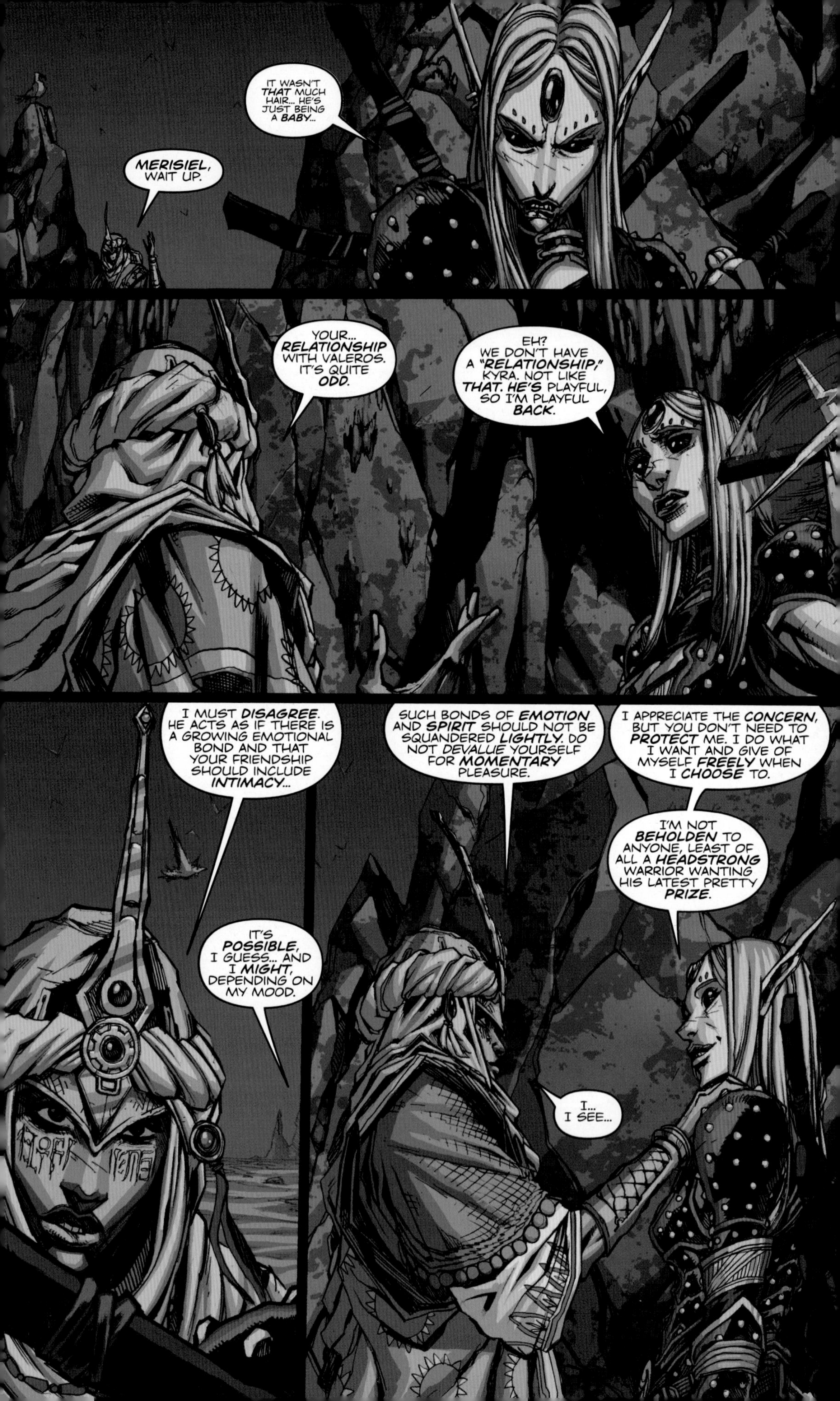
IT WASN'T THAT MUCH HAIR... HE'S JUST BEING A BABY...
MERISIEL, WAIT UP.
YOUR... RELATIONSHIP WITH VALEROS. IT'S QUITE ODD.
EH? WE DON'T HAVE A "RELATIONSHIP," KYRA. NOT LIKE THAT. HE'S PLAYFUL, SO I'M PLAYFUL BACK.
I MUST DISAGREE. HE ACTS AS IF THERE IS A GROWING EMOTIONAL BOND AND THAT YOUR FRIENDSHIP SHOULD INCLUDE INTIMACY...
IT'S POSSIBLE, I GUESS... AND I MIGHT, DEPENDING ON MY MOOD.
SUCH BONDS OF EMOTION AND SPIRIT SHOULD NOT BE SQUANDERED LIGHTLY. DO NOT DEVALUE YOURSELF FOR MOMENTARY PLEASURE.
I APPRECIATE THE CONCERN, BUT YOU DON'T NEED TO PROTECT ME. I DO WHAT I WANT AND GIVE OF MYSELF FREELY WHEN I CHOOSE TO.
I'M NOT BEHOLDEN TO ANYONE, LEAST OF ALL A HEADSTRONG WARRIOR WANTING HIS LATEST PRETTY PRIZE.
I... I SEE...

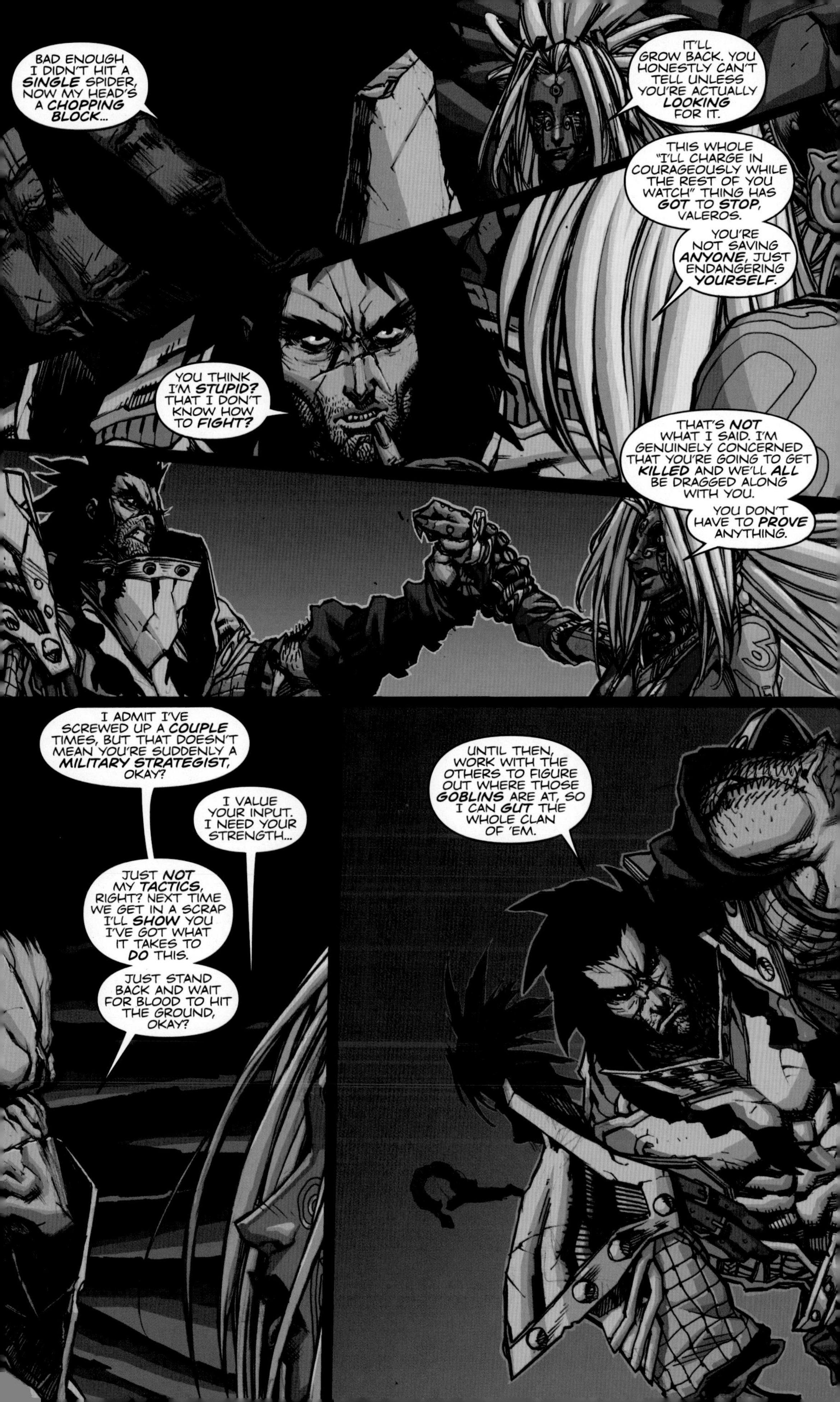
BAD ENOUGH I DIDN'T HIT A SINGLE SPIDER, NOW MY HEAD'S A CHOPPING BLOCK...
IT'LL GROW BACK. YOU HONESTLY CAN'T TELL UNLESS YOU'RE ACTUALLY LOOKING FOR IT.
THIS WHOLE "I'LL CHARGE IN COURAGEOUSLY WHILE THE REST OF YOU WATCH" THING HAS GOT TO STOP, VALEROS.
YOU'RE NOT SAVING ANYONE, JUST ENDANGERING YOURSELF.
YOU THINK I'M STUPID? THAT I DON'T KNOW HOW TO FIGHT?
THAT'S NOT WHAT I SAID. I'M GENUINELY CONCERNED THAT YOU'RE GOING TO GET KILLED AND WE'LL ALL BE DRAGGED ALONG WITH YOU.
YOU DON'T HAVE TO PROVE ANYTHING.
I ADMIT I'VE SCREWED UP A COUPLE TIMES, BUT THAT DOESN'T MEAN YOU'RE SUDDENLY A MILITARY STRATEGIST, OKAY?
I VALUE YOUR INPUT. I NEED YOUR STRENGTH...
JUST NOT MY TACTICS, RIGHT? NEXT TIME WE GET IN A SCRAP I'LL SHOW YOU I'VE GOT WHAT IT TAKES TO DO THIS.
JUST STAND BACK AND WAIT FOR BLOOD TO HIT THE GROUND, OKAY?
UNTIL THEN, WORK WITH THE OTHERS TO FIGURE OUT WHERE THOSE GOBLINS ARE AT, SO I CAN GUT THE WHOLE CLAN OF 'EM.

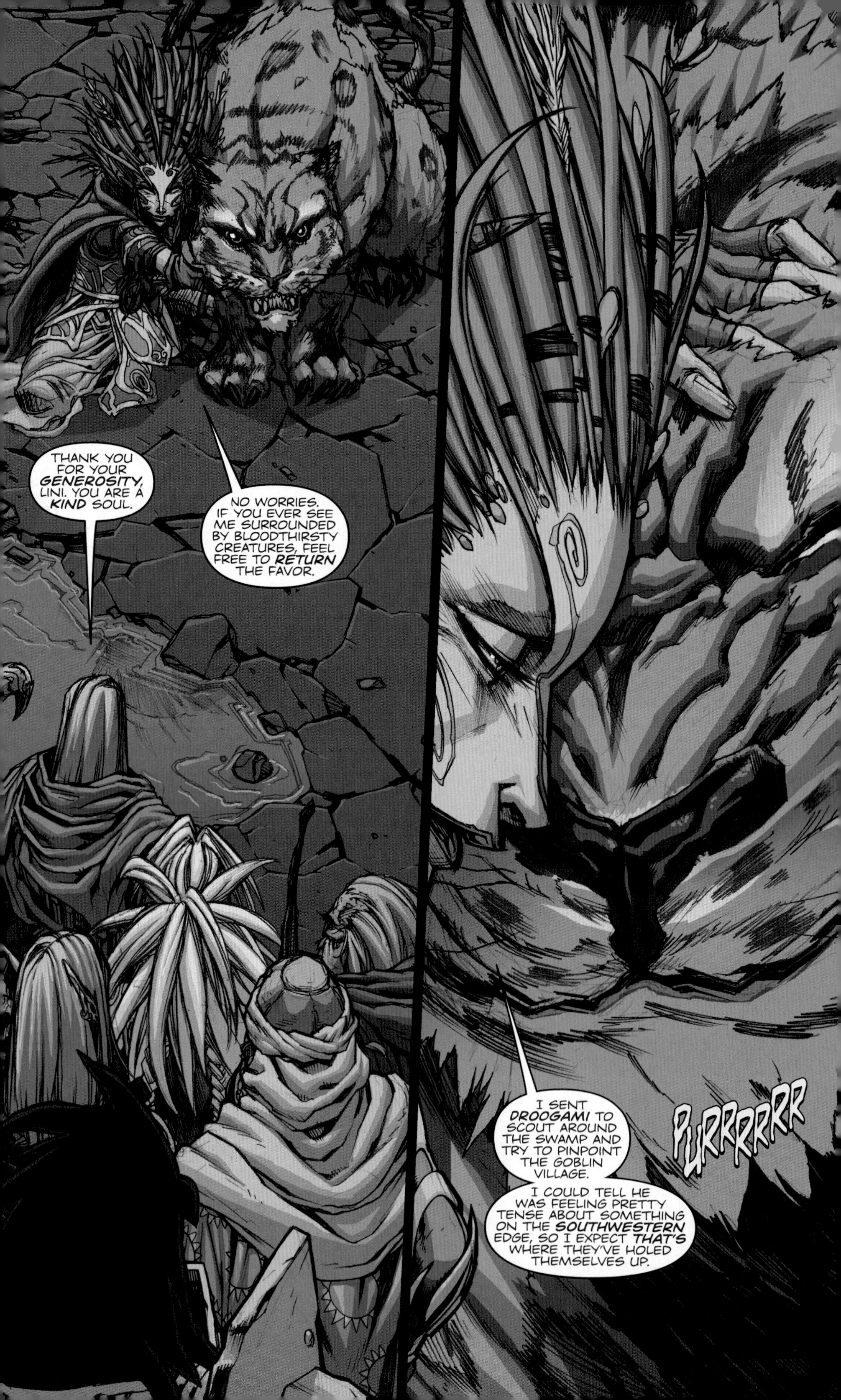
THANK YOU FOR YOUR GENEROSITY, LINI. YOU ARE A KIND SOUL.
NO WORRIES. IF YOU EVER SEE ME SURROUNDED BY BLOODTHIRSTY CREATURES, FEEL FREE TO RETURN THE FAVOR.
I SENT DROOGAMI TO SCOUT AROUND THE SWAMP AND TRY TO PINPOINT THE GOBLIN VILLAGE.
I COULD TELL HE WAS FEELING PRETTY TENSE ABOUT SOMETHING ON THE SOUTHWESTERN EDGE, SO I EXPECT THAT'S WHERE THEY'VE HOLED THEMSELVES UP.
PURRRRRR

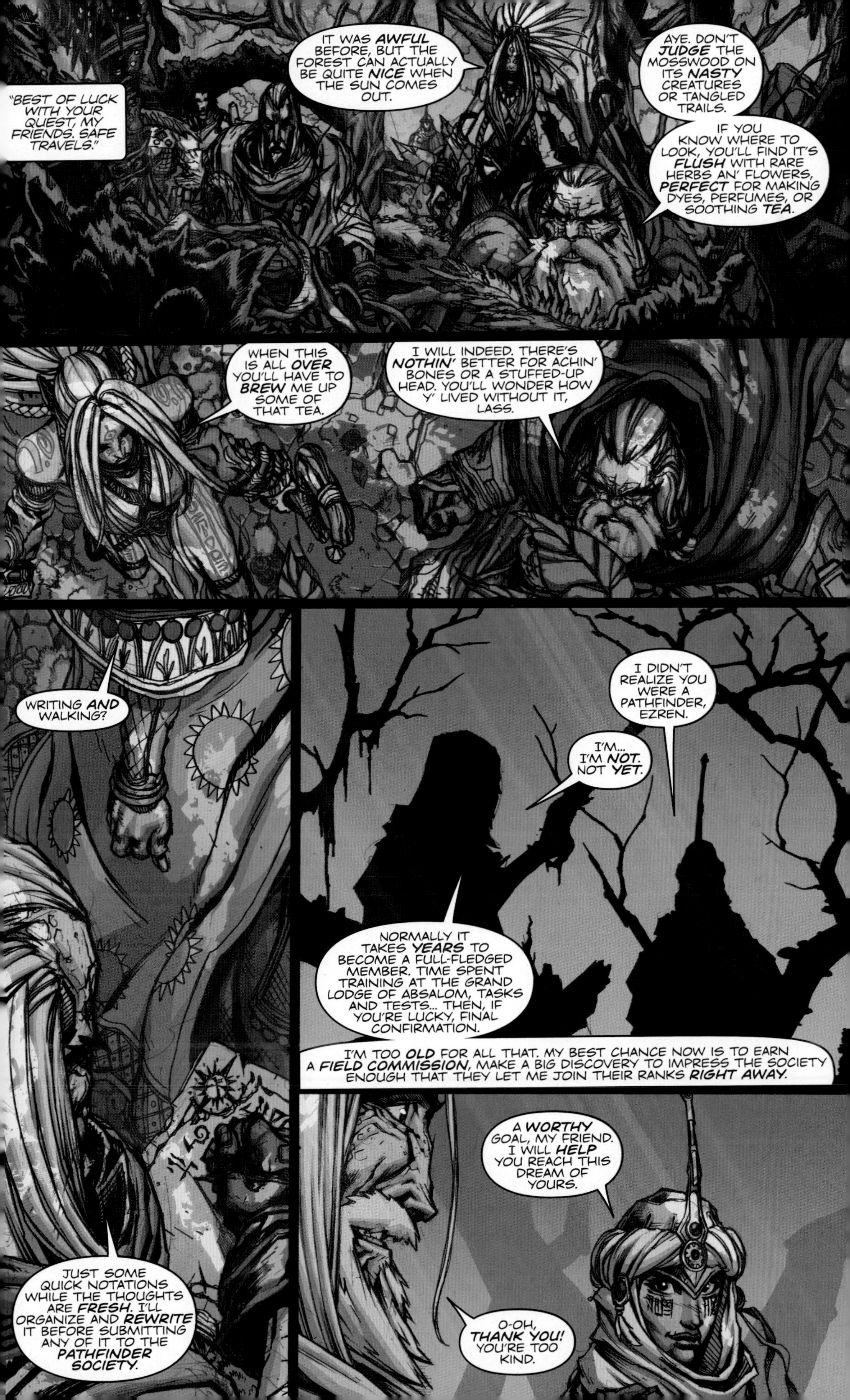
"BEST OF LUCK WITH YOUR QUEST, MY FRIENDS. SAFE TRAVELS."
IT WAS AWFUL BEFORE, BUT THE FOREST CAN ACTUALLY BE QUITE NICE WHEN THE SUN COMES OUT.
AYE. DON'T JUDGE THE MOSSWOOD ON ITS NASTY CREATURES OR TANGLED TRAILS.
IF YOU KNOW WHERE TO LOOK, YOU'LL FIND IT'S FLUSH WITH RARE HERBS AN' FLOWERS, PERFECT FOR MAKING DYES, PERFUMES, OR SOOTHING TEA.
WHEN THIS IS ALL OVER YOU'LL HAVE TO BREW ME UP SOME OF THAT TEA.
I WILL INDEED. THERE'S NOTHIN' BETTER FOR ACHIN' BONES OR A STUFFED-UP HEAD. YOU'LL WONDER HOW Y' LIVED WITHOUT IT, LASS.
WRITING AND WALKING?
JUST SOME QUICK NOTATIONS WHILE THE THOUGHTS ARE FRESH. I'LL ORGANIZE AND REWRITE IT BEFORE SUBMITTING ANY OF IT TO THE PATHFINDER SOCIETY.
I DIDN'T REALIZE YOU WERE A PATHFINDER, EZREN.
I'M... I'M NOT. NOT YET.
NORMALLY IT TAKES YEARS TO BECOME A FULL-FLEDGED MEMBER. TIME SPENT TRAINING AT THE GRAND LODGE OF ABSALOM, TASKS AND TESTS... THEN, IF YOU'RE LUCKY, FINAL CONFIRMATION.
I'M TOO OLD FOR ALL THAT. MY BEST CHANCE NOW IS TO EARN A FIELD COMMISSION, MAKE A BIG DISCOVERY TO IMPRESS THE SOCIETY ENOUGH THAT THEY LET ME JOIN THEIR RANKS RIGHT AWAY.
A WORTHY GOAL, MY FRIEND. I WILL HELP YOU REACH THIS DREAM OF YOURS.
O-OH, THANK YOU! YOU'RE TOO KIND.

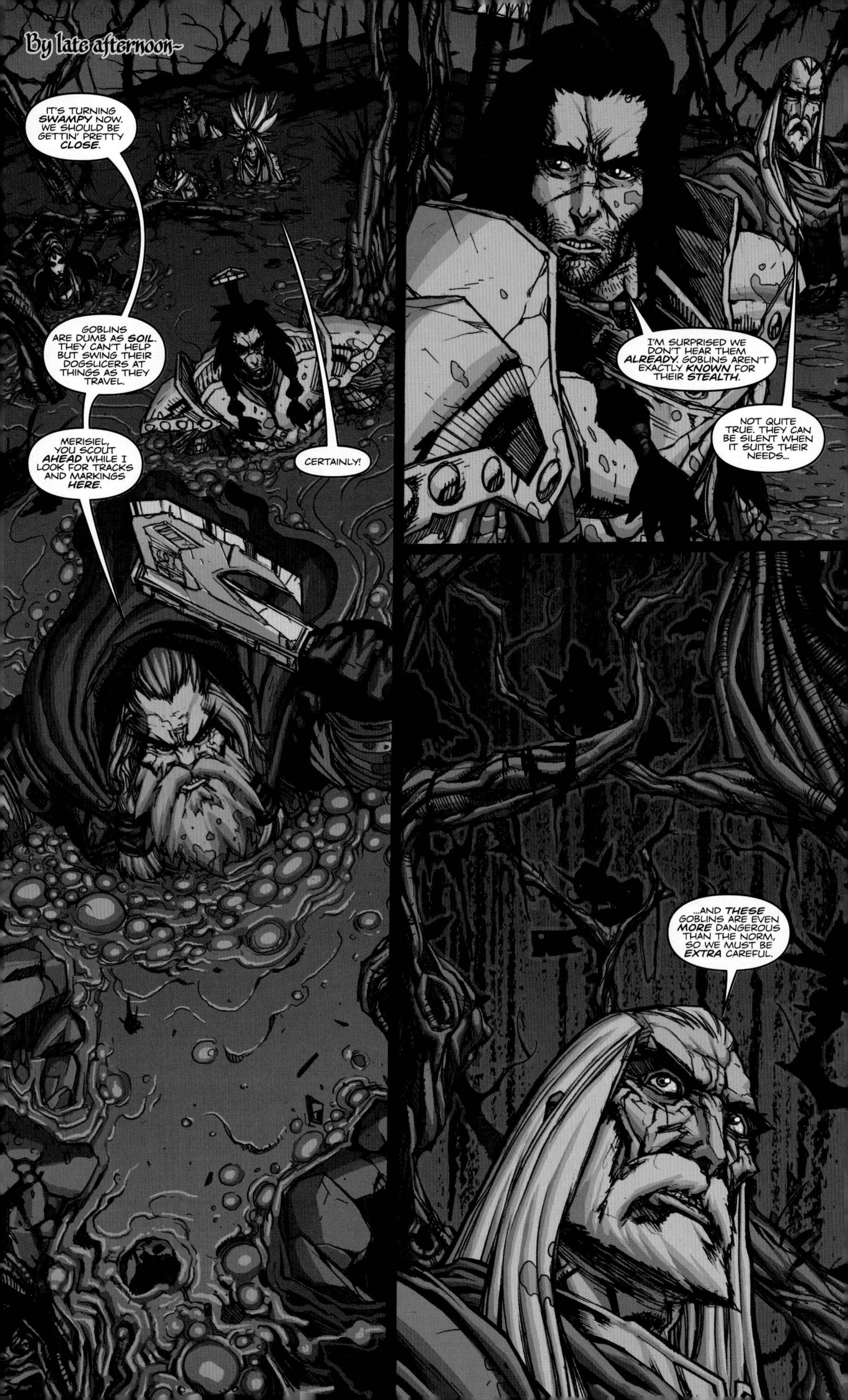
By late afternoon~
IT'S TURNING SWAMPY NOW. WE SHOULD BE GETTIN' PRETTY CLOSE.
GOBLINS ARE DUMB AS SOIL. THEY CAN'T HELP BUT SWING THEIR DOGSLICERS AT THINGS AS THEY TRAVEL.
MERISIEL, YOU SCOUT AHEAD WHILE I LOOK FOR TRACKS AND MARKINGS HERE.
CERTAINLY!
I'M SURPRISED WE DON'T HEAR THEM ALREADY. GOBLINS AREN'T EXACTLY KNOWN FOR THEIR STEALTH.
NOT QUITE TRUE. THEY CAN BE SILENT WHEN IT SUITS THEIR NEEDS...
...AND THESE GOBLINS ARE EVEN MORE DANGEROUS THAN THE NORM, SO WE MUST BE EXTRA CAREFUL.

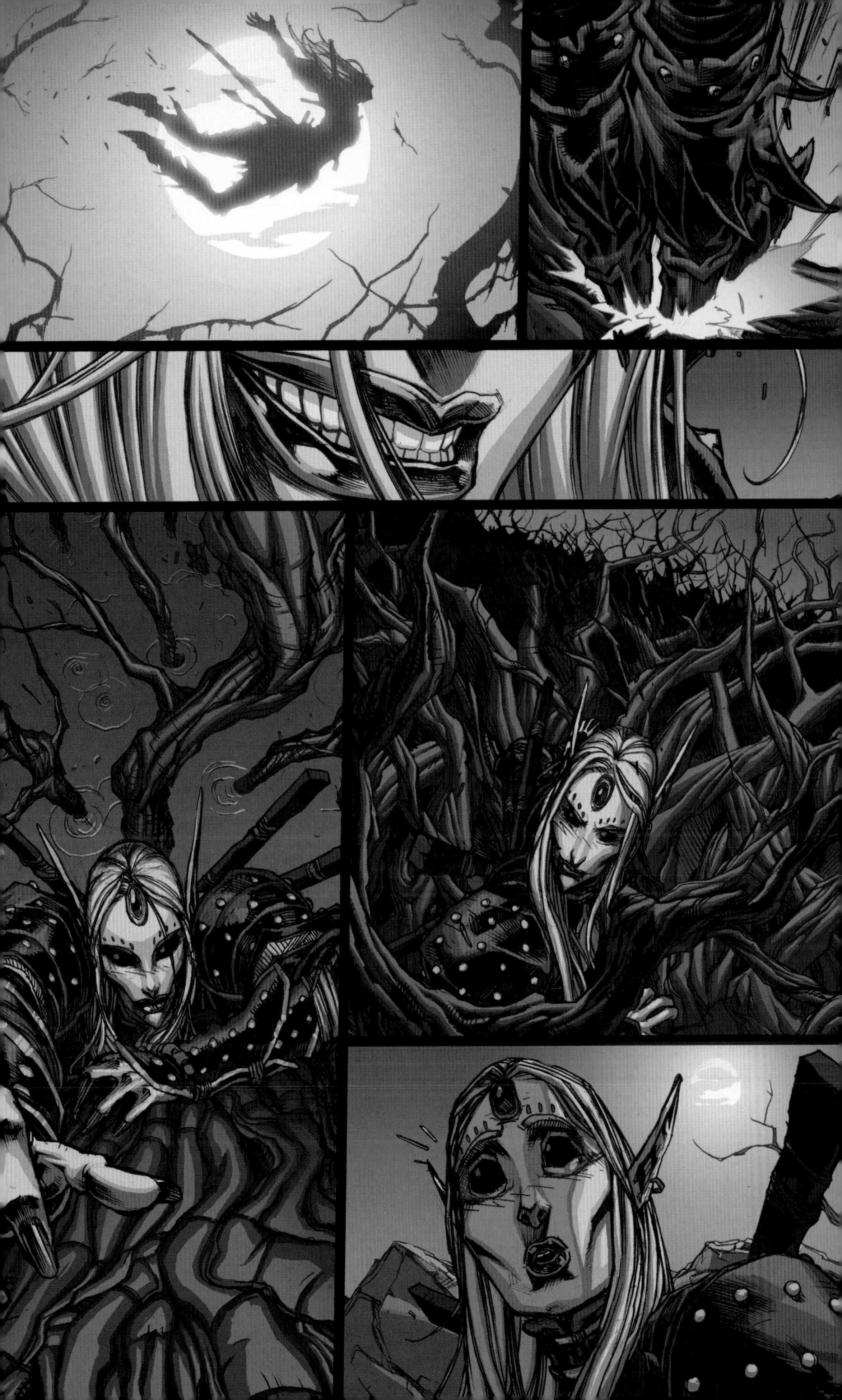

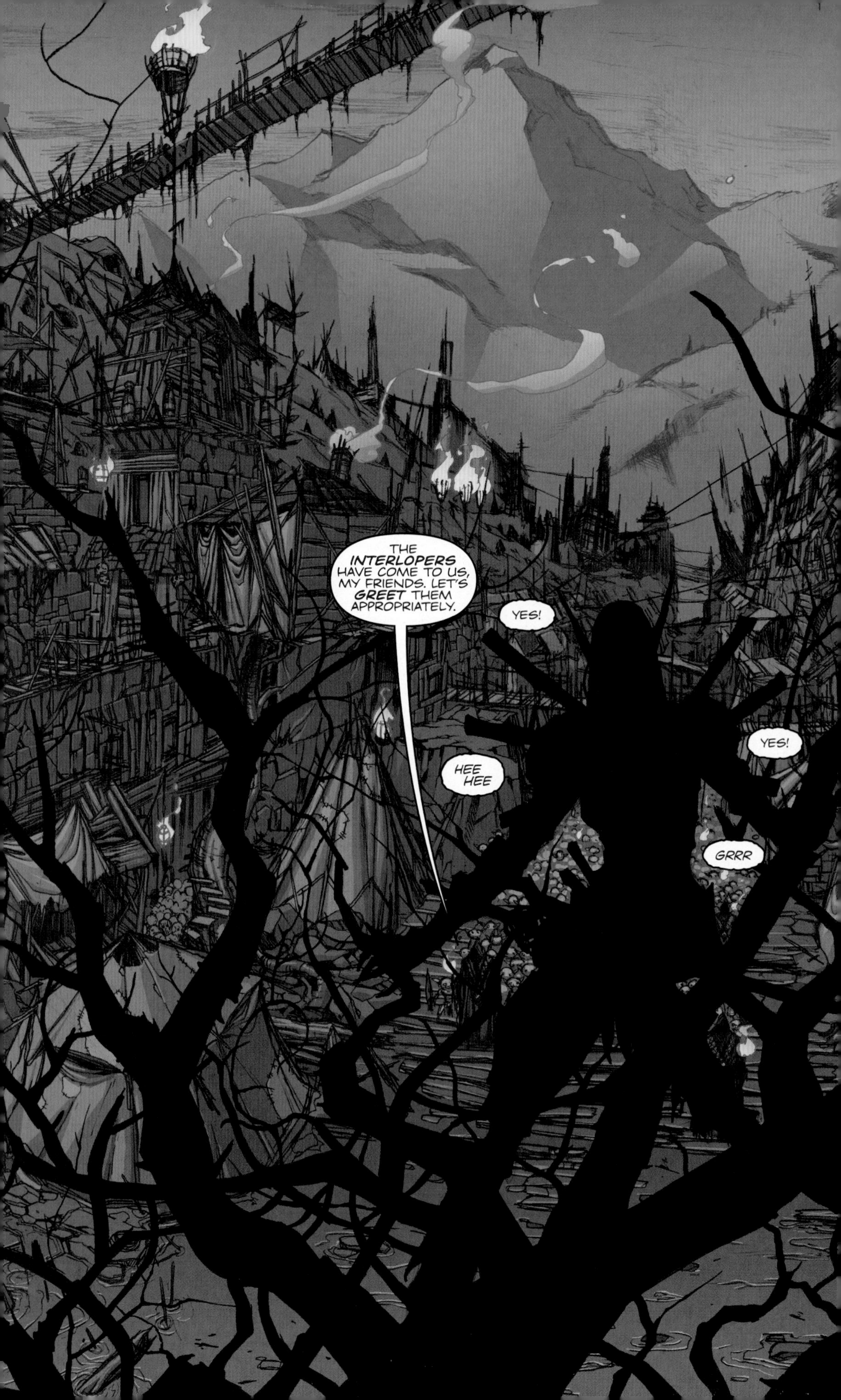

THE INTERLOPERS HAVE COME TO US, MY FRIENDS. LET'S GREET THEM APPROPRIATELY.
YES!
HEE HEE
YES!
GRRR

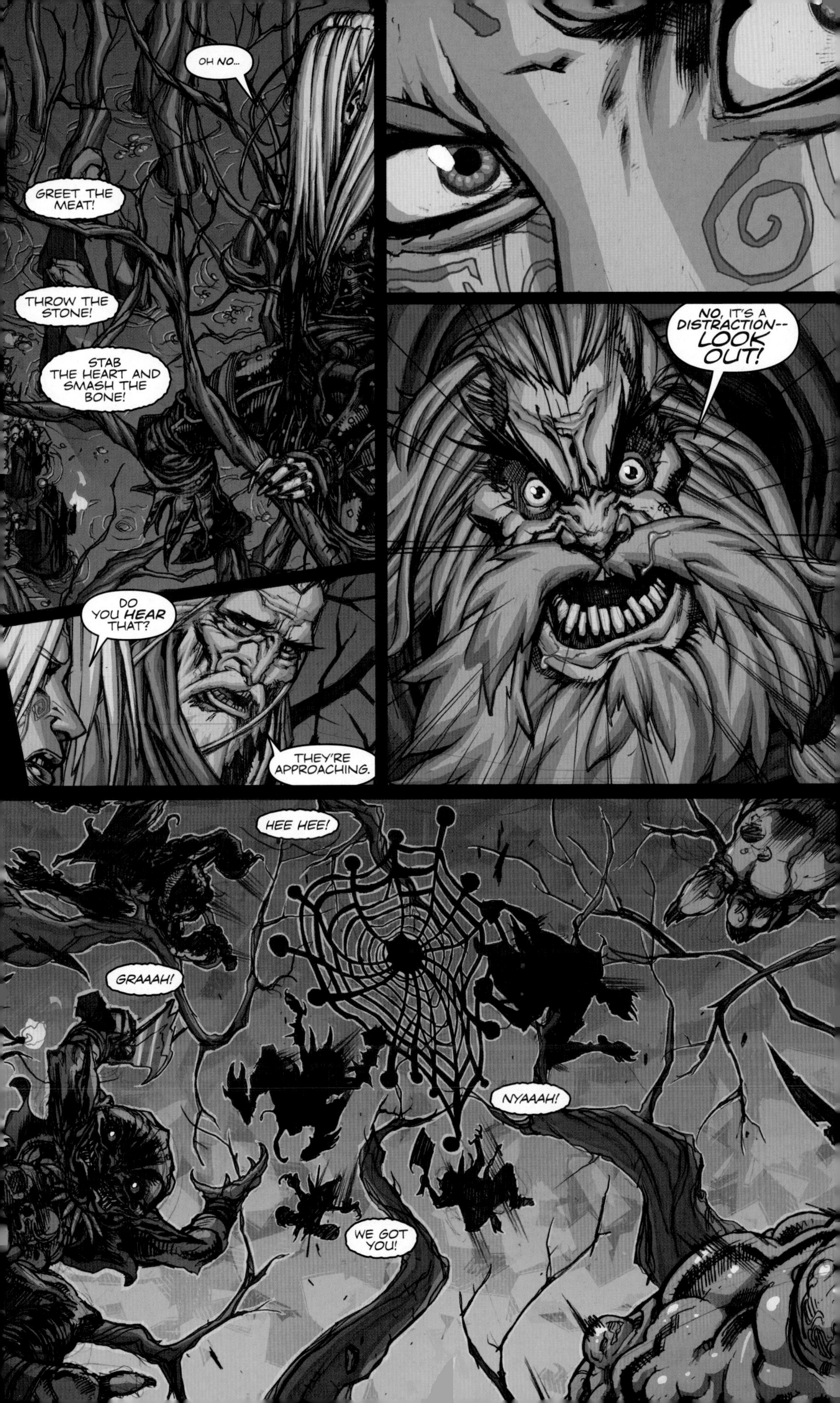
OH NO...
GREET THE MEAT!
THROW THE STONE!
STAB THE HEART AND SMASH THE BONE!
DO YOU HEAR THAT?
THEY'RE APPROACHING.
NO, IT'S A DISTRACTION-- LOOK OUT!
HEE HEE!
GRAAAH!
NYAAAH!
WE GOT YOU!

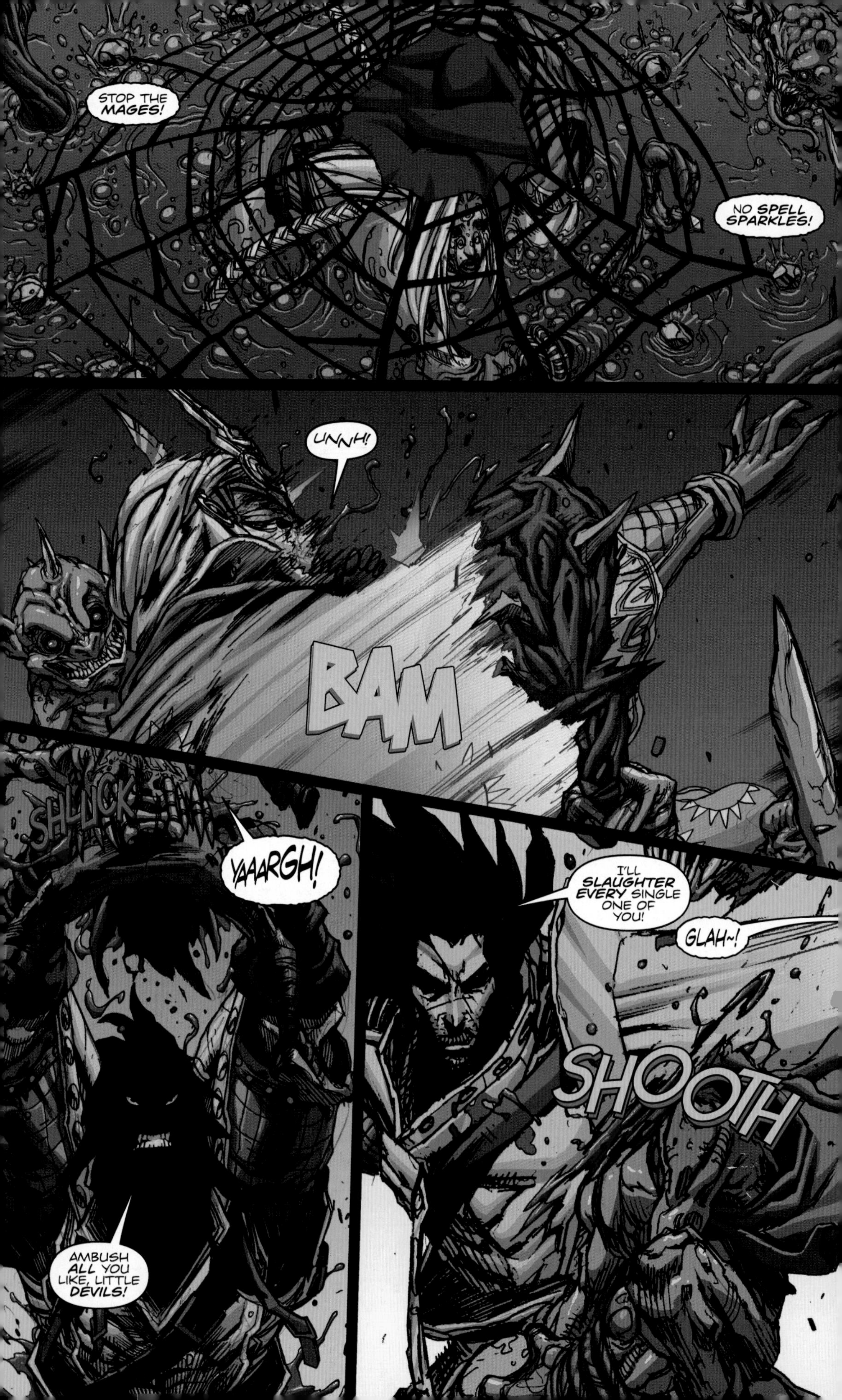
STOP THE MAGES!
NO SPELL SPARKLES!
UNNH!
BAM
SHLUCK
YAAARGH!
AMBUSH ALL YOU LIKE, LITTLE DEVILS!
I'LL SLAUGHTER EVERY SINGLE ONE OF YOU!
GLAH~!
SHOOTH

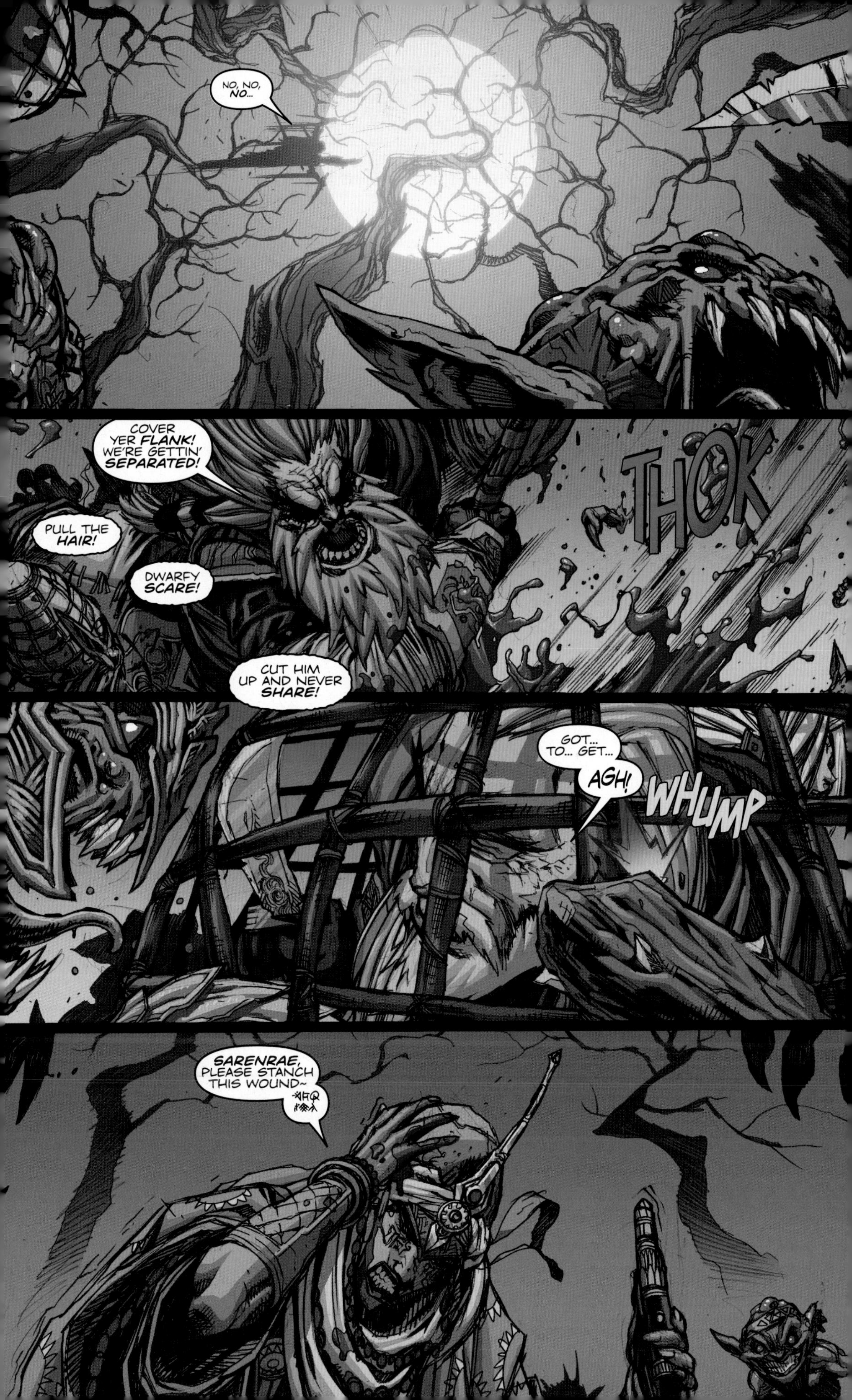
NO, NO, NO...
COVER YER FLANK! WE'RE GETTIN' SEPARATED!
THOK
PULL THE HAIR!
DWARFY SCARE!
CUT HIM UP AND NEVER SHARE!
GOT... TO... GET... AGH!
WHUMP
SARENRAE, PLEASE STANCH THIS WOUND~

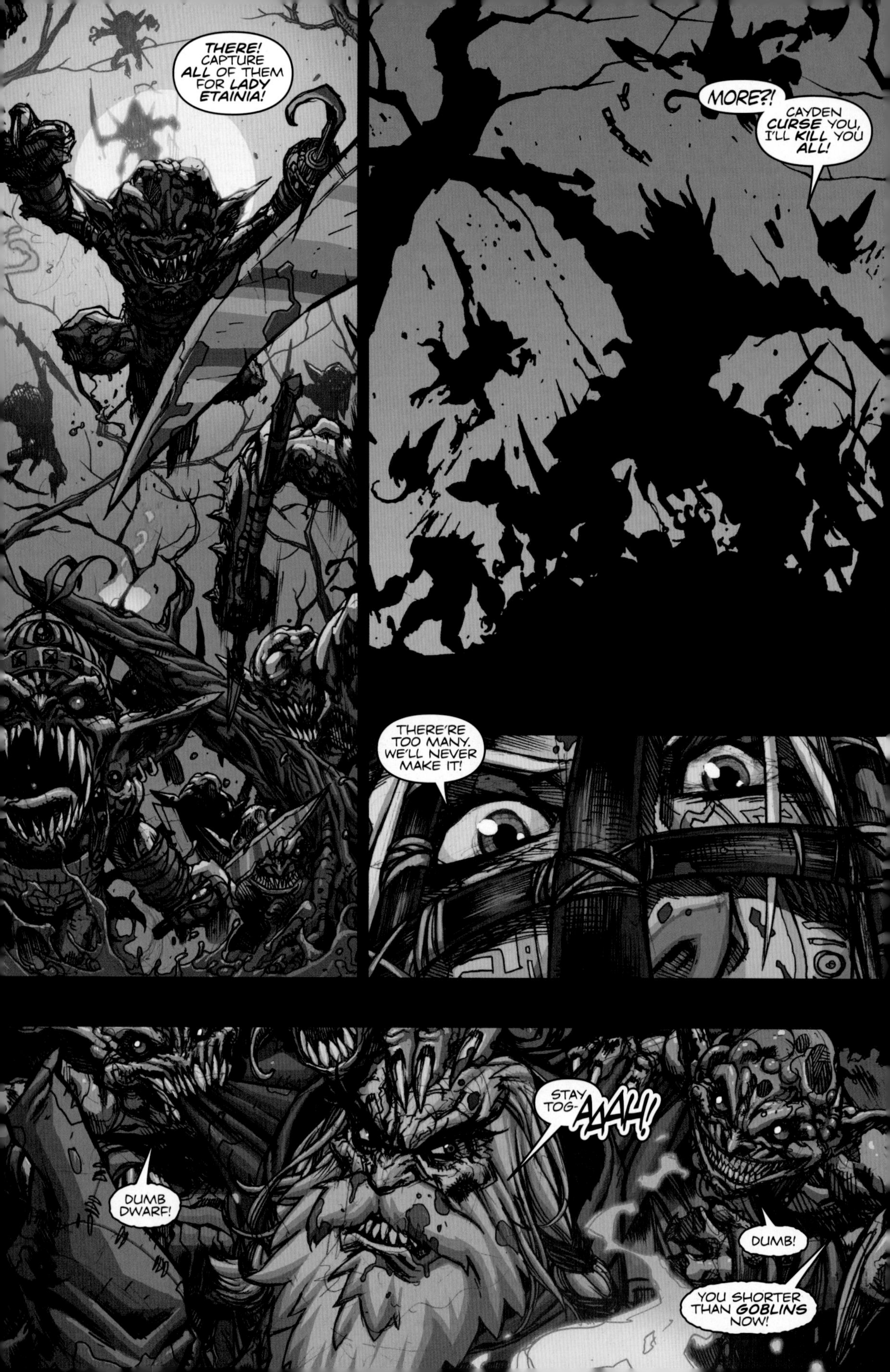
THERE! CAPTURE ALL OF THEM FOR LADY ETAINIA!
MORE?!
CAYDEN CURSE YOU, I'LL KILL YOU ALL!
THERE'RE TOO MANY. WE'LL NEVER MAKE IT!
STAY TOG-AAAH!
DUMB DWARF!
DUMB!
YOU SHORTER THAN GOBLINS NOW!

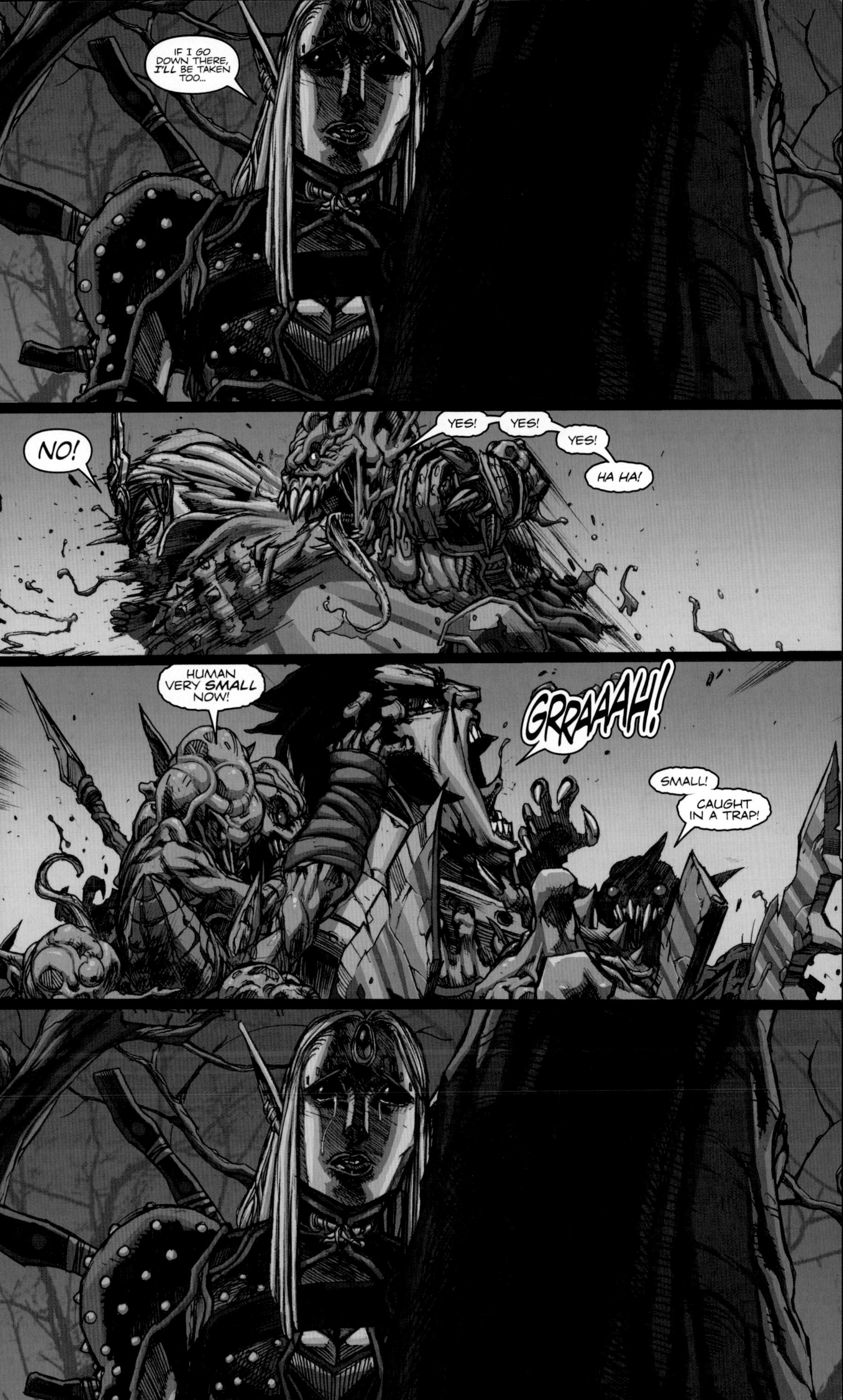

IF I GO DOWN THERE, I'LL BE TAKEN TOO...
NO!
YES!
YES!
YES!
HA HA!
HUMAN VERY SMALL NOW!
GRRAAAH!
SMALL!
CAUGHT IN A TRAP!

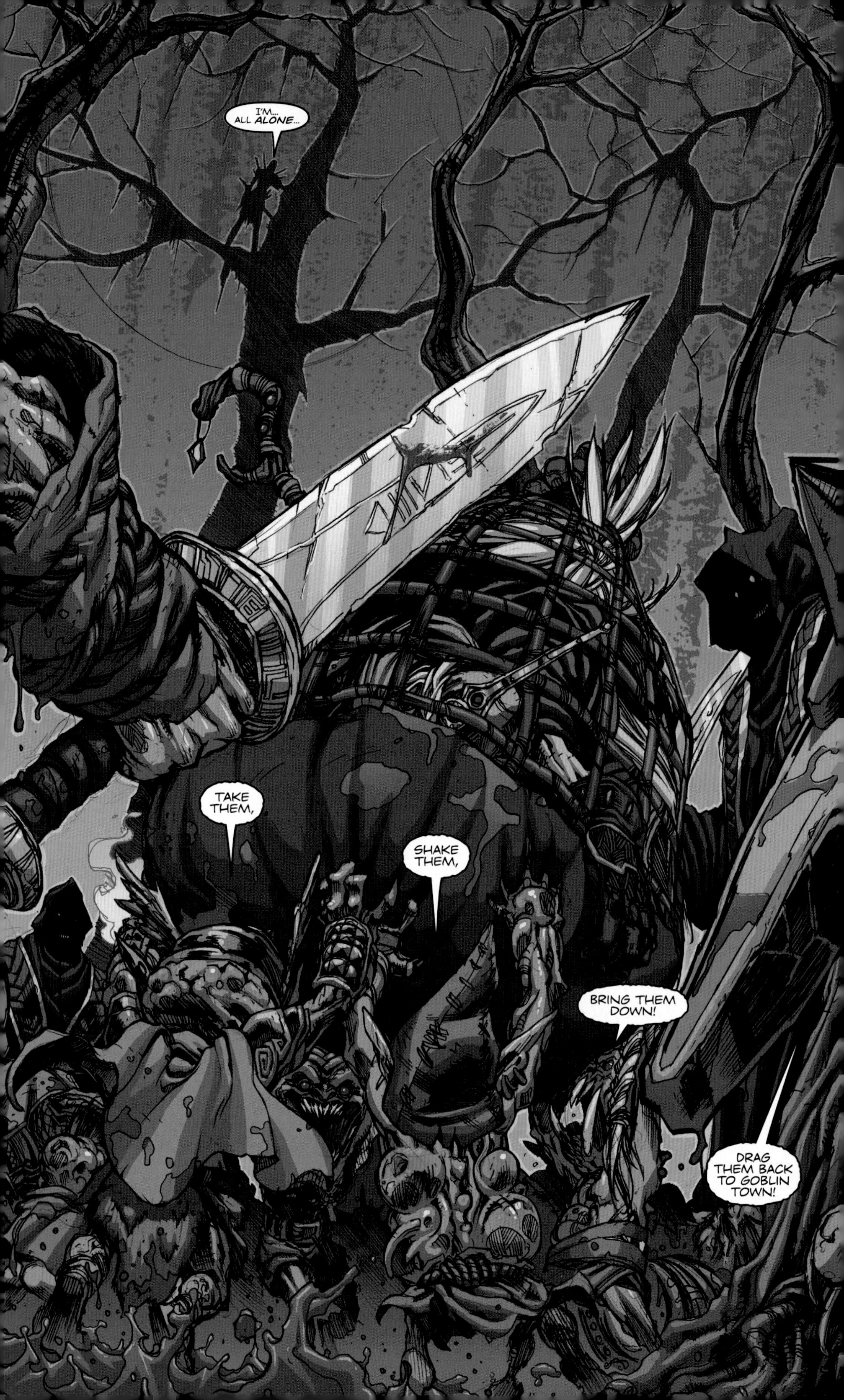
I'M... ALL ALONE...
TAKE THEM,
SHAKE THEM,
BRING THEM DOWN!
DRAG THEM BACK TO GOBLIN TOWN!

CHAPTER 5

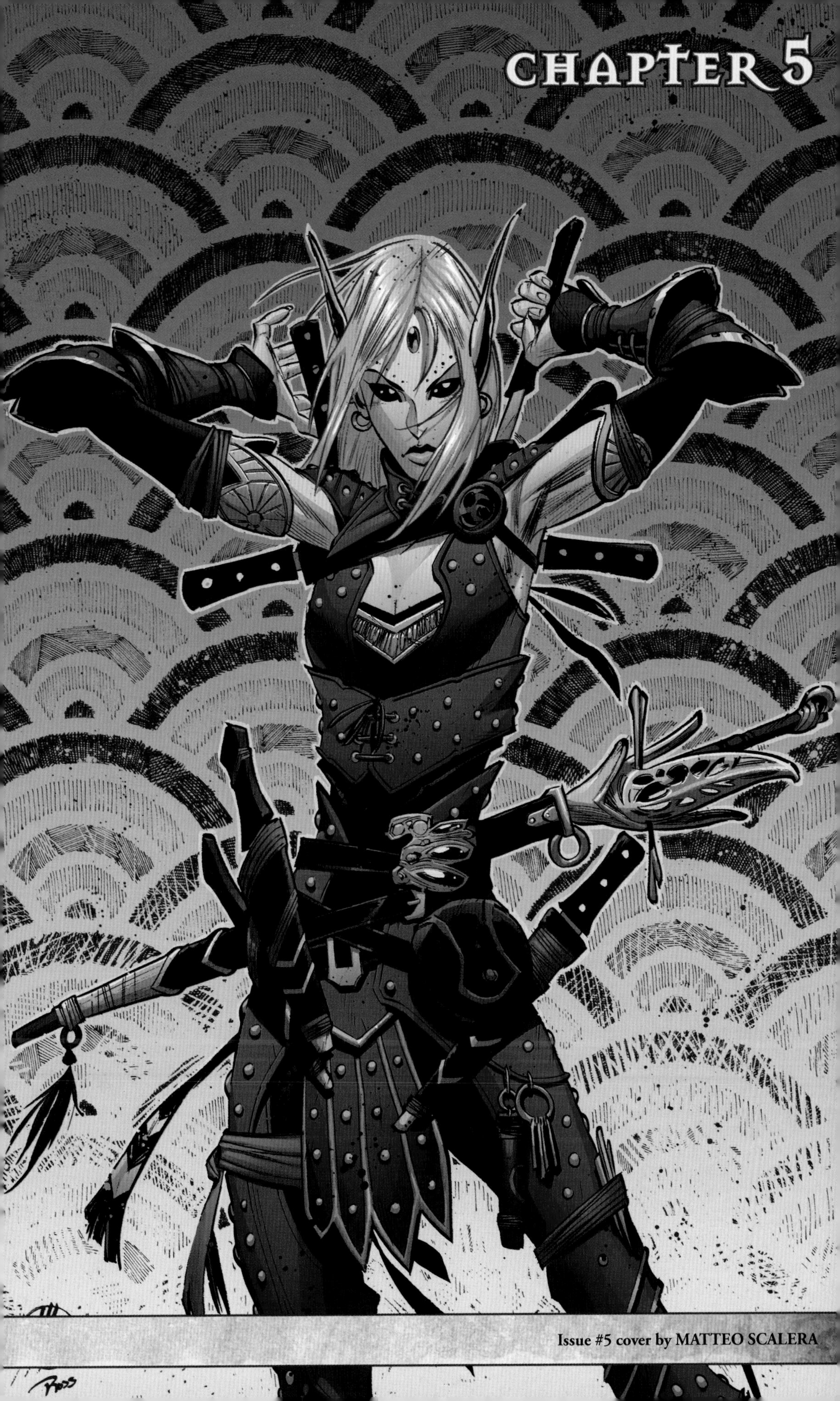

Issue #5 cover by MATTEO SCALERA

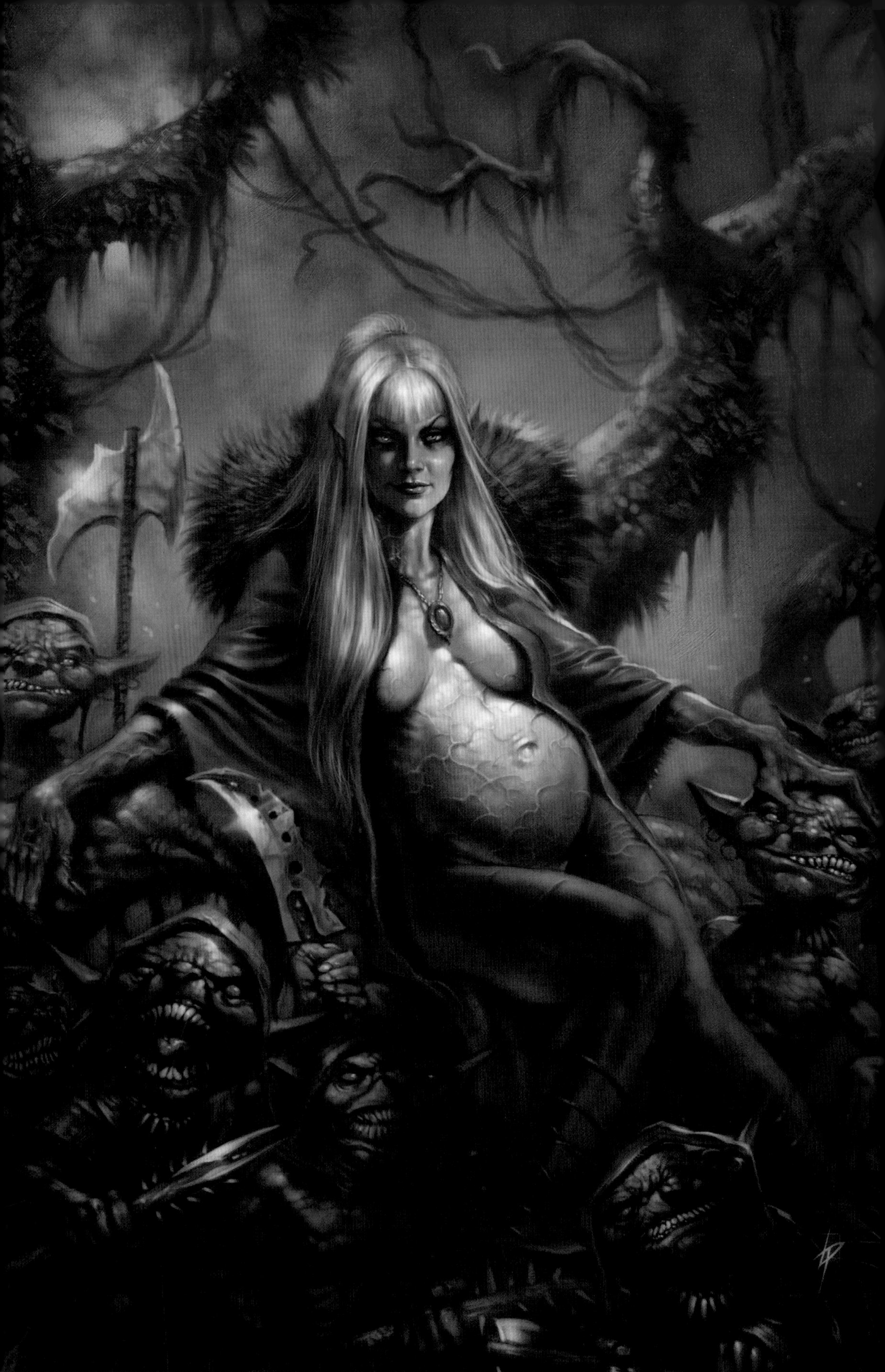

Issue #5 cover by LUCIO PARRILLO

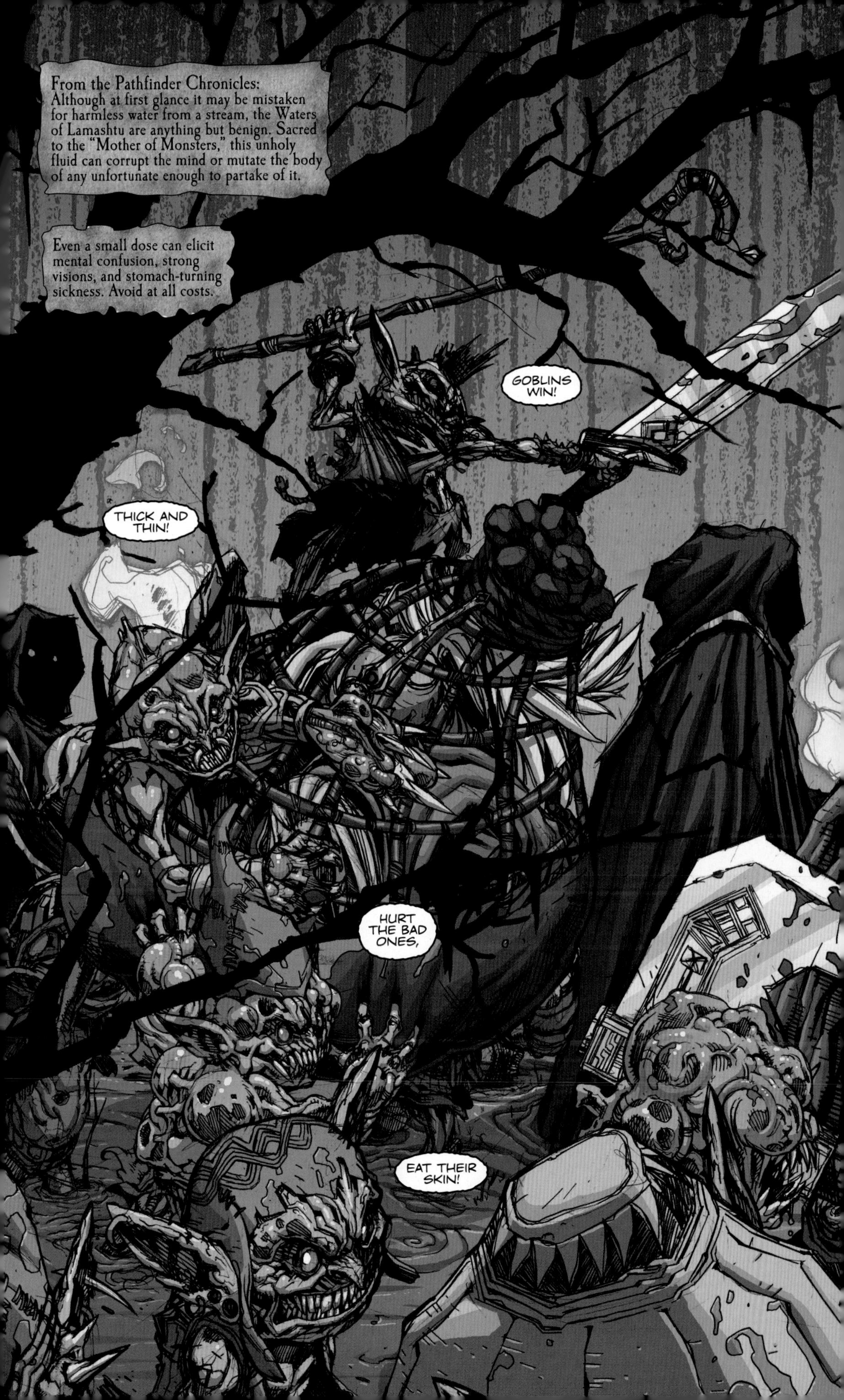
From the Pathfinder Chronicles:
Although at first glance it may be mistaken for harmless water from a stream, the Waters of Lamashtu are anything but benign. Sacred to the "Mother of Monsters," this unholy fluid can corrupt the mind or mutate the body of any unfortunate enough to partake of it.
Even a small dose can elicit mental confusion, strong visions, and stomach-turning sickness. Avoid at all costs.
GOBLINS WIN!
THICK AND THIN!
HURT THE BAD ONES,
EAT THEIR SKIN!

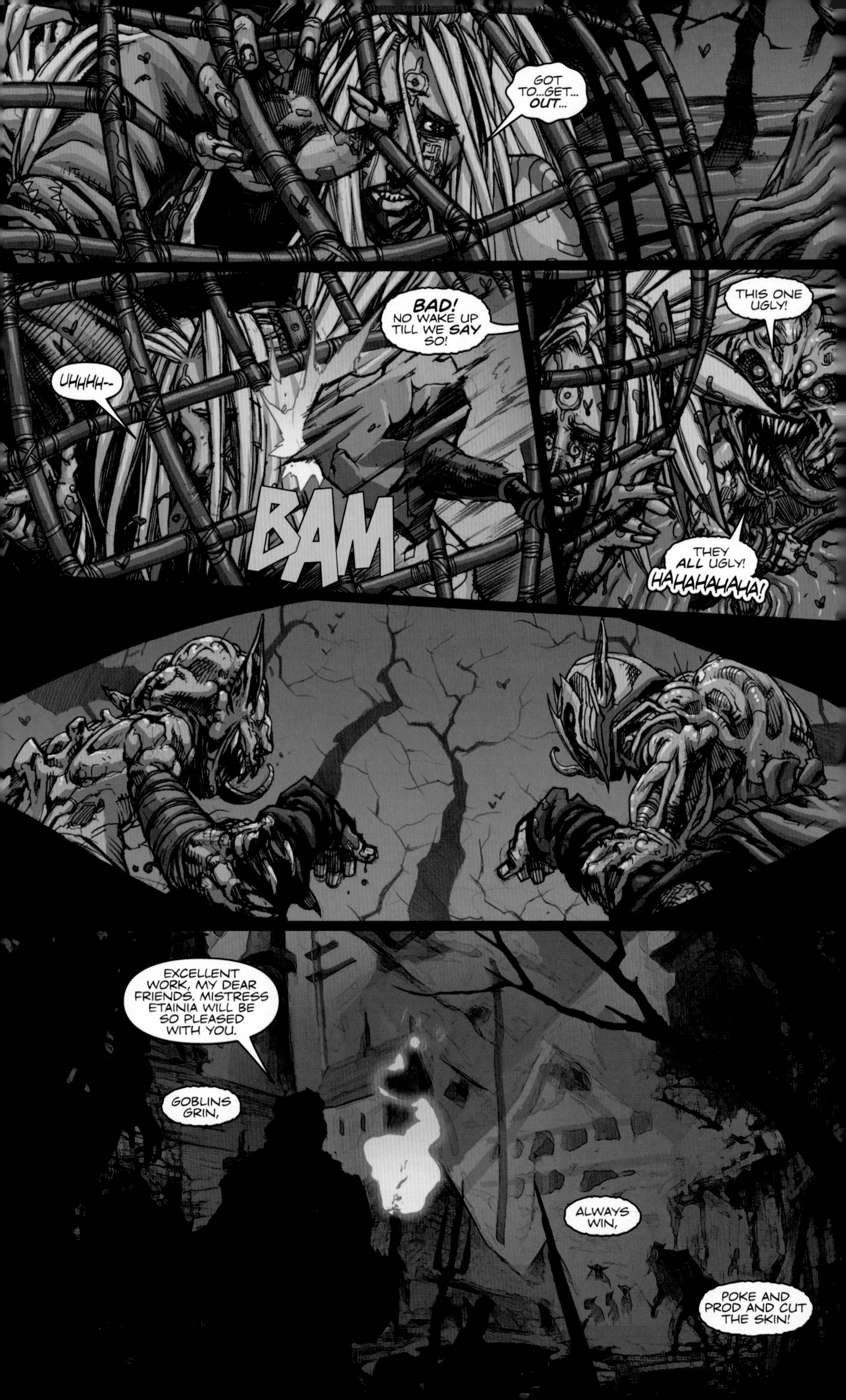
GOT TO...GET... OUT...
UHHHH--
BAD! NO WAKE UP TILL WE SAY SO!
BAM
THIS ONE UGLY!
THEY ALL UGLY! HAHAHAHAHA!
EXCELLENT WORK, MY DEAR FRIENDS. MISTRESS ETAINIA WILL BE SO PLEASED WITH YOU.
GOBLINS GRIN,
ALWAYS WIN,
POKE AND PROD AND CUT THE SKIN!

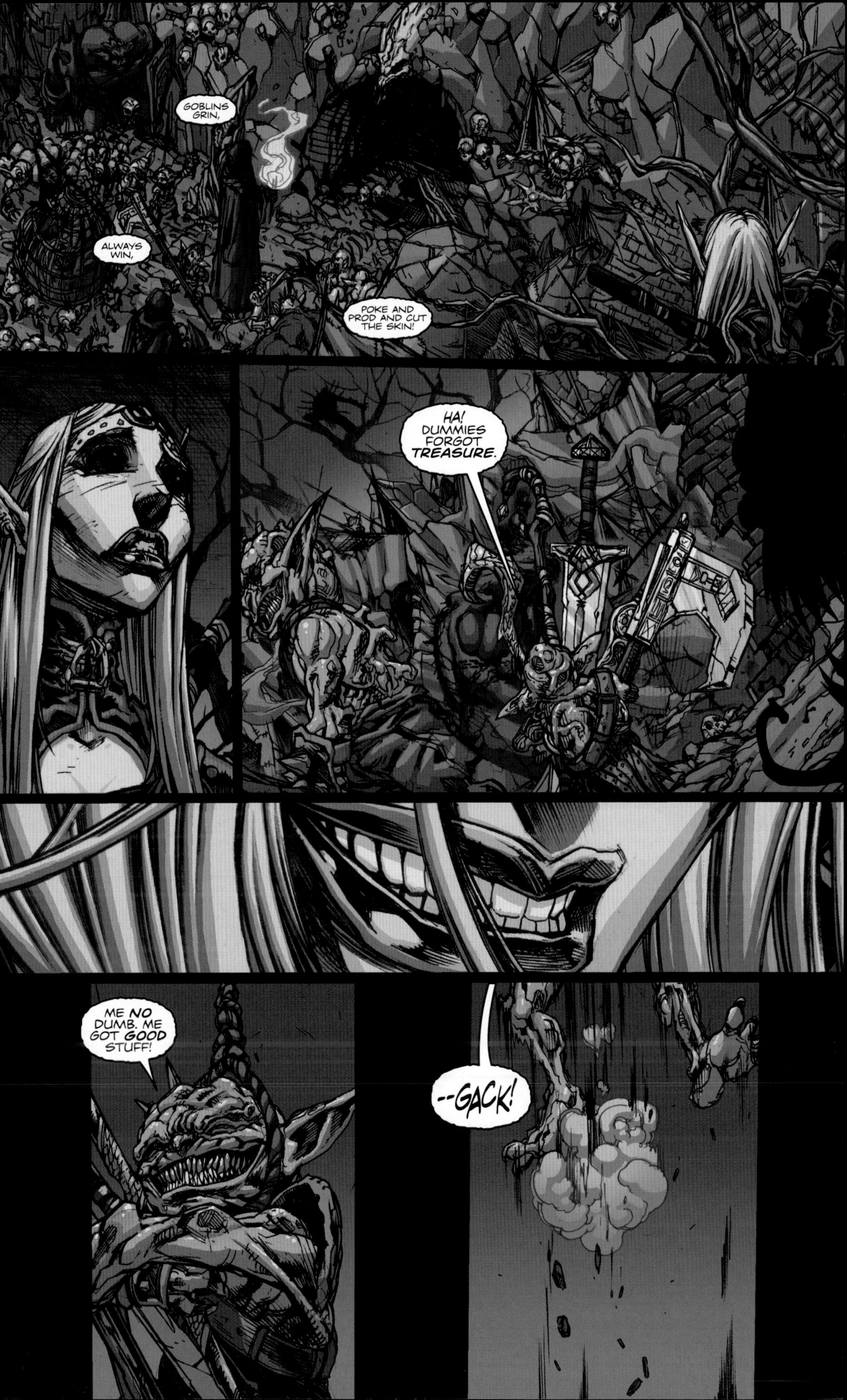
GOBLINS GRIN,
ALWAYS WIN,
POKE AND PROD AND CUT THE SKIN!
HA! DUMMIES FORGOT TREASURE.
ME NO DUMB. ME GOT GOOD STUFF!
--GACK!

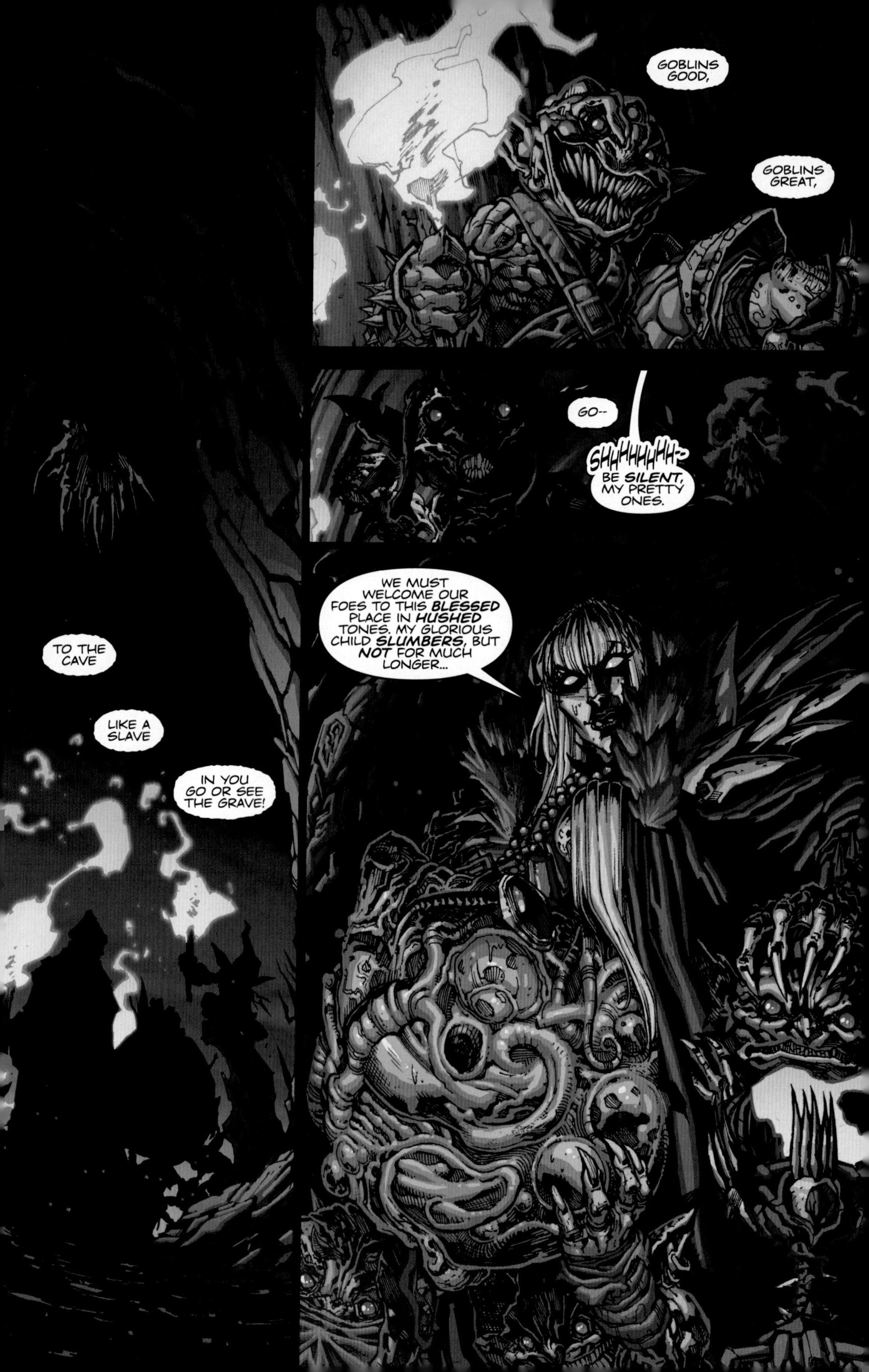
GOBLINS GOOD,
GOBLINS GREAT,
GO--
SHHHHHHHH--
BE SILENT, MY PRETTY ONES.
WE MUST WELCOME OUR FOES TO THIS BLESSED PLACE IN HUSHED TONES. MY GLORIOUS CHILD SLUMBERS, BUT NOT FOR MUCH LONGER...
TO THE CAVE
LIKE A SLAVE
IN YOU GO OR SEE THE GRAVE!

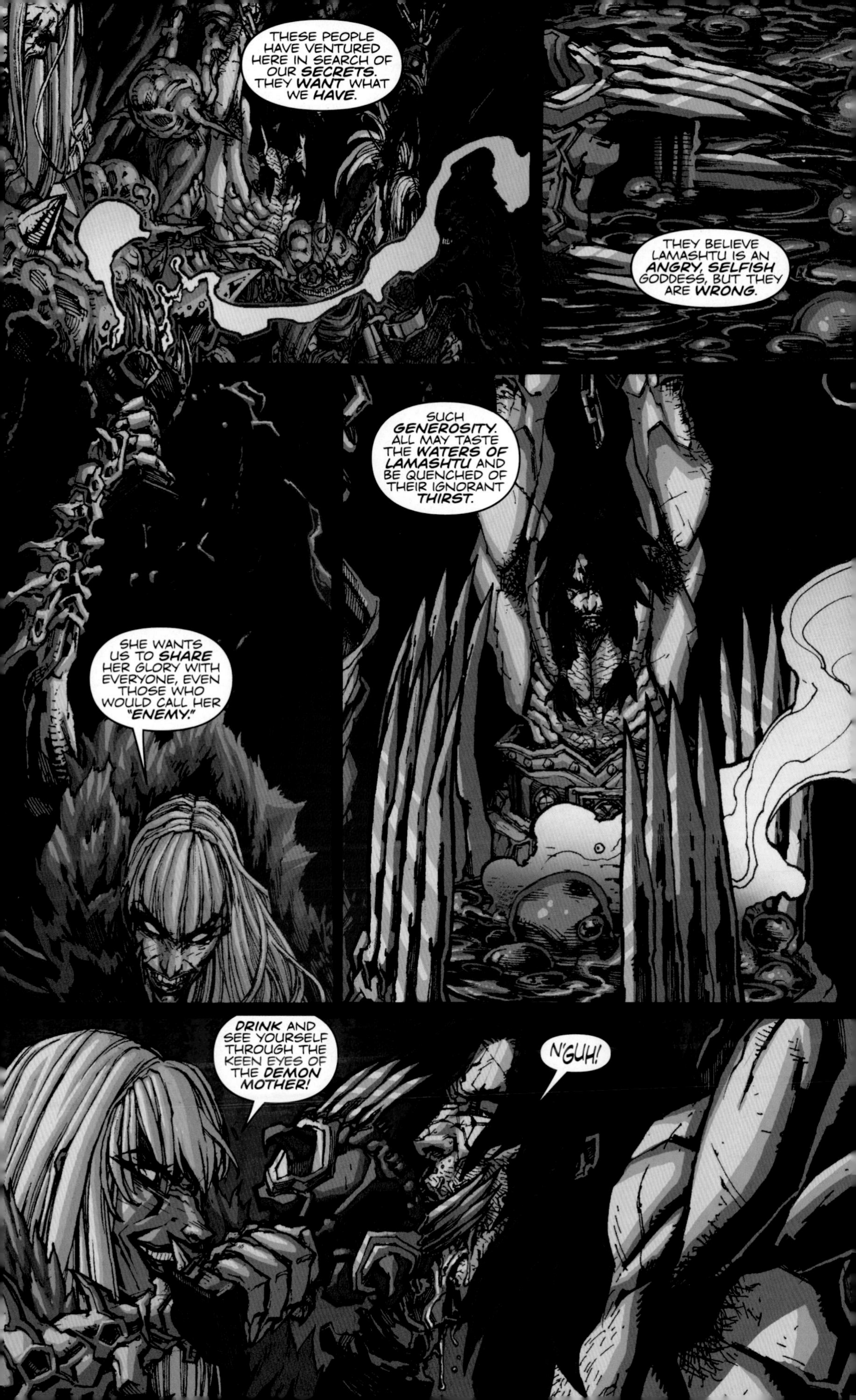
THESE PEOPLE HAVE VENTURED HERE IN SEARCH OF OUR **SECRETS**. THEY **WANT** WHAT WE **HAVE**.
THEY BELIEVE LAMASHTU IS AN **ANGRY, SELFISH** GODDESS, BUT THEY ARE **WRONG**.
SHE WANTS US TO **SHARE** HER GLORY WITH EVERYONE, EVEN THOSE WHO WOULD CALL HER **"ENEMY."**
SUCH **GENEROSITY**. ALL MAY TASTE THE **WATERS OF LAMASHTU** AND BE QUENCHED OF THEIR IGNORANT **THIRST**.
DRINK AND SEE YOURSELF THROUGH THE KEEN EYES OF THE **DEMON MOTHER**!
N'GUH!

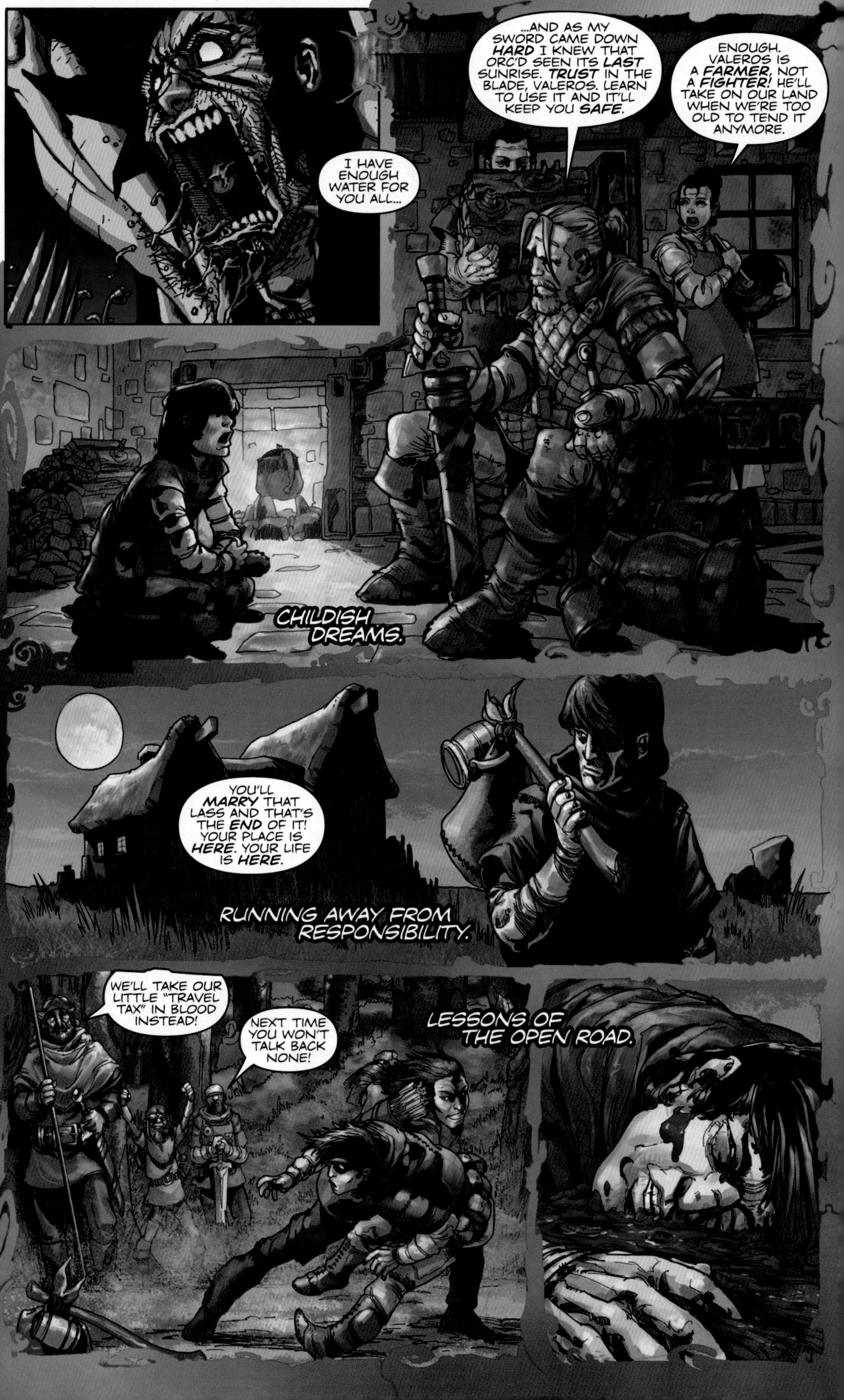
I HAVE ENOUGH WATER FOR YOU ALL...
...AND AS MY SWORD CAME DOWN HARD I KNEW THAT ORC'D SEEN ITS LAST SUNRISE. TRUST IN THE BLADE, VALEROS. LEARN TO USE IT AND IT'LL KEEP YOU SAFE.
ENOUGH. VALEROS IS A FARMER, NOT A FIGHTER! HE'LL TAKE ON OUR LAND WHEN WE'RE TOO OLD TO TEND IT ANYMORE.
CHILDISH DREAMS.
YOU'LL MARRY THAT LASS AND THAT'S THE END OF IT! YOUR PLACE IS HERE. YOUR LIFE IS HERE.
RUNNING AWAY FROM RESPONSIBILITY.
WE'LL TAKE OUR LITTLE "TRAVEL TAX" IN BLOOD INSTEAD!
NEXT TIME YOU WON'T TALK BACK NONE!
LESSONS OF THE OPEN ROAD.

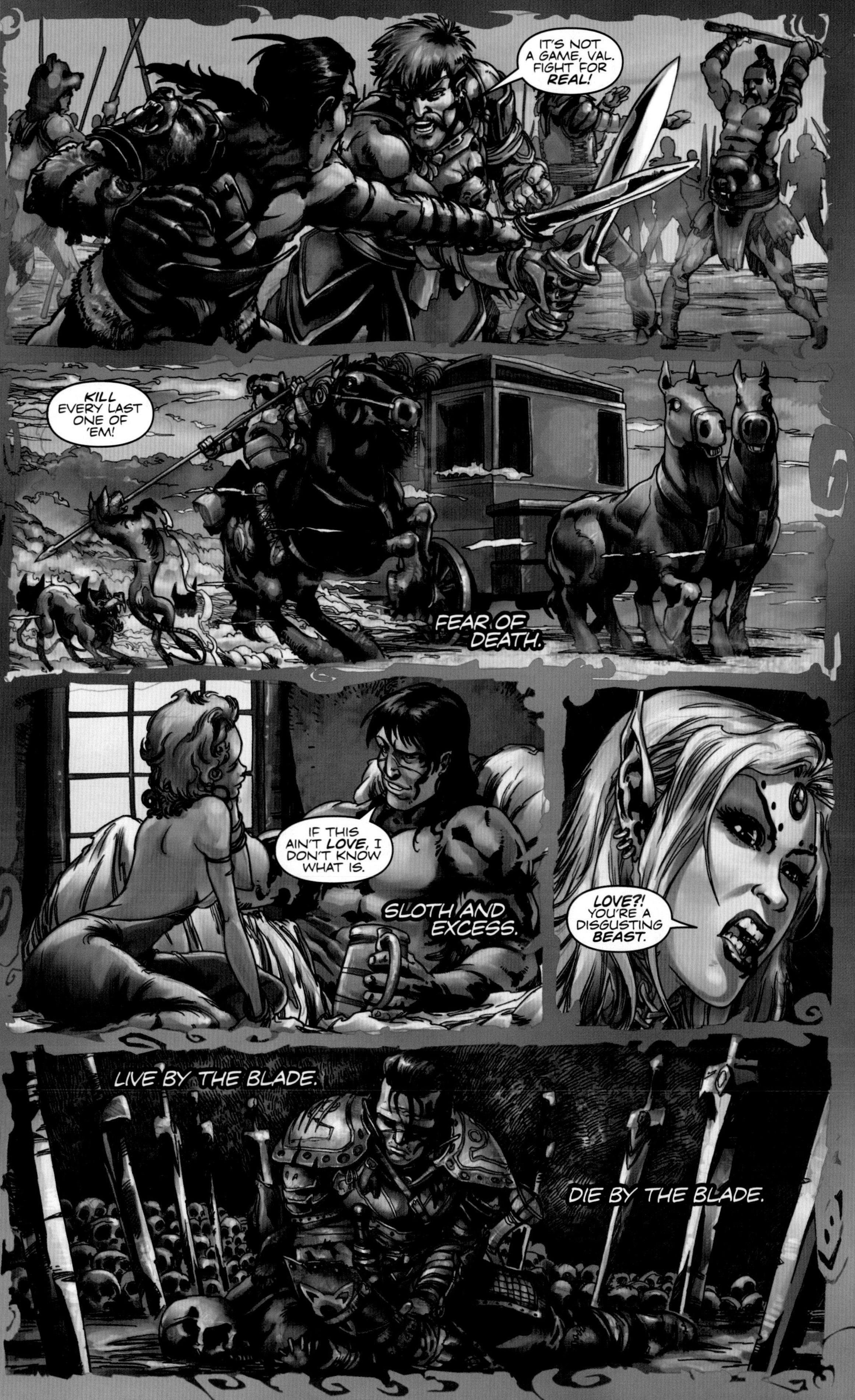
IT'S NOT A GAME, VAL. FIGHT FOR REAL!
KILL EVERY LAST ONE OF 'EM!
FEAR OF DEATH.
IF THIS AIN'T LOVE, I DON'T KNOW WHAT IS.
SLOTH AND EXCESS.
LOVE?! YOU'RE A DISGUSTING BEAST.
LIVE BY THE BLADE.
DIE BY THE BLADE.

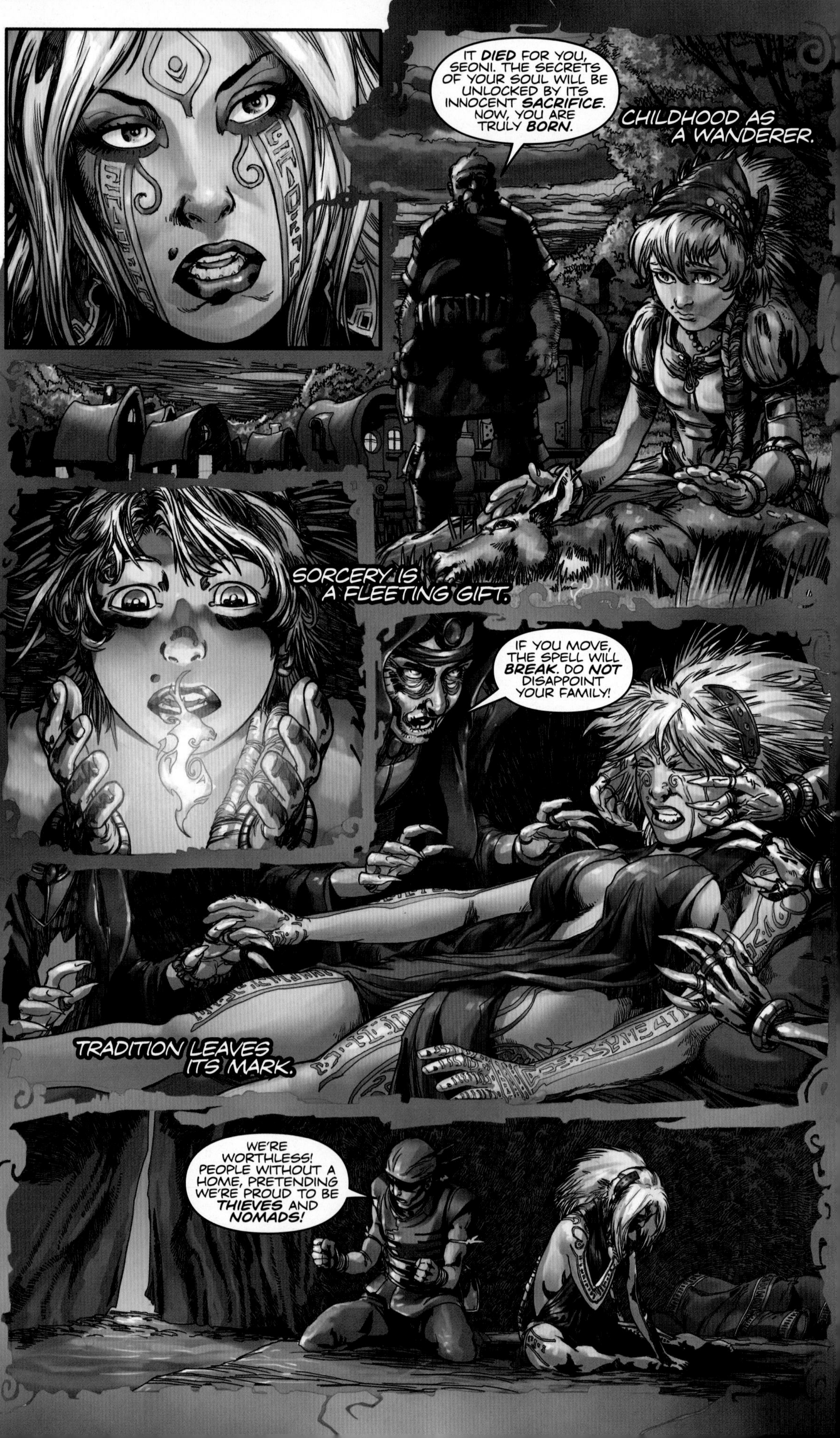

IT **DIED** FOR YOU, SEONI. THE SECRETS OF YOUR SOUL WILL BE UNLOCKED BY ITS INNOCENT **SACRIFICE**. NOW, YOU ARE TRULY **BORN**.
CHILDHOOD AS A WANDERER.
SORCERY IS A FLEETING GIFT.
IF YOU MOVE, THE SPELL WILL **BREAK**. DO **NOT** DISAPPOINT YOUR FAMILY!
TRADITION LEAVES ITS MARK.
WE'RE **WORTHLESS!** PEOPLE WITHOUT A HOME, PRETENDING WE'RE PROUD TO BE **THIEVES** AND **NOMADS!**

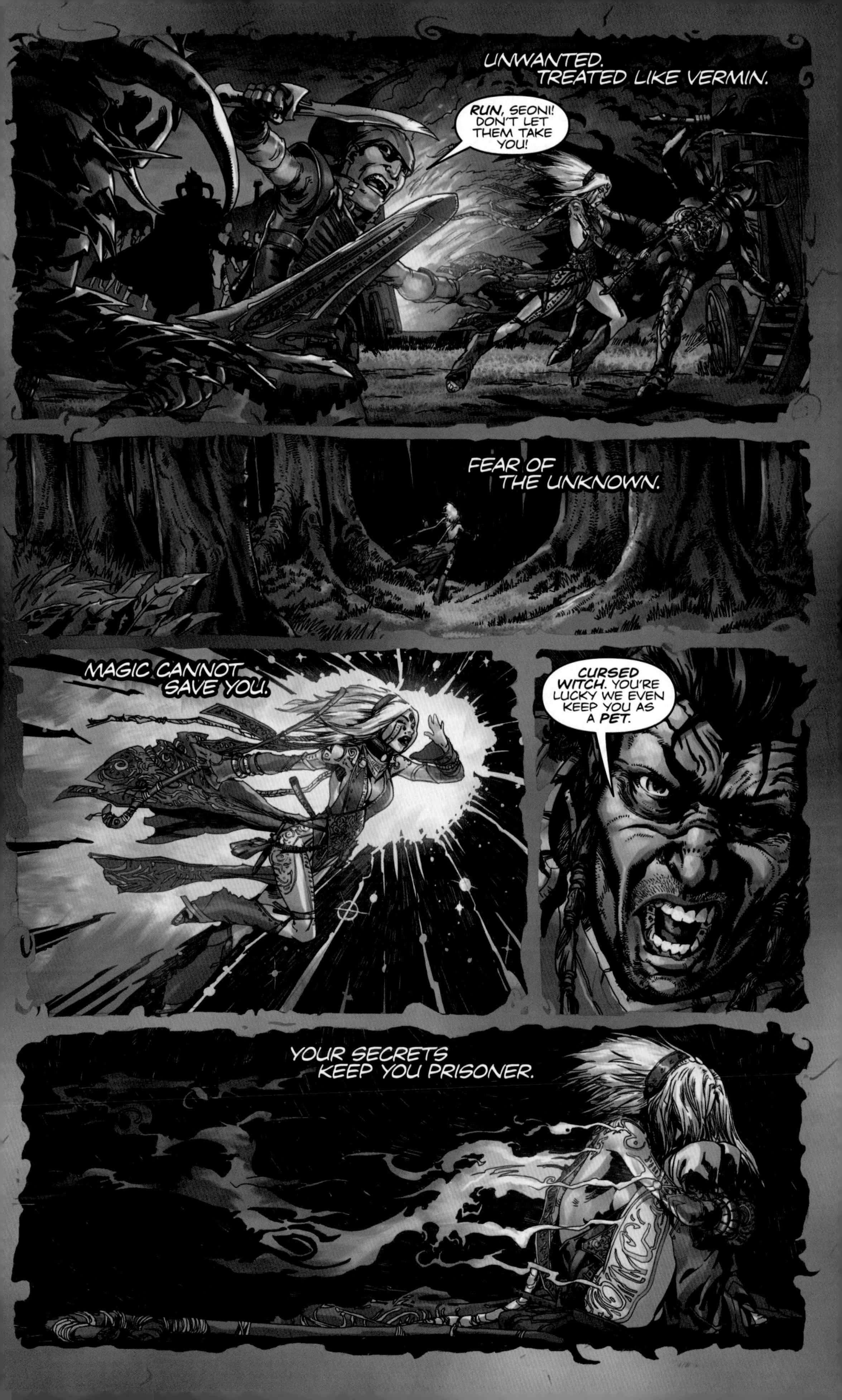
UNWANTED.
TREATED LIKE VERMIN.
RUN, SEONI! DON'T LET THEM TAKE YOU!
FEAR OF THE UNKNOWN.
MAGIC CANNOT SAVE YOU.
CURSED WITCH. YOU'RE LUCKY WE EVEN KEEP YOU AS A PET.
YOUR SECRETS KEEP YOU PRISONER.

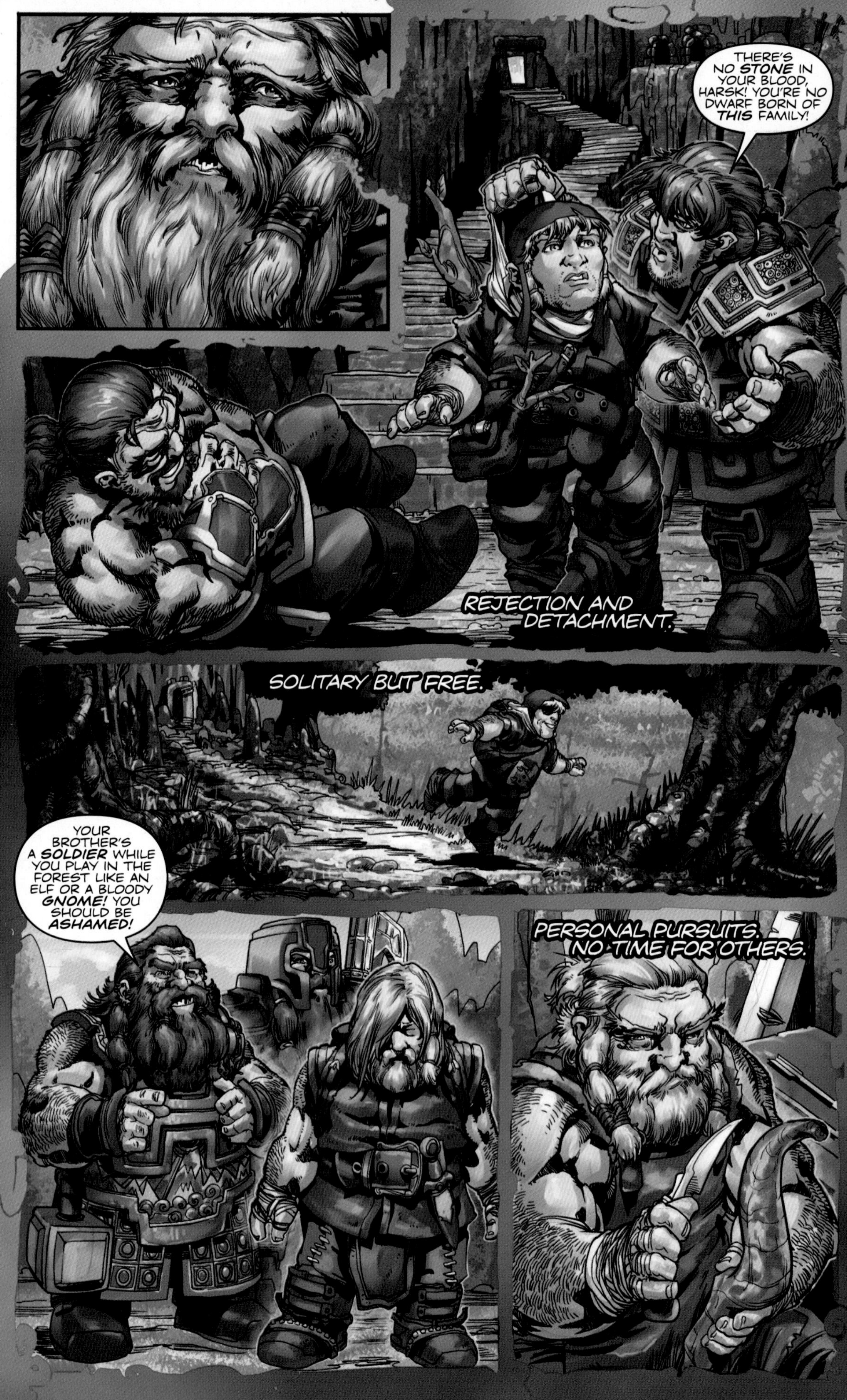
THERE'S NO STONE IN YOUR BLOOD, HARSK! YOU'RE NO DWARF BORN OF THIS FAMILY!
REJECTION AND DETACHMENT.
SOLITARY BUT FREE.
YOUR BROTHER'S A SOLDIER WHILE YOU PLAY IN THE FOREST LIKE AN ELF OR A BLOODY GNOME! YOU SHOULD BE ASHAMED!
PERSONAL PURSUITS. NO TIME FOR OTHERS.

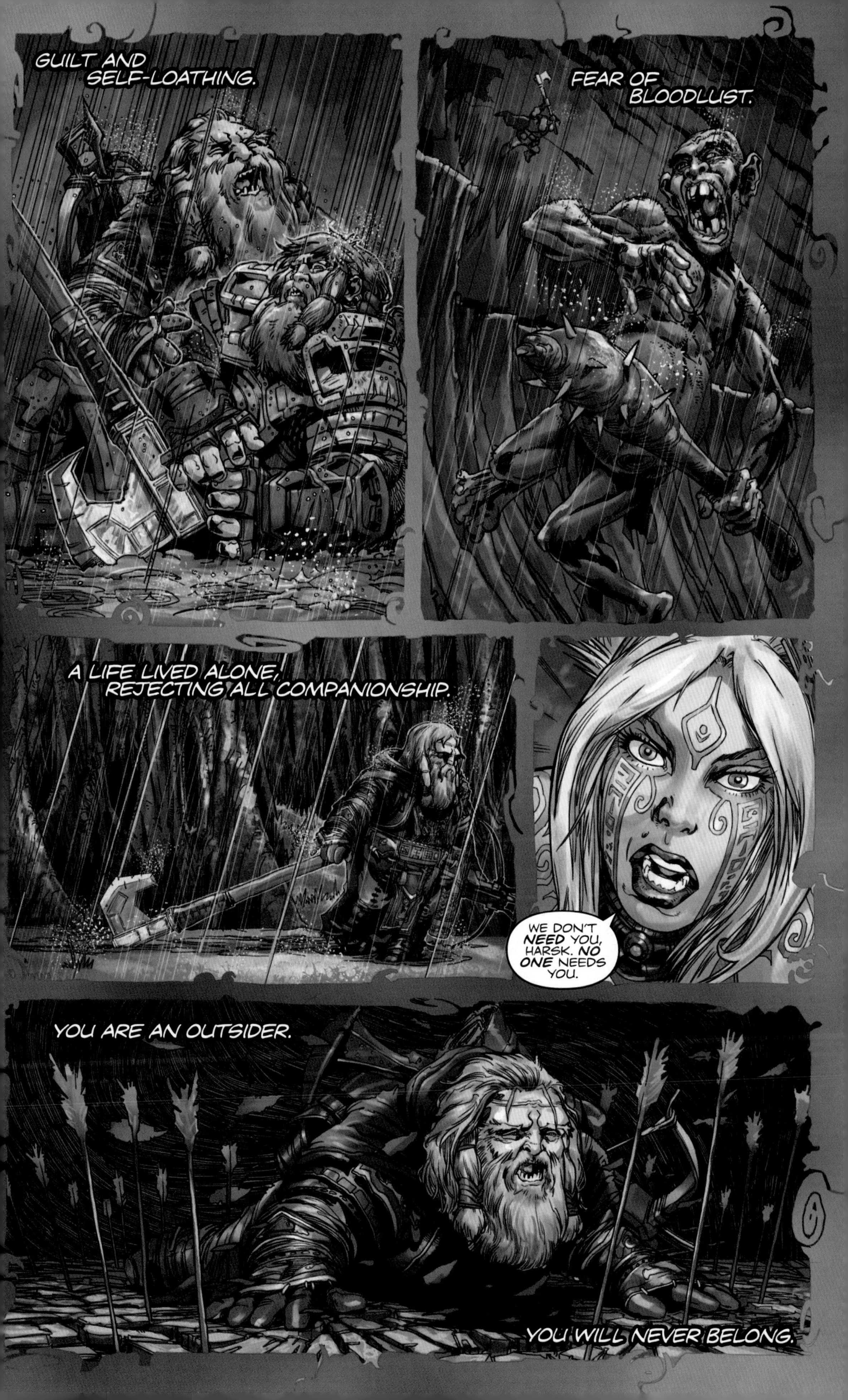
GUILT AND SELF-LOATHING.
FEAR OF BLOODLUST.
A LIFE LIVED ALONE, REJECTING ALL COMPANIONSHIP.
WE DON'T NEED YOU, HARSK. NO ONE NEEDS YOU.
YOU ARE AN OUTSIDER.
YOU WILL NEVER BELONG.

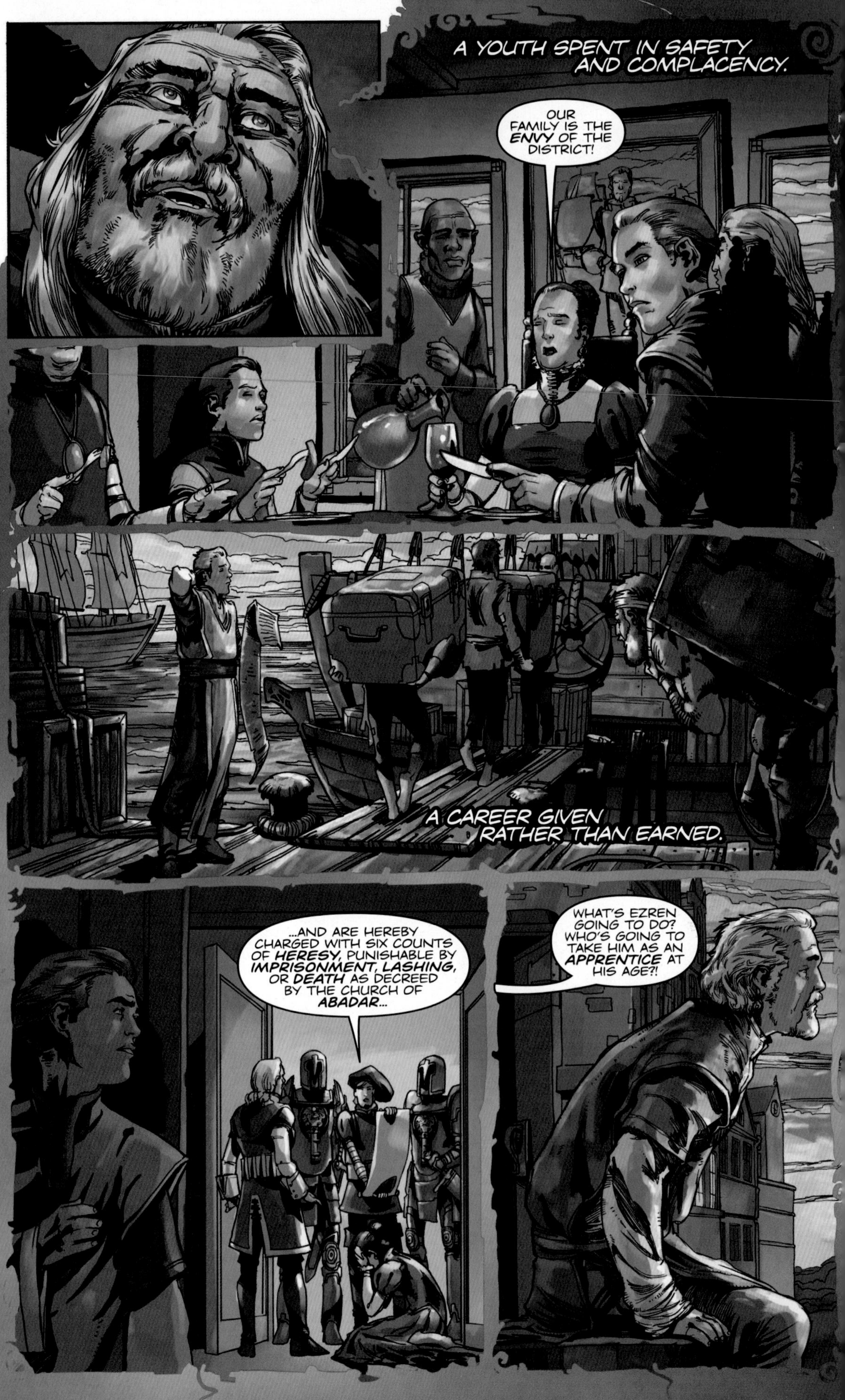
A YOUTH SPENT IN SAFETY AND COMPLACENCY.
OUR FAMILY IS THE ENVY OF THE DISTRICT!
A CAREER GIVEN RATHER THAN EARNED.
...AND ARE HEREBY CHARGED WITH SIX COUNTS OF HERESY, PUNISHABLE BY IMPRISONMENT, LASHING, OR DEATH AS DECREED BY THE CHURCH OF ABADAR...
WHAT'S EZREN GOING TO DO? WHO'S GOING TO TAKE HIM AS AN APPRENTICE AT HIS AGE?!

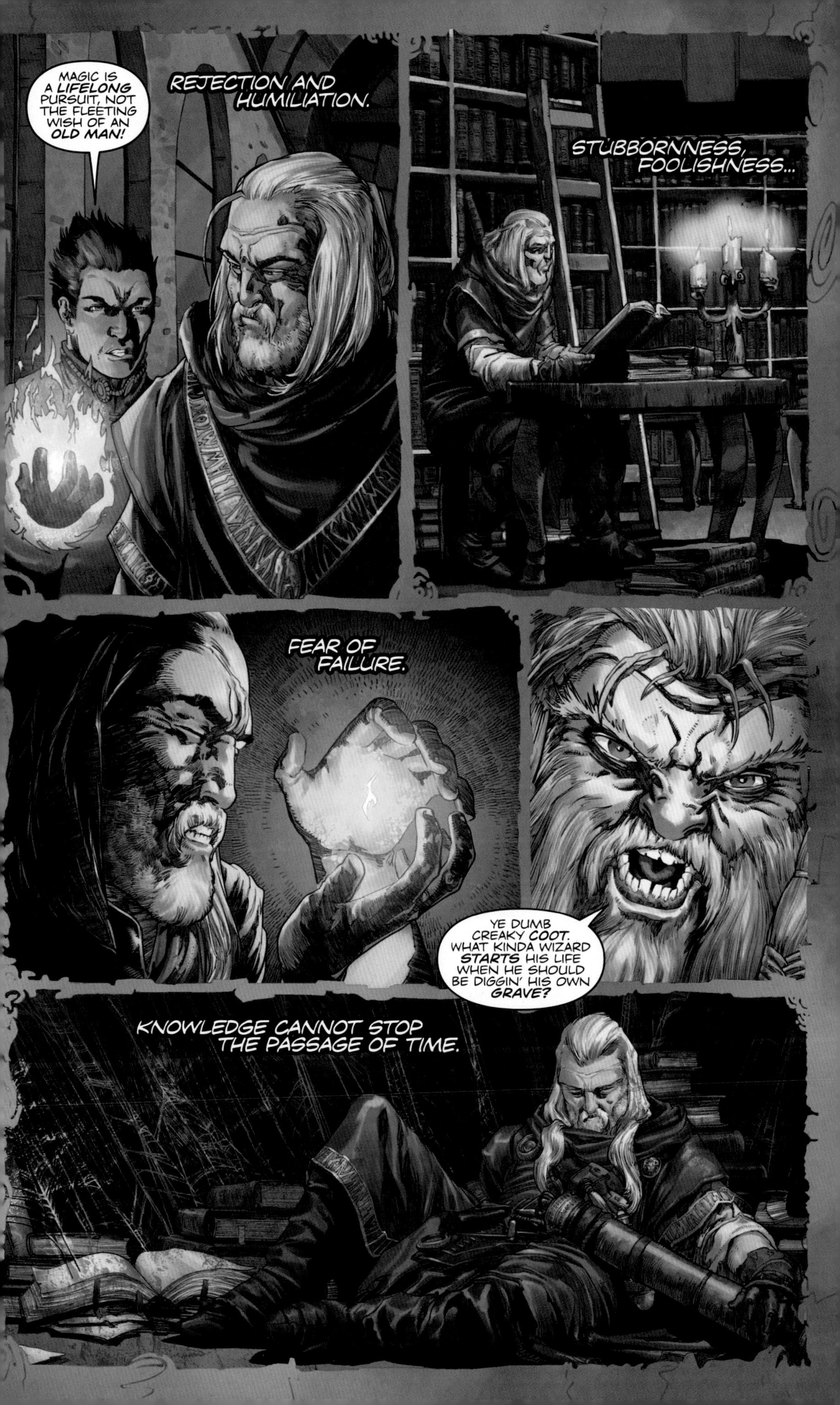
MAGIC IS A LIFELONG PURSUIT, NOT THE FLEETING WISH OF AN OLD MAN!
REJECTION AND HUMILIATION.
STUBBORNNESS, FOOLISHNESS...
FEAR OF FAILURE.
YE DUMB CREAKY COOT. WHAT KINDA WIZARD STARTS HIS LIFE WHEN HE SHOULD BE DIGGIN' HIS OWN GRAVE?
KNOWLEDGE CANNOT STOP THE PASSAGE OF TIME.

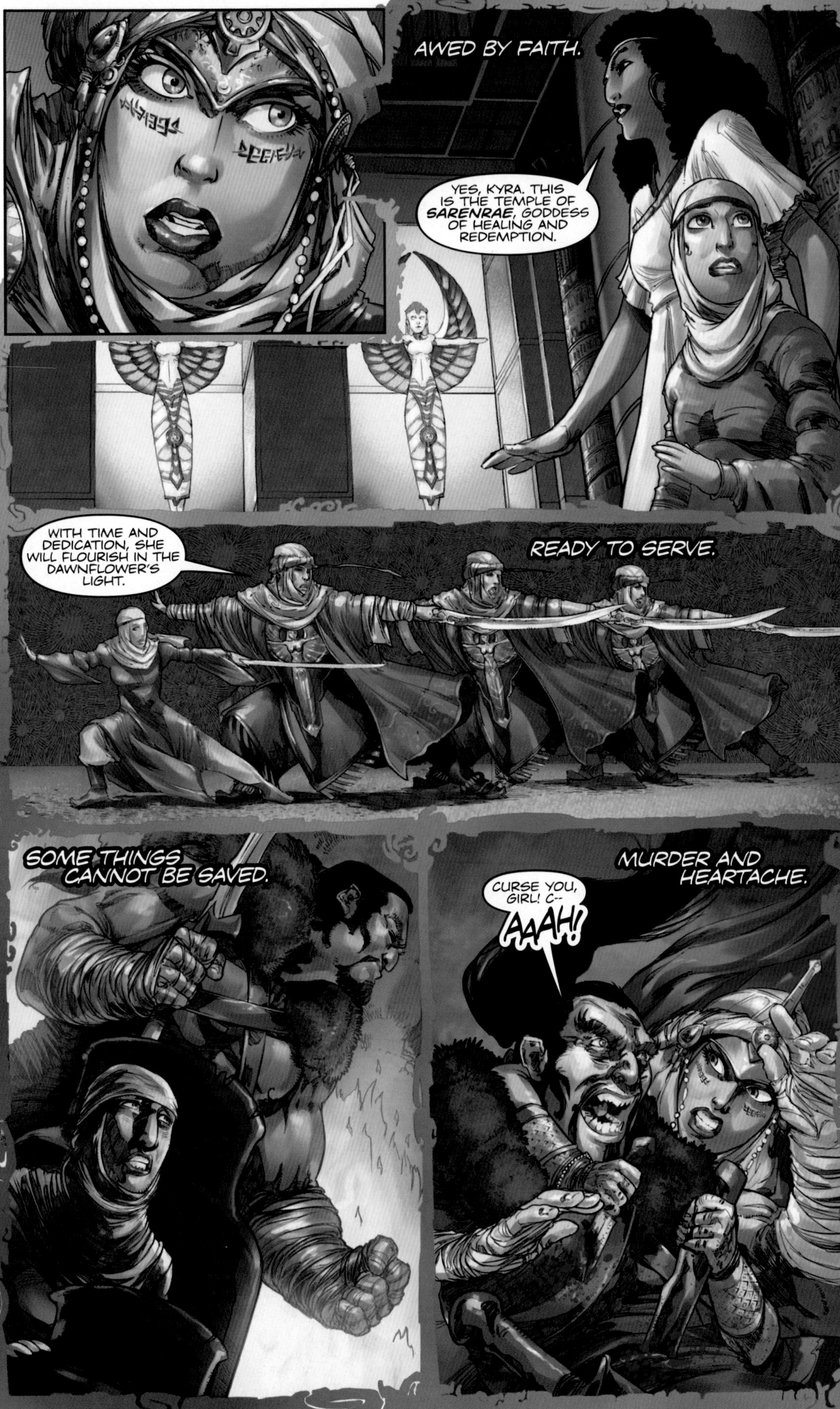
AWED BY FAITH.
YES, KYRA. THIS IS THE TEMPLE OF SARENRAE, GODDESS OF HEALING AND REDEMPTION.
WITH TIME AND DEDICATION, SHE WILL FLOURISH IN THE DAWNFLOWER'S LIGHT.
READY TO SERVE.
SOME THINGS CANNOT BE SAVED.
MURDER AND HEARTACHE.
CURSE YOU, GIRL! C--
AAAH!

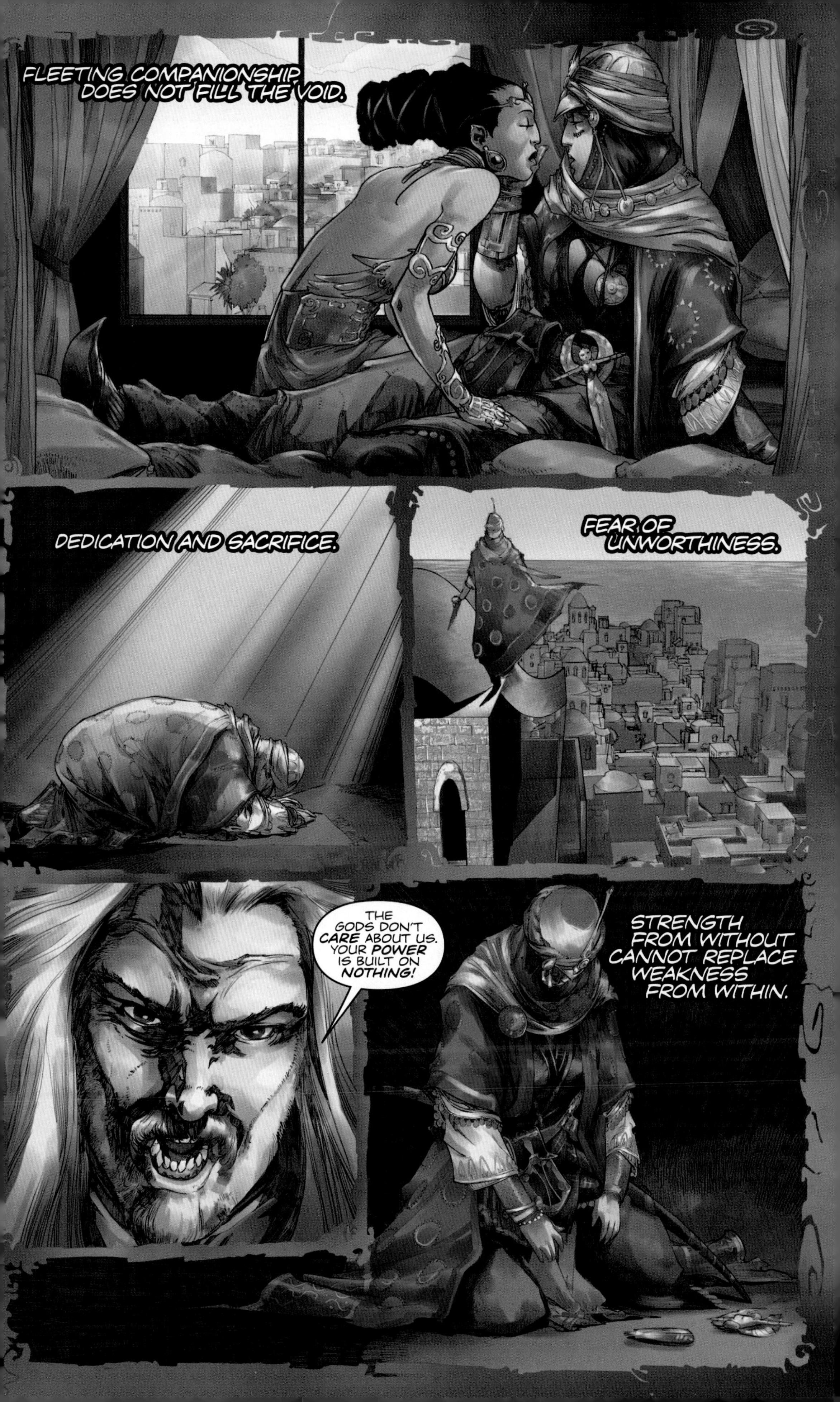
FLEETING COMPANIONSHIP DOES NOT FILL THE VOID.
DEDICATION AND SACRIFICE.
FEAR OF UNWORTHINESS.
THE GODS DON'T CARE ABOUT US. YOUR POWER IS BUILT ON NOTHING!
STRENGTH FROM WITHOUT CANNOT REPLACE WEAKNESS FROM WITHIN.

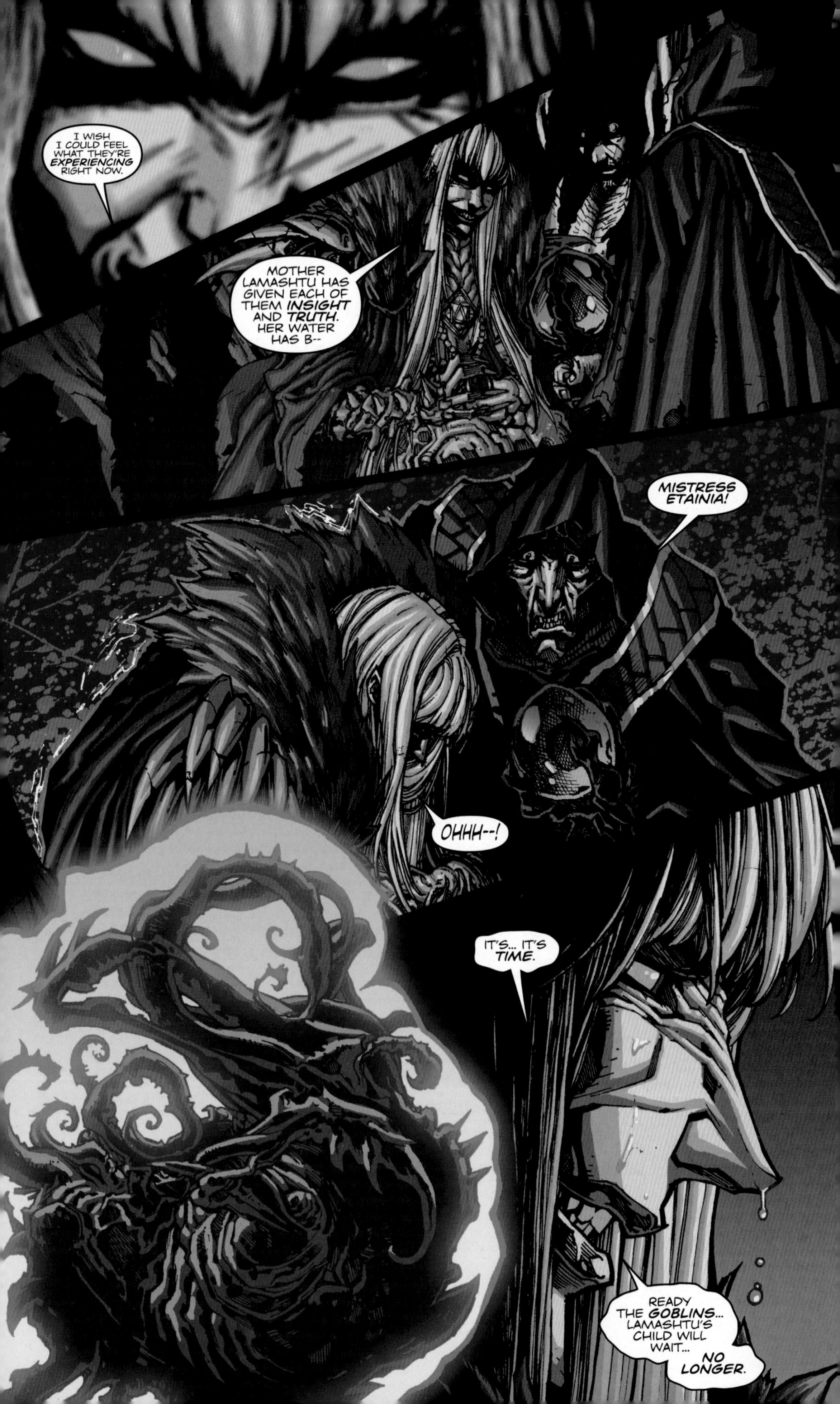
I WISH I COULD FEEL WHAT THEY'RE EXPERIENCING RIGHT NOW.
MOTHER LAMASHTU HAS GIVEN EACH OF THEM INSIGHT AND TRUTH. HER WATER HAS B--
MISTRESS ETAINIA!
OHHH--!
IT'S... IT'S TIME.
READY THE GOBLINS... LAMASHTU'S CHILD WILL WAIT... NO LONGER.

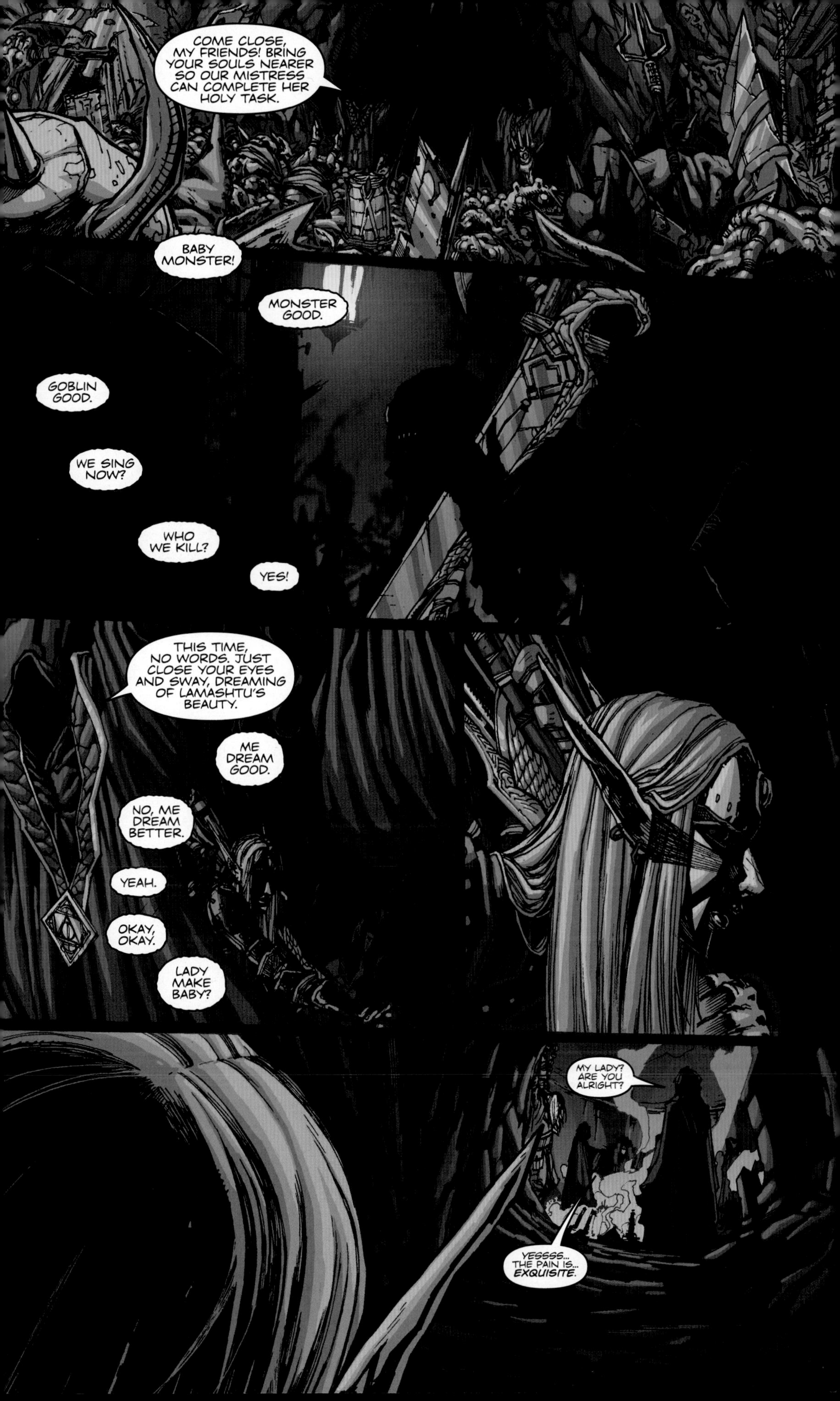
COME CLOSE, MY FRIENDS! BRING YOUR SOULS NEARER SO OUR MISTRESS CAN COMPLETE HER HOLY TASK.
BABY MONSTER!
MONSTER GOOD.
GOBLIN GOOD.
WE SING NOW?
WHO WE KILL?
YES!
THIS TIME, NO WORDS. JUST CLOSE YOUR EYES AND SWAY, DREAMING OF LAMASHTU'S BEAUTY.
ME DREAM GOOD.
NO, ME DREAM BETTER.
YEAH.
OKAY, OKAY.
LADY MAKE BABY?
MY LADY? ARE YOU ALRIGHT?
YESSSS... THE PAIN IS... *EXQUISITE*.

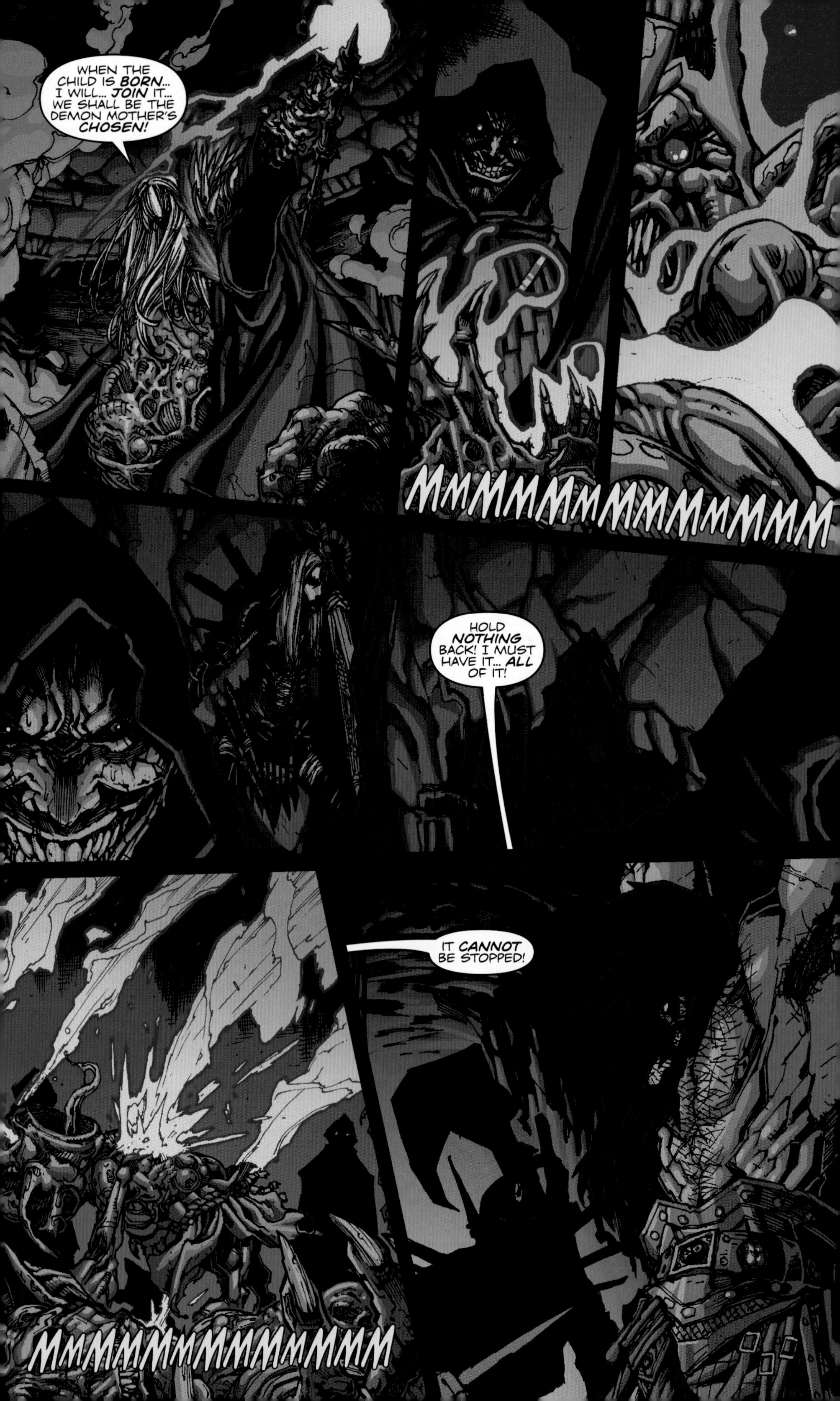
WHEN THE CHILD IS BORN... I WILL... JOIN IT... WE SHALL BE THE DEMON MOTHER'S CHOSEN!
MMMMMMMMMMMMMMMMM
HOLD NOTHING BACK! I MUST HAVE IT... ALL OF IT!
IT CANNOT BE STOPPED!
MMMMMMMMMMMMMMMM

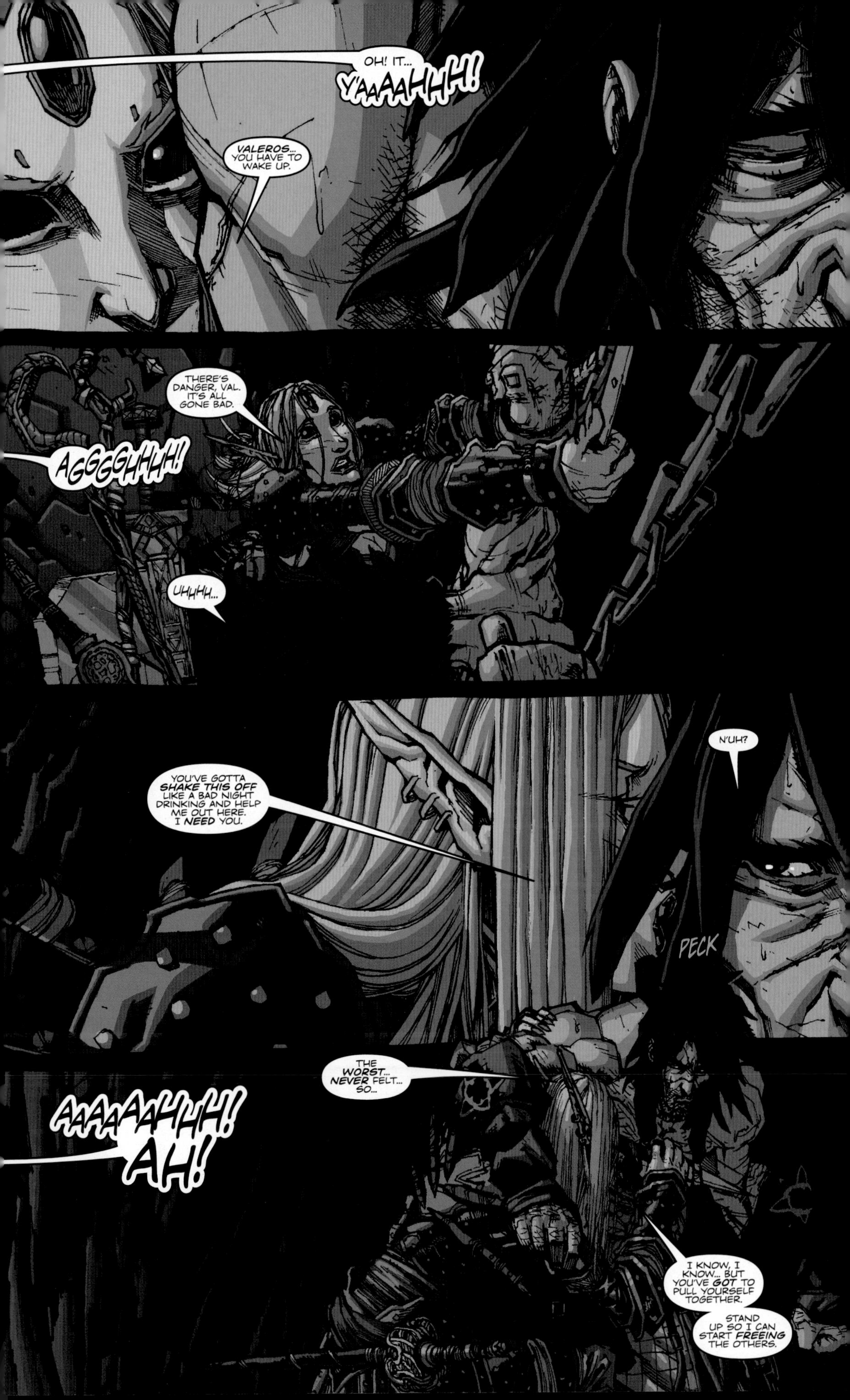
OH! IT...
Y'AAAAHHH!
VALEROS... YOU HAVE TO WAKE UP.
THERE'S DANGER, VAL. IT'S ALL GONE BAD.
AGGGGHHH!
UHHH...
N'UH?
YOU'VE GOTTA SHAKE THIS OFF LIKE A BAD NIGHT DRINKING AND HELP ME OUT HERE. I NEED YOU.
PECK
THE WORST... NEVER FELT... SO...
AAAAAAHHH! AH!
I KNOW, I KNOW... BUT YOU'VE GOT TO PULL YOURSELF TOGETHER.
STAND UP SO I CAN START FREEING THE OTHERS.

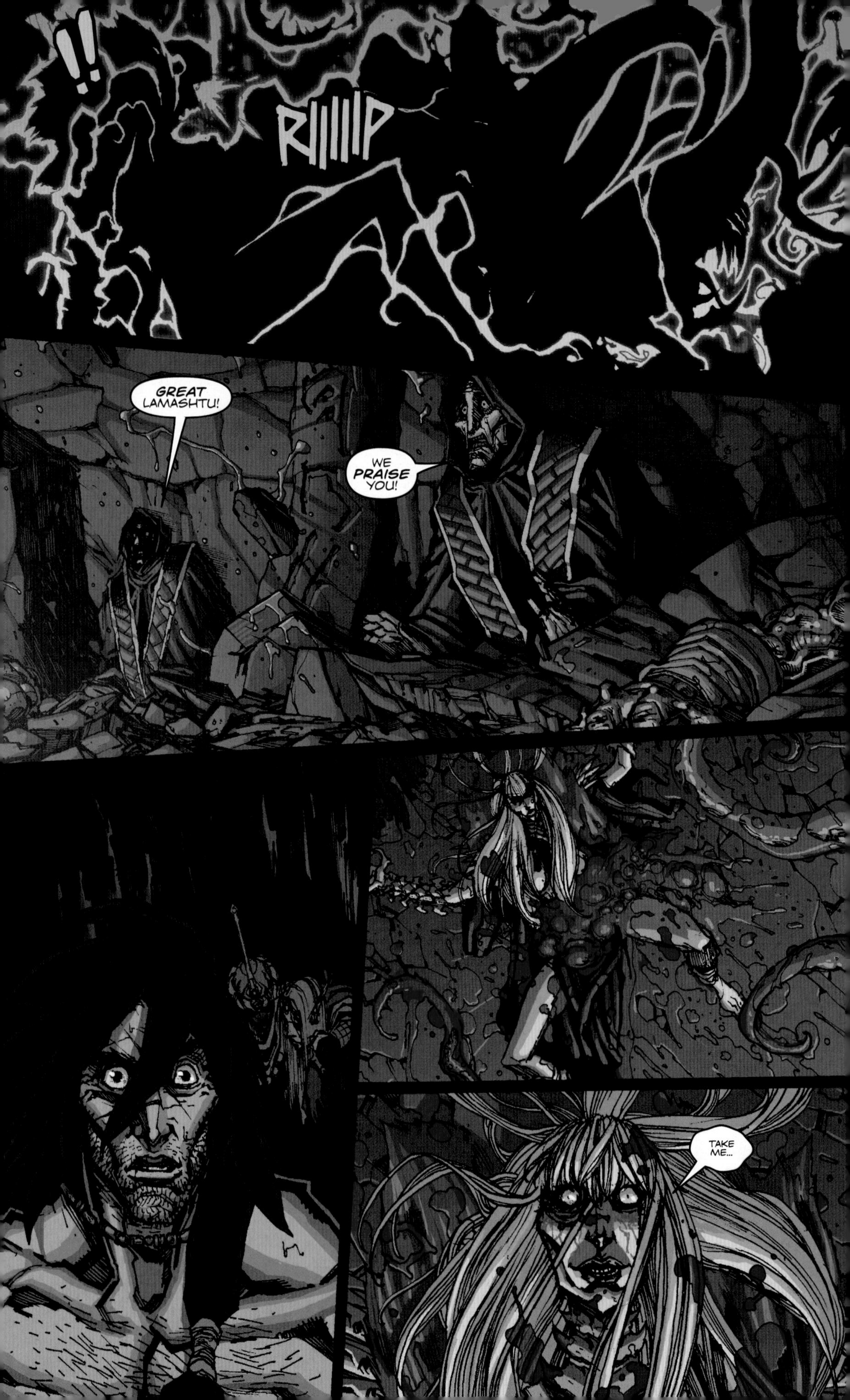
!!
RIIIIP
GREAT LAMASHTU!
WE PRAISE YOU!
TAKE ME...

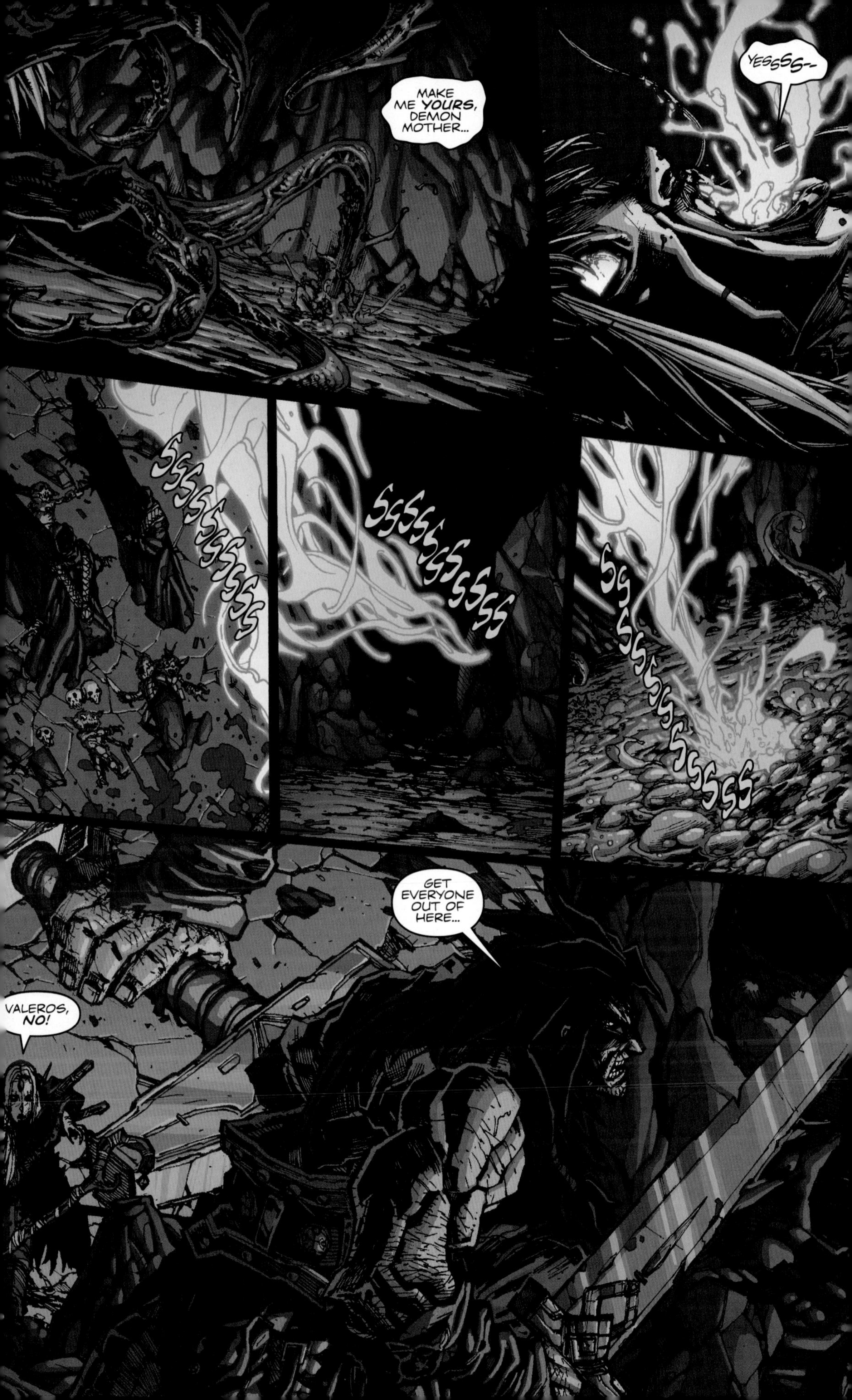
MAKE ME YOURS, DEMON MOTHER...
YESSSS--
SSSSSSSSSSSS
SSSSSSSSSSSS
SSSSSSSSSSSSSS
GET EVERYONE OUT OF HERE...
VALEROS, NO!

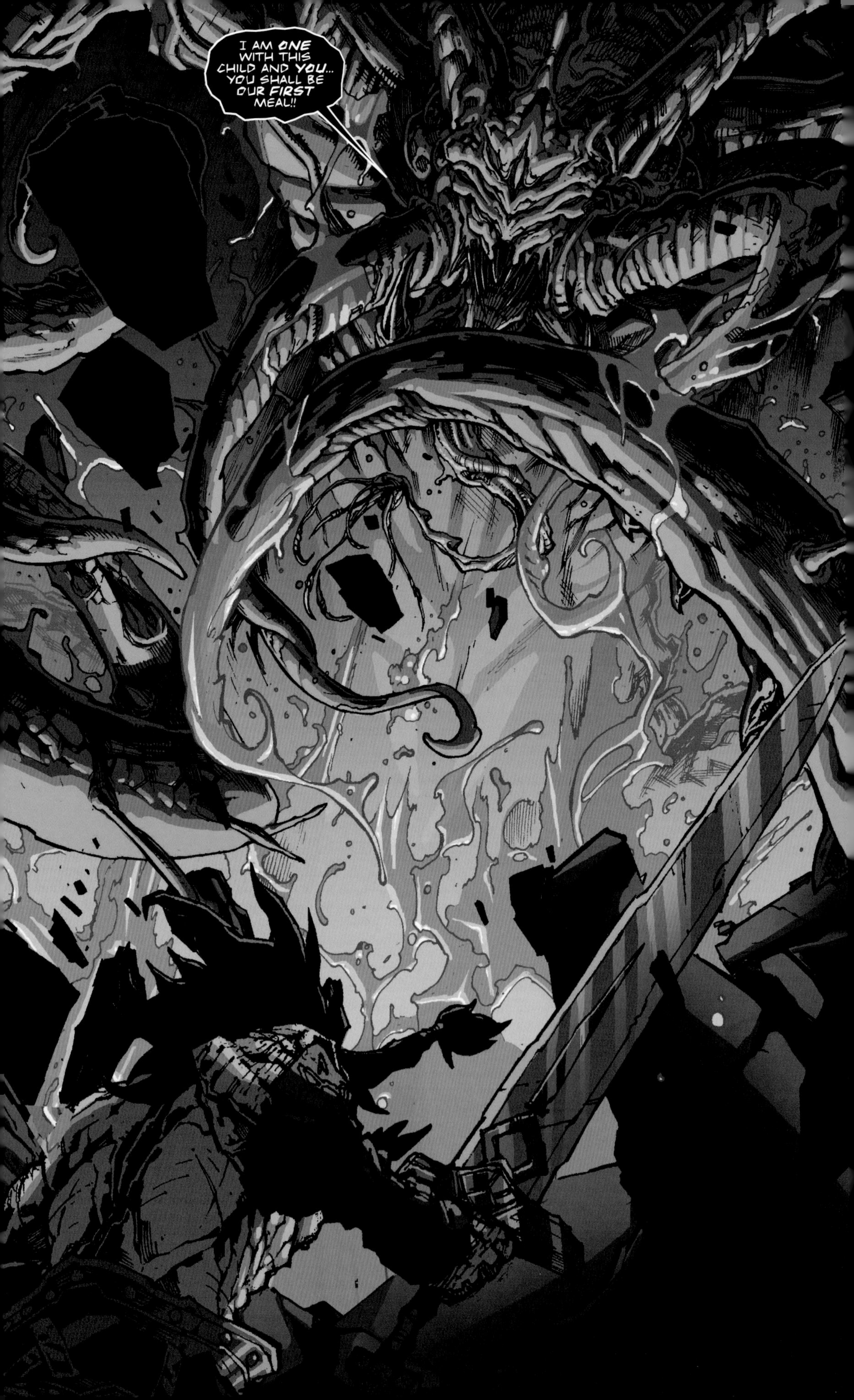
I AM ONE WITH THIS CHILD AND YOU... YOU SHALL BE OUR FIRST MEAL!!

CHAPTER 6

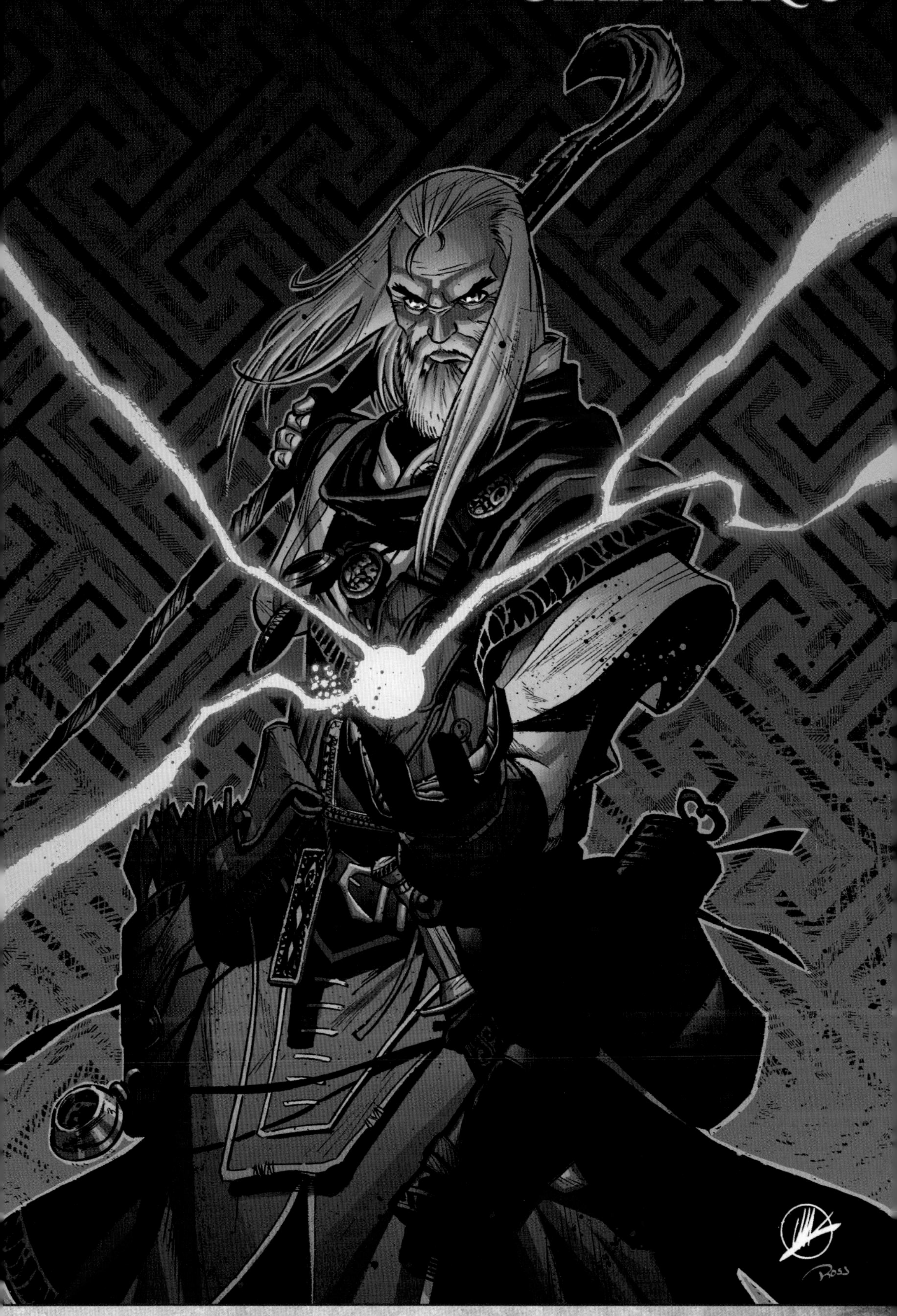

Issue #6 cover by MATTEO SCALERA

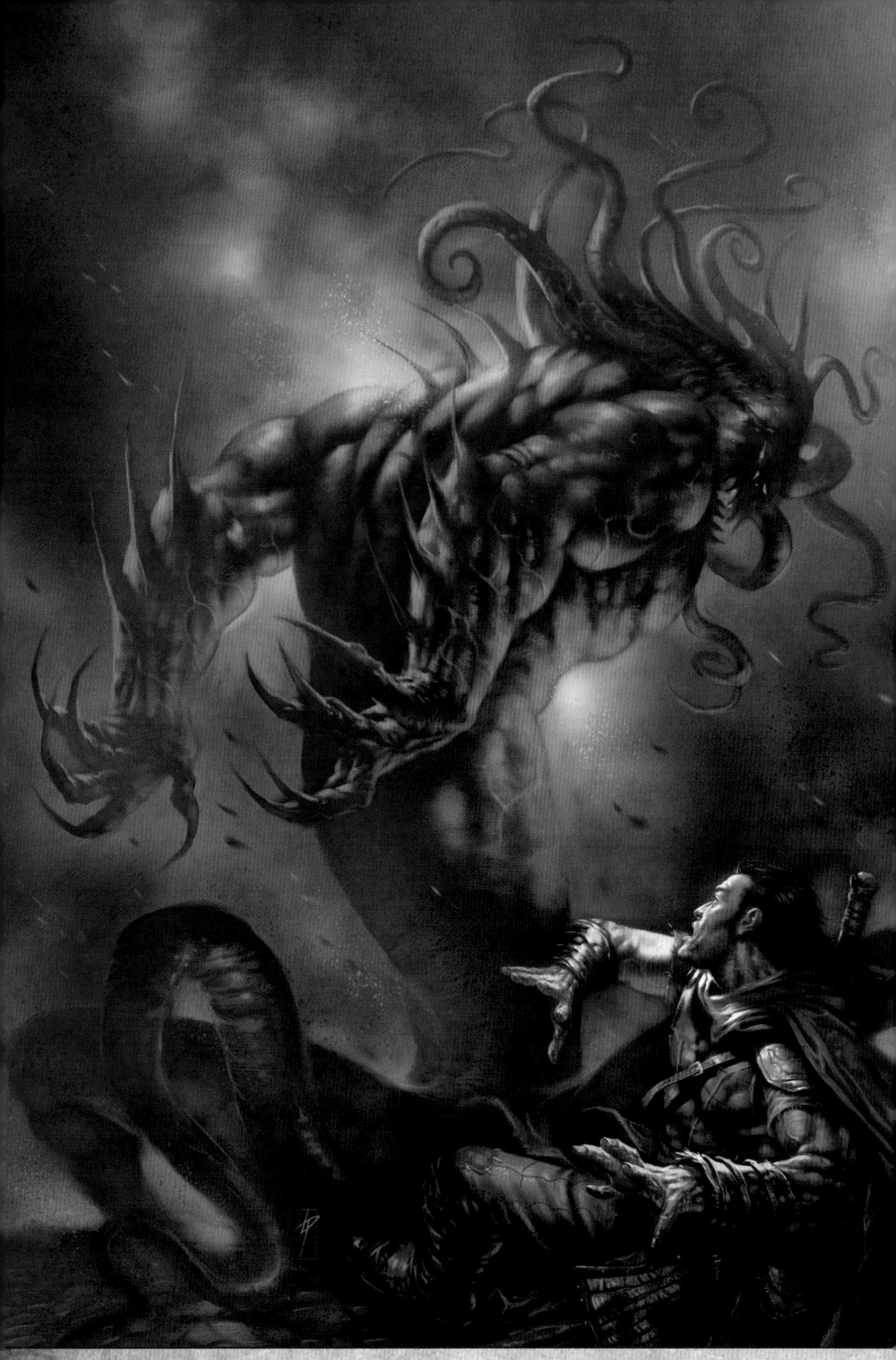

Issue #6 cover by LUCIO PARRILLO

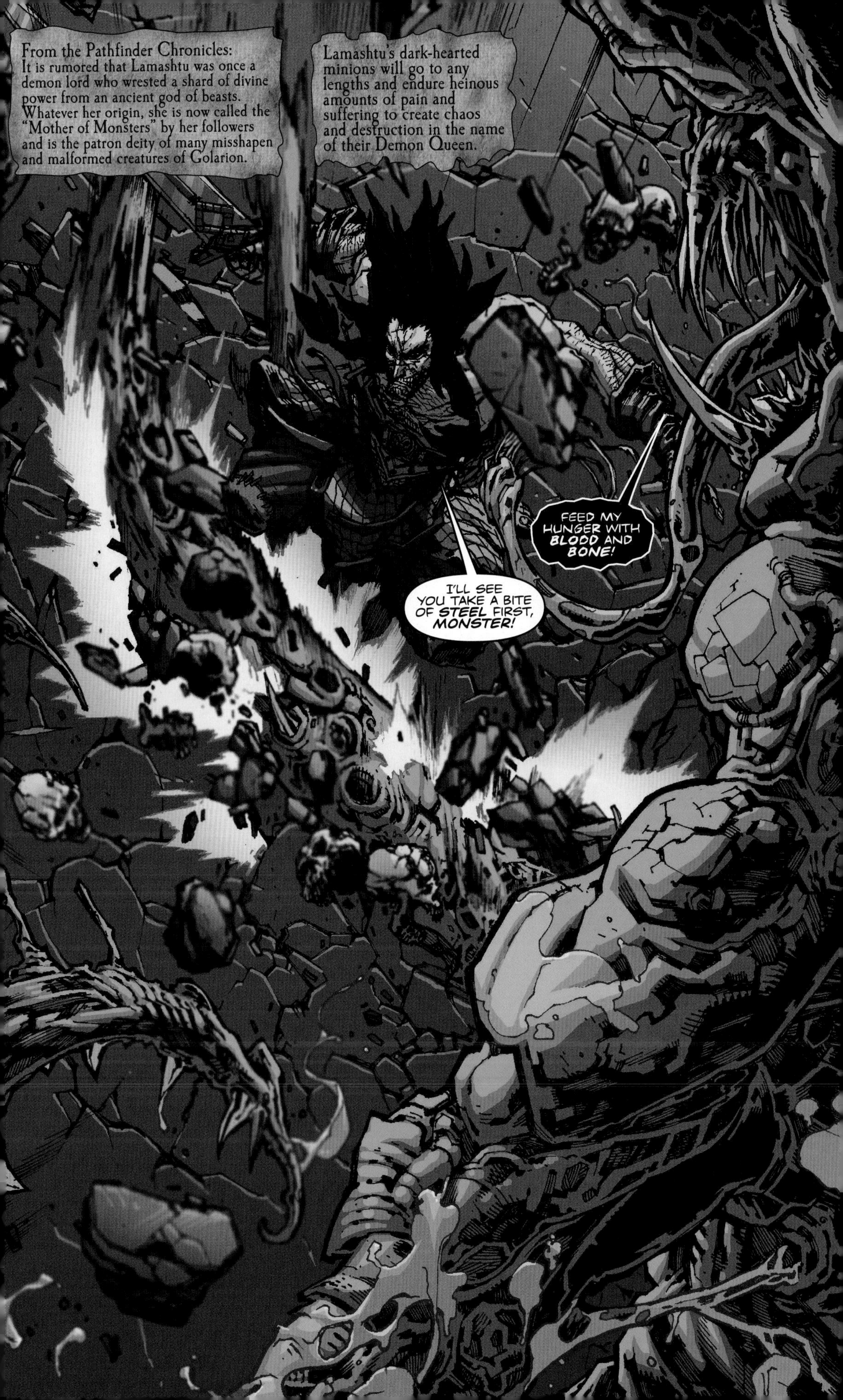
From the Pathfinder Chronicles:
It is rumored that Lamashtu was once a demon lord who wrested a shard of divine power from an ancient god of beasts. Whatever her origin, she is now called the "Mother of Monsters" by her followers and is the patron deity of many misshapen and malformed creatures of Golarion.
Lamashtu's dark-hearted minions will go to any lengths and endure heinous amounts of pain and suffering to create chaos and destruction in the name of their Demon Queen.
FEED MY HUNGER WITH BLOOD AND BONE!
I'LL SEE YOU TAKE A BITE OF STEEL FIRST, MONSTER!

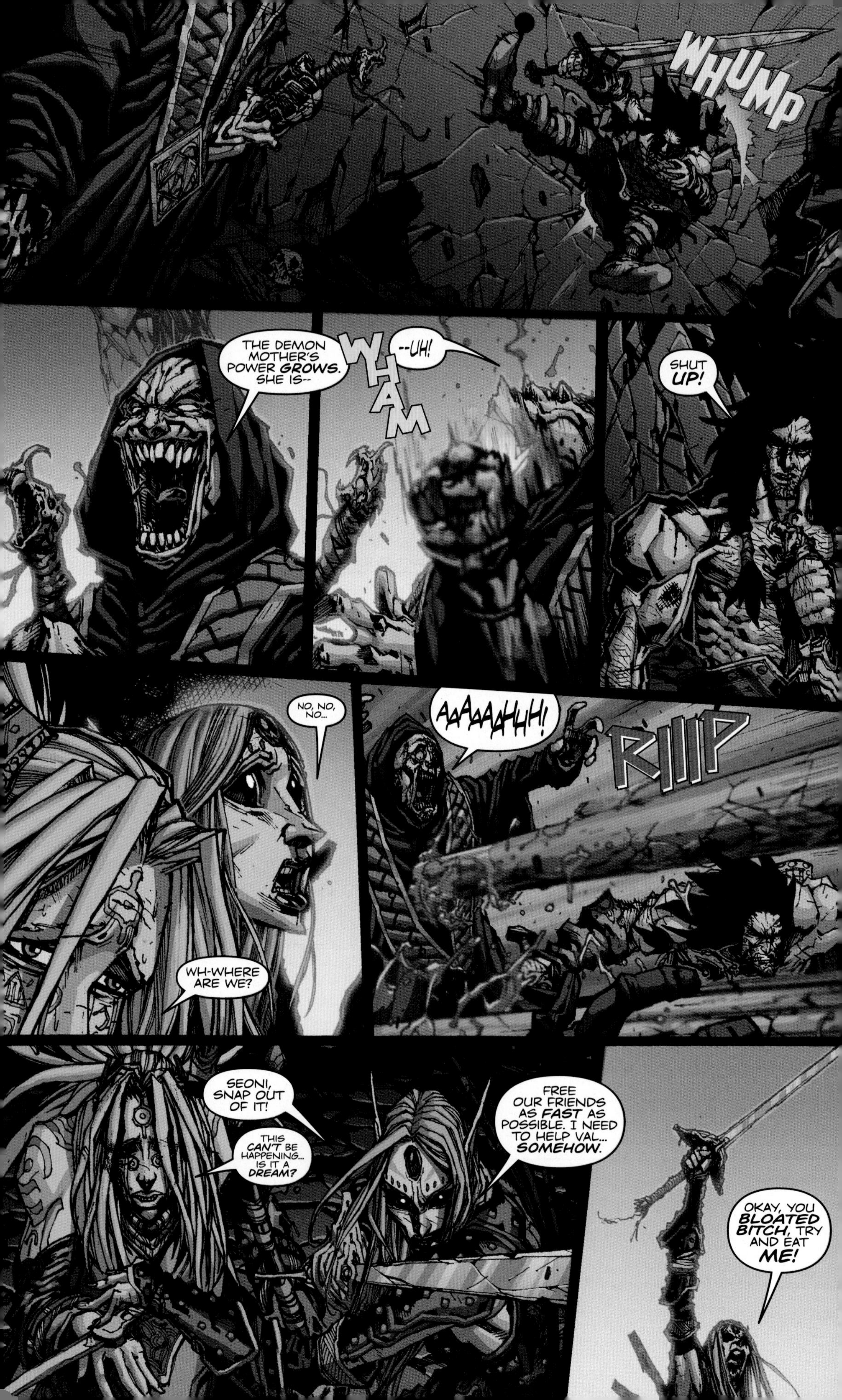
WHUMP
THE DEMON MOTHER'S POWER GROWS. SHE IS--
WHAM
--UH!
SHUT UP!
NO, NO, NO...
WH-WHERE ARE WE?
AAAAAAHHH!
RIIP
SEONI, SNAP OUT OF IT!
THIS CAN'T BE HAPPENING... IS IT A DREAM?
FREE OUR FRIENDS AS FAST AS POSSIBLE. I NEED TO HELP VAL... SOMEHOW.
OKAY, YOU BLOATED BITCH, TRY AND EAT ME!

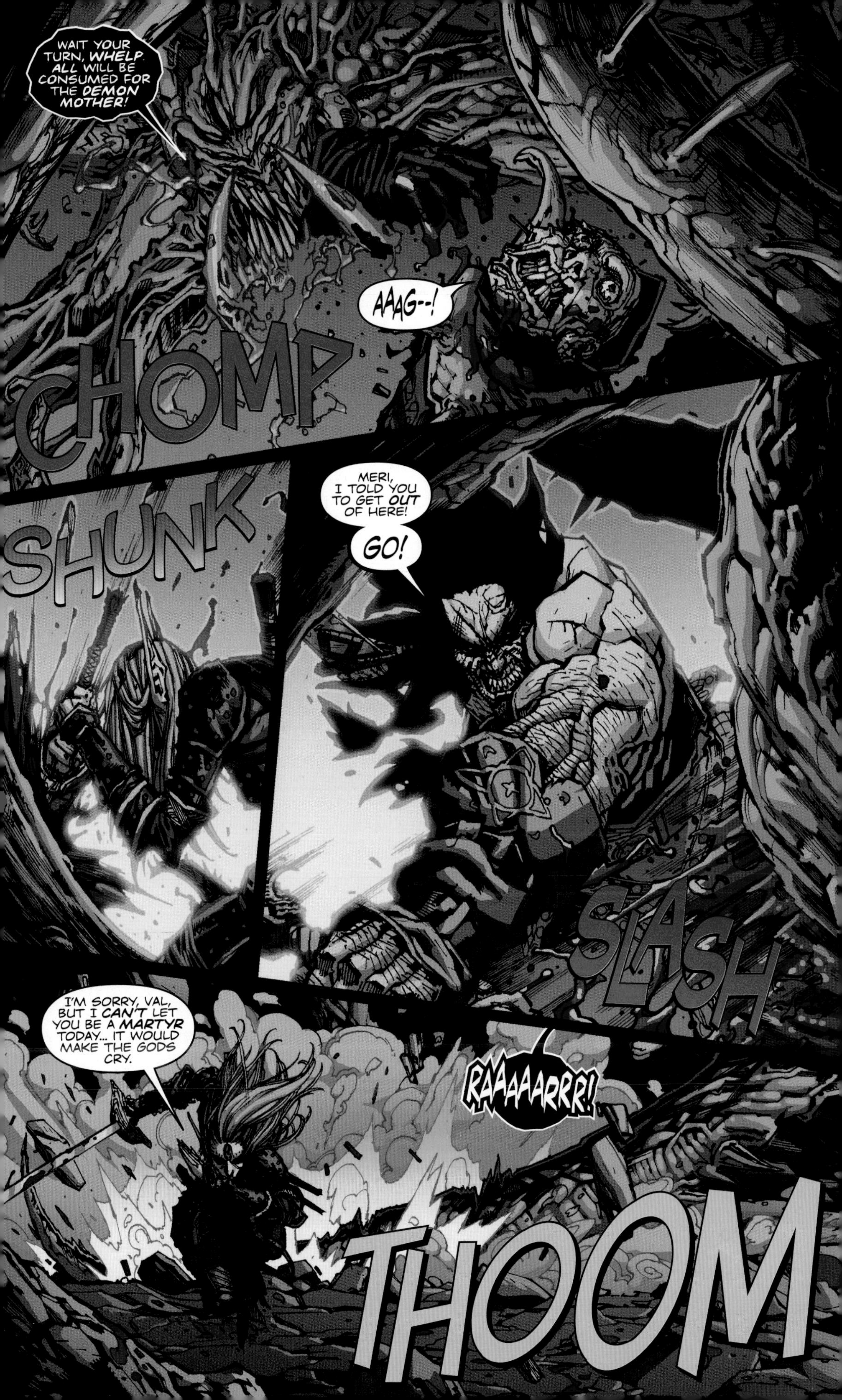
WAIT YOUR TURN, WHELP. ALL WILL BE CONSUMED FOR THE DEMON MOTHER!
AAAG--!
CHOMP
SHUNK
MERI, I TOLD YOU TO GET OUT OF HERE!
GO!
SLASH
I'M SORRY, VAL, BUT I CAN'T LET YOU BE A MARTYR TODAY... IT WOULD MAKE THE GODS CRY.
RAAAAARRR!
THOOM

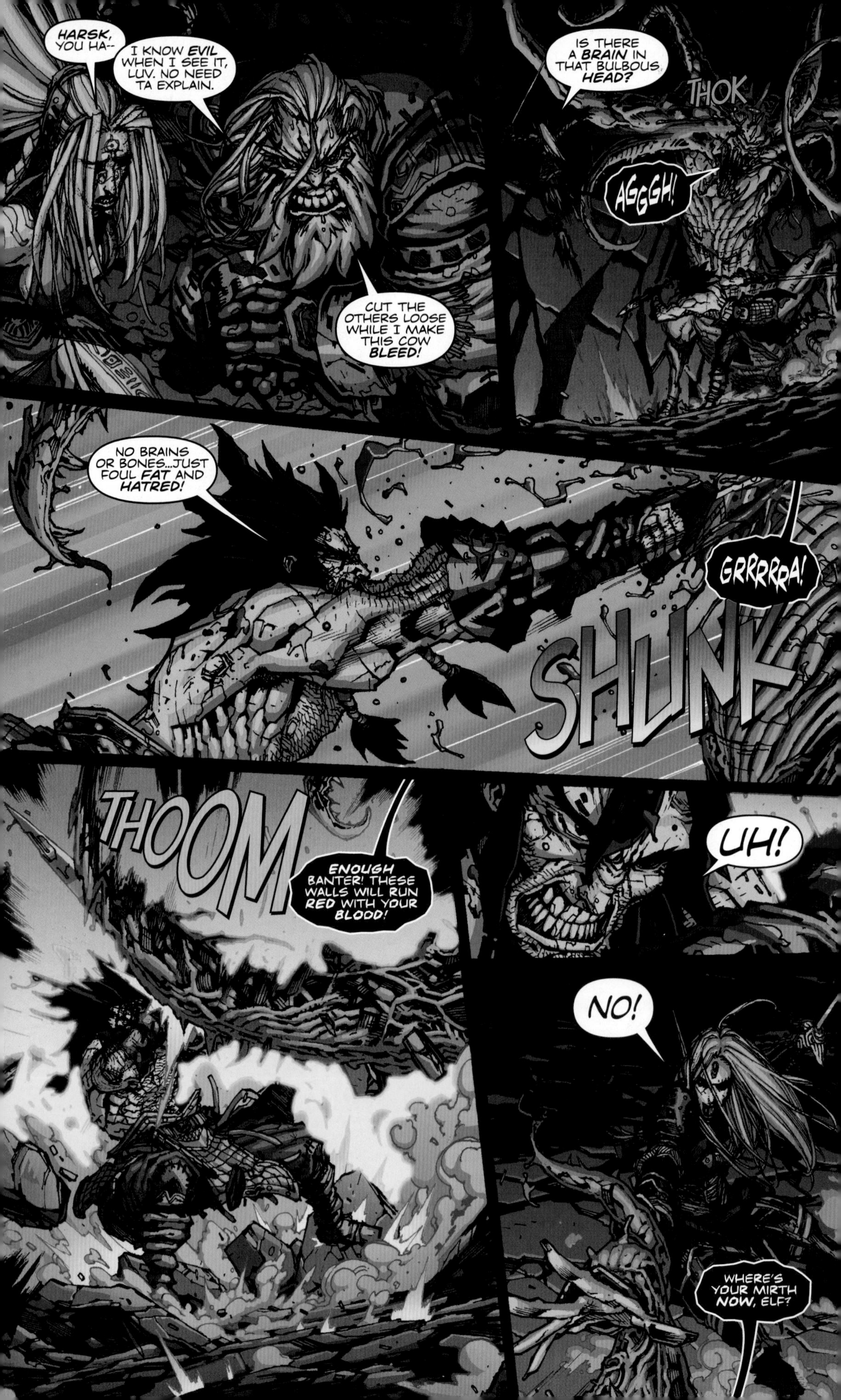
HARSK, YOU HA--
I KNOW EVIL WHEN I SEE IT, LUV. NO NEED TA EXPLAIN.
CUT THE OTHERS LOOSE WHILE I MAKE THIS COW BLEED!
IS THERE A BRAIN IN THAT BULBOUS HEAD?
THOK
AGGGH!
NO BRAINS OR BONES...JUST FOUL FAT AND HATRED!
GRRRRRA!
SHUNK
THOOM
ENOUGH BANTER! THESE WALLS WILL RUN RED WITH YOUR BLOOD!
UH!
NO!
WHERE'S YOUR MIRTH NOW, ELF?

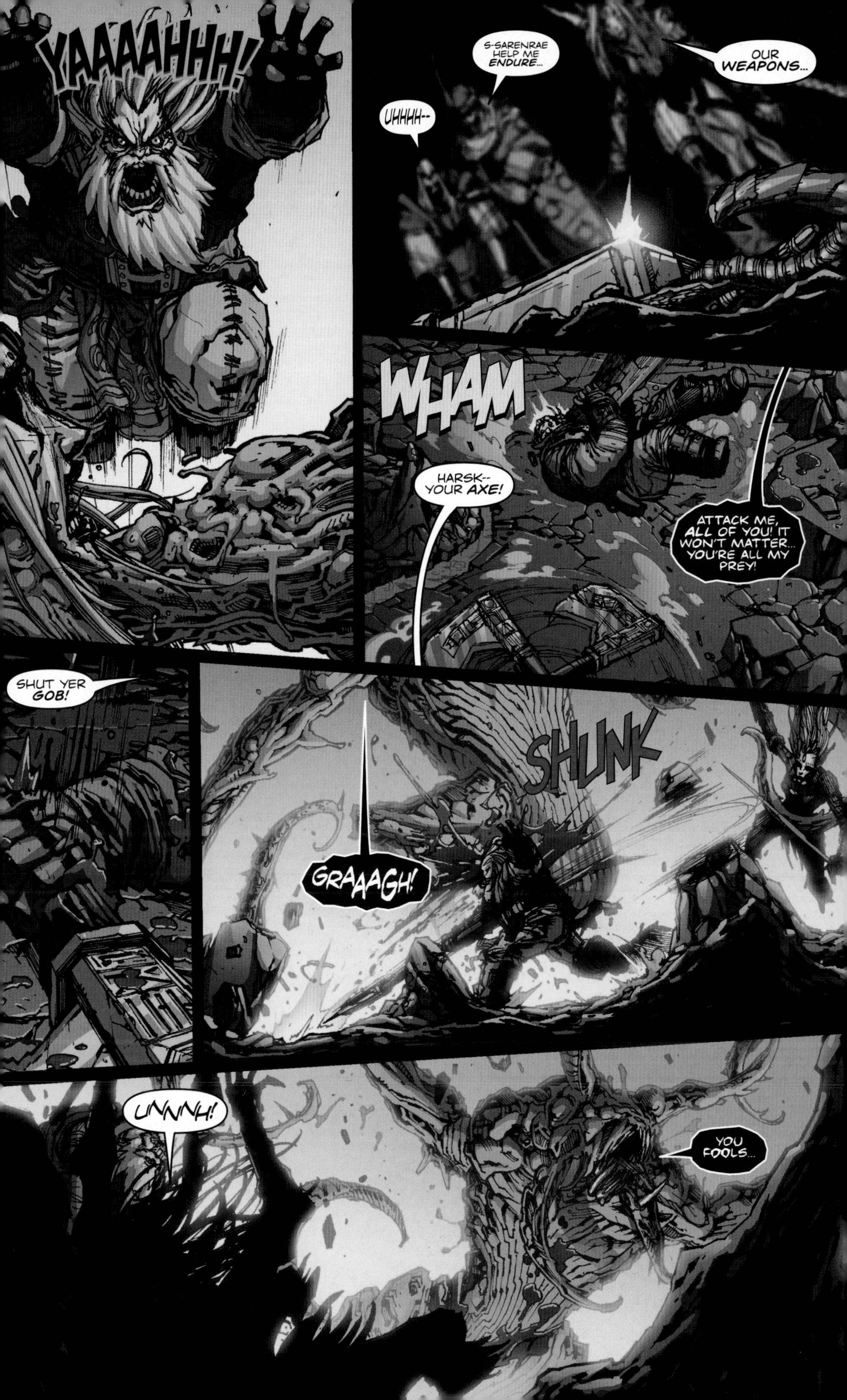

YAAAAHHH!
UHHHH--
S-SARENRAE HELP ME ENDURE...
OUR WEAPONS...
WHAM
HARSK-- YOUR AXE!
ATTACK ME, ALL OF YOU! IT WON'T MATTER... YOU'RE ALL MY PREY!
SHUT YER GOB!
SHUNK
GRAAAGH!
UNNNH!
YOU FOOLS...

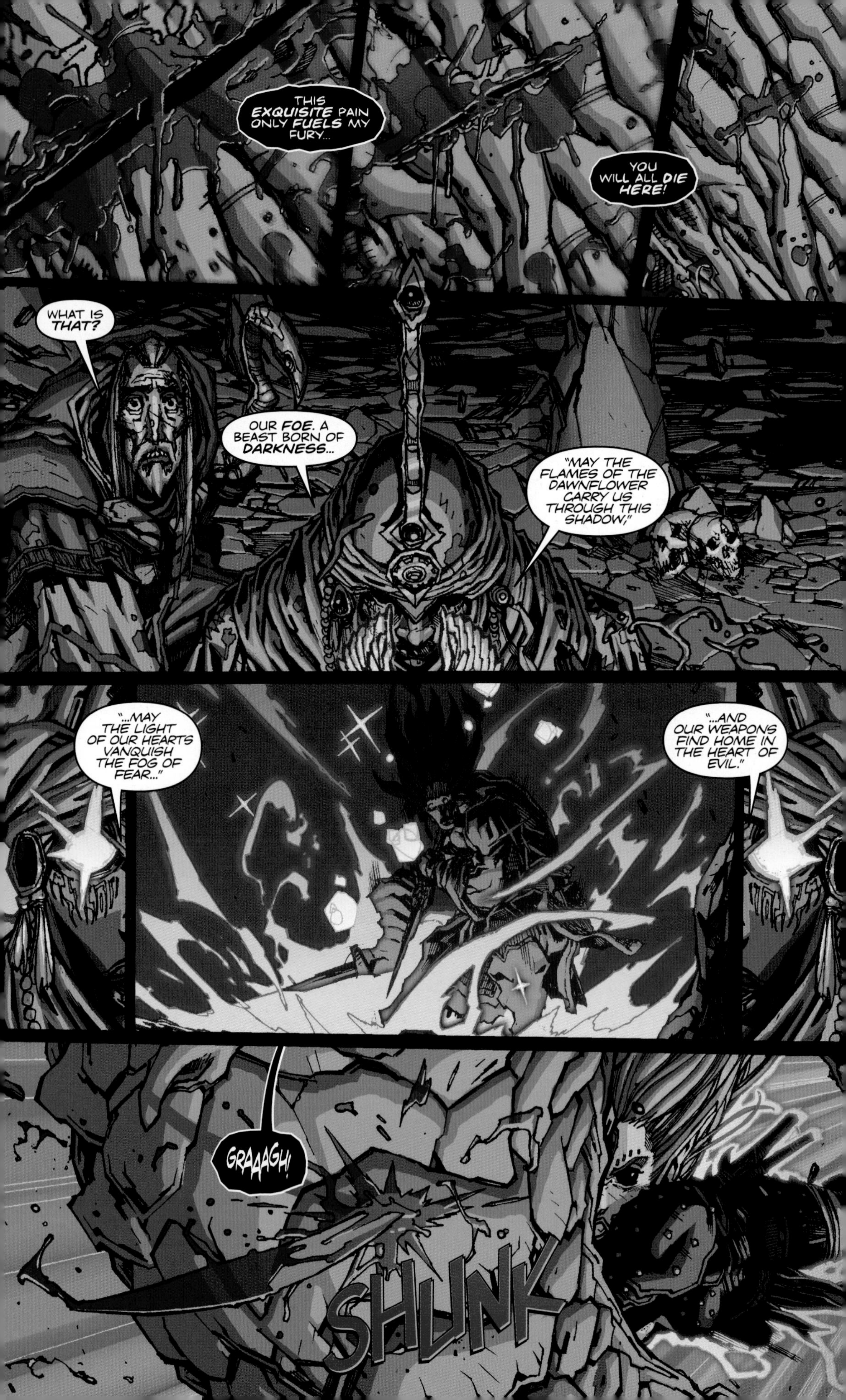
THIS EXQUISITE PAIN ONLY FUELS MY FURY...
YOU WILL ALL DIE HERE!
WHAT IS THAT?
OUR FOE. A BEAST BORN OF DARKNESS...
"MAY THE FLAMES OF THE DAWNFLOWER CARRY US THROUGH THIS SHADOW,"
"...MAY THE LIGHT OF OUR HEARTS VANQUISH THE FOG OF FEAR..."
"...AND OUR WEAPONS FIND HOME IN THE HEART OF EVIL."
GRAAAGH!
SHUNK

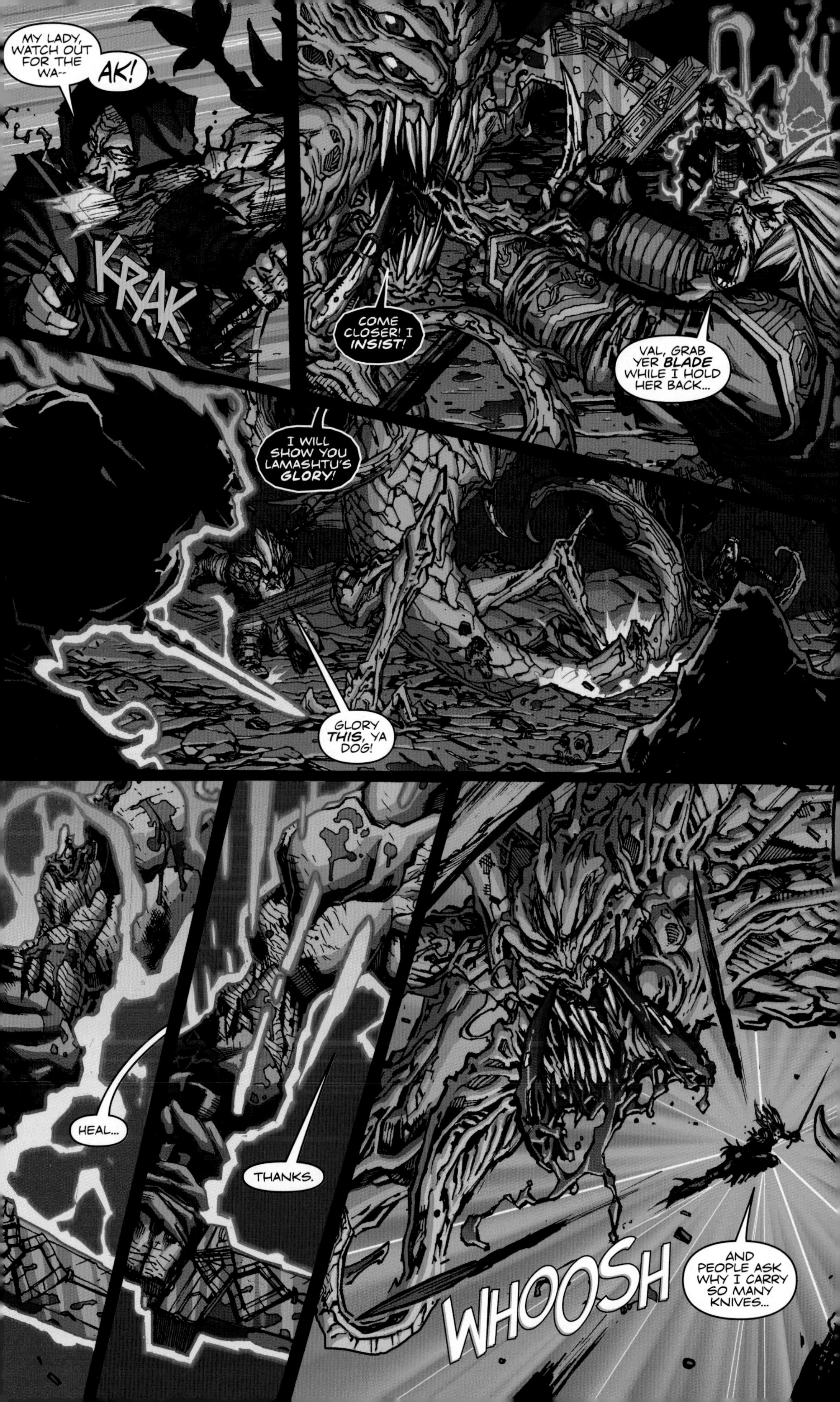
MY LADY, WATCH OUT FOR THE WA--
AK!
KRAK
COME CLOSER! I INSIST!
VAL, GRAB YER BLADE WHILE I HOLD HER BACK...
I WILL SHOW YOU LAMASHTU'S GLORY!
GLORY THIS, YA DOG!
HEAL...
THANKS.
WHOOSH
AND PEOPLE ASK WHY I CARRY SO MANY KNIVES...

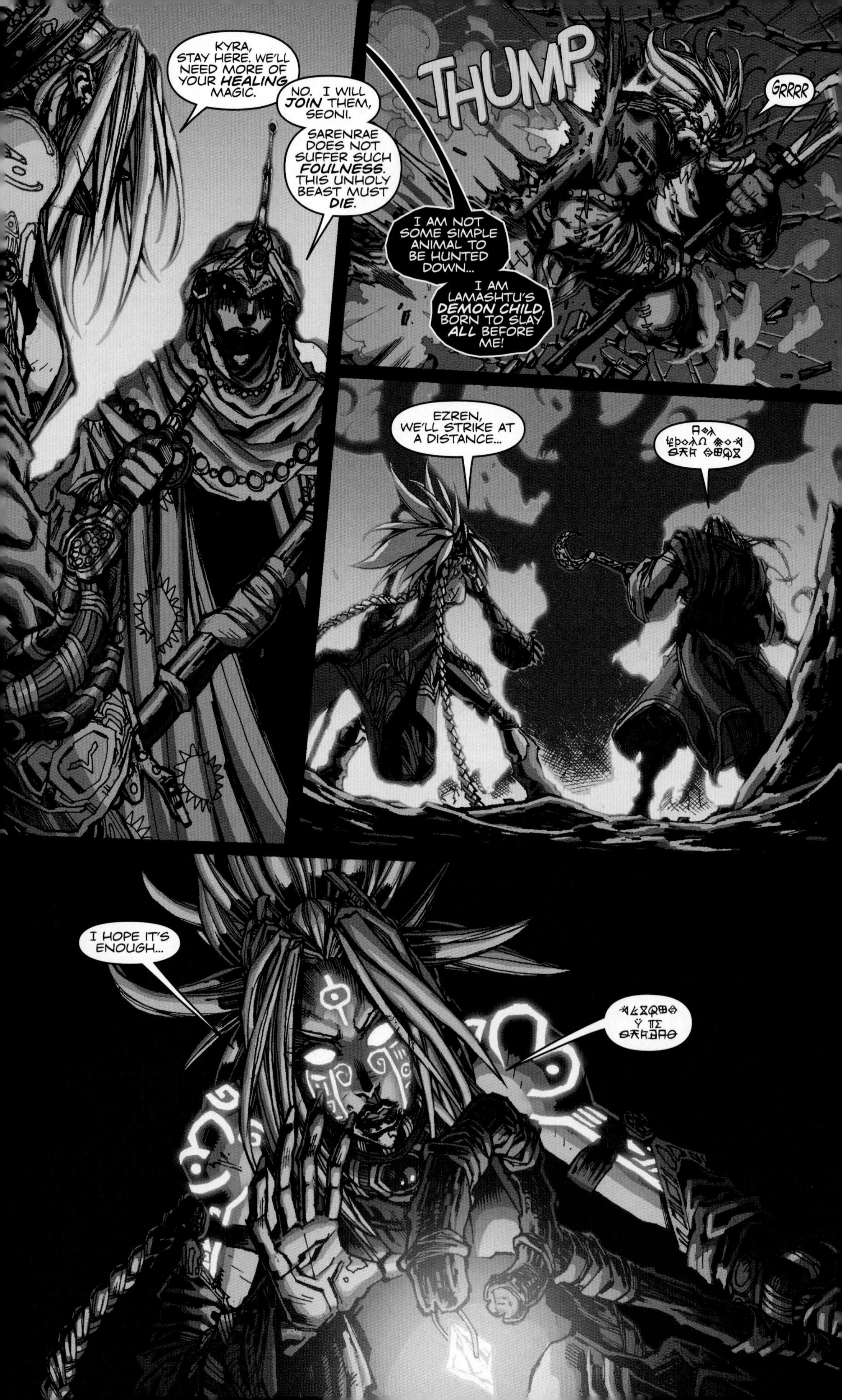

KYRA, STAY HERE. WE'LL NEED MORE OF YOUR HEALING MAGIC.
NO. I WILL JOIN THEM, SEONI.
SARENRAE DOES NOT SUFFER SUCH FOULNESS. THIS UNHOLY BEAST MUST DIE.
THUMP
GRRRR
I AM NOT SOME SIMPLE ANIMAL TO BE HUNTED DOWN...
I AM LAMASHTU'S DEMON CHILD, BORN TO SLAY ALL BEFORE ME!
EZREN, WE'LL STRIKE AT A DISTANCE...
I HOPE IT'S ENOUGH...

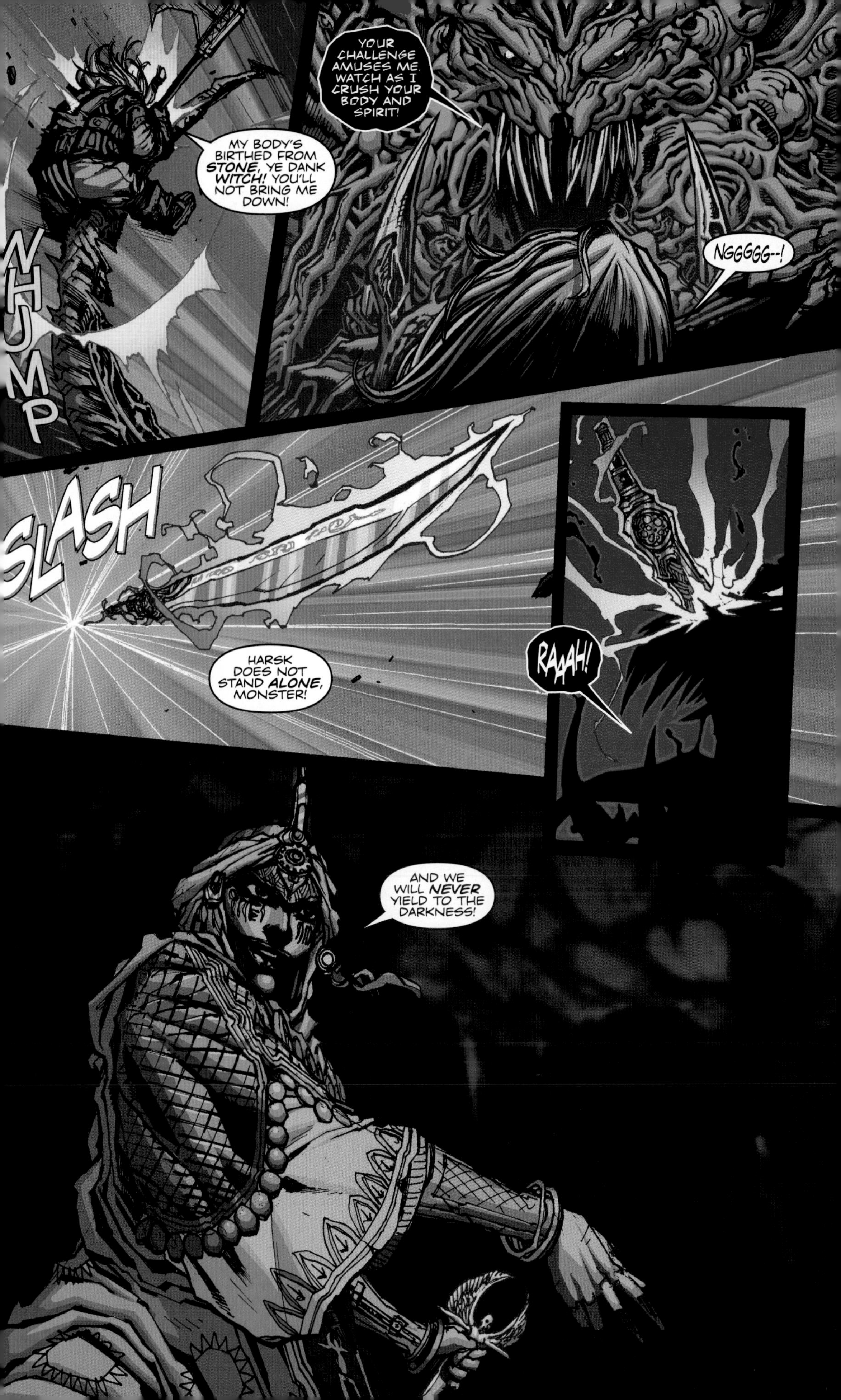
MY BODY'S BIRTHED FROM STONE, YE DANK WITCH! YOU'LL NOT BRING ME DOWN!
WHUMP
YOUR CHALLENGE AMUSES ME. WATCH AS I CRUSH YOUR BODY AND SPIRIT!
NGGGGG--!
SLASH
HARSK DOES NOT STAND ALONE, MONSTER!
RAAAH!
AND WE WILL NEVER YIELD TO THE DARKNESS!

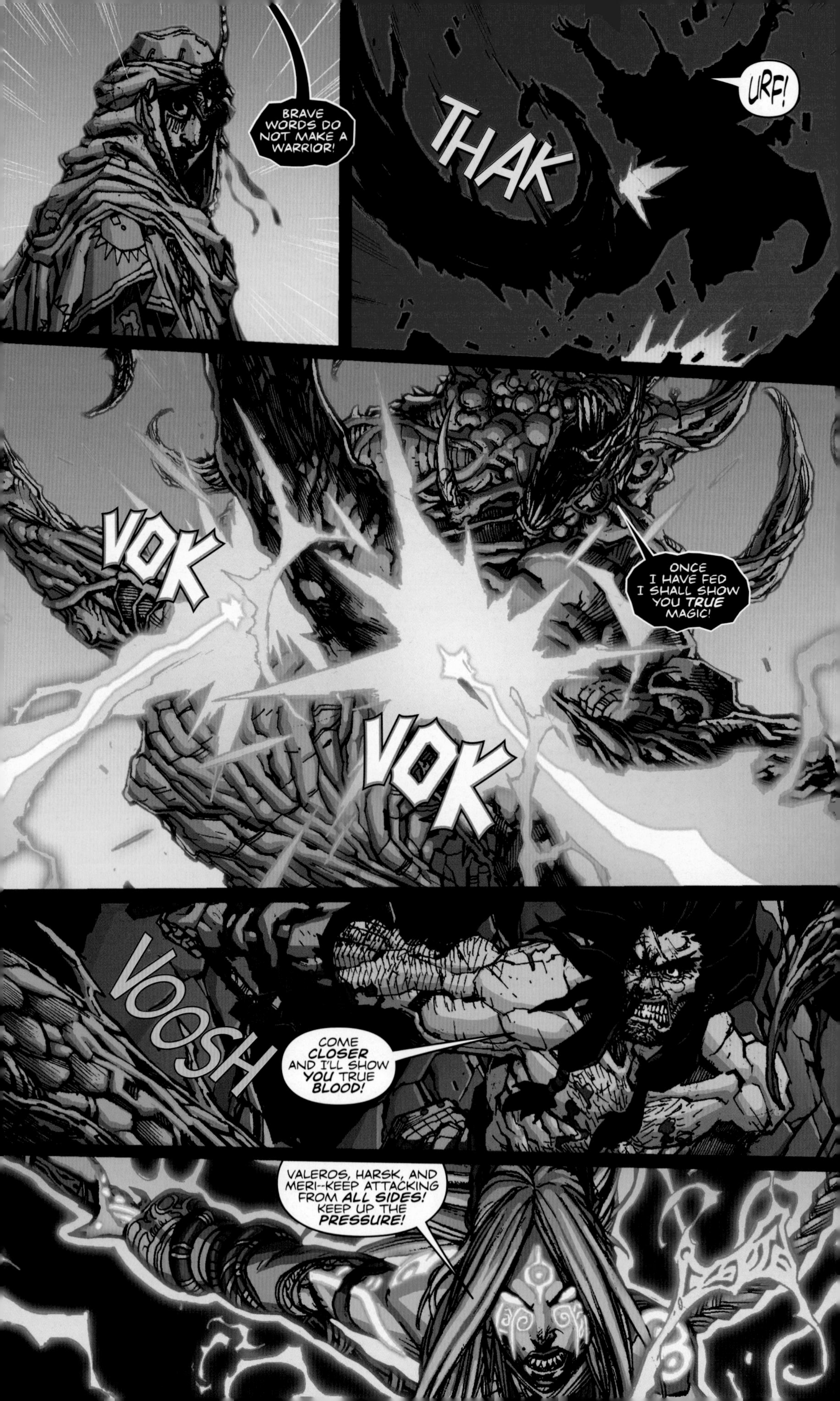
BRAVE WORDS DO NOT MAKE A WARRIOR!
THAK
URF!
VOK
ONCE I HAVE FED I SHALL SHOW YOU TRUE MAGIC!
VOK
VOOSH
COME CLOSER AND I'LL SHOW YOU TRUE BLOOD!
VALEROS, HARSK, AND MERI--KEEP ATTACKING FROM ALL SIDES! KEEP UP THE PRESSURE!

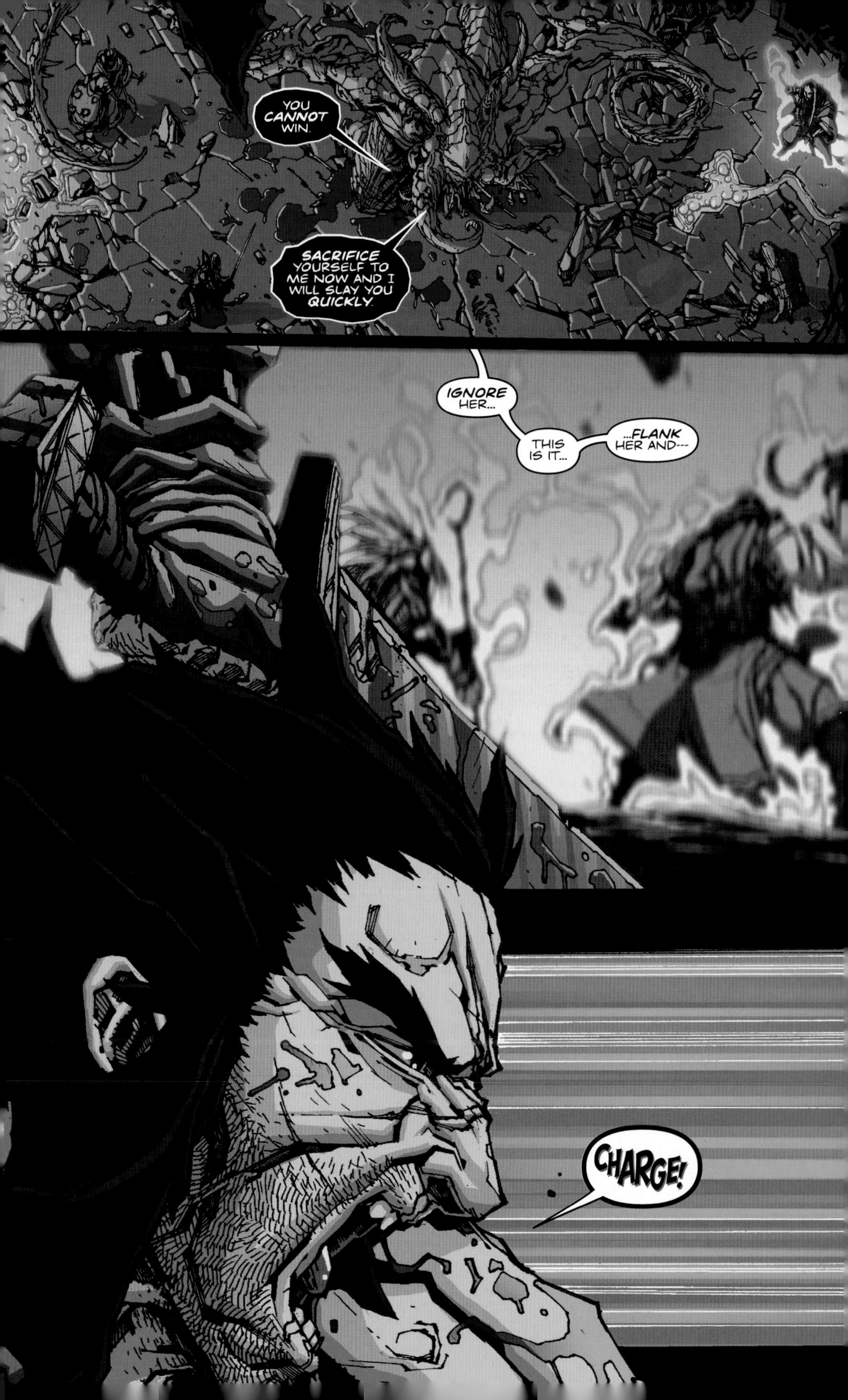
YOU CANNOT WIN.
SACRIFICE YOURSELF TO ME NOW AND I WILL SLAY YOU QUICKLY.
IGNORE HER...
THIS IS IT...
...FLANK HER AND---
CHARGE!

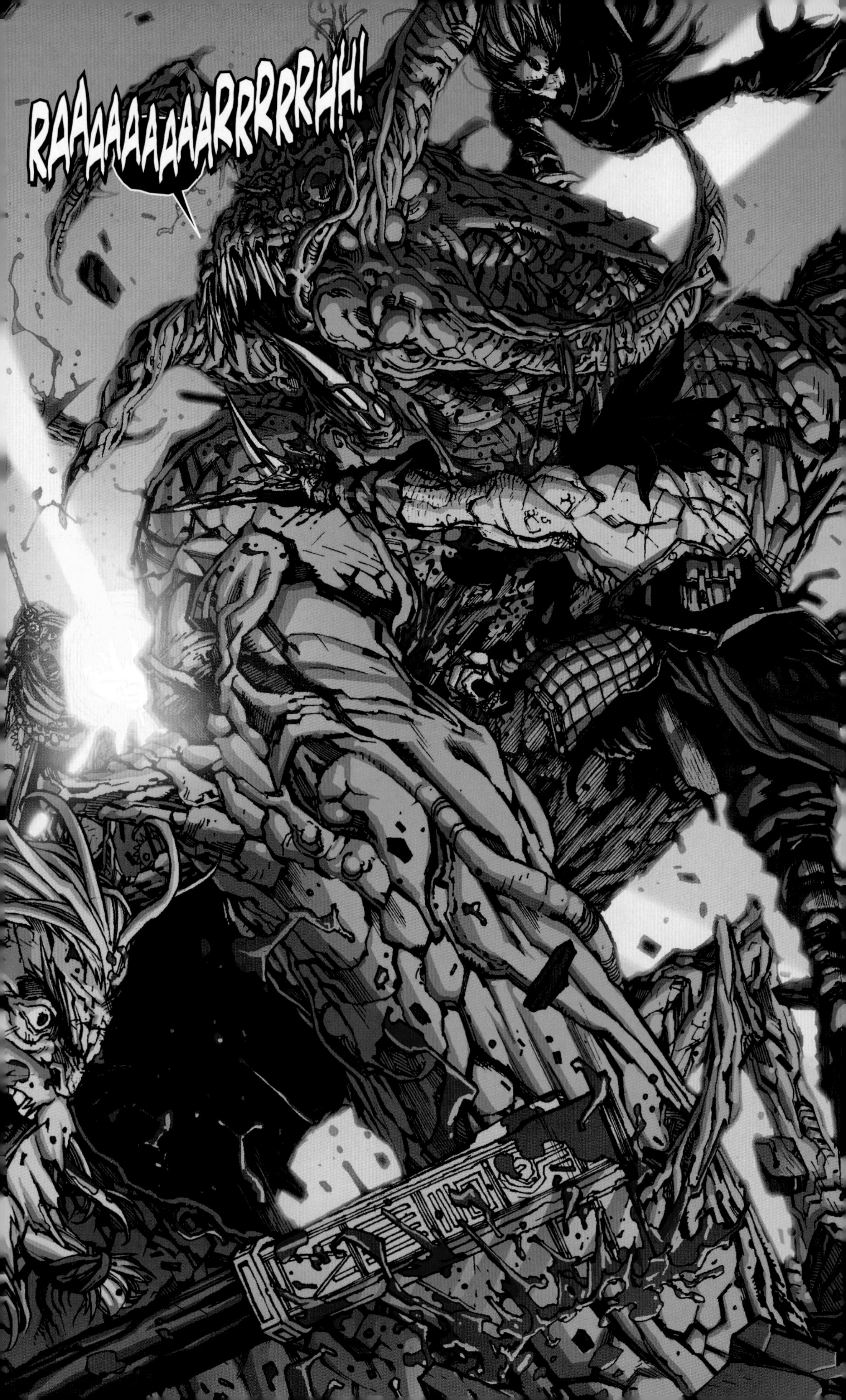
RAAAAAAAARRRRRH!

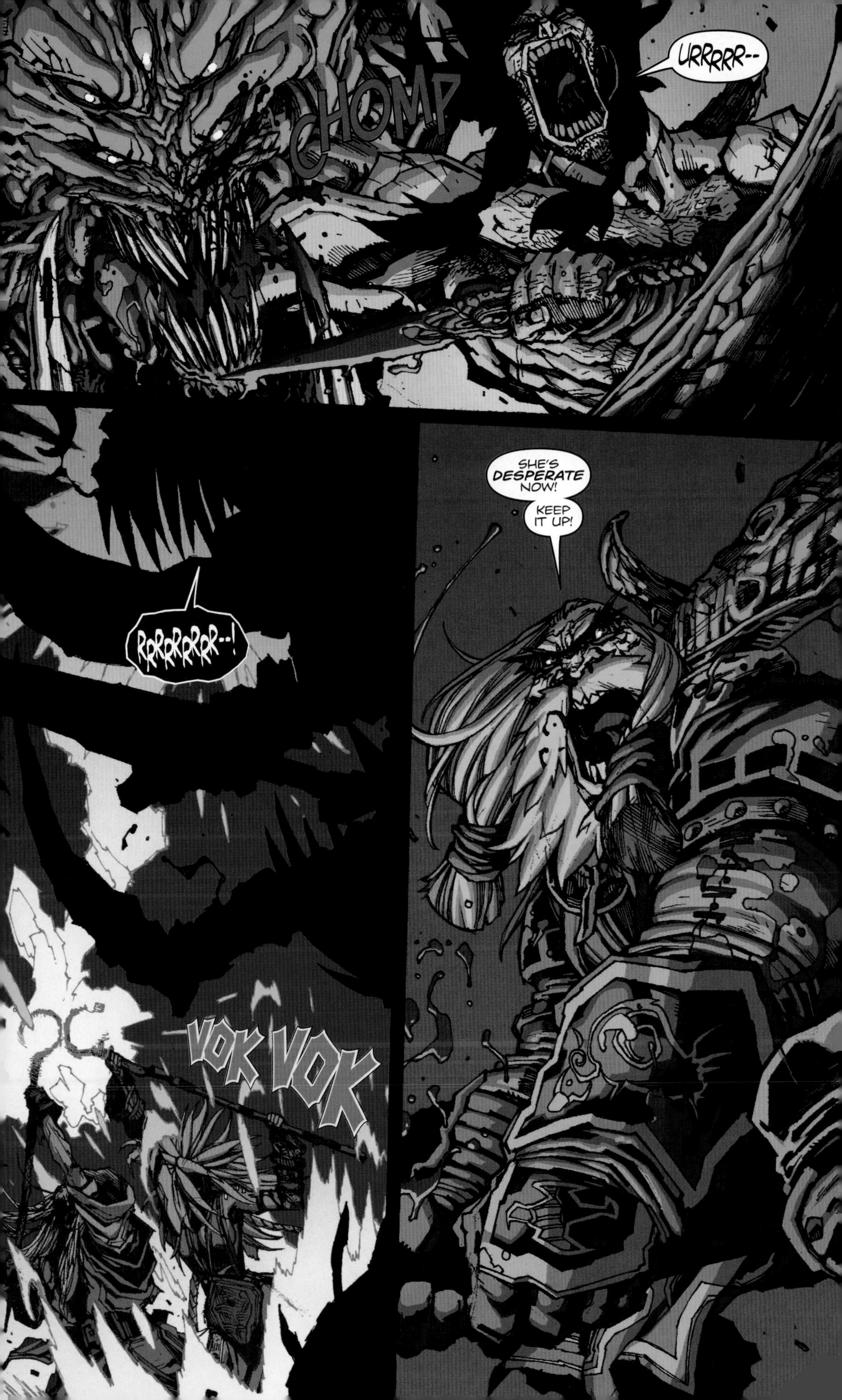
CHOMP
URRRRR--
RRRRRRRR--!
SHE'S DESPERATE NOW!
KEEP IT UP!
VOK VOK

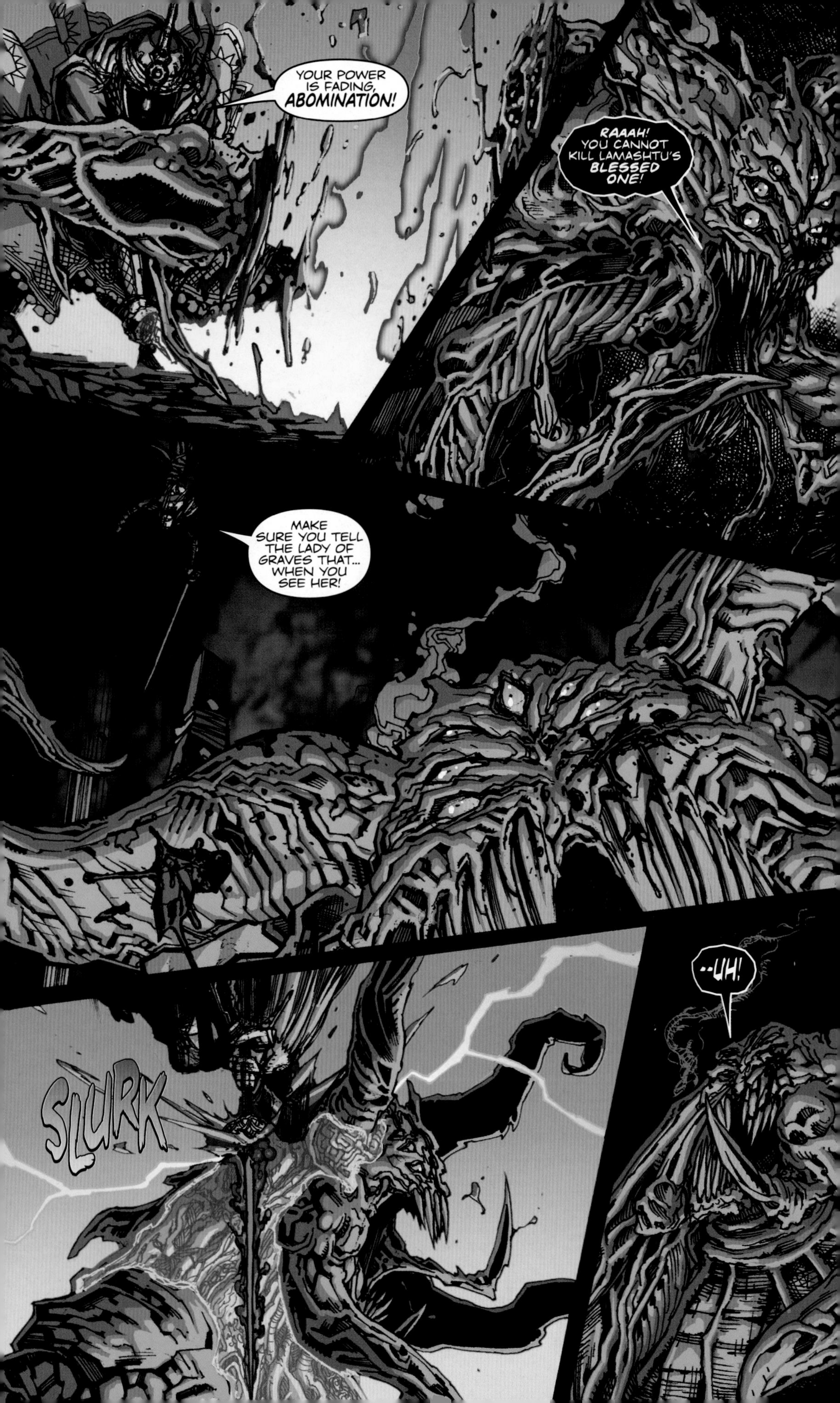
YOUR POWER IS FADING, ABOMINATION!
RAAAH! YOU CANNOT KILL LAMASHTU'S BLESSED ONE!
MAKE SURE YOU TELL THE LADY OF GRAVES THAT... WHEN YOU SEE HER!
SLURK
--UH!

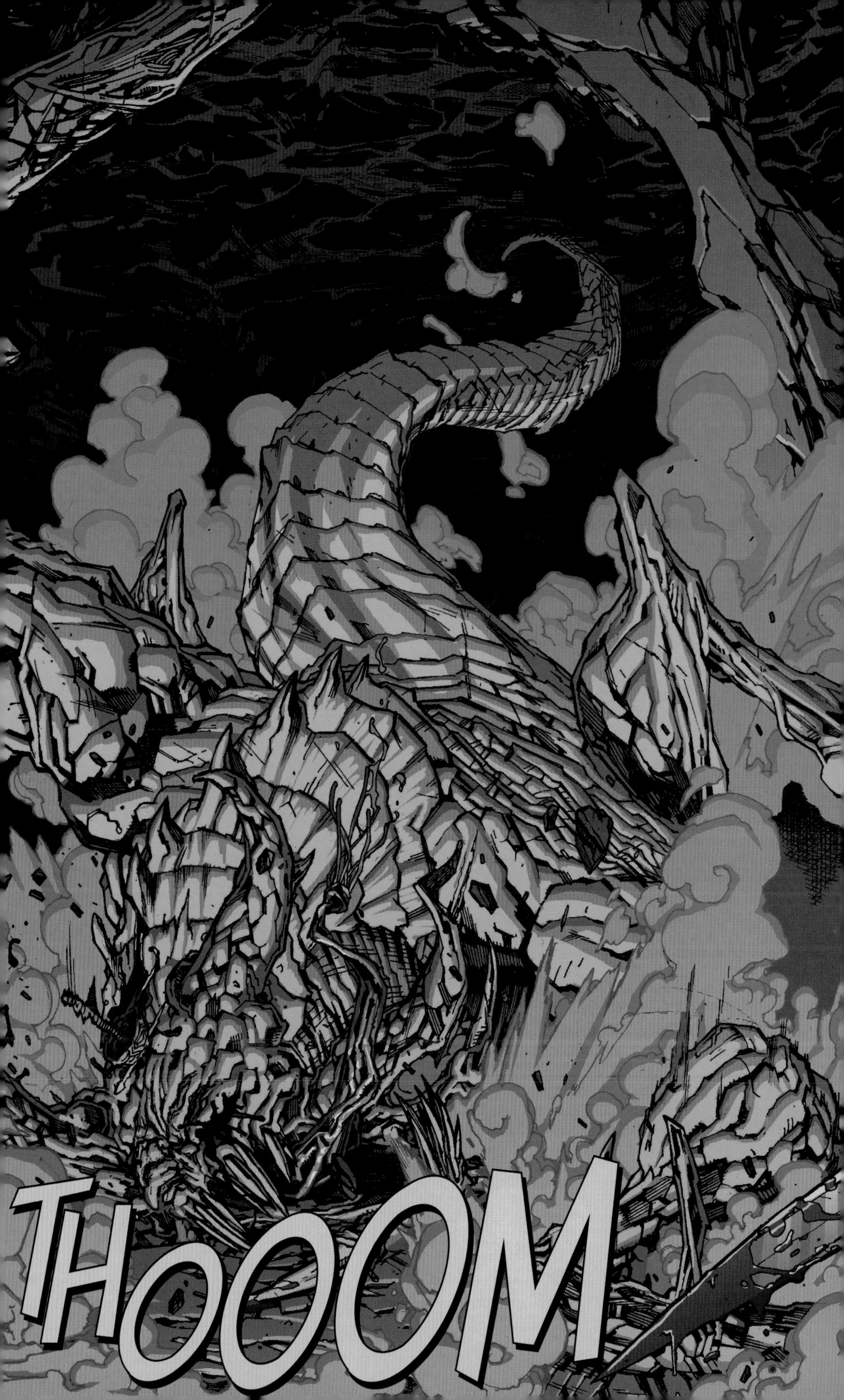
THOOOM

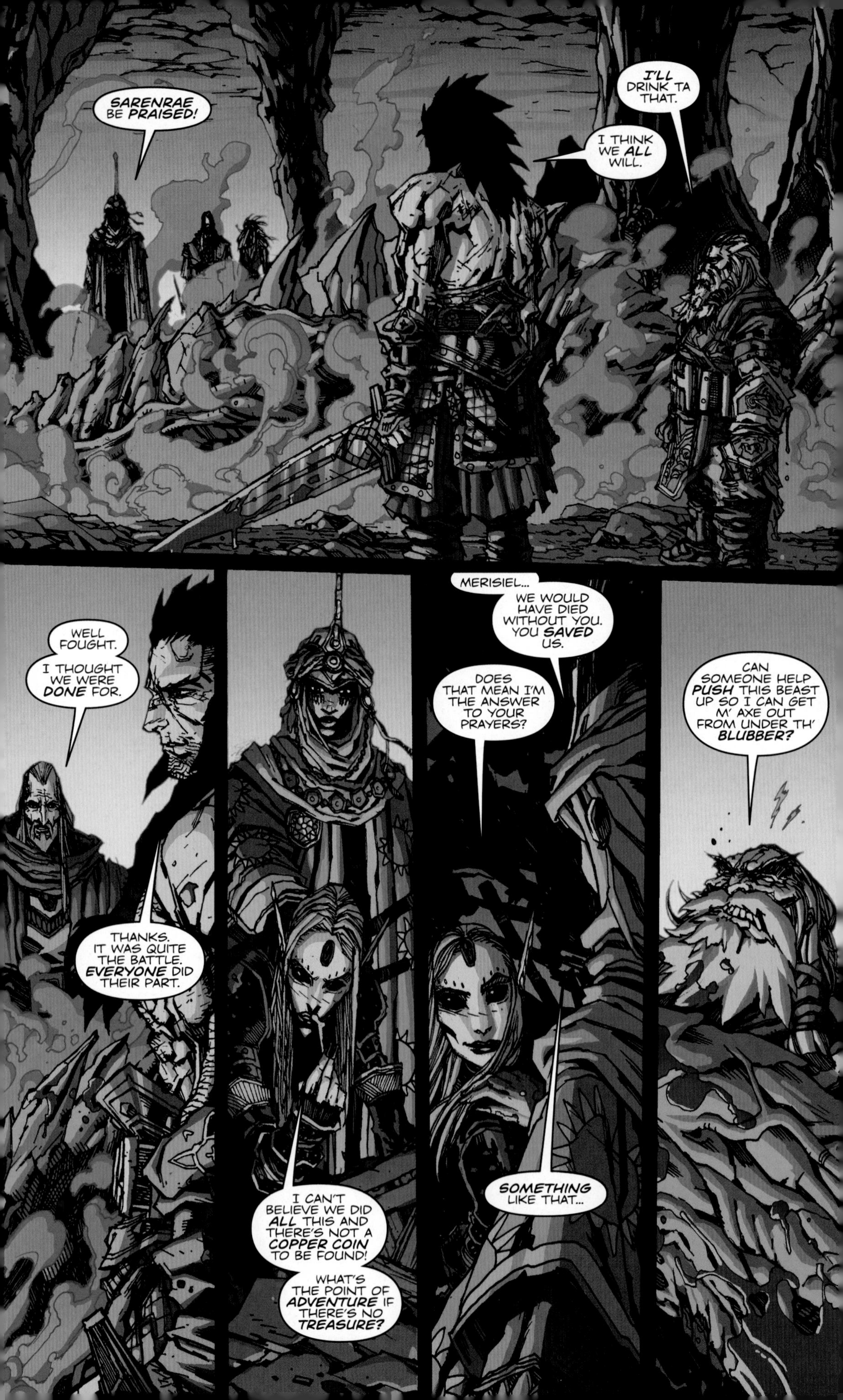
SARENRAE BE PRAISED!
I'LL DRINK TA THAT.
I THINK WE ALL WILL.
WELL FOUGHT.
I THOUGHT WE WERE DONE FOR.
THANKS. IT WAS QUITE THE BATTLE. EVERYONE DID THEIR PART.
I CAN'T BELIEVE WE DID ALL THIS AND THERE'S NOT A COPPER COIN TO BE FOUND!
WHAT'S THE POINT OF ADVENTURE IF THERE'S NO TREASURE?
MERISIEL...
WE WOULD HAVE DIED WITHOUT YOU. YOU SAVED US.
DOES THAT MEAN I'M THE ANSWER TO YOUR PRAYERS?
SOMETHING LIKE THAT...
CAN SOMEONE HELP PUSH THIS BEAST UP SO I CAN GET M' AXE OUT FROM UNDER TH' BLUBBER?

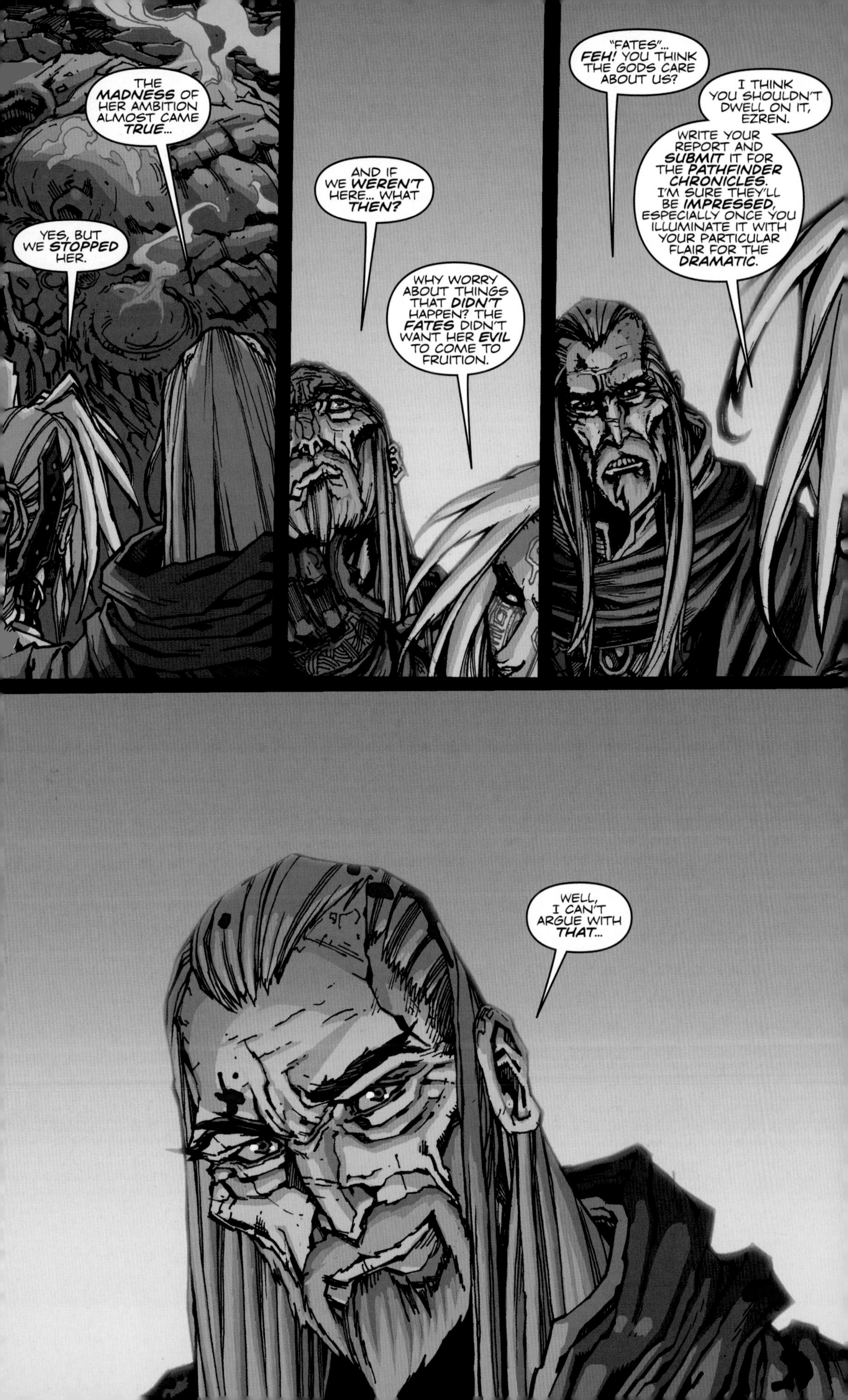
THE MADNESS OF HER AMBITION ALMOST CAME TRUE...
YES, BUT WE STOPPED HER.
AND IF WE WEREN'T HERE... WHAT THEN?
WHY WORRY ABOUT THINGS THAT DIDN'T HAPPEN? THE FATES DIDN'T WANT HER EVIL TO COME TO FRUITION.
"FATES"... FEH! YOU THINK THE GODS CARE ABOUT US?
I THINK YOU SHOULDN'T DWELL ON IT, EZREN.
WRITE YOUR REPORT AND SUBMIT IT FOR THE PATHFINDER CHRONICLES. I'M SURE THEY'LL BE IMPRESSED, ESPECIALLY ONCE YOU ILLUMINATE IT WITH YOUR PARTICULAR FLAIR FOR THE DRAMATIC.
WELL, I CAN'T ARGUE WITH THAT...

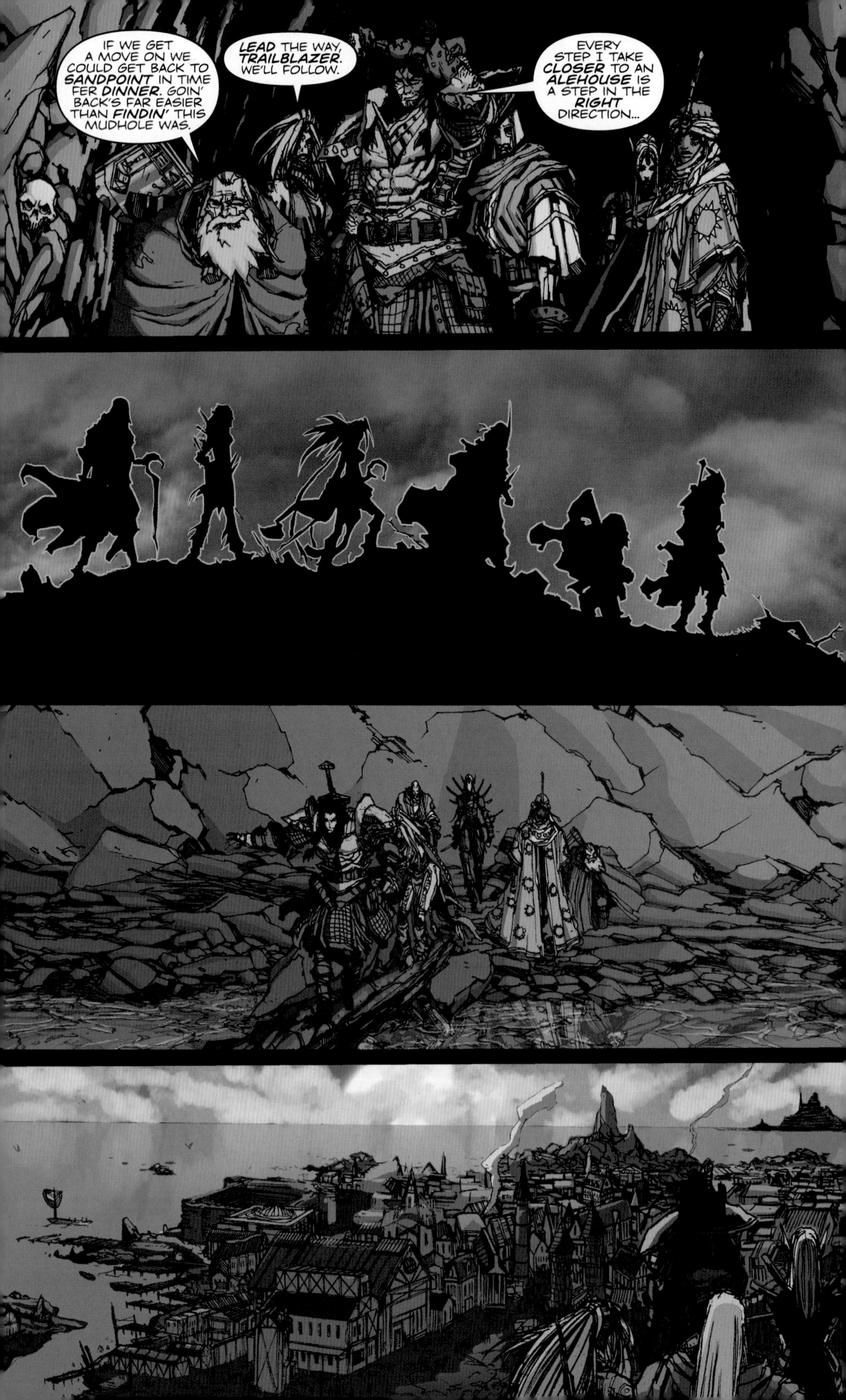
IF WE GET A MOVE ON WE COULD GET BACK TO SANDPOINT IN TIME FER DINNER. GOIN' BACK'S FAR EASIER THAN FINDIN' THIS MUDHOLE WAS.
LEAD THE WAY, TRAILBLAZER. WE'LL FOLLOW.
EVERY STEP I TAKE CLOSER TO AN ALEHOUSE IS A STEP IN THE RIGHT DIRECTION...

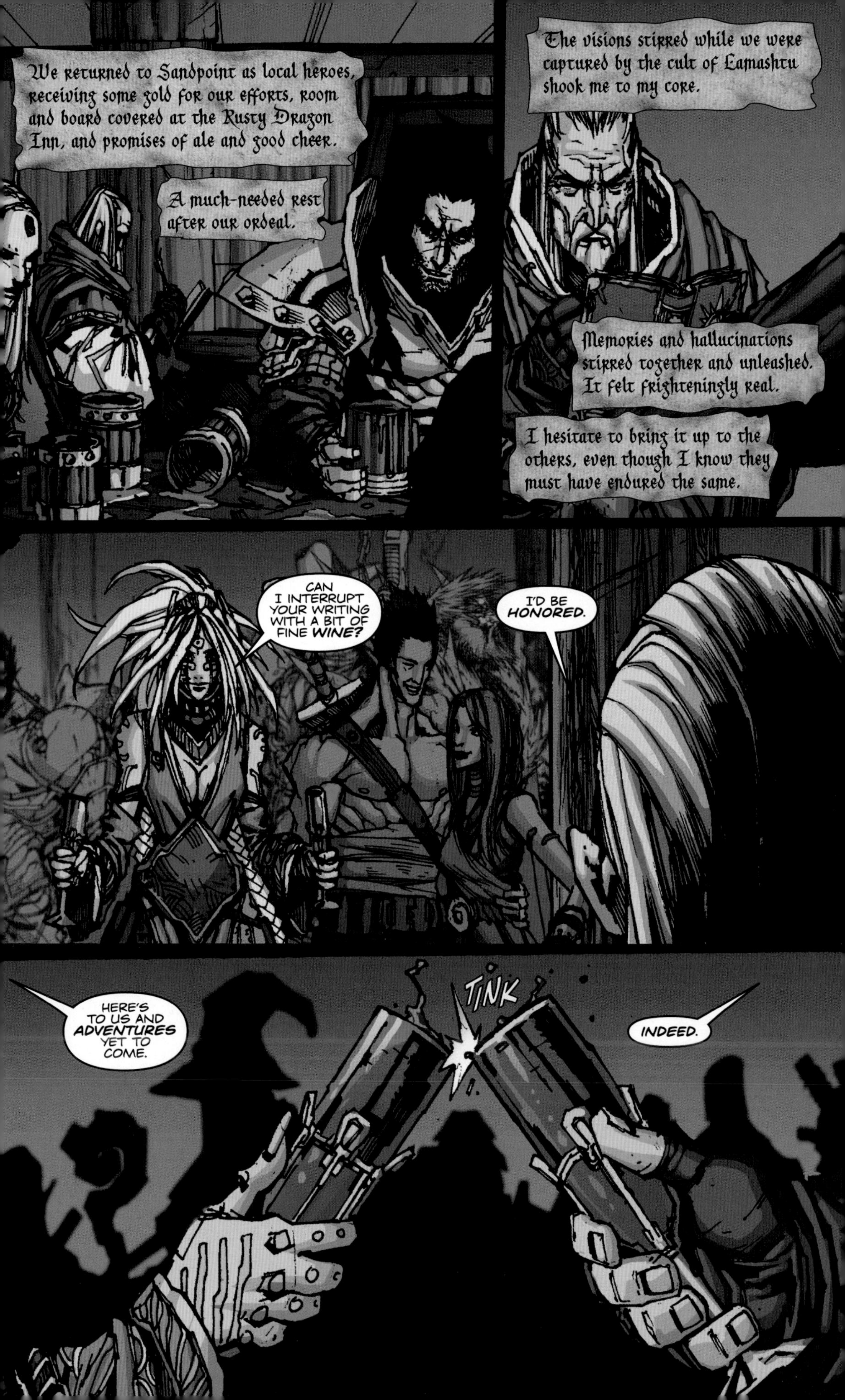
We returned to Sandpoint as local heroes, receiving some gold for our efforts, room and board covered at the Rusty Dragon Inn, and promises of ale and good cheer.
A much-needed rest after our ordeal.
The visions stirred while we were captured by the cult of Lamashtu shook me to my core.
Memories and hallucinations stirred together and unleashed. It felt frighteningly real.
I hesitate to bring it up to the others, even though I know they must have endured the same.
CAN I INTERRUPT YOUR WRITING WITH A BIT OF FINE WINE?
I'D BE HONORED.
HERE'S TO US AND ADVENTURES YET TO COME.
TINK
INDEED.

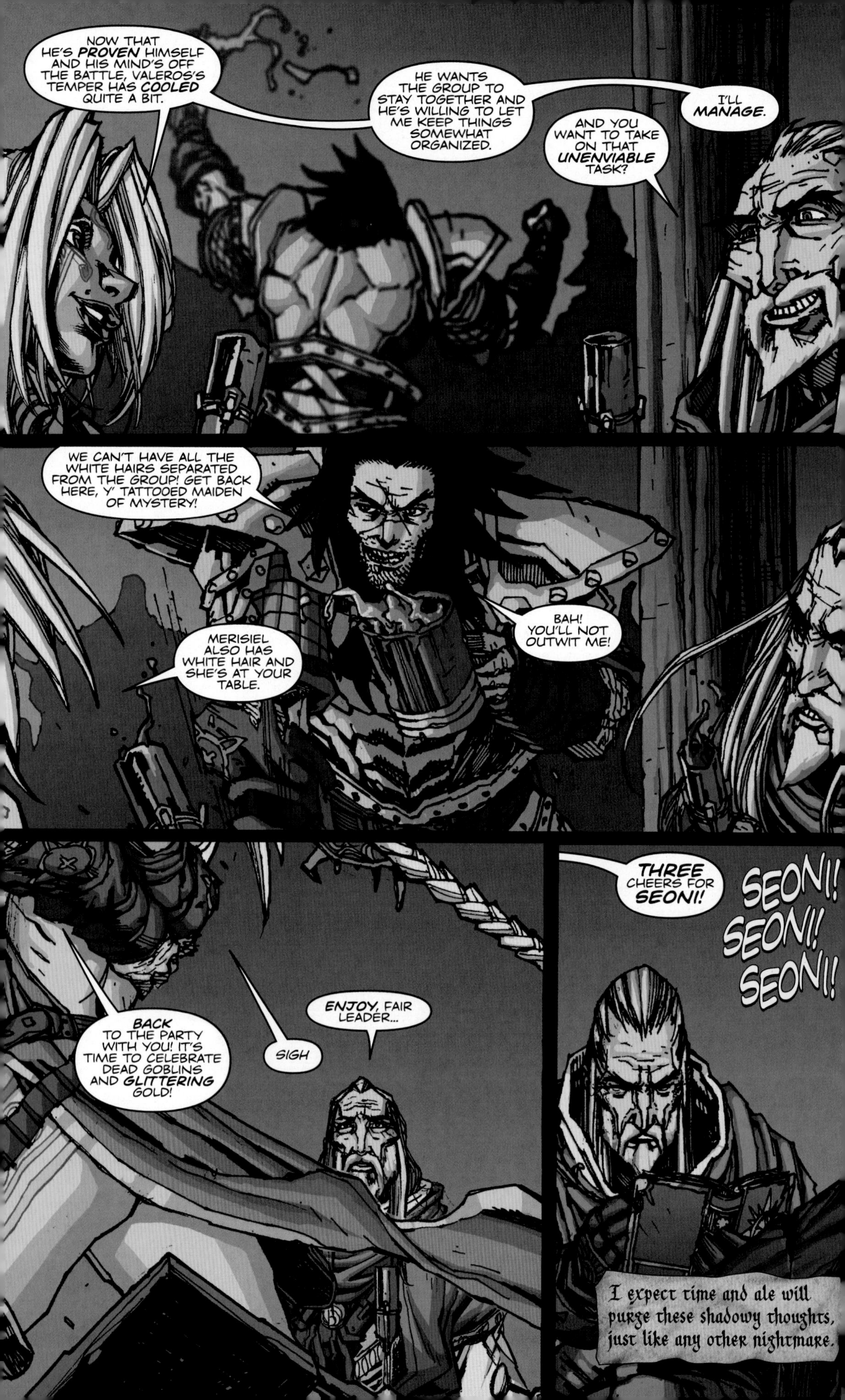

NOW THAT HE'S PROVEN HIMSELF AND HIS MIND'S OFF THE BATTLE, VALEROS'S TEMPER HAS COOLED QUITE A BIT.
HE WANTS THE GROUP TO STAY TOGETHER AND HE'S WILLING TO LET ME KEEP THINGS SOMEWHAT ORGANIZED.
AND YOU WANT TO TAKE ON THAT UNENVIABLE TASK?
I'LL MANAGE.
WE CAN'T HAVE ALL THE WHITE HAIRS SEPARATED FROM THE GROUP! GET BACK HERE, Y' TATTOOED MAIDEN OF MYSTERY!
MERISIEL ALSO HAS WHITE HAIR AND SHE'S AT YOUR TABLE.
BAH! YOU'LL NOT OUTWIT ME!
BACK TO THE PARTY WITH YOU! IT'S TIME TO CELEBRATE DEAD GOBLINS AND GLITTERING GOLD!
SIGH
ENJOY, FAIR LEADER...
THREE CHEERS FOR SEONI!
SEONI! SEONI! SEONI!
I expect time and ale will purge these shadowy thoughts, just like any other nightmare.

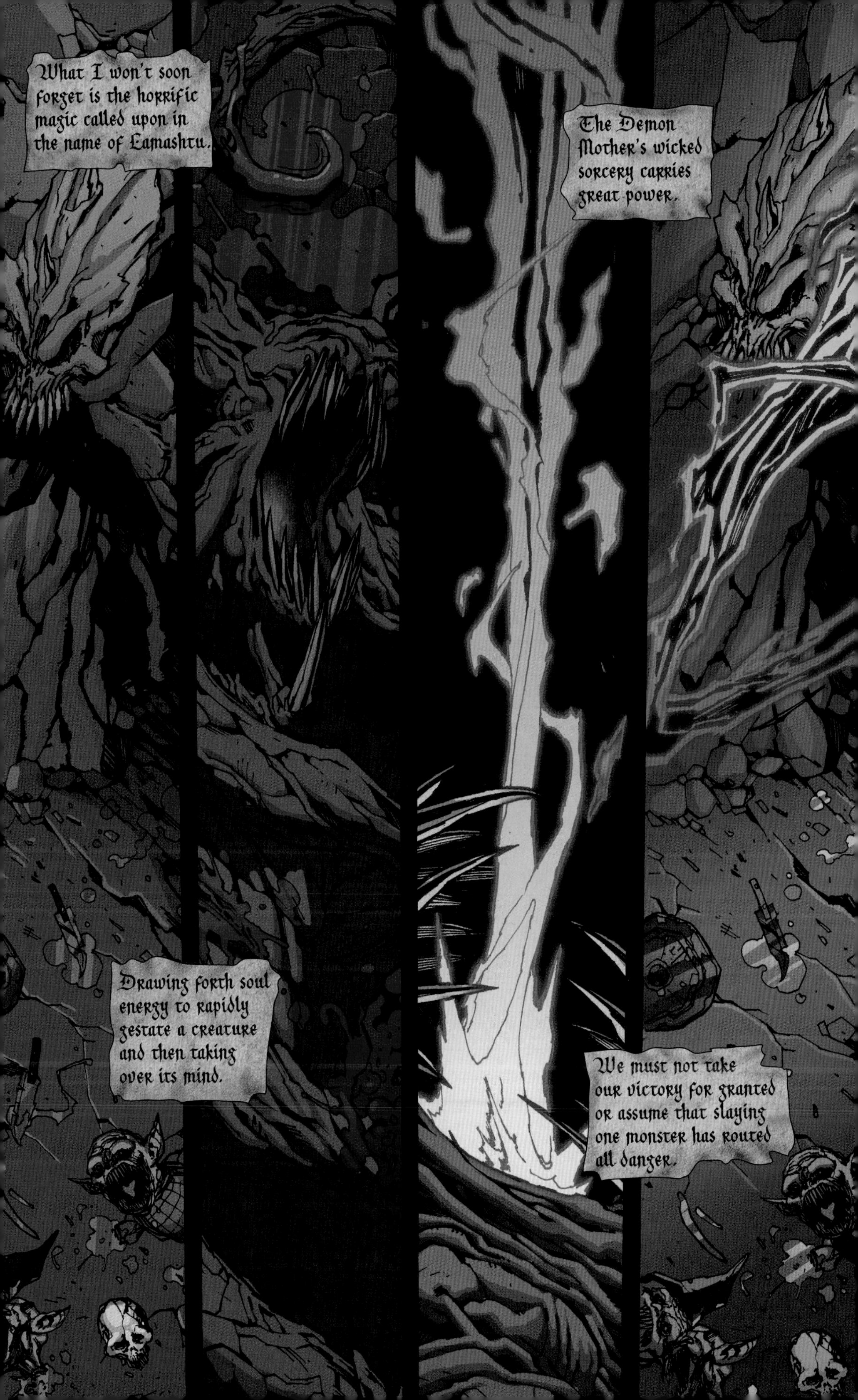
What I won't soon forget is the horrific magic called upon in the name of Lamashtu.
The Demon Mother's wicked sorcery carries great power.
Drawing forth soul energy to rapidly gestate a creature and then taking over its mind.
We must not take our victory for granted or assume that slaying one monster has routed all danger.

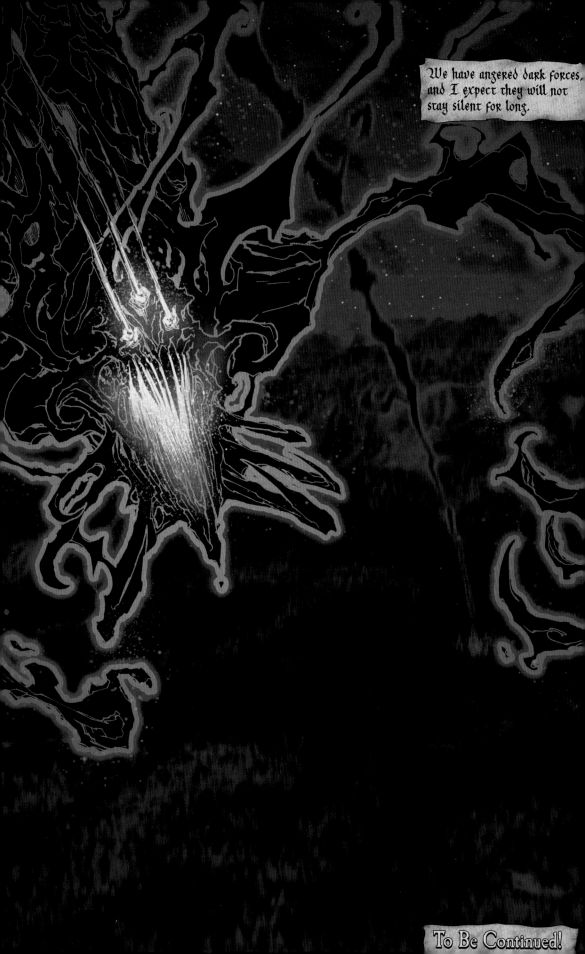

We have angered dark forces, and I expect they will not stay silent for long.

To Be Continued!

The Last Mosswood Goblin

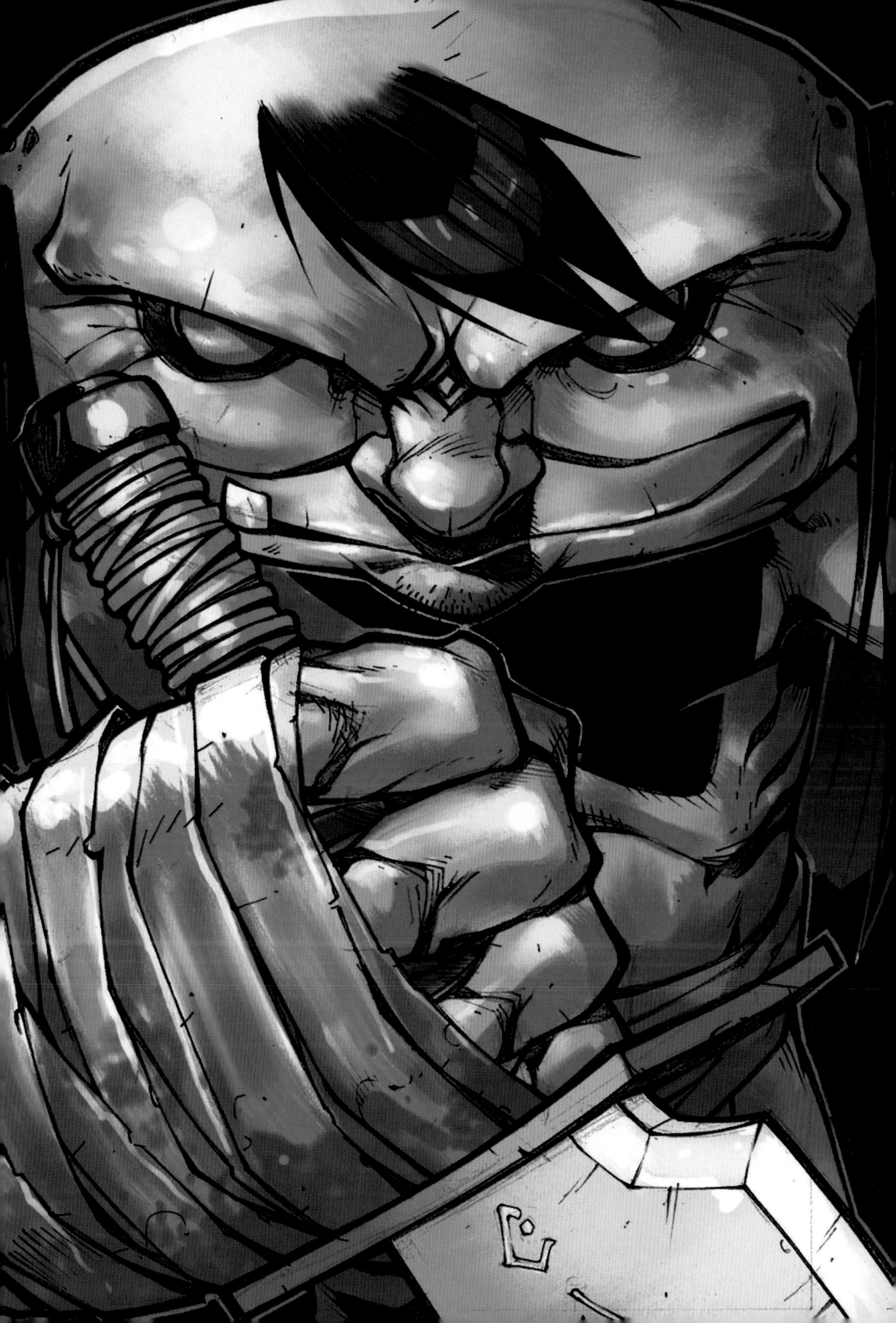

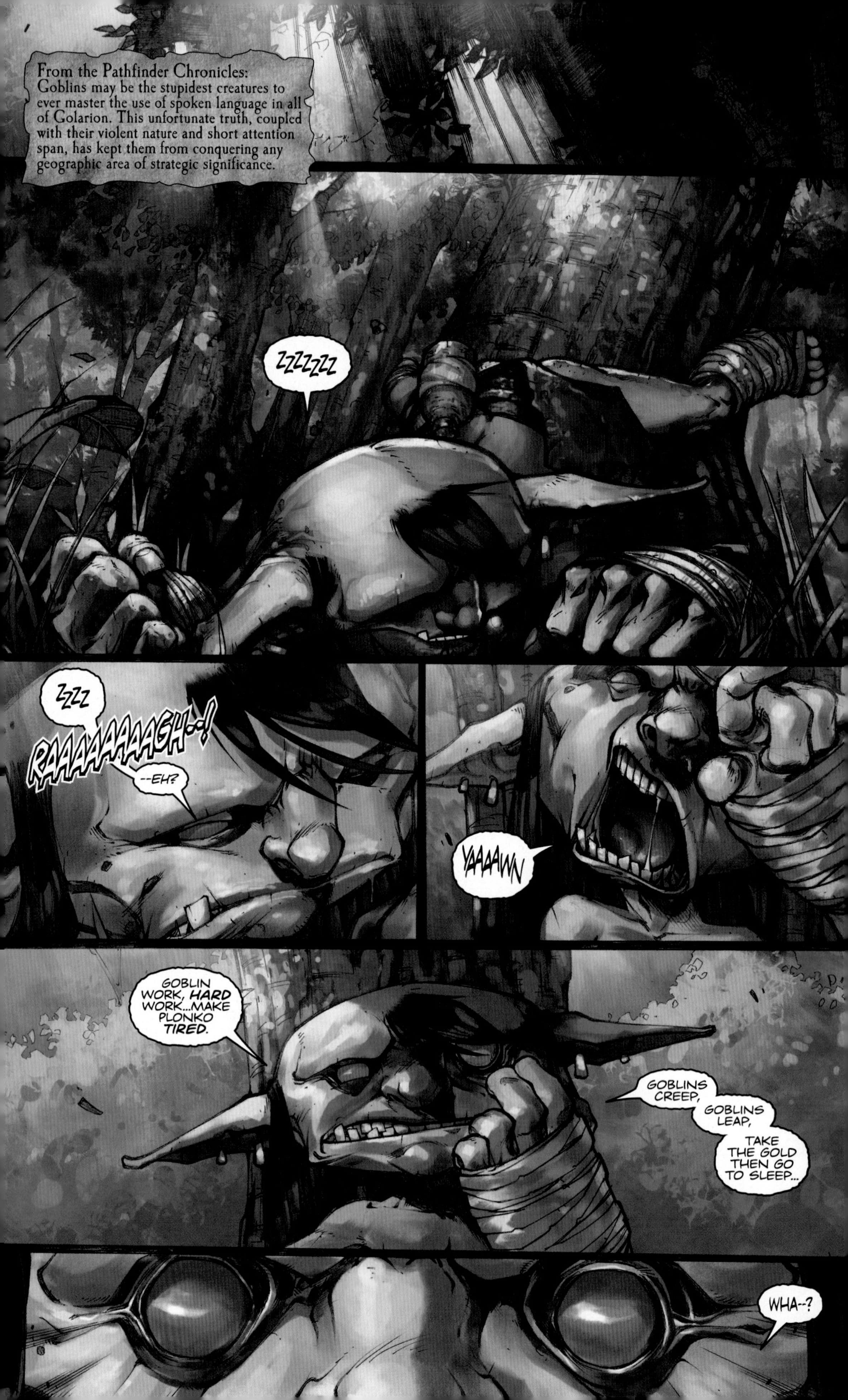
From the Pathfinder Chronicles:
Goblins may be the stupidest creatures to ever master the use of spoken language in all of Golarion. This unfortunate truth, coupled with their violent nature and short attention span, has kept them from conquering any geographic area of strategic significance.
ZZZZZZZ
ZZZZ
RAAAAAAAAGH--!
--EH?
YAAAAWN
GOBLIN WORK, HARD WORK...MAKE PLONKO TIRED.
GOBLINS CREEP,
GOBLINS LEAP,
TAKE THE GOLD THEN GO TO SLEEP...
WHA--?

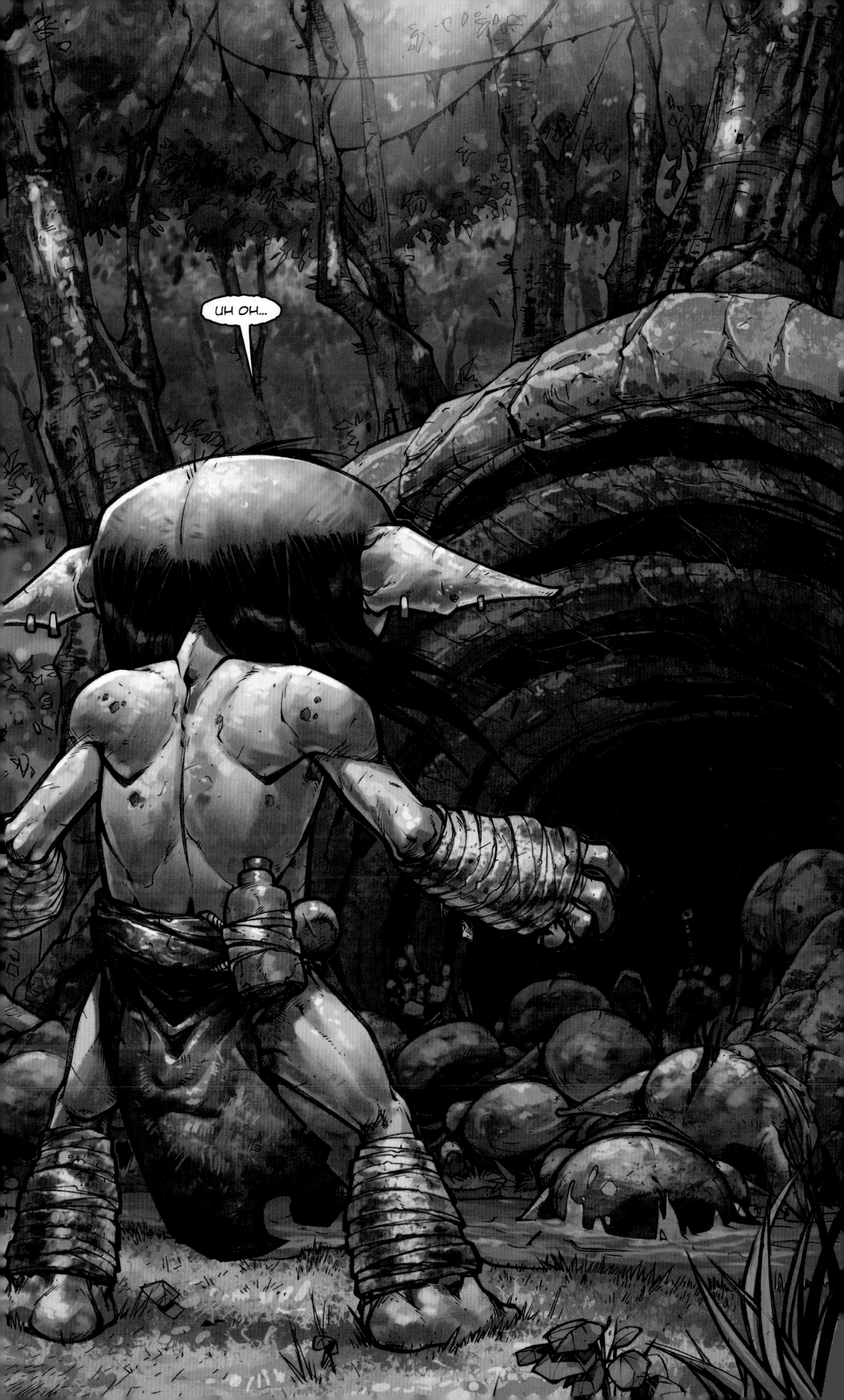
UH OH...

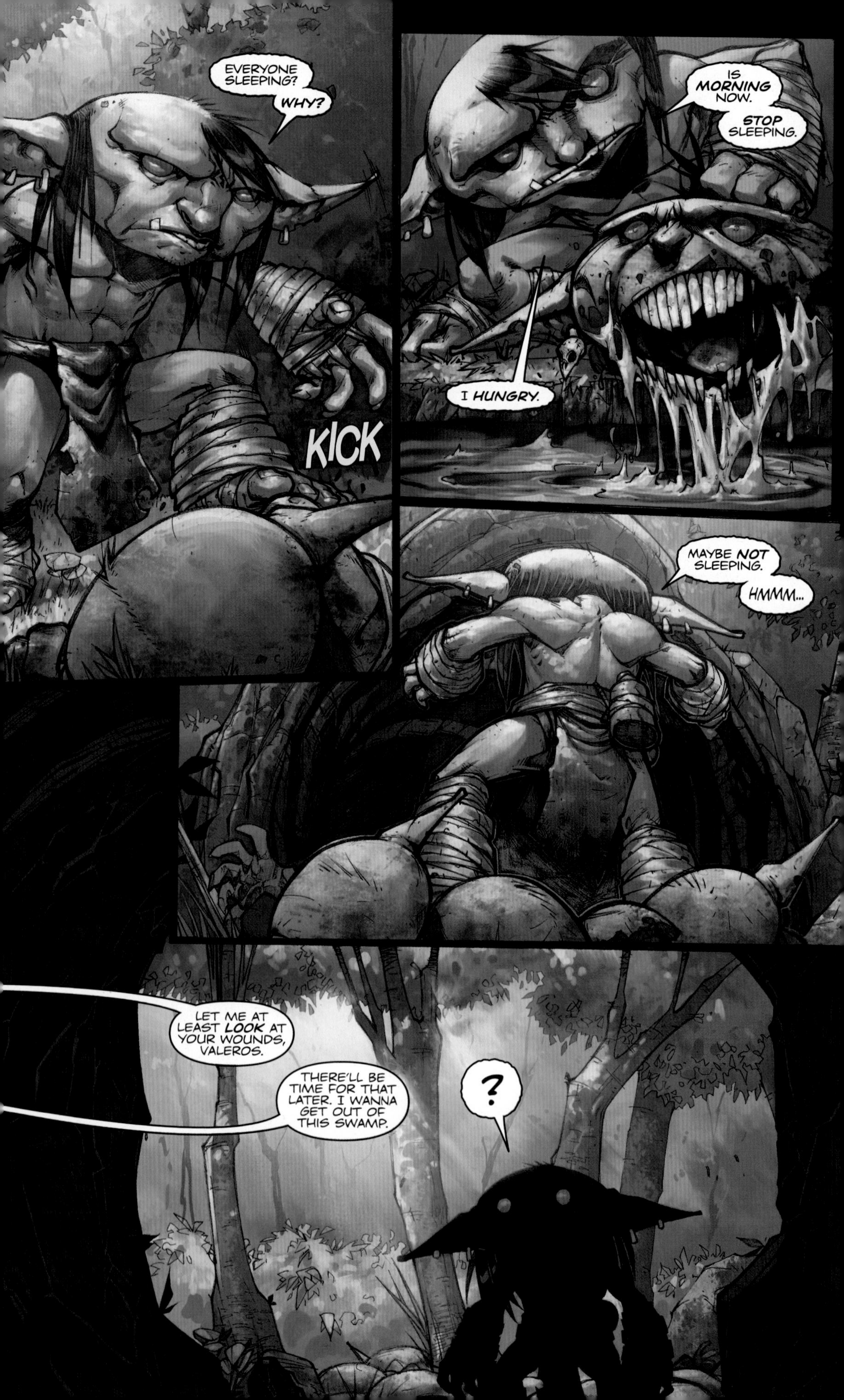
EVERYONE SLEEPING? WHY?
KICK
IS MORNING NOW.
STOP SLEEPING.
I HUNGRY.
MAYBE NOT SLEEPING.
HMMM...
LET ME AT LEAST LOOK AT YOUR WOUNDS, VALEROS.
THERE'LL BE TIME FOR THAT LATER. I WANNA GET OUT OF THIS SWAMP.
?

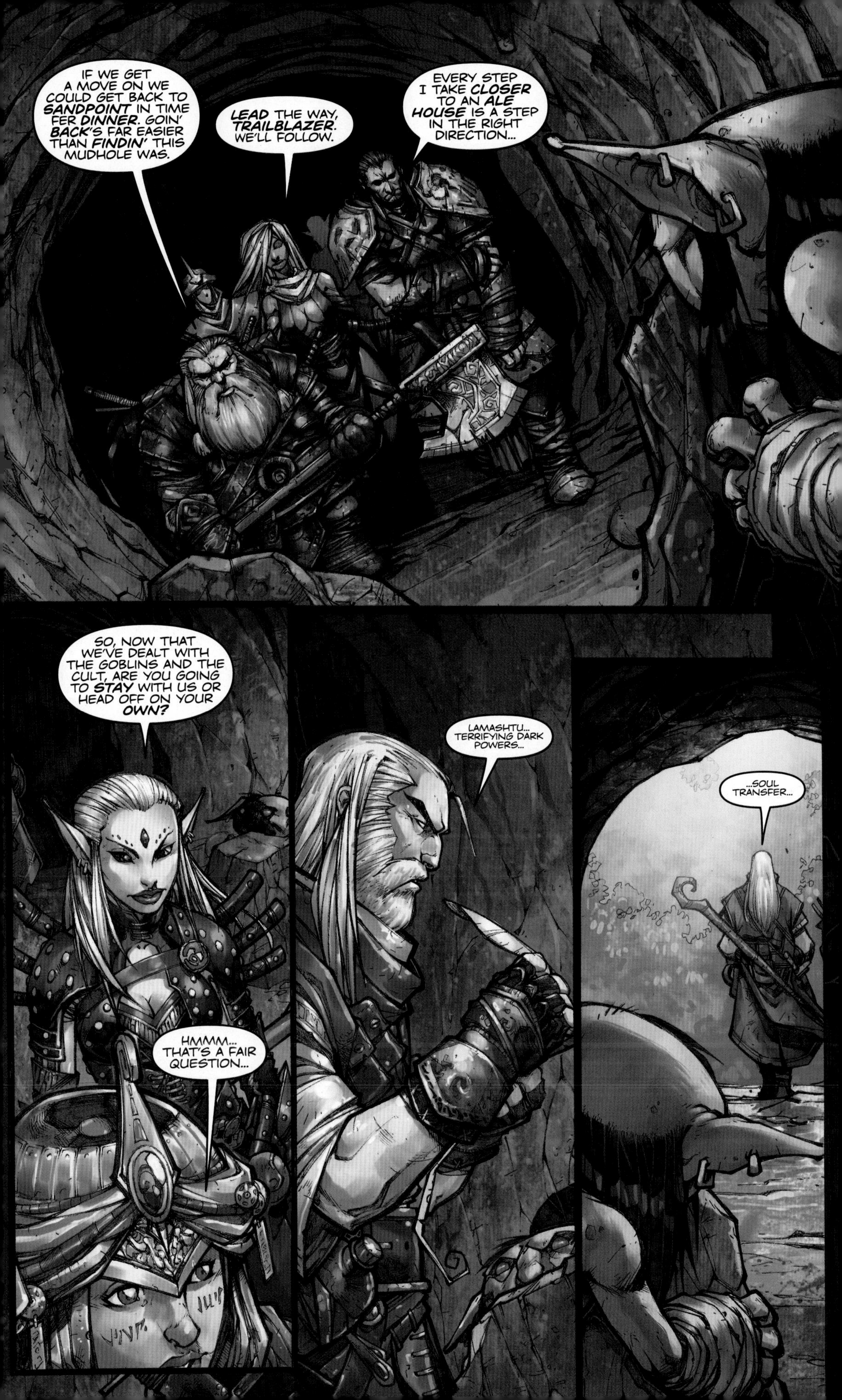
IF WE GET A MOVE ON WE COULD GET BACK TO SANDPOINT IN TIME FER DINNER. GOIN' BACK'S FAR EASIER THAN FINDIN' THIS MUDHOLE WAS.
LEAD THE WAY, TRAILBLAZER. WE'LL FOLLOW.
EVERY STEP I TAKE CLOSER TO AN ALE HOUSE IS A STEP IN THE RIGHT DIRECTION...
SO, NOW THAT WE'VE DEALT WITH THE GOBLINS AND THE CULT, ARE YOU GOING TO STAY WITH US OR HEAD OFF ON YOUR OWN?
HMMM... THAT'S A FAIR QUESTION...
LAMASHTU... TERRIFYING DARK POWERS...
...SOUL TRANSFER...

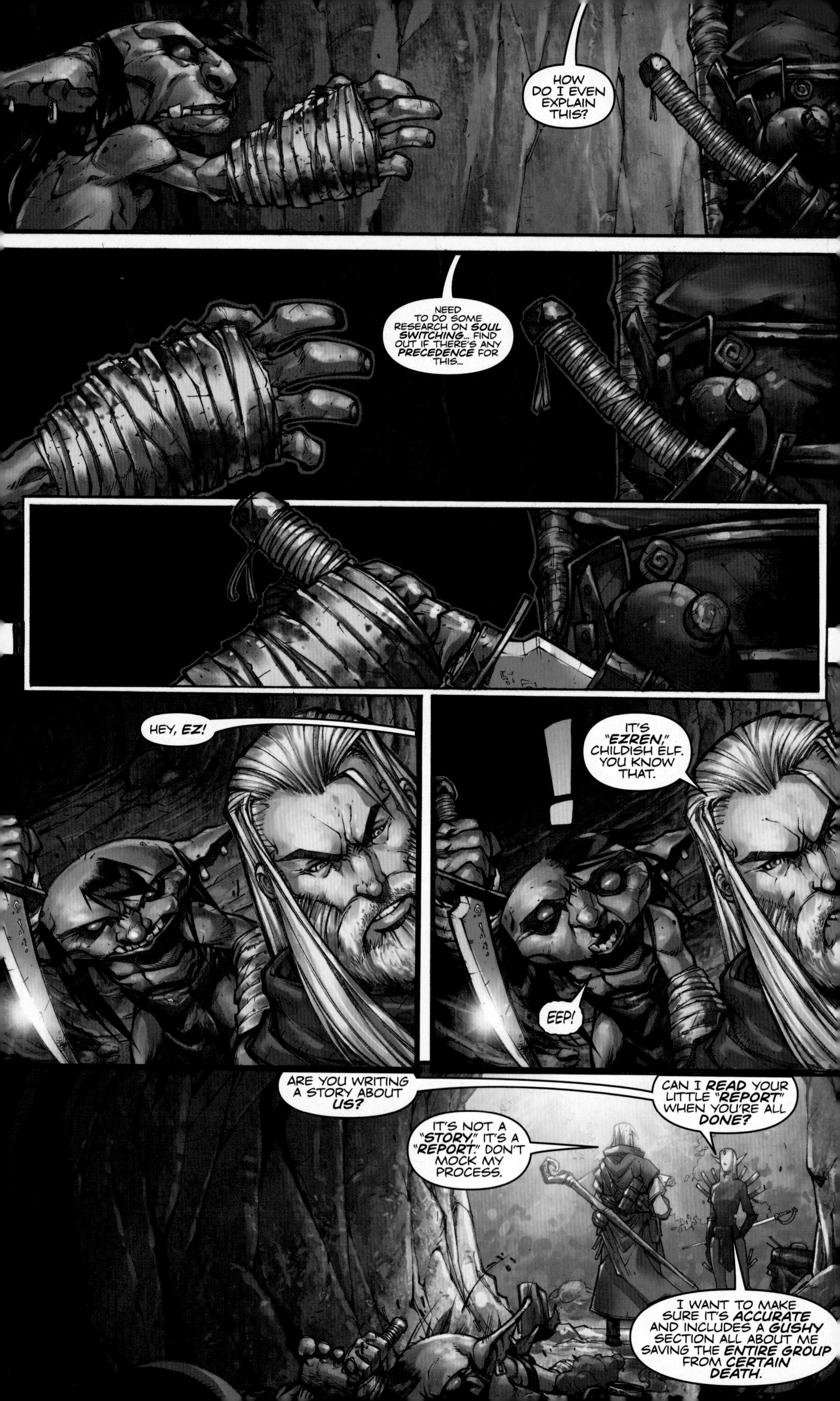
HOW DO I EVEN EXPLAIN THIS?
NEED TO DO SOME RESEARCH ON SOUL SWITCHING... FIND OUT IF THERE'S ANY PRECEDENCE FOR THIS...
HEY, EZ!
!
IT'S "EZREN," CHILDISH ELF. YOU KNOW THAT.
EEP!
ARE YOU WRITING A STORY ABOUT US?
IT'S NOT A "STORY," IT'S A "REPORT." DON'T MOCK MY PROCESS.
CAN I READ YOUR LITTLE "REPORT" WHEN YOU'RE ALL DONE?
I WANT TO MAKE SURE IT'S ACCURATE AND INCLUDES A GUSHY SECTION ALL ABOUT ME SAVING THE ENTIRE GROUP FROM CERTAIN DEATH.

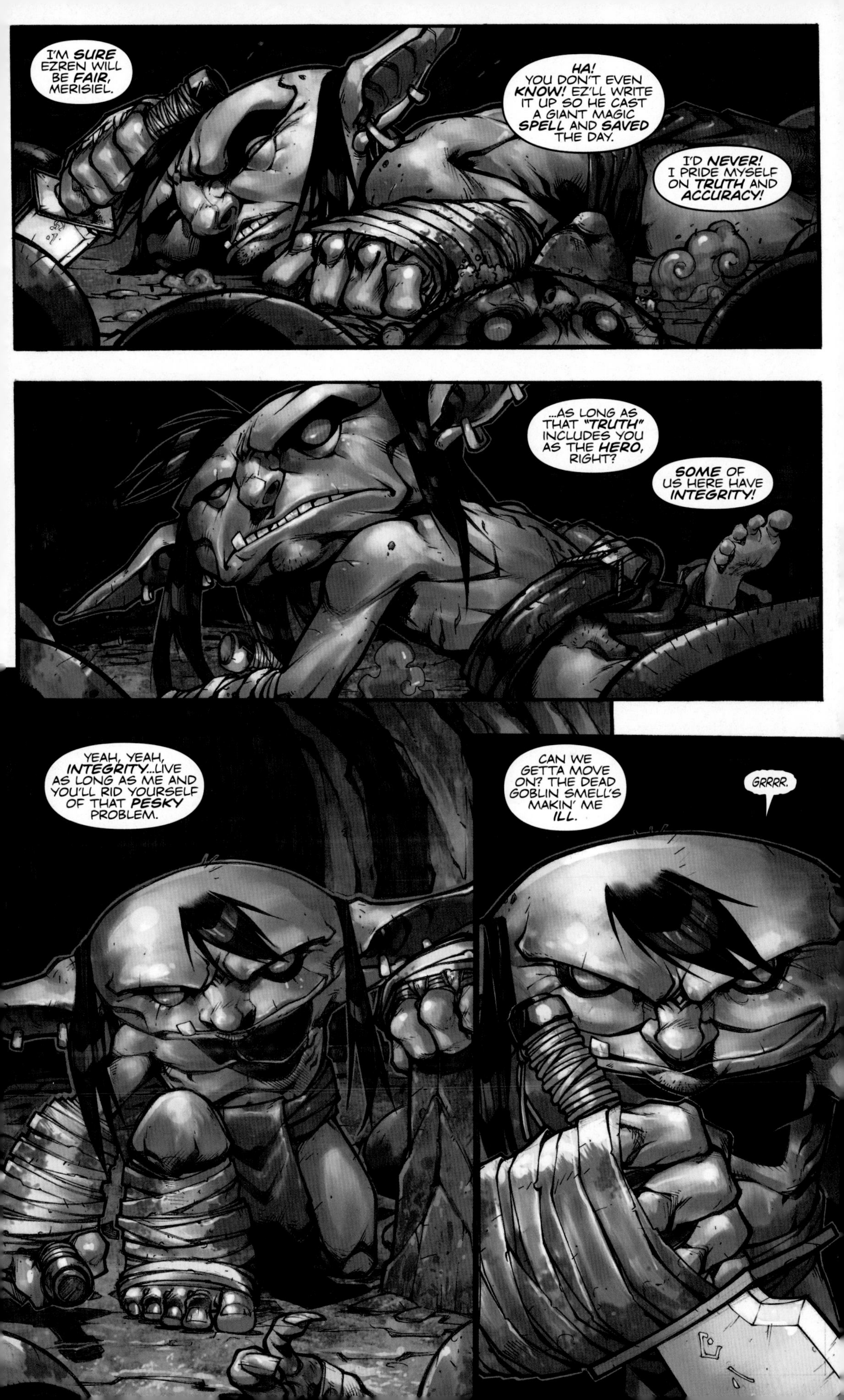

I'M SURE EZREN WILL BE FAIR, MERISIEL.
HA! YOU DON'T EVEN KNOW! EZ'LL WRITE IT UP SO HE CAST A GIANT MAGIC SPELL AND SAVED THE DAY.
I'D NEVER! I PRIDE MYSELF ON TRUTH AND ACCURACY!
...AS LONG AS THAT "TRUTH" INCLUDES YOU AS THE HERO, RIGHT?
SOME OF US HERE HAVE INTEGRITY!
YEAH, YEAH, INTEGRITY...LIVE AS LONG AS ME AND YOU'LL RID YOURSELF OF THAT PESKY PROBLEM.
CAN WE GETTA MOVE ON? THE DEAD GOBLIN SMELL'S MAKIN' ME ILL.
GRRRR.

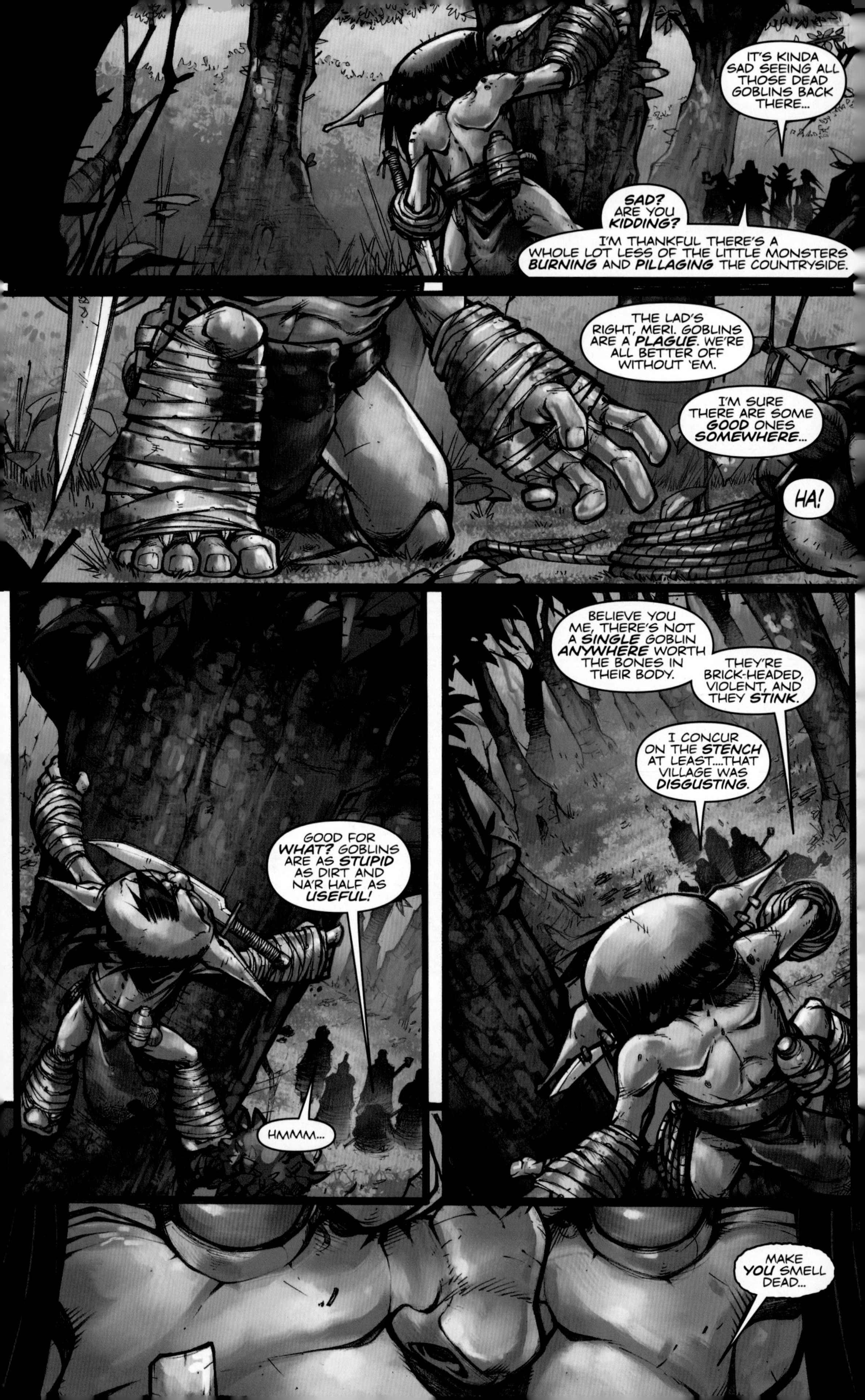

IT'S KINDA SAD SEEING ALL THOSE DEAD GOBLINS BACK THERE...
SAD? ARE YOU KIDDING?
I'M THANKFUL THERE'S A WHOLE LOT LESS OF THE LITTLE MONSTERS BURNING AND PILLAGING THE COUNTRYSIDE.
THE LAD'S RIGHT, MERI. GOBLINS ARE A PLAGUE. WE'RE ALL BETTER OFF WITHOUT 'EM.
I'M SURE THERE ARE SOME GOOD ONES SOMEWHERE...
HA!
GOOD FOR WHAT? GOBLINS ARE AS STUPID AS DIRT AND NA'R HALF AS USEFUL!
HMMM...
BELIEVE YOU ME, THERE'S NOT A SINGLE GOBLIN ANYWHERE WORTH THE BONES IN THEIR BODY.
THEY'RE BRICK-HEADED, VIOLENT, AND THEY STINK.
I CONCUR ON THE STENCH AT LEAST....THAT VILLAGE WAS DISGUSTING.
MAKE YOU SMELL DEAD...

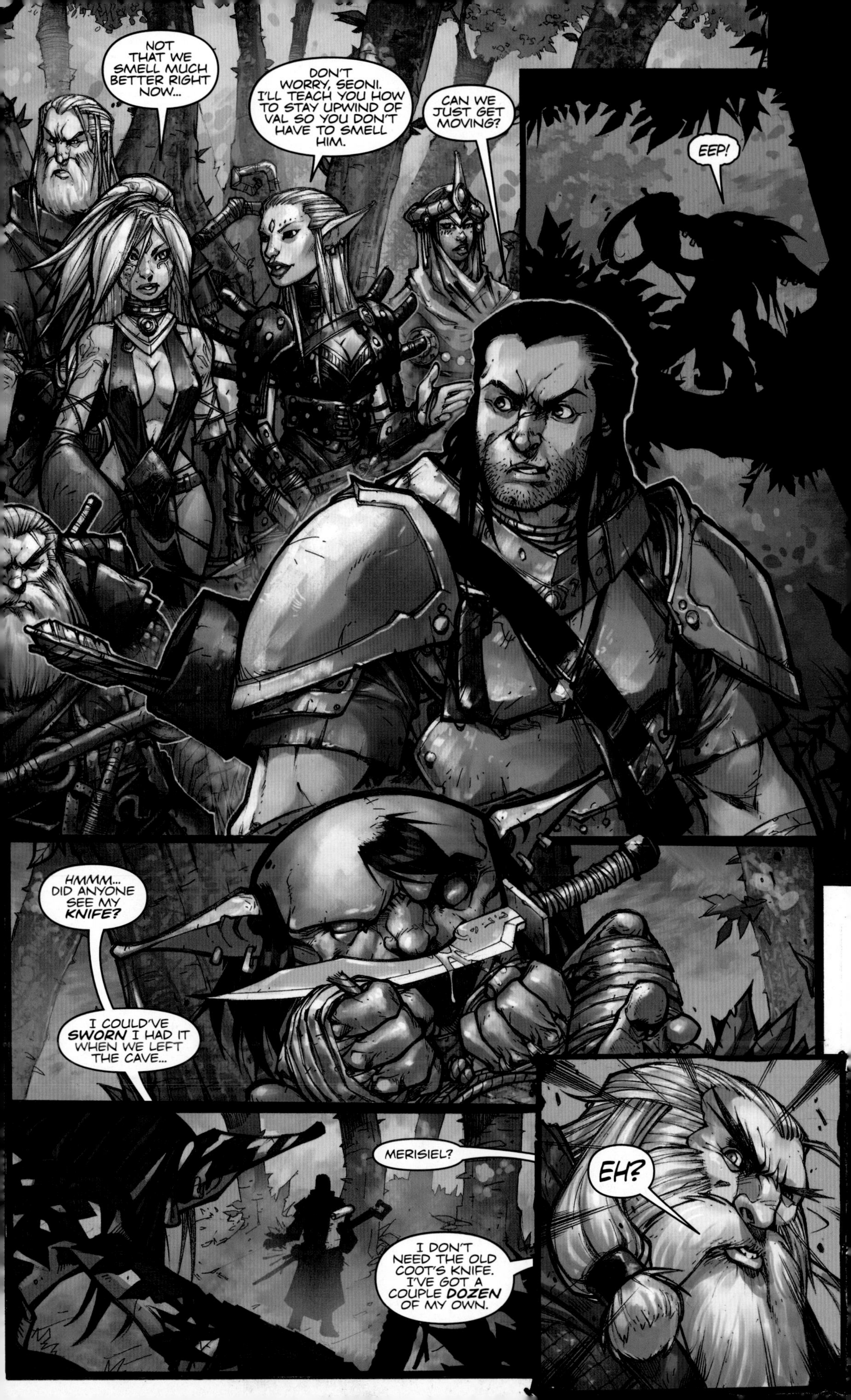
NOT THAT WE SMELL MUCH BETTER RIGHT NOW...
DON'T WORRY, SEONI. I'LL TEACH YOU HOW TO STAY UPWIND OF VAL SO YOU DON'T HAVE TO SMELL HIM.
CAN WE JUST GET MOVING?
EEP!
HMMM... DID ANYONE SEE MY KNIFE?
I COULD'VE SWORN I HAD IT WHEN WE LEFT THE CAVE...
MERISIEL?
EH?
I DON'T NEED THE OLD COOT'S KNIFE. I'VE GOT A COUPLE DOZEN OF MY OWN.

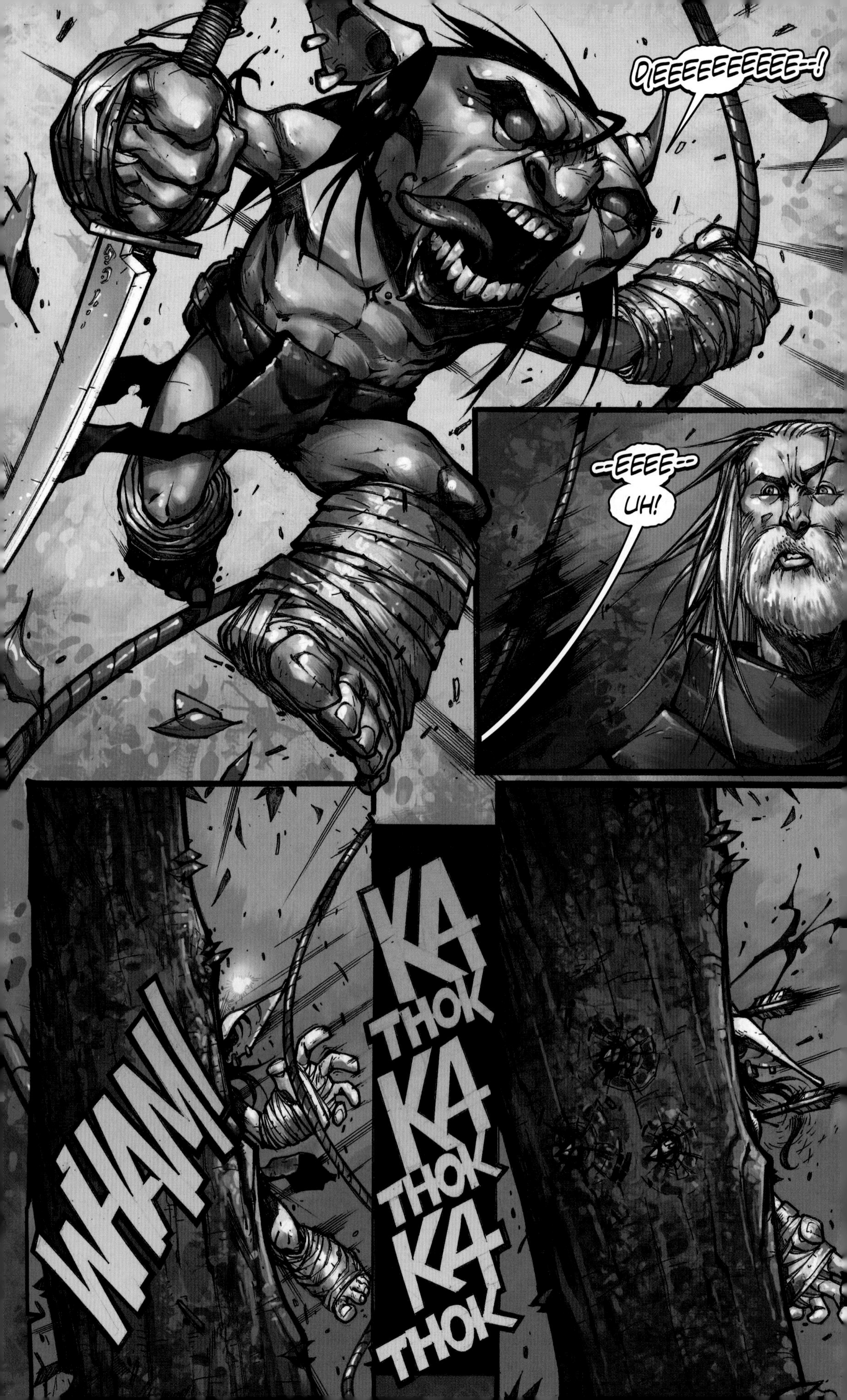
DIEEEEEEEEEEE--!
--EEEE--
UH!
WHAM!
KA THOK KA THOK KA THOK

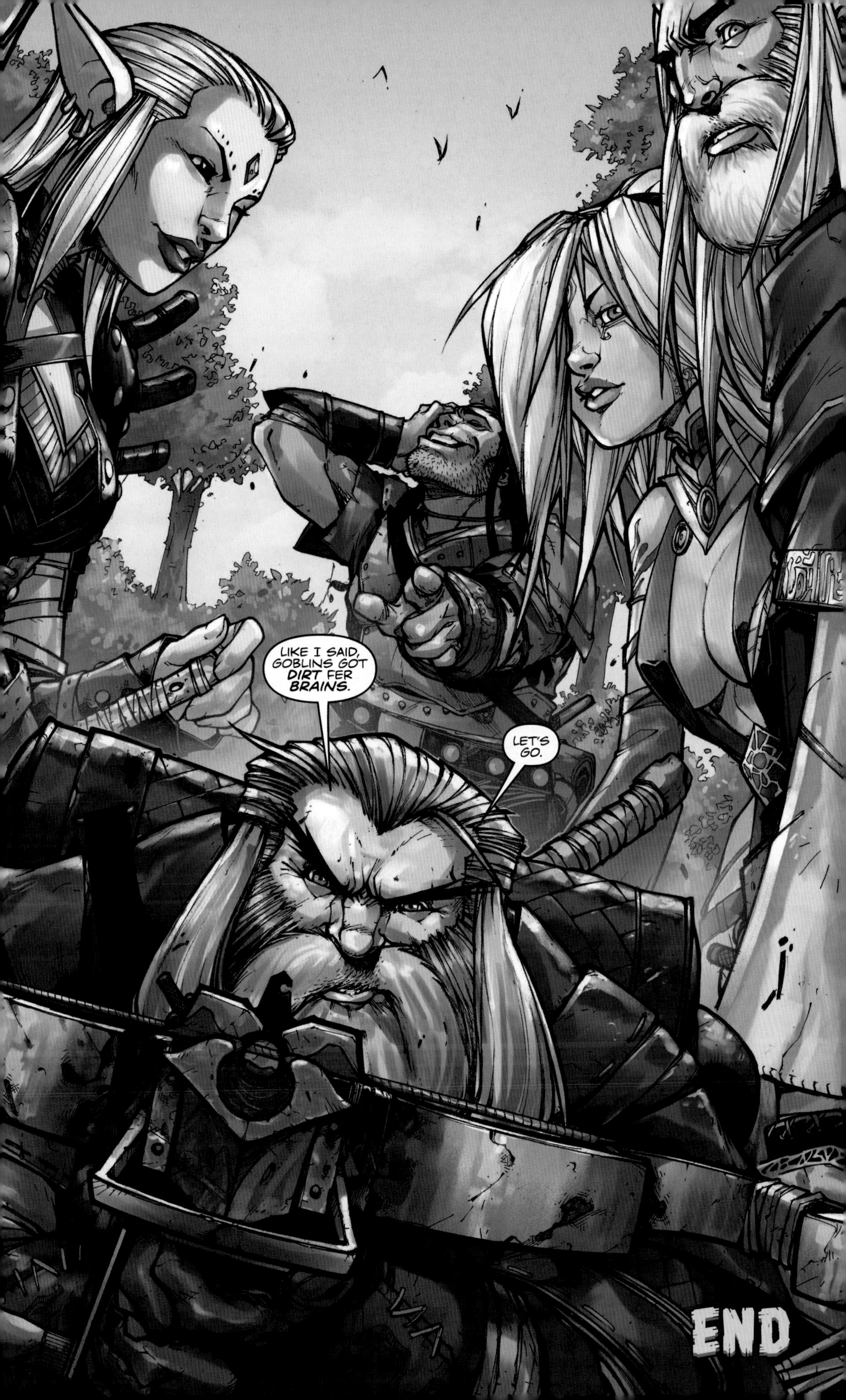
LIKE I SAID, GOBLINS GOT DIRT FER BRAINS.
LET'S GO.
END

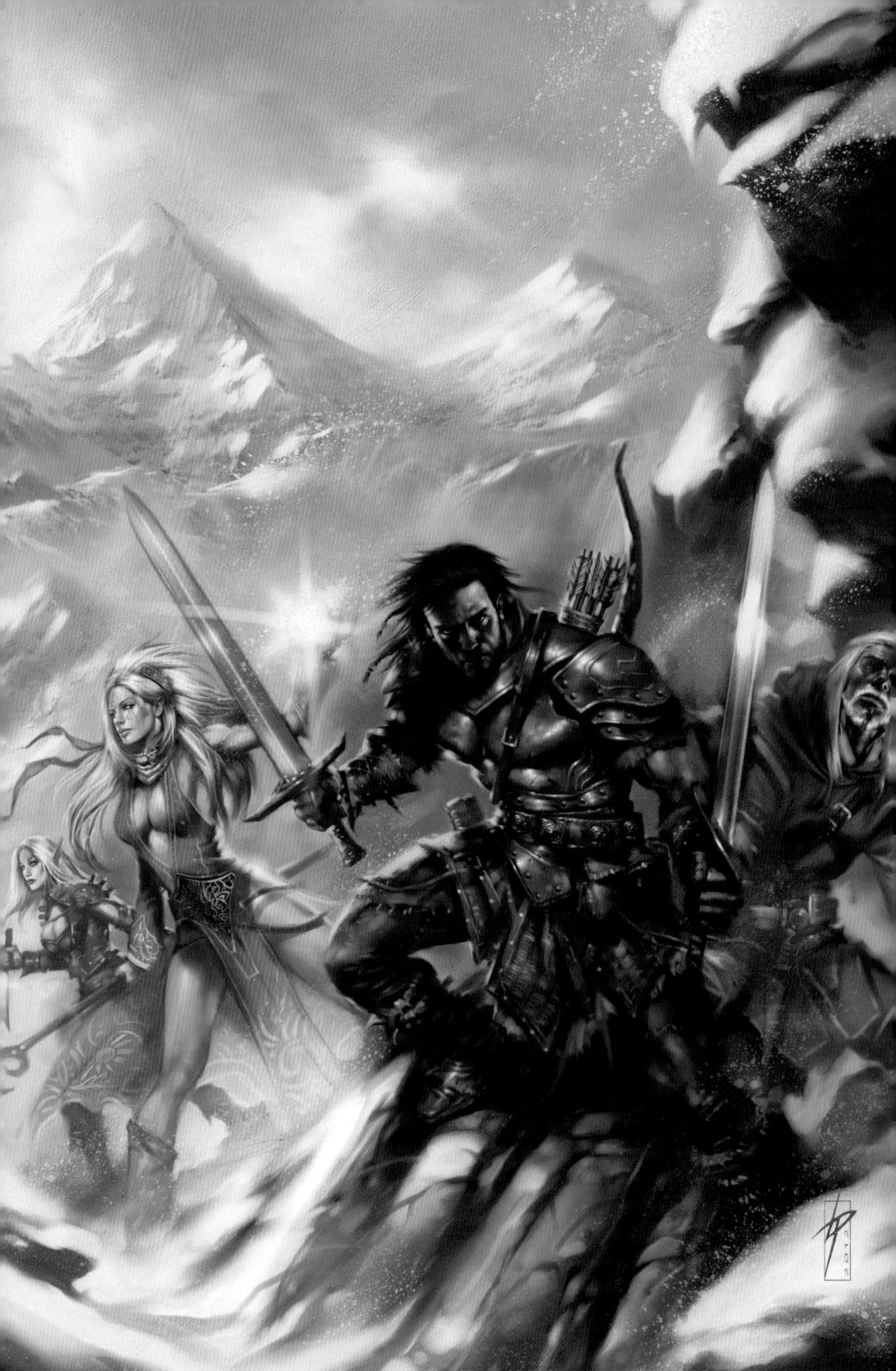

Issue #1 cover by LUCIO PARRILLO

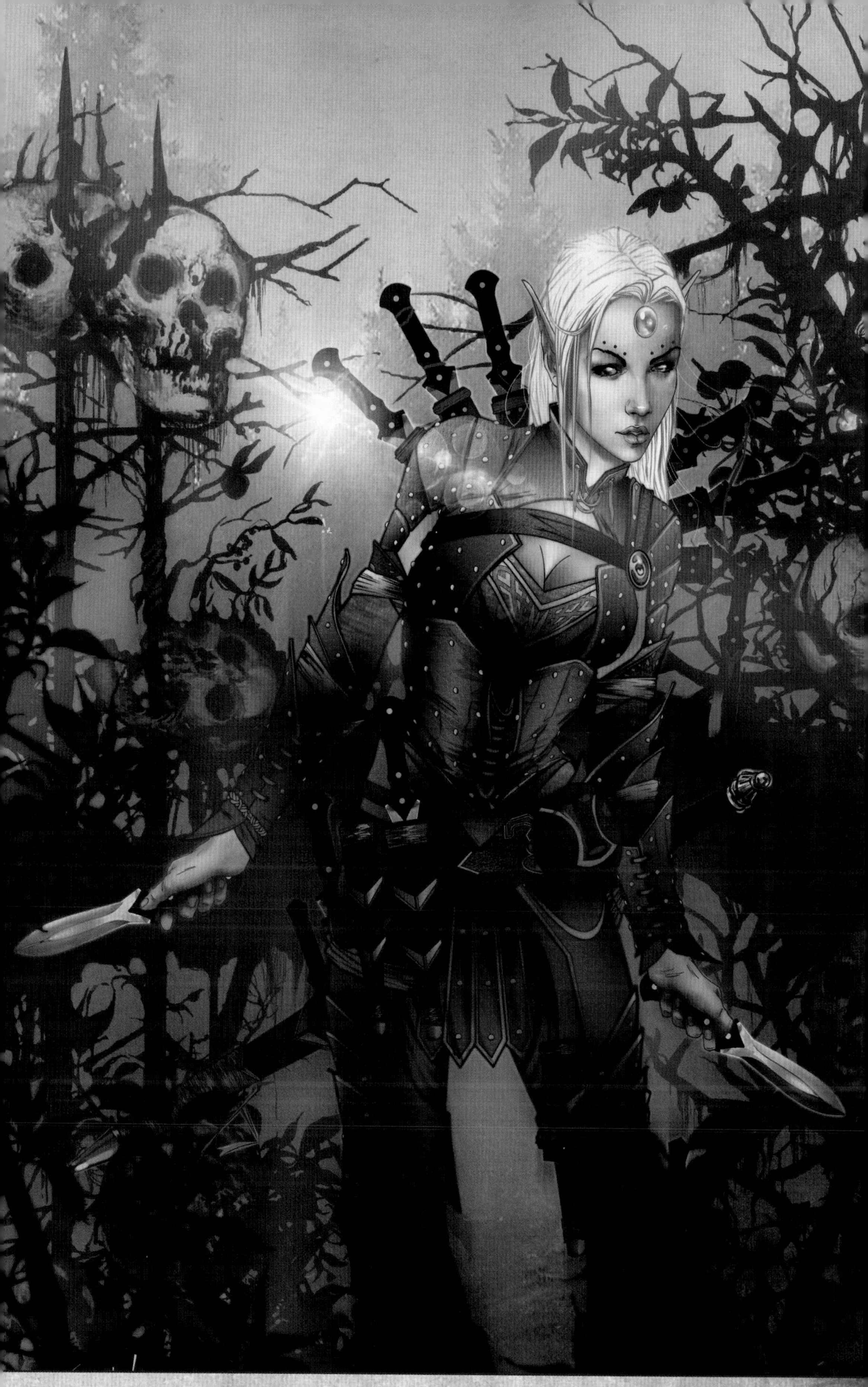

Issue #1 cover by ERIK JONES

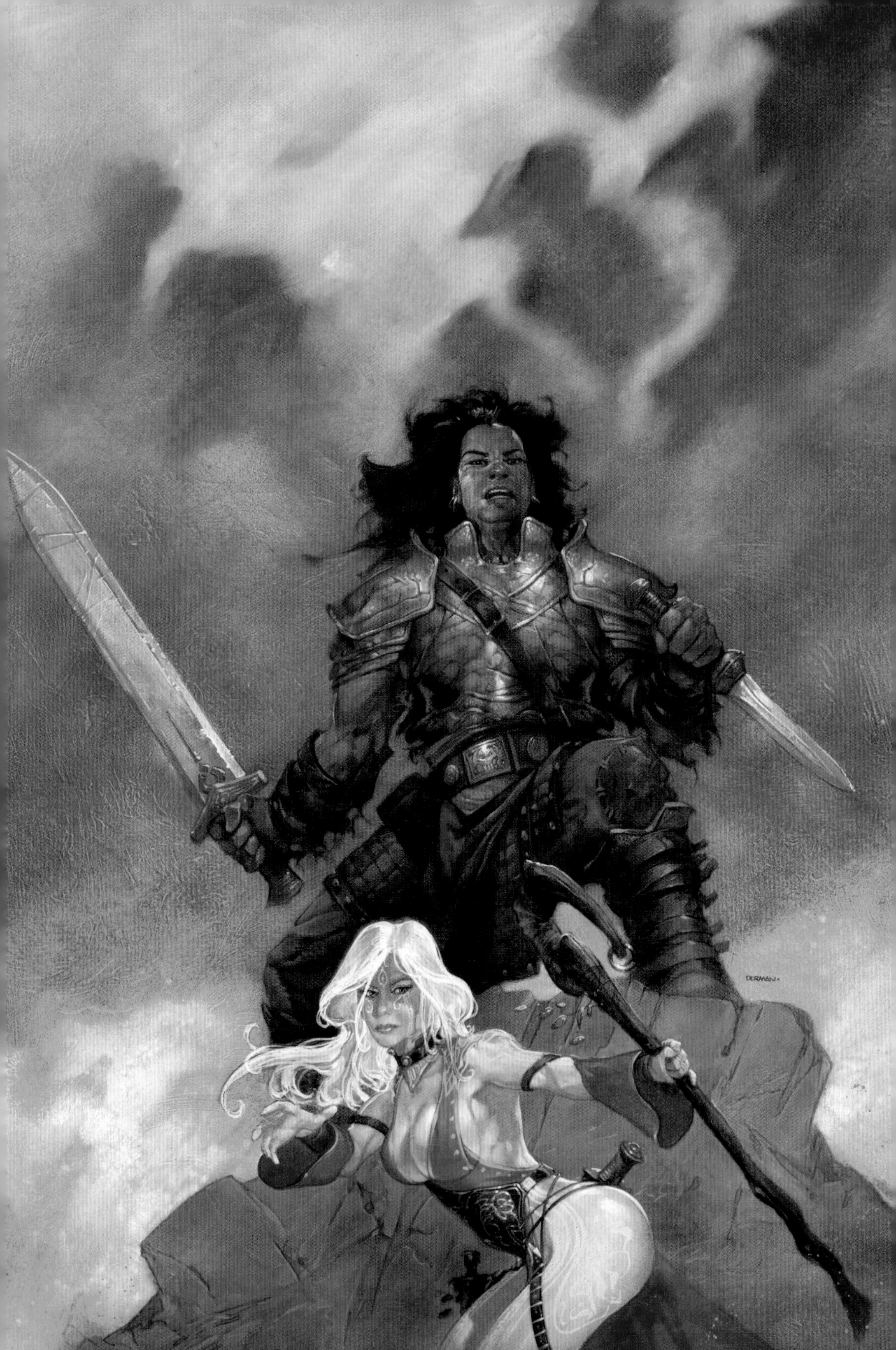
DORMAN

Issue #1 cover by **DAVE DORMAN**

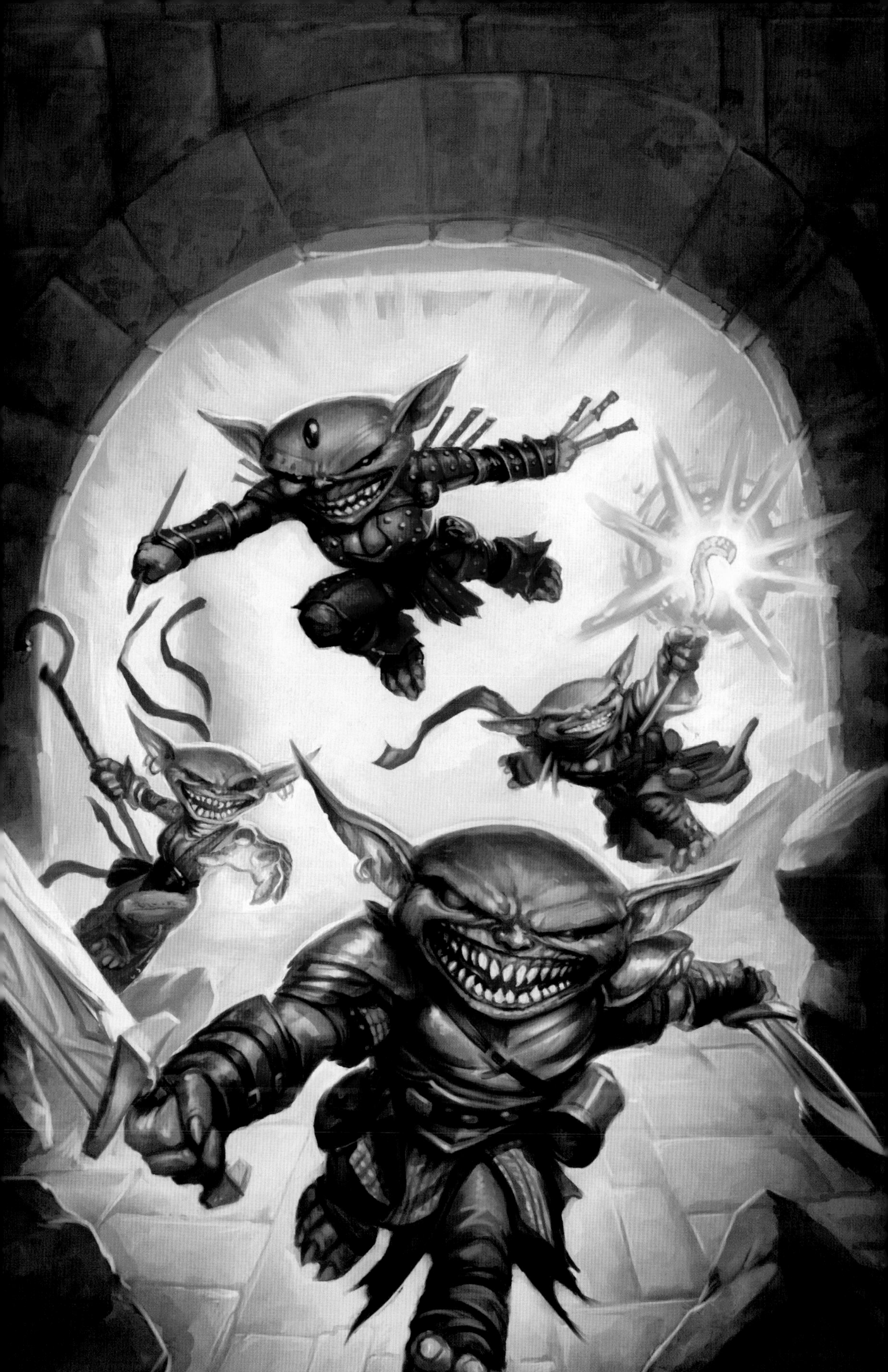

Issue #1 Paizo.com exclusive cover by TYLER WALPOLE

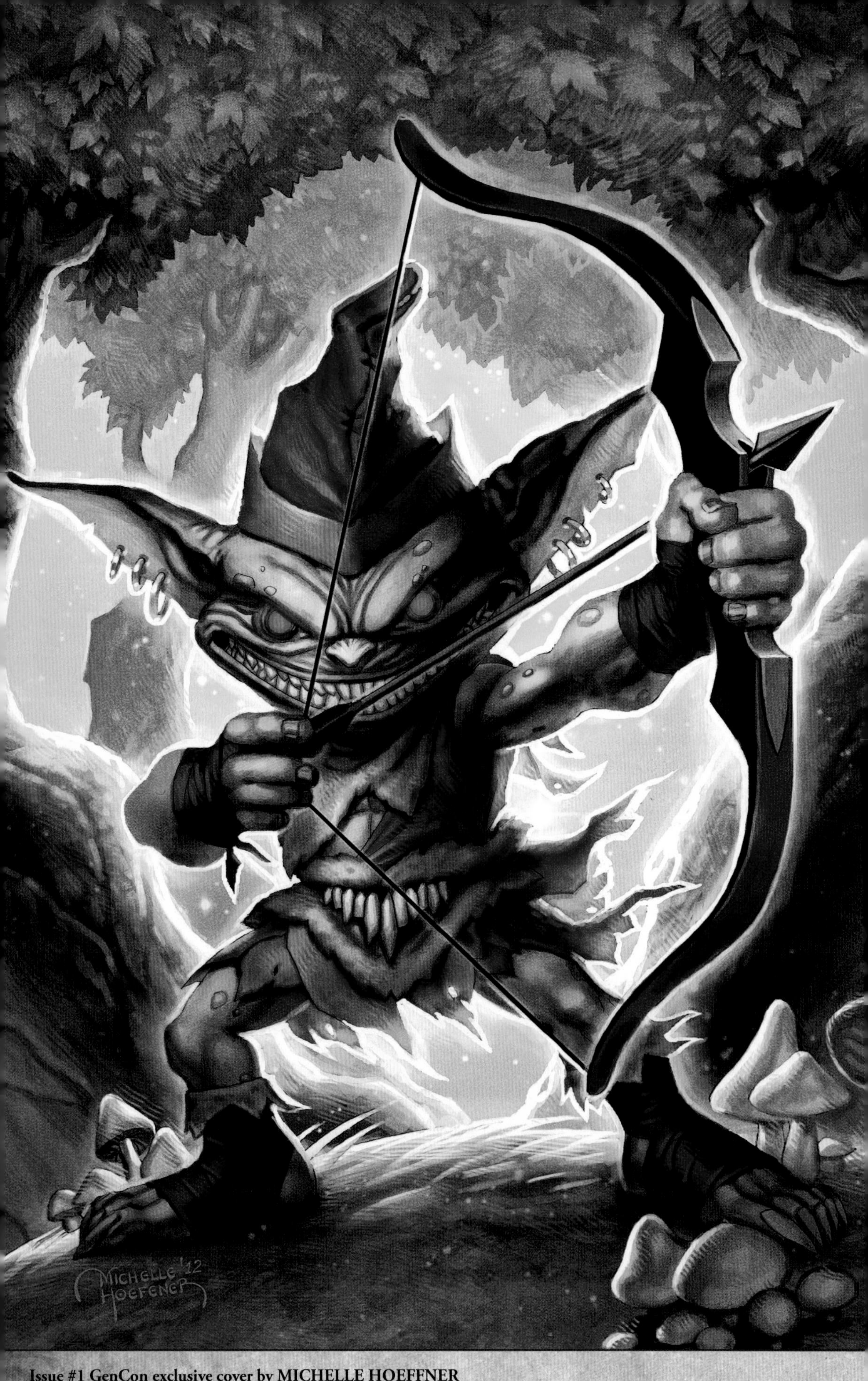
MICHELLE HOEFFNER '12

Issue #1 GenCon exclusive cover by MICHELLE HOEFFNER

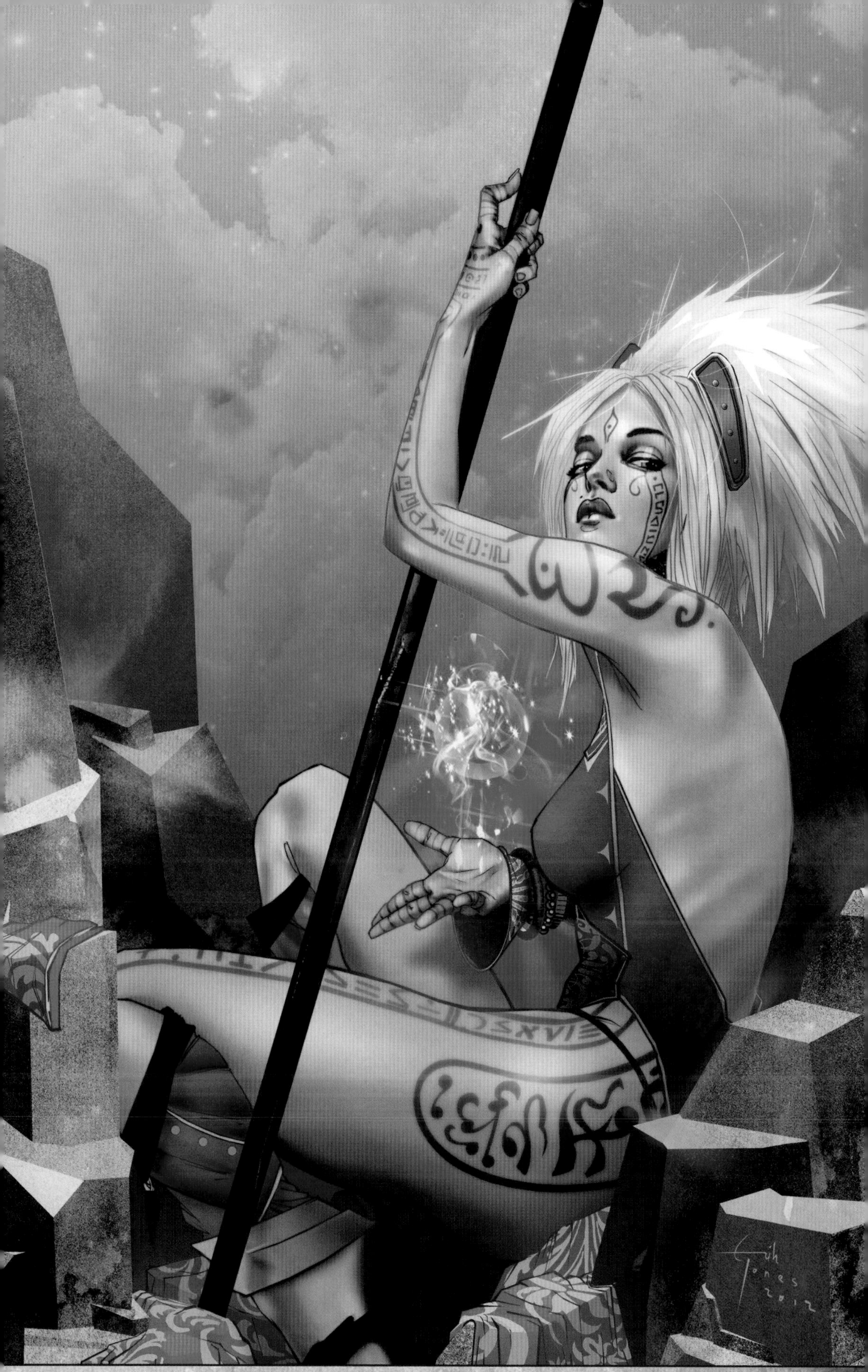
Erik Jones 2012

Issue #2 cover by Erik Jones

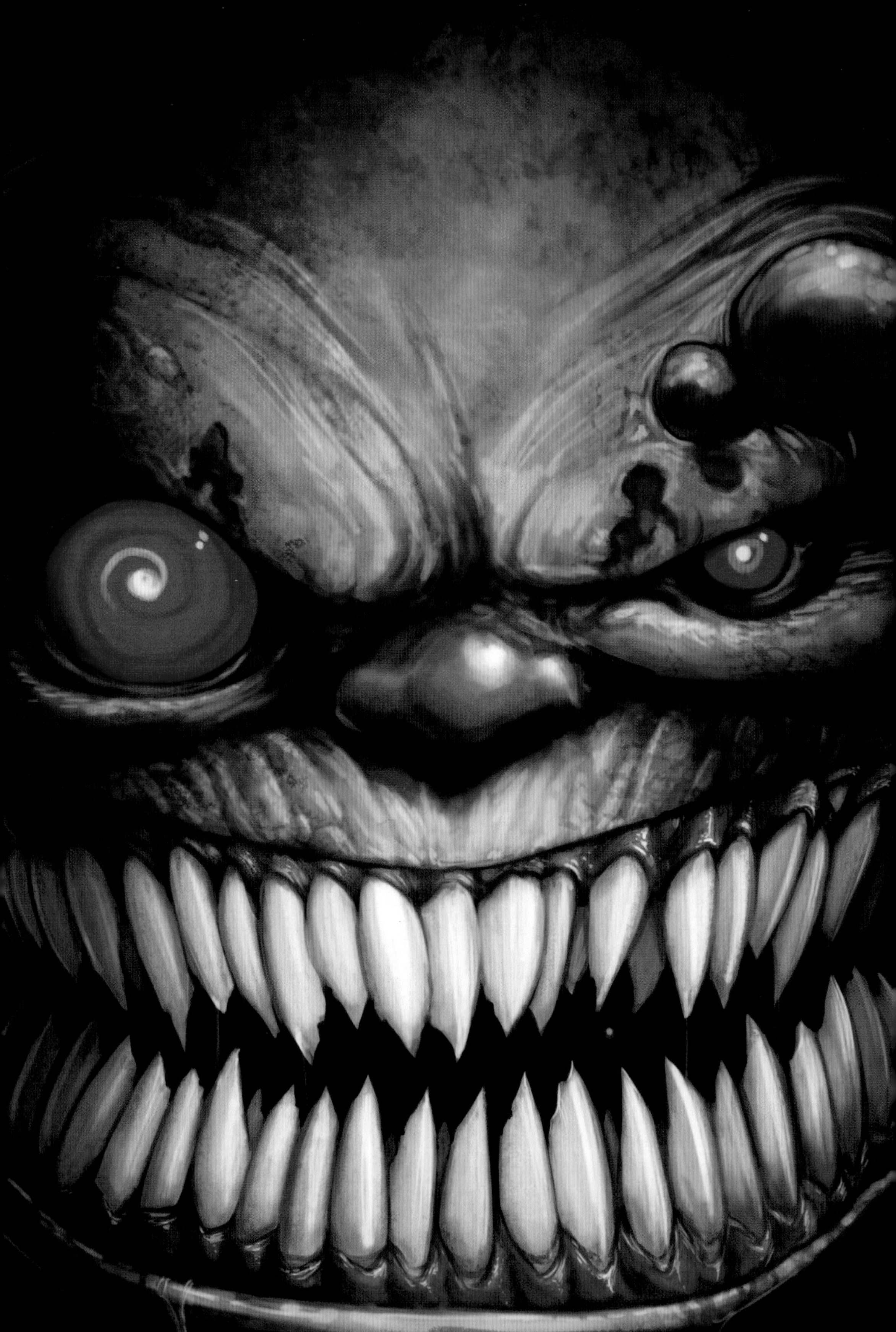

Issue #2 cover by TYLER WALPOLE

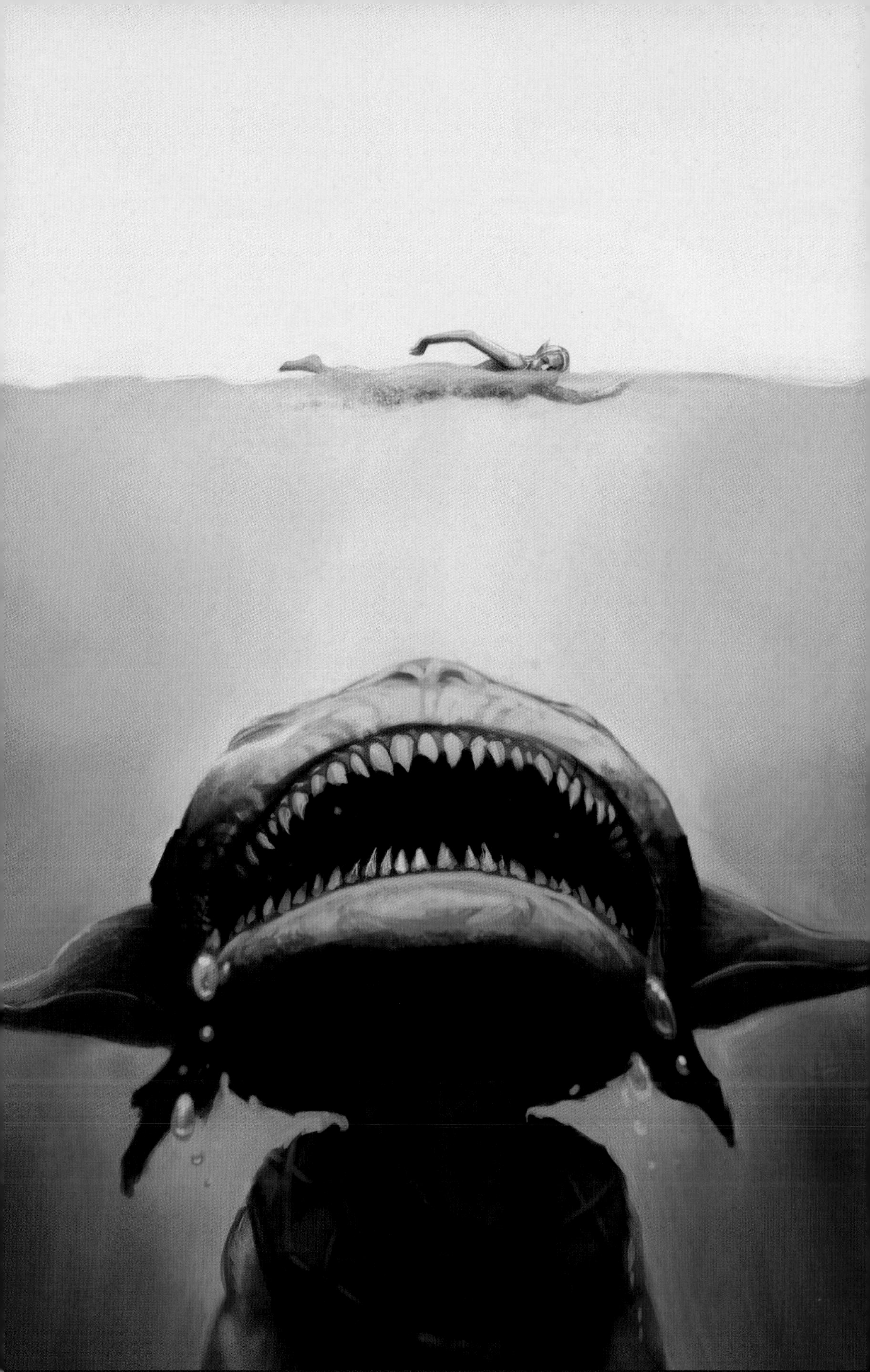

Issue #2 Paizo.com exclusive cover by TYLER WALPOLE

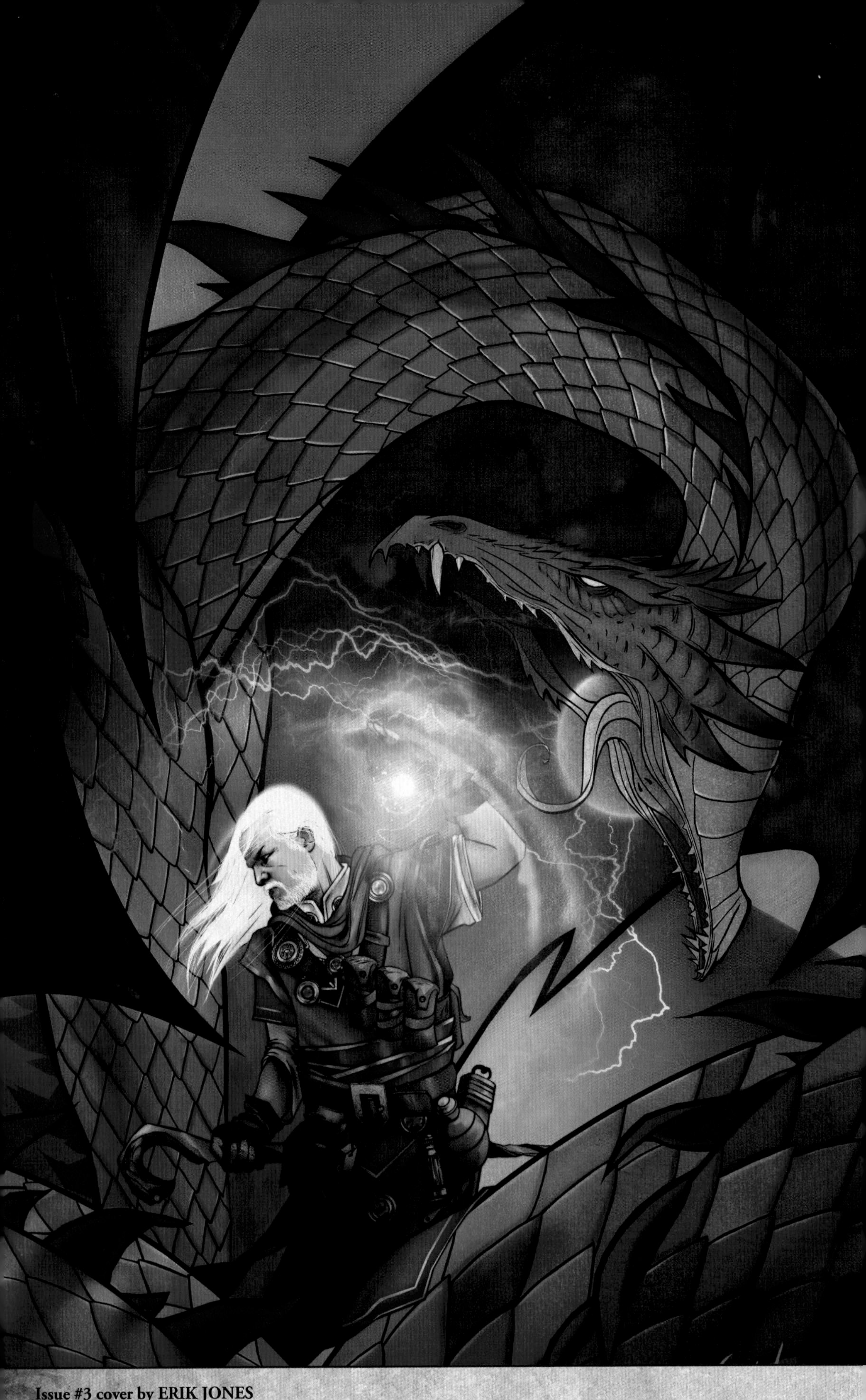

Issue #3 cover by ERIK JONES

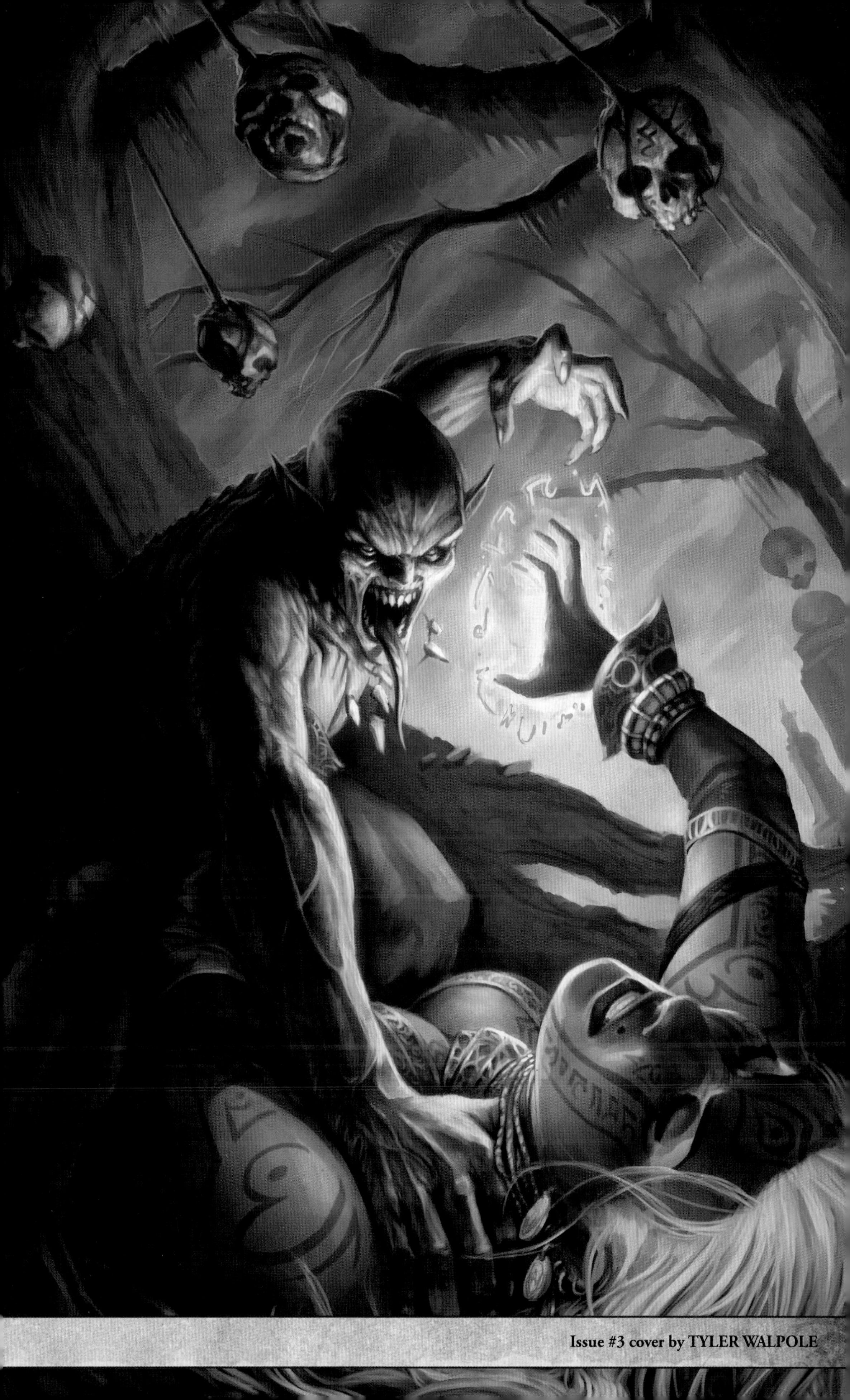

Issue #3 cover by TYLER WALPOLE

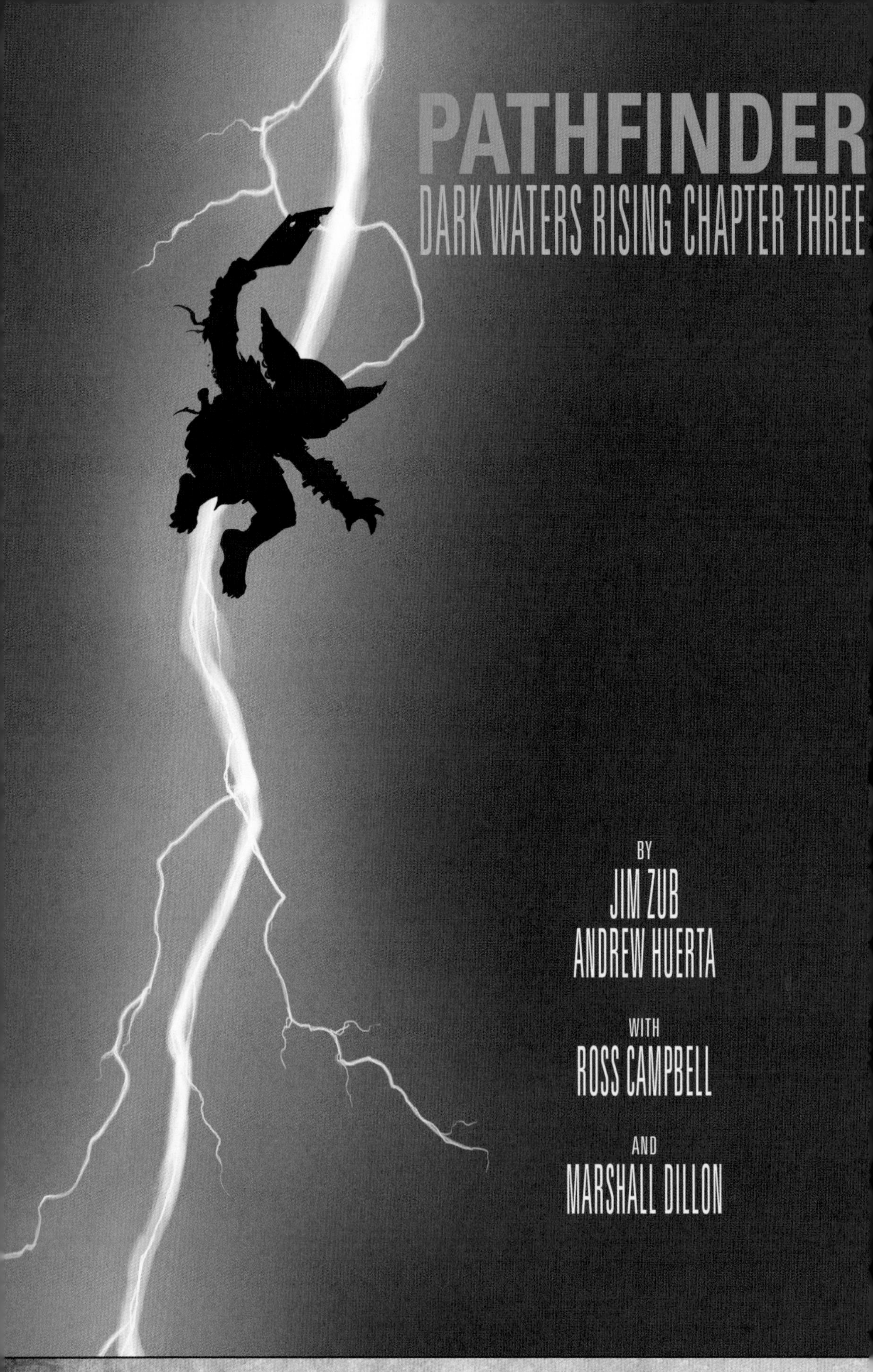
PATHFINDER
DARK WATERS RISING CHAPTER THREE
BY
JIM ZUB
ANDREW HUERTA
WITH
ROSS CAMPBELL
AND
MARSHALL DILLON

Issue #3 Paizo.com exclusive cover by TYLER WALPOLE

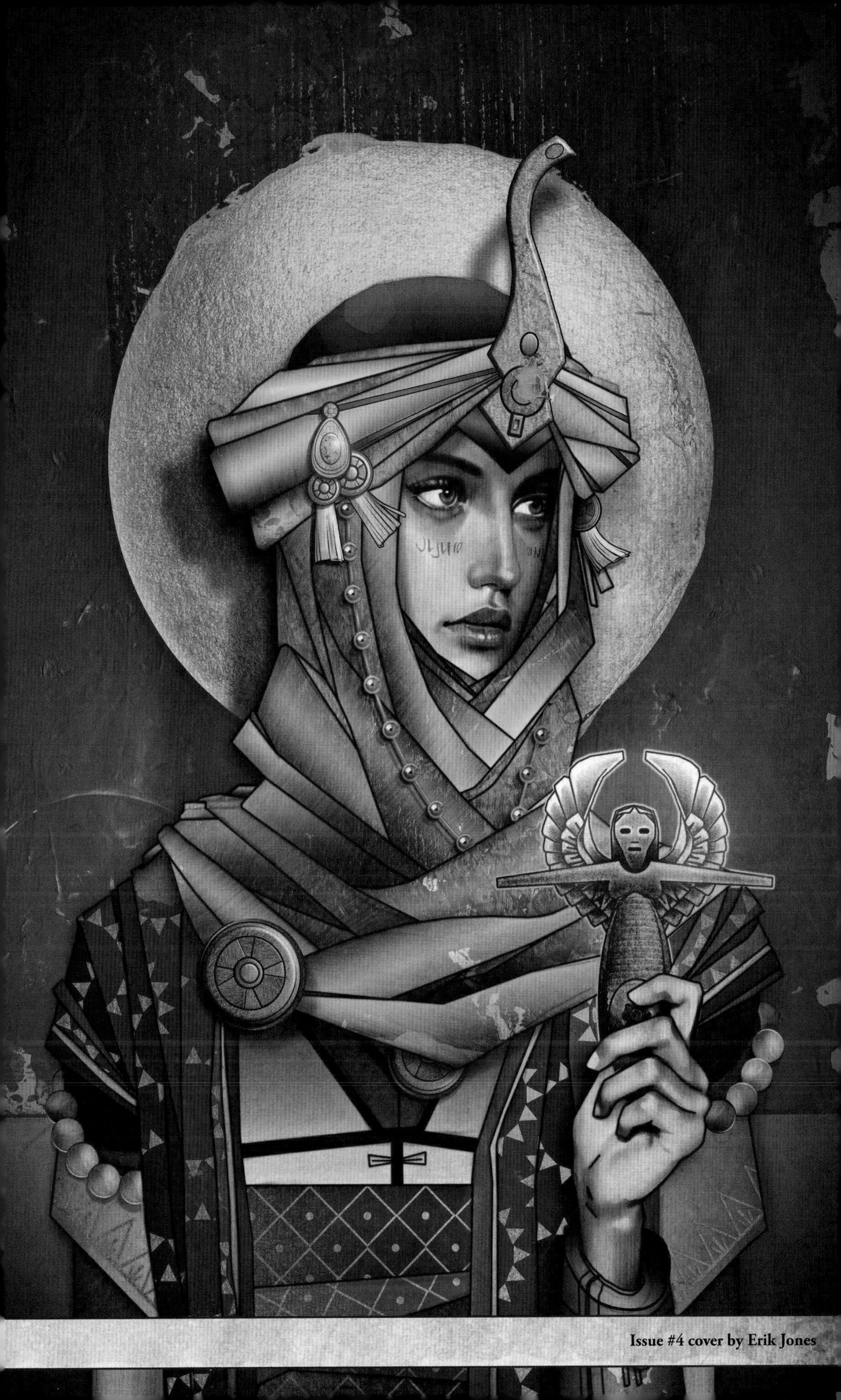

Issue #4 cover by Erik Jones

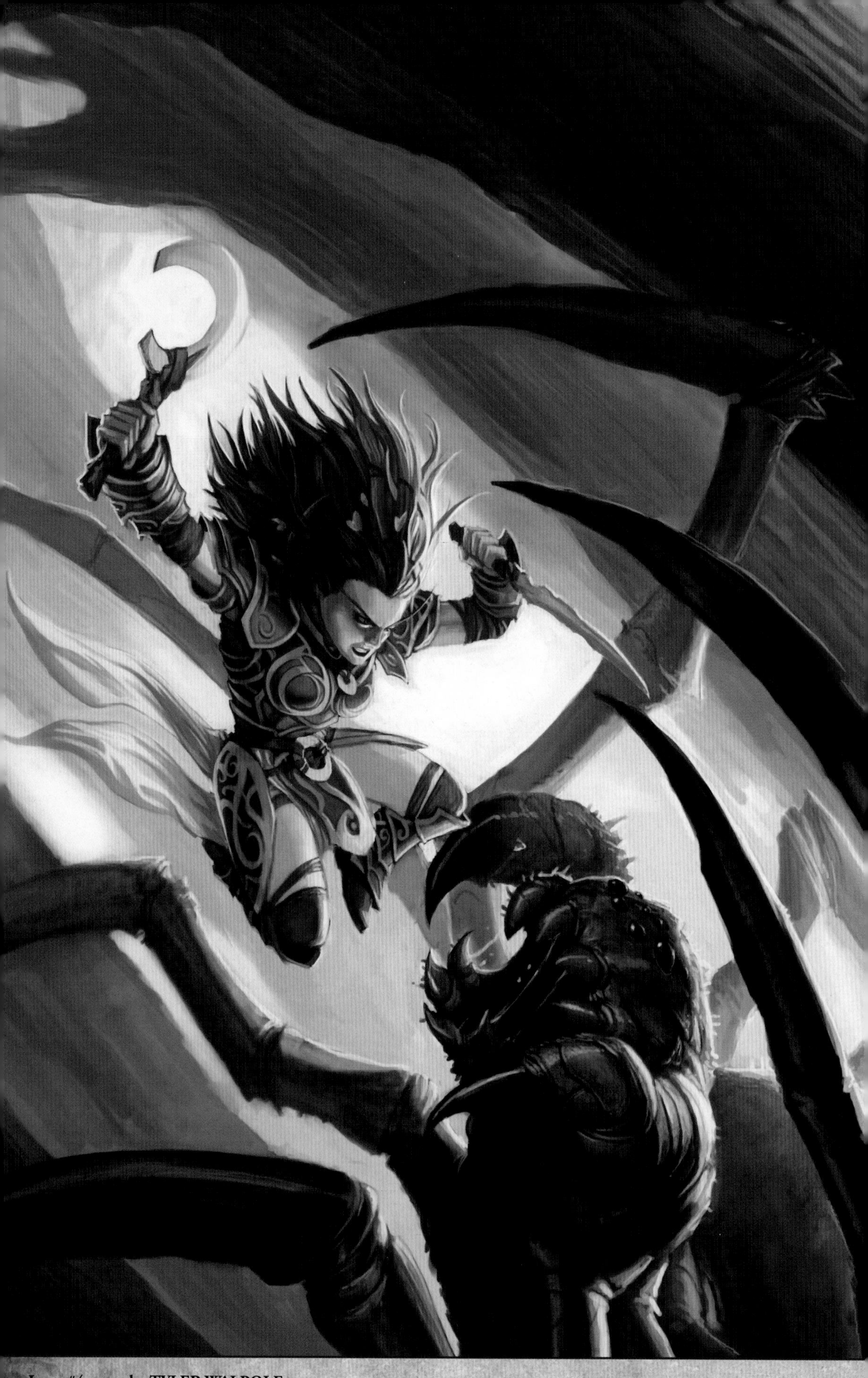

Issue #4 cover by TYLER WALPOLE

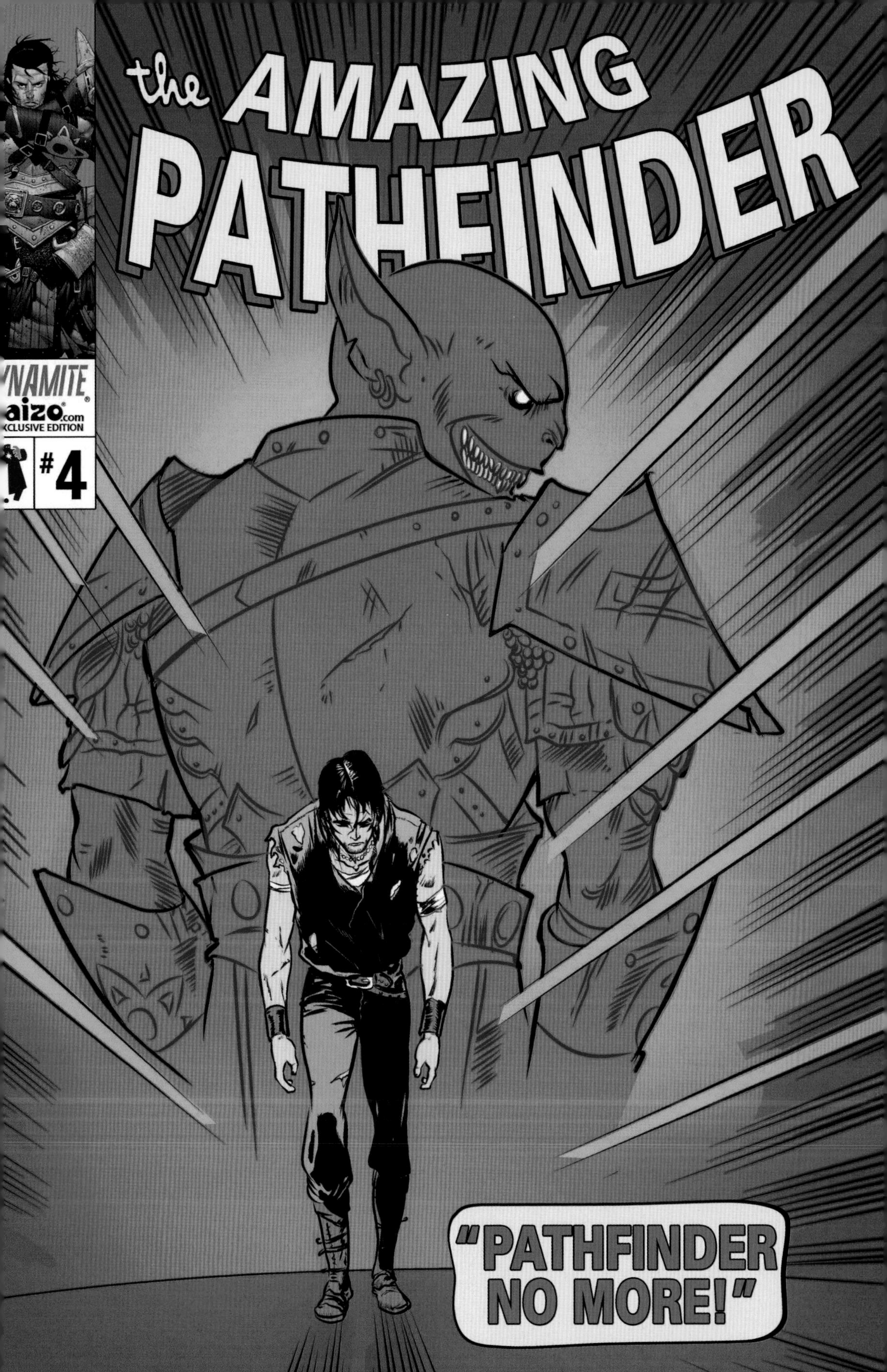
the AMAZING
PATHFINDER
DYNAMITE
paizo.com
EXCLUSIVE EDITION
#4
"PATHFINDER NO MORE!"

Issue #4 Paizo.com exclusive cover by JORGE FARAS

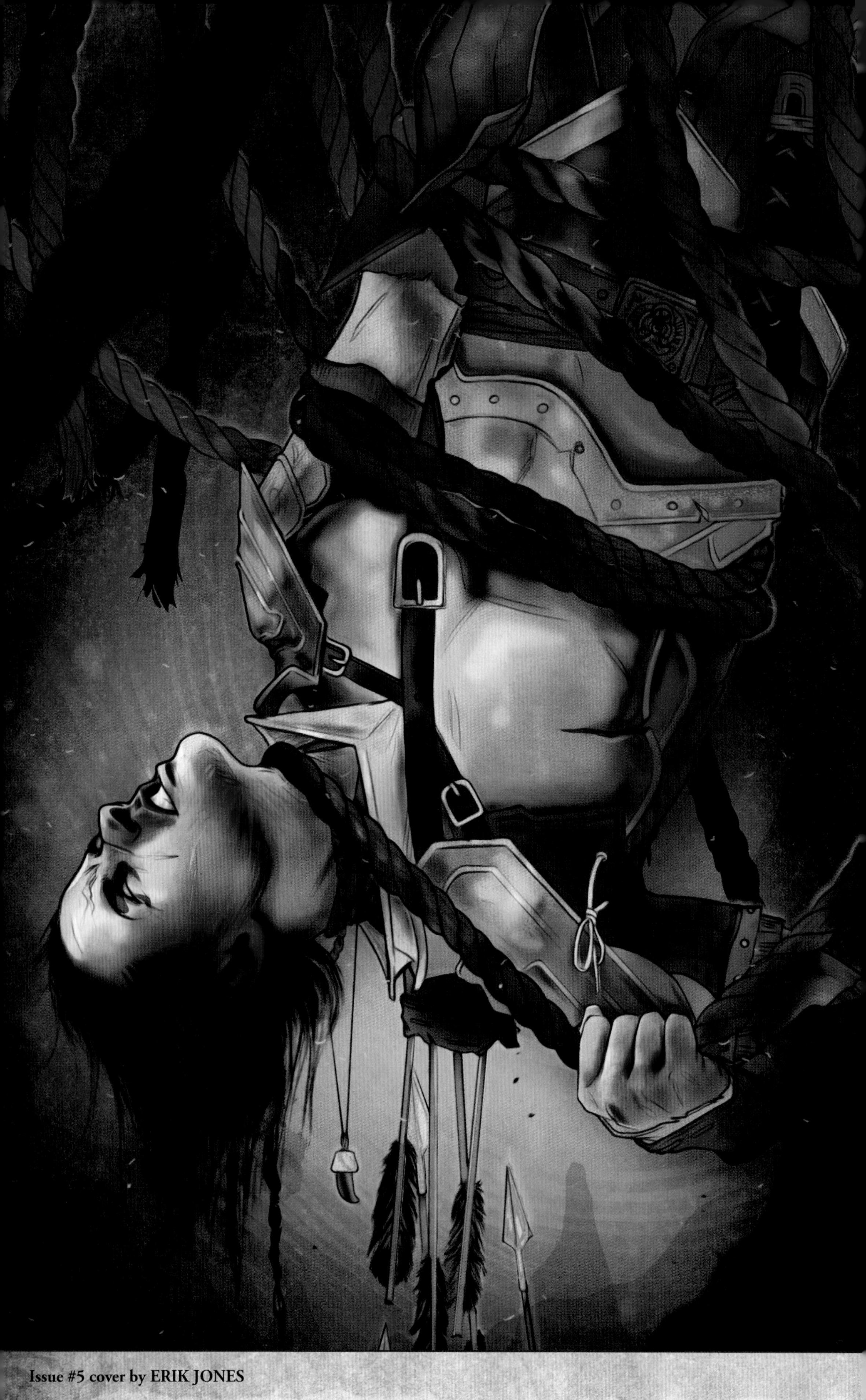

Issue #5 cover by ERIK JONES

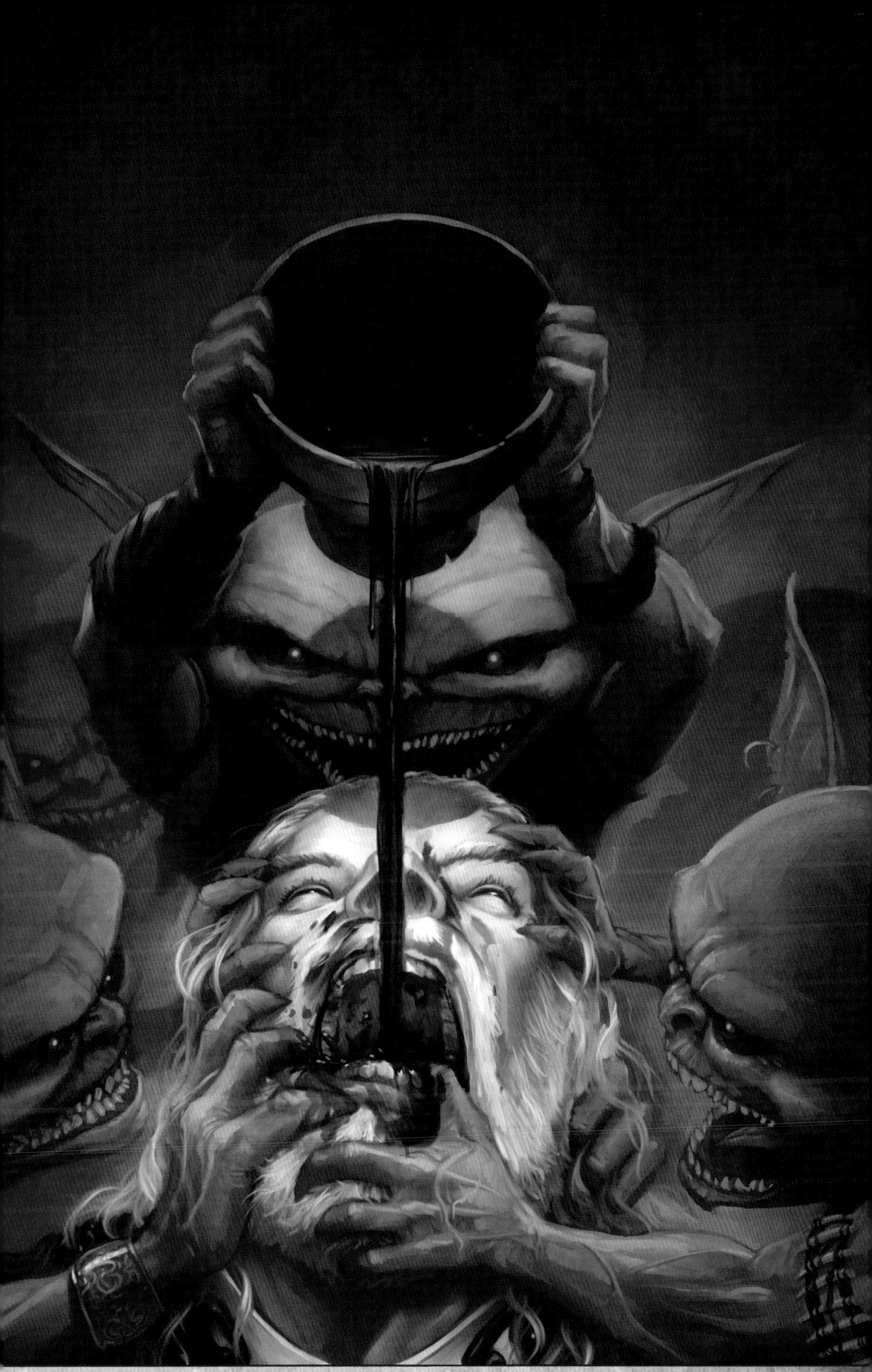

Issue #5 cover by TYLER WALPOLE

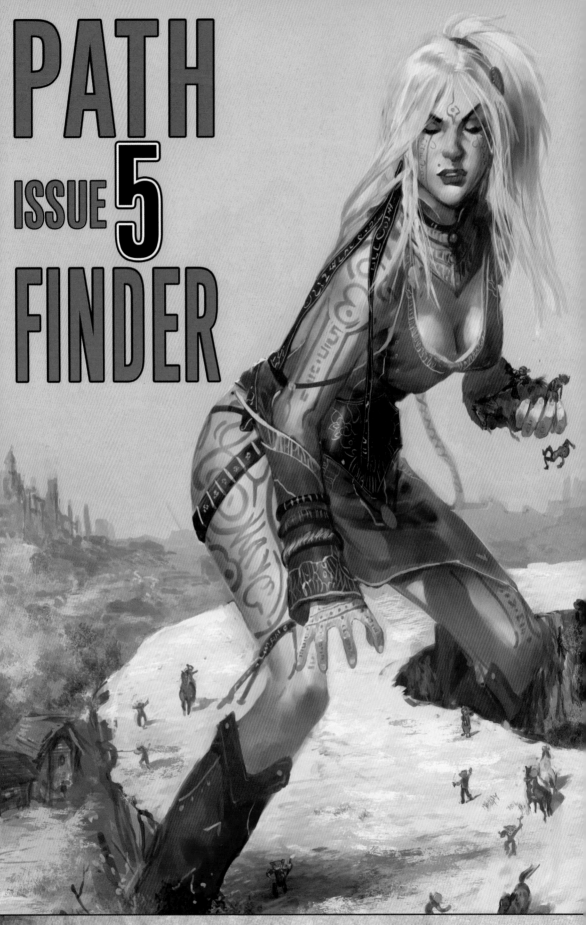

PATH

ISSUE 5

FINDER

Issue #5 Paizo.com exclusive cover by JORGE FARAS

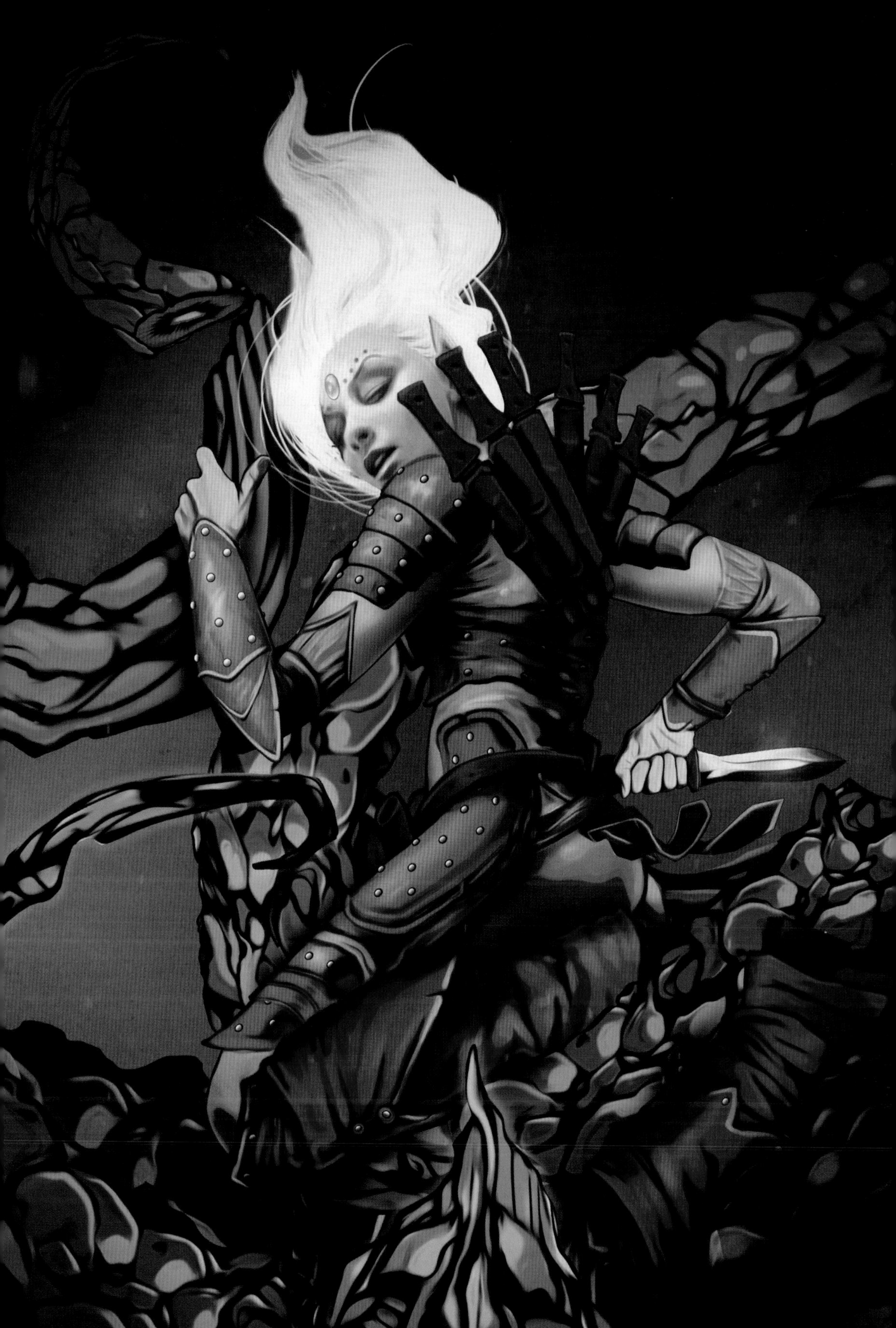

Issue #6 cover by ERIK JONES

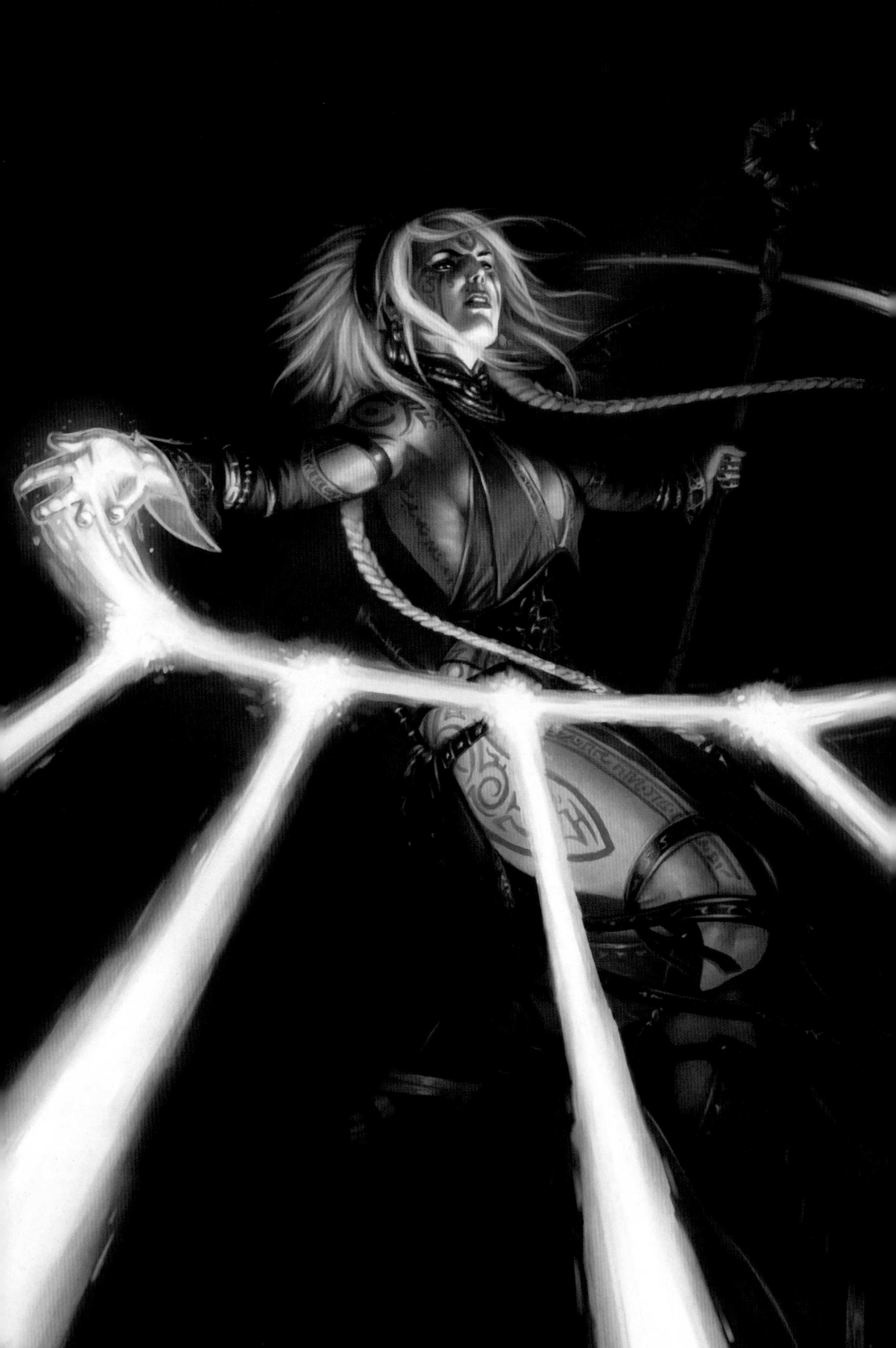

Issue #6 cover by TYLER WALPOLE

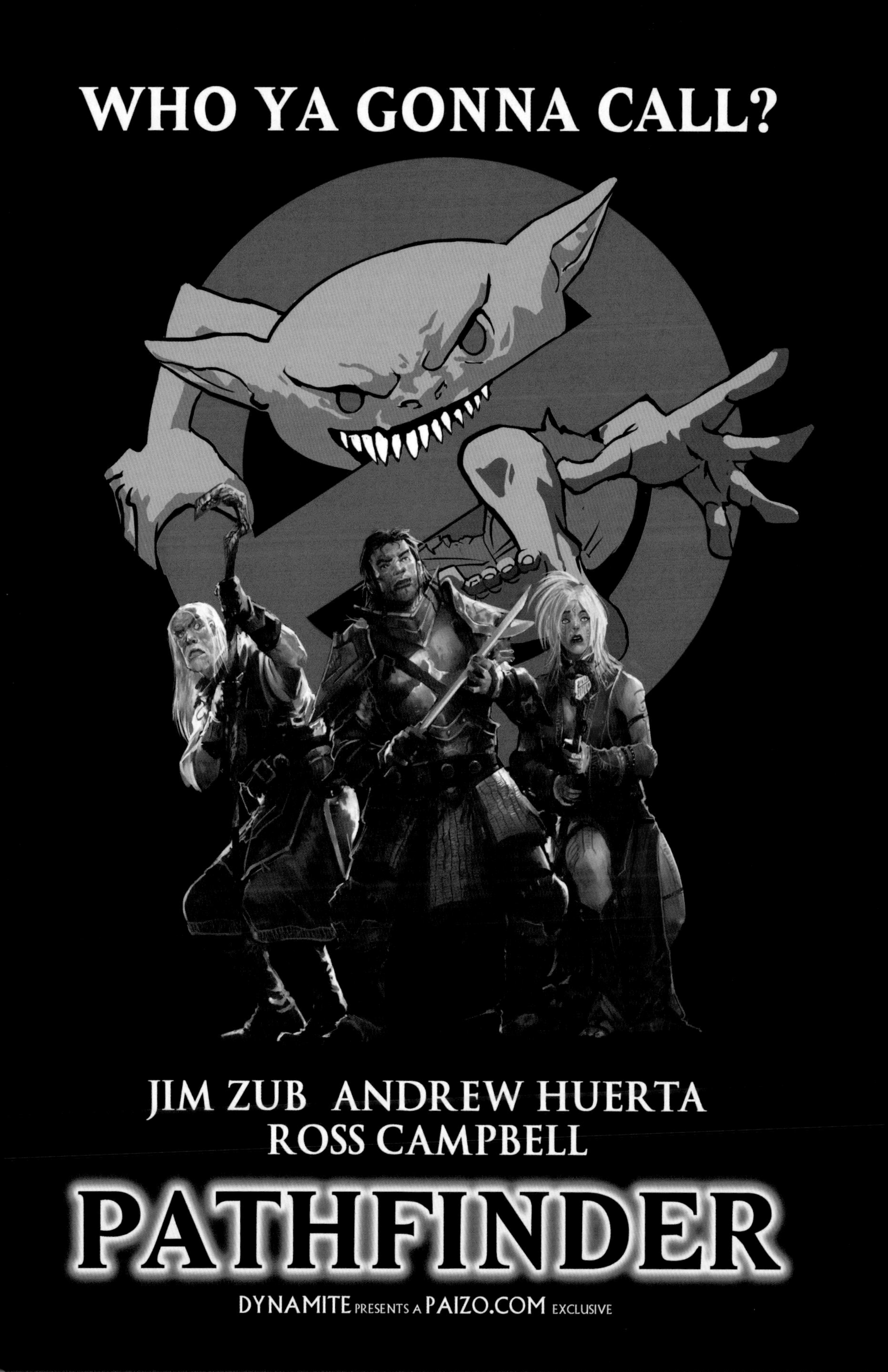
WHO YA GONNA CALL?
JIM ZUB ANDREW HUERTA
ROSS CAMPBELL
PATHFINDER
DYNAMITE PRESENTS A PAIZO.COM EXCLUSIVE

Issue #6 Paizo.com exclusive cover by JORGE FARAS

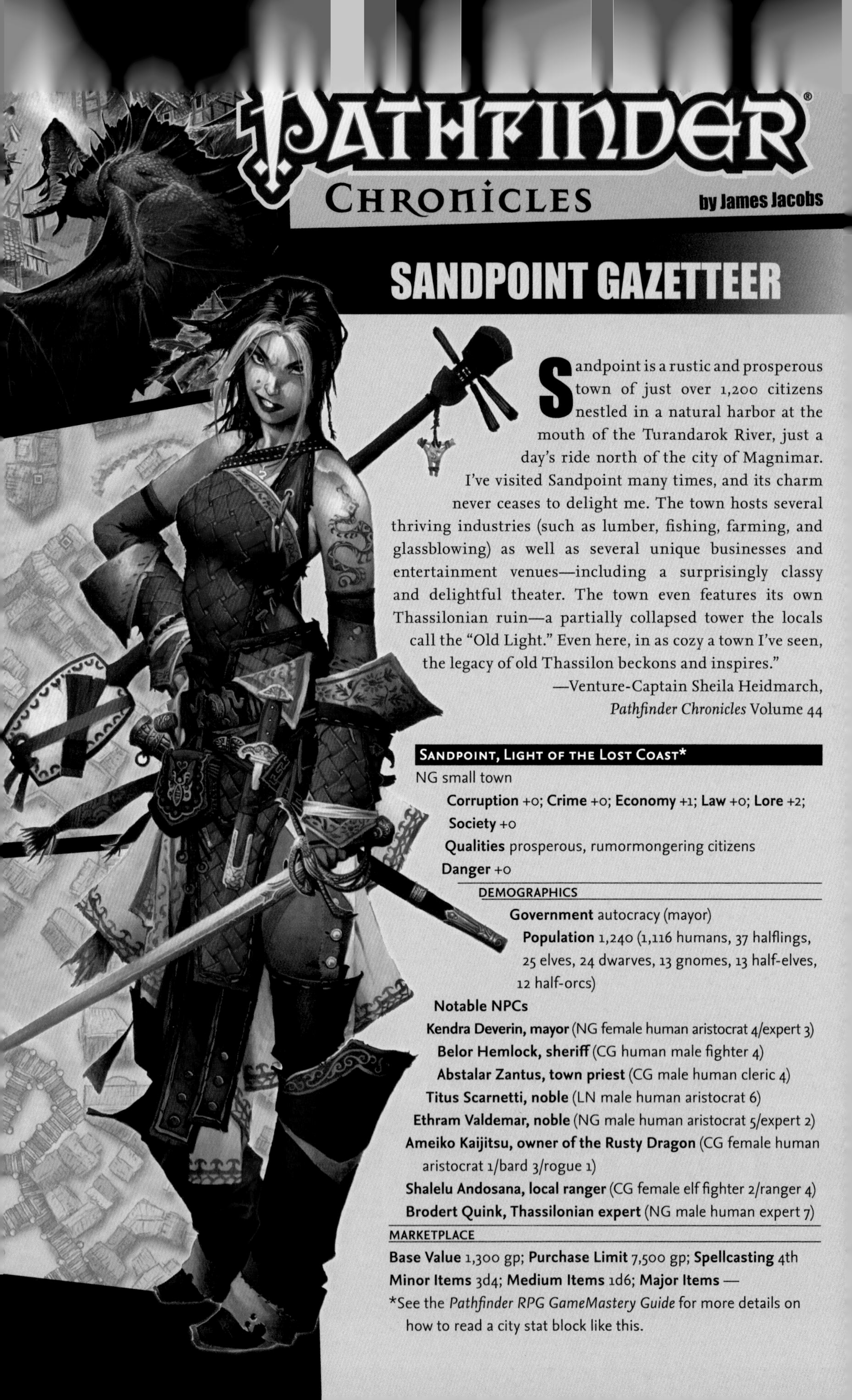

Pathfinder® Chronicles

by James Jacobs

SANDPOINT GAZETTEER

"Sandpoint is a rustic and prosperous town of just over 1,200 citizens nestled in a natural harbor at the mouth of the Turandarok River, just a day's ride north of the city of Magnimar. I've visited Sandpoint many times, and its charm never ceases to delight me. The town hosts several thriving industries (such as lumber, fishing, farming, and glassblowing) as well as several unique businesses and entertainment venues—including a surprisingly classy and delightful theater. The town even features its own Thassilonian ruin—a partially collapsed tower the locals call the "Old Light." Even here, in as cozy a town I've seen, the legacy of old Thassilon beckons and inspires."

—Venture-Captain Sheila Heidmarch,
Pathfinder Chronicles Volume 44

SANDPOINT, LIGHT OF THE LOST COAST*

NG small town

Corruption +0; **Crime** +0; **Economy** +1; **Law** +0; **Lore** +2; **Society** +0

Qualities prosperous, rumormongering citizens

Danger +0

DEMOGRAPHICS

Government autocracy (mayor)

Population 1,240 (1,116 humans, 37 halflings, 25 elves, 24 dwarves, 13 gnomes, 13 half-elves, 12 half-orcs)

Notable NPCs

Kendra Deverin, mayor (NG female human aristocrat 4/expert 3)

Belor Hemlock, sheriff (CG human male fighter 4)

Abstalar Zantus, town priest (CG male human cleric 4)

Titus Scarnetti, noble (LN male human aristocrat 6)

Ethram Valdemar, noble (NG male human aristocrat 5/expert 2)

Ameiko Kaijitsu, owner of the Rusty Dragon (CG female human aristocrat 1/bard 3/rogue 1)

Shalelu Andosana, local ranger (CG female elf fighter 2/ranger 4)

Brodert Quink, Thassilonian expert (NG male human expert 7)

MARKETPLACE

Base Value 1,300 gp; **Purchase Limit** 7,500 gp; **Spellcasting** 4th

Minor Items 3d4; **Medium Items** 1d6; **Major Items** —

*See the *Pathfinder RPG GameMastery Guide* for more details on how to read a city stat block like this.

CRIME AND JUSTICE

Justice and safety in Sandpoint are the responsibility of the town guard, who maintain a presence in the middle of town in a stone garrison built above a small but serviceable prison. The town boasts a dozen full-time guards; these guards patrol the city alone, but with generally not much more than a drunk or a treed cat to worry about, only a few are in service at any one time. The guards are led by Sheriff Belor Hemlock, a man who takes his job quite seriously. He understands the value adventurers bring to town as much as he anticipates the trouble they can cause, and prefers to get on their good side as soon as possible. When a new party of adventurers arrives in town, Sheriff Hemlock makes sure to pay them a visit within the day to pleasantly inquire as to what brings them to town, to guide them toward places where their services may be needed (see Adventure Hooks), and to subtly remind them that while they're in town, they need to be on their best behavior.

Despite the small-town sensibilities, Sandpoint is no stranger to crime. Most of the criminal activity in town is relatively minor, constrained to activities like smuggling, trade of illegal goods, banditry, graverobbing, and pickpocketing. These activities are in large part the domain of the Sczarni, a band of Varisians more interested in profiting off of society than being part of it. The Sczarni are quite adept at covering their tracks and each other—everyone suspects that Jubrayl Vhiski, a regular at **Fatman's Feedbag** who doesn't seem to have any real job or constant source of income, is the leader of Sandpoint's Sczarni, but he and his followers are so adept at walking the line between legalities and shifting blame that Jubrayl's stayed (mostly) out of jail for all the years he's lived in Sandpoint.

Violent crime happens now and then in Sandpoint, but not that often—and when murders do occur, they're usually the result of sudden passions fueled by jealousy or pride. Even then, these slayings are more often accidents than deliberate malevolence. However, this was not the case during the so-called "Late Unpleasantness," a dark time in Sandpoint's recent history when an eccentric artist the town trusted fell under the influence of dark spirits and murdered 26 people before he was tracked down and slain himself by Belor Hemlock. People still whisper stories of the murderer, remembered now as "Chopper," and tales of the crazed maniac still haunt the dreams of those who lived through that dark time.

SHOPPING IN SANDPOINT

At a mere 1,200 or so citizens, Sandpoint is hardly the sprawling metropolis of a city that nearby Magnimar to the south is, yet it's the largest town in about a 50-mile radius. Trade is brisk in Sandpoint, and any of the typical comforts and necessities of urban life can be had. There are even shops that sell weapons, armor, and magical curios, although their selections tend to be somewhat limited. Maps, jewelry, baked goods, clothing, books, and general goods can be found in many shops, and a twice-weekly farmer's market brings fresh produce and goods all the way from Magnimar. **Savah's Armory** is the best place in town to go for high-quality weapons and armor, although Savah's selection tends to be a bit random. Local smith Das Korvut mostly makes tools, but given time can produce fine armor as well. Both the **Pillbug's Pantry** and **Bottled Solutions** sell potions and tonics—with the Pantry being the place to go if what you're looking for is something of a less legal mixture.

And finally, the **Feathered Serpent** is a cluttered curio shop that often sells magical items and strange trinkets.

Injured adventurers often visit herbalist Hanna Velerin if what ails them doesn't require

WELCOME TO SANDPOINT

"PLEASE STOP TO SEE YOURSELF AS WE SEE YOU"

SANDPOINT

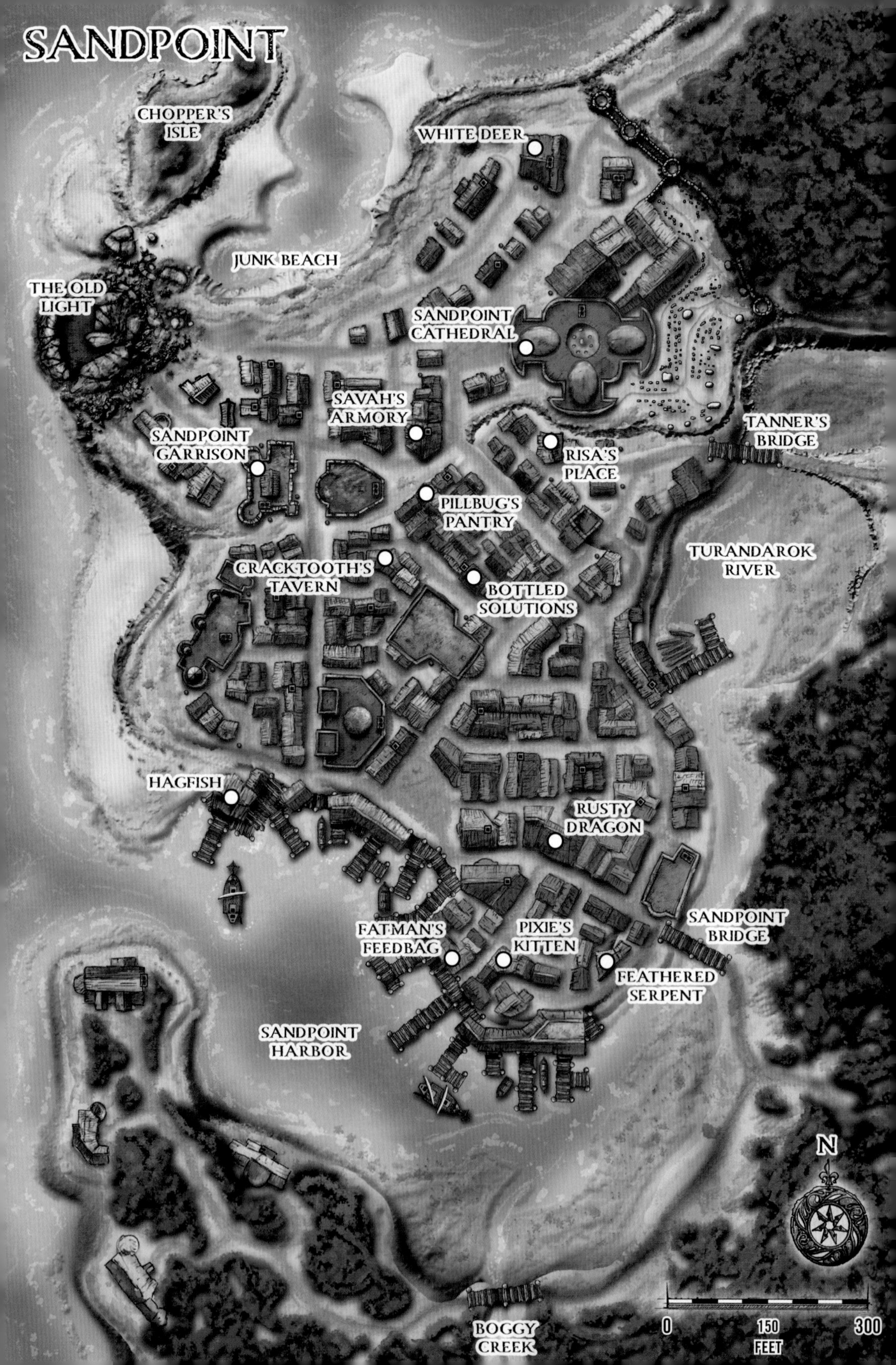
CHOPPER'S ISLE
WHITE DEER
JUNK BEACH
THE OLD LIGHT
SANDPOINT CATHEDRAL
SAVAH'S ARMORY
SANDPOINT GARRISON
TANNER'S BRIDGE
RISA'S PLACE
PILLBUG'S PANTRY
CRACKTOOTH'S TAVERN
TURANDAROK RIVER
BOTTLED SOLUTIONS
HAGFISH
RUSTY DRAGON
SANDPOINT BRIDGE
FATMAN'S FEEDBAG
PIXIE'S KITTEN
FEATHERED SERPENT
SANDPOINT HARBOR
N
0
150
300
FEET
BOGGY CREEK

immediate care, but the **Sandpoint Cathedral** is the best place to go for healing. Tended by Father Abstalar Zantus, a cleric of Desna, the Sandpoint Cathedral is a pantheistic temple that contains shrines to Abadar, Desna, Erastil, Gozreh, Sarenrae, and Shelyn (deities of merchants, luck, hunters, nature, the sun, and beauty, respectively). On a general day, Zantus and his four acolytes can provide healing via spells or channeled energy. Donations in thanks for healing provided (typically 40 gp for *cure light wounds*, twice that for *cure moderate wounds*, and 20 gp per person for channeled energy) are welcome but not required—Zantus generally doesn't charge for healing save for when he has to use a non-renewable resource like a scroll or potion.

Sandpoint offers several places to relax and spend the night, from taverns to inns and even a brothel. The **White Deer** and the **Rusty Dragon** are Sandpoint's two inns—they have comparable prices, but the Rusty Dragon specifically caters to adventurers, and its owner Ameiko (see illustration at the start of this gazetteer) has been known to offer discount rates to adventurers in return for entertaining tales of their escapades (see Adventure Hooks). For taverns and eateries, the visitor can choose between **Risa's Place** (specializes in potato dishes, cider, and stories; particularly valued by the locals since this place isn't well known by visitors), **Cracktooth's Tavern** (specializes in amateur entertainments, ale, and crunchy snacks), the **Hagfish** (specializes in seafood, gambling, and boasting), the **Rusty Dragon** (specializes in spicy and exotic dishes, mead, and adventurers), and **Fatman's Feedbag** (specializes in enormous servings of mediocre food, rum, bar fights, and, for the unprepared out-of-towner, pickpocketing). The **Pixie's Kitten** is Sandpoint's only brothel, but it's run with a sense of style and panache that the rural environs might not suggest.

ADVENTURE HOOKS

Although Sandpoint is a sleepy, relatively safe rural town, there is no shortage of adventure opportunities to be found within the city or in its hinterlands. While several of the town's older and more traditional citizens think of adventurers as little more than rabble-rousers who attract trouble like a lodestone attracts metal, others welcome adventurers with open arms. The **Rusty Dragon**, owned and run by an ex-adventurer named Ameiko Kaijitsu, is perhaps the most popular stop in town for visiting adventurers. Not only does the tavern offer affordable and delicious meals and comfortable rooms, but Ameiko openly encourages adventurers as patrons by keeping a "Help Wanted" board posted with opportunities to help locals with possibly dangerous tasks, and by offering hefty discounts (half the regular price) to anyone who entertains the common room's patrons (and the staff, of course!) with a well-told tale of adventure and mayhem.

Strange Sounds on Junk Beach

Junk Beach has long served Sandpoint as a public dumping ground for refuse and garbage—and as such has also served the Seven Tooth goblins of Shank's Wood as scavenging grounds. See the Pathfinder Roleplaying Game encounter later in this section for more details on this adventure hook.

Awakening the Old Light

The **Old Light** is certainly the first thing most travelers notice as they approach Sandpoint. The Old Light looms atop the town's highest promontory, looking out over the sea. Local legend holds that the circular stone ruin was once an lighthouse from the runelords' ancient empire of Thassilon; some scholars estimate that the light may have once stood as high as 700 feet, given the girth of its remaining

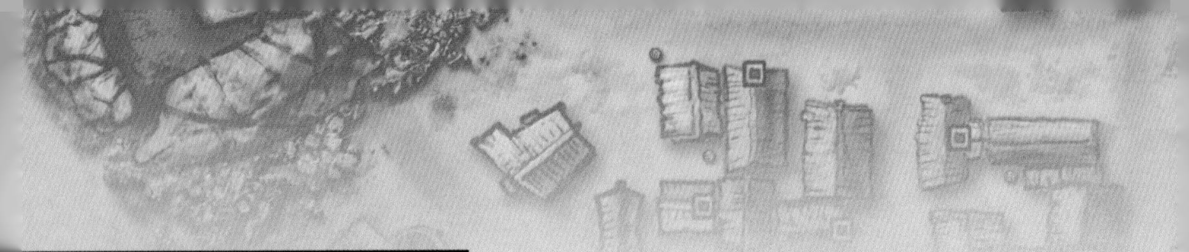

Sheriff Belor Hemlock

Belor Hemlock became the sheriff of Sandpoint not long after the previous sheriff was murdered by Chopper. Belor is a Shoanti, but has abandoned most of the tribal ways of the Hawk Clan to fully integrate with Sandpoint's society—an act his brother Garridan Viskalai does not approve of. Belor is stern and to the point, but also possesses a strong sense of justice and fairness.

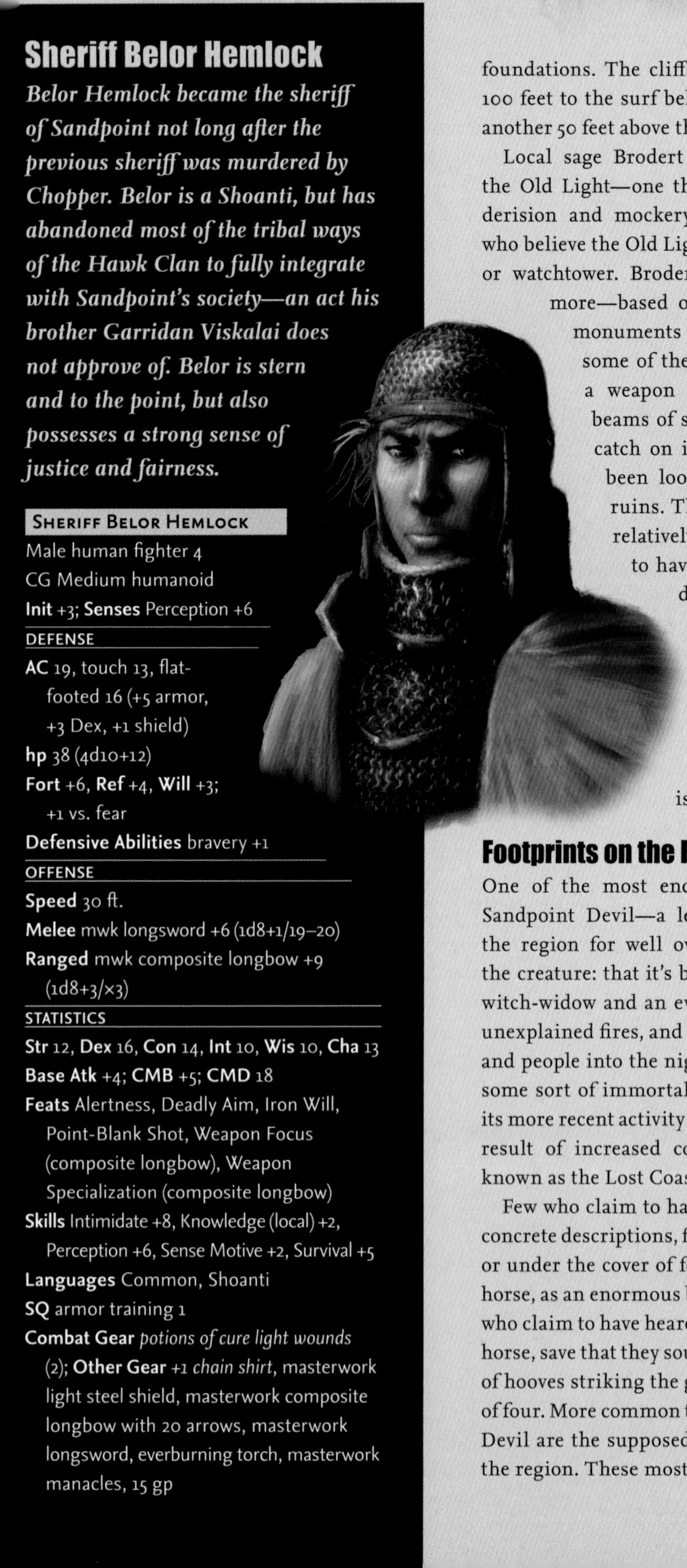

SHERIFF BELOR HEMLOCK

Male human fighter 4
CG Medium humanoid
Init +3; **Senses** Perception +6

DEFENSE

AC 19, touch 13, flat-footed 16 (+5 armor, +3 Dex, +1 shield)
hp 38 (4d10+12)
Fort +6, **Ref** +4, **Will** +3; +1 vs. fear
Defensive Abilities bravery +1

OFFENSE

Speed 30 ft.
Melee mwk longsword +6 (1d8+1/19–20)
Ranged mwk composite longbow +9 (1d8+3/×3)

STATISTICS

Str 12, **Dex** 16, **Con** 14, **Int** 10, **Wis** 10, **Cha** 13
Base Atk +4; **CMB** +5; **CMD** 18
Feats Alertness, Deadly Aim, Iron Will, Point-Blank Shot, Weapon Focus (composite longbow), Weapon Specialization (composite longbow)
Skills Intimidate +8, Knowledge (local) +2, Perception +6, Sense Motive +2, Survival +5
Languages Common, Shoanti
SQ armor training 1
Combat Gear *potions of cure light wounds* (2); **Other Gear** *+1 chain shirt*, masterwork light steel shield, masterwork composite longbow with 20 arrows, masterwork longsword, everburning torch, masterwork manacles, 15 gp

foundations. The cliffs below these foundations drop over 100 feet to the surf below, with the ruined tower extending another 50 feet above that, making for a dramatic landmark.

Local sage Brodert Quink has a strange theory about the Old Light—one that's brought him more than a little derision and mockery from other Thassilonian scholars who believe the Old Light to have been an ancient lighthouse or watchtower. Brodert believes the ruin was something more—based on his studies of other Thassilonian monuments and examinations of faint runes on some of the light's stones, he thinks it was once a weapon capable of emitting not light, but beams of scouring fire. His theories have yet to catch on in Magnimar, and as such, Brodert's been looking for adventurers to explore the ruins. The above-ground chambers have been relatively picked over, but the old sage claims to have located what may be a magical trap door in one of the lower chambers in the Old Light—one that he believes can be opened by an application of magical flame to an ancient set of runes, just as a key applied to a lock can open a door. What lies in the theoretical chambers below the ruin is anyone's guess.

Footprints on the Roof

One of the most enduring local legends is that of the Sandpoint Devil—a legendary monster that has haunted the region for well over a decade. Rumors abound about the creature: that it's bad luck to see it, that it's the son of a witch-widow and an evil spirit, that it's behind any and all unexplained fires, and that it's carried off countless livestock and people into the night sky. Some legends even paint it as some sort of immortal protector of the region, and suggest its more recent activity has skewed toward violence as a direct result of increased colonization of the once-wild region known as the Lost Coast.

Few who claim to have seen the Sandpoint Devil can offer concrete descriptions, for the monster always appears at night or under the cover of fog. It has been described as a strange horse, as an enormous bat, and as a saurian behemoth. Those who claim to have heard it say its footsteps clop like those of a horse, save that they sound strangely sparse—as if the sounds of hooves striking the ground were made by two feet instead of four. More common than actual sightings of the Sandpoint Devil are the supposed signs it leaves behind when it visits the region. These most often consist of deep, hooflike prints

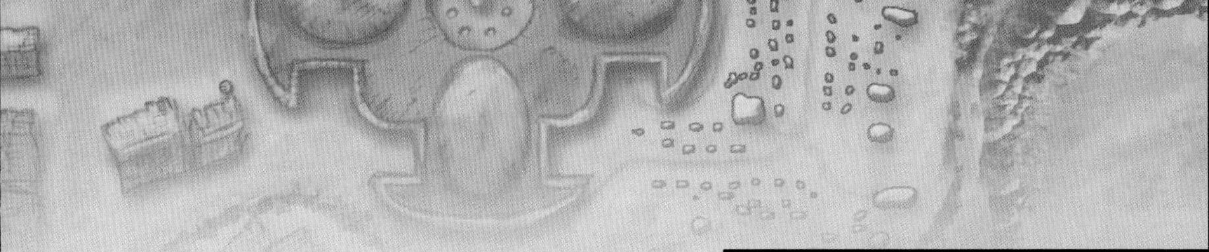

carved or even burned into places no hoof prints should be found, such as on the tops of high roofs, on the decks of ships found adrift at sea, or etched into the sides of cliffs. The Devil is also routinely blamed for missing livestock and strange illnesses. These latter claims hold greater credence in cases where remains of lost livestock have been found, invariably far from the farm and appearing to be partially burnt, gnawed by wolves, or tangled in the high boughs of a tree as if dropped from a great height.

As more people come to dwell in or visit Sandpoint, the mystery of the Sandpoint Devil is spreading. So-called "Devil Hunters" are growing more and more common, and even hoaxes perpetrated by people desperate for attention have begun to spread. Whether the Devil is real or not, the impact of its legend on the land is irrefutable.

The Ghost of Chopper's Isle

Before he was revealed to be a murderer, Jervis Stoot was an eccentric local man whose talent for carving the most lifelike and wonderful images of birds from blocks of wood. "Sporting a Stoot" meant that your home or shop had been chosen by Jervis as a subject for his art. Today, the carved birds have been cut away from storefronts and stoops, for when the people of Sandpoint think of Jervis Stoot, they recall him not as a gifted artist, but as the murderer known as Chopper.

When Sheriff Hemlock (then merely a city guard) led the patrol to Stoot's home atop the small islet just north of town, they found the man dead by his own hand before an altar dedicated to a demonic bird of some strange sort strewn with the eyes and tongues of his victims. The sheriff had Stoot's body burned and his ashes blessed by Father Zantus, and then scattered those ashes at sea, but that hasn't slowed tales that Chopper's Isle is haunted.

It's been several years now, and children who were barely old enough to understand what was happening during the Late Unpleasantness are now old enough to dare each other to climb the sea cliffs to spend the night in the burnt-out shell of Chopper's shack. Few children follow through with these dares, though, since stories of strange lights and unusually large flocks of birds gathering atop the isle persist to this day. Sheriff Hemlock has little to say on the subject, but rumor has it that he's quietly looking for a brave group of adventurers to climb up to investigate the ruins, and the strange stone chambers within the rock itself, to determine whether the ghost of Chopper has come back to haunt Sandpoint.

Father Abstalar Zantus

Caretaker of the Sandpoint Cathedral, Father Zantus serves as the town's moral compass.

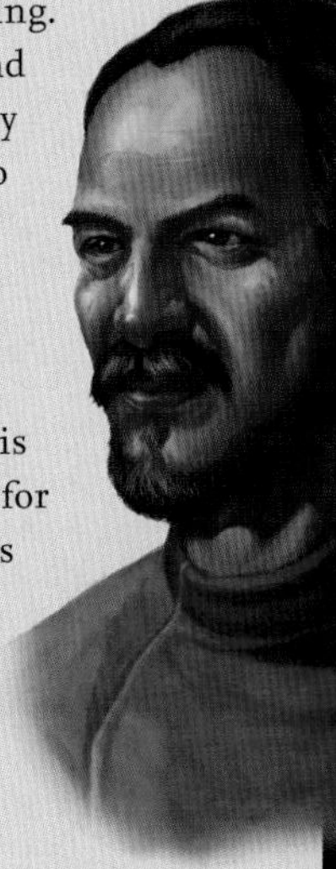

FATHER ABSTALAR ZANTUS

Male human cleric of Desna 4
CG Medium humanoid
Init +1; **Senses** Perception +4

DEFENSE

AC 15, touch 11, flat-footed 14 (+4 armor, +1 Dex)
hp 25 (4d8+4)
Fort +5, **Ref** +2, **Will** +8

OFFENSE

Speed 30 ft.
Melee mwk starknife +5 (1d4–1/×3)
Ranged mwk starknife +5 (1d4–1/×3)
Special Attacks channel positive energy 7/day (DC 14, 2d6)
Domain Spell-Like Abilities (CL 4th; concentration +8)
7/day—bit of luck, touch of good (+2)
Cleric Spells Prepared (CL 4th; concentration +8)
2nd—*aid*[D], *hold person* (DC 16), *lesser restoration, spiritual weapon*
1st—*command* (DC 15), *divine favor, protection from evil*[D], *sanctuary* (DC 15), *shield of faith*
0 (at will)—*detect magic, light, mending, stabilize*
D Domain spell; **Domains** Good, Luck

STATISTICS

Str 8, **Dex** 12, **Con** 13, **Int** 10, **Wis** 18, **Cha** 14
Base Atk +3; **CMB** +2; **CMD** 13
Feats Brew Potion, Extra Channel, Weapon Finesse
Skills Diplomacy +9, Heal +10, Knowledge (arcana) +4, Knowledge (religion) +7, Spellcraft +7
Languages Common, Varisian
Combat Gear *scrolls of cure light wounds* (2), *scrolls of remove disease* (2); **Other Gear** *+1 studded leather*, masterwork starknife, healer's kit, silver holy symbol of Desna, spell component pouch, 21 gp

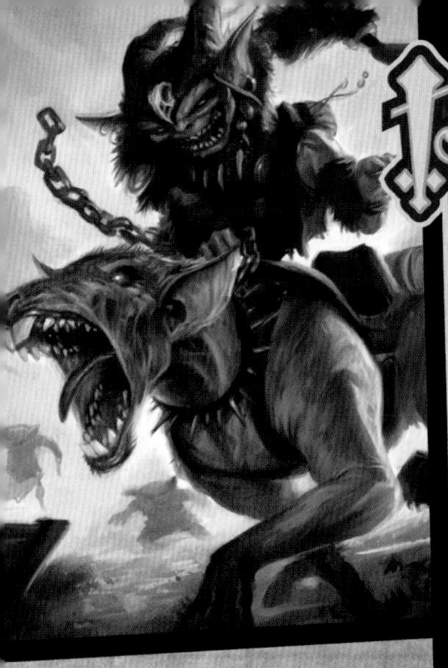

JUNK BEACH

The surging waters of the Varisian Gulf serve Sandpoint in many ways—they keep the town connected to other ports, they provide fishing vessels with their bounty, and they inspire the minds of artists and poets alike. But they also serve a more specialized purpose—they take away the filth and refuse of the city after it's tossed off the northern bluff onto the stained sands of Junk Beach.

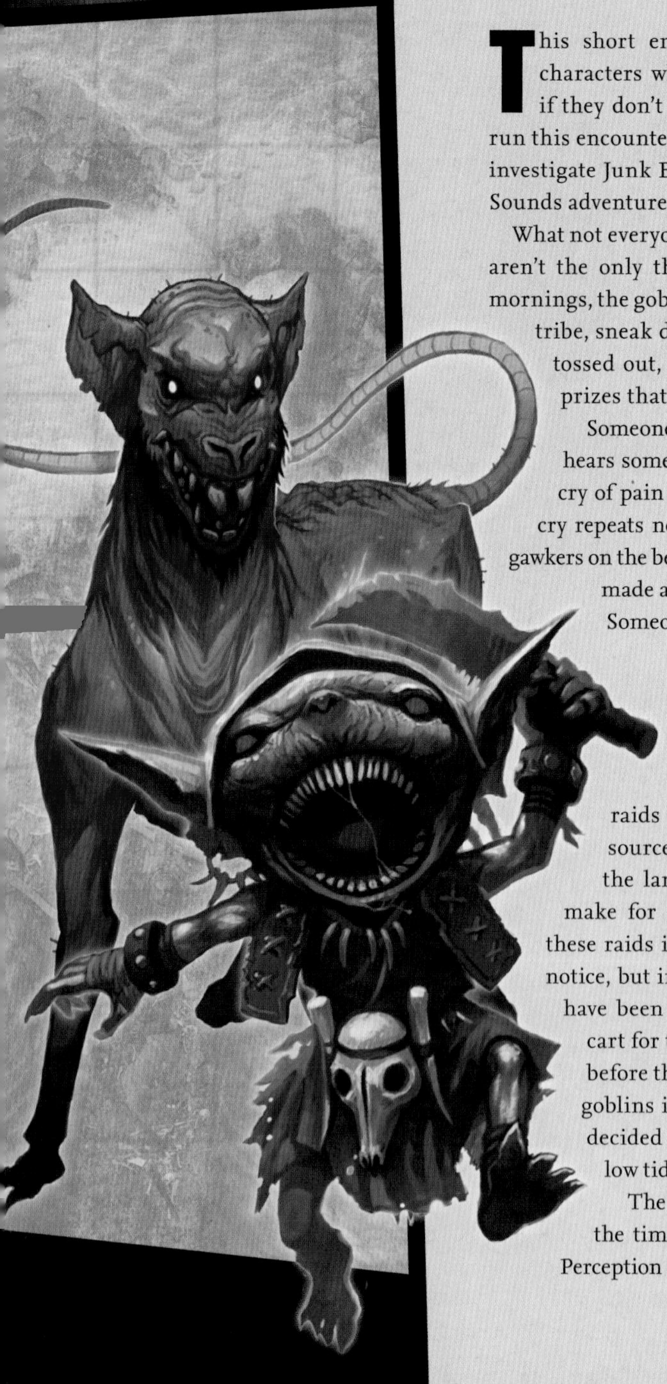

This short encounter works best for a group of 1st-level characters who are well rested and ready for a fight—even if they don't realize the peril they're heading into. You can run this encounter whenever the player characters (PCs) decide to investigate Junk Beach on their own, or you can use the Strange Sounds adventure hook detailed in the "Sandpoint Gazetteer."

What not everyone in Sandpoint knows is that the ocean's waves aren't the only things that take away the garbage. On certain mornings, the goblins of Shank's Wood, known as the Seven Tooth tribe, sneak down the coast to sift through what Sandpoint's tossed out, searching for doubtful treasure and discarded prizes that only a goblin could desire.

Someone, either a player character or one of the townsfolk, hears something strange from Junk Beach—a high-pitched cry of pain that sounds not unlike that of a hurt child. The cry repeats now and then, and has gathered a large crowd of gawkers on the beach above, but no one can see the child, who hasn't made a noise since the tide came in several minutes ago. Someone needs to go down there and investigate!

GOBLINS ON THE BEACH (CR 3)

Raids on Junk Beach are often performed by goblins from the Seven Tooth tribe—these raids not only serve the goblins as their primary source of materials to build homes and weapons, but the large number of seagulls that frequent the place make for good hunting. The goblins normally perform these raids in the early dawn hours, when few are awake to notice, but in this case, a group of eager goblins happens to have been distracted trying to prepare a broken rubbish cart for transport back to the tribe, and the tide came in before they realized they were out of time. There are four goblins in all, along with a lone goblin dog, and they've decided to hide out near the cliff's edge and wait for the low tide at nightfall before they try to sneak back home.

The goblins and the goblin dog have fallen asleep by the time the PCs head down to the beach—allow them Perception checks (penalized by –10 due to their slumber) to

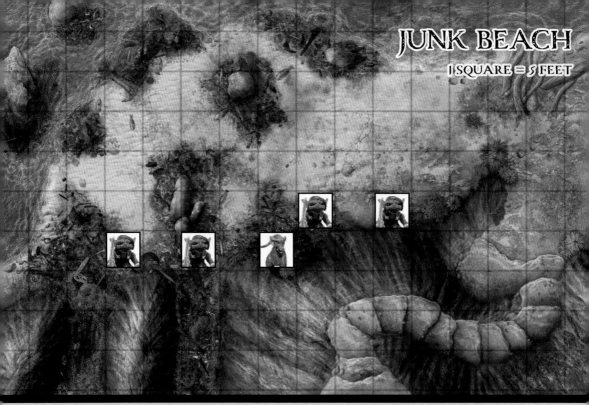

notice the PCs' approach. Likewise, the PCs can notice the snoring and murmuring of the goblins over the wash of the waves with a successful DC 10 Perception check.

	GOBLINS (4)	CR 1/3

XP 135 each
hp 6 each (*Pathfinder RPG Bestiary* 156)
Melee dogslicer +2 (1d4/19–20) or sharp piece of junk –2 (1d3)
Ranged rotted refuse +0 (1d2 plus DC 12 Fortitude save to avoid being sickened for 1d6 minutes)
Miniature *Pathfinder Battles Heroes & Monsters* 1

	GOBLIN DOG	CR 1

XP 400
hp 9 (*Pathfinder RPG Bestiary* 157)
Miniature *Pathfinder Battles Rise of the Runelords* 3

GOBLIN ANTICS

Goblins are easily distracted in battle. Each time a goblin attacks, roll on the following table to determine what sort of action it takes that round. A goblin that's taken any damage adds 2 to the roll.

d8 Roll	Action taken by goblin
1	Attacks nearest PC with thrown rotting fruit, dead fish, or something nastier
2	Attacks nearest PC with a sharp piece of junk
3	Attacks nearest PC with a dogslicer
4	Tries to bull rush a PC into a pile of broken glass and jagged bits of wood (if it's successful, the PC must succeed at a DC 12 Reflex save to avoid taking 1d6 points of damage)
5	Distracts another goblin by laughing at him, throwing sand, or simply by having something yummy looking in its hand (like a half-eaten pickle)
6	Tries to climb onto a rock or a pile of junk in order to leap down onto a nearby PC (the goblin must make a DC 10 Climb check—if successful, he gains a +1 bonus on the attack for being on higher ground)
7	Gets distracted by something shiny in the sand or in the junk
8 or higher	Shrieks in panic and runs away

TREASURE

If the PCs are here to recover the brass spyglass, it's been recovered already and is being used as a weapon by one of the goblins. The goblins have also found several other choice bits of "loot" that they've gathered in a large, nasty-smelling burlap sack near their campsite. An investigation of this treasure reveals 23 gp, 29 sp, a filthy but functional hand crossbow, a copper necklace worth 50 gp, and an awful lot of legitimate garbage.

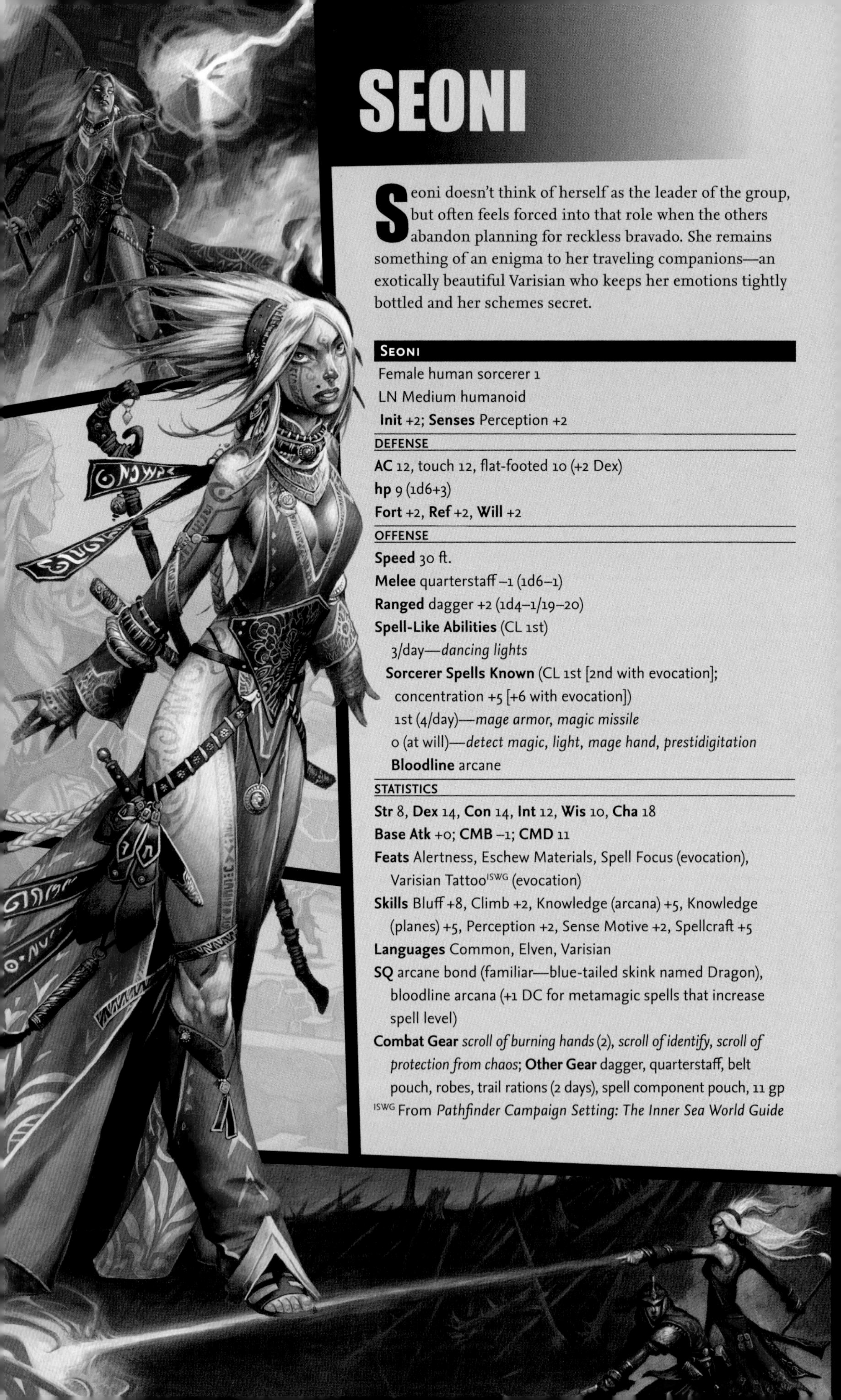

SEONI

Seoni doesn't think of herself as the leader of the group, but often feels forced into that role when the others abandon planning for reckless bravado. She remains something of an enigma to her traveling companions—an exotically beautiful Varisian who keeps her emotions tightly bottled and her schemes secret.

SEONI

Female human sorcerer 1

LN Medium humanoid

Init +2; **Senses** Perception +2

DEFENSE

AC 12, touch 12, flat-footed 10 (+2 Dex)

hp 9 (1d6+3)

Fort +2, **Ref** +2, **Will** +2

OFFENSE

Speed 30 ft.

Melee quarterstaff –1 (1d6–1)

Ranged dagger +2 (1d4–1/19–20)

Spell-Like Abilities (CL 1st)

3/day—*dancing lights*

Sorcerer Spells Known (CL 1st [2nd with evocation]; concentration +5 [+6 with evocation])

1st (4/day)—*mage armor, magic missile*

0 (at will)—*detect magic, light, mage hand, prestidigitation*

Bloodline arcane

STATISTICS

Str 8, **Dex** 14, **Con** 14, **Int** 12, **Wis** 10, **Cha** 18

Base Atk +0; **CMB** –1; **CMD** 11

Feats Alertness, Eschew Materials, Spell Focus (evocation), Varisian Tattoo[ISWG] (evocation)

Skills Bluff +8, Climb +2, Knowledge (arcana) +5, Knowledge (planes) +5, Perception +2, Sense Motive +2, Spellcraft +5

Languages Common, Elven, Varisian

SQ arcane bond (familiar—blue-tailed skink named Dragon), bloodline arcana (+1 DC for metamagic spells that increase spell level)

Combat Gear *scroll of burning hands* (2), *scroll of identify*, *scroll of protection from chaos*; **Other Gear** dagger, quarterstaff, belt pouch, robes, trail rations (2 days), spell component pouch, 11 gp

[ISWG] From *Pathfinder Campaign Setting: The Inner Sea World Guide*

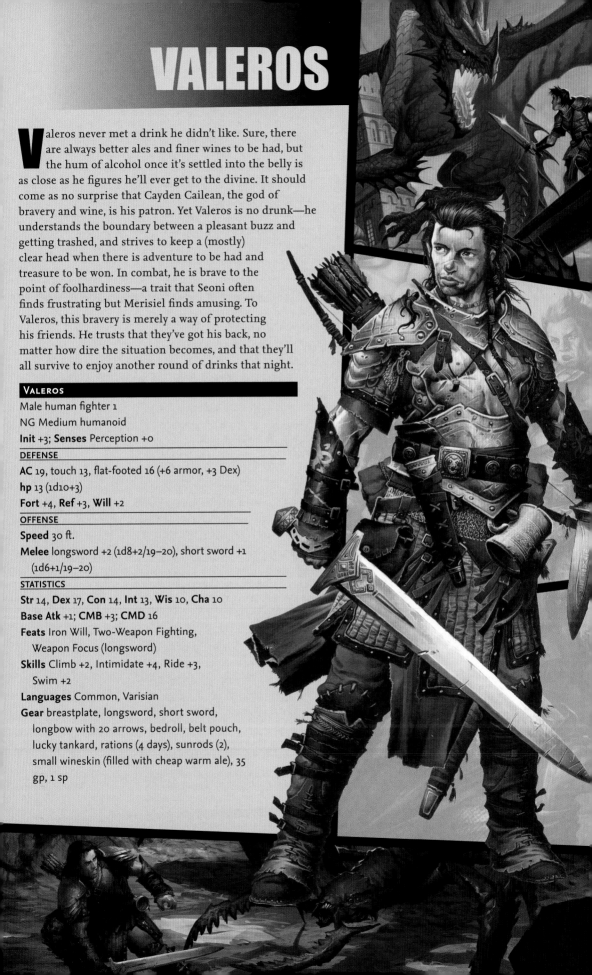

VALEROS

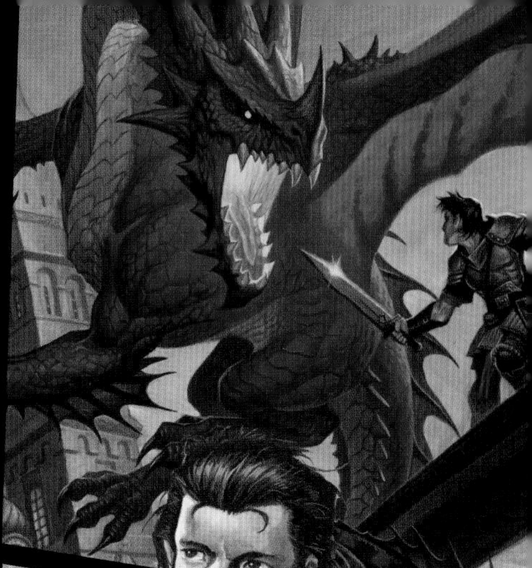

Valeros never met a drink he didn't like. Sure, there are always better ales and finer wines to be had, but the hum of alcohol once it's settled into the belly is as close as he figures he'll ever get to the divine. It should come as no surprise that Cayden Cailean, the god of bravery and wine, is his patron. Yet Valeros is no drunk—he understands the boundary between a pleasant buzz and getting trashed, and strives to keep a (mostly) clear head when there is adventure to be had and treasure to be won. In combat, he is brave to the point of foolhardiness—a trait that Seoni often finds frustrating but Merisiel finds amusing. To Valeros, this bravery is merely a way of protecting his friends. He trusts that they've got his back, no matter how dire the situation becomes, and that they'll all survive to enjoy another round of drinks that night.

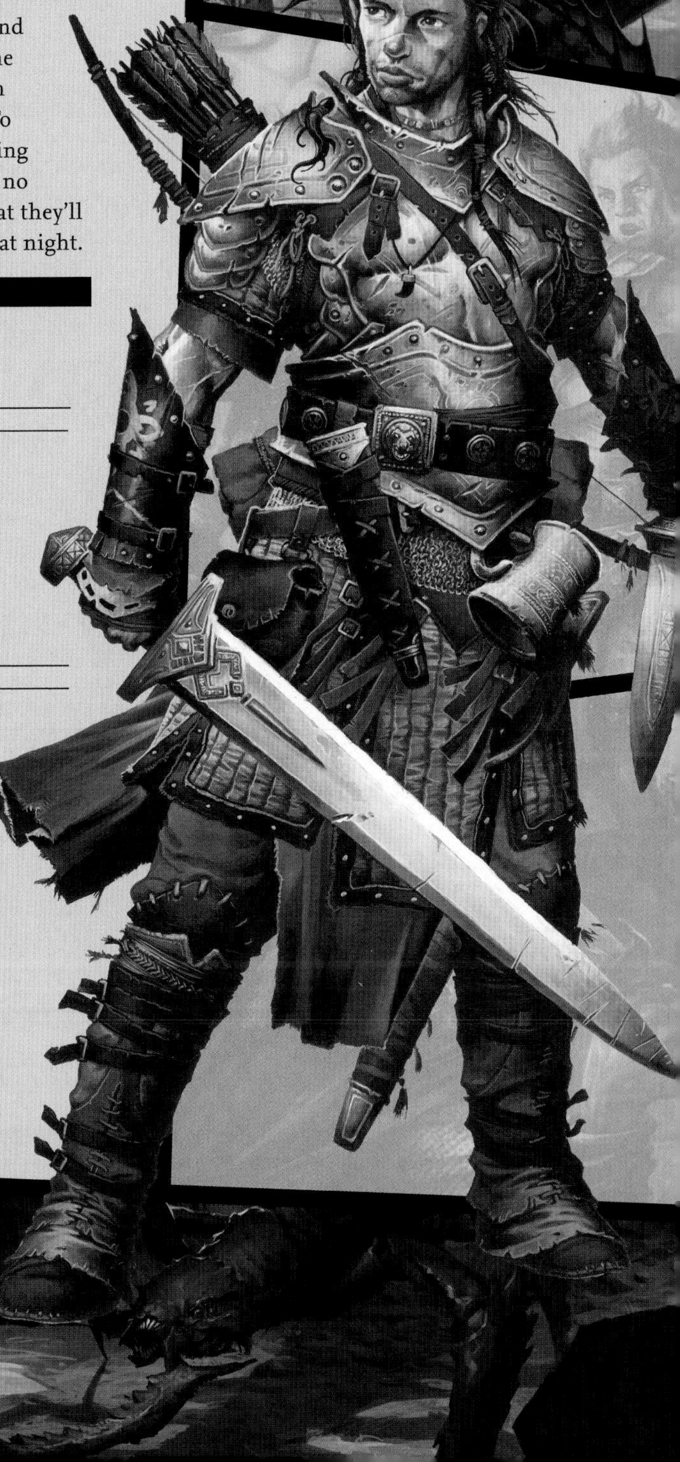

VALEROS

Male human fighter 1
NG Medium humanoid
Init +3; **Senses** Perception +0

DEFENSE

AC 19, touch 13, flat-footed 16 (+6 armor, +3 Dex)
hp 13 (1d10+3)
Fort +4, **Ref** +3, **Will** +2

OFFENSE

Speed 30 ft.
Melee longsword +2 (1d8+2/19–20), short sword +1 (1d6+1/19–20)

STATISTICS

Str 14, **Dex** 17, **Con** 14, **Int** 13, **Wis** 10, **Cha** 10
Base Atk +1; **CMB** +3; **CMD** 16
Feats Iron Will, Two-Weapon Fighting, Weapon Focus (longsword)
Skills Climb +2, Intimidate +4, Ride +3, Swim +2
Languages Common, Varisian
Gear breastplate, longsword, short sword, longbow with 20 arrows, bedroll, belt pouch, lucky tankard, rations (4 days), sunrods (2), small wineskin (filled with cheap warm ale), 35 gp, 1 sp

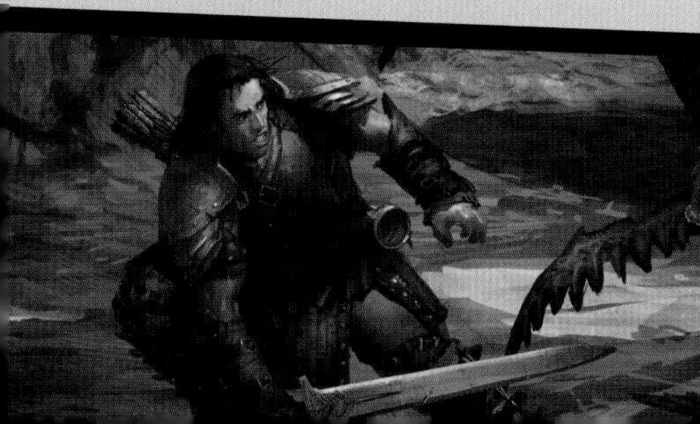

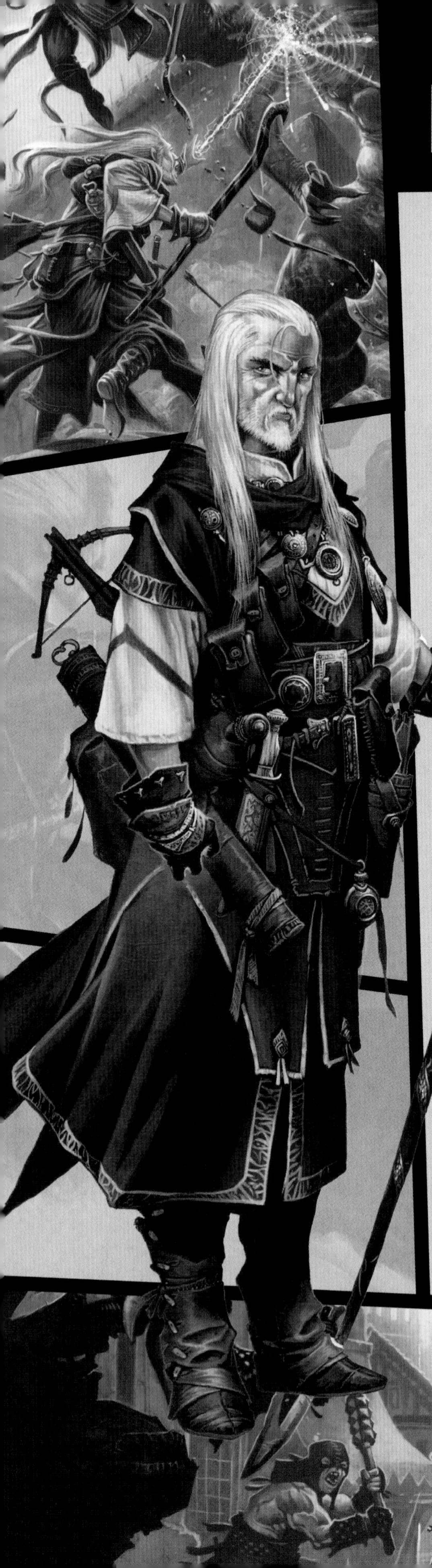

EZREN

Ezren lost his faith in the gods soon after he realized his father, a devout worshiper of Abadar, god of wealth and merchants, was a heretic and a thief. As a result, Ezren abandoned a life of comfort in the sprawling city of Absalom to become an adventuring wizard. His dream today is to be remembered as one of the Pathfinder Society's greatest wizards and explorers. Some (particularly Valeros and Merisiel) may think he takes this goal too seriously, but to Ezren, nothing is more serious than life.

EZREN

Male middle-aged human wizard 1
NG Medium humanoid
Init +0; **Senses** Perception +3

DEFENSE

AC 10, touch 10, flat-footed 10
hp 8 (1d6+2)
Fort +3, **Ref** +0, **Will** +5

OFFENSE

Speed 30 ft.
Melee cane +0 (1d6) or dagger +0 (1d4)
Ranged light crossbow +0 (1d8/19–20)
Special Attacks hand of the apprentice (7/day)
Wizard Spells Prepared (CL 1st; concentration +5)
1st—*magic missile, shield*
0 (at will)—*detect magic, light, mage hand, read magic*

STATISTICS

Str 10, **Dex** 11, **Con** 12, **Int** 19, **Wis** 16, **Cha** 10
Base Atk +0; **CMB** +0; **CMD** 10
Feats Combat Casting, Great Fortitude, Scribe Scroll
Skills Appraise +8, Knowledge (arcana) +8, Knowledge (geography) +8, Knowledge (history) +8, Knowledge (nobility) +8, Linguistics +8, Spellcraft +8
Languages Common, Draconic, Dwarven, Elven, Goblin, Varisian
SQ arcane bond (cane)
Combat Gear *scroll of mage armor*; **Other Gear** cane, dagger, light crossbow with 10 bolts, *wayfinder* (see *Pathfinder Campaign Setting: The Inner Sea World Guide*), pouches (4), traveler's outfit, ink and inkpen, map case, Pathfinder's journal, rations (2 days), spell component pouch, spellbook, 5 gp, 9 sp

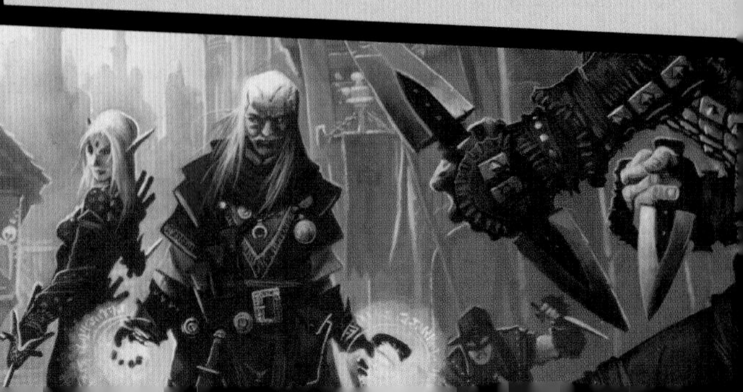

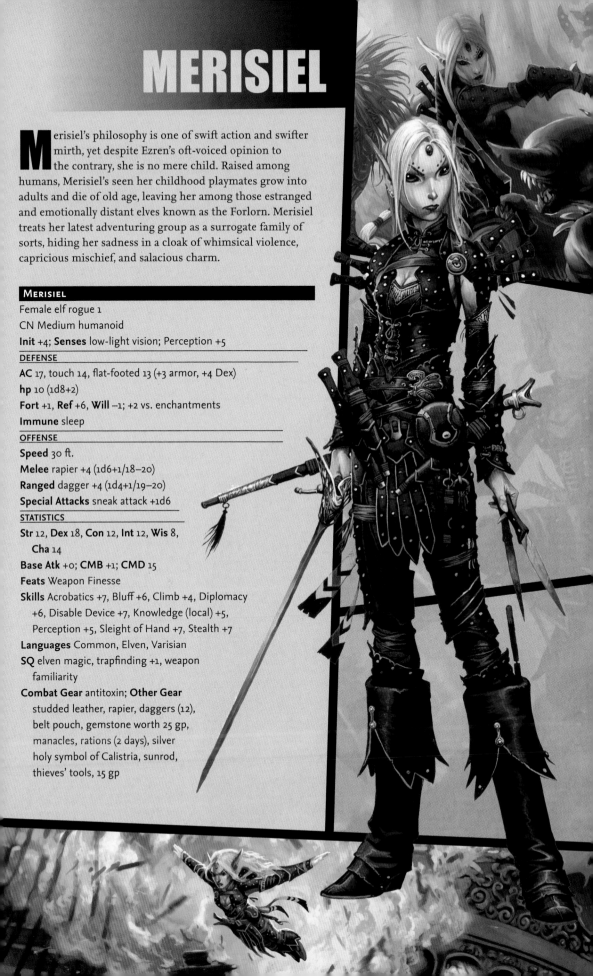

MERISIEL

Merisiel's philosophy is one of swift action and swifter mirth, yet despite Ezren's oft-voiced opinion to the contrary, she is no mere child. Raised among humans, Merisiel's seen her childhood playmates grow into adults and die of old age, leaving her among those estranged and emotionally distant elves known as the Forlorn. Merisiel treats her latest adventuring group as a surrogate family of sorts, hiding her sadness in a cloak of whimsical violence, capricious mischief, and salacious charm.

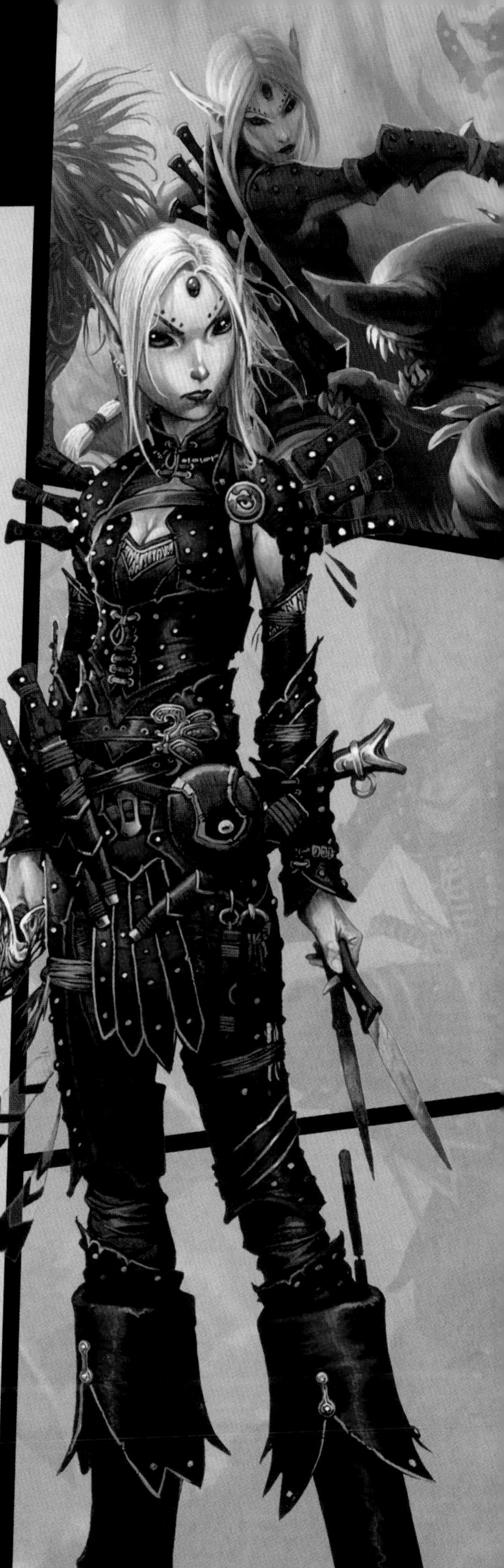

MERISIEL

Female elf rogue 1
CN Medium humanoid
Init +4; **Senses** low-light vision; Perception +5

DEFENSE

AC 17, touch 14, flat-footed 13 (+3 armor, +4 Dex)
hp 10 (1d8+2)
Fort +1, **Ref** +6, **Will** –1; +2 vs. enchantments
Immune sleep

OFFENSE

Speed 30 ft.
Melee rapier +4 (1d6+1/18–20)
Ranged dagger +4 (1d4+1/19–20)
Special Attacks sneak attack +1d6

STATISTICS

Str 12, **Dex** 18, **Con** 12, **Int** 12, **Wis** 8, **Cha** 14
Base Atk +0; **CMB** +1; **CMD** 15
Feats Weapon Finesse
Skills Acrobatics +7, Bluff +6, Climb +4, Diplomacy +6, Disable Device +7, Knowledge (local) +5, Perception +5, Sleight of Hand +7, Stealth +7
Languages Common, Elven, Varisian
SQ elven magic, trapfinding +1, weapon familiarity
Combat Gear antitoxin; **Other Gear** studded leather, rapier, daggers (12), belt pouch, gemstone worth 25 gp, manacles, rations (2 days), silver holy symbol of Calistria, sunrod, thieves' tools, 15 gp

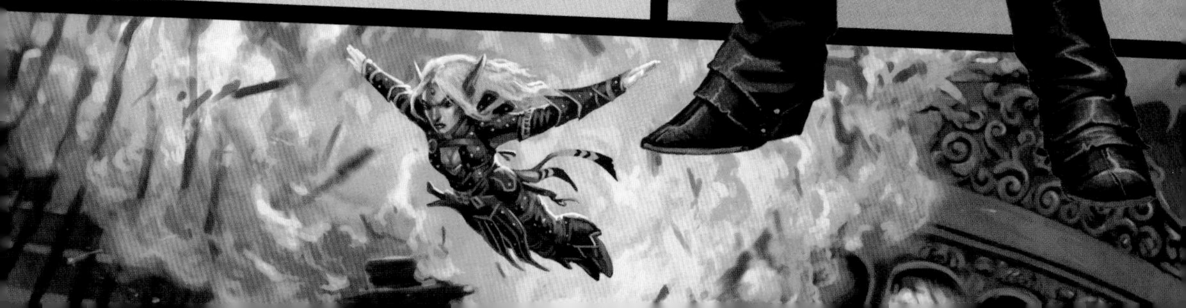

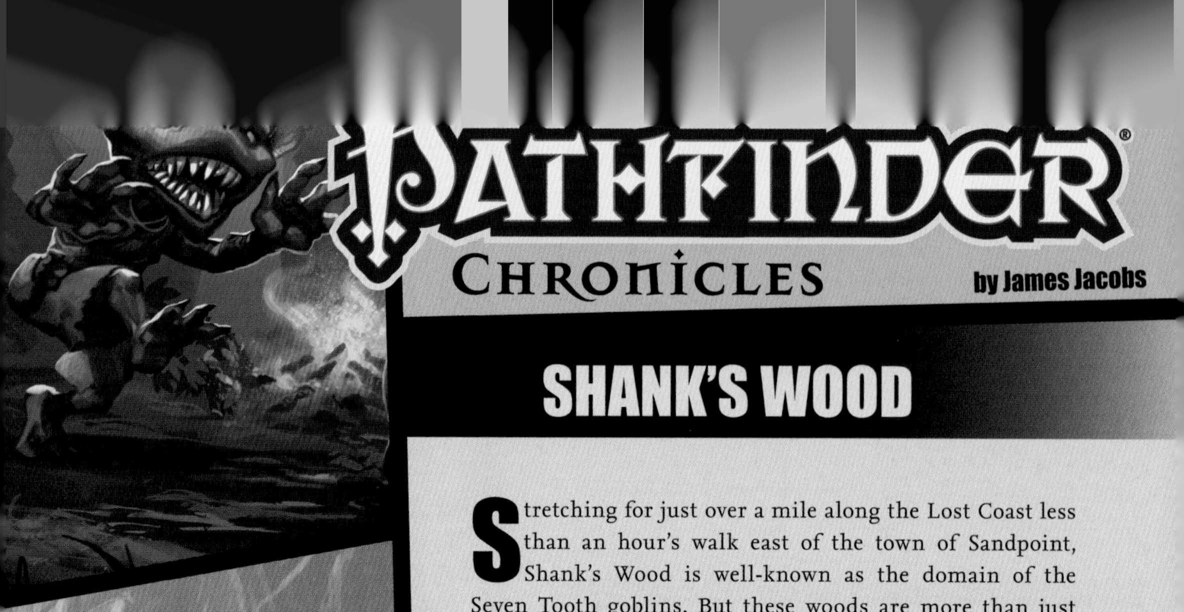

Pathfinder® Chronicles

by James Jacobs

SHANK'S WOOD

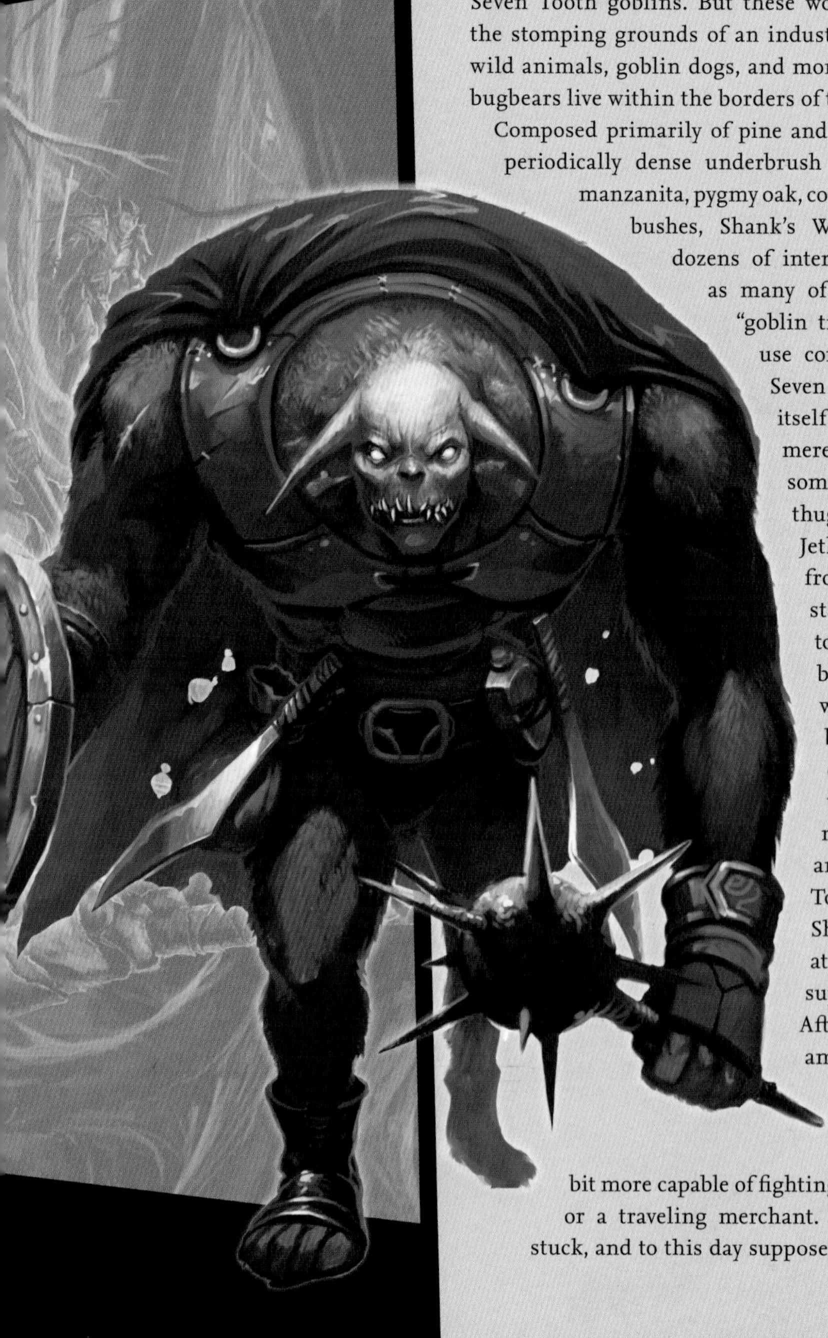

Stretching for just over a mile along the Lost Coast less than an hour's walk east of the town of Sandpoint, Shank's Wood is well-known as the domain of the Seven Tooth goblins. But these woods are more than just the stomping grounds of an industrious tribe of goblins—wild animals, goblin dogs, and more than a few murderous bugbears live within the borders of this woodland.

Composed primarily of pine and eucalyptus trees, with a periodically dense underbrush composed primarily of manzanita, pygmy oak, cottonwood, and blackberry bushes, Shank's Wood is crisscrossed by dozens of intersecting game trails—or as many of the locals know them, "goblin trails" for their common use coming and going by the Seven Tooth goblins. The wood itself was nameless until a mere decade ago, when a somewhat notorious Sczarni thug named Vyron "Shank" Jethezme fled to the woods from Sandpoint after he stabbed his sister's lover to death in a back-alley brawl. Shank lived in the woods for several years, becoming something of a local legend among those who traveled the north Lost Coast Road and among the Seven Tooth goblins alike, for Shank was quite skilled at ambushing both for supplies or just for kicks. After three years, Shank's ambushes tapered off, leading many to suspect he'd finally ambushed something that was a bit more capable of fighting back than a few goblins or a traveling merchant. Nevertheless, the name stuck, and to this day supposed "Shank Sightings" (see

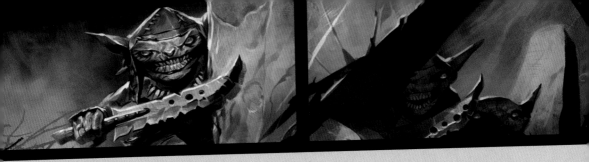

the Shankshack, below) periodically pop up among the local hunters and trappers.

While the goblins and bugbears of Shank's Wood see to it that the majority of the wild animals of the forest are forced to adopt timid lifestyles in order to avoid getting eaten or simply tormented, some wild creatures manage to hold their own. A small number of firepelt cougars dwell in the western reaches of the woods, and wild boars aren't unheard of (although they aren't encountered here with anything near the frequency as they are in Tickwood to the southwest), but apart from these denizens the most dangerous creatures in the woods are the goblins themselves.

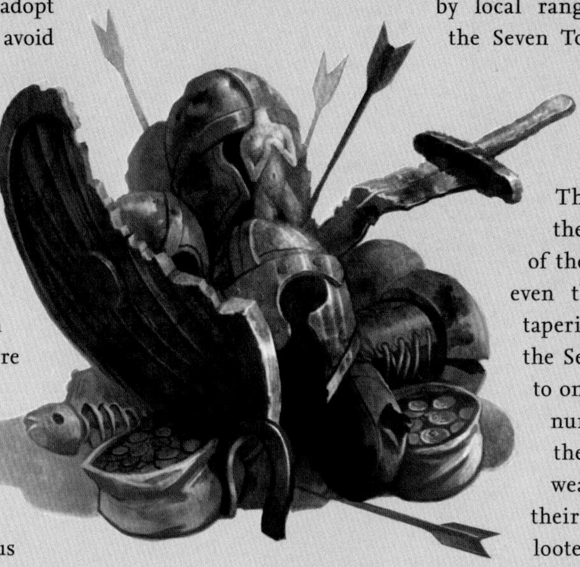

The bugbears of Shank's Wood are low in number, yet in many ways they have come to represent some of the most frightening aspects of the woods. Less than half a dozen of these hulking, silent killers dwell amid the trees, each leading solitary lives and preying as much upon the goblins as they do upon travelers along the roads. The bugbears are canny about their attacks and know better than to draw attention to their homes—when they go stalking, they travel at least a day from the woodland to prey upon farmers and merchants traveling the Lost Coast Road far from Shank's Wood, deliberately throwing off investigations into their lairs. The bugbears do not work well together, and do not go out of their way to support one another, yet neither do they actively meddle in their neighbors' territories. There are, after all, plenty of victims for all.

Although on an individual basis, the bugbears are a greater danger, the Seven Tooth goblins are the most prominent threat facing those who would travel through the tangled undergrowth of Shank's Wood. Perhaps learning from the bugbear tactic of not raiding where you sleep, the goblins have learned to resist the temptation to raid merchants and travelers along the Lost Coast Road—after a series of ill-planned raids resulted in a reprisal attack led by local ranger Shalelu Andosana, the Seven Tooths limit their raids to Junk Beach these days. The harpies of the rocky islets to the north (known as the Three Cormorants) are the primary antagonists of these goblins of late, and even these raids have been tapering off recently, leaving the Seven Tooths the chance to once again build up their numbers and augment their armories with weapons and armor that their best scavengers have looted from Junk Beach. That this gear often breaks doesn't particularly vex the goblins, since there's always more junk to be scavenged.

The Seven Tooth goblins are significantly disorganized—the tribe doesn't typically have a chieftain to speak of, but rather follows the lead of those among them who manage the magical combination of "being mean and pushy" with "somehow managing to not get themselves killed." Now and then, a particularly brutish goblin or (more often) an ambitious bugbear gathers several goblin families to his or her side, but these would-be chieftains have a habit of getting killed by unruly followers before long. This condition of comfortable anarchy makes for a perfect source of minions, as the cult of Lamashtu has recently discovered. The "recruitment" of goblin subjects via the use of strange, mutating magics favored by the cult points to a deeper menace than mere demon worship. Of course, most goblins themselves see little difference between worshiping a demon queen like Lamashtu and a spooky patch of mold growing on a stump that kind of looks like a monster's face—a facet that the cult of Lamashtu has been eager to capitalize upon.

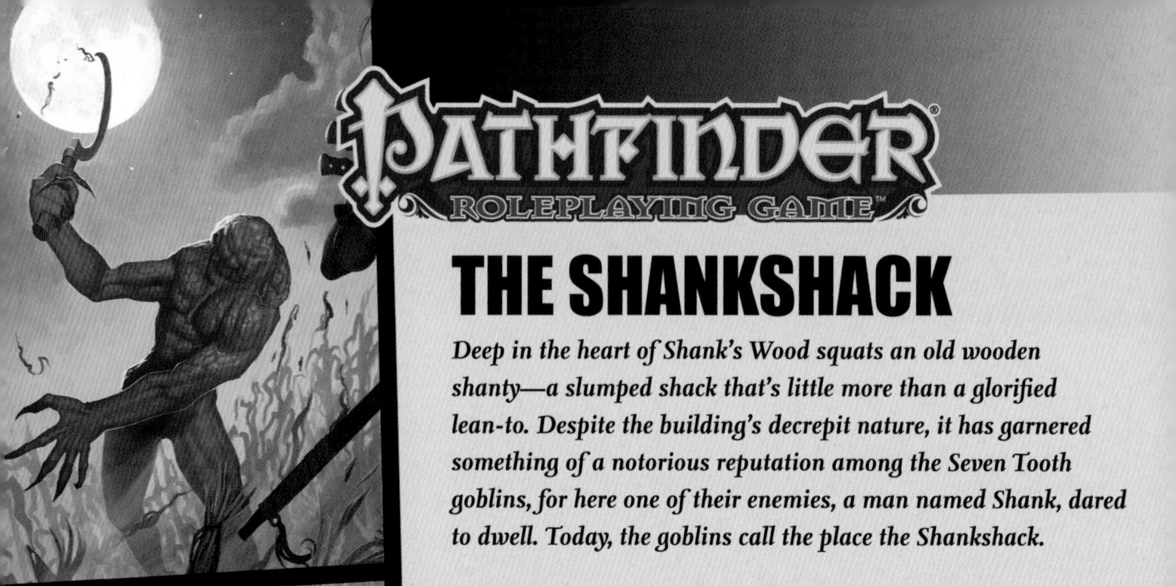

Pathfinder Roleplaying Game

THE SHANKSHACK

Deep in the heart of Shank's Wood squats an old wooden shanty—a slumped shack that's little more than a glorified lean-to. Despite the building's decrepit nature, it has garnered something of a notorious reputation among the Seven Tooth goblins, for here one of their enemies, a man named Shank, dared to dwell. Today, the goblins call the place the Shankshack.

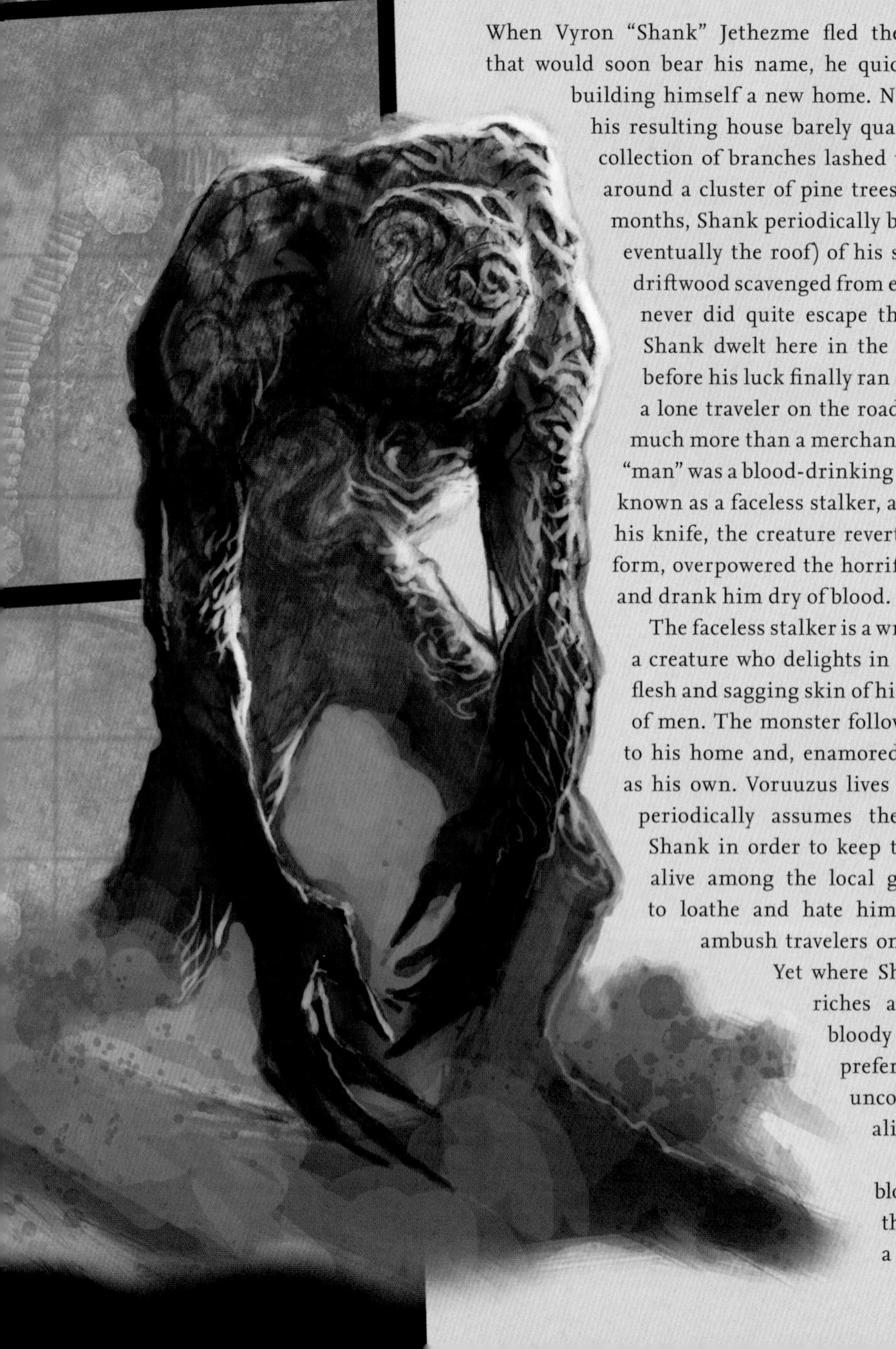

When Vyron "Shank" Jethezme fled the law into the woods that would soon bear his name, he quickly set to the task of building himself a new home. Never one for creativity, his resulting house barely qualified as such, being a collection of branches lashed together to form walls around a cluster of pine trees for support. Over the months, Shank periodically bolstered the walls (and eventually the roof) of his shack with timber and driftwood scavenged from elsewhere, but his home never did quite escape the category of "shack." Shank dwelt here in the woods for three years before his luck finally ran out when he ambushed a lone traveler on the road who turned out to be much more than a merchant. In fact, this apparent "man" was a blood-drinking shapeshifting creature known as a faceless stalker, and when Shank pulled his knife, the creature reverted to its hideous true form, overpowered the horrified Varisian criminal, and drank him dry of blood.

The faceless stalker is a wretch named Voruuzus, a creature who delights in reshaping the wrinkly flesh and sagging skin of his body to ape the shape of men. The monster followed Shank's trail back to his home and, enamored with the lair, took it as his own. Voruuzus lives there to this day, and periodically assumes the form of long-dead Shank in order to keep the legend of the man alive among the local goblins (who continue to loathe and hate him) and to periodically ambush travelers on the Lost Coast Road. Yet where Shank took his victim's riches and left them beaten bloody but alive, Voruuzus prefers to drag his victims unconscious but very much alive back home.

Because fresh warm blood is so much tastier than blood sucked from a corpse.

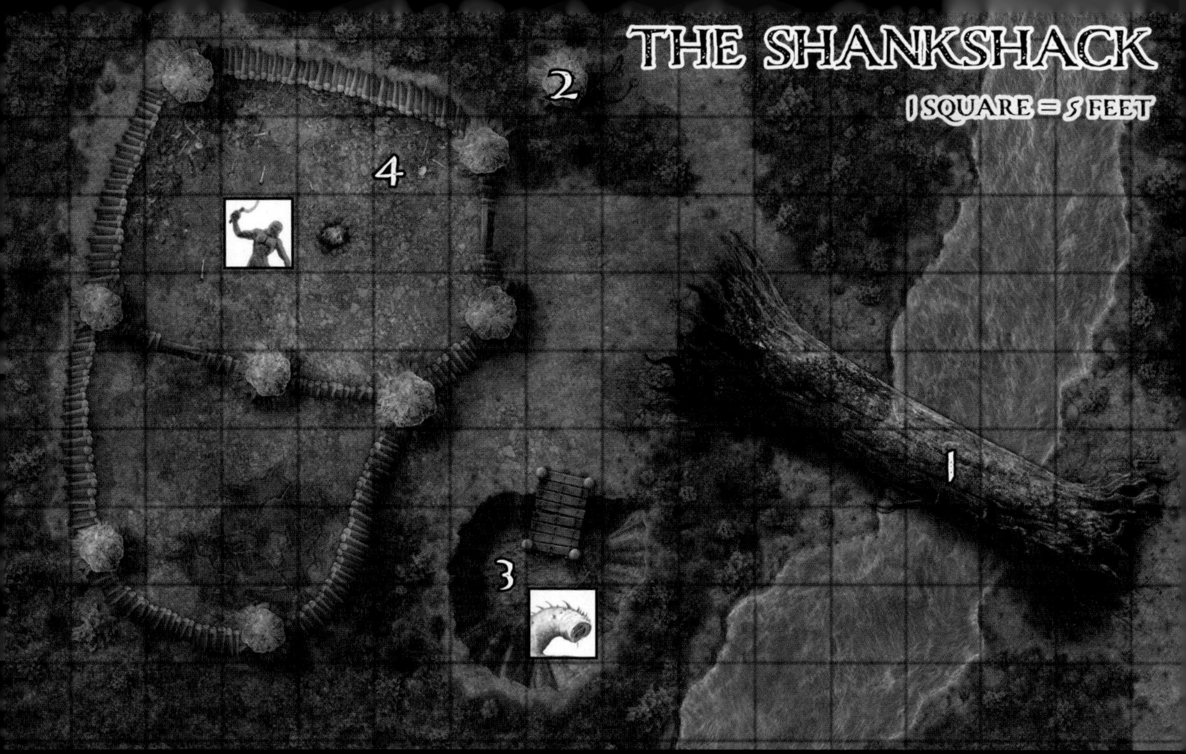
THE SHANKSHACK
1 SQUARE = 5 FEET
2
4
3
1

1. Fallen Log

A huge mossy log serves as a bridge over a nameless, five-foot-deep creek that flows north to the sea.

2. The Hugging Tree

This old pine has lengths of chain affixed to its trunk by long bent nails. The chains themselves are sticky with blood, and Voruuzus's latest victim still remains bound to the trunk by the chains, both arms and legs wrapped around the trunk to give the poor soul the appearance of hugging the tree. If you have the PCs hired to track down a missing traveler, this poor soul can be found here, lashed to the Hugging Tree and lingering on the cusp of death.

3. Leftovers Pit

Once a meal is empty of blood, the faceless stalker tosses the body into this pit. The short wooden walkway leading over the pit is rather unstable—anyone who steps on it finds the old construction giving way. A DC 15 Reflex save is enough to leap back to solid ground, otherwise the victim falls ten feet into a pit of mud and decaying bodies below. This causes no damage in and of itself, but the giant rot grub that dwells within the pit is likely to make up for that—it immediately attacks anyone who falls in.

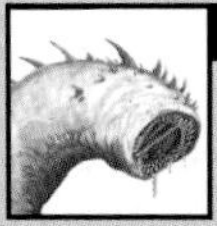

GIANT ROT GRUB **CR 3**

XP 800

hp 34 (*Pathfinder RPG Bestiary 3* 215)

4. The Shankshack

The door to Voruuzus's shack is an ill-fitting one scavenged long ago from the beach (a door that started and ended its life as part of a now-sunken ship). Within, a smoky fire pit helps the faceless stalker fight the clammy cold of the Varisian winters, while a large heap of bones and trash serve it as disgusting decorations. If the faceless stalker heard the PCs approaching (perhaps as they splashed through the creek or dealt with a hungry rot grub), it has assumed Shank's form and waits here to greet the PCs, trying to pull off the disguise long enough to confuse them or set them somewhat at ease before it switches to its true form to attack—the monster's poor understanding of humanity means that it doesn't realize that PCs who have heard of the legendary bandit Shank are unlikely to be put at ease by meeting him in a creepy shack in the woods.

As with the front door, the door separating the back room barely hangs on its shabby frame. Beyond the door is a smaller chamber, where Voruuzus sleeps atop a heap of furs and branches. A DC 20 Perception check made while searching this filthy bed uncovers 34 gp, a masterwork darkwood buckler, a *ring of feather falling*, a *wand of stinking cloud* (8 charges), and a healthy collection of well-fed bed bugs.

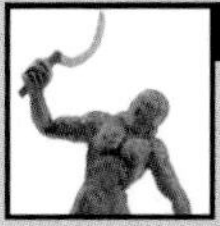

VORUUZUS **CR 4**

XP 1,200

hp 42 (*Pathfinder RPG Bestiary 2* 122)

Miniature *Pathfinder Battles Rise of the Runelords* 6

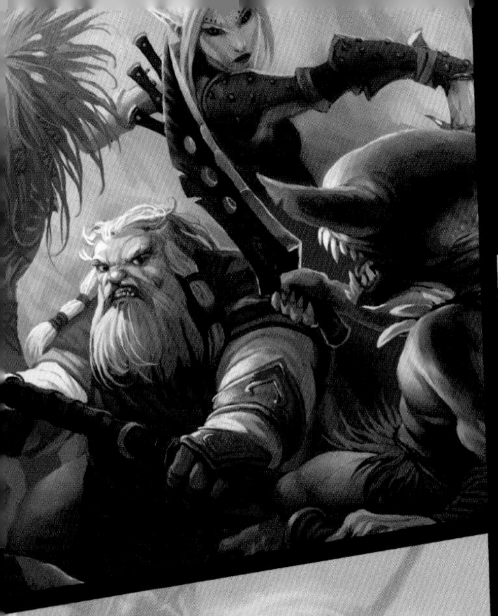

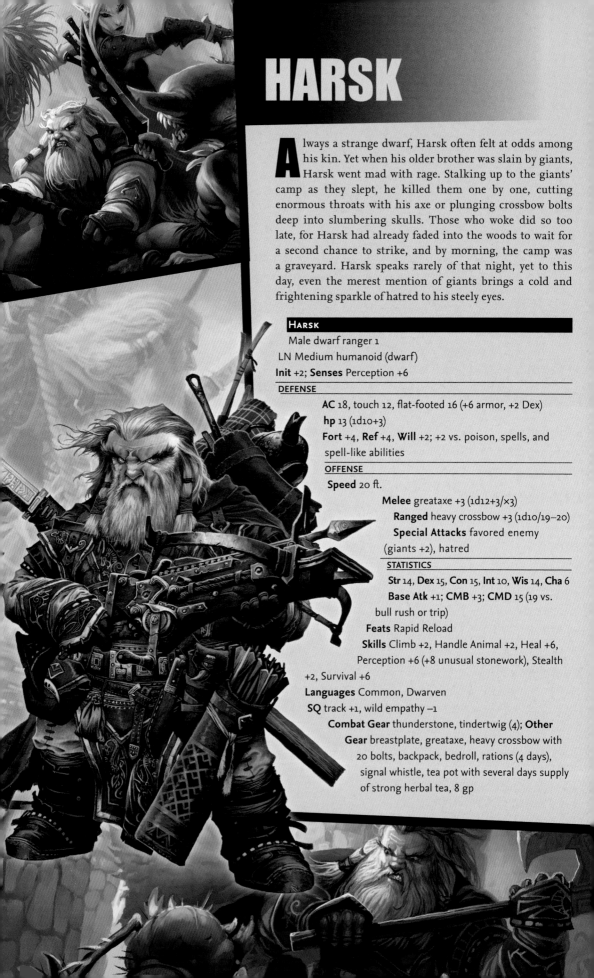

HARSK

Always a strange dwarf, Harsk often felt at odds among his kin. Yet when his older brother was slain by giants, Harsk went mad with rage. Stalking up to the giants' camp as they slept, he killed them one by one, cutting enormous throats with his axe or plunging crossbow bolts deep into slumbering skulls. Those who woke did so too late, for Harsk had already faded into the woods to wait for a second chance to strike, and by morning, the camp was a graveyard. Harsk speaks rarely of that night, yet to this day, even the merest mention of giants brings a cold and frightening sparkle of hatred to his steely eyes.

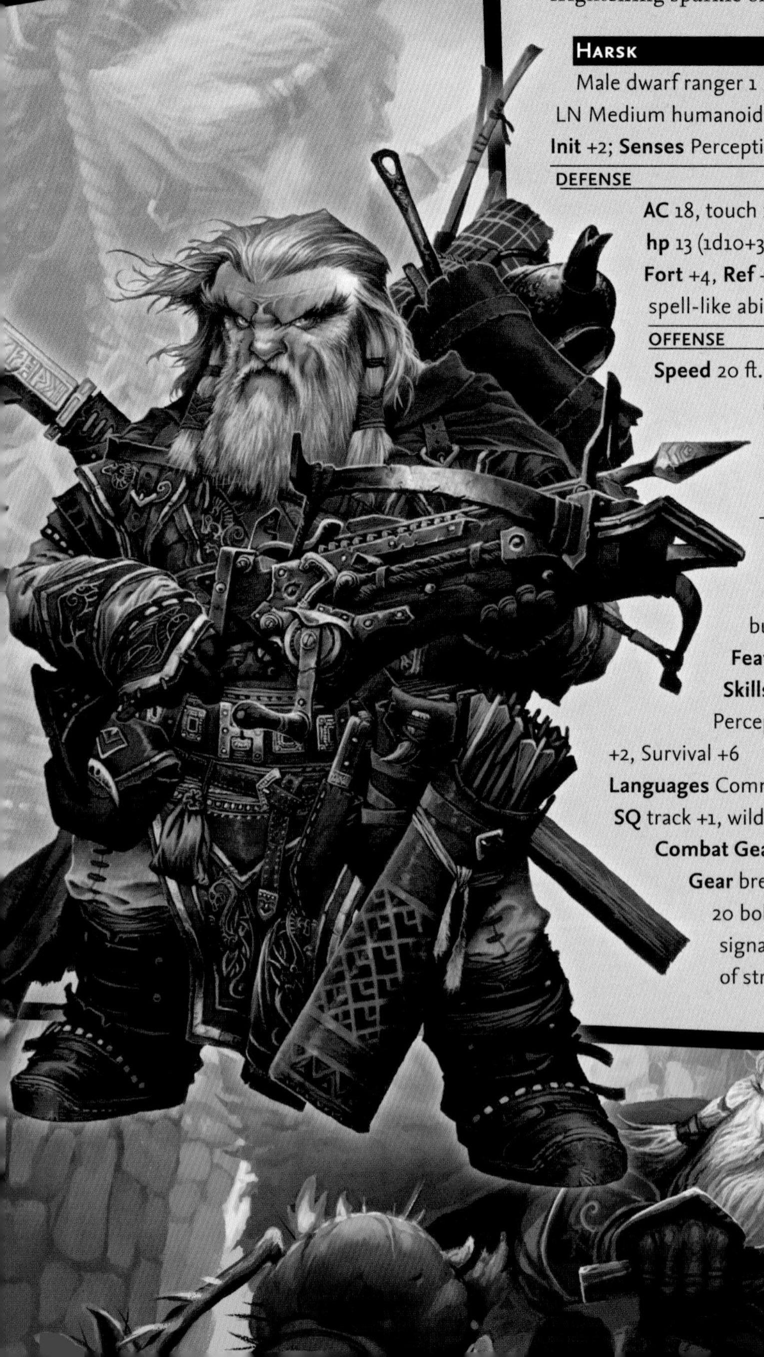

HARSK

Male dwarf ranger 1
LN Medium humanoid (dwarf)
Init +2; **Senses** Perception +6

DEFENSE

AC 18, touch 12, flat-footed 16 (+6 armor, +2 Dex)
hp 13 (1d10+3)
Fort +4, **Ref** +4, **Will** +2; +2 vs. poison, spells, and spell-like abilities

OFFENSE

Speed 20 ft.
Melee greataxe +3 (1d12+3/×3)
Ranged heavy crossbow +3 (1d10/19–20)
Special Attacks favored enemy (giants +2), hatred

STATISTICS

Str 14, **Dex** 15, **Con** 15, **Int** 10, **Wis** 14, **Cha** 6
Base Atk +1; **CMB** +3; **CMD** 15 (19 vs. bull rush or trip)
Feats Rapid Reload
Skills Climb +2, Handle Animal +2, Heal +6, Perception +6 (+8 unusual stonework), Stealth +2, Survival +6
Languages Common, Dwarven
SQ track +1, wild empathy –1
Combat Gear thunderstone, tindertwig (4); **Other Gear** breastplate, greataxe, heavy crossbow with 20 bolts, backpack, bedroll, rations (4 days), signal whistle, tea pot with several days supply of strong herbal tea, 8 gp

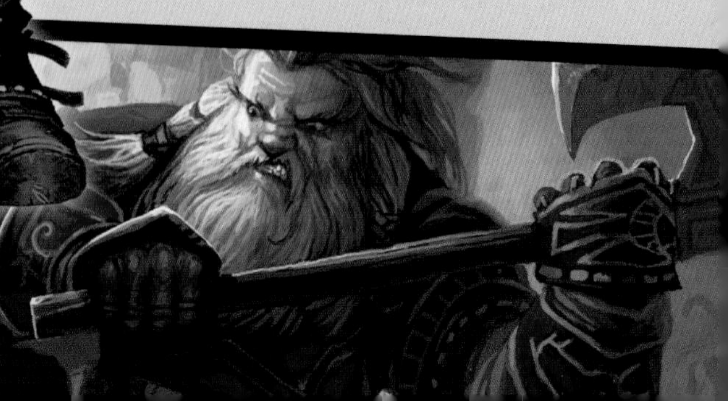

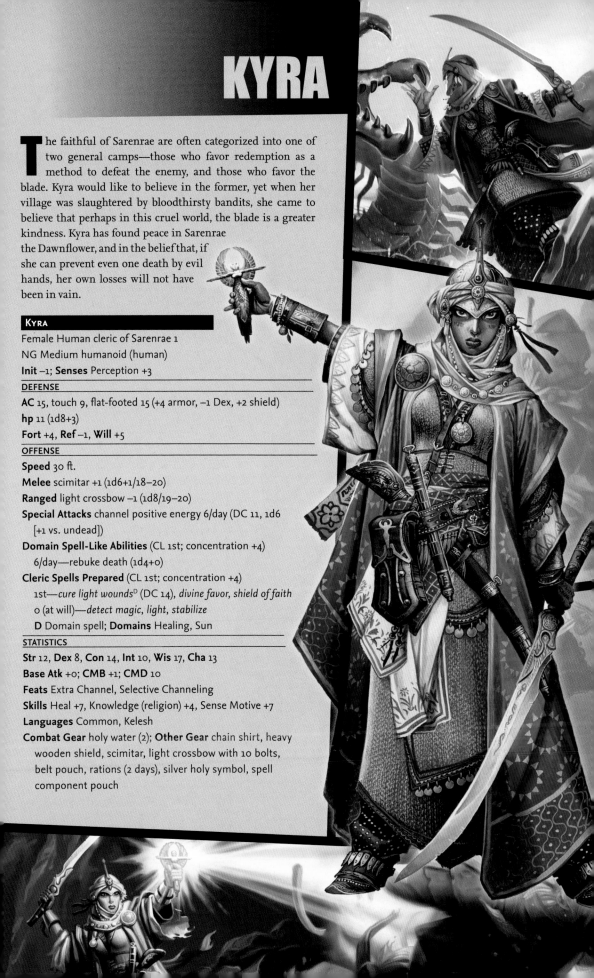

KYRA

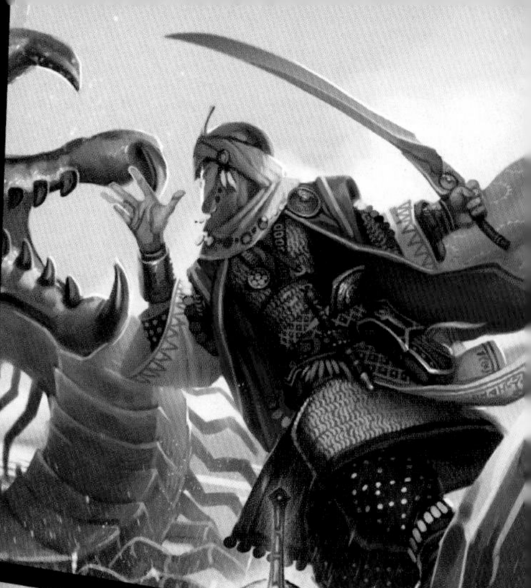

The faithful of Sarenrae are often categorized into one of two general camps—those who favor redemption as a method to defeat the enemy, and those who favor the blade. Kyra would like to believe in the former, yet when her village was slaughtered by bloodthirsty bandits, she came to believe that perhaps in this cruel world, the blade is a greater kindness. Kyra has found peace in Sarenrae the Dawnflower, and in the belief that, if she can prevent even one death by evil hands, her own losses will not have been in vain.

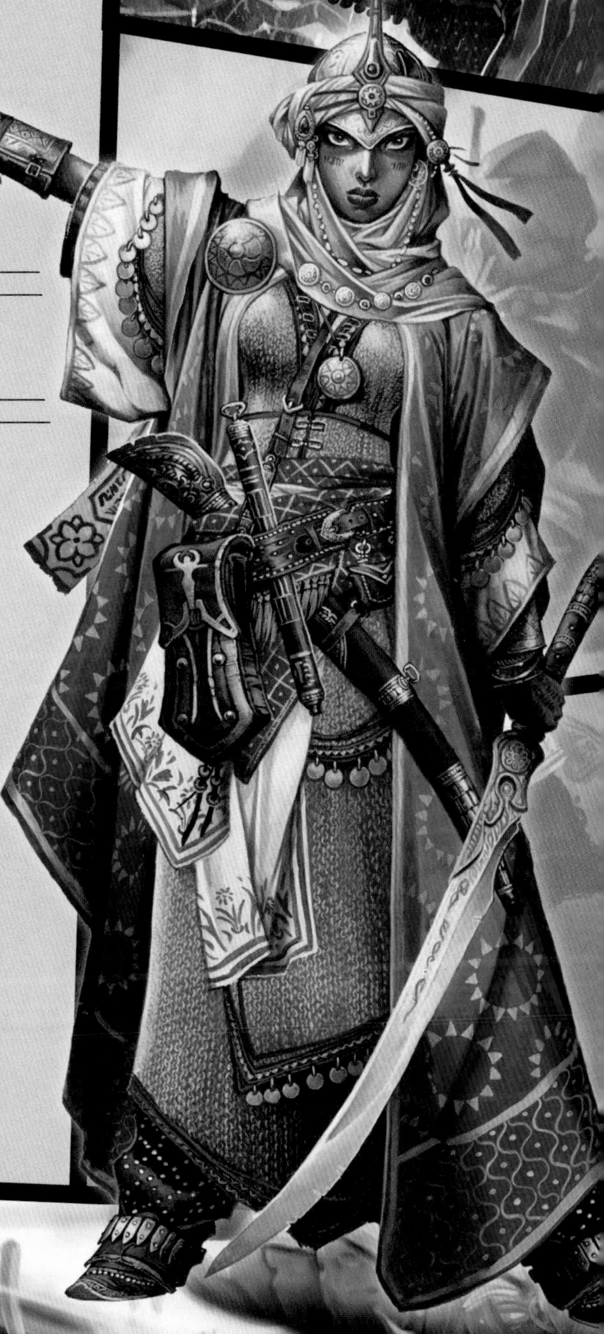

Kyra

Female Human cleric of Sarenrae 1
NG Medium humanoid (human)
Init –1; **Senses** Perception +3

DEFENSE

AC 15, touch 9, flat-footed 15 (+4 armor, –1 Dex, +2 shield)
hp 11 (1d8+3)
Fort +4, **Ref** –1, **Will** +5

OFFENSE

Speed 30 ft.
Melee scimitar +1 (1d6+1/18–20)
Ranged light crossbow –1 (1d8/19–20)
Special Attacks channel positive energy 6/day (DC 11, 1d6 [+1 vs. undead])
Domain Spell-Like Abilities (CL 1st; concentration +4)
6/day—rebuke death (1d4+0)
Cleric Spells Prepared (CL 1st; concentration +4)
1st—*cure light wounds*[D] (DC 14), *divine favor*, *shield of faith*
0 (at will)—*detect magic*, *light*, *stabilize*
D Domain spell; **Domains** Healing, Sun

STATISTICS

Str 12, **Dex** 8, **Con** 14, **Int** 10, **Wis** 17, **Cha** 13
Base Atk +0; **CMB** +1; **CMD** 10
Feats Extra Channel, Selective Channeling
Skills Heal +7, Knowledge (religion) +4, Sense Motive +7
Languages Common, Kelesh
Combat Gear holy water (2); **Other Gear** chain shirt, heavy wooden shield, scimitar, light crossbow with 10 bolts, belt pouch, rations (2 days), silver holy symbol, spell component pouch

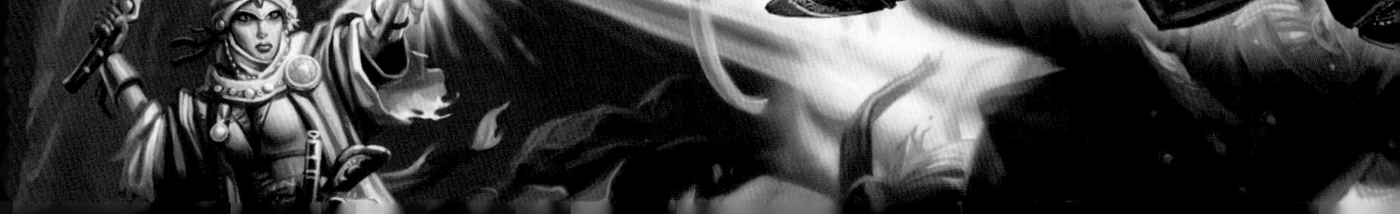

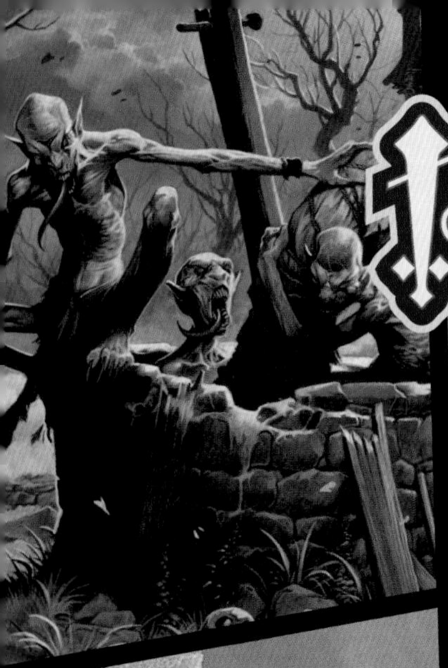

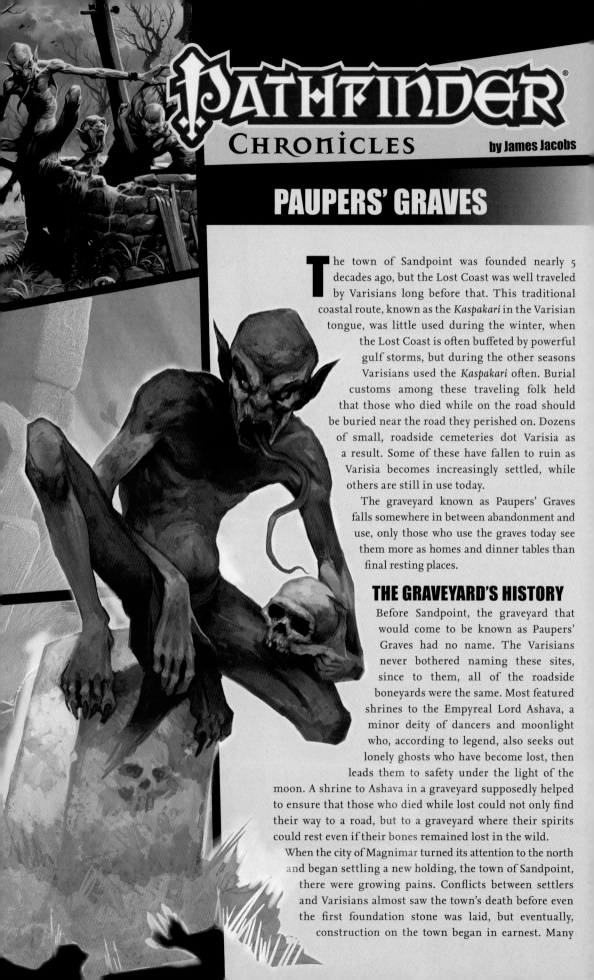

Pathfinder Chronicles

by James Jacobs

PAUPERS' GRAVES

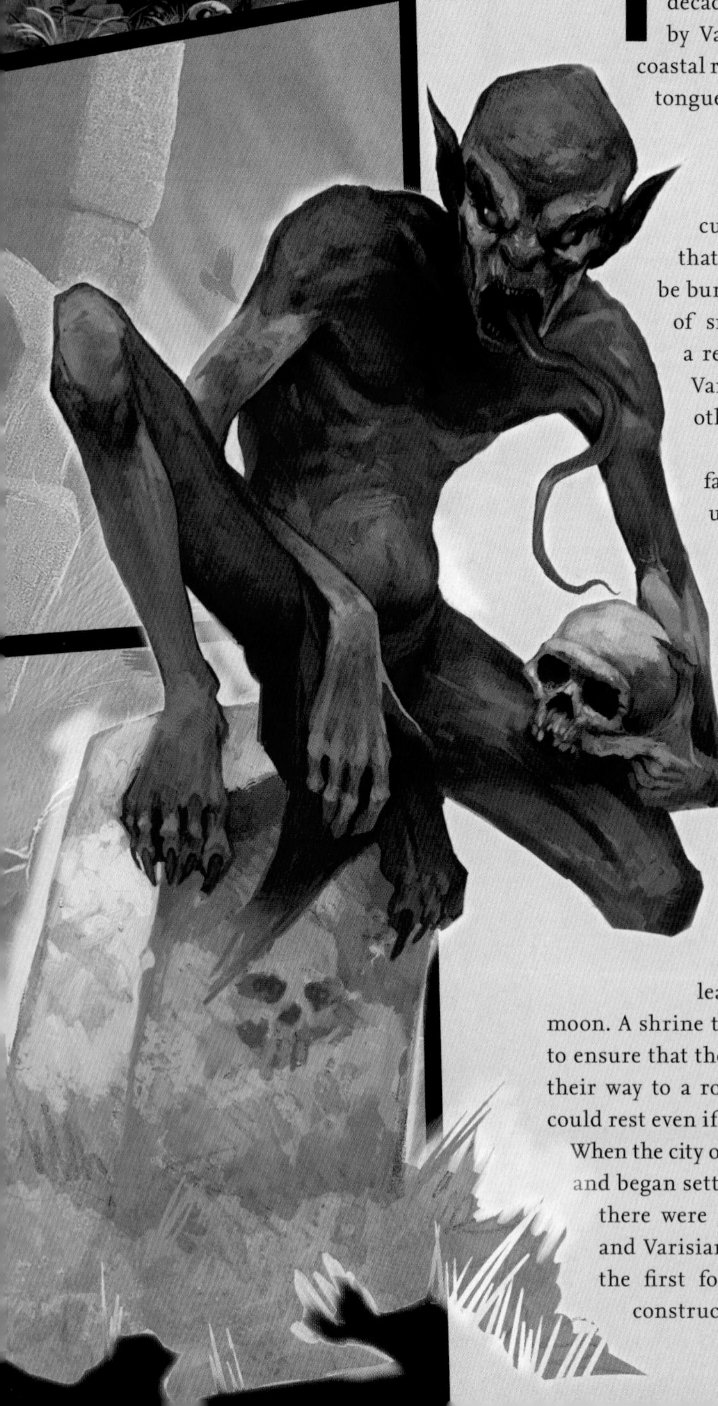

The town of Sandpoint was founded nearly 5 decades ago, but the Lost Coast was well traveled by Varisians long before that. This traditional coastal route, known as the *Kaspakari* in the Varisian tongue, was little used during the winter, when the Lost Coast is often buffeted by powerful gulf storms, but during the other seasons Varisians used the *Kaspakari* often. Burial customs among these traveling folk held that those who died while on the road should be buried near the road they perished on. Dozens of small, roadside cemeteries dot Varisia as a result. Some of these have fallen to ruin as Varisia becomes increasingly settled, while others are still in use today.

The graveyard known as Paupers' Graves falls somewhere in between abandonment and use, only those who use the graves today see them more as homes and dinner tables than final resting places.

THE GRAVEYARD'S HISTORY

Before Sandpoint, the graveyard that would come to be known as Paupers' Graves had no name. The Varisians never bothered naming these sites, since to them, all of the roadside boneyards were the same. Most featured shrines to the Empyreal Lord Ashava, a minor deity of dancers and moonlight who, according to legend, also seeks out lonely ghosts who have become lost, then leads them to safety under the light of the moon. A shrine to Ashava in a graveyard supposedly helped to ensure that those who died while lost could not only find their way to a road, but to a graveyard where their spirits could rest even if their bones remained lost in the wild.

When the city of Magnimar turned its attention to the north and began settling a new holding, the town of Sandpoint, there were growing pains. Conflicts between settlers and Varisians almost saw the town's death before even the first foundation stone was laid, but eventually, construction on the town began in earnest. Many

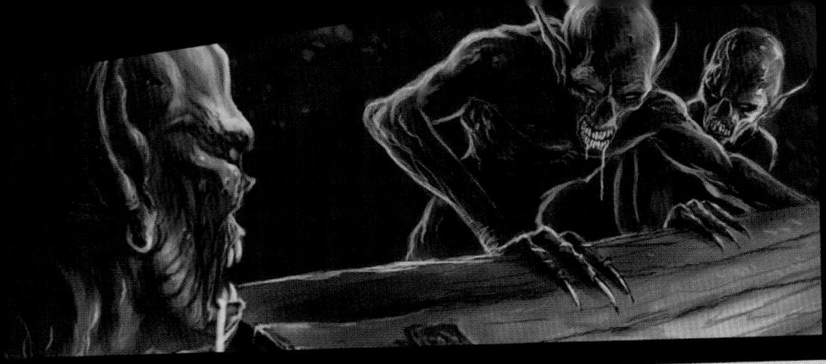

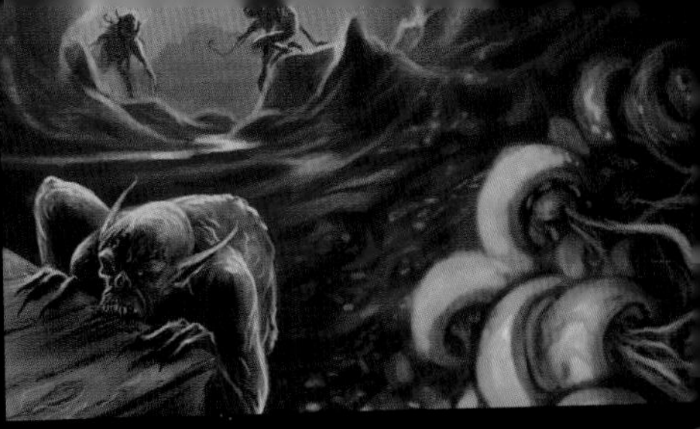

poor and desperate laborers from Magnimar came north to help build the town, following a promise that those who helped in its construction would never want for a home.

But building a town from nothing on the Lost Coast is a dangerous prospect. Disease, accidents, poor judgement, and attacks by creatures both mundane and otherwise saw many deaths, and for several of those early years, Sandpoint didn't have a great solution for its dead. Those survived by kin with coin could pay to have bodies transported 50 miles back south to be buried in Magnimar's Cenotaph or other graveyards, but the poor and indigent who helped build the town had no such luxuries. Burial in unsanctified ground being a poor option at best for many of these superstitious folk, the best option was the small Varisian graveyard just over 3 miles east of Sandpoint.

The local Varisians welcomed the new dead into their graveyard, for despite a few unfortunate incidents with some of the less tolerant settlers, the new townsfolk had quickly become friends, and the graveyard was certainly large enough to serve the town. As more and more of Sandpoint's common folk came to make their final home there, the place became known by the name it is called today—Paupers' Graves.

With the consecration of the original Sandpoint Chapel and its attendant (and more convenient) cemetery, Paupers' Graves grew less and less used. With townsfolk more often electing to be buried closer to home, those who went to Paupers' Graves were increasingly those whose bodies no one cared for or cared to remember. The homeless, the unfortunate, and the desperate became the true heritors of the graveyard. And after the priest of the Sandpoint Chapel opened the Sandpoint Boneyard to all, regardless of financial means, even these destitute dead dried up.

For the next few years, Paupers' Graves lay fallow. Undergrowth encroached and unscrupulous folk increasingly snatched stones from the graveyard walls under cover of night for use in foundations. At best, the graveyard was a dare for teenagers to prove their bravery. But it wasn't until Jediah Kheln came to town that Paupers' Graves truly died.

THE COMING OF KHELN

Freshly broke after losing his wealth to treacherous kin and forced to flee Magnimar after a heist went horribly wrong, Jediah Kheln hoped to use Sandpoint as a base of operations to rebuild his wealth so as to someday return to Magnimar and get revenge on those who had betrayed him. But Kheln's goals were too lofty, and in Sandpoint he soon found that in order to remain inconspicuous (investigators from Magnimar showed up looking for him in town no fewer than five times that first month alone), he was forced to play it straight. He allowed himself no robberies or muggings or even any con games, and as a result spent an increasing number of his nights sleeping in alleys or under piers.

It was in just such a desperate state that a strange and foul-smelling man came to him one morning, an hour before dawn. The man wore a filthy hooded cloak, reeked of strange chemicals, and spoke in a liquescent voice, but what he told the desperate thief made him discount these warning signs. According to the man, a graveyard a mere 3 or so miles east of town held within its overgrown grounds a crumbling statue of a Varisian dancer. No one visited the graveyard anymore, according to the strange man, and so no one would miss the theft of the silver medallion hidden within a secret compartment in the statue's chest.

Kheln asked the strange man why he hadn't stolen the silver medallion himself, and the man only chuckled, observing that the people of town would

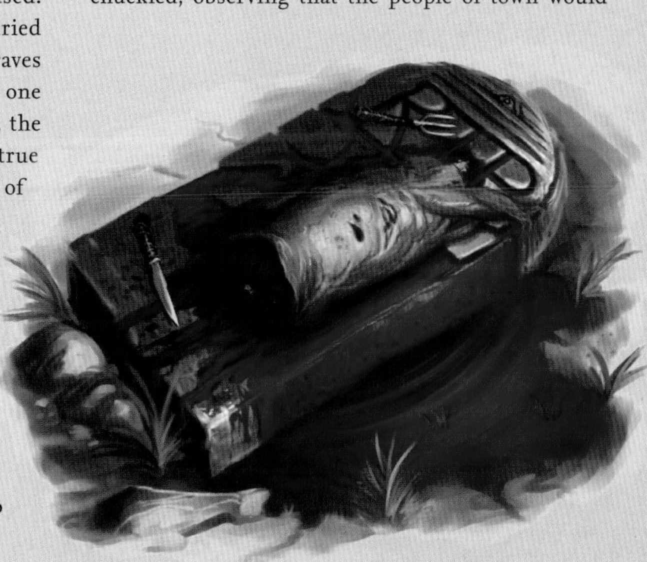

recognize the medallion if he tried to sell it. A trip to Magnimar was beyond the man's endurance, but if Kheln were to travel to Paupers' Graves and steal the amulet then pawn it in Magnimar, the strange old man would be happy to claim a mere 5 percent finder's fee off whatever Kheln could get for the bauble.

Desperation tricked Kheln into accepting the challenge, and he set out for Paupers' Graves that very evening. He found the place exactly as the man had described—deserted, overgrown, and silent. At the graveyard's heart he found the statue—a depiction (unknown to him) of the goddess Ashava. And hidden in her bosom he found the silver medallion—a potent charm that had for centuries warded the graveyard from the fell attentions of evil spirits. Kheln knew none of this, of course, and in removing the charm from the statue, he removed the graveyard's protections.

As Kheln exited the graveyard, visions of handfuls of gold dancing in his head, the strange man met him, stepping out of the shadows with that strangely fluid chuckle. He pulled back his hood to reveal to Kheln the truth—the man was a ghoul. Kheln attempted to flee, but the ghoul leaped upon him and bit him in the throat—a wound enough to paralyze and infect him with ghoul fever, but not enough to kill him. As Kheln lay helpless, the ghoul introduced himself more properly as Kanker, priest of the demon god of graves, Kabriri, and thanked Kheln for doing what he could not—disarming the graveyard's protection. Kheln's payment, Kanker explained as he casually kicked the now useless silver medallion over the side of the cliff and into the surf below, was eternal life as a ghoul. By the time Kheln had regained his mobility, the ghoul was gone.

Hoping against hope that the ghoul had lied, Kheln fled back to Sandpoint, but as he sickened he knew that Kanker had told the truth. Kheln took 7 days to die, and at midnight on the eighth day he rose as a ghoul himself. A ghoul who soon learned that what Kanker had given him was indeed a gift—a gift Kheln intended to repay with eternal loyalty as keeper of Paupers' Graves.

PAUPERS' GRAVES TODAY

Since that fateful day, Paupers' Graves has done more than slide into anonymity; it has become the focus of numerous whispers and fireside tales. Today, people say that Paupers' Graves is no place for living souls, and travelers hold their breath as they hurry past the tangled, forsaken cemetery. By day, the graveyard is foreboding enough, but at night, as the cold fogs drift in from the Varisian Gulf, strange laughter and ominous rustlings echo from the not-so-abandoned graveyard. Those few who visit Paupers' Graves do so for sinister gain, for the place has developed something of a reputation as being a place of power for dark rituals and vile ceremonies, yet even the idle cultist who comes to the graves hesitates to linger long after dark. Locals fear that some day soon, a more powerful cult might find a way to forge a terrible and lasting alliance with the ghouls they say dwell in Paupers' Graves, but what they don't realize is just how infested the place has become.

No bodies remain today in Paupers' Graves, and the ground below is a warren of ghoulish activity ruled by the man who brought undeath to the place—Jediah Kheln has, at long last, found a place to call home.

JEDIAH KHELN

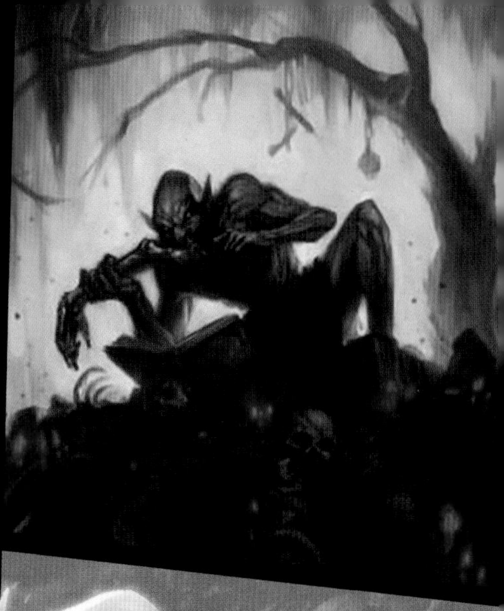

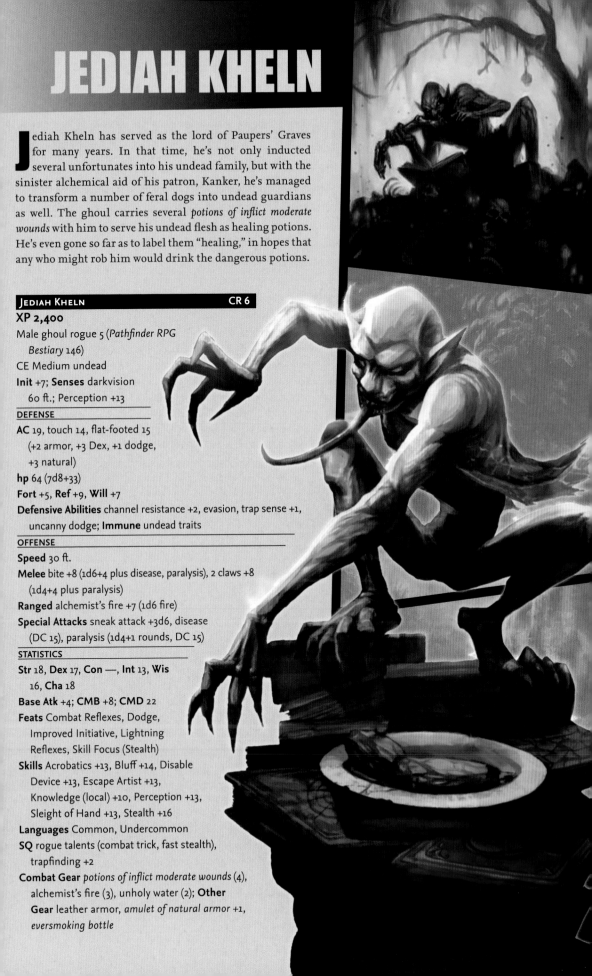

Jediah Kheln has served as the lord of Paupers' Graves for many years. In that time, he's not only inducted several unfortunates into his undead family, but with the sinister alchemical aid of his patron, Kanker, he's managed to transform a number of feral dogs into undead guardians as well. The ghoul carries several *potions of inflict moderate wounds* with him to serve his undead flesh as healing potions. He's even gone so far as to label them "healing," in hopes that any who might rob him would drink the dangerous potions.

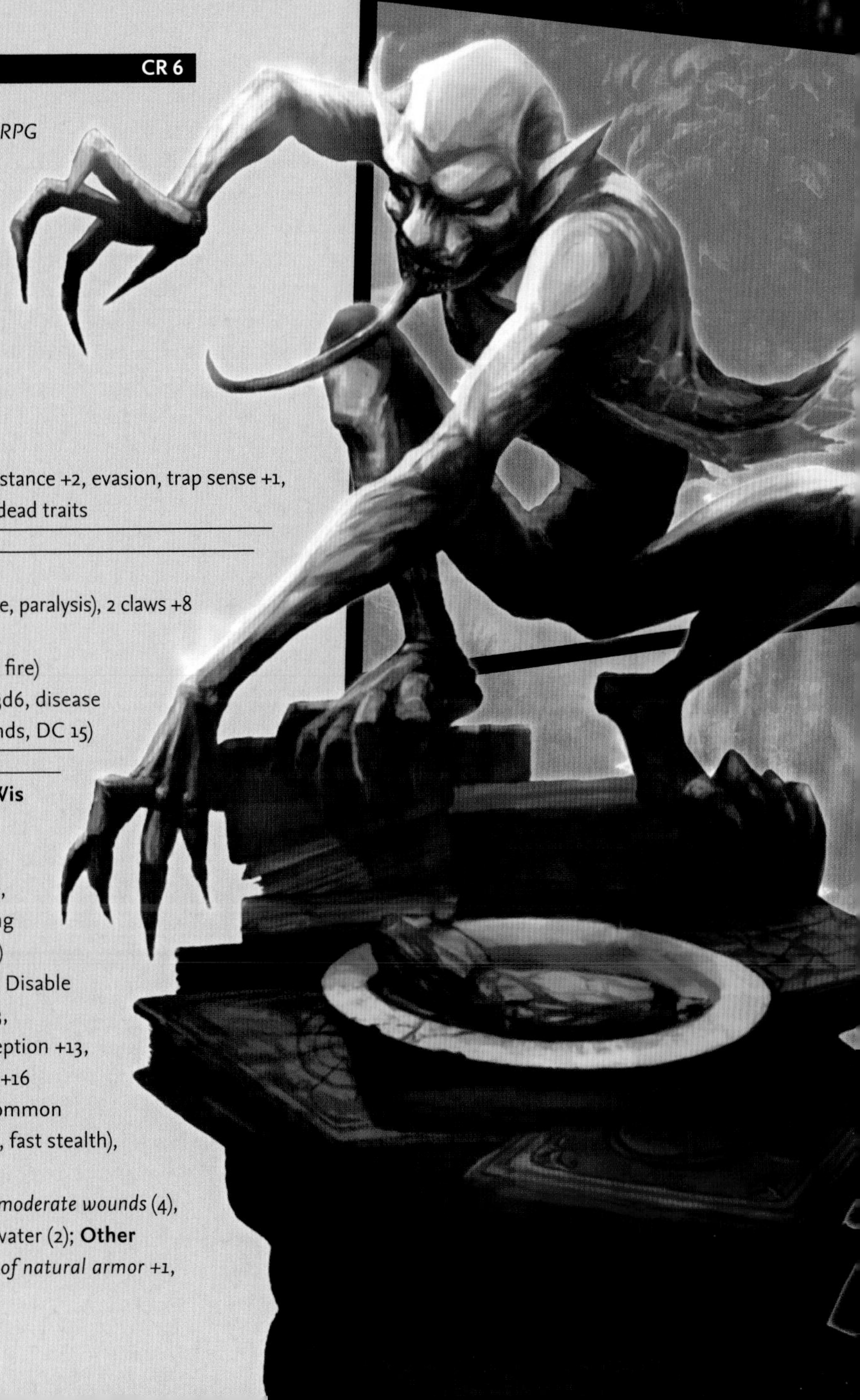

JEDIAH KHELN **CR 6**

XP 2,400

Male ghoul rogue 5 (*Pathfinder RPG Bestiary* 146)

CE Medium undead

Init +7; **Senses** darkvision 60 ft.; Perception +13

DEFENSE

AC 19, touch 14, flat-footed 15 (+2 armor, +3 Dex, +1 dodge, +3 natural)

hp 64 (7d8+33)

Fort +5, **Ref** +9, **Will** +7

Defensive Abilities channel resistance +2, evasion, trap sense +1, uncanny dodge; **Immune** undead traits

OFFENSE

Speed 30 ft.

Melee bite +8 (1d6+4 plus disease, paralysis), 2 claws +8 (1d4+4 plus paralysis)

Ranged alchemist's fire +7 (1d6 fire)

Special Attacks sneak attack +3d6, disease (DC 15), paralysis (1d4+1 rounds, DC 15)

STATISTICS

Str 18, **Dex** 17, **Con** —, **Int** 13, **Wis** 16, **Cha** 18

Base Atk +4; **CMB** +8; **CMD** 22

Feats Combat Reflexes, Dodge, Improved Initiative, Lightning Reflexes, Skill Focus (Stealth)

Skills Acrobatics +13, Bluff +14, Disable Device +13, Escape Artist +13, Knowledge (local) +10, Perception +13, Sleight of Hand +13, Stealth +16

Languages Common, Undercommon

SQ rogue talents (combat trick, fast stealth), trapfinding +2

Combat Gear *potions of inflict moderate wounds* (4), alchemist's fire (3), unholy water (2); **Other Gear** leather armor, *amulet of natural armor +1*, *eversmoking bottle*

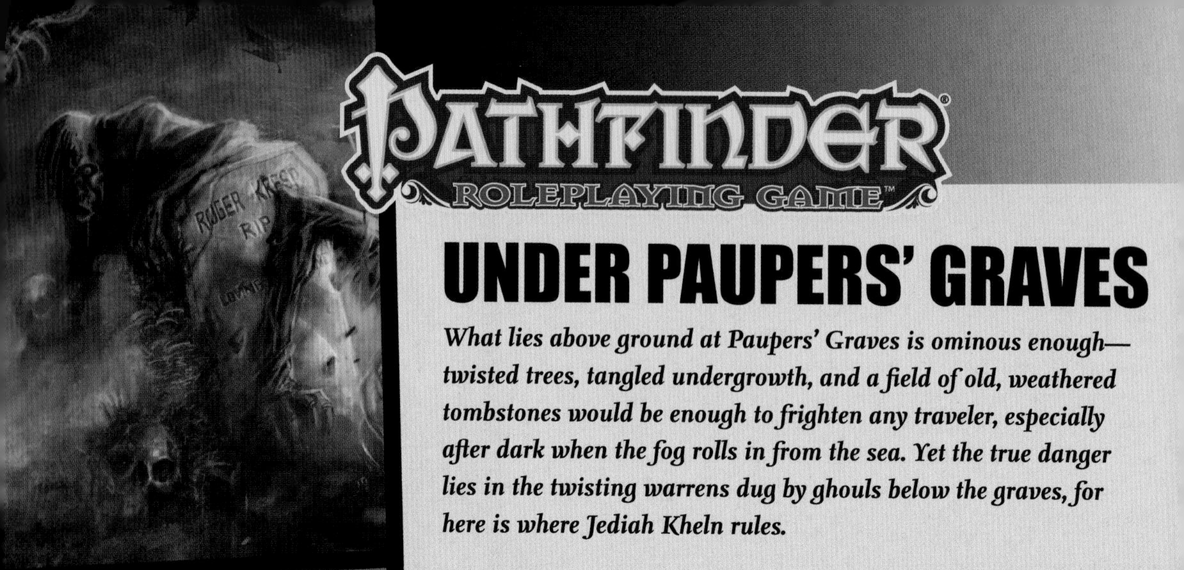
ROGER KREST
RIP

UNDER PAUPERS' GRAVES

What lies above ground at Paupers' Graves is ominous enough—twisted trees, tangled undergrowth, and a field of old, weathered tombstones would be enough to frighten any traveler, especially after dark when the fog rolls in from the sea. Yet the true danger lies in the twisting warrens dug by ghouls below the graves, for here is where Jediah Kheln rules.

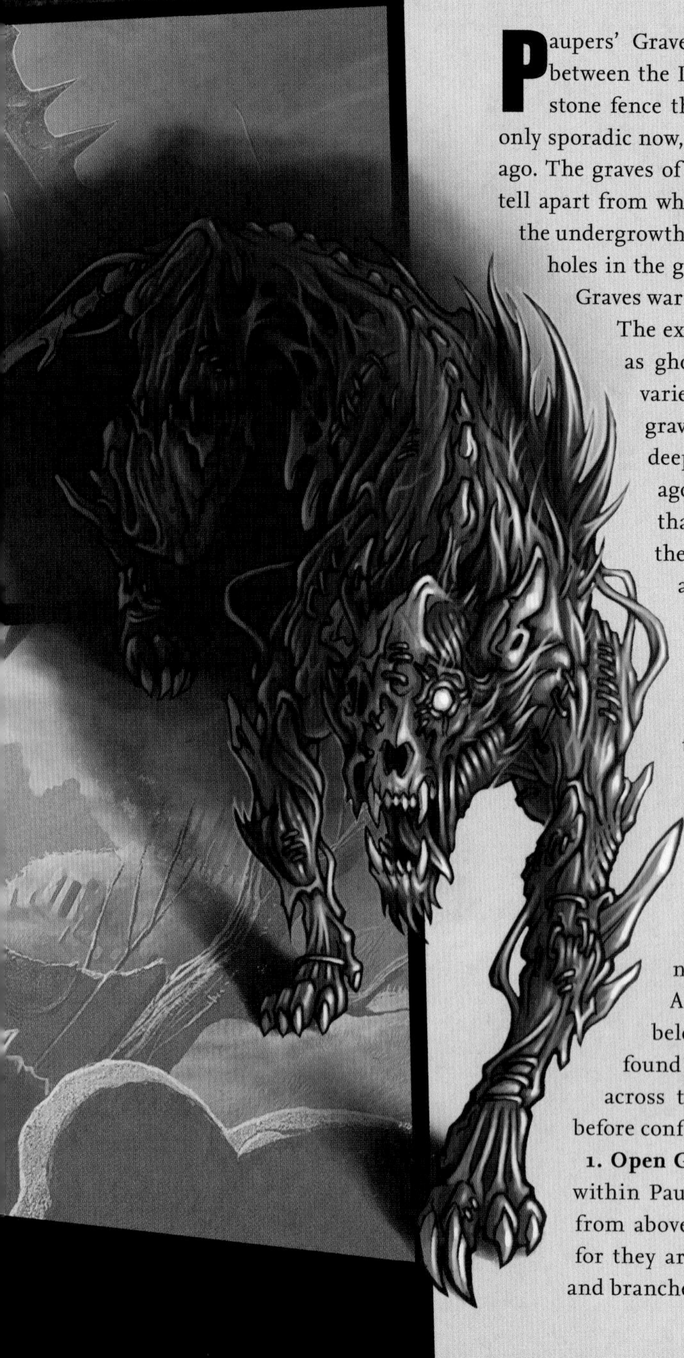

Paupers' Graves itself covers just over three acres of land between the Lost Coast Road and the seaside cliffs. The low stone fence that once defined the graveyard's boundaries is only sporadic now, many of its stones having been scavenged long ago. The graves of the boneyard itself are overgrown and hard to tell apart from what were once trails, but in certain areas where the undergrowth is thickest, graves have been replaced by gaping holes in the ground. These are the entrances to the Paupers' Graves warrens—home of Kheln and his ghouls.

The exact number of ghouls and undead dogs (known as ghoul hounds) that dwell below Paupers' Graves varies considerably, for the warrens below the graveyard extend outward for miles, connecting to a deeper network of tunnels burrowed many decades ago by ghouls much older and more dangerous than Kheln. These tunnels extend southeast to the cavern networks under the escarpment known as Devil's Platter, eventually connecting to an ancient temple devoted to the demon lord Kabriri–and to the alchemist ghast Kanker's lair. New tunnels are constantly being added as well, and explorers may be disturbed to note that some of these "ghoulways" connect to the old smugglers' tunnels below Sandpoint...

Jediah Kheln himself dwells in a small cave network under the center of Paupers' Graves—it is these caves that are presented here. When ghouls start to appear in Sandpoint, tracking them back to the graveyard via their new tunnels invariably leads to these caves. Alternately, PCs could stumble into the warrens below Paupers' Graves via one of the open graves found within the boneyard itself. However they come across these chambers, a group should be 6th level before confronting Kheln in his home!

1. Open Graves: These locations lead up to open graves within Paupers' Graves. Finding one of these entrances from above ground requires a DC 20 Perception check, for they are cunningly obscured by well-placed boughs and branches.

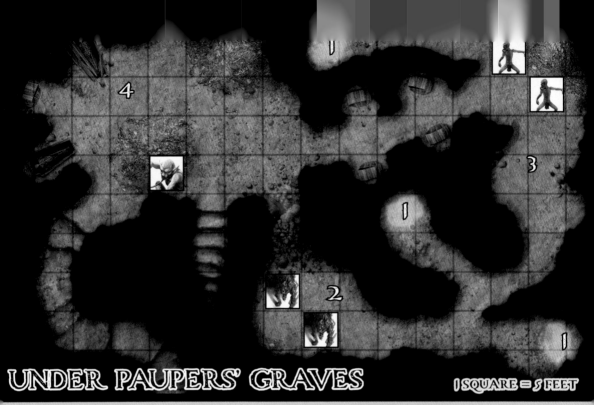

UNDER PAUPERS' GRAVES

2. Kennel: This cavern once connected to Kheln's chambers, but a collapse closed off the northern tunnel several months ago. Today, the room is used to house a pair of ghoul hounds that eagerly attack any who enter.

GHOUL HOUNDS (2)	CR 1

XP 400 each
Variant ghoul (*Pathfinder RPG Bestiary* 146)
Pawn *Pathfinder Pawns Bestiary Box* 85
(Goblin Dog)
CE Medium undead
Init +6; **Senses** darkvision 60 ft., scent; **Perception** +6

DEFENSE

AC 14, touch 12, flat-footed 12 (+2 Dex, +2 natural)
hp 13 each (2d8+4)
Fort +2, **Ref** +2, **Will** +5
Defensive Abilities channel resistance +2; **Immune** undead traits

OFFENSE

Speed 50 ft.
Melee bite +5 (1d6+6 plus disease, paralysis, and trip)
Special Attacks disease (DC 13), paralysis (1d4+1 rounds, DC 13), trip (bite)

STATISTICS

Str 18, **Dex** 15, **Con** —, **Int** 2, **Wis** 14, **Cha** 14
Base Atk +1; **CMB** +5; **CMD** 17 (21 vs. trip)
Feats Improved Initiative
Skills Perception +6, Stealth +6

3. Guardroom: This longer room is typically occupied by a pair of ghouls who serve Kheln loyally. Often, these ghouls are distracted in long and complex philosophical arguments over topics like whether or not flesh is sweeter when infested by graveworms or not, or the correct amount of time one should let a fat corpse versus a skinny corpse ripen before feeding. As a result, the ghouls suffer a −4 penalty on Perception checks to notice intruders.

GHOULS (2)	CR 1

XP 400 each
hp 13 each (*Pathfinder RPG Bestiary* 146)
Miniature *Pathfinder Battles Rise of the Runelords* 5

4. Kheln's Den: The largest chamber under Paupers' Graves serves Jediah Kheln as a grisly banquet hall and meeting place for visits from Kanker's minions. Dirt-caked coffins lean against the wall, often containing fresh bodies scavenged from victims found elsewhere. Kheln himself spends much of his time reading old books while crouched atop a mound of bones, but quickly moves to attack once he realizes his home's been invaded.

JEDIAH KHELN	CR 6

XP 2,400
hp 64
Pawn *Pathfinder Pawns Bestiary Box* 82 (Ghoul)

Treasure: Among the bone heaps in this room lie a few valuables, including a total of 432 gp, a masterwork tower shield, a *+1 whip*, and a filthy but still quite functional *druid's vestment*.

PATHFINDER

CHRONICLES

by James Jacobs

MOSSWOOD GAZETTEER

One of two significantly sized woodlands to the east of Sandpoint (the other being Nettlewood), Mosswood is the less tangled, less dangerous of the two, yet the forest is far from safe. Mosswood's primary inhabitants are goblins, and the Mosswood tribe remains the largest of the Sandpoint goblin tribes today. Part of the Mosswood goblins' tenacity doubtlessly comes from the tribe's chieftain, Big Gugmut, who claims to be the son of a hobgoblin and a wild boar. Mosswood's trees tend to be larger, mostly redwood, but with a many smaller plants like huckleberries, ferns, and smaller trees in the region's undergrowth.

Several sample adventure sites or points of interest hidden within the boundaries of Mosswood are listed below—you can place these locations as you like for any adventure that takes place inside this dangerous woodland.

Hungry Hollow: The carnivorous plants that grow within this long and moist stretch in northeastern Mosswood are notorious among the goblins, for it is a place that, despite even their better judgment, they have a hard time ignoring. All manner of meat-eating plantlife dwells in this not-quite-a-swamp section of the woods, including ravenous slime molds, shambling heaps of vegetation, huge sundews that exude the scent of rotting fish and pickles (a scent most goblins can't resist), and immense pitcher plants augmented by whiplike tendrils that wind out among the undergrowth to form treacherous nooses. Yet amid these ravenous plants are rumored to lie hidden numerous treasures that the goblins of Mosswood are strangely obsessed with. Of course, the fact that every goblin hero that succumbs to the hungry plants only adds to

the treasures when his or her valuables are added to the tangled undergrowth isn't lost on the other goblins. There are increasingly more treasures to be had in Hungry Hollow with each goblin death!

Lost Tors: The Sandpoint Hinterlands feature many rugged hillocks and escarpments—the most rugged of these are the tors. Most of the tors are named after adventurers who explored them, but the ridges within Mosswood are known as the Lost Tors. Unlike the other ranges, these tors remain largely unexplored. This isn't entirely due to their remote location within the woods, but primarilly due to their ill repute—many whisper that the things that live on these densely wooded slopes would just as quickly eat goblins as anything else. On certain nights, when the fog is light and the moon is dark, fires can be spied burning atop the lowest peaks of the Lost Tors, and figures capering and dancing atop them lend credence to tales that ogres dwell in the region. Yet if the Lost Tors do indeed harbor such a tribe, these ogres are unusually secretive and quiet, for no significant ogre raids have ever plagued the region. What might dwell atop the highest of the Lost Tors, where no fires ever burn and strange roars and mournful howls have been known to echo, may even be nightmares and taboo to the ogres themselves.

Mosswood Goblin Families: The goblins that dwell in these woodlands are all part of one large tribe—arguably the largest goblin tribe in the Sandpoint Hinterlands. Known collectively as the Mosswood Goblins, were a single leader ever to rise in power enough to unite them under one banner, these goblins would immediately become the largest threat to the region of all the goblin tribes. Fortunately for Sandpoint, the Mosswood goblins have a long-standing tradition of bickering and biting. The tribe itself is fractured into no fewer than 34 different families, each of different sizes, and each with the conviction that their patriarch or matriarch should be the one leading the rest. Raids, pranks, and even the odd assassination attempt (although these last are only rarely successful) keep the Mosswood goblins busy. Recent rumors that the cult of Lamashtu has infiltrated Mosswood and has recruited several of the goblin families has caused a fair amount of worry

among a few of the region's woodsmen and some of Sandpoint's leaders. With the aid of local adventurers, the hope is that the veracity of these rumors can not only be confirmed, but neutralized if necessary before the cult becomes a significant threat.

Spider Stones: Once a nameless shrine to Gozreh, one of dozens along the Varisian coast, the so-called Spider Stones are one of many places the goblins of the woods avoid. As with most goblin-granted appellations, the Spider Stones are exactly what they sound like—a series of standing stones claimed as a nesting ground for several of Mosswood's more dangerous vermin. Yet the moss spiders that have dwelt among the stones for decades are more dangerous than most, for they are not alone in making this ancient site their home. Turn the page for more details on this location.

PATHFINDER® ROLEPLAYING GAME™

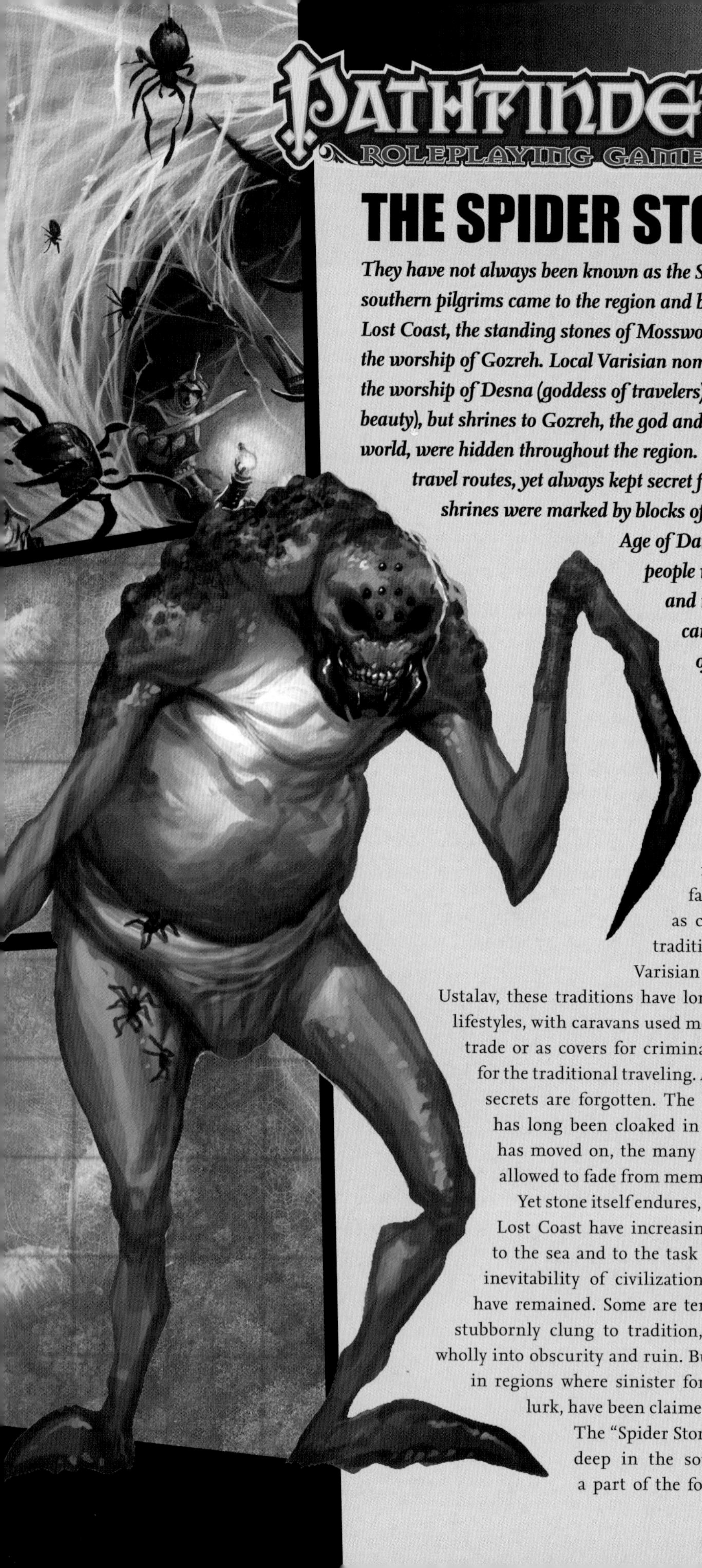

THE SPIDER STONES

They have not always been known as the Spider Stones. Long before southern pilgrims came to the region and brought civilization to the Lost Coast, the standing stones of Mosswoood were a site sacred to the worship of Gozreh. Local Varisian nomads generally preferred the worship of Desna (goddess of travelers) or Shelyn (goddess of beauty), but shrines to Gozreh, the god and goddess of the natural world, were hidden throughout the region. Never far from known travel routes, yet always kept secret from nonbelievers, these shrines were marked by blocks of stone raised during the Age of Darkness, when the Varisian people were struggling to reclaim and retain their roots as they came out from under the rule of the ancient runelords of Thassilon into a new world wracked by darkness and disaster.

For centuries, the people of Varisia have needed nothing more than their families and caravans, but as civilization encroaches, the traditions of travel among the Varisian folk have eroded. In distant Ustalav, these traditions have long been replaced by urban lifestyles, with caravans used more often as instruments of trade or as covers for criminal or darker activities than for the traditional traveling. As older traditions fade, old secrets are forgotten. The nature of druidic worship has long been cloaked in such secrets, and as faith has moved on, the many standing stones have been allowed to fade from memory.

Yet stone itself endures, and while the druids of the Lost Coast have increasingly turned their attention to the sea and to the task of guiding and easing the inevitability of civilization's growth, the old places have remained. Some are tended by hermits who have stubbornly clung to tradition, while others have fallen wholly into obscurity and ruin. But some, particularly those in regions where sinister forces and hungry monsters lurk, have been claimed by new masters.

The "Spider Stones" themselves are located deep in the southeastern Mosswood, in a part of the forest goblins are not eager

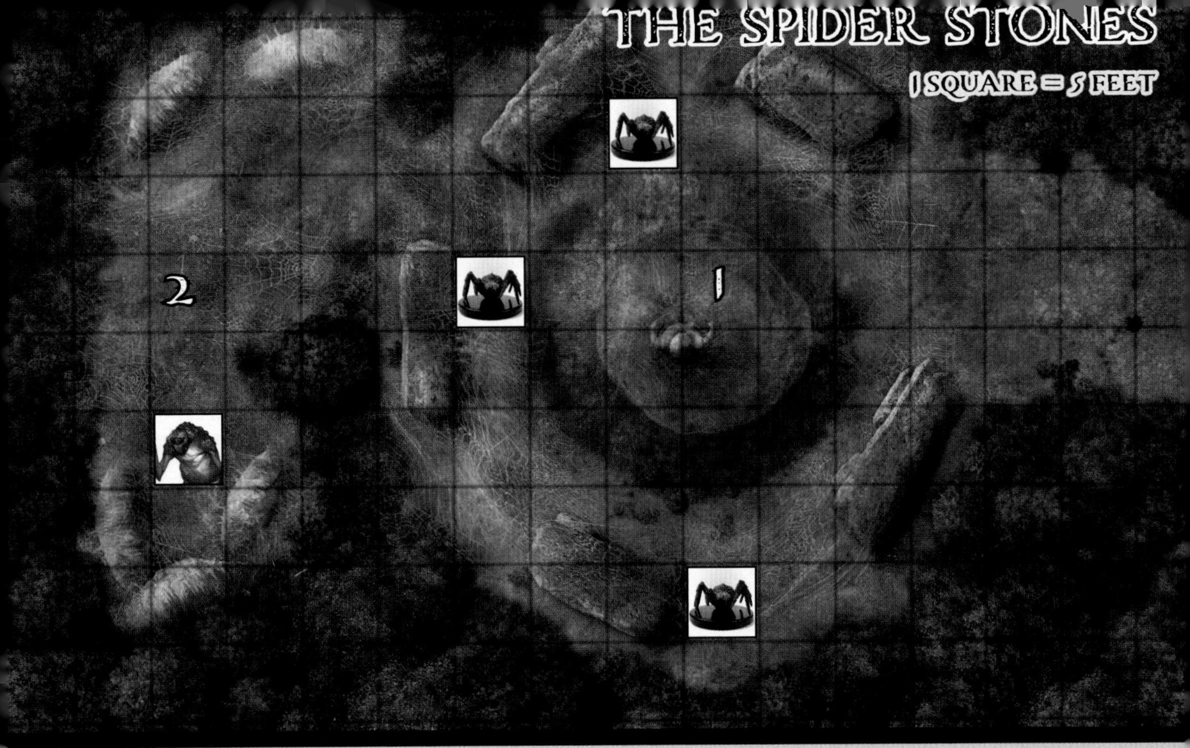
THE SPIDER STONES
1 SQUARE = 5 FEET
2
1

to go. The current lord of the stones is the main reason—a bloated, purple and white ettercap by the name of Citterkith who has turned the stones into a palace of webs.

1. Shrine to Gozreh: The shrine itself consists of five standing stones, each carved from basalt quarried from many miles away, many centuries ago. The stones endure, their inner faces carved with prayers sacred to Gozreh. A statue of Gozreh in his masculine form—that of a stern, bearded man—stands in the center of the stones atop a low mound. All of these, including the undergrowth and canopy above, have been encased in thick sheets of spiderwebs, transforming what was once a clearing in the woods into a web-walled cavern. This is also the den of three particularly creepy crawlies—moss spiders. These arachnids, encountered relatively rarely outside of Mosswood, are unfortunately common in this part of the forest. They are feared by goblins, ogres, hunters, and anyone else with cause to know of them, for unlike the typical giant spider, the bite of a moss spider brings on a particularly agonizing series of convulsions, wracking pain, and if not treated soon, death.

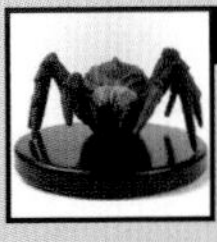

MOSS SPIDERS (3) **CR 2**

XP 600 each

Variant advanced giant spider (*Pathfinder RPG Bestiary* 258, 294)

hp 22 each

Poison (Ex) Bite—injury; *save* Fort DC 16; *frequency* 1/round for 6 rounds; *effect* 1d2 Constitution damage; *cure* 1 save.

Miniature *Pathfinder Battles Heroes and Monsters* 12

2. Citterkith's Den: The ettercap Citterkith thinks of herself as the queen of this little empire of spiders, and often sends one of the moss spiders from area 1 out into the woods to find food to bring back—the ettercap hasn't had a reason to leave these caves for months as a result. She rises up to attack any who dare enter her den, but won't bother coming to the aid of any spiders in a fight in area 1. There appear to be five goblin-sized bodies wrapped in the webby walls of this cave, and while three of these do indeed contain goblins (as well as a total of 153 gp and a +1 *dogslicer*), the other two in fact contain ettercap spear traps (see *Pathfinder RPG Bestiary*).

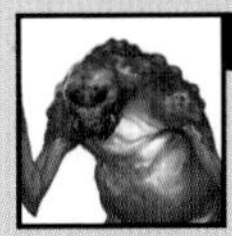

CITTERKITH **CR 4**

XP 1,200

Advanced ettercap (*Pathfinder RPG Bestiary* 129, 294)

hp 38

Pawn *Pathfinder Pawns Bestiary Box* 77

Development: Anyone who kills or drives off the spiders and ettercap, then removes the spiderwebs and helps (over the course of several weeks) restore the balance of nature in this area receives a vision from Gozreh in thanks as a dream—likely of swarms of arachnid eatting birds and healthy animals tearing their ways through webbing. When the dreamer awakens, she does so with the ability to use *commune with nature* as a spell-like ability (caster level equals the dreamer's Hit Dice) up to six times over the course of the next year.

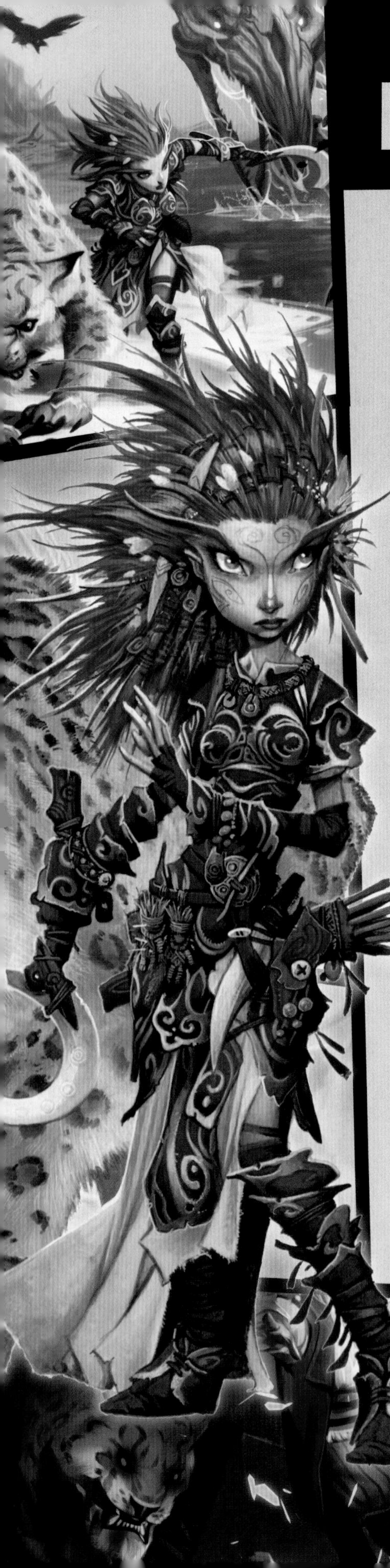

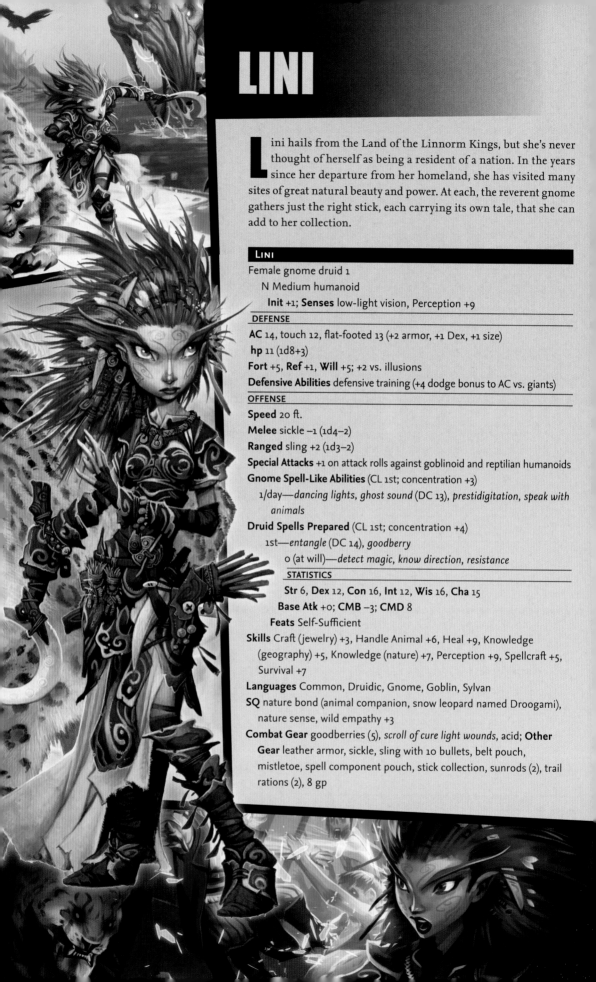

LINI

Lini hails from the Land of the Linnorm Kings, but she's never thought of herself as being a resident of a nation. In the years since her departure from her homeland, she has visited many sites of great natural beauty and power. At each, the reverent gnome gathers just the right stick, each carrying its own tale, that she can add to her collection.

LINI

Female gnome druid 1

N Medium humanoid

Init +1; **Senses** low-light vision, Perception +9

DEFENSE

AC 14, touch 12, flat-footed 13 (+2 armor, +1 Dex, +1 size)

hp 11 (1d8+3)

Fort +5, **Ref** +1, **Will** +5; +2 vs. illusions

Defensive Abilities defensive training (+4 dodge bonus to AC vs. giants)

OFFENSE

Speed 20 ft.

Melee sickle –1 (1d4–2)

Ranged sling +2 (1d3–2)

Special Attacks +1 on attack rolls against goblinoid and reptilian humanoids

Gnome Spell-Like Abilities (CL 1st; concentration +3)

1/day—*dancing lights, ghost sound* (DC 13), *prestidigitation, speak with animals*

Druid Spells Prepared (CL 1st; concentration +4)

1st—*entangle* (DC 14), *goodberry*

0 (at will)—*detect magic, know direction, resistance*

STATISTICS

Str 6, **Dex** 12, **Con** 16, **Int** 12, **Wis** 16, **Cha** 15

Base Atk +0; **CMB** –3; **CMD** 8

Feats Self-Sufficient

Skills Craft (jewelry) +3, Handle Animal +6, Heal +9, Knowledge (geography) +5, Knowledge (nature) +7, Perception +9, Spellcraft +5, Survival +7

Languages Common, Druidic, Gnome, Goblin, Sylvan

SQ nature bond (animal companion, snow leopard named Droogami), nature sense, wild empathy +3

Combat Gear goodberries (5), *scroll of cure light wounds*, acid; **Other Gear** leather armor, sickle, sling with 10 bullets, belt pouch, mistletoe, spell component pouch, stick collection, sunrods (2), trail rations (2), 8 gp

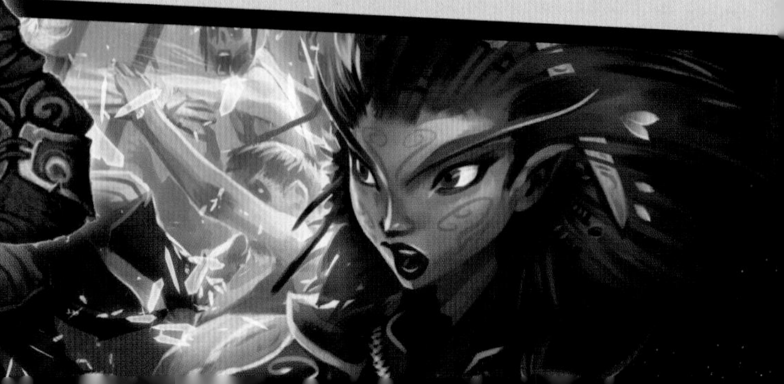

DROOGAMI

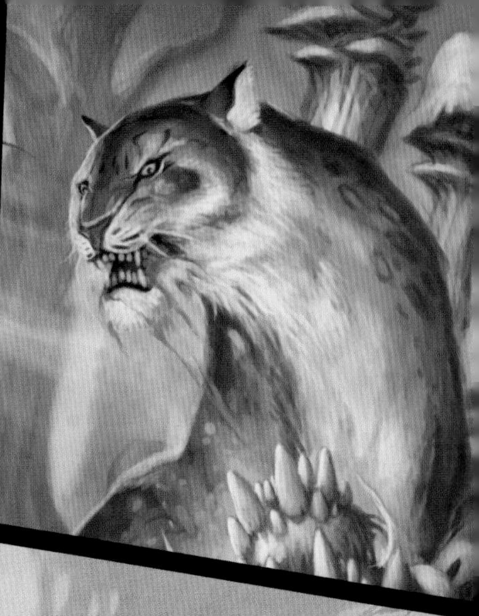

Lini has always had a way with wild creatures. More than once during her childhood, she used this talent to save a playmate from the jaws of a wolf, wolverine, or other predator. Her alliance with the hawks that nested in the region gave her incredible insight into dangers that threatened her kin. When she heard rumors of a snow leopard acting strangely, Lini sought the creature out, only to be shocked when the animal ignored her attempt at friendship and pinned her to the loamy soil in the shadow of a great pine. But as the leopard stayed its claws, and as Lini looked into the leopard's eyes, she heard the voice of nature itself deep within.

She knew then that she had not come to help this particular animal in a time of need. She knew that this creature had been sent instead to help her in her times of need to come. The snow leopard would be her guardian, her mount, her scout, and perhaps most importantly, her friend

Lini left her home not long after, and in the years to follow, while she has travelled with many diverse companions, the snow leopard Droogami has never let her down.

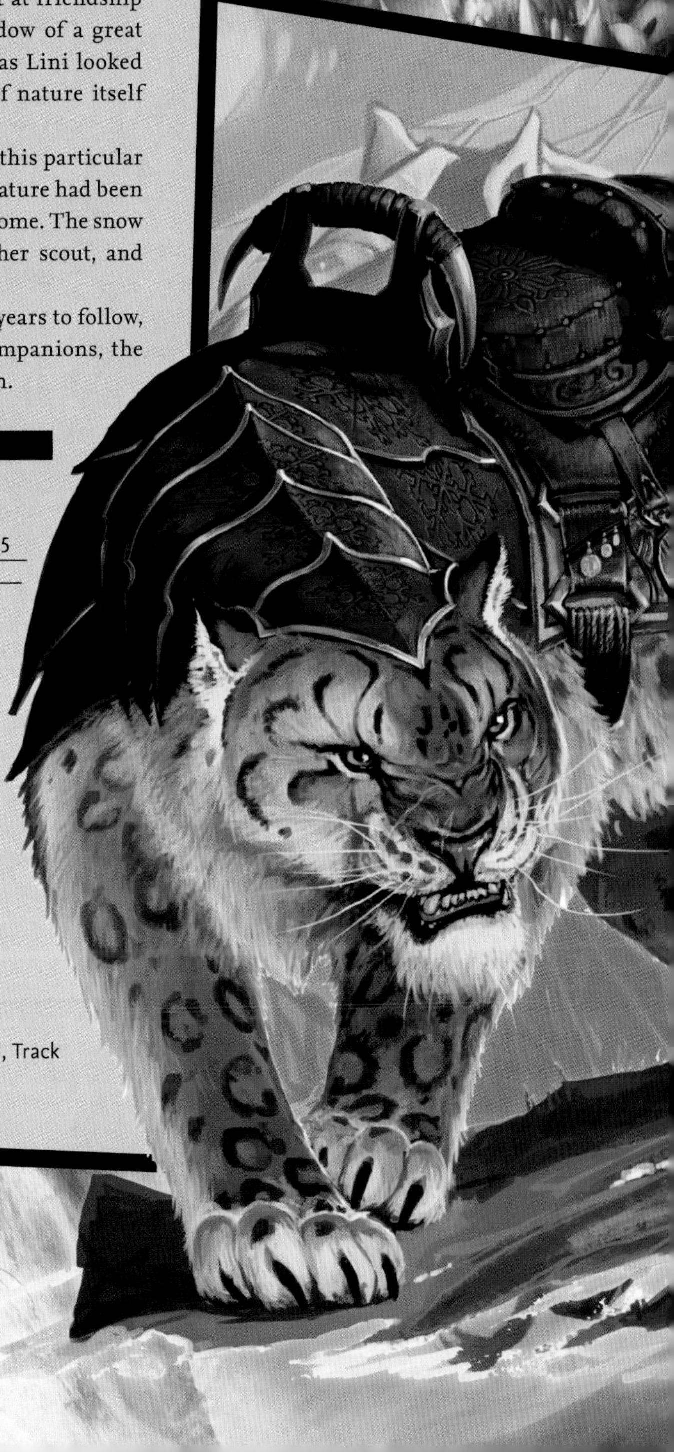

Droogami

Small cat animal companion

N Small animal

Init +5; **Senses** low-light vision, scent; Perception +5

DEFENSE

AC 18, touch 17, flat-footed 12 (+5 Dex, +1 dodge, +1 natural, +1 size)

hp 11 (2d8+2)

Fort +4, **Ref** +8, **Will** +1

OFFENSE

Speed 50 ft.

Melee bite +3 (1d4+1 plus trip), 2 claws +3 (1d2+1)

STATISTICS

Str 12, **Dex** 21, **Con** 13, **Int** 2, **Wis** 12, **Cha** 6

Base Atk +1; **CMB** +1; **CMD** 17 (21 vs. trip)

Feats Dodge

Skills Perception +5, Stealth +13

SQ sprint

Tricks Known Attack, Come, Defend, Down, Guard, Track

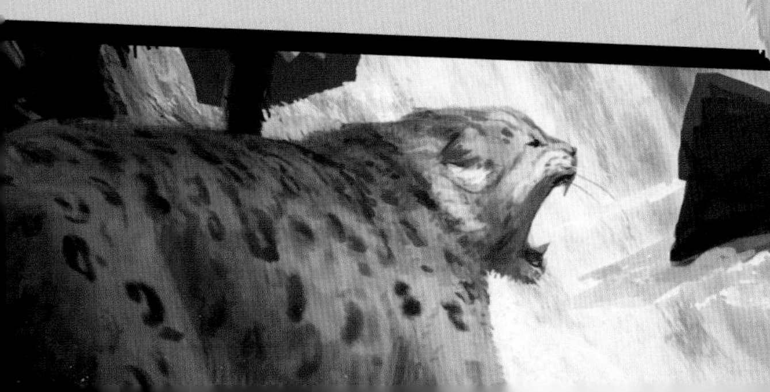

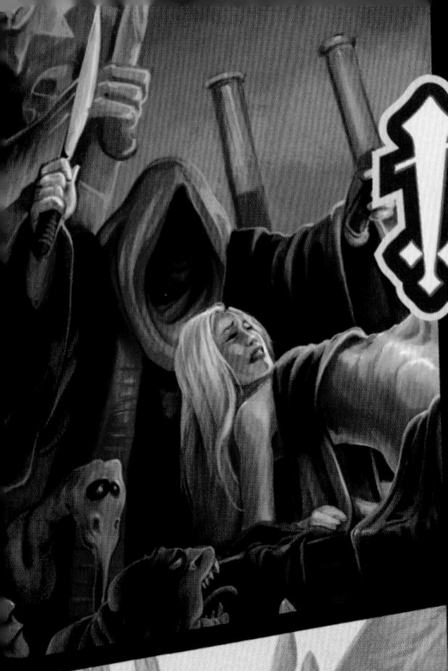

Pathfinder Chronicles

by James Jacobs

THE WATERS OF LAMASHTU

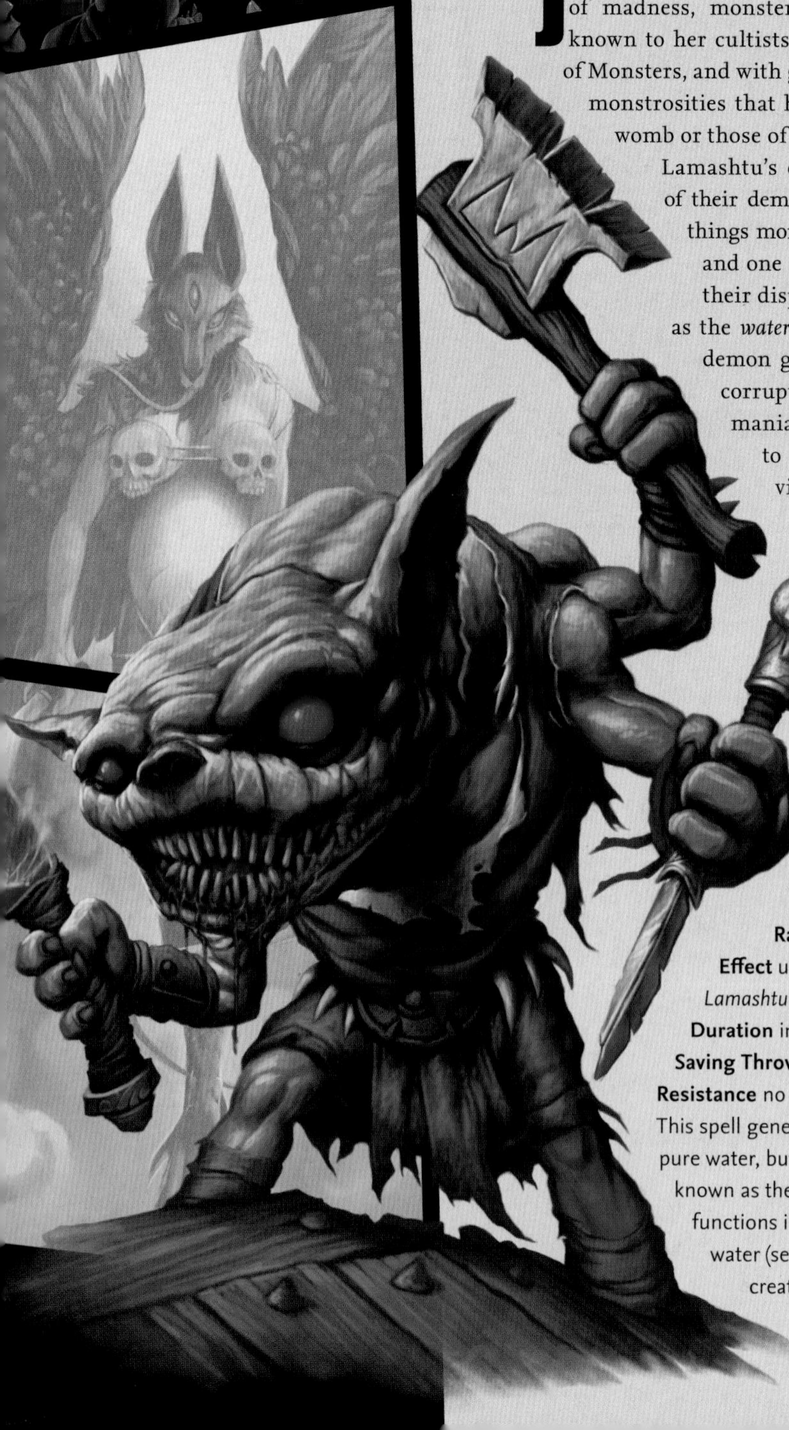

Jackal-headed, three-eyed Lamashtu is the goddess of madness, monsters, and nightmares. She is known to her cultists and enemies as the Mother of Monsters, and with good cause, for legion are the monstrosities that have been spawned from her womb or those of her minions.

Lamashtu's cultists seek to do the work of their demonic patron by promoting all things monstrous throughout the world, and one of the most insidious tools at their disposal is the vile liquid known as the *waters of Lamashtu*. Cultists of the demon goddess—be they evil clerics, corrupt druids, sinister witches, or maniacal alchemists—can learn to call forth these secretions via magic using the following spell (which first appeared in *Pathfinder Campaign Setting: Inner Sea World Guide*).

WATERS OF LAMASHTU

School conjuration (creation); **Level** alchemist 2, cleric 3, druid 3, witch 3

Casting Time 1 standard action

Components V, S, M (250 gp of powdered amber)

Range close (25 ft. + 5 ft./2 levels)

Effect up to 1 dose of the *waters of Lamashtu* per 2 levels

Duration instantaneous

Saving Throw Fortitude partial; **Spell Resistance** no

This spell generates what appears to be clear, pure water, but is in fact a foul secretion known as the *waters of Lamashtu*. The liquid functions in all the same ways as unholy water (see *curse water*). In addition, any creature that is anointed with or drinks this fluid must make

a Fortitude save. (Drinking the *waters of Lamashtu* is particularly effective—a creature who drinks the stuff takes a −4 penalty on the save to resist its effects.) Success causes the creature to become violently ill, vomit the fluid, and become sickened for 1d4 rounds. Failure indicates the water takes root and drives the victim mad (dealing 1d6 points of Intelligence damage) and twists and deforms the body (dealing 1d6 points of Dexterity damage). The subject's Dexterity and Intelligence cannot drop below 1 as a result of this effect. Casting this spell creates approximately 2 ounces of the *waters of Lamashtu*, enough for one dose or use as a thrown weapon (if bottled). The fluid can be created and stored indefinitely, though it cannot be created inside a creature. Extensive exposure to the *waters of Lamashtu* (such as drinking nothing else for months at a time) can have other long-term effects on the target, including the development of monstrous deformities or even total transformation into a beast, at the GM's discretion. Such mutations are rarely beneficial to the victim.

MONSTROUS MUTATIONS

While those who drink the *waters of Lamashtu* suffer potent hallucinations and painful muscle cramps that not only debilitate but often result in madness and deformity, the true perils of the *waters of Lamashtu* lie in overindulgence. To certain creatures—primarily goblins, gnolls, bugbears, and similar bestial humanoids—the waters can have an addictive quality. Unfortunately for such addicts, drinking too deeply of these tainted waters infuses the flesh and mind alike with lasting deformities that in rare cases can actually increase a creature's power, but in most cases merely result in grotesque, painful, and sometimes fatal mutations.

When a creature that is particularly susceptible to the *waters of Lamashtu* drinks more than 2 doses in a 24-hour period, it must make a successful DC 20 Fortitude save or become addicted. (This save DC is not adjusted by the ability scores of the original creator of the water.) Each day that follows without drinking at least 1 additional dose, the addict suffers a −4 penalty on all Will saves

and takes 1 point of Constitution damage from the pain. Rest can keep this Constitution damage from ever progressing to life-threatening levels, but for many addicts, securing additional doses of the water is a better solution

The point at which *waters of Lamashtu* cause mutations varies from drinker to drinker. Fully 80% of these mutations are harmful, resulting in 1d4 points of ability drain to a random ability score as vestigial limbs, suppurating wounds, ingrown pustules, tumors, and bone spurs wreak havoc. In the remaining 20% of cases, the mutations can result in beneficial abnormalities such as fully functional additional limbs or sensory organs, an increase to mental faculties, or even a slight increase to an ability score (usually a +1 inherent bonus). The mutations can even result in new abilities such as flight, water breathing, or poison glands. Such mutants are often heralded as the chosen of Lamashtu and can achieve positions of great power in her cult, but those who lack the support of the demonic cult are more often forced into lives in the shadows of society as freaks and outcasts.

THE BLOODFANG GOBLINS

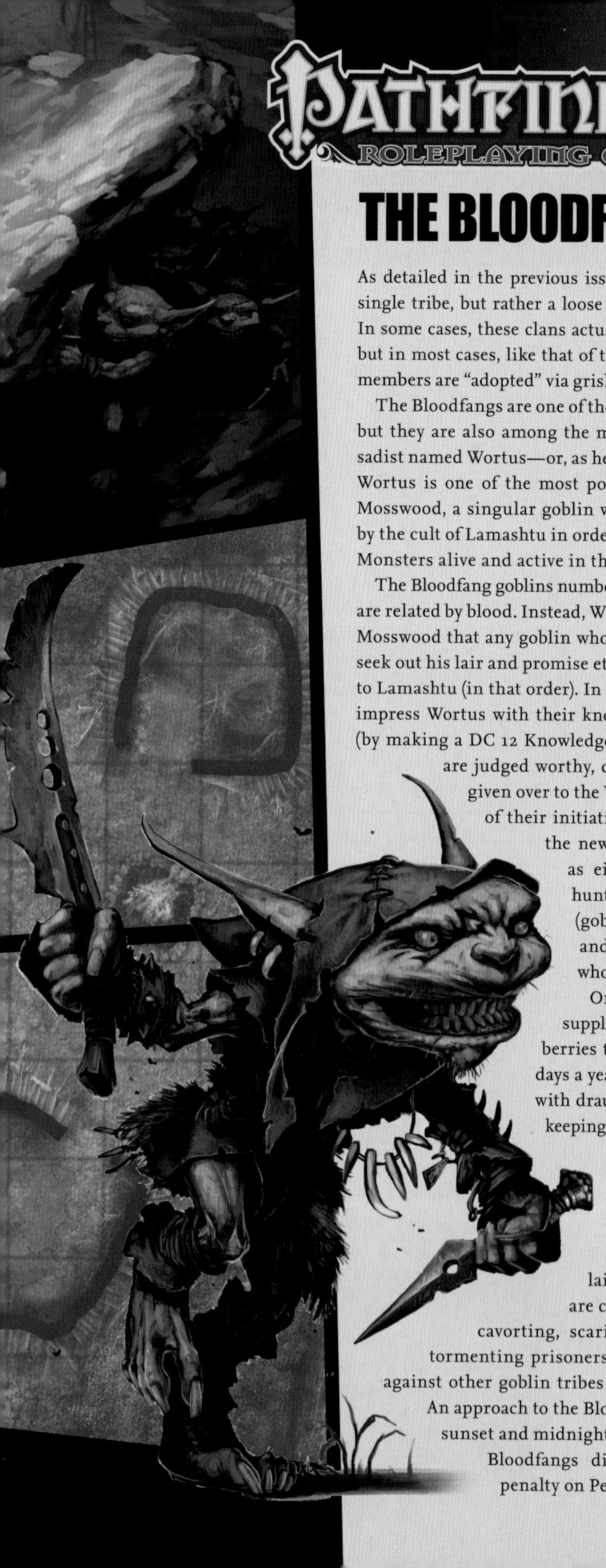

As detailed in the previous issue, the goblins of Mosswood are not a single tribe, but rather a loose collection of extended goblin families. In some cases, these clans actually consist of goblins related by blood, but in most cases, like that of the Bloodfangs, a significant number of members are "adopted" via grisly or dangerous rituals.

The Bloodfangs are one of the smaller goblin families in Mosswood, but they are also among the most dangerous. Their leader is a wiry sadist named Wortus—or, as he prefers to be called, Big Chief Wortus. Wortus is one of the most powerful goblin priests of Lamashtu in Mosswood, a singular goblin who is funded and supported in secret by the cult of Lamashtu in order to keep the interests of the Mother of Monsters alive and active in the region.

The Bloodfang goblins number a mere seven members, none of whom are related by blood. Instead, Wortus has long spread word throughout Mosswood that any goblin who wishes to join his "family" need only seek out his lair and promise eternal allegiance to the Bloodfangs and to Lamashtu (in that order). In reality, however, supplicants must also impress Wortus with their knowledge of the teachings of Lamashtu (by making a DC 12 Knowledge [religion] check). Those who succeed are judged worthy, dosed with the *waters of Lamashtu*, and given over to the Visiondark (see below) for the last stage of their initiation. If they make it through the trial, the new family members can join the group as either stalkers (goblins specialized in hunting and killing humans) or slicers (goblins who build their own dogslicers and specialize in bloodletting). Those who fail either test are eaten.

Once a goblin becomes a Bloodfang, he supplements every meal with bitter-tasting berries that stain his teeth red. On seven holy days a year, the meals are further supplemented with draughts of the *waters of Lamashtu*. Indeed, keeping Big Chief Wortus in fresh supply of the ingredients he needs to create more doses of these magical waters is the most common reason the Bloodfangs have to go raiding

1. Firepit: The focus of the Bloodfang lair is a communal firepit. Clan meals are cooked here, and most nights are spent cavorting, scaring each other with campfire tales, tormenting prisoners, and planning future raids (be they against other goblin tribes or travelers on the Lost Coast Road). An approach to the Bloodfang lair during the hours between sunset and midnight is all but guaranteed to find all seven Bloodfangs distracted and noisy, suffering a –4 penalty on Perception checks.

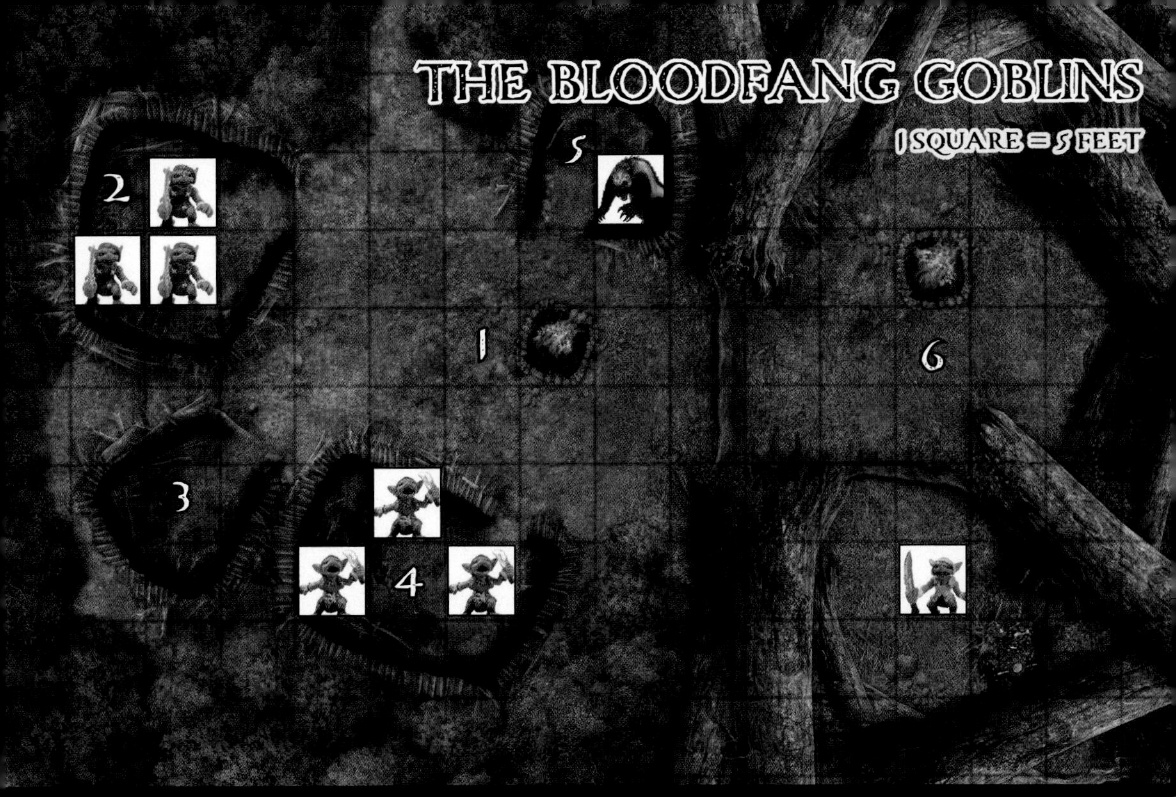
THE BLOODFANG GOBLINS
1 SQUARE = 5 FEET
1
2
3
4
5
6

2. Stalkers' Shack: Goblins who become Bloodfang stalkers stay in the northwesternmost shack, where part of their job is den security. The Bloodfangs sleep in shifts, with one remaining on guard duty at all times, silently patrolling the woods around the clearing save for during firepit moots and meals. The three stalkers keep their stash of treasure inside several polished human skulls—139 gp, three pearls worth 100 gp each, a silver ring worth 140 gp, and a mithral hat pin worth 160 gp.

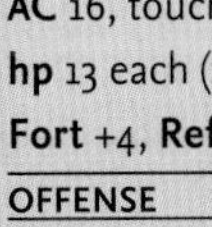

Bloodfang Stalkers (3) **CR 1/2**

XP 200 each

Goblin ranger 1 (*Pathfinder RPG Bestiary* 156)

CE Small humanoid (goblinoid)

Miniature *Pathfinder Battles Heroes & Monsters* 1

Init +3; **Senses** darkvision 60 ft.; Perception +5

DEFENSE

AC 16, touch 14, flat-footed 13 (+2 armor, +3 Dex, +1 size)

hp 13 each (1d10+3)

Fort +4, **Ref** +5, **Will** +1

OFFENSE

Speed 30 ft.

Melee dogslicer +3 (1d4+1/19–20)

Ranged composite longbow +5 (1d6+1/×3)

Special Attacks favored enemy (humans +2)

STATISTICS

Str 13, **Dex** 17, **Con** 14, **Int** 8, **Wis** 12, **Cha** 8

Base Atk +1; **CMB** +1; **CMD** 14

Feats Deadly Aim

Skills Climb +5, Knowledge (religion) +0, Perception +5, Ride +7, Stealth +15, Survival +5

Languages Goblin

SQ track +1, wild empathy +0

Gear leather armor, dogslicer, composite longbow (+1 Str) with 20 arrows

3. Visiondark: This small shack's wooden walls have been coated with numerous layers of pitch, blood, mud, and leaves. While the other shack entrances are typically closed with ratty curtains, this shack's entrance can be sealed with a solid mass of similarly treated planks, transforming the inside into a pitch-black chamber. When new goblins are recruited, they are dosed with the *waters of Lamashtu*, then forced to spend 24 hours in this room with several spears, knives, and dogslicers. During the following day and night, the Bloodfang recruit experiences increasingly realistic hallucinations, and many come to inadvertent harm (or worse) during their thrashings. Those who survive the ordeal never speak of the visions they endured within.

4. Slicers' Shack: The Bloodfang slicers are in charge of plotting raids, tending and tormenting prisoners, and preparing feasts. Typically, their duties work out in precisely that order. The slicers' shack includes two homemade but quite functional sharpening stones for repairing and building new dogslicers. They keep their treasure buried in the southern corner of the shack, wrapped in a black sheet. This treasure consists of 238 gp, an ivory carving of a dragon worth 120 gp, and a *fire elemental gem* that (ironically, considering goblins' love of fire) none of the goblins know is magical.

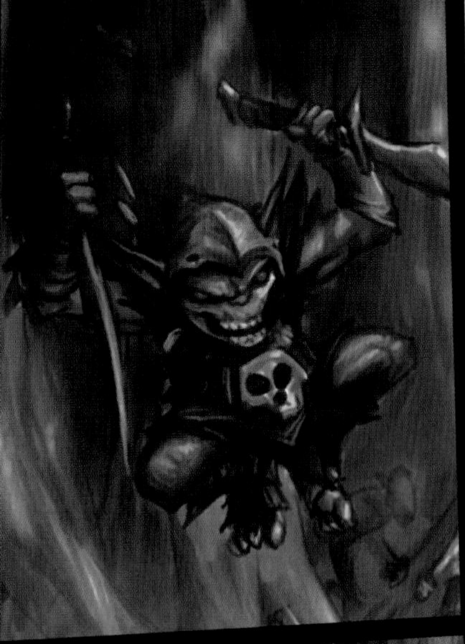
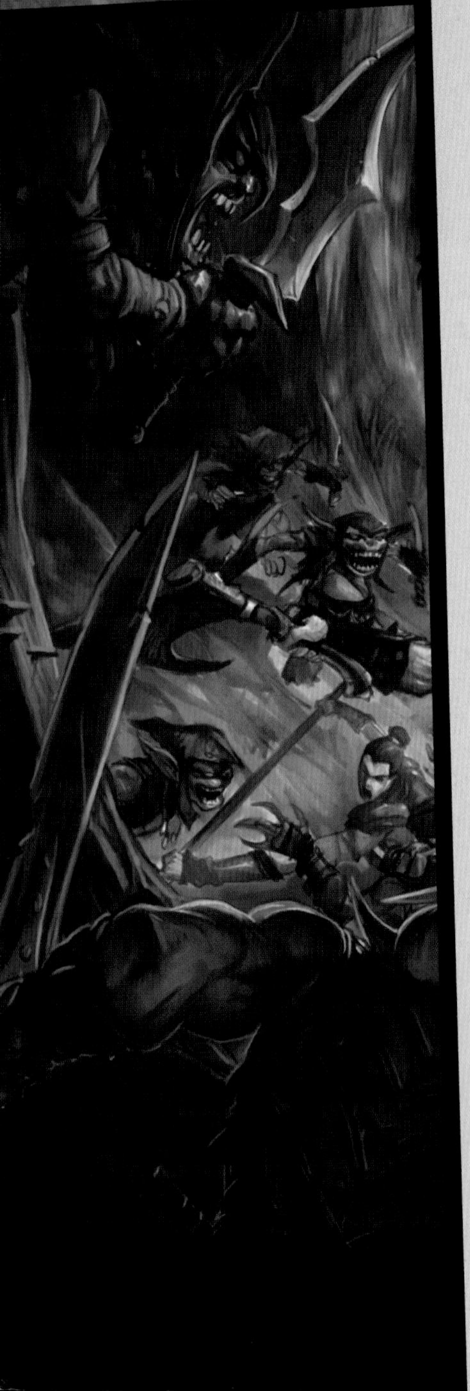

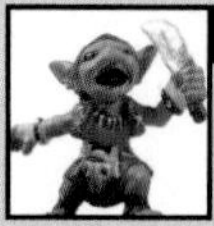

BLOODFANG SLICERS (3) **CR 1/2**

XP 200 each

Goblin rogue 1 (*Pathfinder RPG Bestiary* 156)

CE Small humanoid (goblinoid)

Miniature *Pathfinder Battles Heroes & Monsters* 2

Init +8; **Senses** darkvision 60 ft.; Perception +3

DEFENSE

AC 17, touch 15, flat-footed 13 (+2 armor, +4 Dex, +1 size)

hp 10 (1d8+2)

Fort +1, **Ref** +6, **Will** –1

OFFENSE

Speed 30 ft.

Melee mwk dogslicer +3 (1d4+1/19–20)

Special Attacks sneak attack +1d6

STATISTICS

Str 12, **Dex** 19, **Con** 13, **Int** 10, **Wis** 8, **Cha** 10

Base Atk +0; **CMB** +0; **CMD** 14

Feats Improved Initiative

Skills Acrobatics +8, Climb +5, Craft (weapon) +4, Knowledge (local) +4, Knowledge (religion) +1, Perception +3, Ride +8, Stealth +16, Survival +0

Languages Goblin

SQ trapfinding +1

Gear leather armor, mwk dogslicer

5. Garglegape's Pen: The Bloodfangs' mascot is an ill-tempered wolverine named Garglegape. The beast dwells in this small shack, and while it snaps and growls at anyone who comes close, it's been trained so it doesn't attack goblins. Usually.

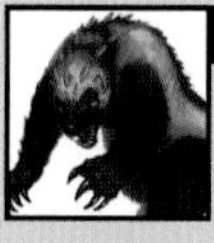

GARGLEGAPE **CR 3**

XP 800

Advanced wolverine (*Pathfinder RPG Bestiary* 279, 294)

hp 28

Miniature *Pathfinder Battles Rise of the Runelords* 10 (Yeth Hound)

6. Wortus's Palace: The leader of the Bloodfangs dwells in a large hollow among several fallen trees—an artificial cavern of trunks and branches. Dead leaves, furs, and the like clog the holes in the roof, making the chamber weatherproof and dark, and the filthy pelts and feathers of slain animals like rats and pigeons carpet the floor. Wortus keeps his own fire constantly lit, resulting in a smoky home, which is just the way he likes it.

As creating the *waters of Lamashtu* requires powdered amber as a material component, Wortus is always careful to keep a stock of the powder on hand. Every few months, a cultist of Lamashtu visits him and he trades the best of the treasures won by his goblins' raids for more powdered amber. Currently, Wortus has 530 gp, seven pieces of jewelry worth 820 gp in all, a *+1 mithral buckler*, and a *wand of acid arrow* (33 charges)—his next meeting with his cult contact is soon!

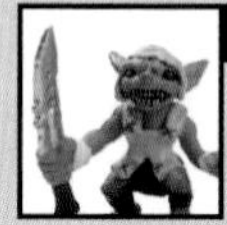

BIG CHIEF WORTUS **CR 5**

XP 1,600

hp 48 (see next page)

Miniature *Pathfinder Battles Heroes & Monsters* 3

BIG CHIEF WORTUS

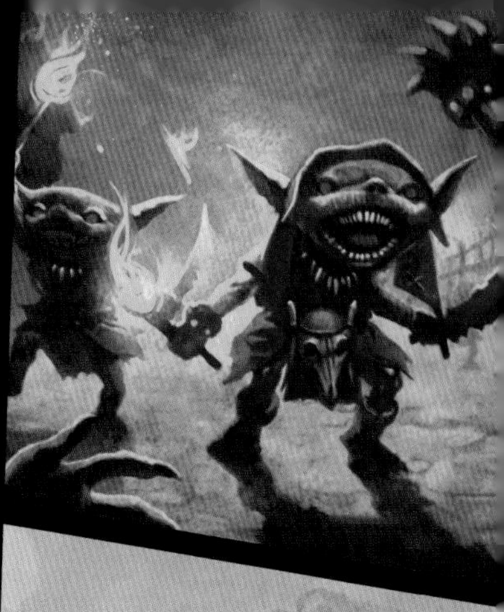

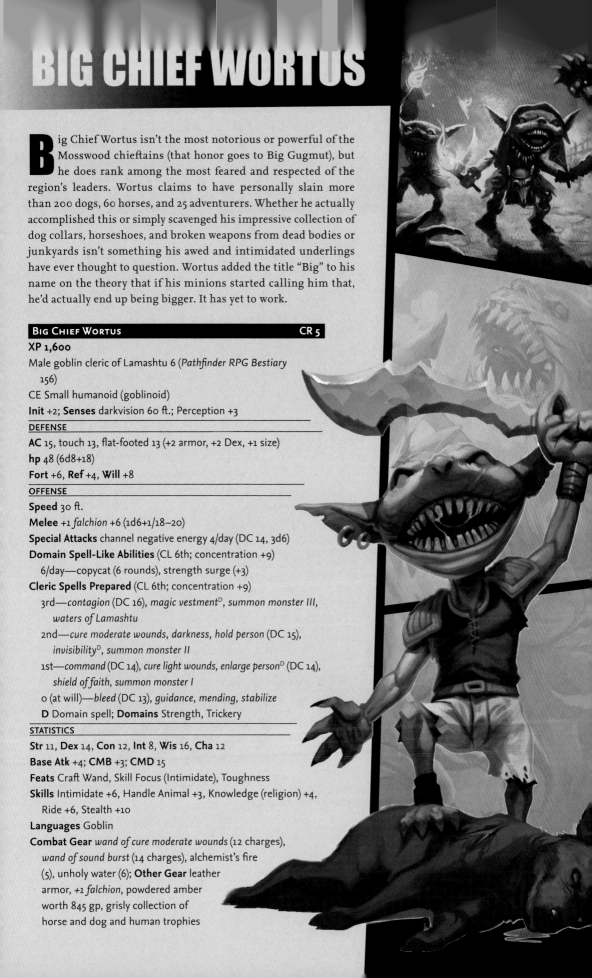

Big Chief Wortus isn't the most notorious or powerful of the Mosswood chieftains (that honor goes to Big Gugmut), but he does rank among the most feared and respected of the region's leaders. Wortus claims to have personally slain more than 200 dogs, 60 horses, and 25 adventurers. Whether he actually accomplished this or simply scavenged his impressive collection of dog collars, horseshoes, and broken weapons from dead bodies or junkyards isn't something his awed and intimidated underlings have ever thought to question. Wortus added the title "Big" to his name on the theory that if his minions started calling him that, he'd actually end up being bigger. It has yet to work.

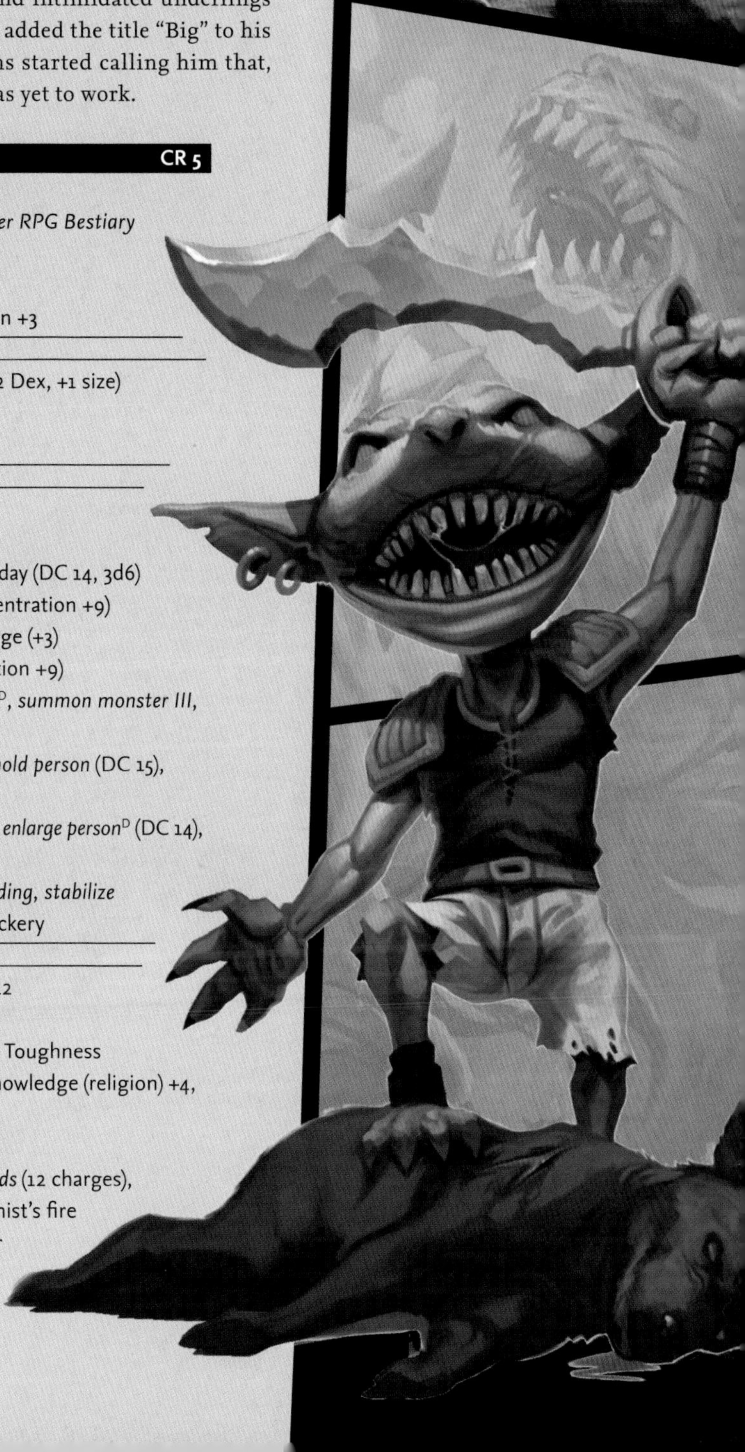

BIG CHIEF WORTUS **CR 5**

XP 1,600

Male goblin cleric of Lamashtu 6 (*Pathfinder RPG Bestiary* 156)

CE Small humanoid (goblinoid)

Init +2; **Senses** darkvision 60 ft.; Perception +3

DEFENSE

AC 15, touch 13, flat-footed 13 (+2 armor, +2 Dex, +1 size)

hp 48 (6d8+18)

Fort +6, **Ref** +4, **Will** +8

OFFENSE

Speed 30 ft.

Melee +1 *falchion* +6 (1d6+1/18–20)

Special Attacks channel negative energy 4/day (DC 14, 3d6)

Domain Spell-Like Abilities (CL 6th; concentration +9)

6/day—copycat (6 rounds), strength surge (+3)

Cleric Spells Prepared (CL 6th; concentration +9)

3rd—*contagion* (DC 16), *magic vestment*[D], *summon monster III*, *waters of Lamashtu*

2nd—*cure moderate wounds*, *darkness*, *hold person* (DC 15), *invisibility*[D], *summon monster II*

1st—*command* (DC 14), *cure light wounds*, *enlarge person*[D] (DC 14), *shield of faith*, *summon monster I*

0 (at will)—*bleed* (DC 13), *guidance*, *mending*, *stabilize*

D Domain spell; **Domains** Strength, Trickery

STATISTICS

Str 11, **Dex** 14, **Con** 12, **Int** 8, **Wis** 16, **Cha** 12

Base Atk +4; **CMB** +3; **CMD** 15

Feats Craft Wand, Skill Focus (Intimidate), Toughness

Skills Intimidate +6, Handle Animal +3, Knowledge (religion) +4, Ride +6, Stealth +10

Languages Goblin

Combat Gear *wand of cure moderate wounds* (12 charges), *wand of sound burst* (14 charges), alchemist's fire (5), unholy water (6); **Other Gear** leather armor, +1 *falchion*, powdered amber worth 845 gp, grisly collection of horse and dog and human trophies

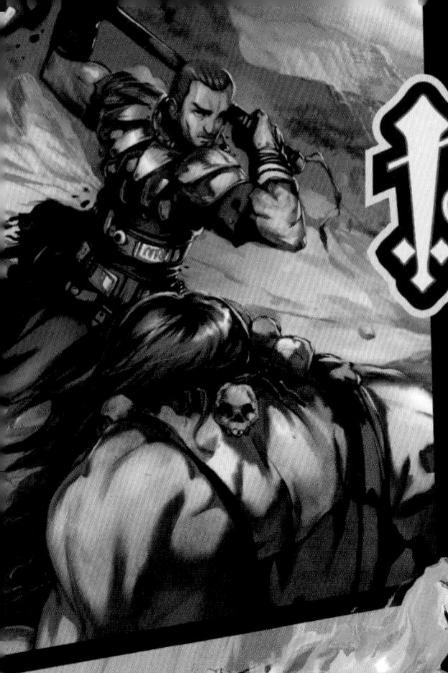

Pathfinder Chronicles

by James Jacobs

HISTORY OF THE LOST COAST

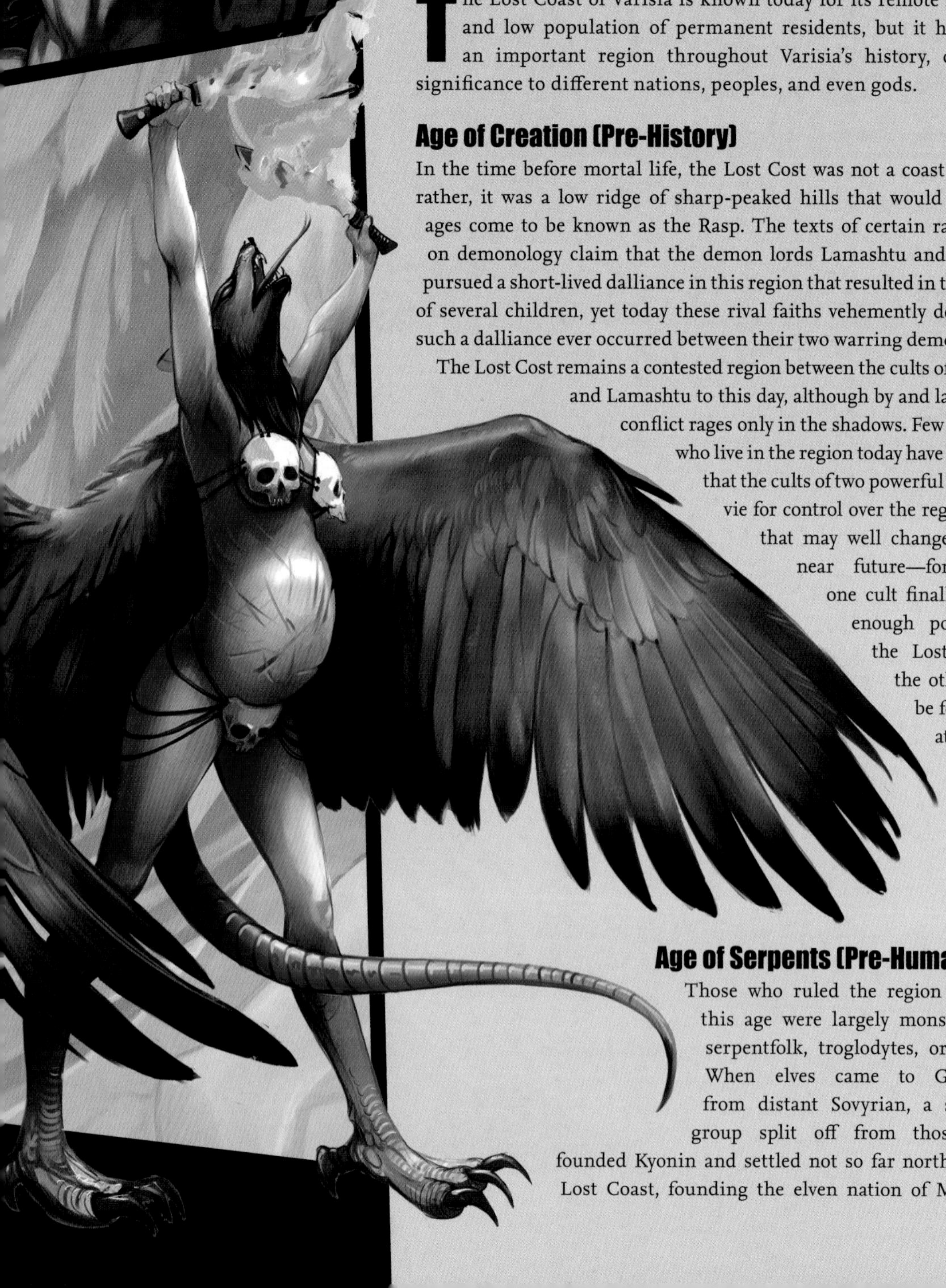

The Lost Coast of Varisia is known today for its remote location and low population of permanent residents, but it has been an important region throughout Varisia's history, of great significance to different nations, peoples, and even gods.

Age of Creation (Pre-History)

In the time before mortal life, the Lost Cost was not a coast at all—rather, it was a low ridge of sharp-peaked hills that would in later ages come to be known as the Rasp. The texts of certain rare texts on demonology claim that the demon lords Lamashtu and Pazuzu pursued a short-lived dalliance in this region that resulted in the birth of several children, yet today these rival faiths vehemently deny that such a dalliance ever occurred between their two warring demon gods. The Lost Cost remains a contested region between the cults of Pazuzu and Lamashtu to this day, although by and large this conflict rages only in the shadows. Few of those who live in the region today have any idea that the cults of two powerful demons vie for control over the region, but that may well change in the near future—for when one cult finally gains enough power in the Lost Coast, the other will be forced to attack.

Age of Serpents (Pre-Humanity)

Those who ruled the region during this age were largely monstrous—serpentfolk, troglodytes, or worse. When elves came to Golarion from distant Sovyrian, a splinter group split off from those who founded Kyonin and settled not so far north of the Lost Coast, founding the elven nation of Mierani.

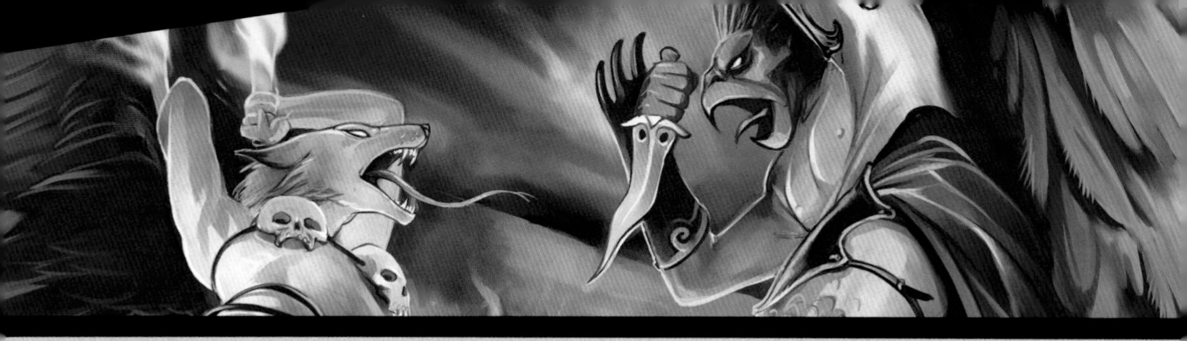

It was their gentle influence that elevated two local human ethnicities from savagery, but once they set the Varisians and Shoanti on their way, the elves stepped back, wisely allowing the human ethnicities to forge their own destinies.

Age of Legend (Pre-Earthfall)

Xin, an exile from distant Azlant, arrived on the shores of Varisia during this age. Impressed with the cultures he discovered there, he chose this region to found his empire of Thassilon and incorporated tribes of Varisians, Shoanti, and giants into the realm. The elves of Mierani proudly—and perhaps wisely—sensed trouble and resisted the advancement of Xin's new nation. Their realm remained a stubborn holdout against Thassilonian expansion until the end, while the region known as the Rasp would become one of the most bitterly contested borders within the empire during the war between Runelord Karzoug and Runelord Alaznist.

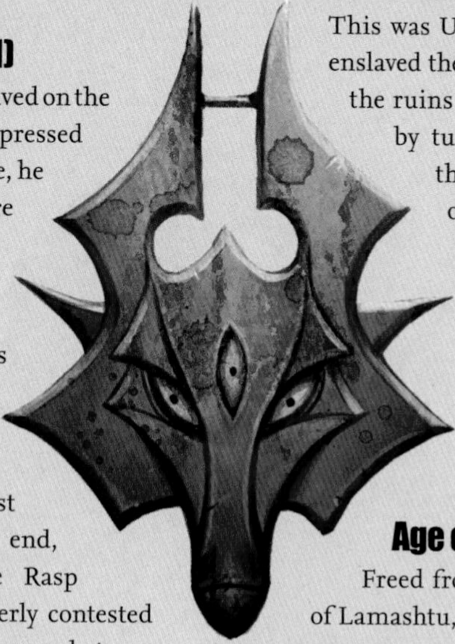

Age of Darkness (–5293 AR to –4294 AR)

Earthfall brought about a great cataclysm that destroyed Thassilon. Far to the northeast, the slumbering volcanoes of the Kodar Mountains awoke to add their ash and fire to an already darkening sky. Stray falling stars from the cluster called down from the sky by the aboleths to destroy distant Azlant peppered Varisia, with significant strikes hitting the Mierani Forest (an event that drove the elves of Mierani deep underground, where many would eventually transform into the first drow). The largest of the falling stars struck the core of Bakrakhan, sinking the bulk of that nation underwater and forming the Varisian Gulf. The easternmost limit of this flooding and devastation stopped at the Rasp and the Fogscar Mountains, creating the region known today as the Lost Coast.

Age of Anguish (–4294 AR to –3470 AR)

Those Varisians who survived Earthfall spent a thousand years struggling for survival, only to emerge from the Age of Darkness and begin rebuilding their society, reverting in some ways to their pre-Thassilonian traditions but in many others retaining the culture and advancements Thassilon had introduced to them. Yet others woke from the darkness as well, including one of the spawn of Lamashtu and Pazuzu. This was Uvaglor, a powerful vrock oracle who enslaved the Varisians just as they emerged from the ruins of the Age of Darkness—it was only by turning to the worship of Lamashtu that the Varisians were able to throw off Uvaglor's rule, a battle that culminated along the new coast once known as the Rasp. In the end, a powerful Varisian priestess of the Empyreal Lord Ashava named Sazzleru managed to not only defeat Uvaglor but lead her people from Lamashtu's clutches as well.

Age of Destiny (–3470 AR to 1 AR)

Freed from Uvaglor's rule and the influence of Lamashtu, the Varisians of the Lost Coast took many years to rebuild their society. In time, the cruelties of the Age of Anguish were all but forgotten, relegated to the stuff of campfire tales.

Age of Enthronement (1 AR to 4606 AR)

Although eager adventurers periodically visited the Lost Coast during the Age of Enthronement, these explorers were rare at best. Traveling Varisians remained the primary movers through the region, with the Kaspakari caravan route serving as a slender artery of relative safety through lands ruled by goblin tribes, ogres, ghouls, and worse. The raising of the *Starstone* in distant Absalom went all but unnoticed by those dwelling on the Lost Coast at this time.

Age of Lost Omens (4606 AR to Present Day)

The Lost Coast spent the first 6 decades of this age in lessening obscurity, a scenic but wild region infested with goblins and far more dangerous perils in its coastal waters, dense forests, and rugged stony escarpments. When Sandpoint was founded in 4666 AR, the Lost Coast began its slow transformation from wilderness into civilization—a process still in its earliest days, and one with a long way yet to go.

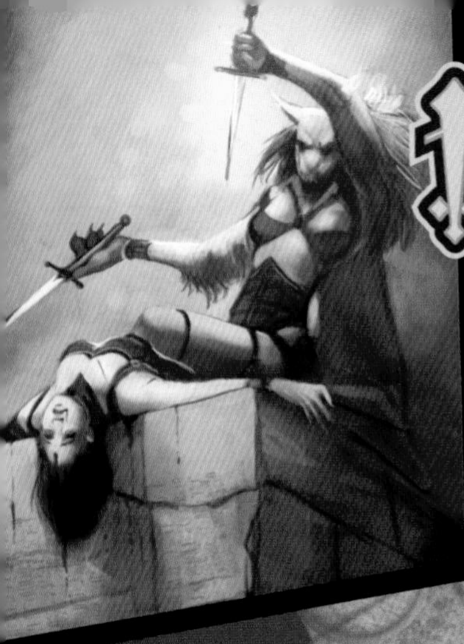

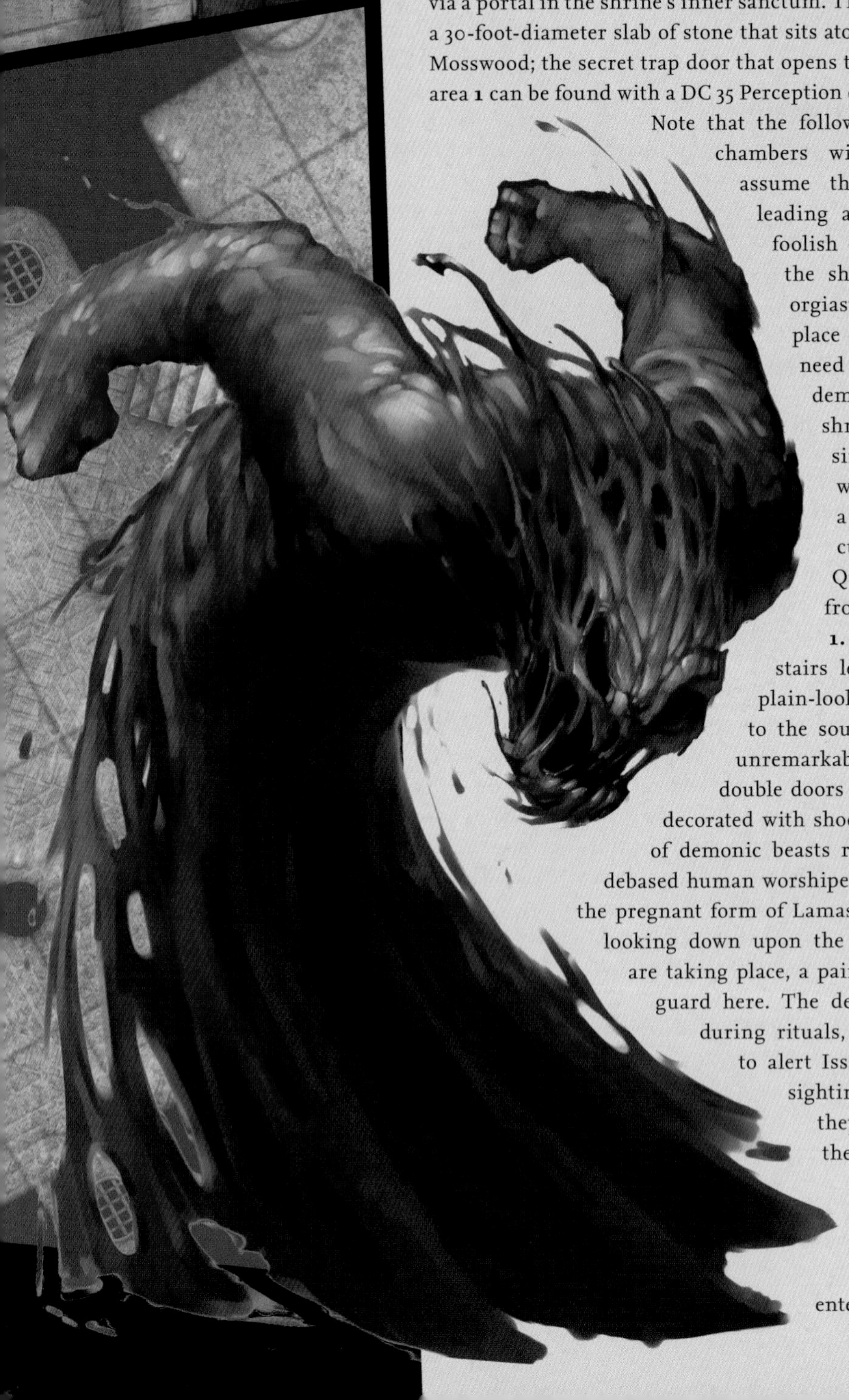

ISSANDRA'S SHRINE

One of the more dangerous of Lamashtu's minions in the Sandpoint Hinterlands is the elven witchpriest Issandra, who tends a small shrine devoted to Lamashtu hidden deep in Mosswood. While a flight of stairs offers access to the shrine, Issandra herself comes and goes via a portal in the shrine's inner sanctum. The shrine is located under a 30-foot-diameter slab of stone that sits atop one of the Lost Tors in Mosswood; the secret trap door that opens to the stairwell leading to area **1** can be found with a DC 35 Perception check.

Note that the following descriptions of the chambers within Issandra's shrine assume that she's not currently leading a ritual. If the PCs are foolish enough to intrude upon the shrine during one of the orgiastic debauches that take place here, they'll not only need to contend with all four demonic guardians of the shrine from areas **1** and **3** simultaneously, but also with Issandra herself and a dozen or more powerful cultists of the Demon Queen who've traveled here from across Western Varisia.

1. Antechamber: The stone stairs lead down to a relatively plain-looking chamber. The door to the south (leading to area **2**) is unremarkable, but the massive double doors that open into area **3** are decorated with shockingly detailed carvings of demonic beasts rutting among a flock of debased human worshipers. Above them all looms the pregnant form of Lamashtu, her three-eyed gaze looking down upon the room. When no rituals are taking place, a pair of babau demons stand guard here. The demons enter area **3** only during rituals, and use their telepathy to alert Issandra immediately upon sighting intruders, just before they attack. (Note that during these rituals, Issandra keeps an *alarm* spell active in this room that triggers a silent mental warning to her as soon as anyone enters this room.)

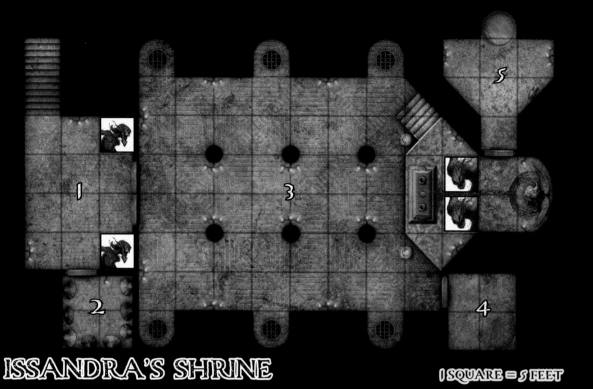

ISSANDRA'S SHRINE

BABAU DEMONS (2)   CR 6
XP 2,400 each
hp 73 each (*Pathfinder Bestiary 57*)
Pawn *Pathfinder Pawns Bestiary Box 54*

2. Robing Room: When Issandra's followers come to hear her sermons and take part in the vile rituals in the shrine itself, they first stop here to don ceremonial robes over their gear. When no ritual is taking place, 16 dark brown bloodstained robes hang here, two to a peg. During a ritual, only a few robes remain, depending on how many participants cavort in area **3**. A character wearing one of these hooded robes gains a +5 circumstance bonus on Disguise checks made within the shrine to pose as a worshiper of Lamashtu.

3. Temple of the Demon Queen: This large shrine features a towering statue of Lamashtu that constantly seeps the *waters of Lamashtu* (see issue #5); these waters run west to a small shrine where they are absorbed and magically recycled back to the statue. Any attempt to harvest this water causes it to suddenly give birth to a loathsome pair of slimy omox demons—likewise, these demons rise up to attack any who attempt to deface the shrine or force their way into area **5** or **6**. The shrine itself is the focus of an *unhallow* spell placed here by Issandra's mysterious superior, an entity known as the Mistmother. This *unhallow* spell functions at CL 20th and is linked to a *freedom of movement* spell that only affects worshipers of Lamashtu; the effect is centered on the altar, and as such encompasses all of the shrine save for areas

1 and **2**. Alcoves along the north and south walls contain gratings that can be lifted to provide access to a flooded dungeon below the shrine that even the cultists themselves avoid.

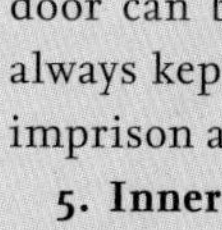

OMOX DEMONS (2)   CR 12
XP 19,200 each
hp 162 each (*Pathfinder Bestiary 2 79*)
Pawn *Pathfinder Pawns Bestiary 2 Box 68*

4. Holding Cell: A filthy heap of straw is this room's only feature. The stout, iron-banded wooden door can be locked (Disable Device DC 40), and is always kept secured when the room is being used to imprison a sacrifice.

5. Inner Sanctum: As with area **4**, the iron-and-wood door opening into this room can be locked (Disable Device DC 40). Issandra uses this plain room to meditate before and after rituals, and can often be found here even on days when no ritual is to take place. The shallow pool of water to the north acts as a portal, but only activates when a dose of the *waters of Lamashtu* are poured into the water—doing so causes a creature standing in the pool to teleport to Issandra's personal lair, a dangerous temple fortress hidden deep in the Fogscar Mountains to the north of Sandpoint. Niches along the southwestern and southeastern walls contain dozens of small urns—9 of these contain powdered amber worth 250 gp (material components for the casting of *waters of Lamashtu*), and one contains 3 doses of *incense of meditation* and a *crystal ball*.

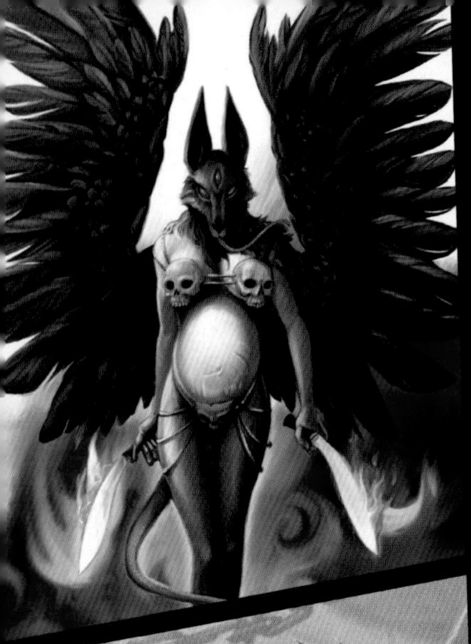

ISSANDRA

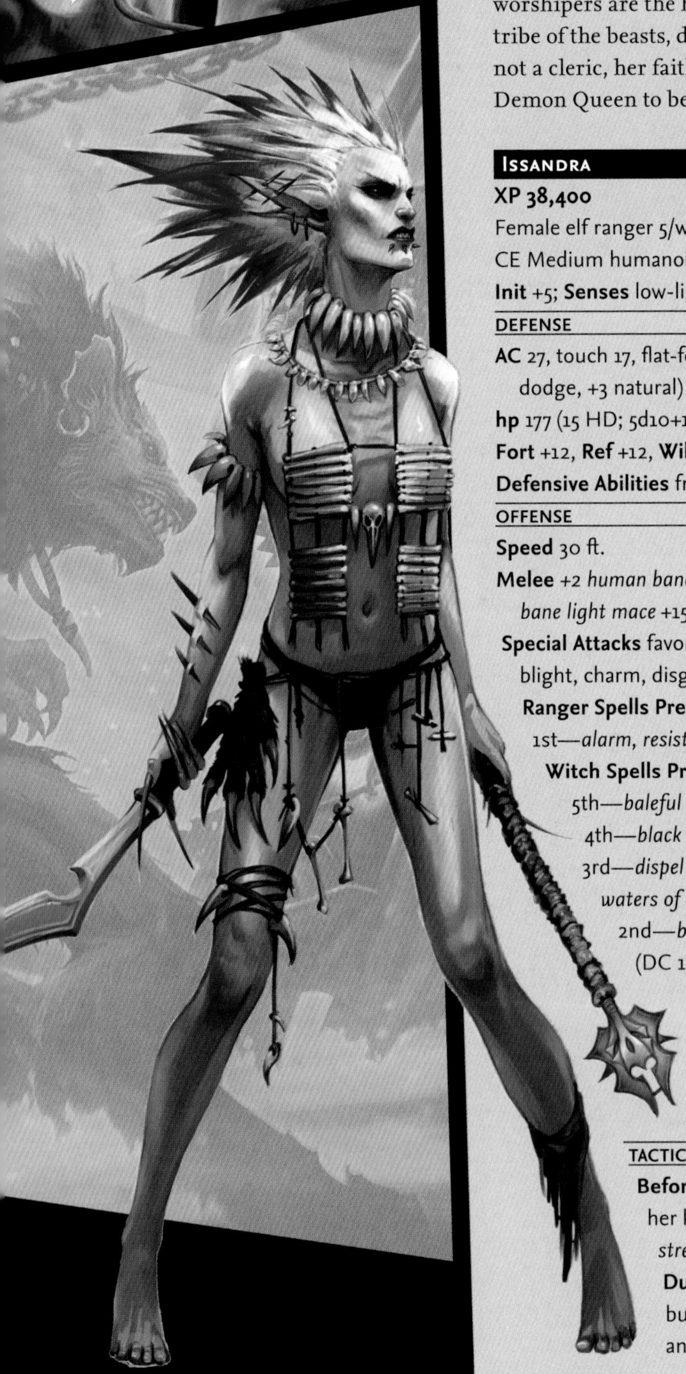

Lamashtu's worshipers along the Lost Coast are legion, but they are spread thin, many of them dwelling in old ruins or hidden lairs in the wilds. All serve an entity known as "Mistmother," yet few have ever met their mysterious patron. The cultist Issandra is one of those few, but she is close-mouthed on what she knows of her sinister superior.

Issandra hails from distant Katapesh, where Lamashtu's primary worshipers are the hyena-like gnolls. There, Issandra ruled a large tribe of the beasts, despite the fact that she is an elf. Although she is not a cleric, her faith in Lamashtu is strong, and she considers the Demon Queen to be the source of all her magical powers.

ISSANDRA **CR 14**

XP 38,400

Female elf ranger 5/witch 10 (*Advanced Player's Guide* 65)

CE Medium humanoid (elf)

Init +5; **Senses** low-light vision; Perception +22

DEFENSE

AC 27, touch 17, flat-footed 21 (+7 armor, +1 deflection, +5 Dex, +1 dodge, +3 natural)

hp 177 (15 HD; 5d10+10d6+110)

Fort +12, **Ref** +12, **Will** +10; ; +2 vs. enchantments

Defensive Abilities freedom of movement; **Immune** sleep

OFFENSE

Speed 30 ft.

Melee *+2 human bane khopesh* +16/+16/+11 (1d8+11/18–20), *+1 human bane light mace* +15 (1d6+8)

Special Attacks favored enemy (elves +2, humans +4), hexes (agony, blight, charm, disguise, flight, healing)

Ranger Spells Prepared (CL 2nd; concentration +4)

1st—*alarm, resist energy*

Witch Spells Prepared (CL 10th; concentration +13)

5th—*baleful polymorph* (DC 18), *feeblemind* (DC 18)

4th—*black tentacles, divine power, dimension door*

3rd—*dispel magic, greater magic weapon, lightning bolt* (DC 16), *waters of Lamashtu*

2nd—*bull's strength, cure moderate wounds, death knell* (DC 15), *hold person* (DC 15), *web* (DC 15)

1st—*command* (DC 14), *cure light wounds* (2), *ray of enfeeblement* (DC 14), *unseen servant*

0 (at will)—*bleed* (DC 13), *detect magic, message, touch of fatigue* (DC 13)

Patron Strength

TACTICS

Before Combat Issandra casts *greater magic weapon* on her khopesh every day. Before combat, she casts *bull's strength* and *divine power*.

During Combat Issandra prefers to fight in melee, but if she's outmatched, she uses flight to retreat and use spells. Note that the *freedom of movement* in her shrine makes *black tentacles* and *web* devastating on intruders when they're fighting multiple worshipers of Lamashtu. She uses Arcane Strike in combat (these modifiers are included in the stats above).

Morale Issandra fights until reduced to 20 or fewer hp, at which point she uses *dimension door* to flee.

STATISTICS

Str 16, **Dex** 20, **Con** 20, **Int** 17, **Wis** 14, **Cha** 8

Base Atk +10; **CMB** +13; **CMD** 30

Feats Arcane Strike, Combat Expertise, Craft Magic Arms and Armor, Craft Wondrous Item, Dodge, Endurance, Exotic Weapon Proficiency (khopesh), Improved Familiar, Toughness, Two-Weapon Fighting

Skills Disguise +14, Fly +23, Knowledge (arcana) +16, Knowledge (local) +13, Knowledge (religion) +18, Perception +22, Spellcraft +21, Swim +7

Languages Abyssal, Common, Elven, Goblin, Varisian

SQ blessed by Lamashtu, elven magic, favored terrain (underground +2), hunter's bond (companions), track +2, weapon familiarity, wild empathy +4, witch's familiar (quasit named Yrogmak)

Other Gear +3 glamered mithral chain shirt, +2 human bane khopesh, +1 human bane light mace, amulet of natural armor +3, belt of physical might +4 (Dex, Con), ring of protection +1, bone unholy symbol of Lamashtu, keys to areas **4** and **5**

SPECIAL ABILITIES

Blessed by Lamashtu (Ex) Issandra has a +2 bonus to Str, Dex, and Con due to overindulgence in the *waters of Lamashtu*.

YROGMAK   CR —

XP —

Male quasit familiar (*Pathfinder RPG Bestiary* 66)

CE Tiny outsider (chaotic, demon, evil, extraplanar)

Init +2; **Senses** darkvision 60 ft.; Perception +7

DEFENSE

AC 22, touch 15, flat-footed 14 (+2 Dex, +1 dodge, +7 natural, +2 size)

hp 83 (15 HD)

Fort +7, **Ref** +9, **Will** +9

Defensive Abilities improved evasion; **DR** 5/cold iron or good; **Immune** electricity, poison; **Resist** acid 10, cold 10, fire 10

OFFENSE

Speed 20 ft., fly 50 ft. (perfect)

Melee bite +14 (1d4–1), 2 claws +14 (1d3–1 plus poison)

Space 2-1/2 ft.; **Reach** 0 ft.

Special Attacks deliver touch spells and hexes

Spell-Like Abilities (CL 6th; concentration +6)

    At will—*detect good, detect magic, invisibility* (self only)

    1/day—*cause fear* (30-ft. radius, DC 11)

    1/week—*commune* (six questions)

STATISTICS

Str 8, **Dex** 14, **Con** 11, **Int** 11, **Wis** 12, **Cha** 11

Base Atk +10; **CMB** +10; **CMD** 20

Feats Dodge, Weapon Finesse

Skills Bluff +6, Disguise +15, Fly +32, Intimidate +6, Knowledge (arcana) +10, Knowledge (local) +10, Knowledge (planes) +6, Knowledge (religion) +15, Perception +19, Spellcraft +15, Stealth +16

Languages Abyssal, Common; empathic link, telepathy (touch)

SQ change shape (bat or jackal; *polymorph*), share spells, store spells

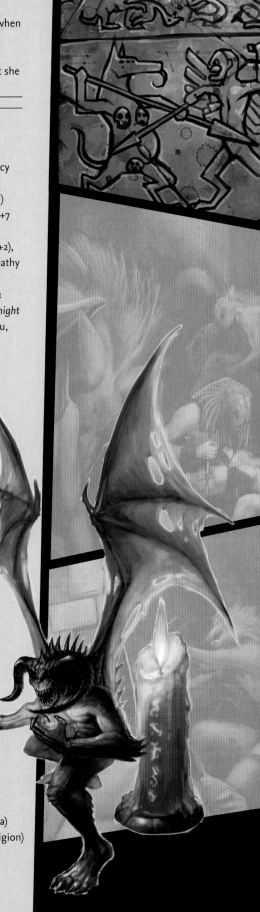

PATHFINDER

HARD-COVER COLLECTIONS
BASED ON THE AWARD-WINNING RPG!

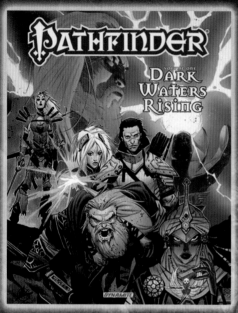

PATHFINDER
VOL. 1: DARK WATERS RISING

PATHFINDER
VOL. 2: OF TOOTH AND CLAW

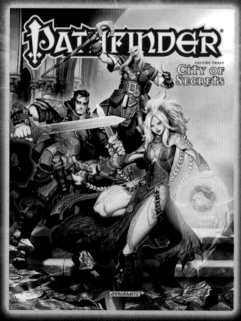

PATHFINDER
VOL. 3: CITY OF SECRETS

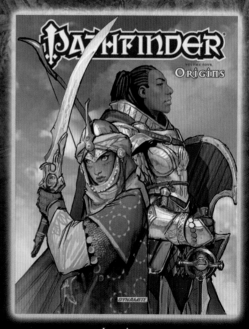

PATHFINDER
VOL. 4: ORIGINS

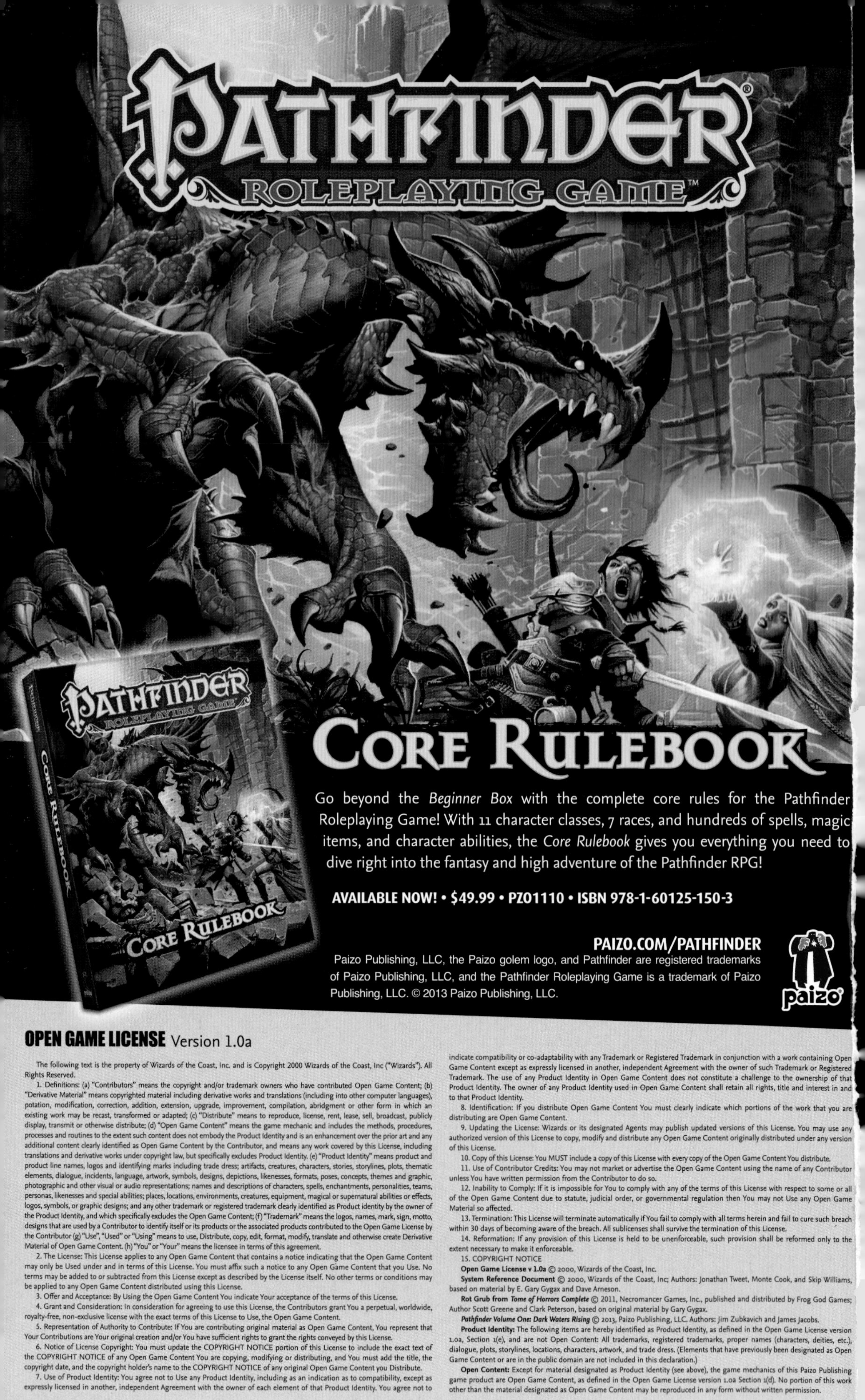
PATHFINDER®
ROLEPLAYING GAME™
PATHFINDER
ROLEPLAYING GAME
CORE RULEBOOK
CORE RULEBOOK
Go beyond the Beginner Box with the complete core rules for the Pathfinder Roleplaying Game! With 11 character classes, 7 races, and hundreds of spells, magic items, and character abilities, the Core Rulebook gives you everything you need to dive right into the fantasy and high adventure of the Pathfinder RPG!
AVAILABLE NOW! • $49.99 • PZO1110 • ISBN 978-1-60125-150-3
PAIZO.COM/PATHFINDER
Paizo Publishing, LLC, the Paizo golem logo, and Pathfinder are registered trademarks of Paizo Publishing, LLC, and the Pathfinder Roleplaying Game is a trademark of Paizo Publishing, LLC. © 2013 Paizo Publishing, LLC.
paizo